1 MONTH OF
FREE
READING

at
www.ForgottenBooks.com

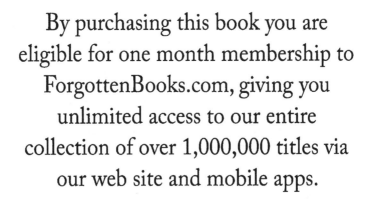

By purchasing this book you are eligible for one month membership to ForgottenBooks.com, giving you unlimited access to our entire collection of over 1,000,000 titles via our web site and mobile apps.

To claim your free month visit:
www.forgottenbooks.com/free161206

ISBN 978-0-483-26896-8
PIBN 10161206

This book is a reproduction of an important historical work. Forgotten Books uses
state-of-the-art technology to digitally reconstruct the work, preserving the original format
whilst repairing imperfections present in the aged copy. In rare cases, an imperfection in
the original, such as a blemish or missing page, may be replicated in our edition. We do,
however, repair the vast majority of imperfections successfully; any imperfections that
remain are intentionally left to preserve the state of such historical works.

BAPTIST PREACHER.

ORIGINAL MONTHLY.

REV. HENRY KEELING,

EDITOR AND PROPRIETOR.

VOLUME III.

RICHMOND:

H. K. ELLYSON, PRINTER.

1844.

CONTENTS OF VOL. III, 1844.

Pages.

JAN. The Value of the Gospel: by Rev. Joseph Walker,
of Hampton, Va, 1
Outlines of a Sermon, by the Editor, 13
Editorial Address, 15

FEB. The Immutability of God: by Rev. Wm. Southwood, of King & Queen Co., Va, 17
Editorial Note, 30

MAR. Christian Union: by Rev. Robt. Fleming, of Newnan, Ga., 34
Note and Extracts, 49

APRIL. Female Piety: by Rev. Robt. Fleming, of Newnan,
Ga., 53
Extract, 67

MAY. The Recording of the Divine Name: by Rev. Wm.
Southwood, 69
The Pressing Claims of the Gospel: by Rev. H.
Keeling, 85

JUNE. The Devoted Pastor: by Rev. S. P. Hill, of Baltimore, Md., 89
Editorial Note, 102

JULY. The Moral Duty of Man: by Rev. M. R. Suares, of
Ga., 105
The Prevalence of Christianity, an Argument for
its Truth: by Rev. Wm. T. Brantly, Jr., of Augusta, Ga., 119

AUG. Ministerial Culture: by Rev. Joseph Walker, 133
The Diffusion of Religious Knowledge, a Precursor of the Millennium: by Rev. J. R. Scott, of Petersburg, Va., 148

SEPT.   The Decline of Spirituality in the Churches: by
             Rev. Thos. Hume, of Portsmouth, Va.,   161
         The Coming of Shiloh: by Rev. R. B. C. Howell,
             of Nashville, Ten.,   167
         Practical Religion, a selection,   179

OCT.   Insubordination: Its Causes, Tendencies and Guilt:
             by Rev. J. Lansing Burrows, of Philadelphia,   181
         Religious Apathy,   191
         Guilt of Unbelief,   195

NOV.   Certainty of Success, a Motive to Perseverance: by
             Rev. Addison Hall, of Lancaster Co., Va.,   197

DEC.   The Mediatorial Reign of Christ, an all-sufficient
             encouragement for the Church to attempt the con-
             version of the world: by Rev. Cornelius Tyree,   217
         A Card,   232

THE
BAPTIST PREACHER.
VOL. III.   January, 1844.   NO. 1.

THE VALUE OF THE GOSPEL:

The Introductory Sermon delivered at the Sixtieth Anniversary of the Dover Association, at Emmaus, in New Kent Co., October 7, 1843, by Rev. Joseph Walker, *of Hampton, and published by request of the Association.*

—

"*For after that in the wisdom of God, the world by wisdom knew not God, it pleased God, by the foolishness of preaching, to save them that believe.*"—1 Corinthians, I: 2.

The desire of knowledge is a distinguishing characteristic of the present age. But it were better to remain ignorant, than to seek merely the wisdom of this world. The mind may be degraded by the objects it contemplates. Being the offspring of the eternal mind, its real dignity requires the consideration of eternal things. Thought, piercing the spiritual world, and taking hold on God, is thought ennobled and divine. It acquaints man with his Creator, stays the arm of rebellion, and begets humility. Every system of education, while it qualifies for the pursuits of this life, should, at the same time, direct the soul to a safe retreat in eternity, where, musing on the inimitable perfections of God and the grandeur of his works, it may be happy forever. The salvation of the soul is of infinitely more importance than a cultivated intellect. While I would not neglect the latter, I would by all means secure the former. Life, eternal life, is the united wish of our race; but the receiving of it, is suspended on the condition, that they gain a knowledge of God and of his Son Jesus Christ. To this truth, he who spake as never yet man spake, testifies, in the following words: "This is life eternal, that they might know thee the only true God and Jesus Christ whom thou hast sent."

From the text, we deduce the following proposition as the theme of the present discourse:

The preached Gospel is the only medium by which to obtain a saving knowledge of God.

1—Vol. 3.   191391

This proposition, we conceive, comprises the real doctrine in the passage. From it we ascertain that human wisdom cannot trace fully, in the works of nature, the character and requisitions of God. The phrase, "in the wisdom of God," stands for external nature. The effect is put for the cause. From every object above, beneath, and around us, shines conspicuously the wisdom of God. Hence a sanctified heart may still exclaim, "O Lord how manifold are thy works, in wisdom hast thou made all." But as the world by their wisdom, could not arrive at a saving knowledge of God, by contemplating his wisdom, or the works of creation, (for this is the *sense* of the text,) he ordained the preaching of the Gospel as the medium of that knowledge.

By the Gospel, we mean that system of principles, precepts, moral duties, and heavenly promises, which were originated by Jesus Christ, and are recorded in the sacred oracles. By preaching, we understand the *means* of communicating this system of truth to man. Whether through the press, by signs, or by oral proclamation and exposition. To make known the Gospel in any way, is to preach it. This, as our proposition imports, is the only way of imparting and receiving that knowledge of God, which *induces* salvation. If it be *not*, then there is some other medium. But where shall we find it? Shall we copy the example of the ancients, and more recently, of enlightened France, and depend on the magic power of reason to unfold the way of life? If the Gospel be *not* the medium of saving knowledge, then indeed, we have no supposable alternative in the universe, save the endowments of the mind. We shall therefore inquire,

I. Whether the mind is able, by the exertion of its powers, *to make one wise unto salvation:*

Solomon says, "that which is to be, hath already been," and as it regards the ability of human reason, as connected with the present state of existence, to discover the true character of God, I think it may be said, that which hath *not* been will *never* be. Reason is uniform in her operations. She draws her conclusions from impressions made on the mind by external objects. Hence under similar circumstances, we may expect her decisions to be the same now as formerly. She contemplates the material universe. The millions of creatures, subsisting in the world, of various shapes, and different habits of life, are subjects for her research. The geological structure of the earth, from its surface to its centre—if man could reach that—furnishes ground for unending speculations. The mountains, piercing the clouds, and the rivers which sweep over the plains, till lost in the soundless deep, interest and astonish the mind. The architecture of the heavens, and other phenomena which might be named, force from it, by involuntary constraint, the admission *that there is a God.* Yea, a God *omnipotent.* And, beholding in all things the adaptation of means to ends, a God *omniscient.* Moreover, if the mind mark the successions of the seasons, seed time and harvest, and the careful provision made for both man and beast, it must allow also a God of *providence.*

These are some of the data, from the consideration of which, reason is to make her deductions concerning the moral nature of God, and man's obligation to him as a holy Being.

But all this testimony has existed from the beginning of time. What has it done in the way of guiding lost sinners to a haven of rest? Has it left on the soul a correct impression of the moral perfections of Jehovah? The super-excellence of his character? His untarnished purity? Matchless holiness? Consummate goodness? No, never since the fall have these sublime qualities been evolved by reasoning skill. Although the heavens have always declared the glory of God, and the firmament hath shadowed forth his handi-work, man by this light alone has never admired the holy nature of God, nor contracted a love for his laws.

The wisest of men, giants in ancient lore, have practiced cruelty, indulged in revelry, and entertained the most absurd notions of the Divine nature. Isolated reason, that "celestial lamp," as some enthusiasts were wont to call it, never taught Greek, Roman, nor Carthagenian a correct knowledge of the true God. Those profound thinkers whom Paul addressed from Mars Hill, were in total darkness touching the real condition of their souls. In science they were adepts. The specimens of art strewed lavishly throughout their cities, bore witness to their claims. They could boast also of philosophers, of poets, and of orators. But, proud of their high distinction, they despised the simplicity of the Gospel. Speaking of Paul, its advocate, in language of the keenest sarcasm—they asked, "What will this babbler say?" To them, those cultivated, boastful Greeks, Paul answered: "Ye men of Athens, I perceive that in all things ye are too superstitious: for as I passed by, and beheld your devotions, I found an altar with this inscription, TO THE UNKNOWN GOD. Whom therefore ye ignorantly worship, him declare I unto you."

Go to the most refined nation on the globe, and if the Bible be wanting, you shall find the people in the ignorance and slavery of sin. Nor has a saving acquaintance with God ever been formed where the word of life has not first been held forth. Judging then of the future by the past, human reason is incompetent to lead us to the rock whence saving comforts flow. If left to her teachings *only,* man must grope his way in the dark, and, in the end, lose himself amid the mazes of his own speculations. Instead of consecrated temples, on whose altars are offered the affections of contrite hearts, this happy country might be studded with pedestals, and images, at which would be practiced the miserable service of idolatry.

II. In the second place we sustain the proposition, *that the*

Gospel is the only medium of a saving knowledge of God.
This will appear, if we notice,

1. The *design* of its doctrines. There are certain *principles*
which form the groundwork of Christianity. They teach man
what he is, his danger, and what has been done for his soul. By
the development of these, the soul is roused from its stupor,
wooed from earth to heaven, and finally made happy in the
Lord.

Firstly, the Gospel defines clearly *the relation* man sustains to
God and a future state. If, through the Old Testament, we look
by faith, on the green fields of Eden, with its rivers and fountains,
its pleasant groves and delicious fruits ;—if in that Paradise, man
appears the noblest of creation's works; the offspring of a just,
holy, and glorious God, loving righteousness, and obeying the
edicts of his Maker with delight ;—in the New *especially,* the picture is reversed. In it he is called the child of the devil, rebellious, obstinate, and hostile to purity and holy worship. His
present relation to God is that of an enemy. The future threatens
him with interminable death ! To be assured of his real condition, his darkened understanding, perverted affections, and the
soul's tendency to irrevocable ruin, *is the first element* of saving
knowledge. Till quickened by the Gospel, man seems uncon-
scious of the *turpitude* of his guilt. Charmed perpetually by
the old serpent, the devil, he is in danger of sinking hoodwinked
down to hell. Hence, to save, is first to *convince* him of his peril.
And not only to convince, but also to arrest him in his course,
that he may survey the path along which he is rushing blindly
into the "bottomless pit." The faithful exhibition of the divine
Word, has often proved competent to this result. Nor need we
wonder, if we consider the momentous truths it discloses in
which we are so fearfully interested. The sentence, "except a
man be born again he cannot see the kingdom of God," is enough
in itself to make one tremble for his safety. While, as if waked
from the torpor of death, he asks, "how can these things be?"
he may well suspect that all is not right. Strange things, indeed,
have sounded in his ears, to which the understanding cannot well
be indifferent. It is more than half convinced that the statement
just made, implying depravity of heart, and, by consequence,
alienation from God, is a solemn reality. If, in connexion with
the affirmation made by the Savior to Nicodemus, the Gospel
thunder,—" Repent, for the kingdom of heaven is at hand ; " and
this again be followed by the ominous announcement, " For we
must all appear before the judgment-seat of Christ, that every one
may receive the things done in his body, according to that he
hath done, whether it be good or bad "—why, the relation man
holds to God and a future state, is clearly developed. Either by
implication or direct teaching, he is every where in the Gospel
exhibited as a wretched, condemned, lost sinner. Liable at

any moment to be struck down and sunk to endless wo!

Here then the sinner is brought into a sad strait. Above, is the sword of Divine vengeance, gleaming ethereal fire; from underneath, are heard the mutterings of that lake which burneth with fire and brimstone; while all around him, there arises an impervious wall of sin. This is the light in which the sinner *must see,* and, to some extent *feel* himself, in order to salvation. Like Isaiah, he must become willing to confess, "that he is a man of unclean lips;" or like Job, that he is "vile;" for such is his exact relation to the "Lord of hosts."

Secondly, through the Gospel we learn *the ground of deliverance from guilt.* By the first item of saving knowledge, the sinner's fears become excited. It cannot be otherwise. Though the convictions, which distress his soul are essential to his acceptance, yet *he* can see in them naught but threatening evil. Behind him is a polluted life; above, he sees a holy God; in front, all is darkness! For the first time in his life he is overtaken by the storm of God's wrath. The tempest increases in fury and blackness! God's fiery indignation flashes deep into his soul. His first inquiry is how he shall be rescued. Surround a man with danger and he attempts escape. Release from peril is the desire universal. When calamity threatens, the mind seeks to avert the catastrophe.

But poor wretch! what shall he do? Whither flee? His *own* righteousness can no longer shield him from the pelting storm. Every step of his way has been stained with guilt. To his astonishment he has found that in him there dwelleth no good thing: Nor can he forget his convictions. As easily could the dying man forget the fever which drinks up his blood. Where shall he obtain relief? Blessed be God! the remedy is at hand. The Gospel, if it kill, can also make alive. If it wound, it can cure. God has "laid help upon one who is mighty to save." Even on Jesus, "the mediator of the new covenant." The cross! suspending the Savior, as an offering for sin, a ransom for ruined man, has all this time been overlooked. The troubled soul, in its agony, has not looked *out of itself.* As soon, however, as it turns to calvary, where Jesus groaned, bled, and yielded up the ghost—an event in which were concentred the patience, obedience, compassion and love of Christ, it *must* relent. In that stupendous scene the sinner sees justice satisfied! He learns that God in Christ can be just, and, at the same time, justify the transgressor. That all God requires is the hearty belief of this great truth. Unwavering confidence in the atonement, as God's method of salvation, will make the moral thunder cease, the clouds of despair to scatter, and the cross of salvation to loom out of the thick darkness!

In no system of philosophy can such help be found. Man, incased in depravity, dreamed not of assistance from *any* source.

This provision for lost souls, had its origin in the Divine compassion. " When there was no eye to pity and no arm to save,'" "God was in Christ reconciling the world unto himself. " Hear testimony on this point. " As Moses lifted up the serpent in the wilderness, even so must the Son of man be lifted up ; that whosoever believeth in him should not perish, but have eternal life. " " And I, if I be lifted up from the earth, will draw all men unto me. " " He was delivered for our offences and raised again for our justification. "

Surely, here is news for the weeping sinner ! " As cold water to a thirsty soul, " so must this be to his troubled spirit ! Here, at the cross, he may sit, wonder, admire, and adore that love, which made so merciful a provision for his poor soul. But,

Thirdly, it is in the Gospel that *Divine aid* is promised *to promote* our return to God. Its necessity comports both with reason and revelation. If needless, it had not been tendered. God has never revealed a superfluous doctrine. To appreciate the importance of the Spirit in the work of conversion, we may only consider our degradation and helplessness. Who that views man, steeped in pollution—waging war against all good, but must see the necessity of Divine interposition to turn him from the error of his ways ? The reclaiming a soul from a life of the deepest corruption to uprightness of heart, is an inexplicable enigma, unless we ascribe the change to the life-giving power of the Holy Spirit. This passage, however, " The wind bloweth where it listeth, and thou hearest the sound thereof, but canst not tell whence it cometh and whither it goeth, so is every one that is born of the Spirit,'" unfolds the mystery. *God, the Spirit is the author of the change.*

With a resurrection voice does he call the corrupting Lazarus from the tomb of spiritual death. Loose him, he says, from the integuments of sin, and let him go. By this power *only* does the soul lift itself from the earth and "arise to newness of life. " " Not of blood, is one born, nor of the will of the flesh, nor of man, but of God. " It is this supernatural agency, operating through the preached word, which discovers to a man his true relation to eternal things ; enables him to repose confidence in Jesus ; sanctifies, and so prepares him for heaven. It is the Spirit who communicates a spiritual taste, enlightens our darkened understandings, and gives simplicity to many passages in the Scriptures, which, without his influence, might appear dark and perplexing.

The doctrine of Divine influence, though opposed by some, towers from the Gospel like the apex of a pyramid towards the sun. While earthly exhalations conceal its base—from its summit, it reflects the rays of heavenly light. To believe this doctrine is not to trust, to idle speculation, but to notice its transforming effects in the life, and on the conduct. " If any man will do his will, he shall know of the doctrine whether it be of God. "

Show me a man, then, whose once ferocious temper is subdued into mildness; who, instead of clanning with the wicked, fills his place in the Lord's house; who, by every act of his life, exhibits humility, and a sense of unworthiness in the sight of his Divine Father; and in him you have an individual, *renovated* by the saving influences of the Holy Spirit. The word was rendered *effectual* by *his* sealing power, and so a soul was taken from the "miry clay," and established firmly on the rock Christ Jesus.

Man's exact relation to God and the future—the ground of his deliverance from "the wrath to come"—and the power by which he is quickened into holiness, are items of knowledge, essential to his happiness and ultimate redemption.

2. That the Gospel is the only medium of saving knowledge, *is plain from the intention of its ordinances.* Connected with the new dispensation are too positive institutions. Baptism, the first, is a rite, denoting a change of heart, supposed to have taken place in the individual submitting to it. A change by reason of which, the understanding is made to acquiesce in, and the affections to harmonize with, the revealed will of God. The immersion of a believer in water, represents the soul cleansed of its guilt—raised from a death of sin, to a life of purity. It is in figure what the burial and resurrection of Christ were literally. It also points to the general resurrection. Human redemption will not be completed till the dead shall be raised at the last day. Though the soul soars to realms of bliss, and is present with the Lord the moment after death, yet till the body glorified shall be united to it, the great end of Christ's mission into the world will not be consummated. The general resurrection, however, will as certainly come to pass as that Christ himself was raised from the sepulchre. "For this corruptible must put on incorruption, and this mortal must put on immortality." When that glorious period shall have arrived, then shall it be said, "Death is swallowed up in victory." His sting extracted, the grave conquered, man will stand disenthralled from the results of the transgression. How accurately, how consolingly, and how beautifully, does the immersion of a believer delineate death and victory in their several forms! Speak we of the burial and resurrection of Christ? the immersion in, and the raising a proper subject out of the water represents them. Or of a death to sin and a resurrection unto holiness? this same ordinance declares them. Or of that day "when all that are in their graves, shall hear the voice of the Son of God and come forth?" In this sublime institution, we have it in figure.

The *Lord's Supper* is both commemorative and prophetic. It looks back to the cross, and forward "to the glorious appearing of the great God, and our Savior Jesus Christ." It stands, at the same time, for the cause and the fruition of our hope. "As oft

as ye eat this bread, and drink this cup, ye do show forth the
Lord's death till he come."

These rites present the professor before the world, as "a new
creature." They imply a death to sin, a resurrection unto life,
and point to Christ as "the author and finisher" of the Christian
faith. Therefore being connected *only* with the Gospel, and
drawing the line between the Church and the world, they testify
to the Gospel as the only medium by which to obtain a saving
knowledge of God.

3. Our proposition is sustained *in the unparalleled success* of
the Gospel. God honors *truth* with the seal of his approbation.
Error, except when aided by persecution, progresses slowly.
Mahomet toiled a long time before the sentiments of the Koran
took root. Nor, till enforced by the threat of arms, did the Arabians receive them. The "Romish Church," by bribery, inti-
midation, and torture, sought to subvert the truth as it is in Jesus.
But his words, " Fear not little flock, for it is your Father's good
pleasure to give you the kingdom," had gone forth. Therefore
her machinations against his cause proved fruitless.

Consult history, sacred and profane, for the effects resulting
from the proclamation of the Gospel. No carnal weapons, no
parade of wealth and lordly equipage;—no artifice and cunning
craftiness were employed:—no Mahomets, Charlemagnes, nor
mitred Pontiffs, were needed to compel acquiesence. The plain,
pathetic story of Christ crucified, and Christ raised from the dead,
was enough to win thousands over to the Christian Faith. The
simple preaching of unpretending men, could heave the bosoms
and start the tear, and extort the cry: "What shall we do?"
"what must I do to be saved?"

In a short while Jerusalem was filled with their doctrine.
First three thousand, then five thousand, and daily such as should
be saved, were added to the Church. By this amazing process,
by men called foolishness, the Divine Message was sent towards
all parts of the earth. Like a fructuous vine, whose roots fasten
in a rich soil, its tendrils took hold on Asia, Africa, Europe, and
finally, America. To this day, as in Samaria of old, the people,
"believing the things concerning the kingdom of God, and the
name of Jesus Christ, are baptized both men and women."
Every week do we hear of revivals and large ingatherings, from
different parts of the world.

What conclusion shall we draw from hence? What other can
we, than that a knowledge and power are communicated through
the Gospel, procurable from no other source. It is emphatically,
though mysteriously, "the power of God unto salvation to every
one that believeth."

The only reasons given, for the adoption of this method in
preference to any other, are the pleasure of God, and the ignorance of the human race. The text supposes the energy and

acuteness of human intellect to have been fully tested. "For after that, in the wisdom of God, the world by wisdom knew not God, it pleased God by the foolishness of preaching to save them that believe."

In whatever aspect we regard the Gospel, whether in the light of its doctrines, ordinances, or success, it plainly exhibits itself, *as the only medium by which to obtain a saving knowledge of God.*

III. Having established our proposition, we, in the last place, proceed to some inferences.

1. If the Gospel be the only medium of salvation, then *it should be preached.* Though it contains all the principles needed to reconcile man to his God, still he must be informed of them, and become interested in them. The Gospel has not *intrinsically* the power either of locomotion or speech. God has originated the plan of-human redemption, taught the doctrines, precepts, and general duties growing out of it, but these will avail nothing unless they be published. Because of this, our Savior when on earth, not only died for the world but sent out preachers to proclaim salvation to all who should believe, to call home the wandering sheep to the Shepherd and Bishop of their souls "How," asks Holy writ, "shall they hear without a preacher?" Preaching, (by which we here mean *oral proclamation,*) is God's *peculiar* method, as explicitly set forth in the text.

2. It ought to be published *in its native purity.* If it be the word of inspiration, then is it perfect. It needs not embellishment, enlargement, nor simplicity. Coming from God who knows what is in man, it must be *in all respects* adapted to our wants. Its doctrines should be assented to, and its ordinances practiced, *just as they are revealed,* without hesitation or doubt. And so doubtless they would be, if the heralds of the cross would maintain uniformly, *a pure speech.* It was the boast of Paul that he could say for himself and his coadjutors: "We are not as many who corrupt the word." Would that the same might be said now. But alas! the interests, ignorance, or prejudices of some, who cry from the watch-towers, influence them either to conceal a part of the message, or, which is the same thing, give it a wrong interpretation. Wo! to that minister who shall mislead immortal souls. Wo! wo! to those blind guides who tamper with eternal things and cause the unwary to err. To perpetuate a pure Gospel among us, as Baptists, two things are required.

1. We want *competent, dauntless teachers:* "Faithful men who shall be able to teach others also." Men who shall possess, not only a stock of general literature, but who can expound the doctrines and ordinances of the Gospel with *clearness and effect.* I object not to a cultivated fancy, a finished style, nor the graces of oratory: these are desirable accomplishments. But, above all, let the *sense* of the text be given. If a man's imagination permit, let him explore the universe, and bring illustrations from her

2—Vol. 3.

abundant treasure-house, but let him also be careful, lest, amid
the flourish of rhetoric, he conceal the CROSS. "Sound
speech that cannot be condemned," is the most efficient preaching.
But in order to that apprehension of the truth, and the exercise of
those dispositions of soul which qualify for the pulpit, the minister
must be a constant, laborious, prayerful, Bible-student. In the
law of the Lord, "must he meditate day and night." The chief
concerns of his heart should be, to give the world an uncorrupted
Gospel, and to rescue dying men from a threatening perdition.
Therefore we remark,

2. That ministers *must be supported.* I mean not that they
shall receive *princely incomes.* That, like the aristocratic prelates
of England, they must have a seat in Parliament, and burden the
people with tithes: but only, that they may be so far relieved
from secular toil, as to give themselves *wholly* to the sacred ministry. I object not to minister farmers, or minister school-teachers,
if necessity compel to these vocations; but certainly, it would
promote the diffusion of an unadulterated Gospel and effective
preaching, if the Churches would disencumber their pastors from
the world.

Compel a minister to some temporal pursuit for the maintenance of his family, and you detract from his usefulness. The
mind, to develope its powers, requires patient and vigorous exercise. It must first *perceive* truth and then study how it may
impart its perception to others with *perspicuity and force.* These
studies comprise its weekly employments for the pulpit. How
can tasks, so arduous, so responsible, be mastered in the broken
intervals of labor and worldly care? Necessarily under such
circumstances, "the man of God" often appears before his congregation, having for it no definite message. He says something
and his audience hear it, but it is thrownoff in such an unconnected, digressive manner, that the understanding, unable to comprehend him, grows weary and indifferent. Thus a Sabbath is lost;
the people disperse unbenefitted, and souls die unreconciled to
Christ!

Morever, compulsion to manual labor, or mercantile pursuits,
subjects the pastor to censure. If he have to present bills, press
accounts, and attend courts, his character will be assailed by the
designing, and the dishonest. Though he were as pure as an
angel, yet would the enemies of Christ impugn his motives,
should his necessary transactions conflict with their interests.
Thus he would lose his influence, and the devil obtain a victory.
Take away his influence, and you render him inefficient. As
well might you wrest from the soldier his armor, and expect him
to conquer in battle, as to expect that a preacher can benefit a
community without influence. The way to perpetuate this moral
power, is to let his intercourse with the world arise mainly from
his official duties.

Then, brethren, as ye love a pure Gospel, and yourselves have felt its power, look out men of honest report; educate and support them; and let them proclaim untrammelled the merits of a Savior's love.

3. The Gospél ought to be diffused *among the destitute.* What so vitally concerns our race should not be withheld. The law of philanthrophy, the cardinal virtue of all christians and the evidence of love to God, incites to the duty of preaching the Gospel. *Disseminate* ought to be the willing motto of the whole Church. To make known the scheme of redemption is the great design of a Church in the world. Life and salvation are to be transmitted through her instrumentality. In view of her relation to the ungodly, she is called the salt of the earth, the light of the world, and a city *unconcealed* on the hill-top. The sphere of her operations is this entire globe. "Teach all nations"—"preach the Gospel to every creature," was the valedictory of Jesus. Hence in what place soever there can be found an unconverted soul, there is work for the Christian. "No one liveth to himself," testifies the word of the Lord. But to carry out this great original plan of our Divine Father two things must be observed.

1. We want *united action.* Heretofore, nothing, like uniformity, in spreading the Gospel, has been attained. Perhaps no Church has yet borne her full proportion of the burden. While some benevolent hearts have contributed beyond their ability, others, equally able, have done nothing. It is unquestionably the duty of *all* to assist in evangelizing the world. Yea, it is as much one's business to spread the word of salvation, as it is to pray for his daily bread, or return thanks for blessings received. I will go farther. A professor who would *confine* the means of grace *to his own Church*, gives not the *best* evidence of a change of heart. How can a liberal spirit, expanding with love divine, place limits to that Gospel of the Kingdom, which is to be preached to all nations? Tell me, what kind of spirit is that, so prevalent among some, which refuses to contribute for the missionary enterprise? It cannot be the spirit of him "*who went about* doing good." It savors strongly of this world. Christ was a missionary—angels are missionaries—the Apostles were missionaries—and if some Christians be *not* missionaries, *surely* they are fighting against God.

Then brethren, let *all* "come to the help of the Lord against the mighty." Let there be some established system by which to draw out the resources of every member. Send the Gospel forth to such as "sit in the regions and shadow of death." Like the rays of the morning sun, let it roll the moral vapors from the earth, and scatter light and heat among the bewildered sons of Adam. But,

2. We must give more attention *to home effort.* While I believe that a really pious heart desires the conversion of *all*

mankind, and that a spirit of missions ought to reach "from the river to the ends of the earth," I believe also, that the destitute around us, *have been too generally neglected.* More regard for our immediate neighbors, would meet a readier response from many in the Church who now do but little if anything. I know, indeed, that a soul rightly exercised, is not fastidious as to persons and places; but nevertheless, there are some who *prefer home labor.* Objections to foreign missions are frequently made on the score of destitution at home. These doubtless are sometimes the evictions of covetous hearts; still, they demand our consideration. Let us present an alternative, and say to our brethren, if you will not give of your substance for Burmah, surely you will for the good of those in your own land, your own State. Have pity on those starving souls, who are bone of your bone, and flesh of your flesh. Give, O! give them "the bread of life." Certainly, they will respond to a request so reasonable.

Again, an ardent solicitude for our own people, would beget a sympathy for the benighted heathen. In proportion as the Gospel is diffused may we expect souls to be converted. These will naturally feel for others still in nature's darkness, and if such cannot be found in our own land, they will be sought abroad.

Every district Association ought at once to turn its attention to home destitution. Every such body, according to its wants and numerical strength, ought to have evangelists actively laboring within its bounds. For want of this, many precious years have been wasted. The elements of moral death have brooded over our State, while the healing balm has not been imparted to check the disease of sin. Here, in this peninsula, there stretches before us "a waste howling wilderness." Error, ignorance, superstition, and prejudice, have drawn the vail of night over its moral horizon. Here, then, is work for this Association. Several of the old Churches, once influential and active, have now scarcely a name by which to establish their identity. I speak not of disruptions, caused by designing religionists, nor of the blamable supineness of brethren, *but of the facts.* Numbers of immortal souls, between Richmond and the blue waters of the Chesapeake, have never known nor felt the Gospel. Many perhaps have not even heard it. This "field is white to the harvest." We need an active, zealous, energetic evangelist to travel and preach between York Town and Fox-Hill. Likely you may need one too, in the upper end of the district. And I doubt not, what is true of our Association, is true to some extent of every other in the State.

The resources of support are *ample,* if Christians would economise in articles of mere luxury. Appearances testify that some professors would rather expend twenty dollars to feast their friends, than to give half that sum to a benevolent enterprise. The superfluities which abound in dress and fare, would be sufficient, no doubt, to support two missionaries in every Association. I repeat, *our resources are ample.* They are sent to us in the dew-drops of the night, and the showers of noonday; in the sun-beams that woo the mists from the soil, and in the golden harvests.

If then there is joy in heaven over one sinner that repenteth, —if heathenish darkness, and soul-destroying ignorance could move God with pity,—if it is his pleasure to save by the Gospel them that believe, let us prove ourselves worthy stewards of that which has been entrusted to our care. Let us "work while it is called to day," and recollect that the fire of the last day, "shall try every man's work, of what sort it is."

4. The Gospel asks *the careful attention* of its hearers. It addresses the intellects, and courts the affections of lost sinners. Though it is God's only method, yet, in order to be saved, we must *heed* its calls. Men must believe it, and "faith comes by hearing." Mark it, my friends, faith *comes.* The faith of the Christian is not that which previously existed in the mind, and is common to man, but it is a divine principle, begotten by the Holy Spirit, and *comes* into the soul through the preaching of the word. But in the arrangement of God; *attention* on the part of the hearer is essential to its reception into the heart. The watchman is "to cry aloud, and spare not;" to lift up his voice like a trumpet, and show the people their transgressions; but his toil will prove unavailing unless the audience *attend.* It is impossible to say, how saving faith communicates with, and is interfused through the soul. We know only the fact on the authority of Holy writ, that "*it comes by hearing.*" Hence our Savior proclaimed in his day: "Whosoever hath ears to hear, let him hear;" that is to say, *attend.* This faith, like the wind, is known only by its effects. "It works by love, purifies the heart, and overcomes the world."

Now then if any in this congregation desire to experience this purifying, all conquering principle, I hope they will ponder well in their minds the word spoken.

This glorious Gospel is to be the means of your redemption, if you slight not its calls. It was sent to reclaim the nations. To be a light to their feet and a lamp to their path. It is to sweep ignorance, hatred, and rebellion from the earth, and establish peace within her borders. Its design is to elevate man to the dignity of angels, and people heaven with redeemed souls: It is to give melody to that song, which shall swell in sublimest strains to the honor of God, the Father, Christ the Redeemer, and the Holy Spirit, the regenerator and sanctifier.

Let us believe, obey, and diffuse this blessed Gospel. Amen!

OUTLINES OF A SERMON:

BY THE EDITOR.

———

The unjust steward.—LUKE, XVI : 1–13.

The apparent designs of this parable, were, to charge the Pharisees with a prevalent vice; and to caution the disciples against
it:—the vice of covetousness. That it was intended to reprove
the Pharisees, appears from the facts that it was spoken in their
presence, and that they so understood it, which our Lord does not
deny. (ver. 14.) That it was cautionary as respects the disciples is
evident, because it was addressed to them, and because certain expressions in the parable imply it. (ver. 8.)

In the case adduced, whether supposed or real, the vice intended is strongly marked. Read verses 1–7. It appears to have
been the ruling passion of the accused, although not his only one.
Indeed no sin is solitary. Gamblers usually drink; swearers violate the Sabbath; and children who disobey their parents are not
apt to pay a strict regard to truth. This man was lazy. "I cannot
dig." And proud. "To beg I am ashamed." Extravagant. He
"wasted" goods. Dishonest. The goods were not his, but his
lord's. He was accessary to the crimes of others.: for he induces his employer's debtors to cheat for his advantage. About to
be discharged for his unfaithfulness, he contracts with them for
a reduction of their bills, to secure himself a retreat, when left
homeless. He had, however, one redeeming quality: "wisdom,"
a prudent regard to the future, but that he perverts. This quality,
in the good application of it, our Lord commends to his disciples
for their imitation. "Make to yourselves friends" &c.

The moral of the parable appears to be contained in the 9th
verse. "Make to yourselves friends of the mammon of unrighteousness, that when ye fail, they may receive you into everlasting
habitations." The unjust steward so used the goods of his employer, entrusted to him, as to secure the friendship of his debtors:
thu: oviding for his own future necessity. Imitate his example.

That this is the moral of the parable, may be inferred from the
parallel. The instrument to be used in both cases is the same:—
wealth. The unjust steward used his master's wealth; we are
advised to use our Lord's. This is the only meaning of the
phrase "mammon of unrighteousness," in contradistinction to the
"true riches." The comparison holds in three particulars. 1.
The steward was displaced. We also shall "fail," or be put out
of office. 2. He made friends of those who could aid him in
future. We are exhorted to do the same in a higher, or moral

sense. God, and all holy beings, approve of a just and beneficent appropriation of wealth. The preposition "of," before "mammon," evidently has the sense of "with," in this place. 3. His motive was a temporary lodge; ours, a permanent abode in heaven.

From the text we make one single inference : that wealth is an invaluable talent.

Perhaps you will say, it is not necessary to insist upon this, because all persons value it sufficiently. But it is not true as is commonly supposed, that all men are eagerly desirous to be rich. If they were, more would become so. The multitude desire to be rich, like they desire to be learned or virtuous; but few so desire it, as to resolve, if practicable, to make the attainment. Fewer still wish to acquire, or possess wealth, that they may employ it usefully.

How much good a rich man may do! From the nature of our institutions, we are not burdened in this country, as certain classes are in Europe, with overgrown fortunes. But there are thousands of Christians in the United States, each of whom might with his mere pocket-money support such a man as Mr. Comstock or Mr Shuck. And many a lady might from her pin-money, educate, year after year, a theological student. We read of some man on the banks of the Mississippi, or of the Ganges, who is blessing the world with his labors, and that man is supported at the expense of $600 or $800 per annum from the funds of some society. Many a Church member who has no talent for such a work, has the means of supporting one or more such men, while men who have the talent, are earning their bread by the ordinary pursuits of life, and the Church and the world are deprived of their services. To "make haste to be rich," is folly; to covet it that we may "consume it upon our lusts" is worse; but to acquire and possess wealth with a view to its lawful enjoyment, and our usefulness, is highly praise worthy.

TO OUR PATRONS.

Two years have passed away, since "The Virginia Baptist Preacher" commenced its evangelical labors, and these labors, we trust, have not been "in vain, in the Lord." In many respects, our success has surpassed our own most sanguine anticipations. As regards material for the Publication, we have had more of it, and of better quality, than could have been reasonably expected. It will be recollected that, of the 24 Nos. we have published, frequently comprising two, and sometimes, three sermons each, one was from Kentucky, and all the rest either from ministers residing in Virginia, or from those who have migrated from this, to other States. Several ministers who promised their aid, and from whom we still expect contributions, have as yet rendered us no aid in this way; and we candidly affirm that we consider the discourses which have appeared, a mere specimen of the capabilities of the Ministry in Virginia.

Of single Sermons we have issued between 50,000, and 60,000. If these have been read, and heard read, on an average, by five persons each, the Preacher has already had more than a quarter of a million of readers or hearers. Some of these Sermons, are of uncommon excellence; they all teach the way of salvation, and press it home upon the conscience. Ought we to fear that so much good seed, has all fallen by the "way side," or in "stony ground?" We cannot fear it. We doubt not, that fruit has been produced, in the instruction, consolation, and increased piety, of many a Christian; and we cherish the thought that salutary impressions have been made on unconverted minds.

It will be perceived from our Title Page, that we have erased the word "Virginia," from our name. The suggestion was first made from the North, by the Editor of the Baptist Record, Rev. L. Burrows, who spoke favorably of the Work, and manifested a desire for its more extensive circulation. In the South, the same feeling was exhibited, especially by Rev. Joseph Baker, Editor of the Christian Index. Of the three names proposed, the one selected will probably combine the views of all, and be liable to the least objections from any quarter. Our "Western" brethren will not complain that the word "Southern" is too local; and "Baptist" is sufficiently comprehensive to include, as suggested by Rev. Dr. Babcock, of the "Baptist Memorial," the whole of our great family in every part of our country, and of the world. And may we not hope that our columns will sometimes be enriched, by the productions even of those, who have gone "far hence to the Gentiles?" But this change, does not imply an abandonment of any one of the objects originally contemplated by this Publication. Our young Ministers will not be the less likely to profit by our pages, from the circumstance that contributions will be made from a more extensive field; nor can it be probable that those who write will be less careful because they expect an increased list of readers.

But, were we, in entering afresh upon our employment, to look no farther than to the improvement of any particular classes, even though they be Ministers, our view would be entirely too confined. We look to the advancement of the religious interests of the denomination, and of the world. We wish to perform our humble part in diffusing abroad truth and righteousness in the earth,—in bringing to pass that glorious era, when none shall have cause to say to his neighbor, "know thou the Lord," but when all, from the least to the greatest, shall know him, whom to know, is eternal life.

THE
BAPTIST PREACHER.

| VOL. III. | February, 1844. | NO. 2. |

THE IMMUTABILITY OF GOD:

A Sermon, delivered at the Meeting of the General Association, in Richmond, June, 1843, by Rev. W. Southwood, *of the County of King & Queen, Va.*

———

"*I am the Lord, I change not; therefore ye sons of Jacob are not consumed.*" Malachi, iii: 6.

———

"Whatsoever God does in the world, he does it as suitable to the highest goodness; the idea and fairest copy of which is his own essence."
Cudworth.

"The transition from a partial exhibition of truth to the adoption of positive error is a most natural one: and he who commences with consigning certain important doctrines to oblivion, will generally end in perverting or denying them." R. Hall.

Every created object which passes before us, and challenges our contemplation as it passes, has the marks of mutability upon it. Do we press the yielding sand, or strike the rock of adamant, and enquire for immutability? The answer is, It is not in me. In every direction, in things animate and things inanimate; in the physical and the intellectual world; we meet with evidences of mutability. The earth and the heavens shall perish, all of them shall wax old as a garment, and as a vesture they shall be folded up and changed. * He who made all things, and who governs all things, is alone immutable, and this we know from his word, which he hath magnified above all his name. † His wisdom and his power are discovered in creation, but revelation was necessary to make known to us the immutability of God. And it is no small consolation to the people of God to know that revelation is made with a special reference to them. Indeed all things are for their sake, ‡ and whether it be creation or revelation they have

---

* Heb. i: 11--12.   † Ps. cxxxviii: 2.   ‡ 2 Cor. iv: 15.
3—Vol. 3.

an interest in all, because they have an interest in Christ through precious faith. All things, says the Apostle, are yours; whether Paul, or Apollos, or Cephas, or the world, or life, or death, or things present, or things to come; all are yours, and ye are Christ's, and Christ is God's. *

That there is an Almighty Being, the light of nature will teach us, and that he made and governs the world, the heathen in all ages have acknowledged; but unassisted reason has drawn sentiments of the Deity from his power and vengeance, and men in their blind attempts to propitiate him have shown that their wisdom is folly, † and that their tender mercies are cruel. Revelation has been given to exalt our reason, to place man upon an eminence, where, in the province of faith, the Almighty might be surrounded by a brightness and a grandeur which the light of nature could not bestow.

The immutability of Jehovah is an attribute of the most exalted nature, and of the purest excellence. In a peculiar manner it distinguishes him from all the creatures that he hath made. Man, his fairest work, fell, because he was mutable; the angels, who kept not their first estate were mutable, ‡ and those who remained faithful stood, not by their own power but because they were elect, ‖ and because they were sustained by him who had chosen them; whose prerogative it is, to be the same, yesterday, to-day, and for ever. §

That the works of God, without his word, cannot sufficiently inform our minds of the unchangeableness of God is clear from this circumstance,—all his works are ordained to mutability. The heavens declare the glory of God, and the firmament showeth his handi-works; ¶ but soon, the heavens shall be rolled together as a scroll, the elements shall melt with fervent heat, the world, and all that is therein, shall be burnt up. ** Then shall the sun start from his place, and the stars shall fall like falling leaves from off a fig-tree: †† then shall the hills melt like wax before the presence of the Lord, ‡‡ and the mountains flee from their stations like chaff before the wind, and like a rolling thing before the whirlwind: ‖‖ then it shall appear, that, all flesh is grass, and all the glory of man as the flower of the field, the grass withereth, and the flower thereof falleth away, but the word of the Lord endureth for ever; and this is the word, which by the Gospel is preached unto you. §§

Jehovah's immutability is the ground of security to the Church of God. He who is unchangeable in his nature is unchangeable in his purposes, and unchangeable in his covenant promises in Christ, to a thousand generations. ¶¶   Though

---

* 1 Cor. iii: 21, 22, 23.   † Rom. i: 22.   ‡ Prov. xii: 10.   ‖ Jude, 6.
§ 1 Tim. v: 21.   ¶ Heb. xiii: 8.   ** Ps. xix: 4.   †† 1 Pet. iii: 10.
‡‡ Isa. xxxiv: ‖‖ Ps. xcvii: 5.   §§ Isa. xvii: 13.   ¶¶ 1 Pet. i: 24, 25.

worldly policy may sneer at such expressions, it is to be feared that the same philosophy, falsely so called, will lead to the denial that one being or essence subsists in three distinct persons, Father, Son and Holy Ghost, who are co-eternal and co-equal in all the properties and perfections of the Godhead; or, at least, to the keeping back of such truths of the Bible, as too antiquated for the popular taste, till on their revival, for revived they must be, they will be so far forgotten that, like the philosophers at Athens, christian congregations will say—May we know what this new doctrine, whereof thou speakest, is? for thou bringest strange things to our ears: we would know therefore what these things mean. *

The visible Church, is, in the context, represented as degenerate and rebellious, and the true children of God among them were not guiltless. But while the Lord says to the formalists, I will come near to you in judgment, and I will be a swift witness against the sorcerers, and against the adulterers, and against the false swearers, and against those that oppress the hireling in his wages, the widow and the fatherless, and turn aside the stranger from his right, and fear not me saith the Lord of hosts, verse 5, he adds for the comfort of true believers the words of our text, *For I am the Lord, I change not; therefore ye sons of Jacob are not consumed.*

For our general instruction, and for the true believer's consolation, let us consider,

I. Those things in which Jehovah shews his immutability:—

II. What advantages result from it to his people:—and

III. Make some reflections which seem naturally to arise from the subject. We are to notice,

First,—Those things in which Jehovah shews his immutability.

And here I would premise that this attribute is common to all the persons of the trinity. As we proceed we shall discover that all those acts of God's grace and love towards his Church come to us entirely through the everlasting covenant in which God the Father, Son, and Holy Ghost are equally engaged. Indeed we can never look at the word, or the acts of God's grace aright, but as we see them in this covenant.† This is the only way to secure a fixedness of attention on Christ, and here he appears gloriously. He is called, The covenant, for he was given as a covenant for his people. ‡ In all God's dealings with us, he acts in and by Christ; and we can only come to God, and behold him in that same way as he is given. ‖ Vague ideas of Christ such as we often hear uttered, in the words—" Our Savior" will do the soul no good. It was such a view of Christ as the Spirit taught which led David, in his last days, when to all believers a correct view of Christ is peculiarly endearing, to lay fast hold on the

---

* Acts xvii: 18, 19, 20.   † Heb. viii: 6.   ‡ Isa. xlii: 6.   ‖ Col. ii: 2, 3.

covenant, and say, This is all my salvation and all my desire. *
And who is there that knows the value of Christ, and has tasted
of his love—who that has a living faith, which triumphs in
Christ, that does not see his election, his calling, his sanctification,
his redemption, and his glorification in this covenant! †

The immutability of God enters so much into all things which
refer to the Lord's dealings with his saints, and into the Christian's
experience, that the mind may dwell on it with the deepest interest
—with increased satisfaction and delight.   Observe,

1. The immutability of his being and essence. He is designed
to be the object of our contemplation in this respect; for when he
commissioned Moses to bring the children of Israel out of Egypt,
and his servant enquired by what name he should make him
known, he replied, I AM, THAT I AM. ‡ I am what I will
be, and I will be what I am. He is an unchangeable being in
himself; he is now, and he will be for ever what he was from the
beginning, the God of Abraham, of Isaac, and of Jacob; the God
of all the families of the earth : the blessed God, in whom those
families are blessed. ‖

I know not, my brethren, in what light this may appear to
you, but I must confess, that to me it is full of all wisdom and
comfort.   It shows the immoveableness of that foundation on
which poor sinners are invited to build their hopes, and the certain duration of all those things which relate to the consummation
of the Christian's happiness and eternal glory; for if our God be
unchangeable in his *being and essence,* he is so "in all his essential properties, his wisdom, his power, his holiness, his omniscience, his all-sufficiency, his love." Here then let us take our
stand, and embrace this unchangeable God as ours.

2. We view God as unchangeable, also, in his decrees.

Ungodly men have not the Lord in all their thoughts. § They
say, Tush, God considereth not, neither is there knowledge in the
most High. ¶   These shew their worldly wisdom by taking
counsel together, by forming themselves into confederacies, and
even against the most High; ** yet they imagine, that the events
of God's great empire are under the influence of fortuitous circumstances,—that all things in this world are guided by chance.
But God sitteth in the heavens, the most high ruleth over all. ††
He declareth his decrees. He saith, his counsels of old are
faithfulness and truth. ‡‡   And the Apostle affirms, He worketh
all things after the counsel of his own will. ‖‖   Hence we learn
that the persons in Jehovah did, as it were, sit in council from the
beginning, and determine absolutely, irrespective of any cause but
his own will, and his own glory, whatever should be, unto the

---

* 2 Sam. xxiii: 5.   † 1 Cor. i: 30.   ‡ Exod. iii: 14.   ‖ Jer. xxxi: 1:
§ Ps. x: 4.   ¶ Ps. lxxiii: 11.   ** Ps. ii: 2.   †† Ps. ciii: 19.   ‡‡ Isa. xxv: 1:
‖‖ Eph. i: 11.

praise and glory of his grace. * All the creatures of his power, angels and men, and whatever should be on the earth, above the earth, and beneath the earth,—the defection of angels and men, the final ruin of the former, † and the redemption of the latter: ‡ the existence, election, and salvation of his Church, and the condemnation and ruin of his enemies;—all these appeared, as in one point, before his view, with all those contingent circumstances that should happen in any connection with them; and these received their unchangeable confirmation by one single act of his will, whereby all things relating to all created beings were determined and settled from eternity to eternity. In reference to this, God hath said, My counsel shall stand, and I will do all my pleasure: ‖ and in relation to this it is also added: Wherein God willing more abundantly to shew unto the heirs of promise the immutability of his counsel confirmed it by an oath: that by two immutable things, in which it was impossible for God to lie, we might have strong consolation, who have fled for refuge to lay hold upon the hope set before us.§

Human wisdom may despise the idea of the divine decrees taking an account of the peculiar circumstances of individual creatures, and providing resources for sinners of mankind. But if God hath made all things for himself, ¶ and for his own glory; and if his glory is most conspicuously set forth in the work of redemption, in which work is called forth the exercise of all the divine attributes, and of such qualities of the Godhead, as were not displayed, either in the creation or preservation of all things; one may well imagine that the divine decrees were worthily occupied in ordaining and carrying on the interests of the Church of God, as well as in forwarding the real benefit of every individual of that Church.

It may indeed be asserted, without "bigoted arrogance," that the concerns of the saints are always the primary objects of the divine regard. If God hath formed his counsels—if he hath declared his decree,—what can be the subject of that council, and what the object of that decree? Is it the solar system—the operations of nature—the regularity of the heavenly bodies in all the universe? Why these are guided by one regular and unchangeable law. Since time first sprang from the bosom of eternity, the sun hath always risen in his place, and hath gone down at his appointed time. ** If to deluge the earth with a flood of waters, the windows from on high have been opened, and the fountains of the great deep broken up, †† yet, when those waters have subsided, the same sun hath shone in the firmament, and the same dry land hath appeared; yea, and God hath sworn by the ordinances of heaven, that the waters

---

* Zech. vi: 13. † Eph. i: 6. ‡ Jude 6. ‖ John iii: 16. § Isa. xlvi: 10. ¶ Heb. vi: 17–18. ** Prov. xvi: 4. Eccl. i: 5. Ps. civ: 19.

should no more go over the earth. * If, for the avenging of Israel, the rays of the sun have not departed from the hemisphere for about a whole day, † yet, at the end of another day, darkness has drawn her sable mantle over the heavens, and day and night have not ceased. The decree which God hath declared for universal nature is, that, as they were made in the beginning, so they shall continue, till the moon shall for ever withdraw itself, and till the sun shall be put out in obscure darkness. ‡

Neither are we to consider God's *decrees* as wholly, or even principally designed to subserve the interests, or to fix the destinies of nations. It is true, he appoints the limits of kingdoms, and determines the duration of empires; he sets up rulers and he puts down the mighty from their seats: he says to the sea, Be dry; and to the waves of the ocean, hitherto shalt thou go, and no farther; ‖ but the bounds of the sea, and the limits of mighty states, and the continuance of the nations, are all decreed to promote the welfare of that kingdom which is an everlasting kingdom, of that dominion which endureth throughout all generations. § Hence, the great image which Nebuchadnezzer saw in his dream, and which depicted the four great monarchies, that should continue in succession, was smitten by the stone,—an emblem of Christ's kingdom, cut out of the mountain without hands so that the iron, the clay, the brass, the silver and the gold were broken in pieces together, and became like the chaff of the summer threshing-floor, and the wind carried them away, so that there was no more place for them, and the stone which smote the image became a great mountain, and filled the whole earth. ¶

What, then, is the subject of these decrees? In the second Psalm, the God-man Christ himself, says, I will declare it. The Lord hath said unto me, Thou art my Son, to-day have I begotten thee. Ask of me, and I will give thee the heathen for thine inheritance, and the uttermost parts of the earth for thy possession. But, behold, these are all by nature in subjection to satan,—by nature they are children of wrath ** Of themselves they will no more turn and seek God, than the Ethiopian change his skin, or the leopard his spots. †† When brought to the knowledge of God, there is in them a law in the members, warring against the law of their minds. ‡‡ They are called to fight against enemies within, and enemies without, ‖‖ and are subject to changes perpetually. The changeable state of the Church then, requires the interposition of the divine decrees; the fearful state of the members of it demands them: and, were it not that the decree is passed, that it is established, and that it remaineth as the faithful witness in heaven, §§ the Church would be blotted out from the world's history and every member would perish. But the foun-

* Gen vii: 11.   † Gen. ix: 14–17.   ‡ Josh. x: 13.   ‖ Gen. viii: 22.
§ Isa. xliv: 27. Jer. v: 22.   ¶ Ps. cxlv: 13.   ** Dan. ii: 34–35.
†† Eph. ii: 3. ‡‡ Ger. xiii: 23. ‖‖ Rom. vii: 23. §§ Cor. vii: 5.

dation of the Lord standeth sure: the Lord knoweth them that are his. * And of all that the Father hath given to Christ he will lose none.† So, then, God's decrees concern those things which, in themselves, are governed by no law of nature, which, in themselves, are subject to change, and which can attain no fixedness but in the divine *fiat*; for God's immutable decree is that he has given his Church to Christ, that all the members of that Church God hath chosen in Christ before the foundation of the world, that they should be holy, and without blame before him in love, having predestinated them unto the adoption of children, by Jesus Christ according to the good pleasure of his will.‡ And that every poor sinner, who hears the sound of the Gospel may hope in God—may not imagine, that pardon, and peace, and salvation, are blessings too high for him to aspire after; it has been absolutely declared, that God hath confirmed his counsel with an oath that they may have strong consolation who have fled for refuge, ‖ to Jesus Christ.

Let none say—The favor of God is not for me!—If you know your need of it—if you feel its value, it is for such as you! it is for you!   And a bright clause in the covenant of grace is, that none are cast out who come to God by Jesus Christ. § Come in, thou blessed of the Lord: wherefore standest thou without? ¶ Thousands have heard the invitation, obeyed the call, have entered into heaven, and, yet there is room. **

3. God is unchangeable in his loving-kindness to his people. If Jehovah hath decreed all things relative and subservient to his Church, the members of that Church ever have been, and ever must be the objects of his unchanging love. See the message concerning the blessings of the New Covenant opened in these memorable words, I have loved thee with an everlasting love, and therefore with lovingkindness have I drawn thee. †† God is unchangeable in his covenant and promise, for they are made in Christ, with his people. It is a covenant of peace, and of grace, and of love; it is founded upon grace; it is full of grace; it is made up of grace from first to last; and therefore is called GRACE. In this covenant are secured to the believer, peace, pardon, justification, and salvation: here he is unchangeably united to a gracious Father, a loving Savior, a divine Teacher: here, for him are laid up blessings in heaven for ever. Hence God says of his Church, I will make an everlasting covenant with them, and I will not turn away from them to do them good. ‡‡ Again, Hear, and your soul shall live; for I will make an everlasting covenant with you, even the sure mercies of David. ‖‖ Again, This is as the waters of Noah unto me; for as I have sworn that the waters of Noah shall no more go over the earth, so have I sworn that I

---

* 2 Tim. ii: 19.   † John xvii: 6.   ‡ Eph. i: 4–5.   ‖ Heb. vi: 18.
§ John. vi: 37.   ¶ Gen. xxix: 31.   ** Luke xiv: 27.   †† Jer. xxxi: 3.
‡‡ Jer. xxxii: 40.   ‖‖ Isa. lv: 3.

will no more be wroth with thee, nor rebuke thee. For the mountains shall depart, and the hills be removed, but my kindness shall not depart from thee, neither shall the covenant of my peace be removed, saith the Lord that hath mercy on thee. *

But may not his people sin against him and forfeit their claims to his favors? They do sin, for there is no man that sinneth not, but yet this shall not break God's covenant; this shall not alter his decree. If his children forsake my law, and walk not in my judgments, if they break my statutes and keep not my commandments; then will I visit their transgression with a rod, and their iniquities with stripes. Nevertheless my lovingkindness I will not utterly take from him, nor suffer my faithfulness to fail. My covenant will I not break, nor alter the thing that is gone out of my lips: once have I sworn by my holiness, that I will not lie unto David. † We sin, and God chastises us because of it, and for our benefit; but still his covenant remains firm and unchangeable. Is not his covenant sealed with blood? And the promises made on the ground and credit of that blood, are all yea and amen in Christ Jesus. ‡ O, what a delightful reflection, that God engages to bring all his people to glory, and to make all needful provision for them by the way. ‖ He not only engages to do all for them, but likewise all in them, so that they may be accounted worthy of his love, being clothed in Christ's righteousness, and renovated by the Spirit's power. For this daughter which the great King hath formed for his own glory, § is not only clothed in wrought gold, but is also all glorious within. ¶ And whether it be the whole Church collectively, or believers individually, nothing for their real interest and happiness here and hereafter shall be wanting.

The triumphant language of the Apostle respecting the unchanging love of God to his saints shall close this head of my discourse. Who shall separate us from the love of God; shall ribulation, or distress, or persecution, or famine, or nakedness, or peril, or the sword? Nay, in all these things we are more than conquerors through him that hath loved us: for I am persuaded, that neither death, nor life, nor angels, nor principalities, nor powers, nor things present, nor things to come, nor height, nor depth, nor any other creature, shall be able to separate us from the love of God, which is in Christ Jesus our Lord. **

II. We are to enquire what advantages result from this attribute of Jehovah to God's people. *Therefore ye sons of Jacob are not consumed.*

Jacob is the supplanter. †† By the immutable decree of God, Jacob had the birthright. Before he was born, God had said, Jacob have I loved; ‡‡ even then it was decreed, the elder shall

---

* Is. liv: 9–10.   † Ps. lxxxix: 30, 35.   ‡ 2 Cor. i: 20.   ‖ Phil. iv: 19.
§ Isa. xliii: 21.   ¶ Ps. xlv: 13.   ** Rom. viii: 35, 39.   †† Gen. xxvii: 36.
‡‡ Rom. ix: 13

serve the younger. * Jacob was the father of the patriarchs, the head of the tribes of Israel; and every object of God's election, every subject of his free grace, and unchanging love, is denominated a son of Jacob.

Let us pause and enquire, are we of this number? They are not all Israel that are of Israel. The children of the promise are counted for the seed. † Have you chosen God for your God? Have you valued the birthright with Jacob? Have you been willing to lay hold on God's covenant? Have you declared yourself on the Lord's side? Have you been born of God—have you overcome the world? Do you follow Christ? Then are ye the sons of Jacob:—then, because Jehovah changes not, *ye are not consumed.*

1. Ye are not consumed with eternal destruction. The sons of Jacob come into the world like others deserving wrath and eternal damnation. Their original corruption renders them subject to death and hell; their actual transgressions prove them individually guilty, and obnoxious to divine wrath; and it is only the unchangeableness of God that has rescued them from deserved judgments. O Christians! feel this truth, and adore that grace, in consequence of which ye are out of hell. Look back on your past course—consider your present conduct—contemplate the future! What were you doing *before you knew God?* Corrupt and abominable, ye committed iniquity with greediness, though perhaps with a fair shew in the flesh. But with what uncleanness were you not stained? Look at the long black catalogue of crimes which have been perpetrated by the lost in hell, and say of which you were innocent? Methinks I hear you say, guilty, guilty; unclean, unclean; yet, you are not consumed. Trace your conduct since you returned to him, from whom you had deeply revolted: had not your heart gone back again? have you not said, I will go after my lovers who gave me my corn, and my wine, and my flax, and my wool? ‡ You have presumed on God's electing love, on his mercy, on his forbearance, on his long-suffering; and this broken staff, has, perhaps, been bound round with a negative, or positive righteousness of your own vain imagination, so that your aggravations since you have known him, have been greater than they were before you knew him. And leaning on some broken reed of Egypt not merely your hand but your soul was pierced. ‖ Think of yourself *now:* your daily forgetfulness, your continual short comings, your misimprovement of talents, your perpetual variableness in all your affections towards God. One hour your heart flames with love to Christ; the next 'tis cold as death. Now you are full of holy desires after Christ, his grace, his glory; and can say, The desire of my soul is to the remembrance of thy name; § but soon there is not one holy

---

* Gen. xxv: 23. † Rom. ix: 8. ‡ Hos. ii: 5. ‖ Isa. **xxxvi: 6.** § Isa. **xxvi: 8.**

breathing in you. To day you delight in God's ways, and have the Holy Spirit within you, leading you to say, Oh how I love thy law; * but to-morrow, and you find no sweetness in one, and no pleasure in the other; you drive on heavily; every duty becomes a burden; and every thought of God oppresses. Now you dread to sin; anon you forget that God seeth you. One, moment you buckle on the armour for the heavenly warfare; but the first temptation carries you away, and you start aside like a broken bow. How frequently do you fall from love to coldness; from faith to unbelief; from holy fear to carnal security; from obedience to rebellion; from delight in God, to neglect of him! And what shall we say of the future? Will it be better with you in future, than it has been in times past? Will you be stronger, holier, more watchful and prayerful, in times to come? Alas! if your salvation depend on this, you are lost for ever. *I am the Lord, I change not.* This is the cause, and shall ever be the only cause why you are not consumed.

2. Ye are not consumed in temporal ruin, nor under present trials. God's love to his saints is the great security both to the Church and to the world. Many a nation hath been delivered for the sake of the righteous that were therein; and so with smaller communities, God said to Abraham, If there be ten righteous in Sodom, I will spare the city for their sake. ‡ And though judgments come upon a people, and all feel the scourge yet the command of the Lord is, Say ye to the righteous, it shall be well with him: ‖ not one hair of their head shall perish. §

3. The sons of Jacob are not consumed with fear, that God should take away his love from them; for he changeth not.

Doth God always act towards his people according to a settled rule? He often changes in his *dispensations,* but never in his *disposition.* His love is some times vailed, but it does not vary; it is sometimes clouded, but never changed. Love under a cloud is still love. The material sun may be eclipsed for a season, but it is still the sun; and though it may be hidden from us many successive days, it does not lose a beam of its light, or a ray of its splendor: when the interposing obstacle is removed, it shines as cheeringly and gloriously as ever. God's anger endureth but a moment; in his favor is life; weeping may endure for a night, but joy cometh in the morning.¶ Who that feels this will not join with the Psalmist, and say, How excellent is thy loving-kindness, O God, therefore shall the children of men put their trust under the shadow of thy wings. ** This loving-kindness is better than life. †† it is to be preferred before many worlds of creature comforts. God's love is all good, all comfort, all happiness; in its fountain, fulness and purity, it is an eternal, never-failing spring

---

* Ps. cxix: 97.   † Hos. vii: 16.   ‡ Gen. xviii: 32.   ‖ Isa. iii: 10.
§ Luk. xxi: 18.   ¶ Ps. xxx: 5.   ** Ps. xxxvi: 7.   †† Ps. lxiii: 3.

of sweetness; an unvariable fountain of delight: in it there is grace, all grace; peace, all peace; joy, all joy; satisfaction, all satisfaction; rest and solace, all rest and solace. O believer! look upon the love of God to you; look, upon it, and in it you will find unsearchable riches, unmeasurable fulness, unfathomable depths; and, which crowns all, eternal unchangeableness. Friends change, comforts change, I myself change, but God's love to me changes not; the believer is for ever in his heart, nor can men or devils cast him out. He sometimes afflicts his children, but never ceases to love them; he sometimes breaks them with breach upon breach;* but yet he loves them. Notwithstanding my sins, which he hates, he loves me; and after a while, in the best time, because his time, I shall bathe in the fountain of his love, and never sin again. Oh! who would not long for this love! He loves his own unchangeably, he pardons, he purifies he makes perfectly holy. A little while, and, however feeble, yet if a child of God, you shall be brought into his presence, and lodged in his bosom.

III. We are to make some reflections which seem naturally to arise from the subject.

1. Believers may rest in his love. God hath made it over to them, in consideration of what Christ hath done, when he was aware they never had deserved it, and never could. Nay, he says, I knew thou wouldest deal very treacherously, and wast called a transgressor from the womb; nevertheless, for mine own sake have I done it; for how should my holy name be blasphemed. †

They may rest in his love, because they have chosen him to be their God. They have joined with Jesus in his covenant, and laid hold on him, and said, We have trusted in thee, O Lord; and in thy word thou hast caused us to hope: ‡ and then he assures them, that he will never turn away from them to do them good. ‖

They rest in his love, because he rests on them. The Lord hath chosen Zion, he hath desired it for his habitation; this is my rest for ever, here will I dwell for I have desired it. § Oh with what confidence may the soul repose in God, when it sees that God delights in his people for Christ's sake! They stand complete in him; in his beauty, in his righteousness, in his completeness: and as he views his own handy-works he says, Behold thou art all fair, my love, there is no spot in thee. ¶

2. We may feel a calm security in that love. Sometimes unbelief may suggest, What though God changes not, I may change from my present purpose; and my interest in him may change. That cannot be. This God is our God for ever and ever. ** "The chief good," says Austin, "which is God, is

---

* Job xvi: 14.   † Isa xlviii: 8, 11.   ‡ Ps. cxix: 49.   ‖ Jer. xxxii: 40.
§ Ps. cxxxii: 13-14.   ¶ Cant. iv: 7.   ** Ps: xlviii: 14.

neither given to such as are unwilling to have him, nor taken away from such as are unwilling to part with him:". and again, "No man does or can lose thee, O God, unless that he is willing to lose thee, and go without thee." O my soul, as long as thou art willing to have God thine, so long he will be thine; yea, more; thine interest in him depends not upon thy willingness of it, but upon his unchangeable love and covenant: and his love and covenant both must change, before thy willingness to cleave to him, and thine interest in him can change.

3. Christians should aim to be followers of God, and to be as steadily fixed in their love towards him, as he is in his love towards them.

Be ye followers of God as dear children. * Be ye imitators of him. Is he unchangeable? Labor after a holy unchangeableness in your spirits, and walkings before him. Christians, whereto ye have already attained, walk by the same rule, and mind the same things. † Seek after, and pray for more fixedness and evenness in your spiritual temper; more consistency and uniformity in all grace and holiness, in all heavenly-mindedness and spiritual obedience; and more uniform perseverance in all acts of duty, and walking with God. It is a great thing to be established, strengthened and settled ‡ in God. Do you begin every day with the enquiry, where is my master Jesus? where is Christ my beloved one? Commence nothing without him. Go not into the world without him as thy companion. Never be seen separate from him! The Father says to Christ, Lift up thine eyes round about, and behold: all these gather themselves together and come to thee: as I live saith the Lord, thou shalt surely clothe thee with them all, as with an ornament, and bind them on thee as a bride doth. ‖ Be thou, Christian, to him as a girdle; then thou shalt partake of his Spirit, and have communion with him for thine abiding consolation.

4. We should be humbled for our changeableness. We live, it is to be feared, more upon the creature than upon God; hence our perpetual changes. We are often happy as we are happy in the creature, and sorrowful, as comfort fails in the creature. We know that every thing but God is empty; that we may take the finger and write vanity of vanities, upon every creature comfort. § We know that God is the only good, and yet we commit two evils, we forsake the fountain of living waters, and hew out to ourselves broken cisterns, that can hold no water. Alas! we drink impure water from many a cistern, when we might have the wine of life dropping from the precious cluster. Let us be humbled for these things, and praise God again for his immutability, who supplies all our need, according to his riches in glory by Christ Jesus. ¶

---

*Eph. v: 1.   † Phil. iii: 16.   ‡ 1 Pet. v: 10.   ‖ Isa. xlix: 18.
§ Eccl. i: 2.   ¶ Phil. iv: 19

5. We may infer from God's unchangeableness, the absolute necessity of a change in sinners. Man is by nature so unlike God, that if he be saved at all, and made eternally happy, there must be a change either in God, or in him. But there can be no change in God; therefore it must be in man. The word of God declares, that Jesus came to save his people from their sins: * that the wicked shall be turned into hell, and all the people that forget God; † that into heaven nothing can enter that defiles: ‡ that without holiness no man shall see the Lord. ‖ So all the Scriptures must be falsified, if man can be eternally happy without a change of heart.

The nature of God forbids it. He hath no pleasure in sin. It is what he hates. What fellowship hath light with darkness? The foolish shall not stand in his sight; he hates all workers of iniquity. § God can as soon cease to exist as cease to be holy; so an unchanged sinner can no more enter heaven than God be absent from it, or cease to exist.

His whole scheme of salvation requires it. Whom he did foreknow, he did predestinate to be conformed to the image of his Son; ¶ and without this, the soul is not justified, cannot be glorified. To enter heaven the soul must be changed; must be justified freely by grace through the redemption that is in Christ; ** and must be renewed by the Holy Ghost. Sinner you have not this change. Hitherto you have sought peace where peace cannot be found. You have sought the living among the dead. †† O seek to God for this divine change; and then being changed into his image, thou shalt enjoy his favor, and see him as he is. ‡‡

6. Lastly, we infer from hence, God's unchangeableness in his punishment of incorrigible sinners, those who reject the only Savior. The unchangeable promises, and the unchangeable threatenings, both come from the lips of him that cannot lie. ‖‖ His love is not more sweet than his wrath is bitter. His love is not more to be desired than his wrath is to be dreaded: and what must be your condition, sinner, if you fall under it? You are now often afraid of the wrath of man; but, who art thou, that thou shoudest be afraid of a man, that shall die, and the son of man which shall be made as grass and forgettest the Lord thy Maker? §§ A little while and man's wrath shall die, but the wrath of God abideth for ever. Foolish creature that despisest God's wrath, as if it were but an inconsiderable thing: hence thy wilful, daily provokings of his anger, and thy unconcern at the tokens of his wrath: hence thy neglect of Christ and his salvation; thy contempt, both of his hatred and of his love. You will sigh and groan upon a dying bed, though surrounded by friends

* Mark i: 21. † Ps. ix: 17. ‡ Rev. xxi: 27. ‖ Heb. xii: 14. § Ps. v: 4, 5.
¶ Rom. viii: 29. ** Rom. iii: 24. †† Luk. xxiv: 5. ‡‡ 1 John. iii: 2,
‖‖ Tit. i: 2. §§ Isa. li: 12, 13,

and the prayers of good men uttered in your hearing, and the invitations of mercy still calling you to the refuge: but what will you feel when pierced by those intolerable torments which make devils tremble?

The days are coming, when sinners in Zion shall be afraid, and fearfulness shall surprise the hypocrite;* when the hardiest sinners as they receive their sentence at the bar of God, as they turn their distracted eyes towards the dread abyss, shall cry out in the language of unutterable despair, Who among us can dwell in devouring fire; who can dwell with everlasting burnings? When the great day of his wrath is come none shall be able to abide it. †

O, sinners! seek for refuge, not in the rocks, on that day, when they shall flee away; but *now*, in the Rock of Ages. ‡ Flee for your life, look not behind you, neither stay ye in all the plain: flee to this mountain, lest ye die. **Amen.**

Note.—It has been said, that there cannot be any reason or motive to pray, or make any petition, to an *unchangeable God*, whose design cannot be altered, and who has fixed all events, without a possibility of any change.

Before any attempt is made to remove this objection, and supposed difficulty, it must be observed, that it equally lies against the *foreknowledge of God*. For if God certainly foreknows every thing that will take place, then every event is fixed and certain, otherwise it could not be foreknown. "Known unto God are all his works from the beginning of the world." He has determined, and passed an unchangeable decree, with respect to all that he will do to eternity. Upon the plan of the objection under consideration, it may be asked, What reason or motive can any one have to ask God to do any thing for him, or any one else, since he infallibly knows from the beginning what he will do, and therefore it is unalterably fixed? Therefore if it be reasonable to pray to an *omniscient* God, it is equally reasonable to pray to an *unchangeable* God. For the former necessarily implies the latter. But in order to show that the objection is without foundation, the following things must be observed.

1. If God were not omniscient and unchangeable, and had not foreordained whatsoever comes to pass, he would not be the proper object of worship, and there would be no foundation, reason, or encouragement to make any petition to him.

This, it is presumed, will be evident to any one who will well consider the following observations.

First. If there were no unchangeable, omniscient Being, there would be no God, no proper object of worship. A being who is capable of change, is necessarily imperfect, and may change from

---

*Isa. xxxiii: 14.   † Rev. vi: 17.   ‡ Mat. xvi: 18.

bad to worse, and even cease to exist, and therefore could not be trusted. If we could know that such a being has existed, and that he was once wise, and good, and powerful, we could have no, evidence that he would continue to be wise or good, or that he is so now, or that he is now disposed to pay any regard to our petitions, or is either willing or able to grant them; or even that he has any existence. What reason or encouragement then can there be to pray to a changeable being? Surely none at all. Therefore, if there be no reason to pray to an *unchangeable God*, there can be no reason to pray at all.

Secondly. If God be infinitely wise, and good, and omnipotent, supreme and independent; then he certainly is unchangeable, and has foreordained whatsoever comes to pass. This has been proved above, or rather is self-evident. But if he be not infinitely wise and good, &c. then he cannot be trusted; he cannot be the object of that trust and confidence which is implied, and even expressed, in praying to him.

Thirdly. The truly pious, benevolent, devout man would not desire, or even *dare*, to pray to God for any thing, if he were changeable, and disposed to alter his purpose and plan, in order to grant his petitions. Therefore he never does pray to any but an *unchangeable God*, whose counsel stands forever, and the thoughts of his heart to all generations. He is sensible that he is a very imperfect creature; that his heart, his will, is awfully depraved and sinful; that he knows not what is wisest and best to be done in any one instance; what is best for him, for mankind in general, for the world, or for the universe; what is most for the glory of God, and the greatest general good; and that it would be infinitely undesirable and dreadful to have his own will regarded so as to govern in determining what shall be done for him or any other being, or what shall take place. If it could be left to him to determine in the least instance, he would not dare to do it, but would refer it back to God, and say, " Not *my will* but ' *thine* be done." But he could not do this, unless he were *certain* that the will of God was unchangeably wise and good, and that he had decreed to do what was most for his own glory, and the greatest good of the whole; at the same time infallibly knowing what must take place, in every instance, in order to answer this end; consequently must have fixed upon the most wise and best plan, foreordaining whatsoever comes to pass. Therefore, whatever be his petitions for himself, or for others, he offers them to God, and asks *on this condition*, always either expressed or implied, *If it be agreeable to thy will*: for *otherwise* he would not have his petitions granted, if it were possible. And he who asks any thing of God, without making this condition, but sets up his own will, and desires to have it granted, whether it be for the glory of God, and the greatest good of his kingdom, or not; and would, were it in his power, compel his Maker to grant his petition, and bow the will of God to his own will; he who prays to God with such a disposition, is an impious enemy to God, exercises no true devotion, and cannot be heard; and it is desirable to all the friends of God that he should be rejected. Resignation to the will of God always supposes his will is unchangeably fixed and established, which it could not be, unless he has foreordained whatsoever comes to pass.

Thus it appears that if God were changeable, and had not foreordained whatsoever comes to pass, there would be no foundation for religious worship, or reason for praying to him; or that there can be no reason or encouragement for prayer and petition to any but an *unchangeable* God.—I preceed to observe,

2. There is good reason, and all desirable and possible encouragement, to pray to an unchangeable God, who has from eternity determined what he will do, in every instance, and has foreordained whatsoever comes to pass.

This will doubtless be evident to him, who will duly consider the following particulars.

First. Prayer is as proper, important, and necessary, in order to obtain favour from an unchangeable God, as it could be were he changeable, and had not foreordained any thing.

Means are as necessary in order to obtain the end, as if nothing were fixed and certain. Though it was decreed that Paul and all the men in the ship should get safe to land, when they were in a storm at sea; yet this must be accomplished by means, and unless the sailors had assisted in managing the ship, this event could not take place, and they could not be saved. Prayer is a means of obtaining what God has determined to grant; for he has determined to give it in answer to prayer, and no other way. "Ask and ye shall receive," says our Savior. When God had promised to do many and great things for Israel, he adds, "Thus saith the Lord God, I will yet for this be inquired of by the house of Israel, to do it for them:" [*Ezek.* xxxvi: 37.] The granting the favors, which God had determined to bestow, was as much suspended on their asking for them, as if there had been nothing determined and fixed about it. There is as much regard had to prayer in granting favors, and the prayer is heard, and God gives them, as really and as much in answer to it, as if there were nothing determined and foreordained respecting them: for the decree includes and fixes the means, as much as the end; the method and way by which events are to take place, as much as those events themselves. The one depends on the other, as much as if there were no decree, and nothing fixed; yea, much more: for the decree *fixes* the dependence and connexion between the means and the end: whereas if there were no decree, and nothing fixed, there would be no established connexion, but all would be uncertain, and there would be no reason or encouragement to use means, or do any thing to obtain an end.—*Hopkins's Sermons.*

THE
BAPTIST PREACHER.

VOL. III.　　　March, 1844.　　　NO. 3.

CHRISTIAN UNION;

OR, THE EVILS OF DIVISIONS AMONG CHRISTIANS,

The Introductory Sermon, delivered at the Session of the Western Association, at Antioch, Meriwether Co. Ga., September, 1843, by Rev. Robert Fleming, of Newnan, Ga.

—

"Only let your conversation be, as it becometh the Gospel of Christ; that, whether I come and see you, or else be absent, I may hear of your affairs that ye stand fast in one spirit, with one mind, striving together for the faith of the Gospel."—PHILIPPIANS, i: 27.

—

The word "conversation" is of copious import. In the text, it means the whole conduct or manner of life, in the "affairs" of religion, and has direct reference to the doings of Christians; so that "whatsoever they do in word or in deed" they are to "do all in the name" and by the authority "of the Lord Jesus." To do otherwise would not "be as it becometh the gospel of Christ." The dancing school, the ball-room, the theatre, the circus, the party of pleasure on the Sabbath, cannot be attended in the name of the Lord Jesus; and therefore cannot be considered as becoming the gospel. The phrase "faith of the gospel," in the text, means *all the doctrines and ordinances of the gospel.* The Scriptures fully teach what we are to believe concerning God, and what duties He requires. "All Scripture is given by inspiration of God; and is profitable for doctrine, for reproof, for correction, for instruction in righteousness; that the man of God may be perfect, thoroughly furnished unto all good works."*

What lesson of instruction is furnished in our text? It teaches us that the Church of Jesus Christ, is one body, which should be always actuated, by one spirit; and that among the various members of the body, the most perfect harmony ought to be cherished. It furnishes then, the following proposition, which, it will be our business to show, is abundantly supported by the Scriptures,

2 Tim. iii: 16.

5—Vol. 3.

and is of great practical import, viz., that DIVISIONS AMONG
GOD'S PEOPLE ARE UNBECOMING THE GOSPEL OF CHRIST.

   1. *They are inconsistent with the feelings of the truly pious.*
   2. *They are inconsistent with Christ's prayer, in John* xvii.
   3. *They are inconsistent with Apostolic precept.*
   4. *They are inconsistent with the happiness of God's people.*
   5. *They are injurious to the spread of the Gospel in ths world,
and are in no sense a blessing, but an evil.*

   1. *They are inconsistent with the feelings of the truly pious.*

   Love to the brotherhood is an essential attribute of the converted soul. Without it we cannot be christians. "He that saith he
is in the light, and hateth his brother, is in darkness even until
now." "We know that we have passed from death unto life,
because we love the brethren. He that loveth not his brother
abideth in death."* The love of God in the soul is not sectarian. The Bible knows nothing of sects, or parties, or branches
in Christ's Church. Christ is not divided. God has taught us,
in our text, that his people should stand fast in one spirit, with one
mind, striving TOGETHER for the faith of the Gospel. God by
his SPIRIT in the heart of the Christian, has taught him the same
thing. The Word of God dees not point one way, and the spirit-
led heart another. The Apostle says to the Thessalonians, "Ye
yourselves are taught of God to love one another." He says to
the Colossians, "Let the peace of God rule in your hearts, to the
which ye are also called in one body." The call of the Holy
Spirit, we clearly discover by this quotation, brings souls together
in one body. It never drives them asunder. Whatever tends to
separate the Lord's people, is inconsistent with pious feeling, and
is not the work of the Spirit of God upon the heart; it is the work
of the enemy, and no Christian can rejoice in it, or pray for it.
Whatever rends the body of Christ, (his Church,) and sets aside
his holy law by infractions on the UNION of the brotherhood,
must be a source of sorrow to the spiritual worshipper. "Rivers
of water run down mine eyes, because men keep not thy law."
O, that the children of God would lay aside all the dogmas of
sectarianism, abandon all human tradition, and come to the simplicity of the Gospel, resolved to carry out the dictates of holy
feeling! O, that they would come with the heart-gladdening
piety of David, exclaiming, "I am a companion of all them that
fear thee, and of them that keep thy precepts." Why should
they not come? The word says *come*—the spirit says, *come*—the
pious feelings of every Christian heart say, *come*—O why not
come that we may all strive TOGETHER for the faith of the Gospel,
and present one unbroken, formidable front against the powers of
Pagan and Papal darkness? Pious Protestant brethren, ye
whose hearts are imbued with the love of God,—you long to see

---

              *1 Jno. iii. 14.

the Gospel triumphant in all lands. When you have looked at the divided state of Zion, you have sat down and wept. Why do ye not arise in the strength of the Lord your God, and, by a stroke of holy indignation, obliterate every vestige of Papal superstition and idolatry? The entire union of the Church of Christ will accomplish it; but without this union the work is impossible. Deem me not presumptious, or officious, or unkind. There is yet a rallying point, and there is yet hope that the watchmen shall see "eye to eye,"—shall look each other in the face as friends,—yea, sing TOGETHER.—sing without a jar. Yes, "There is one body, and one Spirit, even as ye are called in one hope of your calling; one Lord, one faith, one baptism, one God and Father of all, who is above all, and through all and in you all." * This is the Apostolic standard,—a standard erected by God himself. Let all his children rally to it. You love US, and we love YOU as the "children of a royal line." What would we not do to see "the sacramental host of God's elect," embodied and moving forward under the Captain of their salvation, displaying, as they go on to evangelize the world, THE UNITY AND BEAUTY OF THE GLORIOUS GOSPEL OF THE BLESSED GOD.

2. *Divisions are not becoming the Gospel of Christ, because they are inconsistent with his prayer.*—Jno. xvii.

Christ prayed for his Apostles and Ministers, that *they* all might be one. But he says, "Neither pray I for these alone; but for them also which shall believe on me through their word; that they all may be one,—that the world may believe that thou hast sent me." It is certain that the oneness here prayed for, has special reference to all believers AS BELIEVERS, "*that they all might be incorporated into one body.*" † It must, therefore, mean external oneness, and not internal work, for this has been accomplished in their conversion. Then it is to be such a oneness that the world may see it and believe. Religion is to have an outside, as well as an inside existence. The outside is for the world to behold,—that the world may believe that Jesus is the *sent* of the Father. Christ well knew the weakness and corruption of our nature, and he well understood the evil tendency of divisions among his people. He knew that they would spoil the peace, mar the beauty, and impede the progress of his kingdom in this world.

Many professed Christians in the present day, seem to misunderstand one prominent design of CHRISTIAN UNION, or church organization. They make, it would seem, a public profession of religion, (that is, unite with the Church,) for the purpose of adding somewhat to the security of their soul's salvation. Hence we frequently hear expressions like this; "If such and such things were essential, I would do them." Now this kind of language when analyzed, seems to assert that "*Salvation is of works,*" and

---

* Ephs. iv: 4, 6.   † Henry's Com: page 190, Col. 1.

that the individual will do all the things, (if he can only know what they are,) which may secure for him eternal life. All this sort of sentiment is at war with the doctrine of *"Salvation by grace."* No where in the Bible are we taught that the salvation of the soul rests upon our "works of righteousness which we have done," or may hereafter do. When we have done all, we are to consider ourselves as unprofitable servants. Obedience is not the cause of our salvation, but the evidence of it. "In this the children of God are manifest and the children of the devil."* "Whoso keepeth his word, in him verily the love of God is perfected. Hereby know we that we are in him."†

When Jesus uttered this prayer for his Disciples, they were not regularly embodied in a Church organization. It is true they had believed on him, had imbibed his spirit, and had learned lessons of wisdom at his lips, to prepare them for future usefulness in his cause. In order that they might be successful laborers, he prays that they ALL MIGHT BE ONE, and that those who might believe on him through their word might be one,—that the WORLD might see it and believe. He styled them "the salt of the earth,"—"the light of the world." And he commanded them, "Let your light so shine before men that they may see your good works and glorify your Father which is in heaven." The great object of CHRISTIAN UNION is, that the light of the glorious gospel which has shined into the hearts of men, may be reflected upon this sin-benighted world with a brightness as diffusive as the light of the sun. Rays of light have their greatest power at the point of convergency. Let that point, with us, be an ungodly world. The conversion of the world is the great business of the Church. As the children of the light, let us come together in the unity of the spirit, which is the unity of the truth; and let all the affections of the heart, all the powers of the mind, and all the energies of the body, come into holy concert of effort for the enlightening of the WORLD—that the world may believe in Jesus.

The Son of God taught his followers to pray, "Thy kingdom come; thy will be done in earth as it is in heaven." There is no division,—no party interest,—no selfish motive among the redeemed in heaven. Should there be any among them on earth? This prayer of Christ forbids it, and our text exhorts them to labor TOGETHER.

Does the military chieftan exhort his soldiery on the eve of batsle to be united in feeling, and in action? Does he endeavor to infuse into them his mind and his spirit, in order that his commands may be implicitly obeyed, and his designs of conquest accomplished? Christ, the Captain of our salvation, has prayed that his heaven-enlisted soldiers may be united in ONE BODY for the spiritual conquest of the world. Why are they thrown into

---

*1 John iii.   †1 John ii: v.

confusion in their field of warfare? He is not the author of this state of things. He prayed against it, and died without revoking the prayer. He ascended up to the right hand of the majesty on high, where his prayer is still vibrating on his ear. Still,—O, still, it rolls through all the mansions of glory, in all the freshness of that day when it issued from his lips in the land of Judea, and still it breaks upon the ears of earth's dull hearing, divided saints —that they all may be one—that the WORLD may believe.

3. *Divisions among Christians are inconsistent with Apostolic precept.*

Many honest Christians, though certainly not well informed ones on this subject, take for granted what really does not appear in God's Word. They seem to suppose that the Church of Christ was divided into sects, parties and branches in the Apostles' day; and hence, they are quite satisfied, it should be so now. Some have even gone so far in their liberality on this point, as to congratulate the world and themselves that the sects of Christians are so numerous as to permit the different prejudices, prepossessions and notions of men, to be accomodated in making a public profession of Christianity. Our text inflicts a death-blow on such extravagance of opinion. The whole "conversation," or conduct in the "affairs" of religion should be as it becometh the Gospel of Chrrist. Christians should stand fast in one spirit, with one mind, laboring together, (not for parties and for sects,) but "FOR THE FAITH OF THE GOSPEL."

Were we to stop here, we might consider our proposition fully sustained. But the Apostles have said so much on this subject that we feel authorized to indulge in extensive quotations and remarks. Moreover the subject is one in which the happiness of the Church and the interests of an unbelieving world are involved,—deeply involved.

Paul taught, as Jesus prayed. He taught that the Church is one body; and in all his epistles he urges this sentiment; *often* expressing it in the clearest and strongest terms, and *always* reproving Christians for their schisms and divistons; *continually* exhorting them to union, to love, and to good works. In his epistle to the Romans, he says, "We being many are one body in Christ, and every one members one of another."* To the Corinthians he says, "For as the body is one and hath many members, and all the members of that one body, being many, are one body; so also is Christ."† "For by one spirit are we all babtized into one body, whether we be Jews or Gentiles, whether we be bond or free; and have been all made to drink into one spirit. For the body is not one member, but many." "That there should be no schisms in the body; but that the members should have the same care one for anether."‡ To the Galatians

---

* Rom: xii: 6.   † 1 Cor. xii; 12.   ‡ 1 Cor. xii: 25.

he says, "For ye are all the CHILDREN of God by FAITH* in Jesus Christ. For as many of you as have been baptized into Jesus Christ, have put on Christ. There is neither Jew nor Greek, there is neither bond nor free, there is neither male nor female; for ye are all one in Christ."† To the Ephesians he says, "There is one body, and one Spirit, even as ye are called in one hope of your calling; one Lord, one faith, one baptism, one God and Father of all; who is above all, and through all, and in you all." ‡ To the Phillippians he writes as in our text. To the Colossians he says, "Let the peace of God rule in your hearts, to the which ye are also called in one body."‖ To the Thessalonians, he says, "Stand fast and hold the traditions which ye have been taught, whether by word or our epistle."§

Paul not only exhorts Christians to be united, but he sharply reproves schismatics. "Now I beseech you, brethren, by the name of our Lord Jesus Christ, that ye all speak the same thing, and that there be no division among you; but that ye be perfectly joined together in the same mind and in the same judgment,"¶ "Now I beseech you, brethren, mark them which cause divisions and offences, contrary to the doctrine which ye have learned, and avoid them."** Divisions in the Apostle's day were not tolerated; therefore they are not allowable now. They are not as it becometh the gospel of Christ.

4. *Divisions are inconsistent with the happiness of God's people.*

"Behold, how good and how pleasant it is, for brethren to dwell together in unity!" Thue sang the devout David in that day of types and shadows. "I have no greater joy than to hear that my children walk in truth." So exclaimed the aged John, when the Church was in its infancy,—in its primitive simplicity and beauty, before it was loaded with cumbrous traditions, and ceremonies, (brought in by men of corrupt minds,) before these things were rivited upon the religious world by the reign of Papal darkness.

But soon we discover a disposition among men, to be followers of men. And this is the secret of the present torn and divided condition of the christian world. Even in the days of Paul, the Corinthian brethren had to be reproved by him, for this man-following spirit, which had sprung up among them. "It hath been declared unto me of you, my brethren, by them which are of the house of Chloe, that there are contentions among you. Now this I say, that every one of you saith, I am of Paul; and I of Apollos; and I of Cephas; and I of Christ. Is Christ divided? Was Paul crucified for you? Or were you baptized in the name of

---

*Not by birth, nor by baptism. †Gal. iii: 26—29. ‡Eph. iv: 4, 6. ‖Col. iii: 15. §Thess. ii: 15. 1 Thess. v: 9, 11. ¶1 Cor. i: 10. **Rom. xii: 17.

Paul?"* These contentions among the Corinthians were about men,—men who preached the Gospel in its purity too. And yet these divisionists were reproved,—reproved for glorying in men,— for glorying in *good* men, who were laborers TOGETHER with God. † But notwithstanding this cutting reproof, this glorying in men has not ceased. At this day, some glory in Calvin; some, in Luther; some, in Wesley,—all uninspired men. The phrase, "*our church,*" has got abroad in the world, in the room of the Scripture phrase, "*the Church of Christ.*" Some say the "*Catholic Church,*"—some the "*Episcopal Church,*"—some, the "*Presbyterian Church,*"—some, the "*Methodist Church,*"—and some, the "*Baptist Church.*" Hence we hear men of these different denominations, when speaking of their respective sects, say "*our church,*" "*your church,*" *my church.*" All this originates in, and is supported by, men's carnality. Let us all hear what an inspired Apostle has said. "Whereas, there is among you envying, and strife, and divisions, are ye not carnal and walk as men?" The Church as spoken of in the New Testament, is called "*the Church of Christ,*" "*the Church of God.*" Christ is the head of it, and not the Pope, nor the King, nor the Queen of England, nor the Bishops, nor the ruling Elders. It is not "*our Church,*" (no matter who we may be,) and therefore we cannot legislate nor ordain laws for its government. All *we can* do, or should attempt to do, is to "strive together for the faith of the Gospel," and not for the faith of men.

The Church in its organization, is purely congregational, and independent of all other religious bodies. There are no superior orders in the ministry. Jesus Christ has forbid it. "Be not ye called Rabbi; for one is your Master, even Christ, and all ye are brethren. And call no man your Father upon the earth; for one is your Father who is in heaven."‡

In its government the Church is completely republican. The world has never known a purer specimen of democracy than that which is exhibited in the government of the Church of Christ. The first Church conference, which was held at Jerusalem, within ten days after Christ's ascension, may be cited as proof of this assertion. See Acts i: 15—26. But especially see the manner in which the seven deacons were chosen, after this, as recorded in Acts vi: 1—8. It is as follows: "The twelve called the multitude of the disciples unto them and said, It is not reason that we should leave the word of God and serve tables. Wherefore, brethren, look ye out among you, seven men of honest report full of the Holy Ghost and wisdom, whom we may appoint over this business. And the saying pleased the whole multitude, and they chose Stephen, &c., whom they set before the Apostles." The Apostle told "*the multitude of the disciples,*" what kind of

---

*1 Cor. i: 11—13.   †1 Cor. iii: 9, 21, 22.   ‡Matt. xxiii: 8, 9.

men to elect, and allowed them freely to choose for themselves. The Apostles did not think the multitude were too ignorant to be entrusted with this work, and that they therefore ought to take it out of their hands and appoint these officers for them. They (the Apostles,) did not see any danger in permitting the *"whole multitude"* to sit in conference, or church-session. All such discoveries are of later date,—are of uninspired authority,—are the offspring of man's proud heart, in his reaching for power and distinction among his fellows.

But once more. In adjusting a difficult case which originated in the Church at Antioch, we see the same purely republican principles observed throughout the whole investigation. "THE MULTITUDE," that is, the whole church were permitted to sit in determining the case. (See Acts xv: v. 4.) And when they were come to Jerusalem, they were received of THE CHURCH, and of the Apostles, and elders," (ver. 12.) "Then all the multitude hept silence, and gave audience to Barnabas and Paul,"—(ver. 22.) "Then pleased it the Apostles and elders with the WHOLE CHURCH."—(ver. 23.) "And they wrote letters by them after this manner, The Apostles, and Elders and BRETHREN, send greeting unto the brethron," &c.—(ver 30.) So when they were dismissed, they came to Antioch; and when they had gathered THE MULTITUDE, (the Church) together, they delivered the epistle." —(ver. 31,) "Which when they had read, they rejoiced for the consolation."

All the above procedure is in perfect harmony with the doctrine inculcated in Matthew, xxiii: 17. "If he shall neglect to hear them, tell it to THE CHURCH; but if he neglect to hear the Church, let him be unto thee as a heathen man and a publican." This is our Lord's rule; there is no appeal from it. The case ends at the decision of *"the Church."* It is not to be removed up to a Presbytery, Synod, or Conference of Bishops and Elders.

In perfect accordance with our Lord's rule is that of Paul, "If then ye have judgments of things pertaining to this life, set them to judge, who are least esteemed in THE CHTRCH."* What a rebuke upon all modern organizations.

The simplicity and beauty of the Church organization, as given in the New Testament, cannot be easily misunderstood by any one who is disposed to investigate the subject. The Church is required to judge of the fitness of those who apply for membership, and to determine cases in reference to exclusion from her body, and from her decision there is no appeal to a higher judicatory; for she is herself the highest. "Him that is weak in the faith reeeive ye, but not to doubtful disputation."† Paul would teach the Romans that they had a right of Judgment in these cases; but he does not teach that they may receive, into their body, him who

---

* 1 Cor. vi: 3, 4.   † Rom. xiv: 1.

has no faith. In the exercise of their judgment they are to receive him who is *weak*, but not even the *weak*, if there is any doubt or disputation among them in consequence of it. From this, as well as from other passages, we learn that a member cannot be initiated into the Church over the head of any one who may be dissatisfied. The unity of the Spirit is to be preserved in the bond of peace.

CHRISTIAN UNION *can exist only among Christian elements.* Believers,—converted persons,—are the only proper characters for Church membership. The Apostle Peter represents the Church as a body of believers. "Ye also, as lively stones are built up a spiritual house, a holy priesthood, to offer up spiritual sacrifices, acceptable to God by Jesus Christ." * Unbelievers (whether men, women, or children,) cannot offer up "*spiritual sacrifices.*" They cannot be called, "a holy priesthood," in any sense of the word. The conclusion, therefore, is inevitable, that none but BELIEVERS are proper subjects for initiation into the Church of Jesus Christ.

John the Evangelist has instructed us on this point. He says, " He (Jesus,) came unto his own, and his own received him not. But as many as received him, to them gave he power to become the sons of God, even to them that believe on his name; which were born, not of blood, nor of the will of the flesh, nor of the will of man, but of God." † Jesus "*came unto his own,*" that is, the Jews as a nation, who were nationally God's peculiar people. He came unto them, but they, as a nation, did not " *receive him,*" that is, did not believe on him. But as many as received (i. e. believed on him) to them gave he power to become the sons of God; that is, authority to enter his *new kingdom,* the Church, which is declared to be "*a holy nation,*" which were born, not of blood, (as the Jewish nation,) nor of the will of the flesh, (as the Gentiles were,) nor of the will of man, (as all human beings are,) but of God," as all Christians are. The children of Jews were entitled by birth to the privileges of the "*Jewish nation.*" So by *birth from heaven,* individuals are to be admitted into the Church of Christ, the holy nation; and only such have power or authority from God to join the Church, and thus openly " BECOME THE SONS OF GOD."

Paul asserts the same sentiment. " Be ye not unequally yoked together with unbelievers,—come out from among them, and be ye separate saith the Lord—and ye shall be MY SONS AND DAUGHTERS." †

It is designed by our blessed Lord that his holy nation, the Church, shall have holy power in the earth; hence the materials in her organization must be holy. CHRISTIAN UNION can be promoted only by promoting a knowledge of the truth; for a

---

* John i: 11—13.   † 2 Cor. vi: 14—18.

union that is not cemented in truth is not the union of. Christ.
Whenever the truth is set aside by compromise among Christians,
that moment the body loses its only adhesive principle, and falls
into a mass of inanalyzable existence.   It is only when we walk
in the light, as Christ is in the light, that " we have fellowship
one with another. "   He who does not walk in the truth walks in
darkness.   •

What a pity that the bold reformers, who laid hold on the
"mother of harlots " to strip her of the unholy vestments with
which she had decked herself, should bring away, and bring
down to *our day*, those relics of tradition, INFANT BAPTISM, and
DIOCESAN CHURCH POLITY!   The *first* of these has been a
subject of ceaseless disputation.   The *second* has ever been
viewed as assuming power over the liberty and conscience of men,
—as wresting from them that freedom of thought and of judgment
which is the inalienable right of moral agents.   Both of these
relics, being unknown in the New Testament organization of the
Church, are to be rejected.   From the Sacred Scriptures we are
thoroughly furnished unto all good works.   When we pass
beyond the limits of revelation, to explore the regions of the
Fathers, and to examine the decisions of uninspired councils, we
are in a wilderness without a lamp to our feet or a light to our
path.

The people of the Lord should be united.   This is as certainly
the prayer of every Christian, as it is certain that every Christian
prays.   God is not the author of that state of things which sepa-
rates the believing wife from her pious husband at the Lord's table.
Nor can God require any of his children to yield any truth to get
to his table.   Has God granted us the liberty "*not to hold the
truth?*"   Has he allowed us to make an outward show of what
is not an inward reality?   Have Christians peculiarities in their
creed which may be laid down in their approach to the table of
the Lord?   If they have, most assuredly those peculiarities should
never be taken up again.   The Lord's table is easy of access.
The way to it is plain,—is open,—is free.   He has thrown no
bewildering difficulties around it.   *Men* have written volumes
about it ; and have shrouded the subject in all the fogginess of
sophistry.   But Luke who wrote the Acts of the Apostles, has
given us the whole matter in two short verses.   Here it is.
☞ "Then they that gladly received his word were baptized :
and the same day there were added unto them about three thousand souls.   And they continued steadfastly in the Apostle's
doctrine and fellowship, and in breaking of bread, and in
prayers. " * ☜ This Apostolic rule when analyzed simply com-
prizes the four following things, viz.

---

* Acts ii: 41, 42.

1. *Believe, that is gladly receive the word of the Lord.*
2. *Be baptized.*
3. *Then be added to the Church—the same day, if possible.*
4. *Then continue steadfastly, in the Apostles' doctrine and fellowship, in the breaking of bread and in prayers.*

Does any thing in this rule shut the door against a Christian? Is there any thing in it which a minister should not exhort a Christian to do? Is there any thing which prevents a Christian from a free participation in the privileges of the Lord's house? This Apostolic rule throws the door wide open and says,— WHOEVER WILL LET HIM ENTER. The Lord himself has established the laws for the regulation of his house, and he requires all to observe them. All Christians should feel themselves obliged to obey speedily and joyfully.

The simple act of coming together around the Lord's table, if at the sacrifice of principle, is a sinful thing. It never has done away, nor can it do away sectarian feeling and effort. Our text requires that our "conversation" in all the affairs of religion, should be as it becometh the gospel of Christ,—that we should stand fast in one spirit, with one mind, striving TOGETHER for the faith of the gospel. But are all professed Christians doing this? Were we to assert it, the unbelieving world would charge us with weakness, or insincerity.

5. *Divisions, or sects, among Christians, are injurious to the spread of the gospel in the world, and are in no sense a blessing, but an evil.*

We have said that divisions among Christians are incongenial with their pious feelings. We now say, they are injurious to the growth of grace in the soul. They originate, not in the Word of God, but in the corruption of the human heart; and they fall so readily in with the current of men's sinful nature, that they read the Scriptures more, and labor more, to maintain their erroneous positions, than they do to eradicate the roots of bitterness which spring up in their unsanctified hearts. Instead of striving *together*, they are often striving against each other. By their *words*, they are desiring union; but by their *works* they are laboring to remain divided—professing love, but practicing hatred towards each other.

Let any one denomination of Christians get up a religious meeting in a town, and let it become a revival season with them. The rest, for the most part take but little interest in it,—probably speak lightly of it. To them, in their turn under similar circumstances, the same state of feeling and conduct is manifested. Some insinuating, under current is set at work to defeat their progress and prosperity. This is the present state of things in the divided, confused and weakened religious world,—each striving to counteract the other, and to build up its party. O! tell it not, that this state of religious affairs is a blessing to the world, and that God is the author of it. The text forbids it, the pious

feelings of the child of God forbid it,—the prayer of the blessed
Savior forbids it,—the precepts of Apostles forb:d it,—the tears'
and groans of the penitent soul seeking to enter in at the gate of
mercy forbid it,—the perishing condition of the unbelieving world
forbids it. O, then tell it not!—tell it not!!

Look at the facts. The father unites with the Baptists, the
mother with the Methodists, a son with the Presbyterians, a
daughter with the Episcopalians,—is this the kind of union urged
in our text? Is this what God meant when he said by his prophet, "I will give them one heart and one way, that they may
fear me forever; for the good of them and of their children after
them."   No, my friends, never can words so plain be so distorted as to bear such an interpretation. The irreligious world see
these things, and conclude that christianity is nothing but the wild
working of a weak and disordered mind. The beholder is not
struck, at once, with the belief that the Christian religion is from
heaven. In such a state of things religion loses its holy prepon-
derance, and sectarian power is sought more than the salvation of
souls.

One denomination is numerous and strong in a village, another
is small and feeble; and as "weakness invites insult," the dominant party is ready to make a formidable effort to put the feeble
down, if not by reason, probably by ridicule. Who is so dim-
sighted as not to have seen this sort of work? One minister
preaches his views to-day, and another announces that he will
answer him to-night or to-morrow. All the non-religious Church
members are pleased; and infidels, and gamblers and loafers are
ready to witness this unholy war. Many are pleased to see the
sacred sanctuary profaned by the contentions of these self-constituted champions of their respective sects.

A little village scarcely able to support *one* minister, has three
places of public worship, and three sectarian defenders of the faith
to occupy them. The Sabbath comes, and these houses are about
one third or *one fourth* filled with hearers, crying, Lo, here! Lo,
there! What little religion there is in these chapels is made a
sectarian threshing-machine, to beat out and beat down every thing
but its own party. The sectarian doctor—the sectarian lawyer,
—the sectarian teacher,—and not unfrequently the sectarian poli-
tician, is made the idol of sectarian religionists.

Is the Lord in all this whirlwind of confusion? No. Is this
promotive of the religion of the meek and lowly Savior? No, it
has made more infidels than all the writings of infidels themselves.
This language may seem strong; but it is feeble—it is. *feebleness*
itself, when compared with the language of the Son of God on
the subject. "Every kingdom divided against itself is brought to
desolation; and every city, or house divided against itself shall
not stand." * "And if satan rise up against himself and be divi-

---

Matt. xii: 25.

ded, he cannot stànd but hath an. end."* If divisions in the kingdom of satan would overthrow it, what will they do in the kingdom of Christ? Have the advocátes of a divided Church, carefully considered this startling language of the Son of God? Have they had a full view of its import. *A house,—a city,— hell itself, rising up against itself, cannot stand.*

"Divisions, says one preacher, are an evil, but God over-rules them to his glory, and our good." That God exercises a special over-ruling providence in the affairs of his people, it would be weakness in us to dispute. But that we should *"do evil that good may come,"* we utterly deny. *God is merciful,* is not a reason why we should be presumptuous. *Grace abounds,* is not an argument in favor of going on to sin. "Shall we continue in sin, that grace may abound? God forbid." And God forbid that his people should go on to strengthen themselves in an evil work.

Brethren, known as Baptists in the religious world, you perceive the position we occupy. What shall we say in conclusion?

1. *The text requires that we should strive together for the faith of the Gospel.*

We have "made a covenant before the Lord, to walk after Him, and to keep his commandments, and his testimonies, and his statutes." † By the profession we have made, we have declared ourselves on the Lord's side. Shall we continue in sin that grace may abound? God forbid. How shall we that are dead to sin live any longer therein? "Know ye not that so many of us as were baptized into Jesus Christ, were baptized into his death? Therefore we are buried with him by baptism into death; that like as Christ was raised up from the dead by the glory of the Father, even so we also should walk in newness of life. For if we have been planted TOGETHER in the LIKENESS of his death, we shall be also in the LIKENESS of his resurrection." ‡ By the sacrament of the *Supper,* we are taught the doctrine of Christ's death,—his body broken and his blood shed for the remission of sin. By the sacrament of *Baptism,* we are taught *the death, burial and resurrection of Jesus Christ.* In the supper, we show Christ's *death;* in Baptism, his *burial and resurrection.* Jesus Christ has designed that these two sacraments, so strikingly impressive, should be preserved in his Church through all ages. In a recent poem, we have the design of baptism beautifully set forth. Speaking of it the author says,

"———————The import of the rite bespeaks
Its dignity. 'Tis not a senseless thing,
But full of doctrine fashioned to the sight,
In form persuasive, beautiful, distinct.

---

* Mark iii: 26. † Deut. xxii: 3. ‡ "Alluding to the ancient mode of baptism by immersion."—*Wesley.*

'Tis not salvation, but salvation's sign;
'Tis not a conscience sprinkled from its guilt,
But the profession of a conscience pure
And tranquilized.   This is the sacred badge
Of our discipleship, one loud farewell to sin,
The world and every idol lust; our oath
Of duty to the Lord embracing him
As ours forever, and his people ours,
His cause, his cross, and his eternal crown—
It is the blessed gospel symbolized.
Its mighty themes in color, shape and act,
That its evangelizing power may strike
The gazing eye with heavenly argument,
And thence invade and conquer the proud heart.—
Strike down this write, and truth bemoans in tears
A witness slain, a mighty champion fallen.
Destroy it, and a land-mark of the church is gone—
Confused her borders, broken, undefined.
Destroy it, and an avenue of grace,
Instruction, comfort and reproof to men
Is shut, and heaven's bright perfect system marred.
Change it—diminish—circumscribe—its force,
Its import fades; its thrilling eloquence,
So sweet and moving to the pious heart,
So terrible to guilt, to Jargon breaks,
Or in dull empty silence dies away.''—*Index vol.* ii: *p.* 533.

Brethren of this Association.—In common with all who are born of God, you desire the prosperity of the cause of Christ, and regret that state of things which, in these modern days, divides God's people.   You have the witness too, that it is painful to be separated from some of them.   You have the consolation, however, to know that, by the grace of God, you have been able to hold out to the world this changeless apostolic motto, ONE LORD, ONE FAITH, ONE BAPTISM.   But for you, and a long line of predecessors like you, this motto would long since have been destroyed.

"But it shall live; God's faithfulness its life,
Omnipotence its shield.   Long has it braved
The force of time and tortuous argument,
Urged by the erring good and erring vile;
Long braved the fears the silken substitutes,
The wrath and pride of men.———"

2. *You have never believed nor said that Baptism is a soul-saving ordinance.*

While you have labored together to preserve the positive insti-

tutions of Christ's Church in their primitive beauty and simplicity, you have carefully avoided this error. Nor have you said
that Baptism is a means of grace by the observance of which the
tottering soul is propped and its standing made more secure for
the eternal world. The Episcopalian instructs his child to say,
"*In baptism I was made a member of Christ, a child of God,
and an inheriter of the kingdom of heaven.*" And the child is
taught to believe that there are two sacraments essential to salvation; "*that is to say Baptism and the Supper of the 'Lord.*" *
Mr. Wesley, the father of Methodism, says, in reference to the
views of his Church, "It is certain our Church supposes that all
who are baptized in their infancy are at the same time born again,
and it is allowed that the whole office for the baptism of infants
proceeds upon this supposition." † You, brethren, have not so
learned Christ. You have not been made "*inheriters*" of the
kingdom of heaven by baptism; but "*by the holy spirit of God
ye are sealed unto the day of redemption.*" ‡ Baptism and the
Lord's supper are not "*sealing ordinances,*" as some vainly
imagine. Nothing but the Spirit of God can seal us heirs of
heaven. Buck in his Theological Dictionary admits, (what all
Pedo-baptist writers of distinction admit) that "*there are no express examples in the New Testament of Christ, or his Apostles
baptizing infants.*" "*That infants are to be admitted is also
inferred,*" he adds: So infant baptism is supported by inference
and Apostolic tradition, and not by any *express* instructions in the
New Testament. Mr. Wesley, supports it, upon the same foundations, and upon what, "*it is certain his Church supposes.*"
The work of serving God is not regulated by inference, tradition
nor supposition.

It does not follow, however, that we should treat as infidels
those who have embraced this error: by no means. But we
should pray as Christ prayed, and labor as he did, that all his
people might be one. He who prays for CHRISTIAN UNION, and
at the same time labors to perpetuate division, performs an act of
solemn mockery. The uncharitable may endeavor to impress the
public mind with the belief that we esteem ourselves holier than
others, but every well-informed person will certainly view such
representation as unfounded, unkind and unjust. The truth is, *we
deem their Baptism and church polity entirely unsupported by the
Scriptures.* Consequently their CHRISTIAN UNION, or Church
organization, is not that of the Bible. Their piety is not debated.
We love them as Christians; and we *should* love them, and labor
to remove all that hinders Church union.

3. *You have taken the Bible as the only rule of your faith and
practice.*

If divisions are inconsistent with pious feeling,—with Christ's

---

* See Episcopal Cat. ‡ Sermon Vol. i: Ser. 45. p. 405. ‡ Eph. iv: 5, 6.

prayer,—with Apostolic precept,—and with the Church's happiness and prosperity, ought we not to abandon every course and
lay aside every notion, which is unsupported by the sacred oracles?
We do not accuse you, brethren, of holding any sentiment unau-
thorized by the Word of God, nor do we assert that your conversation is not as it becometh the gospel of Christ. But we exhort
you to a careful examination of the Bible, that you may be able to
determine what is truth and what is error, in the professed service
of God. The religion of the Bible is the only acceptable religion in the sight of God. There is no middle-ground between
truth and error. The sectarian may tell you he desires union,
and that he will meet you *"half way."* But truth has no compromise,—no half way point. It is a unit which cannot be frac-
tionized. Like the diamond, it contains but one element.

4. *Guard against all erroneous views of Baptism.*

We have seen among our brethren a kind of rejoicing when
Pedo-baptists immerse persons who unite with them. Now earnest advocates as we are of Baptism, we cannot approve these
instances of Baptism; for it is obvious they do not tend to lessen
the evil of which the Apostle speaks in the text. Do they bring
the people of the Lord nearer together? Not at all. They only
widen the already too widely divided state of Christian feeling
and sentiment. These Baptisms create sects among sects. Our
Methodist and Presbyterian friends always preach against it, and
often ridicule it. They never persuade their members to this
course. They only immerse as an alternative. Now all rejoicing among *you*, brethren, on occasions of this sort, seems to in-
dicatethat you attach some virtue to Baptism,—some soul-purifying
efficacy to the ordinance; than which no sentiment can be more
erroneous. In those cases where individuals, uniting with Pedo-
baptists, feel that *they* must be immersed, it seems obvious that
they attach some undue importance to the ordinance, from the
fact that they do it over all the objections of their ministry, and of
their brethren in the same communion. Our Lord designed that
his Church should be one, STRIVING TOGETHER, walking by the
same rule and speaking the same thing; that there should be *" no
schism in the body."* Hence he gave them, ONE BAPTISM:
—simply one. Baptism is not the putting away of the filth of
the flesh. It is not therefore the soul-cleansing power of immersion, we contend for; but it is the complete union of the Redeemer's flock; that the great truth which baptism is intended sym-
bolically to teach, may be impressed upon the consciences and
lives of others until the WORLD shall believe that Jesus is the
Christ.

5. *Baptists should be the last to be divided among themselves.*

Their Baptism, their Church government, their views of doctrine and of religious liberty, have, with but little exception, been
the same through all ages. The opposition they have endured

from others, should dispose them to unite and sympathize with each other. Bound together by no "*Book of Discipline*," but the Bible;—acknowledging no standard,—nor "*Confession of Faith*," but the Holy Scriptures;—untrammeled with human formulas and creeds; let us "stand fast in the liberty wherewith Christ hath made us free," and labor "TOGETHER FOR THE FAITH OF THE GOSPEL."

> "Christians reJoice! each party name,
> Each different sect shall cease
> Your error, sin, and grief and shame,
> Shall yield to truth and peace." AMEN

NOTE.

That the triumph of Christianity, over irreligion and all systems of false religion, is to be universal, scarcely admits of a doubt. This, seems to be as plainly revealed, as any doctrine in the Bible. But it is taught, as inseparable from the *unity* of the Church,—and is made to *depend* upon it. "I pray that they all may be *one, that the world may believe*," was the prayer of Messiah himself. To suppose that he intended his subjects to be divided into parties is perfectly absurd. To ascribe the fact that they are so, to any obscurity in the scriptures, is equally absurp. The fault must be in ourselves.

In every dispensation of revealed religion, the Church has been *one*. In the wilderness, there was *one* tabernacle, *one* pillar of cloud by day, and of fire, by night. In Canaan, there was *one* temple—*one* altar,—*one* shechinah, *one* holy, and *one* most holy place. The people and service were *one*. That system of religion, confined to one nation, looked forward to the inclusion of all nations,—the middle wall of partition between Jews and Gentiles was to be broken down,—but it was that there might be "*one fold* and *one shepherd.*" Jno. x: 16.

The entire ministerial conduct of the Apostles, co-incided with this principle. The Church *could not be divided*. In all matters of mere personal preference, they might divide;—in choosing fields of labor, or in separation to them, as in the case of Paul and Barnabas, they might divide, the one taking with him, Silas, the other Mark; but the body of Christ, they might not divide. When that perplexing question, concerning the incorporation of the Jewish ritual with Christianity, came up, (Acts xv: and Gal. ii.) what was more natural, than that Paul should form a Gentile *branch* of the Christian Church, leaving the Jewish, to John, Peter and James? But they *durst* not. All who could safely be admitted, into the body of Christ, were *one*. The Church on

7—Vol. 3.

earth, was, in respect of union, like the Church in heaven, admitting,

> "Episcopalian none, nor Presbyter,
> Nor Lutheran, nor Calvinist, nor Jew,
> Nor Greek, nor Sectary of any name."

And yet that Church was not bigoted. They manifested the
utmost forbearance, and liberality, where, as Dr. Campbell expresses it, there was no manifestation of "*pravity of will.*" In
primitive times those who thus withdrew into separate communities, were deemed *sectarians,* not in our sense of the term, as different *names* for the same thing, but *schismatics;* and unfit for
the Church of Christ. The Church and the world, were the
only divisions. But now, a new order of things has arisen.
And how we are to get rid of it,—that is the question. Every
attempt at it, thus far, has proved abortive,—issuing only in the
formation of a new sect. But the thing must not be abandoned,
as hopeless: for the world is to be converted, and the *unity* of the
Church, is to be one of the means.

The restoration of immersion, as the initiatory ordinance, and
its restriction to those who make a credible profession of faith,
could scarcely fail to bring together all Evangelical Christians,
who maintain ministerial parity. There would then be but two
sects of Protestants, Episcopalians and Baptists; and the only
material point to settle between these, would be the authority of
Episcopal power. That this is to share the same fate with mon-
archy, there is the strongest moral certainty. The Church of
England, now very naturally contends, that "lighter carriages
must turn aside to let heavy wagons pass;" but mighty revolutions
are sometimes effected in a very short time. The history of Pu-
seyism shows the instability of English Episcopacy; and that
every change in England is felt in this country. By what means
this great change is to be produced, is beyond conjecture. Logic,
and Biblical criticism, are causes, which will of course produce
their own effects. Probably the extension of love to Christ, to one
another, and to the world, will do more than any other agent, in
melting into fusion, and moulding anew this immense mass.

Whenever an individual mentions Christian union, he is understood as affecting to represent his own sect, and wishing all others
to merge into that. We mean no such thing. That ministerial
parity, and believers' baptism, are destined to become universally
prevalent, we no more doubt, than we doubt the progress of civilization; and that the prevalence of these, in the absence of sectarian feeling would tend wonderly to unite the Church, is beyond
dispute. It is moreover beyond controversy that, the Baptists,
have with them in so far as ministerial parity is concerned, the
sympathy of all Protestant Christendom, except the Episcopalians

and Methodists. They alone are united respecting the proper materials of Church-membership. These two facts place them decidedly in the ascendency; incomparably so. As regards the latter item, there is no harmony but among Baptists. One supposes that the faith of both parents, is necessary to admit an infant to the initiatory ordinance; another, of one only; and a third, of neither. The discordancy is scarcely less, respecting the qualifications of an adult. But, among Baptists, there is no division—all require a credible profession of faith and that only. As regards the former item, no one ever questioned the validity of our Baptism; while the validity of theirs is denied by a large majority of the ablest critics; and the highest ground taken in its defence, is, *that it will serve the purpose intended* Still, we do not suppose that any one sect is to be the rallying point for all; when the consummation shall be effected. Probably all will yield as much as conscience will allow, while nothing of the demands of truth and duty will be compromised.

In the mean time it becomes all Christians to agree in the things in which they can agree, and not unnecessarily to stand aloof from their brethren.   ED.

EXTRACTS.

"There is certainly at the present day a more deep and fervent desire among Christians at large, for an intimate and visible union, than has existed heretofore. This is a happy sign. It appears in every quarter. It is seen in the books which issue from the press, it is breathed from the lips of prayer in the public sanctuary and at the family altar. But this event, so devoutly to be wished, is not to be brought about merely by cogent reasonings, by well-set arguments, by earnest discussion, though in love, nor merely by prayer itself. All these must be connected with an active and hearty co-operation of Christians, on ground that is common for the general good. The principles which are admitted must have wider scope, a free operation in a clear field, before there can be a much greater approach to Christian union. Each must respect the other's independence of mind. Each must really be *jealous* for his brother's freedom of conscience, and then study how both can do the most for Christ's glory, on the ground of common principles, before the mists of prejudice can be dispelled, and the cause of separation dissolved, and heart be bound to heart, in the ties of a real and enduring union. Let this but be done, let the maxim of the text ("Whereto we have already attained, let us walk by the same rule, let us mind the same thing,") thus be practised, and candor will take the place of prejudice, and confidence will take the place of suspicion, and charity will rule in the room of jealousy, truth will be investigated by new lights, with hearts more simple and eyes more single, till ere long, one mind will be seen approximating to another, seeking the same thing, using the same means, and reaching the same end, and so, at last, the full glory of the Lord will appear in Zion, her watchmen shall all see eye to eye, and lift up their voice in perfect harmony.   *   *   *   *

*   *   *   *   *   *   *   All true Christians have attained to the knowledge of some truths which are of eternal worth, and which form the ground of an everlasting fellowship. All such have learned to prize Christianity as the religion of sinners. They have all been convinced of sin by the law, felt and confessed their just condemnation, turned from sin with godly sorrow, trusted in the atoning merits of an Almighty Savior, and feeling their dependence on the Holy Spirit, have panted for his sanctifying influences. All such, wherever they may be, whatever name they may bear, should love each other with pure hearts fervently. No Christian should fail to cherish and acknowledge a cordial fellowship towards any member of Christ's family, on account of the ignorance, or prejudice, or pride, or any infirmity which may mar or deform the image of the Savior, in one whom he must still regard as a brother. He should love him, *in spite of these.* These will all pass away, if the elements of Christian character are there, and that soul will shine in celestial purity on high. Each, therefore, should seek to make the most of the other here, to increase his purity and his usefulness, and to cause all that he has, to redound to the glory of God. Such is the natural tendency of Christian principles when their operation is left unembarrassed. It may be easy for men to raise nice questions on articles of belief, ecclesiastical councils may comprise their creed in two points, in five, or thirty-nine, and say that to receive them all is necessary to church fellowship; yet after all it will be found that those who as lost sinners, have fled to Christ as a divine and atoning Savior, and through the spirit of peace, are seeking to live to his glory, will recognize in each other kindred elements, "the unction from the Holy one," which quickens and enlightens, will feel that *this is true religion;* and though unlearned in every thing except the Bible, will discern here the impress of evangelical Christianity."—*Hague's Christian Union.*

ature
THE
BAPTIST PREACHER.

| VOL. III. | April, 1844. | NO. 4. |

FEMALE PIETY:—
ITS CHARACTER AND INFLUENCE;

A Sermon, by REV. ROBERT FLEMING, *Principal of Newnan Female Seminary, Ga.*

—

'*And on the Sabbath we went out of the city by a river side, where prayer was wont to be made; and we sat down, and spake unto the women which resorted thither. And a certain woman named Lydia, a seller of purple, of the city of Thyatira, which worshipped God, heard us; whose heart the Lord opened, that she attended unto the things which were spoken of Paul. And when she was baptized, and her household, she besought us, saying, If ye have judged me to be faithful to the Lord, come into my house and abide there. And she constrained us.*'—ACTS, XVI: 13–15.

One of the peculiar features of the religion of Jesus Christ, is its transforming influence upon the heart. The systems of religion devised by men, have not only found the heart sinful, but they have been incapable of changing it. However prone mankind may be to boast of their wisdom, it remains a forever settled point, that the world by wisdom, knows not God; and how much soever they may boast of the openness of the heart to the reception of truth, still they are met with this silencing fact, that '*the Lord opened Lydia's heart.*' The heart must be opened for the reception of the revealed word, or the kingdom of heaven will be closed against us in the coming day. Yea verily 'Except we be converted and become as little children we cannot see the kingdom of heaven.' Submission to the will of God, and a reverential regard to his commands, are essential attributes of the child of grace, and they afford the strongest proof that we are converted, —that we are renewed in the spirit of our mind,—*that our heart is opened.*

The holy Spirit is the instrument by which this transformation is produced. 'The love of God, is shed abroad in our hearts by

8—Vol. 3.

the Holy Ghost, which is given unto us.' * It is, therefore, the work of the Spirit,

> 'To pour fresh life in every part
> And new create the whole.'

It is not by baptism that we are made children of God, and inheriters of the kingdom of heaven; but, '*by the Holy Spirit of God we are sealed unto the day of redemption.*' † No other seal than that which God sets upon the heart, can make it 'meet to be partaker of the inheritance of the saints in light.' Where this seal is set upon the heart it becomes a heart of flesh—a feeling, tender heart,—a heart susceptible of holy impressions. 'The fruit of the Spirit is love, joy, peace, long-suffering, gentleness, goodness, faith, meekness, temperance.' ‡

These general remarks respecting conversion, are applicable to all the subjects of it, without distinction of sex; but this discourse invites attention to the consideration

I. Of piety as exhibited in the female character; and

II. Of the influence which pious females exert over others.

1. *Of piety as exhibited in the female character.*

Females, generally, are constitutionally qualified to discharge with more efficiency, the more delicate and tender offices of life, than the other sex. This is apparent from Scripture, and from facts. The feebleness of woman's physical powers, the delicacy of her mind, the tenderness of her heart, and the ardency of her attachments, all indicate that she is designed by the Creator to be 'an help meet for man,'—an auxiliary,—a co-operator with him, in the various duties adapted to her powers.

That the Creator designed the man

> 'To bear the rougher part and mitigate,
> By nameless gentle offices her toil,'

Is not debatable. Nor is it intended here, to discuss the claims to *superiority* in the *one* sex, nor to attempt to show the *inferiority* of the *other*. It is the glory of the female character, as well as our pleasure to know, that she is more sympathetic, more easily moved by the tear of suffering humanity, and less inclined to enter with unyielding purpose into the stern and unholy work of cruelty and oppression, than our own sex. If then she is naturally more lovely in her general character, what is she when her heart is opened and purified by the soul-softening influence of the Holy Spirit? Permit us now to contemplate her character as a devout follower of Jesus Christ.

---

* Rom. v: 5.　　　† Eph. iv: 5, 6, 30.　　. ‡ Gal. v: 22.

Lydia, the female mentioned in our text, whose heart the Lord opened, and whose short history is found in this chapter, was a worshipper of God previously to Paul's preaching to her the gospel. He found her, on the Sabbath day, withdrawn from the bustle of the city of Philippi, by a river side 'where prayer was wont to be made.' He spoke unto her the word of truth, and the Lord opened her heart and 'she attended unto the things which were spoken of Paul.' To open the heart,—to convert,—is *the work of the Lord.* To attend unto the things which are spoken is the evidence,—*the work of the believer.* The sacraments, then, do not appear to be essential to salvation; but an *observance* of them, appears to be essential to an *exhibition* of Christian faith and obedience. Lydia was the first convert of whom we have any account in this city. How did the religion of Jesus Christ appear in her character? It was not displayed in mere profession, nor in unmeaning pomp and noise, but in the simple fact that '*she attended unto the things*' which were spoken by Paul. She became 'a doer of the word.' Her love to the Redeemer, was made known by her obedience to his word and her love to his servants. It was now altogether congenial with her feelings, and perfectly in her line of things, to show them much kindness. It is remarkable in this instance, as well as in all others where the Lord opens the *heart*, that he opens the *house* and the *purse* of the individual. And although the religion of Christ makes its subjects ardent and sincere in their attachment to God's people *generally*, and to his ministers *especially*, yet it does not make them immodest nor vainly ostentatious in the exhibition of their piety. Such was Lydia's attachment to these 'messengers of the Lord of hosts,' that, 'when she was baptized and her household,' she besought them saying, 'If ye have judged me to be faithful to the Lord, come into my house, and abide there.' And she constrained them. Converted persons delight in the society of pious persons. She took pleasure in the company, the conversation, the instructions, and, (more than all,) in the prayers of these holy men, in her family. The hospitalities of her house were freely tendered to them; yea, she *constrained* them, to accept of the temporal comforts with which Divine providence had blest her, and that too, during the whole of their stay in Philippi. Perfectly aware of the ardency of her feelings, and of the strong terms in which they were communicated, she seems to have become fearful lest the Apostles might deem it imprudent to take lodgings at the house of a strange female, of whose character they had had so little knowledge. But she seems to anticipate their objections by prefixing the condition, 'If ye have judged me to be faithful to the Lord.' There is always safety where there is faithfulness to the Lord. I will be faithful to *you*,—my house is *open*,—it is *free*,—I am *able*,—I am *willing*,—I am *anxious* to have you with me.

In all ages of the world, and among all nations, public sentiment has had a powerful influence on the actions of mankind;
but where it is not regulated by the principles of the Bible, it
needs correction. Probably, with us, it needs correction, respecting the liberties and privileges which it allows to females generally, and to religious females particularly. While the female
heart glows with love to God, his cause and his people, there
appears to be a disposition (with some minds at least,) if not to
close, at least not to *open* the channels through which they may be
able to bring into lively and profitable exercise the graces of the
Holy Spirit. And while our sex have claimed superiority of
intellectual powers, they have also, apparently, arrogantly said,
that woman in point of *piety* is inferior to man, and should have
little to *do*, and less to *say* in religion. But we learn from our
text a different lesson. We see the influence of the grace of God
on the heart of a female at Philippi, where the Gospel had never
previously been preached. We see her immediately attending to
the command of God, and giving vent to the holy, heaven-wrought
feelings of her heart, in constraining the Apostles to make her
house their welcome residence during their continuance in the
city.

Paul found Lydia, out of the city, by a river side, where it was
usual for prayer to be made on the Sabbath. She was among the
women who resorted thither. It is probable she was a Jewess,
who worshipped God according to the requisition of the law.
She had not heard of Jesus, or if she had, she had not embraced
the Gospel. But now the Lord opened her heart,—converted her,
and her household. She had come from Thyatira to Philippi to
trade, but she and her family attended to the worship of God on
the Sabbath, according to the knowledge they had of his worship.
It were devoutly to be wished that the *men* who merchandize in
our town and cities would follow her example,—would attend the
worship of God themselves on the Sabbath, and take their families
with them. This was what the world terms 'a business woman.'
She was now what the Scriptures require all Christians to be,—
'diligent in business, fervent in spirit, serving the Lord.' Idleness and gossipping, at any time, but especially on the Sabbath,
are incompatible with the religion of the Bible; and when ever
women or men, (no matter what may be their wealth,) would excuse themselves from the obligation to pursue some honest and
useful employment that might benefit themselves and others, they
are wanting in piety, are at war with the designs of heaven, and
subject themselves to the reproof of all who love our Lord Jesus
Christ. '*No man liveth unto himself*,' should be deeply and
indelibly impressed on every human heart. All are to be *laborers*,
and none *loiterers*, in the vineyard of the Lord. Of them to whom
much is given, much will be required.

Paul had gone to this city a perfect stranger, and had no fellow-christians there to receive him; but he found that the same Lord who had opened other hearts at other places, was ready to open Lydia's heart for his reception. The Christian minister ever finds a home in that house where the word of the Lord finds a place in the heart of its possessor. Christianity is the same in all ages of the world,—'*good will to men,*'—'*to do good and to communicate.*' Eighteen hundred years ago, in the heart of Lydia of Thyatira, it was seen and known by its fruits. The same spirit is found in the heart of every converted female in this community to-day; and by their fruits Christians are known now, as they were then. Lydia's kindness towards the Apostles endeared her to them, and fully convinced them that they were altogether welcome to a liberal participation in the hospitalities of her house. Be not surprised, if the minister should most frequently call at the residence of those whose piety is so well authenticated, and whose constraining entreaties are something more than hollow-hearted formality, or sounding brass or tinkling cymbal.

We have said that the pious conduct of this distinguished individual was such as to secure the decided respect and confidence of the Apostles. In proof of this, we find them, as stated in the 40th verse of the chapter, visiting her house, as soon as they were liberated from prison, and comforting the brethren who composed her household, and who had been so recently baptized. The pre-eminence of her piety is very conspicuous in this instance; for though Paul had been seized by an infuriated mob, dragged before the magistrates of the city, scourged, derided, and imprisoned, still she stands fast in the faith, * and in her vindication of him as a minister of the Gospel. This was a trying time with her and with him; for there was nothing in the popularity of Paul, nor of his religion, at this time in this city, which could induce sycophantic fawning. It is too commonly the policy of carnal spirits to avoid responsibility, and to endeavor to give importance and influence to themselves, by hanging to the skirts of those whom fame with her silvery, though deceitful trumpet, has already proclaimed to be wise, and great, and grand. No such unholy motive could have given rise to the conduct of this woman. Nor could the fear of detracting from her own reputation, by espousing the cause of this despised, persecuted and unpopular minister, deter her, (though a stranger in the city herself and equally exposed to danger,) from the discharge of her duty towards him. It is human nature to shrink from receiving instruction from those who, in public estimation, are degraded and unpopular; and it is too often the case that public estimation is made the '*sine qua non*' of merit. But the grace of God so reigned in the heart of Lydia, that when the Apostle was liberated from

---

* 'For now we live if ye stand fast in the Lord.' 1 Thess. iii: 8.

ᵗthe prison, he found a hearty welcome at her house, and his pious
instructions still fell like the mellow tones of music upon the ears
of the brethren there, and filled their desponding spirits with comfort.   In the holy consolations of spirit-born souls, they dream
not of worldly policy nor of fleshly prudence.   Here is manifested *exalted piety.*   It is not the easiest part of Christian duty to
follow Christ when our reputation, our person, our property, and
our life are endangered by it.   But instances of piety, of a high
order, among females, are not isolated and few.

MARTHA AND MARY, were the intimate personal friends of
Christ.   Lydia evinced her love to Christ by her love to his
Apostles ; but these two amiable sisters had the peculiar honor of
entertaining Christ himself under their humble roof.   They saw
his sympathies as a *man* when he approached the tomb of their
deceased brother Lazarus and wept; but they beheld his power,
as '*the mighty God,*' when he cried, '*Lazarus come forth.*'
These sisters and their brother lived in a retired situation, and
Jesus often visited them.   Retirement is favorable to visits from
Jesus.   Piety is apt to wither in the sickly atmosphere of the
busy, thoughtless world.

MARY MAGDALENE, out of whom Jesus cast seven devils, came
to Jesus as he sat at meat at Simon's house, and washed his feet
with tears and wiped them with the hairs of her head, anointing
them with precious ointment.   What a display of ardent love and
deep humility of soul!   Simon, a pharisee, finds fault, but Jesus
commends her.   The religious zeal and pious labors of females
in our own day, have too often to endure the sulky frowns of some
of Simon's kindred spirits.

DORCAS, a disciple who resided at Joppa, was a woman full of
good works and alms deeds which she did.   She sickened and
died.   Peter was at a neighboring city and was sent for.   When
he came they conducted him into an upper chamber where she
was laid, 'and all the widows stood by him weeping, and showing
the coats and garments which she made while she was with them.'
She was benevolent, and was lamented in death by all the '*saints
and widows.*'   Religion and benevolence are but other names
for *love to God and man.*   They are twin sisters, going hand-in-
hand, ministering to the wants of the widow and the fatherless.

RUTH, the Moabitess daughter-in-law of Naomi, and whose
paphetic history furnishes a beautiful specimen of piety in the
female heart, may be profitably mentioned here.   After the death
of her husband and two sons, Naomi was disposed to return from
the land of Moab to Bethlehem-judah, the place of her nativity
and the land of her kindred.   As she was taking leave of her
daughters-in-law, she pronounces, in the spirit of true piety, her
parting benediction upon them.   'The Lord deal kindly with you
as ye have dealt with the dead and with me.'   'She kissed them,
and they lifted up their voice and wept.'   Orpha consented to re-

turn to Moab, but Ruth said to her Mother-in-law; 'Entreat me not to leave thee, or to return from following after thee; for whither thou goest, I will go; and where thou lodgest, I will lodge; thy people shall be my people, and thy God my God; where thou diest I will die, and there will I be buried; the Lord do so to me, and more also, if aught but death part thee and me.'

We might here introduce with much propriety the name of DEBORAH, the wife of Lapidoth, a prophetess who judged Israel after the death of Ehud; and who led the army of Israel under Barak to successful combat with the army of Jabin king of Canaan, whose army was commanded by Sisera. 'The Lord sold Sisera and his host into the hand of a woman.' She not only judged Israel, but she planned the battle for Barak, and went up with him to Kedish, the field of action, and directed the onset. After this signal conquest, she sung a song of praise to God, ascribing all the glory and honor to him. In all this there is an exhibition of elevated piety, as well as a display of superior mental endowment.

We might mention the names of many other women, whose holy lives are recorded in the word of God for the benefit of succeeding generations. We might speak of Sarah, the mother of Isaac,—of Hannah, the mother of Samuel,—of Elizabeth, the mother of John the Baptist,—of Mary, the mother of Jesus. But time would not permit us to dwell. It is recorded to the imperishable honor of woman, that she was last at the cross and first at the sepulchre of Christ,—last to witness his dying agony, and first to proclaim his triumphant resurrection. We are to consider,

II. THE INFLUENCE WHICH PIOUS FEMALES EXERT OVER OTHERS.

It is not intended here to speak of the influence which pious females exercise over their own sex alone, but over all classes, of both sexes. The wise, energetic, pious woman, occupies a distinguished place in the history of our species, as given in the holy Scriptures. Woman was created to be 'an help meet for man;' and she has proven herself not unworthy the design of her Creator. With a heart and head regulated by correct feelings and principles, she is not improperly styled, 'Heaven's first best gift to man;' or to use the more impressive language of holy writ, 'Her price is far above rubies.' * Let us consider,

1. *Her influence in the family as a wife.*

That she who is 'bone of our bone, and flesh of our flesh,' should have a greater influence over us than any one else, is a point settled by the word of God. 'Wherefore shall a man leave his father and his mother, and, cleave unto his wife, and they shall be one flesh.' † The tender cords that bind the affectionate

---

* Prov. xxxi: 10.   † Gen. ii: 24.

son to his kind father and amiable mother, are loose when compared with those which now bind him to the wife of his virtuous
choice. It is true, he does not cease to love his father and mother,
but he loves his wife more. This is one of the laws of heaven,
stamped upon our existence for purposes wise and good. Thus
the affections of the son and his wife, (as they do not flow back
to the parent,) are concentrated and thrown forward upon each
other and upon their mutual offspring, from age to age, through
all coming time.

The husband is destined to feel the influence of his wife, either
for weal or for woe. The inspired penman has written, 'It is
better to dwell in the wilderness, than with a contentious and
angry woman.' But it is again written, 'The unbelieving husband is sanctified by the wife,' the believing wife.* Who can
estimate the amount of holy influence which the prayers and
godly conversation of a Christian wife may have over her impenitent husband? God has said, 'It is not good that man should be
alone.' The wife was not created merely to help him make
money,—to help him decorate the frail body which is so soon to
fall a prey to the greedy worms of the grave. No; more valuable purposes were to be accomplished in bestowing upon man an
help meet. She is eminently qualified, by piety, to help him make
his calling and his election sure. What pious husband who is
blest with an intelligently pious wife, has not felt the force of this
declaration? How pleasant the family altar, where hearts united
in fearing the Lord, meet to implore his blessing upon their undying spirits! The Almighty himself has fixed, unchangeably,
a price upon the virtuous, sensible, pious woman. We repeat it.
'Her price is far above rubies.' 'The heart of her husband doth
safely trust in her.' 'She will do him good and not evil, all the
days of her life.' '*She will do him good*,'—it will not be an
attempt followed by a failure. The man who can lightly esteem
such a woman, offers insult to the God that made him. And he
who makes piety a secondary consideration in the selection of a
wife, makes religion a secondary object in his own soul. Such
an individual seems to say, *Give me a wife with a plenty of money
and money's pleasures; and religion and religious pleasures you
may give to the winds.*

It sometimes occurs that the wife is religious and the husband
an *unbeliever.* How can she exercise, to the best advantage, an
influence over him? She may do this by her pious *deportment*;
but there is nothing in the word of God, nor in the feelings of a
kind husband, which forbids her praying in his presence in the
family.

But the devotions of the *Christian husband* are aided by the
religious wife. He may be 'cast down,' and feel,—deeply feel,

---

* 1 Cor. vii; 14.

—the need of spiritual help. How seasonable! how pleasant are the prayers of the wife on such occasions at the family altar! Again, he may be confined to his chamber on a bed of affliction. O, who can come around his pillow—who can offer supplication so sincere, so moving, and so availing, as the wife whose holy life has been to him a 'crown of rejoicing' in his healthful days!

2. *Her influence as a mother.*

Just so certain as God designed woman to be a mother, so certainly did he design she should be instrumental in moulding, properly, the mind and morals of her infant offspring. It is painful for us to know that a few, (though very few,) professedly, christian parents have thought it improper to teach *children* the Scrip-tures, from a supposed incapacity, on the part of the child, to understand religious truths. But we would seriously ask, *What are the Scripture examples and precepts on this subject?* Have we forgotten that when God gave the law to the Israelites, he required of parents that his holy commandments should be observed by them and their children after them? 'Thou shalt teach them diligently unto thy children, and shalt talk of them when thou sittest in thy house, and when thou walkest by the way, and when thou liest down, and when thou risest up.' 'And when thy son asketh thee in time to come, saying, what mean the testimonies, and the statutes, and the judgments, which the Lord our God commanded you? Then shalt thou say, we were Pharaoh's bondmen in Egypt,' &c. Deut. vi: 7, 20. By this quotation we prove clearly the importance of religiously instructing children, *in childhood*, that when they shall ask us, in riper years, what these things mean, we may be able to give that explanation which the Holy Spirit may sanctify to their souls' salvation.

But some may say, *This obligation belonged to the Jewish dispensation, and is not binding upon us in the gospel day.* We reply—what has Paul said to Timothy, his son in the gospel? He exhorted him to continue in the things which he had LEARNED and been assured of, 'knowing of whom thou has learned them; and that from a CHILD thou hast known the holy Scriptures which are able to make thee wise unto salvation, through faith which is in Christ Jesus.' Timothy's mother was a Jewess, and his father a Greek. (Act. xvi: 1.) His grand-mother Lois, was a believer; and his mother Eunice had taught him the Scriptures from a child. All we know of his father is, that he was a Greek —not a word is said of him as a *believer.* But the female ancestry of Timothy is mentioned by Paul, with pleasing recollections. He rejoiced that Timothy had been blest with a pious mother and grand-mother. What an inestimable blessing! Some of us have mothers dead and in glory. The many times they kneeled with us to pray for the blessing of God upon our infant souls, are fresh upon the tablet of our memory. To some of us it is the most pleasing recollection of our life, to know that our infantile years were nurtured in the bosom of maternal piety.

Who that has read the history of the Christian Church, is not struck with the ardent piety of *Monica*, the mother of Augustine? She endeavored to instil into his infant mind the doctrines of heavenly truth. Nor were her labors fruitless. He grew up, it is true, without religion; and though eloquent, learned, and esteemed wise, he reached his thirtieth year before he became 'wise unto salvation.' Says he; 'while I was yet walking in sin, my dear mother, in vigorous hope, persisted in prayer to God for me.' A short time previous to his conversion, in his obstinacy, he stole away from his mother at night, and sailed for Rome, leaving her weeping and praying for him on the sea-shore. She soon found that he had gone thither; and, says he, ' *Courageous through piety she followed me through sea and land.*' He was converted before she arived at Rome, and she found him rejoicing in the love of God. He determined to return with her to Africa. While preparations were making for their departure, they were standing together at a window one evening, and expatiating on the blessed condition of the saints, and on the littleness of all worldly things. She said, ' *Son what do I here?* One thing only, *your conversion*, was an object for which I wished to live. My God has given me this—*what do I here?*' Five days after, she took a fever and died.

Mothers, you have religious duties to discharge towards your children, which you cannot neglect without the frowns of God coming upon you. Follow them by your prayers, your tears and a holy life, as did the mother of Augustine. Teach them to pray, —teach them to read the holy Bible,—teach them to remember the Sabbath day to keep it holy,—teach them to attend the Church and be sober,—teach them to live peaceably with others,—teach them to do justice, to love mercy and to walk humbly before God all their days,—let your fire-side circle be itself A SABBATH SCHOOL AND A BIBLE-CLASS. Say to them, as did the Psalmist, ' come, ye children, hearken unto me and I will teach you the fear of the Lord.' How delightful! to behold a father and mother united, heart and hand, in training up the objects of their mutual love in the way they should go! How pleasant it is to spend a Sabbath-eve with such a family! All is order, peace and happiness. The father, mother, sons, daughters and servants, are all cheerful under the influence of a well-regulated religious discipline.

> 'O! how delightful is that dwelling-place
> Where all the members of the household meet,'
> To sing the praises of Almighty grace
> And bow with reverence at the mercy-seat!'

How unlike this, is that family where there is no uniformity, no fixedness of purpose, in these matters! Religious duties in such a family are a task, and the public services of the Church a burden to them.

Are you a widowed mother? Your husband has been accustomed to gather his family together to invoke heaven's blessing upon them. He is dead. How silent! how solitary and desolate the house, under any circumstances, compared with what it was! Evening comes, and the hour of prayer comes, but no song of praise is heard,—no sound of prayer falls upon the ear of the sorrowing orphans. Lonesomeness and gloom reign throughout the desolate mansion. The children, unused to such a state, seem to sigh for the accustomed prayer. Mother of these helpless sorowers, shall they sigh in vain? In the providence of God they are thrown alone upon your arm for temporal and eternal aid. O will you not arise and look to the God of the widow and the fatherless for help? ' *Who will pray for me now,*' said a child to its father, ' *since mother is dead?*' The father had lived without prayer, and the child had never heard him pray; but the question made such an impression upon his heart that he rested not until he found peace with God in prayer. 'Mother who will pray for us now father is dead?' is a question which, we fear, might be asked by the children of too many bereaved pious females. But how can you, Christian mothers, neglect this duty towards your children? God has promised to bless you and them. 'I will give them one heart and one way, that they may fear me forever; for the good of them and their children after them. Jer. xxxii: 39.

We have a model of female excellence given in the 31st chapter of Proverbs, which it would be unpardonable to pass unnoticed in this discourse. 'She opens her mouth in wisdom and her lips are the law of kindness.' 'She eats not the bread of idleness— her children rise up and call her bleased; her husband also, and he praiseth her.' Truly blessed are the children of such a mother; and blest is the husband of such a wife; for when he shall leave her by death, he shall feel that his God, is the God of the orphan children and their widowed mother. Let every female who would fill her station to the glory of God, and who would learn the true science of being happy, amiable and useful, imitate the example of this wife, mother and mistress.

3. *Her influence as mistress in the family.*

She should pray with her household, especially in the absence of her husband. Prayers should not be suspended in the absence of the praying husband. She should read the Scriptures, pray with them, and talk to them daily on the subject of religion. All her demeanor should disclose to them the spirit and temper of a Christian,—of a soul that holds communion with God, and estimates religion as the pearl of great price. Like Lydia she should retire with her family to the 'place where prayer is wont to be made,'—to the Church,—to the prayer meeting. Can we not readily perceive the hand of God in the conversion of Lydia's household through her instrumentality? May we not look back from young Timothy to his mother Eunice, and still back to his grand-mother Lois and find the remote instrumentality of his conversion to the Christian faith? Cannot some of us go back to the days of unpolluted childhood, when we were taught to lisp at a mother's knee, '*Our father who art in heaven,*' and there date the first whisperings of that still small voice which brought us to the fold of God?

4. *Her influence in the Church among her female friends.*

There is power in a holy life, which disarms infidelity itself. And if infidelity is more abhorrent in one class than another, it surely is in that of females. One writer asserts that '*a female infidel is a monster in human form.*' But the pious female in going into the circle of the sisterhood will not encounter such monsters. There she will meet with kindred spirits. There by a holy life, she will kindle a holy fire which will consume envy, hatred, malice, and all the kindred train of evil. She may converse freely on the subject of religion—may unite in prayer with and for them, and thus shed around her an influence which will animate, strengthen and encourage those of her own sex, and diffuse a heavenly radiance over the whole brotherhood. But consider,

5. *Her influence among the brethren.*

By an intelligent and well regulated zeal, she may give life and energy to the services of God's house. The minister himself, while he has indubitable evidence that her heart is lifted up in prayer for him, feels her influence as he breaks to the people the bread of life. When he rises in the sacred desk to enter upon the duties of his high calling, and casts his eye over the assembly, and beholds even *one* whose prayers he knows are ascending to heaven for a blessing on his labors, he thanks God and takes courage,—is strong in the Lord and the power of his might, and feels that he is not working single-handed in the vineyard of his Divine Master. Paul acknowledges the help of some of the devout sisterhood of the Philippian Church. 'I entreat thee also, true yoke-fellow, help those women which labored with me in the gospel.' What those labors were, we are not informed. It must have been in prayer, and deeds of charity and benevolence, that they labored with him; for he did not permit women to preach.

The Sabbath school opens a delightful field of labor for pious females. In this they may co-operate with the brethren, and be efficient laborers with the minister in teaching transgressors the way of the Lord. Who can estimate the amount of good this modern enterprize has already accomplished? It has thrown

light and life into the abodes of darkness and death,—has waked
up the slumbering energies of the Christian world,—is driving
before it the clouds of ignorance and superstition, by pouring into
the youthful mind the wholesome, simple truths of God's Book:
Every Church should be a Sabbath school, and all the brethren
and sisters should, to the utmost of their ability and opportunity,
foster and sustain the glorious enterprize.   Baptists, as they have
ever claimed the Bible as their only ' *rule of faith and practice,*'
and have acknowledged no other book of doctrine and discipline,
should be foremost in the labors of this blessed institution.

6. *Her influence on the world.*

Humanity depraved is so poor a thing, that it is difficult, if not
impossible, to say what it will not do.   Some of our own sex
have such a poor, not to say contemptible, opinion of female intel-
lectuality, as to intimate that all the '*weaker*' vessels are to be
found only among the other sex.   It would be a blessing to the
world if it were so ; but so it is not.   Weakness has not fallen
upon the *daughters* of Eve alone.   That disposition which leads
any of our sex to smile with self-complacency at the claims set
up in behalf of female worth, may be adduced as proof; and
may, very properly, be referred back for its paternity to a more
barbarous and less enlightened age, than the one in which it is
our happy privilege to live.   It is certain that the illiberal abuse
poured upon the female sex is founded in ignorance and folly.
The truly sensible and well informed entertain far better, and far
more just sentiments, in relation to female utility and importance
in the scale of being ; and are ever disposed to ascribe to female
capacity and worth, more than female modesty and wisdom are
disposed to assume or even receive.   No good man has ever
wished to see the female character undervalued or degraded ; and
perhaps very few good women have ever violently coveted
stations and employments which belong peculiarly to men.   The
rivalship and competition of the sexes are altogether ridiculous
and absurd.   Each has its distinct dignity and influence, and
mutual concession is the truest wisdom in the one and the
other.

Let us not conclude, then, that a pious lady is going beyond
the appropriate sphere of her action, when she carries with her
into the world the religion of Christ—that religion which throws
a charm around her by giving softness, gentleness and ease, to her
manners ; and which makes her firm, without stubbornness ;
serious, without sadness ; lively, without levity ; and lovely,
without dissimulation :—that religion, emphatically, which
enables her, in all her associations with the world,

'To tread low-thoughted vice beneath the foot,
And soar above this little scene of things.'

In the circles of her own sex especially, an intelligently pious woman may be eminently successful in assisting and encouraging those who are serious and inclined to unite with the Church. 'A word fitly spoken is like apples of.gold in pictures of silver' —no matter if a *woman* should speak it. It may be sanctified to the spiritual peace of the enquiring soul, and it may dispose the halting convert to halt no more. The woman at the well of Samaria, when she heard the Son of God, ran off in all the raptures of a heaven-born spirit, leaving her water pot and telling the people of her delightful interview—'*Is not this the Christ?*' Many of the inhabitants of the village believed on him, 'because of the words which she spoke.' What a blessed privilege! to speak of Jesus and be owned as an instrument in the salvation of others! Woman may, and should speak of the goodness of God. It is no mark of piety in a woman, (or man either) to be dumb on the subject of religion. For a lady to be able to speak with a kind of enthusiastic fluency in relation to her flower-garden, and to be lifeless and speechless when 'the Rose of Sharon and the Lily of the valley' is the theme, is a reproach to her Christian character. For the *toilet-table* of her apartment, or the *center-table* of her parlor, to be loaded with the books of fiction, or the pamphlets of fashion, and be destitute of the Bible and of religious periodicals, is a reproach,—*a shameful reproach,*—to her head and her heart.

'Religion never was designed to make our comforts less.' Genuine piety does not make its subject gloomy, harsh, or impolite in the society of others. It dignifies, ennobles and elevates the character, and gives to the feelings a tenderness and sweetness which ever render its possessor more lovely to all. How easily, then, may the pious lady approach unconverted females, and, with the tenderness and kindness characteristic of her sex added to the sincerity and warmth of pious feeling, urge upon them the importance of repentance towards God and faith in our Lord Jesus Christ.

That spiritual peace depends much on spiritual deportment and practice, is confirmed by the word of God and the experience of all his saints. Women and men who live lives of practical godliness enjoy most of the life and power of religion in their souls. 'It is good to be zealously affected always in a good thing.' *It is good*—for man or woman. But an eminently pious and zealous woman often appears to the eye of the sluggardly, frozenhearted professor, like an enthusiast. Hence it not unfrequently happens that some of our own delinquent sex are disposed to cry, 'enthusiasm,'—'wild fire,'—'fanaticism'—'monomania,' and the like, when pious females are found ahead of them in holy living—when religion is the *theme of their conversation,* and the work of the Lord, *the business of their lives.* This is doubtless one of the Devil's weapons, put by him into the hands of such professors for their own unholy defence. Disposed, as too many of our own sex are, to undervalue the powers of the female mind, they feel perfectly justified in turning away with a sneer of contempt, believing that public sentiment, (their only rule for determining right and wrong,) will screen them from public odium. Indeed it is to be regretted that it sometimes does. Though it may seem severe, yet we cannot forbear stating it as our decided opinion, that many of the male members of the Churches are not what pious females ought to be—fall far behind that attainment which religious females ought to be expected to make.

Though women are generally more pious and warm-hearted in the service of God than men; yet it is not to be doubted that the standard of *female piety* is too low amongst us. It is probable that at this place, however, it is not below that of many others. But if the standard of female piety is too low, to what *cause* is it attributable? May we not fear that the cause may be found at our door? *We* are not what we should be. *Our* standard is not-occupying that high ground it should, and woman, (ever ready to shrink to the back-ground,) has to occupy at a fearful distance from her true position. Who among *you*, brethren, pray daily in your families? Who among *you* daily read the word of the Lord and bow before him at the family altar? No wonder then that our sisters so rarely do this, when it is so much neglected by those whose more immediate duty it is. While *you* have been remiss, and by *your* example encouraged others to be so, it is probable your pious wife, in her lonely hours of meditation, has said with a deep sigh from her heart a hundred times over, ' *If I were in my husband's place I would try to pray in the family.*' Husband of that godly wife, will you not try to pray? Wife of that delinquent husband, will you not help him? You would most willingly lay your hand to any of his worldly interests to assist him, and surely you would not withhold in helping him to lay up treasure in heaven. Provide the candle, at night, and lay the books before him, and ask him once. Probably this will be enough. It will, if he loves *you*, and his *children*, and his *God*, as he should. What a delightful sight—a father, and his beloved wife and tender offspring, all on their knees, before the Lord their Maker, pleading for the bread of life! And who was instrumental in bringing him to the family altar? YOU, THE WIFE OF HIS HOLY VOW. AMEN.

EXTRACTS.

1. *The manner of Lydia's conversion*—The manner of Lydia's conversion ought not to be overlooked. Her heart was opened. There is something gentle, as well as effectual, in the representation. The Spirit of God not only operates by a variety of instruments, but by a considerable diversity of modes. He descends on Sinai in tempests, and on Calvary in smiles. Some-

times his manifestations are terrible, and sometimes soothing; sometimes he breaks, and sometimes opens the heart. In Scripture we are furnished with illustrations of this diversified operation. Manasseh, who 'made Judah and the inhabitants of Jerusalem to err, and to do worse than the heathen,' and who 'would not hearken' to divine monitions, was taken by the Assyrians 'among the thorns, and bound with fetters, and carried to Babylon.' He who was unaffected, either by mercies or menaces, in his prosperity, 'when he was in affliction, besought the Lord his God, and humbled himself greatly before the God of his fathers, and prayed unto him; and he was entreated of him and heard his supplication, and brought him again to Jerusalem into his kingdom. Then, Manasseh kew that the Lord he was God.' Paul, who breathed out threatening and slaughter against the Christian Church, was suddenly struck to the earth by a miraculous light from heaven, and from a persecutor transformed into an apostle. The Philippian jailer exclaimed amidst his terrors, 'What must I do to be saved?' and was not only prevented from committing suicide, but directed to heaven by the doctrine of his apostolic prisoner, which through grace he cordially received: 'Believe on the Lord Jesus Christ, and thou shalt be saved, and thine house.' On the other hand, Samuel, Timothy, and Lydia, were 'drawn with bands of love.' They heard the whispers of mercy, and felt the attractions of grace. Each of their hearts, like that of Lydia, was *opened*. Passion subsided, prejudice withdrew, ignorance melted away. They were not taken by storm, but 'made *willing* in the day of his *power*.'

2. *The effects of her religion.*—Previous to her embracing the gospel she united business with piety. She was 'diligent in business,' but this did not preclude her being 'fervent in spirit.' As a seller of purple she could only have become *rich*—the acme, indeed, and summit of human wishes, but a miserable barter for real and everlasting happiness; as a hearer of Paul, she might and did become '*wise unto salvation.*'

Every thing is beautiful in its season. We must not wander from our proper business under pretence of religion, nor must we neglect religion upon a plea of business. Religion does not require a relinquishment of our calling and station in society, but no civil engagement can justify a disregard of religion. We may sell our purple—but we must also attend to the instructions of the ministry and the word of God. If we imitate Lydia in diligence, let us not forget to imitate her in piety. It is vain and wicked to aver, that the concerns of this world and those of another interfere; because an ardent religion is not only compatible with worldly occupations, but promotes both their purity and integrity, if it does not secure their success.—*Cox's Fem. Biog.*

THE
BAPTIST PREACHER.

| VOL. III. | May, 1844. | NO. 5. |

THE RECORDING OF THE DIVINE NAME:

*A Sermon, delivered at St. Stephen's Meeting House, King &
Queen Co., Va., on its being first opened for divine worship,
December, 24, 1843: by Rev. W. Southwood, Pastor of the
Church.*

To the members of the Church, by whose Christian benevolence and
liberal subscriptions, the house, for the public Worship of God in the ancient
parish of St. Stephens, was designed and erected, who, from too high an
estimate of his worth, called one so unworthy of such a charge, to watch
over their spiritual interests, as a shepherd under Christ, and to feed them with
divine knowledge, in dependence upon the Holy Spirit:—and, to all who have
rendered their aid in the building: and, to all who are friendly to the effort, to
record the Lord's name in this place, the following discourse is respectfully
inscribed, by   THE AUTHOR.

Vineyard, King & Queen, January 1, 1844.

'*In all places where I record my name I will come unto thee,
and I will bless thee.*' **Ex. xx: 24.**

God, who is at once infinitely lovely, and awfully terrible, encourages man, who has deformed and polluted himself by vices
the most pernicious, and sins the most heinous, to make His name
the wall of his defence, and the wing of His mercy the covering
under which he may repose. All defiled as we are, he who is
of purer eyes than to behold evil, and who cannot look upon
iniquity, hath promised to sprinkle clean water upon us, that we
may be clean; and notwithstanding we have rebelled against him,
he is saying to us who are in arms against his government—
'*Come now and let us reason together;*—and like a tender father
he continues to address us:—'Hast thou an arm like God? or
canst thou thunder with a voice like him? He looketh upon the
earth and it trembleth: he toucheth the hills and they smoke.
The eyes of all wait upon him and he giveth them their meat in

due season;—he taketh away their breath, they die, and return to their dust. Submit yourselves therefore to God. Humble yourselves in the sight of the Lord, and he shall lift you up. Draw nigh to God and he will draw nigh to you.'

Our text, and the circumstances attending its delivery, display the awful grandeur and the infinite condescension of Jehovah. He alarms by the fearful scene which is exhibited on the top of the mount and encourages communion with himself by the words sent down by his servant Moses. But when we think of communion between God, who is holy, just and true; and man, who is sinful and condemned by a most righteous law; we must never lose sight of the absolute necessity of a Mediator. Through the infinite goodness of God, one, in all respects suitable, was revealed at an early period; and in process of time a nation was set apart, and even the family selected, from which he should descend. Moreover, a government was constituted, laws were ordained, and predictions were uttered, so extraordinary in their character, that this Mediator, when he should appear, could scarcely be mistaken by any one who would carefully and honestly compare his claims to the office, with the records of the nation.

A plan, no less wise than gracious, securing the rights of the Divine government, and magnifying all the Divine attributes, is established by the mediation of Him, who was God manifest in the flesh. And this plan, originating in the Divine clemency brings glory to God in the highest, on earth peace, and salvation to men.

All the institutions of revealed religion are intended to glorify God, and secure the highest possible good to man, by leading him to acts of worship, in his earthly courts, as a faint shadow of the worship in heaven, where faith shall be laid aside, for the 'enjoyment of the beatific vision, in the fruition of the object of faith.'

The worship in this lower world, is, often, in its outward habits, the covering for dispositions, which, if the veil were stript off, the service, and the votary, would exhibit a striking contrast. But although this may, unhappily, be the state of things in the Church, it should not deter the sincere Christian from engaging in acts of faith, and religious worship; nor from benevolent efforts for the erection of buildings for the accommodation of those who wish to go where the way of life is pointed out by the preachers of the gospel: for by such means, instituted by Divine authority, sanctioned by Divine example, and encouraged by Divine promises, sinners may be brought from east, and from the west, from the north, and from the south, to sit down with Abraham, Isaac and Jacob, in the kingdom of God.

When Stephen, that eminent saint of God, stood before the grand council of the Jewish nation, on the day of his martyrdom, he gave a brief epitome of the history of that remarkable people, from the call of Abram to the death of Christ; whom he by way of eminence styles 'the *Just one*,' while the council itself, he denounces as his '*betrayers and murderers.*' An extract of this persecuted saint's defence against the malicious charge of blasphemy, will bring us to that part of their Exodus where Jehovah was pleased to give to Israel the words of the text. 'God spoke to Abraham in this wise, That his seed should sojourn in a strange land; and that they should bring them into bondage, and intreat them evil four hundred years. And the nation to whom they shall be in bondage will I judge, said God: and after that they shall come forth and serve me in this place.' Acts vii: 6, 7.

.. When the emancipated tribes had proceeded about fifty days on their journey from Egypt, the land of their bondage, towards Canaan, the place referred to by this eminent saint, and first martyr to the Christian cause, they came to the mountain in the desert of Arabia Petræa, with the two memorable peaks, Horeb and Sinai, before which Israel encamped.

And surprising as was the display of the Divine power, when Moses struck the rock in Horeb, whence refreshing streams gushed forth from the opening flint; a scene of a much more wonderful character was now to be exhibited on the adjoining mount.

The cloudy pillar which had been their guide in the wilderness, now rested upon the summit of Sinai, and Moses went thither to receive the Divine commands. The Angel which spake to him in the mount, directed him to return to the people and inform them that Jehovah intended to make a solemn covenant with them; and that if they would obey him he would confer upon them privileges and honors such as no other nation could enjoy. When Moses had delivered his message to the people, they replied: 'All that the Lord hath spoken we will do.' Now the lively oracles were received, now the covenant was ratified between God and Israel, and the form of their government constructed. Never before had there been a display of the Divine presence so august and overwhelming to the beholders. So appalling was the sight that the people petitioned that the details of their law might not be spoken to them, but given first to Moses, and by him to the nation. And the Gospel tells us that 'so terrible was the sight, that Moses said, I exceedingly fear and quake.' Indeed the whole scene was so tremendous that Divine support alone could sustain a creature constituted as man is. The great lawgiver of Israel has himself depicted it:—'And it came to pass on the third day in the morning, that there were thunders and lightnings and a thick cloud upon the mount, and the voice of the trumpet exceeding loud; so that all the people that was in the camp trembled. And Moses brought forth the people out of the camp to meet with God; and they stood at the nether part of the mount.' 'And all the people saw the thunderings, and the lightnings, and the noise of the trumpet, and the mountain smoking: and when the people saw it, they removed, and stood afar off.—Ex. xix: 16–19. xx: 18.

The Ten Commandments, written with the finger of God, on two tables of stone, were delivered amidst such awful grandeur. And now, lest the people might suppose that God who had displayed this magnificent scene before them would be pleased with pomp and show in the worship which his people should offer to him, hoping thus to appease his anger, or obtain his favor, he commanded them to observe the greatest simplicity in erecting the altar, on which they should sacrifice to him, and our text is a gracious declaration and promise connected with this command. 'In all places where I record my name I will come unto thee and I will bless thee.'

In discoursing from the text, it is my intention,

I. To examine the import of the expression '*my name*;' as it is here used;

II. To show how this name is to be '*recorded*' in any place; and

III. To consider the *promise* connected with the recording of this name.

According to the order proposed, I am

I. To examine the import of the expression, '*my name*,' as used in the text.

We can see much of the great first cause, the Supreme Being, in the works of creation. The wisdom which contrived, and the power which executed such a plan can never be deceived nor resisted. Infinite in his comprehension and in his working, he ever continues the same. His name is impressed where ever his beneficence is seen, or his government felt. 'The invisible things of him from the creation of the world are clearly seen, being understood by the things that are made, even his eternal power and Godhead.' Rom. i: 20. But David says, 'He hath magnified his word above all his *name*.' Ps. cxxxviii: 2. Amidst the splendor and variety of created objects, men, in their fallen state, 'professing themselves to be wise, became fools, and worshipped and served the creature besides (para) the Creator.' Rom. i: 25. To lead men from the debasing practice of idolatry, towards which there seems to be a natural propensity in the human heart; and to draw attention to the Messiah, who was to come into the world, to make an atonement for transgression, and establish a kingdom of a purely spiritual character, are the great objects for which the old Testament was given, and the Jewish nation set apart under its peculiar, but temporary government. In these we find a gradual developement made of that eternal, and incomprehensible Being whose mode of existence cannot be described; from whom all beings derive their existence and support; and who needs nothing, can receive nothing, from any of his creatures. It is here that he hath unfolded his will, and instructed us in his nature and character more plainly and more fully, than 'by the things that are made.'

The perfection of this glorious Being, no creature, however

high can comprehend: and should he reveal himself to man in any other way than he has already done, it would still be only what the exhibition of the most delicate, and complicated piece of machinery would be to the gaze of the wild untutored savage. And there is nothing which can be formed, no resemblance made, which can convey to the mind, any idea of him. He has prohibited all attempts at such a resemblance, in compassion perhaps to man's ignorance, as well as being jealous of the glory and honor of his name: for, what fools have men made of themselves where idolatry has existed! And if we would see the nature of the crime of image-worship, it is only necessary to read a few verses in the 33d chapter of Exodus, where, for this great sin, 3000 Israelites were in one day put to death. But he has been pleased to make himself known by *names*, and by such appellations as can belong to no other being than himself.

1. When the fulness of time was come, and Messiah was exercising his Divine mission, one of the very important lessons which he taught, was, that ' Moses wrote of him.' And how soon do we find this declaration confirmed on turning to the writings of the great Jewish lawgiver. In the very first sentence of his history, one of the names which can belong to no other than to the Supreme Being occurs, a name throughout the Bible applied to each of the three persons in the Divine essence. In the Hebrew ELOHIM, which, in our Bible is translated God, the most learned and pious men, not only Christians, but Jews themselves, most confidently assert, that it must, without contradiction, teach a plurality of Persons in the Divine essence. Mr. Romain, whose learning and piety are worthy of the highest respect and confidence, says, when speaking of this word, ' It belongs to the covenant of grace, and is descriptive of the acts and offices of the eternal three in the glorious plan of man's salvation.' And again—' It is a relative word descriptive of the gracious offices of the eternal three in the economy of man's redemption. And neither the personality expressed by its being plural, nor its meaning, is retained by our translators in the singular word, God.'

The thoughts conveyed by this NAME should enter into every act of religious worship;—in every exercise of that faith, which *purifies the heart and works by love, and overcomes the world,* it must be found;—for ' he that cometh to God must believe that he is;'—that he is what he is,—what he is revealed to be;—a Triune God. What he is revealed to be, is his *name*; and this can only be comprehended by himself. He has not revealed himself that we should comprehend him, but that we should adore him. That we should adore those perfections which compose his *name*.

2. To the patriarchs he was known by another name also. ' I appeared unto Abraham, unto Isaac and unto Jacob, by *the name* of God Almighty.' Ex. vi: 3. Here his all-sufficiency is set forth in his *name*, that when the patriarchs are called upon

to trust their covenant God with their own lives, and to believe
that events the most extraordinary and wonderful shall be accomplished in their descendants, he condescends to encourage them by
the assurance that he is all-sufficient—all-sufficient to explain, in
due time all mysteries, and accomplish all promises. This was
given for their faith to rest upon; as if he had said to them, I am
all-sufficient, though you cannot comprehend all my plans, or
penetrate my purposes. Thus, his *name* was to them a strong
tower, into which they might run, and feel entire security.

3. When Moses was called to present himself before the faithless monarch of Egypt, and demand the liberation of Israel, he
anxiously enquired by what *name*, he, who had charged him with
such an unheard-of commission, should be made known to those
to whom he was sent?   The answer given is, ' I am, that I am. '
' Thus shalt thou say unto the children of Israel,' ' I am' hath
sent me unto you. '   In this name, He, who proclaims himself by
it, declares that he is *The Being;* The eternal one; The Infinite; The Unchangeable ; The Independent one.   I will be,
what I will be!   Who can think of this *name* without involunta-
rily exclaiming, in the words of Elihu, ' Touching the Almighty
we cannot find him out. '   Job. xxxvii: 23   May we not venture
to suppose that this *name* was intended to convey encouragement
to Israel?   Moses was about to say to them, ' The God of your
fathers hath sent me unto you,' and he anticipated an enquiry
which they might make—*What is his name?* Now may not the
answer given in these mysterious words, ' I am that I am,' (if
Moses leading Israel out of Egypt, in their way to Canaan was
typical of Messiah leading his Church from this world to heaven,)
be found explained in the xx Ps.; ' The *name* of the God of
Jacob *shall* defend thee ; in the *name* of our God will we set up
our banner.   Some trust in chariots and some in horses: but we
will remember the *name* of the Lord our God. They are brought
down and fallen ; but we are risen and stand upright.'   That
which God was to Abraham, Isaac and Jacob, that he would be,
and that he was, to Israel; and all the promises made to the
fathers should be, and were, fulfilled to them, their children; for
this is his *name*, ' I AM, THAT I AM. ' And was there not great
reason why they should sing in a subsequent part of their history,—' When Israel went out of Egypt, the house of Jacob from
a people of a strange language: Judah was his sanctuary and
Israel his dominion. The sea saw it and fled: Jordan was driven
back.   Not unto us, O Lord, not unto us, but unto thy *name* give
glory for thy mercy and for thy truth's sake. ' Ps. cxiv. cxv.

4. Jehovah is likewise a *name* by which the Most High is
known, and is perhaps, the most expressive ; and now on Israel's
deliverance, about to be used in a way peculiarly appropriate ; so
much so that he says, ' I appeared unto Abraham, unto Isaac, and
unto Jacob by the name of God Almighty, but by my name
Jehovah was I not known to them ;' that is, not in the way in

which he was now about to make himself known to Israel. He had made promises that he would take them into covenant with himself, and go before them; drive out the heathen before their face, and establish them under a peculiar constitution; now he was about to give *existence* to that singular form of government, so long ago, and so repeatedly promised, not that it should be carried into effect in the days of Abraham, Isaac and Jacob when the promises were made, but with their posterity. And as all this was done without any cause in them, so when he gave it effect, when he brought the covenant established with the patriarchs, into *existence*, he would be known by his great name JEHOVAH, which signifies *existence*—existence without a cause. ' *I am that I am*,' may be regarded as an explanation of this. But the *name* of the Lord always has reference to the covenant of grace, just as all the sacrifices offered upon the Jewish altar pointed to the great sacrifice Christ; and, hence the expression ' *my name*,' here, is connected so immediately with building the altar, which altar was typical of the human nature of Christ, upon which ' he made his soul an offering for sin.'

We shall see how the *name* of the Lord is expressive of his Divine perfections in the work of Redemption, if we look into that magnificent passage in which ' the Lord proclaimed his *name* to Moses, when he descended in the cloud, and stood with him upon the mount. The Lord, the Lord God merciful and gracious, long-suffering, and abundant in goodness and truth, keeping mercy for thousands, forgiving iniquity and transgression and sin, and that will by no means clear the guilty.' Ex. xxxiv: 5, 6, 7. By comparing this passage with that to which it relates, in the preceding chapter, (xxx: 19,) ' I will make all my goodness pass before thee,' you will see that it is but an amplification of what had been previously promised; a glorious cluster of the most precious declarations ever made to man, shewing how God could be ' gracious to whom he would be gracious.' This proclamation opens up to the believer's mind the covenant of redemption. Here, by faith, he sees Christ suffering as his people's surety; mercy and truth, righteousness and peace, meeting together, in him. Ps. lxxxv.

It is viewing *Jehovah* as a covenant God that the believer understands how every one who calls upon the *name* of the Lord shall be saved. Joel ii: 32. Not that the uttering of a word, or name however great can save. He has prohibited the ' taking his name in vain; and there it stands in the imperishable code, an awful warning to ignorance and rashness; but the knowledge of God in covenant is the way to acceptance, and salvation. Isa. liii: 2. John xvii: 3. When knowledge and piety separated from ignorance and idolatry in the days of Enos, ' then began men to call upon the *name* of the Lord,' (Gen. iv: 26.)—to worship him as a God in covenant, as Abel did; relying upon he promise, that the seed of the woman should bruise the serpent's head.   Gen. iii: 15.   And the language of all true believers ever will be, 'the desire of our soul is to thy *name*, and to the remembrance of thee.' Isa. xxvi: 8.   The *name* of the Lord imports what the Father, Son and Holy Spirit have graciously covenanted to do for the salvation of sinners.   This *name* was made known in various ways under the Old Testament dispensation: and Paul was chosen to bear the *name* of the Lord before the Gentiles, and kings, and the children of Israel, and for the sake of this *name* he was to suffer great things.   Acts ix: 15, 16.   And in the course of his labors he informs us, 'the Holy Ghost witnesseth in every city, saying that bonds and afflictions abide me.   But none of these things move me, neither count I my life dear unto myself, so that I might finish my course with joy, and the ministry which I have received of the Lord Jesus, to testify the gospel of the grace of God.'   Acts xx: 23, 24.

Here we see that the '*name*' of the Lord, which Paul was to make known, was, 'the gospel of the grace of God.'   This is the *name which is above every name*.   And this is the *name* which, in dependence on grace divine, we hope to record in this place, waiting upon the King in Zion, who has said, in language exactly corresponding with what our text imports: 'Where two or three are gathered together in my *name*, there am I in the midst of them.'   Matt. xviii: 20.

This leads me to show,

II. How the *name* of the Lord, is to be *recorded* in any place.

The Lord recording his name under the Old Testament dispensation always had reference to what was to take place when the Messiah should come.   Previous to his coming, the Church was in its minority; the Mosaic ritual was its schoolmaster, instructing it by types and shadows, until the fulness of time should come.   At first the Tabernacle was the place where God recorded his name. This was a fabric formed according to the divine plan given to Moses in the mount, and the cost of its construction was met by the voluntary contributions of the people; and so zealous were they, that it is said,—'The people bring much more than enough for the service of the work; so the people were restrained from bringing.'   Ex. xxxvi.   Here was the altar, and here their sacrifices were offered; here communion with the Most High was sought, and by virtue of the promise in our text was obtained; 'and the glory of the Lord filled the Tabernacle.   Ex. xl.

Here the Lord recorded his name.   But the Tabernacle itself, the altar, the sacrifices, all had reference to Christ, and if we seek communion with the Father it can be obtained only through that Mediator.   From Abel to the last of the Old Testament saints all paid their homage to God, and expected the blessing, through faith in the promised Messiah.

The same Divine Architect which gave the plan of the Tabernacle, caused this structure to be superceded by another of a much more magnificent character, and more permanent in its location. In this, the sacred utensils used in the worship of God, corresponded in their character with those of the Tabernacle, and in size with the larger edifice in which they were used. The Temple now became the centre of the Mosaic institution; and here, as well as in the Tabernacle, all the offices of worship had reference to the covenant of grace, and the whole dispensation was subservient to the coming of the Messiah, who is 'the end of the law;' and whose death, by the wicked hands of treachery and violence, was a sure presage that this edifice, with all its splendor, should meet with such an utter overthrow, that 'not one stone should be left upon another.' In all the types, whether in persons or in things, *the Lord recorded his name.* The bleeding victim, at once exhibited, to the eye of faith, God's hatred of sin, as well as the atonement to be made by the *Lamb of God for the sin of the world.* On various parts of the covenant of Sinai, believers under the Old Testament looked, and were refreshed in their spirits, and rejoiced, by faith; for they discovered 'a more excellent ministry, a better covenant, which was established upon better promises.' It was such persons, and such persons only, who saw Jehovah's name recorded in the symbolical service. The sacrifices were confined to the altar, and the services of the High Priest to the Temple; yet notwithstanding this, in every synagogue where a copy of the law was deposited, where the Prophets were read, where the solemn worship of God was observed, there also the Lord *recorded* his name as the God of salvation. Hence, perhaps, it was that there was such a laudable desire among the Jews to multiply synagogues. We are told that there were thirteen at Tiberias, in the days of our Lord, and four hundred in Jerusalem. In each of these places the law was expounded, and the writings of the Prophets read every Sabbath day. Thus, the hopes of all Israel were animated by having attention called to the Messiah.

And now, under the New Testament dispensation, in which all in the Old has its accomplishment; wherever the doctrines of the gospel are preached;—wherever christian obligations are set forth;—wherever the discipline of the church is enforced;—wherever the ordinances of the gospel are observed;—wherever the promises of a covenant-God, in Christ Jesus, are held up for faith to lay hold upon;—wherever spiritual worship is engaged in;—there the name of the Lord is now *recorded,* and the King in Zion declares,—' Where two or three are gathered together in my name, there am I in the midst of them.' Matt. xviii: 20.

The bleeding sacrifices have now ceased to be offered. The altar has been thrown down, never more to be built. The vail of the Temple is rent, never to be repaired. The High Priest has lost his censer and his breastplate. But Christ has become all this, and more than all this, to us. He has offered himself once for all, and by his one offering forever perfected them that are sanctified. He is now the altar whereof we eat; the High Priest who has entered into heaven itself, there to appear in the presence of God for us, perfuming all our works of faith and labors of love with the rich fragrance of his own obedience and blood ; so that believers can now approach the mercy-seat through the rent vail of the flesh of Him who carries his Church as a seal set on his arm, as a seal set on his heart.

The purposes for which that wonderful theocracy was established in Israel have been accomplished, and the Angel of the covenant, (mentioned by St. Stephen,) who spake to Moses the words of our text, expressly calling himself Jehovah, who is so styled by Moses likewise, has appeared, clothed in our nature, made like his brethren, in all things except sin! This wonderful spectacle, this great mystery of godliness, God manifest in the flesh, utters from lips truly human, and with a voice really ours, ' *Where two or three are assembled in my name, there am I in the midst of them.*' The entire spirit of this passage and the text are the same. It may seem, to persons, too much under the influence of local attachments, and whose imagination is apt to linger about spots once the scenes of remarkable occurrences, or which awaken, by associations, our sympathies, that those places, sacred to memory, on account of events which have transpired, would be the honored places where God would make the most remarkable displays of his power and goodness,—record his name,—be in the midst of the assembly. But no!—

" ——————Where'er *believers* meet,
There, they behold thy mercy-seat;
Where'er they seek thee, thou art found,
And every place is hallow'd ground."

For wise and gracious purposes, God has hid, in merciful obscurity, many places which would otherwise have become the scenes of debasing idolatry and superstition, as they had formerly been of the displays of Divine mercies or judgments. The Jews had long been accustomed to have their religious thoughts absorbed by forms and localities. They had lost the spirit of their worship, in an inordinate attachment to places and ceremonies, relying upon his promised blessing in certain places and accompanying certain ceremonies, notwithstanding they might write Ichabod upon all their sacred observances. While their Temple yet stood, and their religious rites were still performed, the sacred fire had gone out, the Schechina had departed, Urim and Thummim were lost, the spirit of piety had almost entirely disappeared, the name was all that they retained of being the people of God. And when Messiah came, whom they had expected,— most of them alas! with a superstitious rather than an enlightened joy!—there was no beauty in him, that they should desire him.

When he told them that Jerusalem would be no more sacred than other places; that it should be destroyed and trodden down of the Gentiles; that his kingdom was not of this world, but that he was for salvation to the ends of the earth, and that the true worshippers must worship God in spirit and in truth; and that whosoever imbibed this doctrine should be saved; they said '*we will not have this man to reign over us.*'

There is this difference between *recording* the *name* of the Lord under the *first* and the *second* covenant. That dispensation was exhibitive, this is aggressive; that was confined with all its blessings to one nation, this is the power of God unto salvation to every one that believeth; that prefigured the essential doctrines and blessings, in what the Apostle calls carnal ordinances, which we under our aggressive, gospel system, proclaim to the ends of the world, and render victorious by weapons which are not carnal but mighty, to the pulling down of strong holds. And our blessed Lord when he ascended up on high, gave such gifts to men as qualified them for the work of recording his name, for the perfecting of the saints, for the work of the ministry, for the edifying of the body of Christ. Ep. iv. The Lord is still qualifying men for the work of the ministry, that they may record his name; and that that blessed promise spoken by Malachi may be fulfilled: 'from the rising of the sun even unto the going down of the same my name shall be great among the Gentiles; and in every place incense shall be offered unto my name, and a pure offering; for my name shall be great among the heathen saith the Lord of hosts.' Ch. ii: 11.

If we would record the name of the Lord now, in any place of worship, the great truths of the gospel must be explained and enforced. As to the place, nothing can make one place more sacred than another, but as gospel truths are for the time present recorded there.

I should esteem it a pleasing duty—a profitable exercise—at present to exhibit before you some of the great doctrines of holy writ, but our time will not admit. On future occasions, as Providence may open the way, and as grace may enable me to perform the task, I hope I shall not be backward in endeavoring to lead you into a knowledge of these doctrines which the Bible teaches, and which it has been the glory of the true Baptist Church firmly to hold, and fearlessly to profess and teach, through evil report, and good report, in all periods of its history.

On this occasion I remark that the doctrines of the Trinity,—election,—justification in Christ's righteousness, by faith alone,—the final perseverance of all *true believers* to eternal life,—when these are scripturally taught, in any place, there the name of the Lord is recorded. But the name of the Lord is not thus recorded in all places where the gospel is professedly preached, nor by all who profess to preach it.

The doctrine of the Trinity is the foundation of the christian fabric. Take it away and the whole building totters and falls. To honor the Father, the Son, and the Holy Spirit, the personal names given in the New Testament, to Elohim, the plural term by which Jehovah was made known, 'In the beginning,' is a very important consideration with all who would rightly serve God, and promote his cause.

What would become of Christianity without the Divinity of Christ? What without the personality and divinity of the Holy Spirit? What without the unity of the Godhead? Our obligations to revelation bind us to acknowledge with reverence, and to teach with trembling, that though there is but one God, yet in the Godhead there are three distinct persons; nor is this to be denied because we cannot comprehend the manner of their existence: then might we deny also the eternity and all the perfections of God.

There is also the great, and glorious doctrine of justification, through the imputed righteousness of Christ, by faith putting forth the hand as influenced, by the regenerating spirit of love in the heart of a sinner, till now in a state of condemnation. But the first motion of faith, towards Christ is that which secures the justification of the sinner, without the help of any previous work, or waiting for any work to follow. This is the great scripture doctrine of justification. The justification preached at the reformation, and the only justifying righteousness in which a sinner can stand at the last day. A doctrine which lies at the very threshold of the Christian Church.

The doctrine of election has reference to the subjects of God's special love, and his mere good pleasure in choosing them to salvation, through sanctification of the Spirit, and belief of the truth. Intimately connected with this, was that transaction called the covenant of grace, entered into between the sacred three, in which the Father chose, the Son undertook to redeem, and the Spirit to sanctify. Thus bringing many sons unto glory, (Heb. ii:) from that dreadful state of ruin in which the whole human family was plunged by sin.

Though believers have many enemies without, and the remains of sinful nature still struggling for the mastery within, and the work of the Spirit is much impeded in its progress, yet the covenant entered into with Christ, on behalf of his people is *ordered in all things and sure.* Where the precious seed has been sown in the heart, fruit to eternal life will be brought forth. And our blessed Savior says, 'I give unto them eternal life, and they shall never perish, neither shall any man pluck them out of my hand.' John x: 28. And upon this subject the Apostle Paul is not less plain in his declaration to the Philippians—'He who hath begun a good work [of grace] in you, will perform it unto the day of Jesus Christ.'

It is not intended by this little sketch of these doctrines, or by any remark connected with them, to convey an idea that they should be recorded in lines so prominent as to obscure in the least the lustre of other doctrines, dear to every believer; and which all together form the glorious galaxy of gospel truth. But because they are much more neglected than they ought to be, when their great importance in our holy religion is considered: and because, in some places, some of them are entirely overlooked, and in others only touched upon incidentally.

There are two classes of objectors to these doctrines. One class says they are contrary to human reason; to the best, the most equitable, and most merciful systems of human polity, and, therefore cannot form any part of the plan of the all-wise, and all-merciful God. Persons who talk thus seem to forget that the Author of reason, is also the Author of faith, and that he hath assigned appropriate spheres for each to operate in. Our intellectual faculties are necessarily confined to this world. To ascend above the material universe is mere speculation. We have no clear conception of any thing immaterial but that it exists. But faith ascends higher; it pierces the skies; and becomes familiar with things which the tallest intellect would never reach. 'Eye hath not seen,' says Paul, 'nor ear heard, neither have entered into the heart of man the things which God hath prepared for them that love him; but God hath revealed them unto us by his Spirit.' Here the Apostle informs us that revelation has opened up to faith, what no human intellect could discover. That faith soars above, and sees, what reason, (the idol of these objectors,) though it has eyes, sees not. Let human reason, and human sympathies fall down in profound reverence before that faith, which stands in fearless confidence upon the word of God.

The other class of objectors to preaching these doctrines, say that, prudence and expediency forbid that they should make a part of the preacher's labors. At least they must not be made prominent in preaching the gospel. But what gospel can we have without the Trinity? How can we preach the God of the Bible without it. The Athenian Philosophers in their speculative devotions dedicated an altar, by an inscription,—'*To the unknown God.*' St. Paul seeing this, benevolently proclaimed, '*Whom ye ignorantly worship, him declare I unto you!*' Here was no concealment; no doctrine of expediency, in operation in the Apostle's mind, to bar the truth; he had not taken satan's hush money to close his mouth against popular error, and moral delinquency, and 'pious fraud.' But like an ambassador, he boldly declares Him whose servant he was. And he declares him not only as he was, the Creator, as Moses said, when he called him by that plural name; but he also on the same occasion speaks of his predestinating purpose, and foreknowledge, '*having determined the times before appointed,*' &c. Acts xvii. What is this prudence, this expediency, which hides from the view of any, and all of the fallen race of Adam the righteousness of Christ imputed to sinners when they believe, for their justification? Why any concealment of the doctrines, (which some are afraid to touch,) from any persons, as the Puseyites do, who say, that, *until they have first been prepared for receiving the faith in its fulness, by insisting first of all upon repentance and judgment to come; by urging such assistances to poverty of spirit, as fasting and alms, and the necessity of reverent and habitual prayer, and that nothing* EXPLICIT *need be known of Christ, Now all this comes from the doctrine of 'Reserve' of the 'secret,' of what they [the Puseyites] call 'Economy.'* There is an admirable sermon by Bishop M. Ilvaine, against the doctrine of the Oxford tracts, which I feel pleasure in recommending. This doctrine has been gaining ground for many years in the Episcopal Church, and now it is shaking it to the very foundation. Those in that communion who feel their danger are now falling back upon those doctrines which have lain concealed, in a great measure for a length of time, as the only weapons of defence by which their citadel can be saved.

Hiding the great doctrines, of which I have been speaking, under the bushel of expediency, instead of proclaiming them upon the house-top, is the insidious working of a sly, selfish spirit, which will by-and-by, break forth with a power which nothing but those insulted, imprisoned truths, in the hand of the Holy Spirit, will be able to resist. In the opinion of the Pastor of this Church, the concealment of the great doctrines of grace has led to the present distraction in the Episcopal communion; and he here, at the opening of this house for gospel instruction and worship, raises his humble voice of warning, that, if those doctrines should be concealed by a considerable number of any other communion, a Pusey may arise among them and the same consequences may follow in another communion as are now seen in the Episcopal. The relation between God and the sinner is always to be considered in the recording his name in any place.

A guilty and condemned world at the feet of a just God; a crucified Jesus and pardon through his blood; a quickening spirit, and regeneration by his power; faith, repentance, conformity to the image of Christ; all belong to *recording* the *name* of the Lord. To these belong the holiness, the benevolence, the glad tidings of the gospel. Where prayer is wont to be made, and offered in a spiritual manner; where the praises of the Lord are sung with the spirit and with the understanding also; where the purity of the Church is preserved, not only by the doctrines preached, but by the discipline enforced; *there* the Lord's name is recorded.

Upon this extensive subject I may add, and that in few words; where the two standing ordinances of the gospel are rightly administered, there is the sacred name of the King in Zion recorded. In this place we hope to record his name in eating bread and drinking wine, in remembrance of the sufferings which he endured, and the atonement which he made.

'We see the blood of Jesus shed
Whence all our pardons rise,
The sinner views th' atonement made,
And loves the sacrifice.'

But in the ordinance of Baptism the name of the Lord will be recorded in another place, a place as sacred in itself as this, where those who have believed through grace, exhibit the delightful spectacle of being baptized *into the death of Jesus Christ.* There the Lord's name will be recorded in his three fold character of person,—by their baptism into the name of the Father, the Son, and the Holy Ghost. Baptism rightly performed is not merely a duty, or a recognition of certain christian doctrines, but an act of adoration addressed to each of the divine persons in Jehovah, and to the recording of the name of the Lord in this manner, his promised presence is annexed: 'Lo! I am with you always, even unto the end of the world.'

This leads me to consider,

III. The promise contained in the text—'*I will come unto thee, and I will bless thee.*

'*I will come unto thee,*' signifies more than his omnipresence, for in this sense he is, and must be, every where; but in its largest acceptation it signifies his *spiritual presence.* He was visibly with Israel in the cloudy pillar, and in the pillar of fire. He appeared also between the cherubim which were over the mercy-seat, in a visible manner. But there have been places under both the old and new dispensation where his spiritual presence has been felt and enjoyed in all its power, as the God of grace and salvation; not in public only; but in pious families and by individual saints. May we, diligently seek to record his name in this place; in all families where we visit; and in all places wherever we go. May our life be a life of faith, a running record of the fear of God, and that we live in the expectation of the second coming of Him, who, by his spiritual presence, now walks in the midst of the golden candlesticks, but despises not the humblest shed, where his name is recorded in an *act of faith.* —'*I will come unto thee.*'

The blessing promised in our text is experienced in *all* places —in all communities—where knowledge and piety are *extending*: —where the ministry is enlightened and wholly devoted to the work, and sustained by the people;—where moral courage prevails over selfishness and the fear of man;—where there is unity and peace, the body one, in action and love;—where a missionary, an aggressive spirit prevails;—where the spirit is poured out as a spirit of prayer, joy, and love;—where converts are made and added to the Church.

These I can only name *now* for want of time; and must hasten to conclude.

In conclusion, I would say to the Church which is expected to

interest in the great work of making known the gospel of salvation.   It is the common cause of Christ's Church.   The only
separation which an humble follower of Christ will know is a
tseparation from error and sin.   The spirit which leads to separa-
ion the apostle attributes to carnality and childishness.   The
Corinthians had attained to very little experimental knowledge of
gospel truth.   Carnal policy seems to have been the governing principle.   So long as they could build up Paul, or Apollos, or Cephas,
the authority of Christ, whose command is—'*Go out into the
high-ways, and hedges, and compel them to come in,* was of
little account.'   You brethren have heard this command and
obeyed it.   Having begun in the spirit of the gospel never adopt
the unholy maxim of trying to become perfect by the wisdom of
the flesh.   See, brethren, that the whole arrangements of the
Church in this house be under the direction of the Master, who
said,—'*My kingdom is not of this world.*'
    To members of other Churches, allow me the privilege of
saying:—We respect whatever of piety, or knowledge, or benevolence—whatever of any part of the Christian character you
may exhibit.   The more plainly you reflect the image of our
blessed Lord, the more we admire you; the least of you we love
for the Master's sake; and hope to cultivate towards you the best
Christian feeling which grace may enable us to exercise.
    To our neighbors and friends, who are not professors of reli-
gion, I would beg to address a word.
    We wish your highest happiness in this life, and in
heaven hereafter.   Here, where the Lord's name will be recorded, and his blessing felt, according to his sure word of promise, we shall be happy to see you, and tell you about Christ, and
salvation through him.   And though it may be in a plain style, it
should not be forgotten that simplicity is the most striking characteristic of gospel truth.   Jesus himself was the plainest of men,
and taught his doctrines in the most colloquial manner.   You
have a common interest in the seats of this house, and whether
rich or poor, we cordially invite you to occupy them.
    Permit me to drop a word to the young.   You are our hope;
we who are your seniors must leave these benches, and this pulpit
to you.   May the Lord endue you with vigorous understandings
and pious hearts; that when the cause of truth shall be committed
to your hands the change may be advantageous to the cause of
God and truth.   It should be among the chief delights of a Christian life to lead youth into the sublime and sanctifying truths of
the gospel of Christ.
    And I would address a word to the servants.   You clearly
perceive that this place of worship has not been built without
regard to your accomodation, and comfort.   While you occupy
the comfortable seats prepared for you, may God of his infinite
mercy make the prayers, the singing, and the preaching, a blessing to you and to your children.

Finally,—May all who shall have any part in carrying forward the religious services of this house, guard against the errors which darken, and the practices which deform the professing Church. And here may the Lord for many years to come record his name, by the faithful preaching of the gospel, and all the institutions of his holy word. And fulfil those promises made to the Head of the Church and his people in him. 'I will pour water upon him that is thirsty, and floods upon the dry ground: I will pour my Spirit upon thy seed, and my blessing upon thine offspring. and they shall spring up as among the grass, as willows by the water-courses. One shall say I am the Lord's; and another shall call himself by the name of Jacob; and another shall subscribe with his hand unto the Lord, and surname himself by the name of Israel.' Amen.

THE PRESSING CLAIMS OF THE GOSPEL:

A SERMON BY REV. H. KEELING.

—

'*Behold now is the accepted time; behold, now is the day of salvation!* 2 Cor vi: 2.

It is not wonderful that mistakes have existed concerning religion, even among those possessing the Bible, and perusing it with care. Under similar circumstances, the appearances of nature, have been misunderstood and the volume of inspiration can scarcely be expected to be plainer. Religion in its fundamental principles, is plain; but as a science, whose laws may be investigated, or as an art whose principles are to be practised, it involves much intricacy. It is precisely so, of subjects which claim our daily attention. Law is an abstruse subject: but no one is in danger of a criminal offence, through mere mistake. Morality is more so. Yet men rarely err through their ignorance. Few things are more complicated than machinery; and yet the mechanical powers are resolvable into three or at most six.

Among the most common mistakes of modern times, is this: that religious discourses are intended to be mere orations, delivered either for amusement or instruction, or at most to convince of some one great truth or duty and to persuade to its belief or performance; and that such discussion may be safely left for future action, when the interview has passed.

It is clear, that the gospel has to do with but two classes of men,—the Church, and the world; and the objects it proposes are likewise two,—the edification of the Church, and the conversion of the world. It claims the immediate conversion of every sinner to whom it addresses itself.

My business here to-day, is with the latter class. I am come on a distinct errand. Although I am not an Apostle, or a prophet,

'I have a message;' and to each one present, I affirm, that although I am come on a very different errand from that, of Ehud to Eglon, yet 'I have a message from God, unto thee.' My object is perfectly intelligible and it deeply concerns you. My business with each, is particular and exclusive, as if he and I were alone. I am not come, to prescribe a remedy for a disease, otherwise mortal; nor to vindicate rights of person or property; nor by my testimony to wipe off reproach from injured reputation. I am here to tell you, how you may be saved; upon what conditions; and why you ought without delay, to comply. The documents are ready; your signature is requisite. Our Master makes a just, reasonable, benevolent proposition. It is for you to agree or disagree, and abide the consequence. Accordingly then, I am to show you,

I. The *precise thing*, the gospel requires you to do, that you may be saved. On this subject the Bible is explicit, but the public mind confused. Repentance, faith, love, trust in God, external obedience, each of these, and of many other things, is supposed by many, to be the *hinge* upon which salvation turns. But if you carefully compare all that the Scriptures teach, you will find, that they reduce all mankind to *one* class, and suspend the salvation of every rational creature, to whom the gospel comes, on *one* condition. All, whether Jews or Gentiles are reduced to one class. Skepticism, idolatry, worldliness, profligacy, morality, ambition, thoughtlessness, love of pleasure, it matters not, what predominates, if obedience to Christ is withheld,—they are all so many different aspects of the same thing,—*a heart opposed to Christ and to God.* All stand on the same level before the Omniscient judge—all guilty, and exposed to hell. As the *disease* is *one*; so the *remedy* is *one.* That is, a *cordial reception of Jesus Christ as the only Savior.* This is the pascal lamb—the brazen-serpent—the floating ark—the altar—the sacrifice—the priest:—every allusion, every service, every truth, every duty, everything looks to Christ. And whatever we are required to do, it all amounts to nothing, except as connected with our cordial reception of him as our only Savior. The figure is changed, but the idea is always the same. I am to show,

II *When* this thing is required to be done. Our text is to the point. ' *To-day*,' ' *now*' is the time. In every view you take of the Gospel it claims instant regard.

Invitation. Does it invite? The guests are expected to accept. Not to accept is insult. What else is meant by the parable of the supper? 'Ho, every one that thirsteth.'

Command. 'God commandeth all men everywhere to repent.' Is the command *present* expecting future obedience? Is God to be served on credit? It might as well be by proxy. 'To-day if ye will hear his voice, harden not your heart.'

Warning. 'Generation of vipers, who hath warned you.' 'The axe is laid at the root of the tree, every tree that bringeth not forth fruit is hewn down and cast into the fire.'

Remonstrance. 'Turn ye, turn ye, why will ye die?' 'What more could I have done to my vineyard, than I have done in it?'

All possible objections to the ground I take, are resolvable into three: the refutation of which leaves the claims of the gospel undisputed.

1. This view of the case makes personal religion *instantaneous,* and therefore *easy,* whereas the Scriptures teach differently. Can I enter these walls a 'vessel of wrath,' and return an heir of glory? The answer is easy. In one aspect of it, piety is progressive; in another instantaneous. The formation of character is necessarily progressive; but its beginning must be at some instant. To become learned in the school of Christ requires your life; but to enter as a pupil is the act of a moment. Your thoughts may retrospect with the rapidity of lightening your whole past history; and you may be for years planning to come to Christ; but whenever your affections do centre in Christ it will be *at some moment.* If you postpone it till the hour of your death; and then should not be hardened to steel, but repent, it will be as sudden as if it occurred this minute.

2. It takes the work of salvation from the hand of God and places it in the hand of the sinner—and of course dishonors grace and gives glory to sinful man. I deem it important, (in reply) not only to *admit,* but to *maintain* that the whole work of salvation is of the Lord. He institutes the means, and gives them efficacy. But these means include our own acts, and the acts of others as instruments. 'He worketh in us, to will, and to do.' But this implies our *willing* and our *doing.* There are many things in metaphysical science, and theological doctrine, beyond our comprehension. But these two truths are axiomatic: when you turn to God, he has inclined you to it, and your turning to him is nevertheless *your own act.* My business here to day, is not to tell what God does, but what the sinner himself does, that he may be saved.

3. It attaches an importance to means which does not belong to them. The force of this objection depends npon the import of the *word* means. Many persons think that if they place themselves in the house of God under the ministry of the Gospel, and where prayer is offered by others, they are using *the means* of grace, and that their duty extends no farther—that spiritual worship is beyond the range of their obligation. The supposition that a heartless service, excluding faith, and love, and every holy exercise, is a divinely appointed means whereby enemies of God may expect to be coerced into friendship for him, is altogether preposterous. The gospel requires a holy service or none—and so does the law. And it is precisely as easy for a sinner to become reconciled to God, by an immediate act of his own, as it is, with a heart totally opposed to God, honestly to use means of reconciliation. Having thus briefly, but fairly stated *what* the

gospel requires you to do that you may be saved; and *when* you
are to do it; I proceed,

III. To, offer some reasons *why* you should instantly comply.

1.   Every thing that you hold dear in the universe, is at stake.
The loss threatened, is *yourself.* If it were your mortal life, it
would be a comparative trifle; but it is your eternal life. Were
your fortune confiscated,—your body threatened with the loss of
a single faculty, as seeing or hearing,—or your liberty endangered
—you would turn pale, and tremble or weep. When our kindred die, we sorrow, and put on the habilaments of woe. But for
such a loss as this, there are no sighs fit to be sighed, no tears fit
to be wept, no habilaments ⸜of mourning fit to be put on. Man,
are you dead, or are you insane, that you can believe the declarations of the Bible, be unprepared for the coming account, and yet
feel easy? It is not wonderful my Christian brethren, that when
we reflect on the condition of our unconverted friends, we are
nervous, and feverish, and sleepless.

2.   Your increasing danger requires it. God is unchangeably
the same. The gospel is the same now as when Paul preached
it. Your relation to God is the same, as when you first heard it.
But *you* are *not* the same. Every act of unbelief darkens the
cloud of your guilt. Every hour's delay to submit to Christ,
throws you in a moral progression farther from God. You rush
with accelerated velocity, from an immeasurable hight of prive-·
lege to the vortex of ruin. Or as the Bible expresses it; you
'heap up wrath against the day of wrath, and the revelation of
the righteous judgment of God.' Your mere habit of unholy
action renders your salvation, momently less and less probable.
When you first heard the thunders of Sinai you shuddered with
fear—when you first listened to the story of the Savior's love,
your heart melted with grief—but now you are *adamant.*

3.   If you perish you have no excuse; nor alleviation of your
guilt and folly. If you had been born in a heathen land—or
under the old dispensation—or at the dawn of gospel day;—the
case would have been different. Or if God had given you no
heart, or no conscience;—or if the way of salvation had been
hard;—or if you had not been prayed for, and preached to, and
wept over;—you had had some apology. But now, none, absolutely none. You saw the volcano sending forth its lava, and
rushed to the ruin. You do not refuse to build an ark that you
may be saved, but to enter that ark when built: and that too
when you see the fountains of the great deep broken up and the
windows of heaven opened If in this voyage you suffer shipwreck,
it will not be on the trackless ocean, in a hurricane, but in sight
of land, stubbornly steering in awrong direction, and yourself at
the helm.

THE
BAPTIST PREACHER.

| VOL. III. | June, 1844. | NO. 6. |

THE DEVOTED PASTOR:—

A sermon, by Rev. Stephen P. Hill, *of Baltimore.*

—

' *We preach not ourselves, but Christ Jesus the Lord and ourselves your servants, for Jesus' sake.*'—2 Cor. iv: 5.

The institution of the gospel ministry, although at first sight, it appears a feeble and insignificant instrumentality, is notwithstanding, the means, which God in his infinite wisdom has selected for the salvation of the world. It hath pleased Him by what is deemed 'the foolishness' and weakness 'of preaching to save them that believe.' Not that all men who assume the sacred office are called and qualified of God to preach the gospel. There were many in the time of the Apostles, who professed to be public teachers, and who from various motives of a selfish and unholy character, thrust themselves like 'fools' into the place 'where angels fear to tread.' Some like Simon Magus had no higher view of the awful work than that it was to be purchased with money. Some like Diotrephes, strove for it that they might have the pre-eminence. Some preached Christ from envy and strife and contention, supposing to add affliction to the Apostle's bonds. Such were 'false Apostles, deceitful workers, transforming themselves into the Apostles of Christ:—and no marvel, for Satan himself is transformed into an angel of light.' The truth is there was never any thing good, that was not capable of being counterfeited. There are not only hypocrites in the Church, but hypocrites in the Ministry. It was a remark of that venerable man, Abraham Booth, that 'he feared there would be found a larger proportion of wicked ministers than of any other order of professing Christians.' Certainly the Lord Jesus Christ includes this number among 'the many' that will say to him in that day, 'Lord, Lord, have we not prophesied in thy name? and in thy name cast out devils? and in thy name done many wonderful works? And then will I profess unto them, I never knew you: depart from me, ye that work iniquity.'

Personal piety in the Minister of the Gospel is the first qualification to be sought. The questions to be asked, are not, Is he

talented? Is he eloquent? Is he possessed of rare and remarkable gifts? Is he capable of attracting crowds? But, Is he pious?
Has he grace? Does he love God? Are his motives pure? Has
he a simple and single desire to honor Christ, and to do good to
his fellow men? Nor, should a Minister take his own piety for
granted. He should examine himself. He should deal very
rigidly with his heart. He should weigh well his motives in the
balances of the Sanctuary. He should act independently of flesh
and blood and try to please only God, who trieth the secrets of
the inmost soul, who judgeth not as man judgeth, but who looketh
in the heart. He must take heed to *himself.* He must be pre-
eminently a man of prayer. Luther's remark was that Three
things made a divine, prayer, meditation and temptation. And it is
related of the celebrated Austin of Hippo, that being asked what
was the first thing in religion, he said 'humility.' When asked
what was the second, he answered 'humility.' And what was
the third, he still returned the same answer, 'humility.' Now
this is the point on which we would insist, in describing the character of the true Minister of Jesus Christ; and the example of
the Apostles and primitive Ministers is before us, to this end, 'we
preach not ourselves, but Christ Jesus the Lord and ourselves
your servants for Jesus' sake.'

Let us consider,

I. WHAT THE APOSTLES DID NOT PREACH, *or what is implied in preaching ourselves;*

II. WHAT IS IMPLIED IN PREACHING CHRIST; and

III. THE FACT THAT MINISTERS SHOULD CONSIDER THEM-
SELVES *as the servants of the people for Jesus' sake.*

I. WHAT THE APOSTLES DID NOT PREACH, *or what is implied
in preaching ourselves.*

1. *We preach ourselves if we preach to gain a living.*

In saying this, I would not be understood to say, that Ministers
should not have a living as well as others. For ' so hath the
Lord ordained that they which preach the Gospel, should live of
the Gospel." 'It is written in the law of Moses, thou shalt not
muzzle the mouth of the ox that treadeth out the corn. Doth
God take care for oxen? Or saith he it altogether for our sakes?
If we have sown unto you spiritual things, is it a great thing if
we reap your carnal things?' 1 Cor. ix. Indeed no plainer
proposition can be made out, either from the Scriptures, or from
common experience, not only that the pulpit, is worth more than
it costs, but that nothing has such righteous claims to a generous
and adequate support. When we look at all that religious institutions have done for us, temporally as well as spiritually, we must
feel convinced that ' the pulpit is not in debt to the people, but the
people to the pulpit;' and when we carefully read the word of
God, we shall learn that nothing is in stricter accordance with his
will, and that no principle is clearer laid down than that 'the

laborer is worthy of his hire.' But if he be a *mere hireling*, who has desired to be put into the priest's office that he may get a piece of bread, if he chooses the ministry as he would a profession, or a trade, because thereby he may have the means of subsistence, if he takes the oversight of the flock for filthy lucre's sake, and makes the work of God a sinecure:—then truly he may be ranked first in the description of those who preach themselves; whose aims are selfish; whose motives are mercenary. ' They prophesy for reward, and divine for money:' and under a cloak of sanctity they hide a heart of covetousness. ' Woe unto them for they have gone in the way of Cain, and ran greedily after the error of Balaam for reward.'

2. They preach themselves, who preach for popular applause.

Alas! how many it is to be feared preach from this miserable motive, and what a lamentable tendency there is in the people to feed this pernicious flame! 'to have men's persons in admiration,' and to waft perfumes to the idol of popular favor! Now if a man preaches for fame, if he preaches to display his talents, his fine voice, or fine person, or his commanding eloquence, he evidently preaches *himself.*

'Either vain
By nature, or by flattery made so, taught
To gaze at his own splendor, he exalts
Absurdly, not his office but himself......
......In man or woman but far most in man,
And most of all in man that ministers
And serves the altar, in my soul I loathe
All affectation. 'Tis my perfect scorn.
What! will a man play tricks, will he indulge,
Or will he seek to dazzle me with tropes,
When I am hungry for the bread of life?'

It is of course necessary to the successful ministration of the Gospel, that the preacher should be possessed of some gifts; that he should have learning: the more the better. He should be especially mighty in the Scriptures; and he may be an eloquent man. He may even employ in his preaching, the aids of elocution and the graces of style. But let him make all his acquirements, subservient to the great *end* of his Ministry, the salvation of souls. Let him use the ornaments of literature and learning as the surgeon does the polish of his instruments. Let him beware lest he pervert the use of these things by making them minister to his own vain glory. It is a great matter to be able to say with the Apostle: ' For neither at any time used we flattering words as ye know; neither of men sought we glory, neither of you, nor yet of others.'

3. Preaching ourselves implies again, that we preach to build up ourselves, or our sect or party.

This is a motive which cannot be right in the sigat of God. We see much of this species of zeal in our times. ' 'Men speaking perverse things to draw away disciples after them.' The Apostle saw it in his time and rebuked it. The spirit of sectarianism, the spirit of party zeal, the spirit of supposed superiority, the spirit of selfseeking on the part of the Minister, and the spirit of favoritism on the part of the people: 'Now this I say that every one of you saith I am of Paul, and I of Apollos, and I of Cephas, and I of Christ. Is Christ divided? Was Paul crucified for you? Or were ye baptized into the name of Paul? Ye are yet carnal, for whereas there is among you envying, and strife, and divisions, are ye not carnal and walk as men? Who then is Paul? and who is Apollos? But ministers by whom ye believed?' How preposterous, in this view, do those arrogant claims appear, which are set up exclusively for our particular Church as though no moral excellence or salvation could exist out of it: and how vain to suppose that certain forms and ceremonies are essential to the true office of a Christian Minister. The pastors of primitive times, were only the brethren of other Christians; and though they were to be esteemed very highly in love for their work's sake, yet they possessed, they assumed no power over the consciences, or the liberties of the people. Their influence arose from their character, and from the pious and humble manner with which they performed the functions of their sacred office. In the New Testament the pastor is a plain man surrounded by a number of individuals who form themselves into a voluntary society, that they may mutually enjoy the ordinances of Christ, and who have appointed him to be their officiating Minister. In this view of the subject Christianity fully manifests its character as a religion of the heart, as distinguished by its simplicity and spirituality, and as being the choice of those who really love its name. The moment the idea of secular greatness and magnificence was suffered to possess the mind of Christians, the gold changed, and the most fine gold became dim. Then the Ministerial office ceased to require personal qualifications, and assumed powers, which the Apostles neither exercised nor professed. Personal piety, and holy zeal for the salvation of men, ceased to be regarded as necessary for the sacred office; and successive corruptions, subverted its spirituality and its sacred design.

II. But let us pass to notice *what is implied in preaching Christ Jesus the Lord.*

It is, in other words, to preach the truth of the Gospel. In this the Lord Jesus has a prominent part. The Gospel concerns him from first to last. He is the author and he is the finisher of our whole faith. He is the sun of the whole system, and is emphatically the truth. So that in preaching the truth, we must preach him; and he who does not preach him, does not preach the Gospel. This is the grand theme of the Christian Ministry.

The topics on which we are to dwell, the subjects which are to employ our meditations, are his person, his character, his work, his laws. In view of these the Apostle with all his pre-eminent abilities and gifts, declared that he counted all things but loss for the excellency of the knowledge of Christ Jesus his Lord. And so rapt was he in the sublime discoveries of the Gospel; so completely superior was he raised by them above all selfish considerations and personal aims; that he determined to know nothing among men save Jesus Christ and him crucified. This was the subject matter of the Apostle's preaching. Not that he undervalued the moral precepts of Christianity, or that they did not find a place in his ministrations: for these were important parts of the Gospel, but still subordinate and not the essential parts of it. They revolved around it like planets and satellites, but He was the central luminary that gave them all their beauty, and light. and life. To preach then Christ Jesus the Lord, is to preach the *whole* truth, in distinction from a part, or a single part, on all occasions. A person for instance may preach the *morality* of the Gospel, and if he preach nothing else he cannot be said to preach the Gospel any more than the physician can be said to be master of the healing art, who would recommend one, and the same prescription to every patient, no matter what the nature of his disease. It is also to preach the whole truth on proper occasions in distinction from the whole on *every* occasion. Christ himself never unfolded all his truth, nor what he did unfold, at one time. ' I have many things,' said he to his Disciples ' to say to you but ye cannot bear them now.' What should we think of a physician, who being called to visit the sick, should administer the whole quantity of his medicines at one time? But the truth at proper times, and under proper circumstances, is to be unfolded, as it may be adapted to the case of the people. I need not say. that this includes the being and perfections of God; the character and condition of man; the atonement and divinity of Jesus Christ; His glorious character, and perfect righteousness, and availing blood, as the only ground of a sinner's hope; the blessings of the salvation he has procured; its comforts, its privileges, its duties, its requirements, its prospects and rewards, with the awful guilt of rejecting it, and the fearful punishment of the impenitent. Nor should we omit to teach very clearly and strenuously the nature and necessity of the work of the Holy Spirit as the glorious and efficient agent of the regeneration, and of the progressive sanctification of the soul. We must distinguish between his operations on the heart, and the mere movements of animal passion; between true and false, or spurious religion; warn against the ever varying dangers that are around the flock; lead them into the pastures of safety and feed them with knowledge and understanding. The whole truth, must also in order to be preached faithfully, be *applied* to the conscience and to the heart.

It is not enough that it be preached merely, it should be *fastened* and *clenched* to the heart.   Its adaptedness to the wants and con-dition of men must be shewn; the lights and shades of different characters must be drawn; and the nature and peril of particular sins be exposed.   The truth must be separated from *error*, a dis-criminating line must be drawn between them at the place where their varying colors mingle.   The beauty of holiness, so apt to be-come dim in the heart of even the best, must be brought out till it is seen and felt, in contrast with the hatefulness of vice.   The corrup-tions that gather around the truth must be removed, like the earth that conceals and buries the gold in its mountain bed, and the precious ore be refined of its dross and alloy, and applied to a valuable purpose.   All this, and much more than this, is implied in preaching Christ faithfully, and all this is to be done in every possible way.   The duties of the pastoral office are so diversified that an enumeration of them would be impossible.   They lie in every department of labor, and are often of the most arduous and depressing kind.   If an inspired Apostle, in view of the impor-tant trust committed to him, exclaimed, 'Who is sufficient for these things,' with what a crushing weight must it fall upon the shoulders and heart of those not similarly privileged.   Besides preaching the Gospel, the truth of God, faithfully, impartially, entirely; besides illustrating, enforcing and applying the word of life in the pulpit, he must follow it up with anxious and prayerful, and exemplary piety, at all other times.   Not only in public, must he declare the whole counsel of God, but in private, he must study the peculiar circumstances, the individual wants of his flock, adapting himself with heavenly skill, to each particular case. There are the self-righteous, the indolent, the careless, the self-sufficient, the spiritually proud, the formal, the worldly, the back-slider, the inquirer, the tempted, the afflicted, that require instruc-tion, reproof, and advice, adapted to the minute and diversified forms which their several cases may assume.   There is the Con-ference Room, the Bible Class, the Sabbath School, over which he must cast the light of an affectionate superintendence.   There are duties all along the retired walks of domestic life.   The Pas-tor is a sympathising friend.   He rejoices in your prosperity, and he weeps in your adversity. · In the hour of bereavement, and sickness, and death, he is near with the balm, the only adequate one, of consolation.   He seeks to guide, and that in every way, your feet, and the feet of your children, in the way of peace, and in paths of everlasting life.   What an aggregate of labor!   Who can rightly estimate it?   '*He watches for your souls as one that must give account,*' Chrysostom says, he never read these words without being shaken as with an earthquake; and Quesnel remarks, that 'the pastor who trembles not at these words, should tremble at his own blindness and insensibility.'

> ' 'Tis not a work of small import
> The pastor's care demands;
> But what might fill an angel's heart,
> And filled the Savior's hands.'

Now when you take in connection with this amount of duty, the time the Pastor must find for the professional and for the devotional reading of the Scriptures; the attention that must be given to the interests of religion beyond the field of his own immediate labors; the time that must be given to the physical and moral wants of his own family; the allowance that must be made for his health and the care that he must take of his own heart and the labor he must use over his own soul; you will feel that his is indeed a work under which he would certainly sink, were not the arms of Omnipotence pledged to uphold him.

III. But we notice lastly the view in which Ministers should regard themselves: '*ourselves your servants for Jesus' sake.*'

Ministers are not the servants of the people in such a sense as implies inferiority, or their having authority over him. On the contrary, what authority there is, is on the other side: ' Obey them that have the rule over you, and submit yourselves: for they watch for your souls, as they that must give account, that they may do it with joy, and not with grief. for that is unprofitable for you.' Heb. xiii: 17. But they are the servants of the people, inasmuch as their whole time and powers are required to be devoted to the spiritual good of their flock. Is the Minister a *watchman*? He is required to hear the word from Jehovah's mouth and warn the people from Him. He *watches* for souls as one that must give account. Is he a shepherd? He is sent to seek the lost, to restore the wandering, to feed the flock of God, the *sheep* and the *lambs* of Christ. Is he a *steward*? It is required in him that he should be found faithful. Is he a ruler, a guide, an overseer? He is bound to train, to regulate, and direct the Church of God. It is his duty to preside in the Church. And this requires the utmost prudence and wisdom. Amidst a variety of different spirits and tempers, how arduous the labor of keeping things in proper order! How much righteousness, and godliness, and faith, and firmness, and meekness, and patience, and forbearance, and love, need we here! The less of self-importance and tenaciousness in carying a point we manifest, and the more of respect and disinterested regard for our brethren, the better we shall succeed. Is he a *laborer*? He must work with all diligence in his Master's vineyard, until the night of death shall bring his reward. Is he a builder? He must be very careful of what materials he builds the spiritual temple, since every man's work must be tried of what sort it is. Is he a pilot? How well acquainted should he be with his chart, and how vigilant in his trust! Now it is necessary that the people should feel that their pastor is in all various ways laboring for their good. They must if possible be constrained to feel a conviction, that in all that he does, he is actuated by no mercenary views, or selfish purposes; that money, or fame, or the gratification of his personal pride, is no part of his object; that he habitually and sincerely seeks not their wealth, or their applause, but their salvation. Our rejoicing should be this, 'that in simplicity and godly sincerity, not with fleshly wisdom, but by the grace of God, we have had our conversation in the world, and more abundantly to you-ward.' We should be able to say boldly and without fear of contradiction 'we seek not yours but you, and I will very gladly spend and be spent for you, though the more abundantly I love you, the less I be loved.' 'For we are manifest unto God and we trust also are manifest in your consciences.' Let us then in this connection, consider the *mutual ties* subsisting between a pastor and his flock. These are expressed throughout the Epistles in many terms of endearment, remarkable for their tenderness and force. It is obvious from these passages,

First. That they are created by the love of Christ. We cannot love him that begat, without loving those that are begotten. We cannot love the original which we have not seen, without loving the image which we have seen. We cannot love Christ without loving his people. They were objects of infinite love by him, long before a single principle of attachment towards them was implanted in the hearts of others. He loved them with an everlasting love. He loved them to the death. '*I am the good Shepherd,*' he says, 'the good shepherd giveth his life for the sheep.' Like him it will be our anxious endeavour 'to seek and save that which is lost.' The love of Christ constraineth us to lay down our lives for the brethren. The soul is an object of inestimable value. The sufferings and death, of 'the Lamb of God,' have endeared it to the affections of all his true servants, and stampt on it an importance which transcends every other. Those whom he has redeemed by his blood, are so dear to him, that he has identified their interests with his own; and his Ministers will also feel that they are identified with theirs. How beautiful was this affection exemplified in the case of the great Apostle, who had once breathed out '*threatnings* and *slaughter* against the same holy brotherhood.' What does he say to the Corinthians? That 'out of much affliction and anguish of heart, I wrote unto you with many tears; not that ye should be grieved, but that ye might know the love which I have more abundantly unto you.' 'And I will very gladly spend and be spent for you, though the more abundantly I love you, the less I be loved.' In what terms does he write to the Galatians? 'My little children, of whom I travail in birth again, until Christ be formed in you.' In what to the Ephesians? 'For this cause I bow my knees unto the Father of our Lord Jesus Christ—that ye being

rooted and grounded in love may be able to comprehend with all
saints what is the breadth and length, and depth, and height, and
to know the love of Christ which passeth knowledge.' How
does he address the Philippians? 'For God is my record, how
greatly I long after you all in the bowels of Jesus Christ.' And
what his language to the Thessalonians? 'We were gentle
among you, even as a *nurse* cherisheth her children, so being affectionately desirous of you, we were willing to have imparted
unto you not, the Gospel of God only, but also our own souls,
because ye were dear unto us. And ye know, how we exhorted
and comforted and charged every one of you as a *father* doth his
children, that ye would walk worthy of God who hath called you
unto his kingdom and glory.' Thus the tenderness of a *father*,
of a *nurse*, is made to represent the affectionate solicitude which
a pastor feels for his people. The same tender care has been
beautifully expressed in poetry under another similitude.—

'And as a *bird*, each fond endearment tries
To tempt its new fledged offspring to the skies,
He tries each art, reproves each dull delay,
Allures to brighter worlds, and leads the way.'

Secondly. The ties of such a relationship are strengthened by
exercise. This is a natural result. The minister who has been
long accustomed to labor for a people's good;—to watch and
weep and pray for them, under all the changing occurrences of
life, becomes more and more attached to the objects of his love,
in consequence of their continual action on his heart. The
mother, finds her affections insensibly fastening themselves stronger and closer around a beloved child, in consequence of her frequent anxieties and watching and efforts for its welfare. Just so,
the pastor, that has the best interests of his people at heart, will
acquire a sensibility for them, more intense than any with which
he feels for himself. In the different scenes which he is called to
witness and to soften, whether it be in domestic prosperity or
affliction, his heart is open to sympathy. It is his privilege to
impart relief. His very character, as a messenger of divine
mercy, makes it his duty to minister in spiritual things. He is to
operate on the affections. His office implies every thing tender,
attractive, and endearing; and he will be successful in his ministry of benevolence, in proportion to his lively sense of the differ-
ing circumstances of his flock. He is supposed to be acquainted
deeply with the experience of the heart. He studies and feels its
wants—kindles with its hopes—struggles with its fears—endeavors to understand and to explain the causes of its disquietude—
to know and to tell where it may find repose. Hence the endearment of his relation and the strength which it continually acquires.
An affecting illustration of this tenderness is exhibited in the part-

ing interview of Paul with the Church at Ephesus. His appeal
to them on that occasion cannot be too often considered. ' Ye
know from the first day that I came into Asia, after what manner
I have been with you at all seasons, serving the Lord with all
humility of mind, and with many tears and temptations, which
befel me by the lying in wait of the Jews, and how I kept back
nothing that was profitable unto you, but have showed you, and
have taught you publicly, and from house to house. Therefore
watch and remember, that for the space of three years, I ceased
not to warn every one night and day with tears.' Such was the
Apostle Paul, the living example of ministerial tenderness and
fidelity. Such were the grounds on which he appealed to the
sympathies of his ministerial charge.

*The Minister is the servant of the people in view of the benefit
and consolation derived from God's providential dealings with
him which they derive from his very afflictions.* 'Blessed be God,
even the Father of our Lord Jesus Christ,' says the Apostle
Paul, 'the Father of mercies and the God of all comfort, who
comforteth us in all our tribulation, that we may be able to comfort them which are in any trouble, by the comfort wherewith we
ourselves are comforted of God. For as the sufferings of Christ
abound in us, so our consolation also aboundeth by Christ. And
whether we be afflicted, it is for your consolation and salvation,
which is effectual in the enduring of the same sufferings, or
whether we be comforted, it is for your consolation and salvation.'
Such was the spirit of faith with which the Apostle regarded even
the most painful tribulations of his life; such was his confidence
in their author, and such his satisfaction with their end, that he
bursts out in praise while reviewing, nay even in the midst of
those very tribulations. Nor for himself alone is he grateful, but
for those to whom he ministers, as having mutual participation
with him in the consolations as well as sufferings which he is
called to experience. And he intimates that one great design of
his own afflictions, is, that he may be able to comfort them which
are in any trouble, by the comfort wherewith he himself is comforted of God: That is to say, the benefit of his personal experience in suffering is reflected upon others who are called to suffer, in that he is made more capable of sympathising with their
trials, and of communicating to them the consolation which
aboundeth to himself by Christ. Thus whether he was afflicted,
it was for their present and ultimate good, not only for the former
reason, but because the patient endurance of the same sufferings
which he also suffered, had the same happy and saving tendency
in them; or whether he was comforted, it was, for similar reasons,
for their consolation and salvation. On these reasons we need
not now enlarge. Every one who perceives the operation of
moral causes, can readily understand why these afflictions of the
Ministry were calculated to work such beneficial effects in 'the

body of Christ.' If sanctified by the Spirit of God to Minister and people, the blessed influence of these dispensations will be manifest to all. Their mutual prayers will evince their mutual interests, and common sufferings will create common sympathies and ties. And let it be observed, that *these ties extend beyond this life, to eternity.* Not only is it, writes the Apostle, for your present consolation, but for your future salvation, that we thus suffer. Sent by the same Author, designed for the same end, borne with the same patience, sanctified by the same Spirit, endeared by the same Redeemer's blood, and sweetened by the joys of a mutual faith,—'our afflictions,'—'though not for the present joyous, but greivous,—are yet 'but for the moment, and work out for us a far more exceeding and eternal weight of glory.' In this heavenly discipline, selfishness has no place. The anxiety of a faithful minister for himself is swallowed up in his anxiety for the eternal happiness of his people. 'For what is our hope, or joy, or crown of rejoicing? Are not even ye in the presence of our Lord Jesus Christ at his coming? For ye are our glory and joy.' And thus, to use the words of Rutherford to his flock, 'my witness is above, that your heaven would be two heavens to me, and the salvation of you all, as two salvations to me.'

These views of the Gospel ministry will sufficiently account for the extreme anxiety and tenderness of those whose honor and privilege it is to share it; and of the deeply affectionate regard towards such of those who are the subjects of its ministration. In former times, nothing could be stronger, than the endearing bond of attachment, which united a faithful shepherd to his charge. Read the Epistles of the great Apostle—we would say again to all—if you would behold an exhibition of ministerial endearment. Consider what praises, what prayers, he offers on behalf of the saints, for their mercies and for their tribulations. See how ready he is at all times 'to rejoice with those that rejoice, and weep with those that weep.' Reflect on his 'longings after them in the bowels of Jesus Christ.' Think of the anxiety of his sleepless nights, implied in Heb. xiii: 17; his 'watching often,' his 'labors even to weariness,' his 'striving as in a conflict,' that they may be comforted and enlarged. 'Taken from them' sometimes 'in presence:' but never 'in heart,' he 'longs to see them that he may impart to them some spiritual gift;' and whether seeing them, or hearing 'of their affairs,' he can at no time be satisfied unless assured 'that they stand fast in one spirit, with one mind, striving together for the faith of the Gospel.' And to such an extent did he carry his sympathies toward them, that he declares, 'if he was offered up,' if his life was made a sacrifice 'upon the service of their faith, he should joy and rejoice with them all.'

'How beautiful and holy,' then, in the language of Bloomfield, 'in all its perfection of obligation, is the spiritual connexion

which subsists between a faithful Minister of Christ and the flock
which he is appointed to feed.   How many are the methods by
which that bond of affection may be more closely drawn!   Many
an anxious care does the faithful and vigilant Pastor experience
for the welfare of those who are endeared to him by the sacred
sympathy of spiritual affinity; many a sorrow for failures in
which the world thinks he has no interest; and many a joy for
blessings which he alone perceives descending upon the heads of
those whom he loves in the Lord.'

Finally. I come to ask you to turn with me aside a moment,
to witness a scene of more than ordinary solemnity.   It is the
death-bed of a Christian Pastor.   He desires, before his voice is
forever silenced, to address to you one word more of affectionate
exhortation.   His heart, before it is forever still, would throw
before you, once more, its tenderest sympathies.

He who thus seeks you, sincerely loves you, and has your
truest interests at heart.   He watches for your soul, as one that
must give an account, and he trembles under the dreadful responsibility of his charge.   The subjects, on which he is anxious, in
the simplicity and godly sincerity of the truth, to speak, are
eternal realities.   They deeply concern your happiness, for the
present and for all future periods.   He is commissioned from God,
with a message to you, and as God's faithful ambassador he
would deliver it, as the last he will ever have to communicate, in
the conviction of its immeasurable importance.   And oh! if it be
true, that 'a death-bed is the detecter of the heart,' you may be
sure, that the words which he will speak are the words of honesty and soberness.   Let us approach the spot.   It has nothing
repulsive.

> 'The chamber where the good man meets his fate,
> Is privileged beyond the common walks
> Of virtuous life, quite in the verge of Heaven.'

God smiles on him, and he smiles on death.   He is in near
prospect of perfect purity, everlasting freedom, full and uninter-
rupted joy.   The doctrine of the resurrection, and faith in his
happy interest in that doctrine, sustain him in his final hour, and
make him rejoice in the sacrifices which he made to attain to this
triumphant consummation.   Reclining on his last pillow, his
heart is possessed with 'the peace of God which passeth all
understanding.'   The termination of his earthly toils and conflicts hastens on, and like the weary laborer, at the close of day,
he waits to quit the field and go to be 'forever with the Lord.'
Hear his language—'I am now ready to be offered, and the time
of my departure is at hand.   I have fought a good fight, I have
finished my course, I have kept the faith.   Henceforth there is
laid up for me a crown of glory, which the Lord, the righteous

judge, will give me at that day.' But to you, over whose spiritual interests I have watched, I am anxious to address a final appeal. My motives for assuming the responsibilities of the sacred office, as far as with the closest self-examination, I have been able to know them, were love to Christ, and an ardent regard for your eternal welfare; it was indeed 'in weakness and in fear, and much trembling,' that I ventured on such holy ground. Yet made willing by divine grace, to forego the gratifications of a world that perisheth; I spurned the allurements of ambition, and the pursuit of pleasure, and 'chose rather to suffer affliction with the people of God, than to enjoy them, for a season.' 'What things were gain to me, those I counted loss for Christ.' And as worldly inducements had not influenced me in my choice, so neither could worldly discouragements, afterward, lead me to swerve from it. The scoffs of the wicked, the unkindness of false brethren, depressed spirits, a broken constitution and a premature grave— 'none of these things moved me.' I panted for usefulness, and under a weight of conviction which I could not shake off, I felt that 'necessity was laid upon me, yea woe was me if I preached not the Gospel.' Trusting in him 'who had called me by his grace,' I went forth, and 'ye yourselves, brethren, know our entrance in unto you, that our exhortation was not of deceit nor of uncleanness, nor in guile. But as we were allowed of God, to be put in trust with the Gospel, even so we spake not as pleasing men, but God, which trieth the heart.' 'And we were gentle among you, even as a nurse cherisheth her children, so being affectionately desirous of you, we were willing to have imparted unto you, not the Gospel of God only, but our own souls also, because ye were dear unto us.' Now therefore, once more suffer the word of exhortation. The *welfare of your soul*, as it has been the object of anxious solicitude in life, so is it the absorbing desire in death. Believing in its immeasurable worth, and its alarming exposure to perdition, how can it be otherwise, than that the tongue should employ its latest power of utterance, in warning you to 'flee from the wrath to come.' If the value of a thing is to be estimated, by its susceptibility of pleasure or of pain, and by the length of its duration, then the *soul* must be of all things most valuable. This is the seat of life and of feeling, and it can *never die*. The body is but a perishable tenement erected for its temporary abode. Its best and brightest properties are fading and corruptible. If then you look upon this, to admire its strength or beauty, which at the best, are but the advantages of an hour, how much more, should you prize the nobler, the imperishable attributes of the soul! The inhabitant, and not the habitation; the essential being, and not the mere outward veil that covers it. When you remember too, how soon and how suddenly sickness may wither all your earthly comforts and hopes, how can you build with confidence upon them? When you see the emptiness and delusion of the world, how can you pursue, with so much ardour, its miserable pleasures? Why give your affections to objects so uncertain of attainment, so unsatisfying even if gained?—to riches, when they take to themselves wings, and flee away; to fame, when it vanishes like a shadow from the grasp; pleasure, when its gayest scenes, only load the hours of reflection, with self-reproach and agonizing shame? Alas! 'the fashion of this world passeth away,' and he alone is wise, who seeks an inheritance in the world that is to come. I see you pursuing phantoms, blinded and led captive by the father of lies, at his will. I warn you of your infatuation and danger. I address your reason and your conscience. I place before you the counsels of heavenly truth, unfolding the sad, but true description of your character, pointing you to pardoning blood, and a reconciled God, —bringing 'life and immortality to light,' and setting before you alike the promises and threatenings of Him who is almighty, in the one *life*, and in the other *death*. 'And now behold, I know that ye all, among whom I have gone preaching the kingdom of God, shall see my face no more. Wherefore I take you to record this day that I am pure from the blood of all men, for I have not shunned to declare unto you all the counsel of God.'

Such, however imperfect, may be supposed to be the dying appeal of a faithful Pastor. How tremendous is that account, which he will have at least to give of himself, and of those over whom he has labored in the Lord. He is 'a sweet savor of Christ, in them that are saved, and in them that perish, To the one, he is the savor of life unto life; and to the other of death unto death. And who is sufficient for these things?' Happy will he be, if when the chief Shepherd shall appear, he may behold the countenances of his flock beaming in glory, and hear their voices raised in the praises of God and the Lamb; and bowing with them before the everlasting throne, 'may present every man perfect in Christ Jesus.'

———

Note.—It is a part of the plan of this work, to publish in each No. one long sermon or two short ones, making from twenty to twenty-four pages. In the progress of the 3d vol. thus far, we have frequently failed of our object, from the want of MSS. of suitable dimensions. This is our apology for the issue, mostly, of single sermons, for the last several months, and for the insertion of so many of our own notes. The remaining Nos. of the vol. will contain more matter. But we gladly occupy the blank of two pages, left us, for suggesting a few thoughts co-incident with the foregoing excellent sermon.

The author in fixing his title to his sermon, does not use the phrase 'Devoted Pastor,' in the popular, but in the proper sense,

as the sermon itself shows. The phrase in common parlance'
means, a Pastor who has no other employment besides his pastoral charge. Our author uses it to mean, one who does his work
faithfully and assiduously. It may happen that a Pastor who has
no other business to occupy him, may do this very negligently;
while another, may perform an incredible amount of Ministerial
duties, although in the mean time burdened with other labors for
his own support, and thus perhaps sink under accumulated cares.
May the Lord hasten the period when every Minister of the Gospel, liberated from his school-room, his farm, and every secular
pursuit, shall make the Ministry his sole employment,—attending
to none other except as it may be *subservient* to his great work, as
learning and science.

Obligations and privileges are always reciprocal. A devoted
Pastor deserves a devoted people; and a devoted people deserves
a devoted Pastor. 'Let him that is taught in the word, communicate unto him that teacheth in all good things.' Gal. vi: 6.
The wisdom and justice of this arrangement, are inculcated
throughout the Bible; evident from the nature of the Ministerial
office, and the wants of every Church and community; implied
in that great secret of success in all other enterprizes, division
of labor for unity of object; and seen in its good effects where it
is observed, and its bad ones when it is disregarded.

But this subject demands another view. We solemnly fear, the
Pastoral relation is not half appreciated or understood, even by
those of us, who have studied it most. Notwithstanding the light
which blazes from the pulpit and the press, the spirit of this *quid
pro quo* age, is constantly assimilating this relation to others,
whereas there is none like it on earth. That of preceptor and
pupil, properly understood, perhaps approaches it nearest. The
tuition fee is not the reward, to which the faithful preceptor looks,
nor to merit it the object at which he aims. Nor does the intelligent and grateful pupil purchase his instruction and counsel, like
he does a garment or a horse. It would break the heart of a
wise and good teacher to conduct a class on this principle. We,
for ourselves, should greatly prefer the spade or the plough. Not
that these are dishonorable; but the instruction of youth is more
honorable.

We shall never forget, how we felt shocked, when an aged
Minister from one of the Northern states, mentioned in our
presence some few years ago, 'Every Pastor among us, expects
now, in accepting the call of a Church, to resign in two or three
years.' Such an expectation is in our judgment an extinguisher
of both pastoral, and Church, usefulness and pleasure. If we had
fifty lives to live over again, we would never accept of one charge,
with such an expectation. It requires that length of time to
become acquainted. Give us the pastor, to whom we can go as a
tried and well proved friend, for advice in every case of difficulty,

and comfort in every trouble. To whom we can confide every secret of our hearts, as to a father or a mother. And were we again to enter the field of labor, give us a flock with the little ones of whom, around the fire-side and in the Sunday School, we could form attachments never to be broken, not by death itself. We could love the Minister who sojourns with us for a month, or for a few years, but it would only be as a visiter, not as a resident.

One of the greatest faults in the Methodist ecclesiastical polity, is, that it destroys the pastoral relation. Itinercy, for a sparse population, has its advantages: but these, especially if the change is annual or frequent, must be subject to many draw backs. Want of acquaintance between the parties renders intimate friendship and confid nce impossible; change from one field of labor to another abridges the necessity of study, and produces a barren mind; and novelty of person and voice, is substituted for newness of idea and thought.

We almost fear it may have been indiscreet in us to glance at so important a subject, when brevity forbids us to say what is in our heart. Editor.

DIVINE INFLUENCE.

'Let' the spirit be poured from on high' on the ministers of the Gospel; secular aims vanish, the mind rises superior to mortal frowns or smiles; zeal for the salvation of men glows like the perpetual fire on the altar of the Lord, and a missionary passion is inspired. Let the holy influence descend on a Church of Jesus Christ; its members will abound in love; they will fear the Lord, and speak often to each other. Prayer meetings will become crowded; an anxiety will generally be felt for the conversion of sinners, associated with desires to become useful in the world. The hand will be opened to communicate to the relief of the poor, and for the spread of the Savior's kingdom; and circumspection and holiness mark the life and conduct. Let it descend on a family; parents become affectionate, children respectful, servants obedient, while the domestic altar flames with a sacrifice morning and evening to Him in whom 'the families of the earth' are 'blessed.' Does it descend on the ungodly? hypocrisy hurls away her mask, sabbath breaking is ended, swearing is no more; falsehood and deceit, envy and malice, are supplanted, and their seats in the heart occupied with integrity and good will; infidelity hides its head, confounded; youth relinquishes its vain expectations and follies, and age its obduracy and avarice. This blessed influence is the rod of Moses on the rock, which produces penitential streams: it is the shadow of Peter, that 'passing by,' heals all manner of disease: it is the sling of David, before whose energy the enemy of Zion falls. Sacred Spirit! forgive these low allusions! it is thyself brooding on the face of the waters.' *Dr. Staughton.*

THE
BAPTIST PREACHER.

VOL. III.	July, 1844.	NO. 7.

ON THE BENEVOLENCE OF THE MORAL DUTY OF MAN, TO
LOVE GOD SUPREMELY, AND HIS NEIGHBOR AS HIM-
SELF: A SERMON, BY

REV. M. R. SUARES, OF GEORGIA.

—

*"Thou shalt love the Lord thy God with all thy heart, and
with all thy soul, and with all thy strength, and with all thy mind:
and thy neighbor as thyself."*—LUKE x: 27.

Obvious as the truth is, that there is a God, yet there have been
men in all ages, who denied his existence, and ascribed the fair
proportions of this universe to chance. Bewildered in the dark
regions of speculative subjects, and rushing from things profane,
to things divine, they have clothed the fairest truths in the darkest confusion. It is not strange therefore, that we should be goad-
ed with the baneful systems of atheism and infidelity; and that
the fair prospect of man's immortality should be reduced to a
system of pure materialism. Siezing with avidity every circumstance that may seemingly invalidate the existence of God, they
have published it to the world, with the voice of a trumpet, ere
its truth could be fully established. The commixture of good
and of evil; the prosperity of the murderous and oppressive;
the depression of the benevolent and the good; constitute, in their
estimation, an infallible argument, that there is no moral distinction; and that consequently, there can be no moral government.
Sentiments like these, have weakened the religious principles of
those whose imbecility of mind has made them the sport of 'every
wind of doctrine.' Few, however, unaided by the light of revelation,
can fail to gather from the storehouse of nature, some evidence of
an original and benevolent power. The child of nature, rude
and unpolished, whose soul has never glowed with the kindlings
of science,

"Sees God in clouds or hears him in the wind."

But if with revelation combined, any can be found who conscientiously disbelieve the existence of God, it will form a singu-

lar example in the history of mind. Not unfrequently, men
adopt the principles of infidelity, not from a conviction of their
truth, but because they are more congenial with their habits and
feelings. Man, though he be ever so vile, will think it below his
dignity not to be governed by principles, whether they be the
natural or artificial convictions of his mind. In surveying the
wide field of speculative subjects, one is astonished at the diversity of theories. Many groping [their way in the dark regions
of abstractions, are scarcely perceptible. The further they proceed, the more dim is the object of their pursuit, until they find
themselves wrapped in darkness, impervious to the ways of truth.
The mists of prejudice, which have thus been gathered and con-
densed, hanging awfully over the light of revelation, have concealed these foul theories in the intensity of their blackness. It
is not surprising therefore, that when a pall is thrown over divine
truth, the systems of men should conflict with each other, and exhibit the strangest confusion. The origin of man has been ascribed by one to plants—by another, to the race of monkeys—
and a third, to oysters. More in accordance with the principles
of reason, is the Bible's account of the formation of man.

Human arrogance has not been satisfied at aiming its shaft at
man's origin; but it has dared to question the validity of the
Scriptures. Like the fabled giants, building mountain upon
mountain, in order to reach heaven, to know its mysteries, or to
be as Gods; so man would pile objection on objection, until he
had proved, or imagined he had, that there is no God—no heaven—no hell—no state of retributive justice,—and consequently
the Bible, purporting to be the word of God, is the production of
fiction, and no way binding upon the moral sense of man. Such
a system as this, was introduced into the world by Epicurus; and
for ages, this theory, dark and foul in its features, was embraced
with the fondest devotion. The passions of men gathering around
it, audibly proclaimed it the true secret of human happiness. Silencing all remonstrances of conscience, they pressed closer to
their bosom the illusions of a false hope. Thus armed, they
could lie as sweetly as on beds of roses, amid the thunderings of
Sinai. They could smile at the drawn sword of God's justice—
they could hear, unmoved, the wailings of the lost; for they were
only the creations of a diseased mind, or the fumes of a heated
imagination. All the sublime and awful truths of the Gospel
were considered by them the results of a superstitious fancy.
The practical tendencies of such sentiments, are too obvious to
need a passing notice. Their characters are too deeply and
painfully written in the history of France. The gradual and silent infection produced by the wide diffusion of infidel sentiments,
poisoned the fountain of her moral character. The materials of
vice which were gathering for ages, poured their awful contents
in every direction, affecting those who felt as well as those who

witnessed their awful explosion. Costly indeed was the lesson taught by this example; and therefore the more likely to be remembered. The tragical scenes that succeeded, will constitute a monument, cemented withblood, teaching all future generations the folly of man in subverting all laws of justice between God and his creatures; and substituting a religion of fancy for that of the Bible. With feelings of unmingled pleasure, coming ages, gazing upon the edifice of divine revelation, and enraptured with the beauty of its structure, will wonder at the philosophy of those materials that compose it, which so far from being defaced by the assaults of men and time, have only acquired additional lustre and glory. And this will ever constitute an infallible evidence, that like its original, it is divine, and the more it is tried, the more illustrious it becomes. 'Thou shalt love the Lord thy God with all thy heart, and with all thy soul, and with all thy strength, and with all thy mind: and thy neighbor as thyself.'

In the discussion of the subject before me, I shall consider several points.

And *first*,—That there is a God, and that He is benevolent.

Secondly—That the creation of man is a blessing; and he, therefore, is under moral obligation to love God supremely.

Thirdly—That He who could thus create man, susceptible of so much enjoyment, is the only being worthy of his (man's) affections; and there is none more qualified to appreciate it.

Fourthly—The rule by which we may determine the supremacy of our affection for God.

Fifthly—Who is our neighbor? and what is to be understood by the expression, 'Love thy neighbour as thyself.'

Sixthly—That the permanency of our happiness is inseparably connected with the observance of this command, 'Thou shalt love the Lord thy God with all thy heart, and with all thy soul, and with all thy strength, and with all thy mind: and thy neighbor as thyself.'

You perceive that I have marked out for myself, a very wide and extensive field. I cannot gather every flower and go through the tedious process of analyzing them for you. I can show you only a few of each class, and ask you to examine the rest for yourself. And, *first*,—There is a God.

The existence of God has never been questioned, except by those, who seeming to be wise, have become fools. Who, in gazing on this planet, its mountains, its rivers, its lakes, its volcanoes, and understanding what part they act in the physical economy, can fail to perceive, that it is the production of an intelligent agent. Were it not for the mutual accommodation of laws, visible in every department of the physical universe, the most serious results would succeed. For if the earth's progress around the sun were seven times greater, it would overcome the power of gravitation, and consequently, neither man, nor beast, nor any creature could inhabit it. Now, to regulate it by a law, so that its velocity shall be precisely such, as, acting in harmony with other laws, shall produce a beneficial result, surely it would be contrary to all principles of reason and analogy, to suppose it to be the production of any other than an intelligent agent. To say the least, it cannot be the effect of chance. Should some novel machine be presented to us, after understanding the relation which the parts sustain to each other, and the laws by which motion is produced, we immediately conclude that it is the production of an intelligent agent; because it betrays design. For if it be not the work of an intelligent mind, it must be the work of chance; and if so, then chance, which made it one thing to-day, may make it another thing to-morrow, so that it may become a perfect Proteus. The planet, of which we are the inhabitants, as well as our constitution, abounds with evidences of design. If the earth had no motion, its ability to support its inhabitants would cease. If there were no light the eye would be useless— if there were no air the lungs could not move. Now, for the action of the planet to be such as to destroy stagnation; for the eye to require just such rays as are essential to produce vision: for the lungs to require just such air as is requisite to produce respiration; is a coincidence solvable on no other supposition that that it is the result of an intelligent, a superior mind. With an air of triumph, and conclusions truly philosophical, the Psalmist has said: 'Shall he who made the eye not see; shall he who made the ear not hear; shall he who gave man knowledge not know.' Exceptions have been taken to some defect, connected with our physical organization. It has been said, that the eyes are sometimes a source of pain. This, however, does not invalidate the position, that the eye was designed for use. A pen-knife may sometimes cut a man's finger, but he never would presume to say that the knife was made for that purpose. Therefore the failure of any organ to perform its function, is no proof of the want of design. But again—

It is a principle in philosophy, that inanimate matter cannot move itself; and unless it be moved, it must remain in a state of rest. It must also be admitted, that the earth was created before man. The question is, does the earth move? The answer is, it does. The next question is, who moved it? It could not have been man: for, according to the principles of mechanics, he had not the power. Besides, man was made, adapted to the earth, and consequently the earth must have been governed by those laws which now regulate it, prior to its inhabitation by man. Therefore, as the earth does move, and its motion was not produced by man, it must have been made by some agent superior to man— that agent is God. By a similar course of reasoning on moral subjects, we can arrive at the same conclusion; but time forbids me to indulge much longer on this topic. The relation which one moral law sustains to another, and their final results, incontestibly prove, that laws which are so comprehensive in their design, adapted to all the complicated relations of life, could have originated with no other than an infinitely wise and benevolent being. For the moral economy of God's government carries with it more features and evidences of design, than his physical; or to say the least, it throws more light on the deep and profound workings of his incomprehensible wisdom. To anticipate moral changes, and form laws suited to every exigency, prove not only design, but benevolence—and hence we arrive at the second proposition of our subject; that the creation of man is benevolent.

Men have ever exhibited a strange aversion in acknowledging the extent of their obligation. Any consideration, how forced soever, and unnatural, that can be adduced to lessen their responsibility, will be readily and cheerfully adduced. The love of responsibility is not natural. It is not a native plant of the human mind, though it may be seen flourishing in the more fruitful portions of it. These spots, however, form an exception to the general character of the soil, and should not be regarded as an authorized rule in determining the character of the rest. The love of curiosity may sometimes be mistaken for responsibility. Curiosity is natural, because it is connected with knowledge. It is the very key to knowledge, and its indulgence a source of pleasure; for knowledge is pleasing. Responsibility, on the other hand, though assumed, because it must fall on some member of the human family, is a source of care and anxiety, and therefore not natural; for it is incongruous with the principles of our constitution to impose burdens and duties on ourselves, without the prospect of an equivalent. Motives of ambition, or a sense of duty, may impel to the assumption of responsibility, because of some ulterior good; but no native disposition is sufficiently strong to force us to assume it. Hence, men have always striven to lessen their obligation; and this just in proportion to the responsibilities involved. As the relation we sustain to God is the most important of all relations, the obligations arising from that relation are equally so; (i. e. important) and hence from this native indisposition to assume responsibility, men have questioned, though falsely, whether they are under any obligation to love God with all their minds, and their neighbor as themselves; inasmuch, say they, as God has forced these responsibilities upon us, without our consent; or, in other words, that God has made us and the duties consequent upon that relation without first consulting us. A little reflection will convince us, that although man was not consulted, yet his creation is a blessing, and the duties arising from that relation are in the highest degree beneficial.

Viewing man as he is, we find him a singular piece of machinery, combining in himself the elements of a compound being.

His physical constitution acting in harmony with his moral; and his moral with his intellectual; present to the reflecting mind a production too benevolent in its conception, and admirable in its execution, not to excite investigation and praise. To know something of that master workman; to arrive at some information of Him, who produced so fine a specimen of art, would be a subject of solicitude to a thoughtful mind. The frequency of the object, it is true, has detracted from its beauty, but the merit of the production is the same. Man considered as the work of art is unrivaled. But if we shall endow him with the principle of locomotion, by which he can change his position at pleasure, we shall add utility to the beauty of his structure. If, in addition to this, we shall invest him with numerous organs, such as the eye, to gaze on scenes of beauty, and the ear, to hear sounds of melody, we shall possess a production, combining in itself, beauty, utility, and pleasure. Besides, he has a moral and an intellectual nature, harmonizing with each other, both of which are sources of pleasure. The enjoyments of his moral nature are too numerous to be defined; and those of his mental will ever mock the efforts of man. But if we shall endow these several constitutions with perpetuity; with an increased susceptibility of enjoyment; if the physical organization shall become a glorified one; if the moral affections of the soul shall increase forever; if the intellect shall ever progress, and find no limit to its developments; if such be the result of that strange production, man; if such be his destination, he is unquestionably the master-piece of God's skill. He is the crowning jewel in the diadem of his creative power; and all nature, if vocal, would say—

> "For man kind nature wakes her genial power,
> Suckles each herb, and spreads out every flower;
> Annual for him, the grape, the rose renew,
> The juice nectareous, and the balmy dew;
> For him the mine a thousand treasures brings,
> For him health gushes from a thousand springs;
> Seas roll to waft him, suns to light him rise,
> His foot-stool earth, his canopy the skies."

The production of man was the result of benevolence. The sources of his enjoyment are infinite; and the obligation consequent upon this gift is equivalent to his supreme affection for God. Men, however, looking at the evils of life, and regarding them as the absolute condition of our existence, have questioned the benevolence of man's creation. In their estimation, they can trace but few features in the whole relation of man, which they regard as benevolent. The sufferings perceptible in every department of human life, preponderate so much in comparison with the few blessings common to it, that they would do violence to their judgment to suppose life any other than a curse. This assertion is in opposition to truth, and derogatory to God. How poor soever a man may be; a subject of the severest affliction; destitute of friends; not having where to lay his head; yet his existence is a treasure which he values too highly to barter for the cessation of his sufferings. The pleasures of a conscious existence; the satisfaction of having lived; of knowing there is such a world; peopled with such an order of beings; is a blessing with which all the sufferings of life, when contrasted, seem like an atom, compared with the immensity of infinity. Man is always partial to himself; and hence his conclusions are frequently erroneous. He looks at objects, not in their natural position. The rays of selfishness are too numerous and rapid in their convergency to admit those of truth; for this reason, and no other, he regards human existence a curse; and therefore feels himself under no obligation to love God with all his strength, and his neighbor as himself. A little reflection will convince us, that the unavoidable sufferings of life, are essential ingredients to the right enjoyment of it. A poet, unknown to me, has no less beautifully than philosophically said—

> And if life's joy had no alloy,
> We'd but half enjoy it,
> We prize it now, because we know
> Time may soon destroy it.

Those who have reflected upon the laws of physical nature, cannot fail to perceive the utility of those changes peculiar to it. They seem like so many blood vessels carrying the principle of life to every part of the system. The mountain torrent, rushing to the ocean, is again supplied by the principle of evaporation. The ocean is agitated by the silent, yet powerful influence of the moon. The clouds are constantly moving, and purifying the atmosphere by the explosion of their electric properties. The emboweled materials of the earth, are silently gathering strength, and displaying their power in the eruption of volcanoes. All nature is active; and its activity is essential to its healthy existence. By a careful investigation into the philosophy of that moral system under which we live, we cannot fail to perceive, that the necessary ills of life are essential to the production of re-action, on which depends the right enjoyment of life; for the action of one moral quality on another is as requisite to the vital condition of the moral universe, as the action of one particle of matter on another. The ills which arise from the violation of moral laws, are injurious in themselves, as well as to others. The horrors of war; the inconveniences of idleness; the sufferings of drunkenness; and the pain consequent upon many offences too numerous to be mentioned, are the effects of our folly. To as-

cribe them to God, and say He made us miserable, when we have
made ourselves so, is an act of injustice.   A faithful observance
of those laws under which we are placed, will conduct us to happiness ; and we are to form our estimate of things, not by what they
are, but by their obvious intention and design; by what they are
capable of becoming.   Hence we attach so much importance to
man, because of the elements of greatness that are in him.   God
having made man susceptible of the highest degree of improvement; should man through negligence, or carelessness, plunge
himself in misery, no fault can be ascribed to God; and man is
just under as much obligation to love God supremely, as though
he had arrived at that point of happiness of which his nature is
susceptible; which was the second point to be proved.   But this
leads me to the *third* consideration of my subject, that God is
worthy of man's supreme affection.

The powers of man can never fully comprehend the nature
and character of God.   His works are the best representatives of
him.   They speak with a tongue too eloquent to be misunderstood ; that "He who made them is divine."   God's power can
never be withstood, either by men or angels.   He said, " Let
there be light, and there was light."   The dark and confused
mass of chaos became order aud beauty ; and the whole universe,
with all its countless variety of grandeur was created by the
breath of his lips.   The moral qualities of God are commensurate with the greatness of his power.   He is not a creature, of a
sudden impulse, but firm and inflexible, governing the universe
which he has made, with a strict impartiality, aiming at general,
not particular good.   Benevolence is the most prominent feature
in his character.   It is legibly inscribed upon all his works.
But more especially is it illustrated in the noblest and best of all
gifts, His Son.   This is the consummation of all benevolence.
It is the crowning gem in the diadem of His glory.   Coming
generations will gaze upon it as if lost in silent abstraction, wondering that God should so love the world as to give His son to
die for it.   Men may boast of their benevolence.   Their acts of
self-devotion may be heralded, till vale and mountain shall echo
with the sound; yet no form of benevolence bears any proportion
to that which is embodied in the person of Christ.   He is the
sun of our moral existence, and we are the planets that reflect his
glory.

In addition to this comprehensive benevolence, peculiar to God,
He is infinitely just.   Remotely removed is it from his character
to practice any imposition.   Justice is one of those pillars in the
edifice of his character, without which, it would be imperfect,
and incomplete.   In the administration of His government, there
is no partiality.   The rich and the poor, the bond and the free,
are dealt with according to their offences.   ' The soul that sinneth,
it shall die,' and ' he that doeth these things shall live.'   No ex-

ceptions are made. Party influences have no agency in the direction of his mind. In a government where there is no justice, there can be no safety, either to person or property. To the wicked; the extortioner; the violent; such a system may be desirable; because they can plunder with impunity, and enrich themselves with the spoils of others. But to the virtuous and the good, such a government would be far from being eligible. An inflexible adherence to justice, is the only method by which the general good of society can be promoted. This disposition is strikingly exemplified in the character of God. His eyes are so pure, that he cannot approbate sin in the slightest degree. The very angels are said to be guilty of folly, when viewed in the light of his purity. It is not within the bounds of human power to make laws suited to every individual act; but God being infinite in wisdom, has a code of moral laws, as comprehensive as the universe, suited to every exigency, simple or complex. Hence, no one who lives worthily shall fail of his reward.

Far short of the excellency of His character shall we fall, if we shall limit our conception of Him to his power, his benevolence, and his justice. He is equally eminent for the infinitude of his veracity. Truth is one among the brightest ornaments in His character. Its influence upon the conduct of men, is that which adds lustre to the greatness of its glory. The conviction, that he is true; that His promises will never fail; has fortified the bosoms of those who were about, with their own blood, to seal their testimony to the truth. As in the ordinary relations of life, he who is most veracious, enjoys our confidence and regard; so God, being infinite in truth, is deserving of the unqualified affection of men. Truth is the foundation on which rests the superstructure of His glory. Earth may pass away, but His word shall endure forever. If in addition to this, we shall endow Him with immutability; with a power to effect with a single thought, what shall invariably be for the highest happiness of his creatures; with long suffering and kindness; with an unwillingness to see any of His creatures perish; but with the disposition of an aggrieved parent, entreating them to be reconciled to Him:—surely a being, so incomparably omnipotent; so infinitely benevolent; so inflexibly just; so scrupulously veracious; so impartially affectionate, is deserving the supreme affection of man: and there is no object more worthy of it; which was the third subject under consideration. But this conducts me to the fourth proposition: the rule by which we may determine the supremacy of our affection for God.

No parent is at much loss to determine the difference in the moral disposition of his children. The obedient and disobedient are classed off with much system. Their conduct is the rule by which this knowledge is attained. How eloquently soever a child may plead in asserting its affection for its parent, and
16—Vo. 3.

will give no practical proof of it, all of its confessions will amount to nothing.   The rules which God has laid down for the regulation of our conduct, are founded upon the best principles of wisdom and justice; and a faithful observance of them, is the only rule by which we can determine our affection for God.   If, therefore, the commands of God are not observed by us, we can make no pretensions to love for Him.   If only a part of his commands are observed, we have no supreme affection for Him.   If it be our habitual desire to keep the laws of God, and the violation of them at any time occasion regret and sorrow; if our sentiment be, whom have I in Heaven but thee, and there is none upon earth I would desire in comparison with thee; such a disposition of mind will constitute the strongest evidence of the supremacy of our affection for God.   Foreign from my intention is it to insinuate, that a sinless life is inseparably connected with loving God with all our strength; for if this be our only rule, then there are none who have this affection for God, since there is no man that liveth and sinneth not.   Admitting, with feelings of regret, that good men are liable to sin, I shall maintain, that they do it from necessity and not from choice.   They that are after the Spirit do mind the things of the Spirit.   The rule by which we may determine, whether we love God supremely or not, may be summed up in this.   When our sinful passions clamor for the indulgence of one sin, and the law of God forbids it, do we obey the law of God?   When the world is alluring us to follow its fashion, and the law of God requires that we be crucified to the world, do we obey the law of God?   When the pleasures of life are inviting us to themselves, and the law of God requires that we deny ourselves, do we obey the law of God?   When fame is wooing us to itself, and the law of God forbids that we seek the praises of men, do we obey the law of God?   When our selfish feelings would urge us to live for ourselves, and the law of God requires that we live for Him, do we obey the law of God?   If so, then we prefer the will of God to all others; and he is the only object of our affection.   This is the only sure criterion.   'If ye love me, ye will keep my commandments.'

This devotion of our affections to God will not be without a corresponding advantage.   Them that honor me, says God, I will honor.   Them that honor me with their affection, I will honor with mine.   I will be their God, and they shall be my people.   I will be their friend.   I will be their guardian angel. I will soothe their sorrows.   I will raise their desponding spirits. I will fortify them against the ills of life.   I will deprive death of his sting, and the grave of its victory.   They have honored me with their affection, and I will honor them with mine.   I will honor them with my smiles.   I will honor them with my confidence.   1 will honor them with my society.   I will honor them with a crown of imperishable glory.   They shall be honored, for they have loved me with all their minds. Hence our affection for God is inseparably connected with our happiness. But this leads me to the fifth consideration of my subject : who is our neighbor, and in what sense we are to love him as ourselves.

Human wisdom will find itself but poorly prepared to comprehend all the moral relations of life ; nor indeed is it her province. She may comprehend a few, and these may give her some impression of those that are unintelligible; and as the few within the limits of her knowledge carry with them evidences of benevolence, the presumption is, that those which are beyond her reach, are equally so; (i. e. benevolent.) There are no data upon which any other conclusion can be based. To love our neighbor as ourselves, may seem a task almost too arduous; but nevertheless, it is a moral duty. The moral law of God has never been abrogated. It is as binding on the consciences of men now, as when it was first delivered amid the thunderings and lightnings of Sinai. Nay, more so; for Christ has invested it with additional dignity and glory. He has made it more honorable. His atonement has superseded the necessity of no law but the ceremonial. Men are under no obligation to observe the external rites of the old covenant; but its moral principles remain. God no longer makes his presence a condition of offering sacrifice at Mount Gerizim, or Jerusalem; but requires the devotion of a pure and holy affection. Thou shalt love thy neighbor as thyself, is a command frequently introduced, enforced, and insisted upon. It seems to be the soul of all the other commands contained in the second table of the decalogue. Hence we account for the frequency of it in the writings of the New Testament. Numerous are the instances in which the Saviour inculcated it. Scarcely, if ever, did he make a public address, without recommending the observance of this command. The Apostle Paul, faithful to the example of his Lord, has not been wanting in inculcating this duty. In his epistle to the Galatians, the 5th chapter, and 14th verse, he says : For all the law is fulfilled in this word; even this: Thou shalt love thy neighbor as thyself. In his address to Timothy, he says: Now the end of the commandment is love out of a pure heart and a good conscience, and of faith unfeigned. In his epistle to the Romans, after enumerating the prohibitions of the first commandment, he says: If there be any other, it is comprehended in this, namely: Thou shalt love thy neighbor as thyself. The Apostle James was no less anxious to enforce the same duty. In the 2nd chapter of his epistle, and the 8th verse, he says: If ye fulfil the royal law according to the Scriptures—Thou shalt love thy neighbor as thyself, ye do well. The frequency with which this duty is inculcated, shows its importance; and it never would have been thus urged, unless it was beneficial; and experience teaches us that it is emphatically so.

It would be a perversion of the term neighbor, to suppose it applicable to those only who reside in our immediate neighborhood.   Moral obligations recognize no localities.   They are neither more or less binding by nearness or remoteness ; and consequently every man is our neighbor.   This is in accordance with that beautiful illustration given by our Saviour in the parable of the good Samaritan, To do to others, what you would wish that they, under similar circumstances, should do to you, is considered the extent of the obligation involved in the command, Love thy neighbour as thyself.   The interpretation is rational, and in harmony with the laws of our nature.   If this simple command was faithfully observed, what a vast amount of sufferings would be obviated ; and what incalculable benefits would succeed.   Rapine, murder, and injustice would find no soil in which to germinate. Hatred, malice, and revenge would find no food to satiate their fiend-like appetite.   The iron messengers of death would no longer belch their fires of destruction.   The whole face of the world would be changed from on Acheron to a paradise.   The voice of wailing would be changed for exultation.   All would be peace, tranquility, and enjoyment.   Parents would be affectionate to their children, and children obedient to their parents.   Masters would be kind to their servants, and servants faithful to their masters. Rulers would regard the rights of the ruled, and the ruled would respect the authority of the rulers: Such would be the condition of society, if this simple command was faithfully observed.   Let no man presume to say, that it is impossible.   The rule which a monarch gave to his son who wished some information in the government of his subjects, may materially assist you in fulfilling this command, of loving your neighbor as yourself.—Says he to his son: 'In petitions, or remonstrances on the part of your subjects, place yourself in their condition, with all the circumstances in question, and what you would expect your monarch to do for you, that do you for them.'   A hearty recommendation of the same rule may here be appropriately introduced. Our happiness is so blended with each other, that whatever would be beneficial for one, will be so for another.   In promoting the interest of my neighbor, I do virtually advance my own—so intimately are our interests interwoven with each other.   Hence we perceive the reasonableness, the benevolence of the command to love our neighbor as ourselves.   But I must hasten to notice the sixth subject under consideration, viz : That the permanency of our happiness is inseparably connected with the observance of the command of loving God with all our strength, and our neighbor as ourselves.

The duties of life are numerous—some civil—some domestic, and some social; yet they are all moral duties.   Experience, the most faithful schoolmaster we have, has long since taught us, that there can be no permanency in any institution which is not based upon principles of morality and justice. That, where these fundamental principles are wanting, there can be no durability to human systems. That how beautious soever may be the super-structure, there is nothing solid on which it can rest. That it carries within itself the elements of destruction, and sooner or la-ter, these will work its ruin. No one who has reflected upon moral subjects, can fail to perceive the relation which God has established between justice and permanency, between virtue and happiness ; and that without these, nothing can be permanently useful. Hence we account for nations arising to a very high state of national prosperity ; and maintaining it for a time ; and then declining. These changes are not the result of necessity, as maintained by some. The supposition, that nations, like indi-viduals, have a beginning, a perfection, and an end, is fallacious. Moral results can no more exist, without their antecedents, than physical. The rules which conduct a nation to prosperity, if persevered in, will continue that prosperity ; but if departed from, will effect a declining. Hence we see, that Persia, for more than two centuries, enjoyed a degree of unrivaled glory, so long as she adhered to the simplicity of her jurisprudence ; but so soon as she departed from it, her glory fled,

"Like the baseless fabric of a dream."

And Greece, too, the land of poetry and philosophy ; and Rome, the proud mistress of the world ; and others, whose memo-ries lie hid in the chronicles of other times—they will ever con-stitute imperishable memorials of the truth, that nations tend to decay in proportion as they decline in virtue and intelligence. Hence, Phocian, in substance, has judicially said, that nations have never ceased to be prosperous, but by departing from those institutions to which they owed their prosperity.

Now the same laws which will apply to nations, will to indi-viduals—for we cannot suppose a nation without individuals. Besides, moral results can differ only in degree, and not in kind. He therefore, whose rules, for individual government, are not strictly moral and just, can never experience any permanent en-joyment ; for, like an unjust and oppressive nation, he will be at war with every one ; he will carry in his bosom the elements of destruction ; and these, sooner or later, will work his ruin. Hence, moral principles are essential to the permanency of indi-vidual happiness. And in proportion to the purity of those prin-ciples, will be the degree of enjoyment. As God is infinitely holy, just, and benevolent, whatever proceeds from Him, in the form of laws, must be of the same character ; and hence this command, Thou shalt love the Lord thy God with all thy heart, and thy neighbor as thyself, being a pure, holy, and just com-mand, the observance of it, from a moral necessity, must give permanency to our happiness; which was the last point to be proved. I would pursue the subject further, but I have already detained you too long.

In discussing the subject before me, I mentioned some of the ill effects arising from the disbelief of the existence of God, and the rejection of the Bible, as a divine revelation. After which, I briefly considered some arguments in favor of the existence of God; and showed, that He not only exists, but that He is benevolent. I next observed, that the creation of man could be none other than a favor; and man therefore, is under moral obligation to love Him supremely. I further stated, that He, who could thus create man, is alone worthy of his supreme affection; and a preference for His will is the only rule to determine man's affection. In further consideration of the subject, I observed, that every man is our neighbor, and that to do for him what we would expect him to do for us, under similar circumstances, is all that is implied in the command. In conclusion, I stated, that the permanency of our happiness is inseparably connected with the ebservance of this command: Thou shalt love the Lord thy God with all thy heart, and thy neighbor as thyself.

In whatever light the subject is viewed, it is filled with moral congruity. Its observance is the secret of human happiness. It is a rich and valuable treasure, over which many materials are thrown, and the more they are removed, the stronger becomes its attraction. It brings us in closer proximity with God It multiplies the sources of our moral discoveries. It unfolds to us scenes of beauty and grandeur, moving in harmonious succession; all illustrating the wisdom and benevolence of its incomparable Author. Viewed through the mists of natural religion, or the dark vapors of pagan philosophy, it may seem an arbitrary command, prejudicial in its consequences. But contemplated in the reflected light of the Gospel, and the experience of ages, it appears in its native beauty and loveliness—the magnet of philosophy; the pivot on which hangs the destinies of the world; the only sure touchstone to an imperishable weight of glory.

> "Such is thy glorious law, O God!
> 'Tis for our light and guidance given;
> It sheds a lustre all abroad,
> And points the path to bliss and heaven.
>
> "It fills the soul with sweet delight,
> And quickens all its dormant powers;
> It sets our wandering footsteps right,
> Displays thy love and kindles ours."

THE PREVALENCE OF CHRISTIANITY

IN THE WORLD FOR NEARLY TWO THOUSAND YEARS ONE
OF THE HIGHEST MORAL
PROOFS THAT IT IS A DIVINE REVELATION,

Preached as a Commencement Sermon, before the University of Georgia, Athens Ga., July 30, 1843, *by* REV. WM. T. BRANTLY, JR., *pastor of the Baptist Church in Augusta, Ga.*

—

"And now I say unto you, refrain from these men, and let them alone: for if this counsel or this work be of men, it will come to nought: but if it be of God, ye cannot overthrow it: lest haply ye be found even to fight against God."—ACTS v: 38, 39.

You remember the occasion of this advice. Very shortly after the return of our Lord to heaven, the preaching of the gospel by his Apostles, was attended with such extraordinary success as to excite the apprehension of the Jewish rulers, lest the new religion should supplant the faith of their ancestors. They had already given orders to the heralds of the cross to quit Jerusalem, and to desist from the publication of their offensive doctrines. But acting from the highest convictions of duty, the Apostles persisted in preaching Christ crucified. Perceiving that their injunctions were disregarded, a council was convened to devise a plan for the suppression of the troublesome heresy. After some deliberation, it appeared to the assembly that the most effectual method of extinguishing this religion was to put to death its preachers, the obstinate advocates of its claims. They were about to carry this measure into effect, when as we are informed by the narrative, Gamaliel a doctor of the law, held in high reputation among the people, urged the adoption of a different course. He reminded the council of several impostors, who had previously risen up and caused them much trouble by seducing the people; but who, having been put to death, their followers were in a short time dispersed. He brought to their notice the case of Theudas who had enlisted in his cause about 400 disciples who continued faithful during the life of their leader, but who were disbanded shortly after his death; he adverted also to Judas of Galilee, who in the days of the taxing drew away much people after him, but who were scattered when he died. From these cases he inferred, that if Jesus Christ was really an impostor, inasmuch as he had been crucified, the believers in what he published would soon be dispersed and there was no necessity for shedding their blood. If they were not thus disbanded they might take it for granted that he was no deceiver. In view of these facts, I say unto you, refrain from these men, and let them alone: for if this counsel or this work be of men it will come to nought: but if it be of God ye cannot overthrow it lest haply ye be found even to fight against God.

The advice of Gamaliel, though agreed to in this instance, was soon forgotten. These men were not let alone. Every conceivable obstacle was thrown in their way. Ridicule, wit, learning, wealth, secret treachery, open malice, industrious violence, were all excited against them. Persecution in its multiplied forms, torture of every species, the most malignant passions of the human heart, have been arrayed against this work, but has it been overthrown? What has been the result of this contest? At the lapse of nearly 2000 years since Gamaliel gave this advice, have the developments of this long period, permit me to ask, evinced this to be the work of man, or have they demonstrated it to be the power of God? I put the question this morning: Has the combined hate of its uncounted foes been sufficient to accomplish its annihilation? No, my hearers. The trophies of redeeming love in every age cry, NO. The unnumbered multitudes who through faith in the cross of Christ, this day exult in the hope of a blessed immortality,—cry NO! the tens of thousands now in glory, from their exalted abode echo back the cry, NO! NO!! In vain have the kings of the earth set themselves, and the rulers taken counsel together. Victorious over every foe, trampling down every obstacle, this despised gospel has lived, and still lives, and will continue to exert its saving power when time shall be no more.

Christianity, then, is a fact whose existence demands explanation. When I find it flourishing in the world notwithstanding the opposition which it has encountered; when from century to century I see it subject to the most rigid scrutiny—tried by the severest tests which man or devil could devise; when I look at its advocates hunted down with the most unsparing fury ; when, notwithstanding every effort which has been made for its suppression, I find that the religion of Christ still triumphs, I can account for that triumph but from one consideration. And that is— that it has been preserved in the world by the power of Almighty God. He who can resist the force of evidence like this, I must pronounce hopelessly sceptical. He would not believe Christianity to be a divine revelation though one should rise from the dead and assert the truth. His unbelief is as wilful and as obstinate as that of the man, who, at mid-day, should plunge into the dark mines of the earth, and contend in the face of truth and of reason that the sun did not shine.

With these remarks, I invite you to the consideration of the theme suggested by the text. It is this:—*The prevalence of*

Christianity in the world for nearly 2,000 *years, constitutes one of the highest moral proofs that it is a divine revelation.*

And I do not propose this subject at the present time because I deem it essential to the conviction of any who may be sceptical upon this point. I presume that the greater portion of those to whom I now speak entertain no doubt of the truth of the proposition which has been announced. Whilst however, you may feel perfectly satisfied that you are not following a cunningly devised fable,—that your faith stands in the power of God and not in the wisdom of man—it cannot be uninteresting to review those considerations by which we should be at all times ready to give a reason of the hope that is in us. Our proposition is sustained if you consider—

I. That Christianity has found in every unrenewed man an uncompromising opponent of its claims. Had the religion of Jesus imposed no restraint upon the tempers of a depraved nature; had it thrown no curb upon the passions of the human heart; had it called upon men to encounter no self-denial; to undergo no hardship; to make no sacrifice; then the argument supporting its divine original, drawn from its protracted life, would be very materially invalidated. Being a religion at least inoffensive, its harmlessness might have shielded it from assault, and it might have been allowed to stand or to fall by its own merits. Were such its character, the caviler might contend that it owed its existence to accident, or that it was protected by the imbecility of its doctrines. But even in this case, its preservation in the world for so many centuries, amidst the revolutions of kingdoms, the ceaseless fluctuation of human opinions, and the ravages of time, would be very powerful presumptive evidence that it had been defended by an omnipotent energy. If besides imposing no restraint, Christianity had coincided with man's corrupt propensities; if it had fostered the pride of his heart, encouraged him in his sinful pursuits, and taught him how he might gratify ambition, revenge, malice, and all the degenerate desires of fallen humanity; had such been the character of the Christian religion, then I admit that no argument in favor of its being a divine revelation could have been derived from its extended prevalence. With such principles it could need no supernatural power to sustain it. Being of the world, the world very naturally would love its own and strive to keep it in the world.

But the religion of Jesus Christ has ever been directly at war with the darling passions of depraved nature. From its earliest appearance it has been the determined enemy of every sinful indulgence. Its doctrines were the most unpalatable to the carnal mind which could possibly be conceived. There was scarcely a feature in the whole system adapted to secure for it the least popularity in a guilty world. Its very presence was a rebuke to sin-loving mortals. To man disposed to trust in his self-righteousness, to extenuate his offences, and to laud the virtues and excellencies of his own character, Christianity declared that, as a creature, he was mean—as a sinner, he was vile; that his moral character was radically disordered; that a deadly taint had seized and corrupted the breath of every desire; that from the crown of the head to the sole of the foot there was no soundness. It published the humiliating truth, that that heart which he cherished as the seat of so many fine affections and elevated dispositions, was deceitful beyond all comparison, and desperately wicked. It sounded in the ear of those inflated reptiles of the dust who, swollen with vanity, would lift themselves up and be of consequence,—"He that exalteth himself shall be abased,"—"Pride goeth before destruction and a haughty spirit before a fall,"—"Except ye be converted and become as little children, ye shall not enter into the kingdom of heaven." To man in love with ease and indulgence, said Jesus, deny thyself, deny thyself. If any man will come after me, let him deny himself and take up his cross and follow me. He who would be my disciple, must crucify the flesh with its affections and lusts. It called upon those who were prosecuting with inexpressible eagerness the vain objects of time, not to labor for the meat which perishes, but for that which endureth forever. To the man inflamed with envy, hatred, and revenge, and burning to gratify these unhallowed tempers, Christ preached a doctrine which confounded the philosophy of this world; a doctrine as novel as it was repugnant to those who heard it. "Love your enemies, bless them that curse you, do good to them that hate you, and pray for them which despitefully use you, and persecute you." Christianity thus being in direct opposition to the whole current of man's natural desires, it is not surprising that he should have hated it. It is not extraordinary that its preaching should stir up the most violent opposition, of those whose pleasures it abridged, and whose practices it condemned. There were soon seen innumerable proofs that Paul spoke the truth, when he declared "the carnal mind is enmity against God." Every unconverted man was the enemy of the Gospel. He looked upon it as the censor of his morals, and the opponent of his cherished gratifications. He regarded his very happiness as identified with the extermination of a religion so objectionable in all its provisions. And the early history of Christianity, is a history of the industry manifested by men in the adoption and execution of such measures as they thought best calculated to effect this desirable consummation.

But how is it that we still find in the world this religion, so long a stumbling-block to human pride and ambition? Why has it not long since been banished from the earth? When its enemies have ever been so much more numerous than its friends, when it has met on every hand such unrelenting hostility, how comes it to pass that Christianity is still triumphant? How is it, that a religion so universally hated, has achieved such wonders in subduing pride, in breaking up hard hearts, and in melting into contrition and penitence stubborn natures? How is it that the phenomenon, of a man to-day breathing out threatening, and slaughter, and maddened with rage against this religion, and to-morrow, its most ardent supporter, has found a parallel in every age of the Church? Whence has the gospel this soul-subduing energy? By what might has Christianity effected all this? I answer by the *power of the living God.* Leave divine interfer-ence out of the question, exclude from all this the hand of God, and the fact that on this, the 30th day of July, 1843, there is such a religion prevalent in the world as the Christian religion, is itself a miracle far more astonishing than any of the wonderful mira-cles said to have been wrought by its divine founder in support of its claims.

II. If you look at the means which have been employed to promote the extension of Christianity, you will perceive that these must have been unavailing unless seconded by an almighty pow-er. We could conceive that a religion as objectionable to the pride of man's heart, as is the religion of Jesus, yet protected at all times by the strong arm of civil power, or recommended by the imposing forms of learning and of grandeur, might attain a currency to which it was by no means entitled. Indeed all spurious religions, which have ever gained much popularity in the world, must ascribe that popularity to secular support, or to their acquiescence in man's corrupt propensities. For it has been universally found that where the former has been withdrawn, or when they no longer chime in with the carnal mind, these false systems have declined and ultimately become extinct. There have ever been some peculiar circumstances of an accidental and secular character to which they have been indebted for their ex-tension. Look, for an illustration of this remark, at the sects which existed in the world antecedent to the Christian era, and contemporary with Christ. The leaders of the different sects of philosophy secured for their opinions, very considerable circula-tion, but did not their authors and patrons render themselves commendable by means and arts either merely specious, or posi-tively sinful? The followers of Plato were numerous, but it is well known that they courted public favor by their skill in the sublime science of geometry. How was it that the peripatetics acquired such celebrity? It was because the pupils of this school devoted themselves to the study of plants and of animals, and by their extraordinary proficiency in natural science, exhibited to the people many of the secrets of nature and thus acquired their esteem and veneration. Whence the popularity of the Stoical doctrines? The Stoics were distinguished for their learned subtleties in disputation, and being able to confound their opponents, they acquired a reputation for wisdom. What was there so facinating in the doctrines of Pythagoras as to secure the attention of such multitudes? It is well known that the Pythagoreans charmed their hearers with lofty speculations respecting the soul, the enchantments of harmony, and the origin of all things. We need not stop long to account for the popularity of the doctrines of Epicurus. His doctrines are not entirely obsolete at the present day. These systems were defended by some of the most powerful and eloquent writers which have ever lived, and this no doubt, in a very material degree, contributed to their currency. The temporary success which attended these and all other systems of religion which were in the world prior to the Christian religion, can be accounted for entirely on natural principles; we need look no farther than this world to learn the secret of their triumph.

The same remark is applicable to the false systems of modern times. Take for instance that popular defection, Mohammadism. The origin and the extension of this delusion can easily be accounted for. Mohammadism has been propagated by the sword: it is indebted for its success to the craftiness and hardihood of its founders; to the lenient eye with which it has ever looked upon human infirmity and depravity. It is moreover a religion in very considerable accordance with the perverted tastes and passions of men. By holding up a heaven of sensual delight, it has excited the pursuit of the groveling, and secured a numerous train of followers. If you advert to the different systems of paganism now existing in the world, it will be seen that they owe their propagation to the support of civil power; to the slavish fears of their subjects; or to the fact that they pander to the debasing appetites of those whom they would secure as their votaries.

But to what is the success of Christianity owing? Who can account for its origin and extension upon any principles of human calculation? Who will explain its existence as he would explain the progress of any of the counterfeit religions of the world? The success which has attended the preaching of the gospel must be accounted for on principles widely different from any of these. Look at its early advocates,—men selected from the most humble avocations in life,—without distinction of birth, without learning,—without refinement,—without the smallest pretensions to greatness—save that which they derived from being the advocates of an unpopular religion. Look at its doctrines. As we have already seen, most unpalatable to the carnal mind; such as must have excited all the opposition of which it was capable. To one class, the Jews, who were expecting a Messiah clothed with temporal power, the fundamental doctrine of Christianity, that its founder had been put to death as a malefactor, was an absolute stumbling block; whilst in the estimation of the Greeks, who were in quest of wisdom, it was the veriest foolishness. Look at the class of people upon whom they proposed to operate. These, in the view of the world, were as insignificant as those who preached to them. Other religions had aimed to reach the opulent, the learned, the great of this world, neglecting those in the humble walks of life. Christianity aimed to save the vilest, to recover the meanest from their degradation. Indeed it was the peculiar glory of this religion, that the poor had the gospel preached unto them. Whilst the wise, and the prudent, and the proud of this world looked with disdain upon its doctrines, the humble rejoiced in the saving efficacy which they imparted. Other religions, as we have already seen, owed their extension to secular support, or to some contingencies. But Christianity has had no such support. It has been for the most part, opposed by those very influences which have been exerted to sustain false religions. Some of the most enlightened governments have only tolerated it, (which indeed is all that it asks,) designing in no way to touch the question of its merits; while in a great majority of cases, the kings of the earth have planted themselves against it, and the powers of this world have been leagued with the powers of darkness to " blot out its memorial from under heaven. "

But how is it, I ask again, that Christianity is still triumphant? How comes it to pass that with men so illiterate and obscure for its advocates; with doctrines so offensive ; with people so poor and despised for its adherents; with the strongest powers ever known in the world, exerted to arrest its progress; how comes it to pass, that the religion of Jesus yet prevails, and that successive centuries have only rendered more and more resplendent the lustre which encircles it ? Upon what principles of historical calculation can we account for all this? What human reasoning will explain it? For my part I can assign but one reason, the protection of Almighty God. Its existence under circumstances such as I have described, is powerful proof that it is a divine revelation. Well may we change the phraseology of Gamaliel and say: If this counsel, or this work had been of man, long since would it have come to nought; if it had been some scheme like that of Theudus, or Judas of Galilee, or like that of Plato, or Pythagoras, or Epicurus, or Aristotle, or Mahomet, or Juggernaut, long since would it have perished. But having God for its author, truth without any mixture of error for its subject, and salvation for its end, it has prevailed and must prevail. It will continue to add victory to victory until there shall not be found one enemy, not one heart a stranger to its saving power. Infidelity may as well attempt to teach the stream to forget its nature and to roll up the mountain side; or it may as soon hope to hurl the earth from its orbit, or to pluck the sun from the firmament, as to stay the mighty progress of the religion of Jesus.

III. The success of Christianity in exterminating the false philosophy, and the false religions of the world, is another fact

supporting the proposition before you.   It is a common observation, that "man is a religious being."   And there is much truth
in the remark.   Our hopes and our fears, our love of pleasure,
and our dread of pain, our sense of right and of wrong, the vast
longings of our nature, all dispose us to seek a religion of some
sort.   Now if Christianity had found the world in utter destitution of every thing which could be called religion, it might have
been contended that inasmuch as this was the first and the only
system presented to the world, that the religious nature of man
would dispose him to embrace a religion which he secretly despised, rather than to be without any religion.   Under such circumstances, it might be maintained, with some plausibility, that
no argument supporting the divine authority of Christianity could
be deduced from its success.   But let it be borne in mind that the
religion of Jesus found the minds of men pre-occupied with systems and creeds which they held in the highest veneration, and
which were adhered to with all that tenacity with which the
enlightened disciple now clings to his faith.   It was therefore
requisite that much error should be dissipated before the world
could be prepared for the reception of the truth.   The minds of
men must be liberated from the ignorance which had enslaved
them, and the delusions under which they had been laboring must
be exposed, before they could be qualified to listen to the gospel
of the Lord Jesus.   To do this was a work replete with difficulty.   They had to convince those who did not wish to be convinced,
and whose idolatry impelled them to fortify themselves against all
the assaults of the truth.   There is nothing about which a man
is so sensitive as about his religious belief, and though that
belief be false and pernicious in the extreme, it is hard to persuade
him that such is the case and to induce him to abandon it.   When
the Apostles of the Savior went forth upon their work, they were
instantly met and opposed by the mythology of the pagans and
the philosophy of the Greeks, which had for centuries
enslaved the minds of the people, and entrenched themselves behind the sanctity of established customs and long
venerated opinions.   The religion of Christ was the decided
antagonist of both these popular systems.   It met the system of
paganism with the declaration that it was entirely false, and
charged it with teaching precepts directly at variance with those
moral principles which Deity had implanted in the human bosom.
Paganism held, that religion consisted in part, at least, of impure
observances and unbridled excesses.   Christianity taught, that it
was the pure in heart alone who could see God.   Paganism
embodied the Deity in sensible forms and represented him under
images which human hands had made.   Christianity condemned
such representations, teaching that God was a Spirit, and requiring
those who would worship him acceptably, to worship in spirit
and in truth.   Paganism inculcated the worship of many deities.

Christianity preached one only living and true God.

Such was the discrepancy between Christianity and paganism. Nor were its doctrines less strikingly in contrast with the philosophy than with the religion of the age. Whilst one sect of these philosophers declared that matter was eternal, that the world had no beginning and could have no end; Christianity proclaimed that God spake and it was done, that he commanded and it stood fast, and that the world is to be one day destroyed by fire. Another sect held, that the world owed its origin to the fortuitous concurrence of atoms, and that the same chance which had created it, preserved it in existence. Christianity taught, that the world was created and preserved by a Being so particular and designing as to number the very hairs of the head. Instead of the doctrine held by many, that the wise man might defy the gods; Christianity taught that all created things are in God's sight but as the small dust of the balance; that we are sinners against him, and that we can only approach unto him in the exercise of penitence, humility and faith. Whilst pagan philosophy relied for its support upon the authority of man, the *autos ephe* of the Master, Christianity claimed to be a revelation from the supreme God, supporting that claim by incontestable miracles.

Such was the religion of Jesus, and with all the opposition which it encountered from the false worship and the false philosophy of the age, mark how rapidly the truth was circulated. In the language of another,* soon we hear they have filled Jerusalem with their doctrine. The Church has commenced her march. Samaria has with one accord believed the gospel. Antioch has become obedient to the faith. The name of Christ has been proclaimed throughout Asia Minor. The temples of the gods, as if smitten by an invisible hand, are deserted. The citizens of Ephesus cry out in despair, great is Diana of the Ephesians. Licentious Corinth, is purified by the preaching of Christ crucified. Persecution puts forth her arm to arrest the spreading superstition. But the progress of the faith cannot be stayed. The Church of God advances unhurt amidst racks and dungeons, persecutions and death, yea, smiles at the drawn dagger and defies its point; she has entered Italy and appears before the walls of the eternal city. Her ensign floats in triumph from the capitol. She has placed upon her brow the diadem of the Cæsars!

And whence, I inquire again, this success in surmounting obstacles so formidable? By what power has it achieved a victory in comparison with which the proudest victory ever achieved by man dwindles into insignificance.

The sceptic may seek an explanation in ordinary causes, he may ascribe it to accident, or chance. I ascribe it to the power of the Lord God of hosts. Tell me that *chance* has done this!

---

* Wayland.

I would as soon believe that chance turns the earth upon its axis or moves the planets in their orbits.

IV. I remark, finally, that the severe ordeal to which Christianity has been subjected, must have destroyed it but for divine preservation. Whatever may be said of the sufferings to which the early believers in Jesus were subjected, it is certain that they prove this much: that those who submitted to them were firmly convinced, that what they believed was true. Hypocrisy might make a profession, when that profession costs nothing. It might be willing to enter the Church, when the path to be traveled was one of flowers and of sunshine ; when it was cheered on by an approving world. But when it comes to the fire and the sword, to the dungeon and the rack, hypocrisy will flinch and run away from the trial. There were not many hypocrites in those days. They were sincere men. And if these men were convinced, then the evidence for the truth must have been sufficient for this purpose, for it would have been consummate folly and madness to have staked their lives upon an uncertainty. It is difficult to conceive of more terrible tortures than those which were employed to compel believers to renounce their faith. The mind sickens at the recital of the horrible cruelties by which the enemies of the cross strove to effect their fiendish designs. The early history of Christianity, is a history of persecutions, distresses and tortures, by which the followers of Jesus were destroyed. A Roman lawyer wrote seven volumes, in which he attempted an ennumeration of the various punishments with which it was judged that Christians should be afflicted. A favorite practice, we are told, was to pelt them to death with stones ; multitudes were sent out of the world in this way. At one time, the flesh was torn and lacerated with saws, and the torment was continued until they were literally cut to pieces and destroyed. Again, it was the agony of the rack, an instrument which effected the death of its victim by tearing asunder the limbs from the body ; at another time, it was to be shut up in a loathsome dungeon, where in gloomy darkness, the believer in Jesus was left to meet death in all the horrors of starvation ; and again, as if to impart a terrific variety to their tortures, their victims were subjected to the inexpressible misery of the scorching flame encircling the body of the sufferer and literally burning away the foundations of life. It would seem as if man's diabolical ingenuity had ransacked the very magazines of hell, to devise modes of consummate torture. In the language of an eloquent defender of our faith : The most furious efforts of fanaticism ; the concentrated strength of kings and of empires ; have been frequently and perseveringly applied to blot from under heaven the memorial of Christianity. The blood of her sons and of her daughters, has flowed like water ; the smoke of the scaffold, where they wore the crown of martyrdom, in the cause of Jesus, has ascended in thick volumes to the sky. The tribes of persecution have sported over her woes, and erected as they supposed, monuments of her perpetual ruin. But Christianity still lives. She has lived to celebrate the funeral of kings, and of kingdoms that plotted her destruction. When her persecutors have gone to their reward, she rears her head in triumph and tramples upon their ignominious dust. She lives when the puny arms which were raised to stay her progress, have palsied in death and now lie mouldering in the grave.

And whence this victory? Whence this wonderful conquest? How comes it to pass that amidst the faggot, and the fire, and the dungeon, and the rack, and the blood, the religion of Jesus still lives? How let me ask, has it been enabled to survive unhurt, the fires of persecution and the fierce hostility of her foes? I answer, because this work and this counsel was of God, and could not be overthrown. Divinity was enstamped upon it. The signature of omnipotence was clear and legible. Though storm after storm has for centuries been beating upon it, still it remains unshaken. Like the tempest which strengthens the sturdy oak of the forest and forces it to strike its roots deeper and wider in the earth, the fury of its opponents has only implanted it more firmly and immoveably in the affection of those who know its saving power. Well has it been said, that "opposition, like the wind from heaven blowing upon a conflagration, instead of quenching it, has only blown it into a brighter blaze." The very blood of her sons and of her daughters which has flowed so freely, has only enriched her soil, and drawn from it a multiplied host of followers.

I ask then, may we not most confidently assert, that the prevalence of Christianity in the world for nearly 2000 years, constitutes one of the highest moral proofs that it is a divine revelation.

My Christian brethren, what abundant reason have we to exult that our faith stands in the power of God. Can we ever be sufficiently thankful for such a religion, and for all the evidence which we possess of its being a divine revelation. With the bright hope of the Gospel, how is every ill of life alleviated, every tempest of this stormy pilgrimage assuaged. With this in our hearts, we may smile on suffering, tribulation, adversity of every species, and even on the last enemy himself. Wrest from us this hope and we are undone. We are plunged into uncertainty and darkness. With this we may ask,

"What is the bigot's torch? the tyrants chain?
I smile on death, if heaven-ward hope remain."

If we be stript of this support,

" If the warring winds of nature's strife,
Be all the faithless charter of my life,
If chance awaked—inexorable power—
This frail and feverish being of an hour,
Doomed o'er the world's precarious scene **to sweep,**
Swift as the tempest travels o'er the deep—
To know delight but by her parting smile,
And toil, and weep, and wish, a little while,
Then end ye elements that formed in vain
This troubled pulse and visionary brain—
Fade ye wild flowers—memorials of my doom—
And sink ye stars that light me to the tomb. "

But thanks be to God, this religion can never be wrested from us. You may heap suffering upon the disciple of Jesus. You may subject him to the keenest torture, you may tear from him his very heart, but you cannot wrest from him the faith which he has received from the Holy Ghost. We have this hope as the anchor of the soul sure and steadfast. It is the solace of our lives,—let it pass into fruition and be the perfect bliss of heaven.

What shall I say to him who is refusing to receive Jesus Christ and his religion? You are fighting against God, impenitent hearer. You refuse to acknowledge the claims of his Son, and this is opposition enough to destroy you. Do not tell me that you have not been fighting against God, when I see you resisting his Spirit, refusing the calls of his grace, tearing from you the cords which a merciful being has thrown out to draw you to himself. What an unhallowed war you are waging. Wo unto him that striveth with his Maker. Who hath hardened himself against Him and has prospered. In such a contest expect defeat, expect ruin, expect to be covered with eternal shame. But desist, desist. Come over to the Lord's side. Enlist with the soldiers of the cross. Fight the fight of faith, and a glorious victory shall be yours. When you come to die, as you look back upon the fading scenes of time, and look foward to the realities of eternity, you can say in the language of one of old: " I have fought a good fight, I have finished my course, I have kept the faith, henceforth there is laid up for me a crown of righteousness. "

I have left myself but a moment to speak a word to those * who are about to go forth from this venerable Institution to engage in the more public duties of life. My brothers, I am not a stranger to the emotions which this morning pervade your bosoms. It is but a few years since my circumstances were similar to your own, and the feelings with which I was then exercised are yet vivid in my recollection. In view of the inter-

---

* The Graduating Class.

esting position which you now occupy, what can I say to you? This is not the time for any protracted advice. I can only exhort you to cherish the elevated sentiments of virtue and of truth, which I doubt not have been again and again impressed upon your attention by those to whom has been confided the important work of training your intellects, and of guiding your morals. Those who have been distinguished for any thing very great or good in this world, have generally had some particular maxim, some leading truth to which they have looked as to the polar star of their being. Permit me to suggest one maxim for your guidance in all future life. It shall be that which an inspired man addressed to a youth dear to his heart, when he was about to enter upon the responsible duties of his vocation,—"Study to show thyself approved unto God." This advice has a stronger claim, because it is the dictate of revelation. If you enter any of the learned professions, let this study form a part of your daily studies, and let it adorn the profession which you may choose. Should your life be devoted to the pursuits of commerce, let this study incite you to write *holiness to the Lord* upon your merchandise; and should you engage in the ancient and respectable business of agriculture, let this study shed its sacred influence over this vocation. That is a most shallow and miserable philosophy which excludes God from its calculations. The time has gone by when the vituperation of Christianity passes for superior shrewdness and penetration. Believe me, gentlemen, the way of transgressors is hard. Believe me, nay, believe inspiration, That wisdom's ways are ways of pleasantness, and that all her paths are peace. Study to show thyself approved unto God. Do this then, my brother, anp whatever thou mayest fail in hereafter, you will not have failed in the one thing needful. Neglect it. Then in whatever else thou mayst succeed, life will be to thee an utter failure! May God bless you!

THE WORK OF THE MINISTRY.

" The obstructions which the gospel meets every time it is preached, are the accumulations of centuries, and the result of no small part of the plans of men. It is the profoundest scheme in this world of sin, the most gigantic enterprise that men ever formed, to go through this world committing sin every day, and yet evading remorse of conscience; indulging in guilty passions, and yet escaping the thunders of law, gaining as much of the world as a man pleases, and yet not harrowed in his solitary moments by the accusings of conscience; passing amidst the blightings of God's indignation, and yet not terrified; and hearing all the time the appeals of mercy and yet not moved. Never was there so vast a scheme of wickedness, so complicated, elaborate,

and compacted on any other subject. Philosophy here has lent
its aid; poetry its charms; eloquence its appeals; false theology
its alliance; learning its skill; age its experience; and youth its
ardor, in forming plans to oppose the obvious claim of the gospel.
And it is complete. While this influence governs the sinner,
what cares he for the groans of Jesus Christ; or the offers of
mercy; or the judgment seat of God; or the glories of heaven;
or the pains of hell? What cares he that we appeal to him by
every thing that is sacred in heaven, terrible in despair; that is
tender in love, and bleeding in mercy, or that is infinite in the
interests of his own soul, or terrible in the future scenes of woe?-
To all these appeals he is indifferent.

The ministers of religion must be qualified not merely to de-
claim, but convince; not only to weep and plead, but to stand up
against philosophic men and convince them they are wrong: to
show that the fatalism of the Stoic, and of the better kind of
deists; the sensuality of Epicureans, and of the mass of infidels;
and the dogmas of a theology founded on ancient and false philosophy, are as much in the face of true science as they are of the
bible. If in this pursuit we are drawn into the regions of metaphysics, the fault is not ours but that of those who led us there.
If the sinner like hunted game, will flee to dens and hiding places
we must follow him; and he should be the last to complain that
we preach to him metaphysics. It must be *proved* to men that
they *are* wrong. The time has gone by when declamation can
be substituted for argument. Dark dogmas, however pompous,
statuary, and solemn, will not supply the place of evidence in an
age of light. Men will think and reason, and draw their own
conclusions; and this must be fully understood by the ministry.
Man must be made to feel that God's view of sin is just. That
what *he* has expressed is the true measure of human guilt. That
the dying agonies of the Redeemer were but a fair expression of
the guilt of men. That God has a right to affix the penalty to
crime; and to declare that these shall go away into *everlasting*
punishment. Men must be *roused*, and severed—however rudely
—from earthly things; and hurried onward, and thrown into the
deep solemnities of a universe, where the God of justice reigns,
where every thing is full of God, and where voices from earth
and heaven and bell, mingle, and fall on his ear, and tell him
to hasten away from his delusions, and be prepared to die. Man
must be brought to a willingness to arrest his plans of wickedness where they are; to abandon the unfinished scheme; to stop
in his career of pleasure; to relinquish a plan of gain however
flattering, and a scheme of ambition however imposing, and
pause, and turn to the living God. The purpose must be one
that shall be executed now. "—*Chris. Spec.*

THE
BAPTIST PREACHER.

| VOL. III. | August, 1844. | NO. 8. |

MINISTERIAL CULTURE:—

A sermon, preached before the Virginia Baptist Education Society, at its Fourteenth Annual Meeting, in the First Baptist Church, Richmond, June 3, 1844, by Rev. Joseph Walker.

———

"Study to show thyself approved unto God, a workman that needeth not to be ashamed, rightly dividing the word of truth."
2 Tim. ii: 15.

The education of which we are to treat in this discourse, is that of the intellect. It may be thought, as our subject is *Ministerial* Culture, that we should unite the moral with the intellectual, and thus contemplate the improvement both of the understanding and the heart. But such a course, while it might serve to flatter settled prepossessions, would be irrelative to the designs of the Education Society. This Institution has for its *main* object the development of the mental powers, rather than the tuition of the religious affections. And though conducted on principles strictly moral, it neither proposes to convert men, nor teach them theology. The former is taken for granted; the latter is to be prosecuted in a different institution, and depends for its success mainly on the ardent prayers and patient researches of the student. Young men of approved piety, "apt to teach," selected and sent hither by the Churches, are the only ones received in the character of Ministers. The prime object in sending them, is to aid in the cultivation of their natural endowments. *Fitness*, therefore, will confine our remarks on this occasion to the advancement of the understanding.

It is a reflection on the intelligence of the present age, that discourses on education, are deemed at all necessary. The naked fact that sermons must be preached, setting forth the value of educated mind, implies a fearful amount of ignorance and indifference on the subject. And the objections raised against the *education of Ministers*, carry on their face, in legible characters, the stamp of barbarism. Oppose education and you declare

19—Ve. 3.

war against the philosophy of the human mind. You wring
from man, with a sacrilegious hand, the capacity to learn, and
rank him with the brute creation. You close every avenue to
the soul, and shut out *forever* those sublime emotions, arising
from observation and reflection. In short, you make his appetite,
his lust, and a blind instinct, the only incentives to action. In the
absence of mental training, what becomes of logic? of poetry?
of eloquence? of political science? of painting and sculpture?
of the mechanic arts? of refined intercourse? and, I may ask, of
civilization itself? But it is not so much for education in general that we shall plead to-night, as for its *degrees.* A man having the susceptibility, surrounded bv the magnificent scenery of
nature, and holding intercourse with his fellows, is obliged, in
the nature of things, to learn something. He begins his education at his mother's breast. And, however loudly some may
inveigh against it, yet every man is to a certain extent educated.
It is for a greater expansion of the mind, dependant, in a great
degree, on its own endeavors, that we contend in this discourse.
The mind is a perpetual motion, possessing the singular power
to enlarge its perceptions, treasure up ideas, and distribute them
to kindred minds. This power is to be excited by study; and the
effect of mental toil, will be for weal or wo, just in the ratio that
a man studies to subserve the cause of Christ, or the selfish purposes of man. Hence the Apostle exhorts: "Study to show
thyself approved unto God, a workman that needeth not to be
ashamed, rightly dividing the word of truth.

I. In the first place, *we shall explain the design of study.*
Every particle of matter, as well as every attribute of mind has a
relation to some end. The end of study is, 1. *Simply, to increase
our knowledge.* The man who for the first time sees a steam
engine and inspects carefully its cylinders, its rods, its valves and
its levers; knows, as by intuition, that it was designed by some
man and made for a certain purpose. In the same way the phi-
losopher, intent on the phenomena of mind, concludes that perception, abstraction, comparison, reason and memory, were created by an intelligent, adequate cause, and must have respect to
some noble design. The question now arises, for what purpose
were these faculties furnished? This can only be solved by a
trial. This mental machine must be put in motion, and then we
shall see that it moves the man, as the engine does the ship.
What gives impulse to the mind, is beyond the province of philosophy, or metaphisics to search out. This, however, is apparent
to every one who has the least experience on the subject: that he
can abstract his mind from things and extraneous events, and pursue a train of reflections which enlarge his knowledge, mature
his judgment, and establish his memory. This is study. Thus
the intellectual succeptibilities are strengthened, and the measure
of knowledge is increased. God creates a soul, a full apparatus

with which to make experiments in every department of moral, physical, or mental science. Having supplied that soul with its several faculties, there he leaves it. It must now shift for itself. It has the power to think—there are objects of thought—and for the full development of its capabilities, there must be patient, persevering effort. God has dealt with the soul as with the body. Those members and organs which contribute to its sustentation and comfort, *must be used* or the body famish. So there must be mental energy or the surprising achievements of which mind is capable, will be forever concealed like the unsculptured statue in the quarry.

Study directs the mind in its researches after the essences of things, leads it to perceive the connexion and agreement of ideas, and thus to extend the sphere of its information. Doubtless there is a degree of knowledge acquired necessarily from the nature of our organization. As for instance, he who can hear, *must* have an idea of sound; or he that is not blind, knows *unavoidably* that the earth presents a variety of appearances; but that knowledge which makes the statesman, the teacher, or the Gospel Minister, is the result, not only of a capacity to admit, but also of a power to search for, try, and retain such ideas as may be needed for future use.

2. The design of study *is the diffusion of knowledge among our fellow beings.* The man who uses not his information for the good of others, lives to little purpose. If his acquirements terminate in himself, the world could easily have spared him. Knowledge, like the sun, is given to shine, and succeeding generations walk by the light of their fathers. The strugglings of mighty minds in days of yore, gave an impulse which is felt in the present day, and the scholars of this age, are to send an influence into the distant future. The discovery of Greek and Roman manuscripts, by such men as Poggio, under the patronage of the De Medici, was as a resurrection of literature in the fifteenth century. Europe was introduced, as by magic, to intellects long since swept away in the waste of time, but still speaking to the world in the dignified tones of metaphysics and philosophy. The thirst for learning soon became highly enthusiastic. These relics of antiquity, elaborated and mystified, it is true, formed nevertheless the bases of purer thought, and were the harbingers of more enlightened times. The master spirits of the age, by investigating former systems, marking well their tendencies, discarding error and retaining only truth, supplied the understanding with a better induction.

Ancient genius, therefore, bewildered and misdirected as it may have been in some things, was, notwithstanding, the beginning of that light which has since flashed in brilliant radiance over many portions of the globe. It was then by the labors of our forefathers that knowledge was handed down to us, and it behoves us

to repay their kindness by sending it forward to our posterity.
The life of man is too short for every generation to furnish its
own literature.   As the farmer subsists on the crop of the past
year, so the scholar profits by the works of his predecessors.
We study to improve, and we improve to impart.   In the case of
the Minister, the wisdom of this world should be made to advance
the cause he advocates.   The salvation of his species, and the
honor of his Creator should be the leading motives, prompting
him to diligence in the pursuit of an education.   So teaches the
text: "Study to show thyself approved unto God," &c.

II. *Secondly,* we offer some remarks *on the best method of
study.*   To guide us on this point, we have no directions in the
text.   We only learn from it that study is essential—that it is
pleasing to God—and that great advantages are consequent thereon.
Doubtless it is left optional with the individual to choose his own
plan according to his circumstances and opportunities.   This,
however, is certain, that some methods will facilitate the progress
of education more than others.   In a matter of so much importance to the world, if we consider the brevity of human life, that
mode of instruction should be adopted, which will secure an
education with the greatest possible despatch.   The governing
maxim with all students should be to save time.   The inquiry
should not be altogether what a man *may* do, but also *how soon*
it can be done.   One may, by extraordinary labor, instruct himself.
With a sprightly genius and a determined spirit, he may outstrip
the alumni of the college.   He may scale the summit of literature, and thence look down with conscious superiority on professors and tutors.   Yet this would not prove his method of acquiring information to have been the best.   It would only prove him
to belong to that class of men whose perception is as the lightening's flash—who leap from premises to conclusions as by instinct,
and who despise scholastic rules only because their genius will
not be fettered by them.

Self culture, while in some instances, it answers our most sanguine expectations, in most cases, is too tardy for extensive usefulness.   If by travelling on foot for his goods, the merchant lose
both time and money, why not take the cars and procure them at
once?   So if by an increase of knowledge, we may benefit the
world, let us speed to the temple of education by the shortest
route.   Should the preacher blend the literary with the theological, and go plodding through grammars and elementary works
when his time is needed for pulpit preparation, and pastoral duties, he will rarely be a ripe scholar, or a profound theologian.
Experience has taught that mind can assist mind.   The streams
of literature, issuing from the colleges of the land, and nourishing
the intellects of surrounding communities, are standing testimoni-
als of this truth.   Institutions of learning, in which the student
has the benefit of vigorous, well trained minds, are the places to

store the understanding with useful knowledge, and form the mental habitudes of the Christian preacher. The instruction of able professors, conducts the student by a direct course to the object of his pursuit. Instead of digging for ore in uncertainty, he grasps at once the pure metal. If he will but attend, the pain of severe application will change into a pleasure, and the several branches of learning by the aid of teachers, will salute the mental eye, beautiful and soft, as the colors of the rainbow. Delighted with the rapidity of his progress, he becomes the more inquisitive—masters one difficulty after another, and will be satisfied with nothing short of a thorough education. Daily do we see a marked difference between him who recites at the tap of the college bell, and those who grope their way along the dark mazes of self-teaching. The reason of this difference is plain. The alumnus has the advantage of experienced instruction. He is bound by the rules of the institution to be regular and unremitting in his recitations. He has the benefit of books and polished conversation. Moreover, he is impelled to perseverance by that laudable rivalry always excited in a college class. Who does not perceive in this method of tuition, invaluable auxiliaries in the attainment of knowledge? On the other hand, the self-instructing student is abandoned to his own resources. No mind coming in contact with his to evolve light! No preceptor to sooth the troubled brain! Hence he moves at the caprice of his spirits. To-day, he applies himself as if he would be a scholar in a week; to-morrow, from a depression of spirits, he neglects his books. Thus for want of stability he loses the next day, what he had treasured up the day before. And supposing he should retain the ideas which have passed into his mind, still he fears to trust his judgment as to the correctness of what he has acquired. Therefore he cannot use his information with that confidence which will bring respect. We need be at no loss then in deciding on the superiority of academical over private study. By the former method much precious time is saved, which may be appropriated to active usefulness, and the student is better educated. This considered, we have done wisely to form societies and erect colleges for the improvement of the rising Ministry. Doing thus, we have fallen in with the policy of the age. That policy is to accomplish much in a little time. If therefore a young man desire the office of a bishop, and you would qualify him for that good work, let him first enter a college. His vocabulary of ideas must be enlarged. These are to be his stock in trade, in his transactions for the souls of men. In the college he may select the implements for his vocation. There let him gird on his intellectual armor and march against the foe. There let him become familiar with language, science, and the powers of his own mind, that he may give a proper direction to the minds and morals of his fellow men. If Paul exhorts the young preacher to study, that he may obtain the approval of God, let us point our licentiates to the seminary as the surest way to comply with his injunction.

III. In the third place, we offer some reflections *on the noblest end of study.* Under this head we do not urge the necessity of mental contemplation because it brings pleasure to the student, or elicits the applause of the great, but because it is the will of God, and may contribute to the melioration of the human race. To please the Creator, and rescue man from his degraded condition, is the noblest, and should be the chief end of intellectual toil. "Study to show thyself approved unto God," &c., is the instruction in the text. Most men study. The mind *will not* be inactive. If it would, *it could not* be totally indifferent to what it sees and hears. Thousands there are who at this moment are abstracted in severe thought. The history of past ages abundantly testifies that so it has been from the origin of man. Eyes have dimmed in the midnight lamp long before we were born. Temples have throbbed from the commotion within. Ideas have rushed into the brain from all points, waiting the decision of the judgement, and, being rejected, have given way to new ones. The machinery of mind in a man awake, like the pulsations of the heart, admits of no suspension. To what purpose has been this intellectual warfare? For what end these nightly lucubrations? With a few exceptions they have served only, to cater for the baser passions, and win the flattery of a vain world. In some instances, too, the mental faculties have been used to rob God of his glory, and scatter confusion throughout the fair domain of heaven. The world has had her Paynes, her Gibbons, her Volneys: prodigies of mind—transcendent geniuses—of some service, also, to literature and science, but, I ask every candid man, have not these degraded their powers by using them against God and the Bible? Yes, these beams of light have turned against the sun! But we have our Bulwers, Coopers and Scotts. By the magic of whose pens the eyes flash and the cheeks burn. The heart flutters and the tears start. Now we pity, now hope, and anon, we are indignant. Hour after hour glides on, and still we read. Neither business, duty, hunger nor thirst, can break the spell. But we are gotten through. The novel, the romance, or the play is at last read. What have we learned? How much is the heart made better? Alas! is not the heart worse? Are not the affections vitiated? the passions more assailable? and the soul in more danger? This is the influence of mind perverted. I exhort no one to such a use of his endowments. It is as if one would clean the street with silver shovels. But what says the text? Study to show thyself approved unto *men?* No, but unto God. Especially should the Christian Minister have this end in view. He ought to be a finished workman in sacred things. Let us see in what respects college tuition can advance the Ministerial profession.

1. *It will establish patience.* To acquire knowledge on any subject is no easy task. Music, even with all its entrancing powers, when studied scientifically, demands intense application. There must be repeated trial, or there can be no proficiency. Like the miner delving for the precious metals, the student must often strike into the same pit. Most minds from indolence or a natural obstinacy, are wanting in docility. They must be kept to the subject under consideration with some severity, or there can be but little success. I have heard of some mechanists, who were surrounded with models—had on hand always a number of machines partly completed, but could never make any one of them answer exactly the purpose for which it was designed. So in the studies of some preachers; almost every shelf and drawer contains the unfinished skeleton or manuscript of a sermon. Why are not these carefully reserved for future use? Why have we the head without the body? I am persuaded the reason is, not so much for want of genius or talent, but for *lack of patience.* This will appear evident if we examine the manuscripts. Here then is the exordium. It conducts us with ease and dignity to the subject. The subject is just that which arises naturally out of the text. The argument, so far as it goes, is sound. The style is graceful and the language chaste, and we are convinced, from this specimen, that the man who could proceed thus far, *might* have gone much farther. But we are stopt in the dark! The train of thought, like the trail of a comet, is lost in the mist We can trace it no longer. Why this abrupt termination of so noble an enterprise? Ah! the mind became wearied. Truth could not be found without painful reflection. The mind begged a respite, and a respite was ingloriously granted—in other words, there was a lack of *patience.* Now, making due allowance for the difference of natural temper, I maintain that patience is to a great extent acquired. It becomes strengthened and confirmed by habitual perseverance. What can settle better this essential quality in the mind of the young Minister, than the instruction of the college? In the college, study is made a business for a term of years. This lays the foundation of that patience which he will need all his life. At first, the mind, perplexed with the intricacy of language and science, may be fretful; but soon it is soothed and reconciled to the investigation of the most abstruse subjects. As the ox bends to the yoke, and toils steadily all the day, so the mind, accustomed to severe exercise, will contemplate in the deepest abstraction, till truth is found, and the topic for discourse thoroughly understood. Robert Hall, it is said, possessed the power of abstracting his mind at pleasure in an eminent degree. Doubtless this became a habit through constant discipline and matured patience. A good workman can complete what he undertakes. Patience is essential to this end.

2. College instruction *matures the judgment.* Wanting a

clear judgment, a Minister cannot be approved unto God.   The
scantiness of our knowledge obliges us to decide in regard to
many things by the aid of reason.   When, after mature reflection
and a careful comparison of ideas, the mind assents to the truth or
falsity of a proposition, this assent is called judgment.   The mind
decides, though not with the certainty of demonstration, that the
matter under consideration is true or false, according to the evidence in the case.   An accurate and speedy judgment between
truth and error, is of the greatest importance to the Minister of
Christ.   He is often called to his official duties, when there has
been no time allowed for previous preparation; and yet, it will be
expected that he shall "speak the words of truth and soberness."
He is to teach his fellow men what is the mind of the Spirit—the
exact will of God concerning them.   He must lay bare the
depths of human depravity,—portray the purity and divinity of
Christ,—the richness, efficacy and sufficiency of his atonement,—
the inflexible justice as well as the tender mercy of the Eternal
God, and the felicity of heaven.   The doctrines involved in the
foregoing expressions, ought to be as familiar to the mind of the
Christian teacher, as is the sun to the natural eye.   His judgment
in relation to all matters connected with his sacred vocation,
should be fully matured on the authority of revelation.   He must
be able at any time to confront the captious objector with the
reasons on which his views are founded.   Moreover, "a good
workman" will have an easy, perspicuous method of communication.   He is "rightly to divide the word of truth."   This is absolutely requisite, that he may be intelligible to his audience.
His thoughts should preserve a natural connexion, which the
mind of the listener perceiving without labor, he is led step by
step through the discourse, so that at its close, he carries home,
not only the text, but *the whole sermon* with pleasure and profit to
himself.   Show me a preacher who observes not order; who
commences his discourse in the middle, and ends at the beginning
—who, before you can catch what he would wish to say, will
throw in two or three parenthetical phrases—then jump to a new
sentence before the first is finished; and I ask: To what purpose
does he preach?   Confusion, whether in ideas, arrangement, or
speech, will neither entertain nor enlighten any one.   All such
irregularity arises from a weak judgment.   And a sound judgment
can only be formed by a constant and patient exercise of the
reasoning faculty.   It is thus that correct principles are formed,
and thence that legitimate consequences are deduced.   Now we
maintain that college tuition will best direct the mind in the principles of sound reasoning, and hence to the formation of a lucid
judgment.   Dependent as the judgment is on accurate comparison, what can better establish it in the mind, than the study of
language?   Though the student forget his Latin and Greek, as
many do, the first year after he leaves college, yet, it cannot be

denied that this branch of education greatly aids the discrimina-
ting powers. The careful comparison of the corresponding words
of different languages, matures the habit of close observation.
Thus the discerning faculties are improved and the exact import
of words is ascertained. It is by this and similar studies that the
pupil gains a clear view of ideas and reasons coherently through
a discourse. How important this is to the man of God!

3. College teaching acquaints with *the correct use of words.*
If it be essential to perspicuity that every word should represent
a distinct idea in the mind of the speaker, it behooves him to select
such as are least equivocal. In our language there are sometimes
several words used indiscriminately to convey the same idea, but
usually, from among these, one might be selected, which
would express the sentiment in a more felicitous and stronger
light to the mind of the assembly, than any of its synonymes could.
This word *must be used* if the speaker would be effective. A
determinate idea in the mind, and a fit word to convey it, may be
regarded as the ground work of that power, which holds the attention, and enforces truth. No congregation can be interested or
much benefited, if the speaker's ideas be obscure, or his words
ambiguous. Reproach men for nodding in church! it is often
the darkness of the pulpit that overshadows them. If you would
prevent a soporific influence, you must set the intellects of your
hearers in motion. Let truth flash vividly into the understanding,
so that the idea is perceived, as soon as its symbol is pronounced.
Let the expression be as apt as the sense is striking; then will it
seize on the soul, enlist the affections, win the heart and with a
pleasing anxiety, prepare the mind for the next truth to be uttered.
Words without meaning are contemptible. Mere sound can be
produced by an irrational creature as well as by a rational. But
when they dart into the mind of the listener a thrilling sentiment:
" They are truly as apples of gold in pictures of silver." It is
lamentable to reflect on the time which has been wasted in the
pulpit in bandying mere words about. An ignorance of the
import of words, is the stem on which many of those prolix, dry,
unintelligible sermons grow. The preacher having neither settled thoughts nor words to express them if he had, feels notwithstanding that he must make an effort of some sort to entertain his
congregation. Hence instead of a proposition stated and dis-
cussed; an argument presented and enforced; we have wordy cir-
cumlocution, violent gesture, and boisterous declamation. The
effective speaker, however, is he who first thinks for thought, and
then for words to send it to the mind and hearts of his hearers in
the happiest and most striking manner. But one may not always
have time to select suitable words. He might be called on unex-
pectedly, having made no preparation whatever, and shall he not
be excused, if under these circumstances, he use such words as
first present themselves, though they be feeble and somewhat in-

appropriate? *Most certainly not.* To meet this very emergency, he should *familiarise* his mind to the words in common use, with the ideas of which they are signs, that he might be ready on the shortest notice, to draw on his vocabulary and meet the exigency of the most unlooked for occasion. The audience make no allowance for non-preparedness, and they ought not. A blunder in the choice of words, may subject the speaker to ridicule, and leave a wrong impression on the auditory. But this view of the subject supposes an accurate discrimination in the selection of proper signs. Of words whose power and tendencies have been well considered. Where so well as in the academy can we become familiar with their variety and customary use? Is not the standard of accuracy in language, found in the practice of our best speakers and writers? And do we not know that ripe scholars and experienced professors, have the best established reputations for correctness and elegance in speech? If then an extensive and precise knowledge of words will promote the usefulness of a Christian Minister—and that may more easily be acquired in a literary institution: Let every—ye very licentiate prepare himself by passing, if possible, through a collegiate course.

4. College tuition *imparts confidence.* I must not be understood as meaning here, that overweening trust in their own abilities, which is not unfrequently seen in beginners; but a consciousness in the mind of the preacher, that what he is about to say, has undergone due investigation, and will bear the test of criticism. The mechanic, master of his craft, cares not who sees him operate. He knows when and how he ought to strike and where. Whether the plain farmer, or the governor of the state be a looker on, it is all the same to him. Conscious of his ability, he is secured against all trepidation. So let the Minister's mind be well stored, and well trained from habits of diligent study; and he will show himself approved unto God, nor quail in the presence of man. Let him have settled, well defined principles, understanding his subject in all its details—feeling conscious too, that his views are according to the scriptures, and cannot be refuted—and withal that his literary attainments are as great, at least, as those of his Church and congregation, and he will speak appropriately, and reason soundly to the end of his sermon, though a Felix give him audience. This sort of confidence—that the subject is mastered and understood, is needful to the efficiency of a Gospel teacher. We hear of failures—such an one has failed, say the people. Made a complete failure. Why, there are but two causes which will justify an entire failure. The one is natural infirmity; the other, the sudden attack of disease. Let a man study to show himself approved unto God and he will neither fail, nor be ashamed. Be sure that you know your business and you can do it. The college, as we have seen is the place where an education can best be obtained. A

thorough education, united to deep piety, will give the preacher a confidence and earnestness, which will make the beggar crouch in the street, and the king tremble on his throne. Perhaps this was the reason of Paul's intrepidity on so many trying occasions. Behold the monk of Erfurth! with a nervous arm does he nail his thesis to the Church door; he grapples with the Pope's legate—he stands before the Diet at Worms; he is ready to preach Christ, and to defend the cause against all opposers at any time, and in any place. What gives him this honest boldness? Why does he not give way to his enemies? Ah! he understands his calling. Education has given power to his mind, and Grace has sanctified his heart. He is a workman that needeth not to be ashamed. He has by hard study found the truth, and he will divide it rightly among his fellow men, though beasts of Ephesus beset him, and thrones frown blackness. Study leads to truth, and truth gives a holy confidence—is mighty and must prevail. Rely on it, ye who are preparing for the Ministerial office—in proportion as the intellect is improved—if the man be holy, in that proportion will he have courage to preach Christ without fear or favor.

IV. In the last place, we inquire: *Who will be held responsible for the neglect of Ministerial Education?* If, as we have seen, the mental faculties must be cultivated to make an able Minister of the New Testament, then, if these be neglected, a weighty responsibility must rest somewhere God will not hold him guilty, who is content to pass his life in inert supineness. But of whom will he demand account?

1. *Of the student.* Much, very much will depend on *his* perseverance and assiduity. To him the address, "Study to show thyself approved unto God," is made in a direct manner. Colleges will avail nothing if the student be indolent. Better, by far, he had continued at the plough, or in the work-shop, then to loiter away his time at studies for which he has neither taste nor ambition. To enter the ministry, and refuse to task the mental powers for the advantage of the cause of Christ, is sinful in the sight of God. The difference in improvement between men of the same measure of natural capacity, is attributable to a proportional difference in application. The mind like the truant schoolboy, wanders constantly from its task. To keep the attention to a question until the mind has viewed it on all sides, requires no ordinary struggle. Hence when the brain begins to throb, and the eyes to blear, many throw their books aside. But at this very point they should make an extra effort. It is the crisis—the "tug of war," another attempt and the "Rubicon" is passed. Those splendid productions in science and literature, which reflect the genius of their authors, as the setting sun does his glories, are the fruit of the severest mental toil. It is a mistake to suppose that great mental achievements are the result entirely of natural genius.

While I am not among those who maintain that all minds might produce the same developements if an equal amount of labor were bestowed, yet, it is as apparent to my mind as the light of a sunbeam, that genius must be kept actively employed, or "the mountain will only produce its mouse." In our fallen state the mind travails in pain for every valuable acquisition. And it would seem too, that the fatigue is increased in proportion to the worth of the thing sought. Gold is taken in small parcels, and by much labor, out of the Earth; while iron lies in great abundance on its surface. Pearls lie concealed in the Ocean, and diamonds are fastened to craggy rocks, or rest in deep and dangerous pits. Hazard and effort are the harbingers of success in every noble undertaking. The mind collects knowledge, as the bee its honey, from extraneous objects. There must be a perpetual activity or but little can be effected. You may tell the world that you have been at college—you may speak of classmates, and show your diploma; but unless your time while there has been well employed, they will easily discover that you have *only been there.* I am no despiser of diplomas when they have been deserved, yet unless the ideas represented by that term, be deeply settled in the mind, you unrol the parchment in vain. It will do you about as much service as would the notes of a defunct bank. They are the vouchers in the brain which give the graduate a safe conduct with the public. It is entirely possible to secure a degree without the student's having a clear view of any branch of science which has engaged his attention during his collegiate course. But let him be assured that he will receive the rebuff of the community, should he attempt to pass as a finished scholar. There will always be some who will see through the web of his pretensions, and expose his pedantry. I say then to every candidate for the sacred office, God will hold you accountable for the improper use of time while you attend college. To all I say, "Study to show yourselves approved unto God." You owe this to your own honor—to the Churches that gave you license—to lost sinners, and the glory of God.

2. *Churches may lay themselves liable for the neglect of Ministerial Culture.* In many of them there are promising young men, who might prove a blessisg to the cause of Christ, if they could be aided in their endeavors to obtain an education. "To the poor the Gospel is preached," and it is remarkable that the poor generally preach the Gospel. "Not many wise men after the flesh, not many mighty, not many noble are called to this work." The brightest stars that ever graced the Ministerial galaxy, have risen out of the mist of earthly obscurity. Shall I name John Reuchlin the bailiff's son, who by his extraordinary progress in Hebrew literature, snatched the ancient scriptures from the darkness of the fifteenth century, as our own printer-boy did the lightning from the thunder cloud? Or the heroic

Luther, and his accomplished "yoke fellow," Melancthon, the last, the son of an armorer; the first, of a miner? Or shall we scale the cloud piercing Alps, and thence admire the amiable and highly gifted soul of Zuingle the shepherd? This catalogue of master spirits, who emerged from the deepest poverty to an eminence towering high above the mightiest princes, surpassing them in intellectual power and influence, and shaking their thrones to their centre, might be increased almost "in infinitum." It is a scripture truth, confirmed by observation, that God takes the "base things of the world, and things which are despised, to bring to nought things that are." That is, he chooses the poor of this world, to carry out his designs in the diffusion of Gospel light. It is also a fact, that many of those worthies of past ages, whose weapons of warfare, were mighty through God to the pulling down of strong holds," had been assisted in their preparative studies by the munificence of benevolent friends. This striking duty: "Let him that is taught in the word communicate unto him that teacheth in all good things," is what I would urge on the Churches of the Old Dominion. Donbtless there are fine capacities, susceptible of the highest cultivation, allied to hearts, burning as the suppressed flames of a furnace to make known "the unsearchable riches of Christ," at this moment lying dormant in the Churches. Why are they not preparing for the Ministry? Why are they left to mouth out their crude ideas in their attempts to speak, to the embarrassment of themselves, the discomfort of their hearers, and the injury of the cause they would benefit? Ah! I fear they are neglected by the Churches. The belief that no "good can come out of Nazareth," still prevails; and it is this, backed by a covetous spirit, that shackles the intellects of our youth, and shuts the college door on those who would do honor to their patrons, and be ornaments to our blessed religion. I verily believe that there are at this hour, scores of young men in the Virginia Churches of approved piety, "apt to teach," who ought now to be at our college; but who, for want of funds, are doomed to an inglorious ignorance. While it is expedient to keep back an ambitious aspirant, who would use the Ministerial office only as a passport to popularity, and to secure "filthy lucre," retiring modesty, indicating usefulness, ought to be encouraged. How cruel to withhold aid under such circumstances! I maintain that the Churches, who are able, are responsible to God, for the neglect of Ministerial education.

1. *Because they possess the means.* It would be difficult, I apprehend, to find the Church that could not do a little for this enterprise. We do not require an impossibility, nor does God, but we do claim *something* from *every* Church, to defray the expenses of Ministerial instruction. "For if there be first a willing mind, it is accepted according to that a man hath, and not accor-

ding to that he hath not." God, too, in the distribution of wealth, occasionally drops a fortune or two, in the different societies of the brotherhood. How ought this property to be disposed of? To be consumed on our lusts, and so exert an evil influence among the brethren, and before the world? " I trow not." A portion of it, at least, should be appropriated to the benevolent institutions of the age, and of those, one is for the education of Ministers. Who can compute the amount of good a Church might bring about, by qualifying only one young man, the better to preach the Gospel. She might thus put a ball in motion which would roll onward and onward to eternity. " The gold and silver are the Lord's," and if they be applied to unrighteous purposes, while the cause of Christ is left to bleed, the stewards will have to answer for this misappropriation at the judgment.

2. *The Churches will not hear an uneducated man.* It is a modern fact, that even the most covetous Churches testify to the worth of education. The first question propounded when a Minister is recommended to a Church, is: "*Is he educated.*" A strong-minded, common-sense preacher, well read in the Scriptures, is frequently set aside for the novice hot from the college. And though he may not be able to sustain himself in his new position for a single month, yet because he is a graduate *he* must be taken, and the other left. I cannot say that I would always approve this preference, still, it proves that Churches know the value of education, if it can be had without previous cost. Then let every Church educate. Why import? Most likely every Church might furnish her own preacher, out of her own membership.

3. By educating their Ministers. *the Church would educate the mass of the community in which they are located.* A large portion of those who attend service, have no means of instruction, except as they hear it from the pulpit. They have neither time nor money to enable them to improve in the use of language. They speak as their neighbors speak—" Murder the king's english," and violate the plainest rules of grammar. But let them attend the ministry of one whose thought is accurate, address chaste, and pronunciation good; and there will be a manifest improvement of that community. Here is the *reflex* influence of an educated Ministry. The very individuals who in the first instance furnished the education, now reap a harvest from it themselves. The pulpit is the high school which craves no additional tax.

4. In conclusion, we shall not spend time in refuting objections. The time for that necessity no longer exists. That God approves education is too manifest to admit of a doubt. His choice of those possessing, not only good native powers of intellect, but a settled purpose to improve those powers, to effect deliverances and establish reformations in the world, sets all doubting on the subject at rest. If the Israelites are to be brought out of Egypt, he will call a Moses, " skilled in all the wisdom of the Egyptians,"

to the work. If prophets are wanted to make known his mandates, they must take a course of study in the school of Elijah. If he will call Apostles to spread and confirm Christianity, they must be instructed three years by the ablest master the world has ever known. If the scriptures are to be translated, He will stir up the spirit of a Tyndal, a Judson, or a Wickliff. In fine, if he would have an able and successful servant for *any* department of the divine office, that servant "must study to show himself approved unto God, a workman that needeth not to be ashamed, rightly dividing the word of truth."

Need I say more of the utility of education, of the ardor with which young men should seek it, and of the duty of the Churches to encourage and sustain it? Brethren, let us foster our society, so laudable in its designs, and withal so useful in giving reputation and success to the rising Ministry. In it and similar organizations, are comprised our liberties, our wealth, our virtue, our happiness, and as a powerful auxiliary, our salvation.

It has not been my intention, in this discourse, to undervalue the services of those whose opportunities for mental improvements have been limited. " God forbid !" Jehovah himself has affixed to their " labors of love" the broad seal of his approval, in having made them instruments in the conversion of many immortal souls. My object has been to provoke young Ministers to emulation in the pursuit of knowledge. I know that the Clergy of present age, *must* have enlarged views, and well trained minds, as well as sanctified hearts. The march of mind is onward, and still onward. Its susceptibilities are never satisfied. Like the daughter of the " horse-leech," they cry: " Give, give." The *mass* is being educated, and they will receive instruction from none but educated teachers. The free Schools at the North are doing wonders in the diffusion of knowledge. It is in vain that the people of the South, dispute the palm with the North on the subject of general education. The general intelligence there, by reason of the free schools, compared with that in the South, is as the sun shining against a cloud. But similar schools will be established among us. The South will be redeemed, and the mass will be enlightened. This is the strong argument for the immediate education of our Ministry.

Young men, brother Ministers in Jesus, let me urge it on you " to study to show yourselves approved unto God." Difficulties you will have in abundance, but if your souls be once lighted by the torch of knowledge, you can master them all. If you cannot enter college, employ a private tutor. Should you be too poor to do this, and your Church refuse you aid, then draw on your own resources, and do the best you can alone- Neither be discouraged nor intimidated by what any one may say or think. That stereotyped phrase, " drink deep or taste not," has more in it of pedantry than of charity or good sense. I say taste, and drink as deep as

you can. Taste to-day, taste to-morrow, taste while you live. Thus
shall you be a finished workman in sacred things, and receive the
approbation of your Heavenly Father. AMEN.

THE LATTER DAY GLORY TO BE BROUGHT ABOUT THROUGH
THE DIFFUSION OF RELIGIOUS KNOWLEDGE :

A Sermon, delivered before the Va. Baptist Sunday School
and Publication Society, June 4, 1844, in the Second Baptist
Church, Richmond, by Rev.* J. R. SCOTT, *Pastor of the Market St.
Baptist Church, Petersburg Va.*

" *Many shall run to and fro, and knowledge shall be increased.*"
—DAN. XII.: 4.

The great body of Evangelical Christians are united in the
belief, that, before the final consummation, this world is destined
to witness an era of moral splendor, as yet unparalleled in its history.   It is to be an era in which the Gospel shall have triumphed
over every form of false religion ;—the jarring sects of Christendom shall have been merged into the one only true and perfect
Church,—the nations, joined in one common brotherhood, shall
learn war no more, but in the pursuits of peace, seek each other's
prosperity hardly less than their own,—and all the lesser circles
of society shall be pervaded by those mellowing, ennobling, joyous
influences, the natural products of genuine piety and benevolence.
It is to be an era that shall teach what the angels meant by the
welcome they sang to the babe of Bethlehem, in their sweet carol,
" glory to God in the highest, and on earth peace, good will towards
men."

This expectation has been excited by the study of those glowing
pictures thrown by Prophecy's inspired pencil upon the canvass of Revelation ; by the contemplation of those significant
promises by which the Father assured the Son that he should see
of the travail of his soul, and be *satisfied;* by the witness of the
inherent tendency of Christianity; and by the observation of the
results, so vastly greater than the most sanguine could have anticipated for the outlay,—which have followed the efforts already
put forth for the extension of the Redeemer's Kingdom.

These brilliant anticipations form not merely a cheering perspect-
ive, with which the Church is privileged to regale herself, when
she would turn from the gloomy scenes around her, but an end for

---

*As portions of the discourse, and the conclusion entire, were not written
until after its delivery, the author cannot profess to give the sermon more
than *substantially* as preached.

which she is to strive. As such an end, we are happy to say, they are coming to assume a more and more definite shape in the view of the faithful; they are becoming more and more settled in their position, and distinct in their outline; and attracting towards themselves a steadier and steadier gaze. The people of God are beginning to take it for granted, not only that this end must, and cannot fail to be realized, but also, that it is to be accomplished through their own instrumentality; and that the Church cannot withhold her energies from its prosecution without forfeiting the character of being that body which Jesus constituted when on earth, and to which he committed, along with the care of his ordinances, the business of conducting to complete and final victory the triumphs of his cross.

The means which are to be employed in this stupendous and honorable work are various. There is one, however, which stands forth the most prominent of all; which may, indeed, be said to lie at the foundation of the rest; to which, at least, the others may be regarded as in some sense but subsidiary. I refer to the diffusion of faithful evangelical instruction. To this subject, in its bearing on the arrival of the glorious era so fondly anticipated, I would call your attention in the present discourse. It will be my aim on this occasion to impress your minds with the fact so clearly revealed in the word of God, that *the universal diffusion of religious knowledge by the Church, is the great prominent means by which the latter day glory is to be brought about.*

This, I am aware, my friends, sounds very much like an axiom; and the query may arise, why should a truth so familiar,—one implied in the very existence of every association formed for the spread of the Gospel,—be made the theme of discourse on an occasion when every one is eager for novelty? Would to God, brethren, the *action* of our Churches indicated that they *did* regard our proposition as self-evident. Readily as its truth is accorded, there is but too much ground to apprehend either that christians are not aware how much is involved in it, or that their pure minds are sadly in need of being stirred up by way of remembrance. Could I but hope by this discourse barely to impress on your minds more deeply what you already know and concede, and thus far to stimulate you to vigorous and consistent action, my chief solicitude on this occasion would be disposed of.

To proceed. The slightest inspection of the prophecies which foretell the triumph of the Redeemer's kingdom, must convince every one of the truth, and of the importance of our proposition. The era which that triumph shall introduce, is to be one of *intelligence,*—a period in which religious knowledge shall be every where disseminated. Indeed, what but this,—the prevailing acquaintance with sacred truth,—is it, which must be regarded as the very basis of the millennial structure? True, the happiness of our race will be the crown of the love and obedience which

mankind shall then universally render to their Maker.   But will
it not be, because men every where *know* the Lord, that Jehovah
shall *be* every where loved and obeyed ? People are not to be
obedient and happy in spite of ignorance.   Their felicity is not
to be by a law of necessity, irrespective of causes naturally adapted to produce it.   Its explanation will be the fact, that the
KNOWLEDGE of the Lord covers the earth as the waters cover the sea.

It is equally interesting and instructive to see how generally
the prophets, when they refer to the latter day glory, speak of the
prevalence of religious information, not merely as a particular
feature of that glory, but as its *cause.*   The passage just adverted
to from Isaiah, affords an illustration in point.   The prophet had
been describing the amazing transformations that would be effected under the Messiah's reign: the wolf should dwell with the
lamb; the leopard lie down with the kid; the calf, and the young
lion, and the fatling together; and a little child should lead them;
none should hurt or destroy in all the Lord's holy mountain. He
then assigns the reason ; and what is it ? " For the *knowledge of
the Lord* shall cover the earth as the waters cover the sea."

An example very similar occurs in the book of Habakkuk:
" For the earth shall be filled with the knowledge of the glory of
the Lord as the waters cover the sea."   This fact is indeed adduced
as the ground on which the judgments denounced in the connection,
would surely fall on the sinners to whom Habakkuk was sent;
but it is clearly implied that those judgments were to be a source
of instruction and warning, in consequence of which a better day
would be expedited, which should declare the glory of Jehovah's
mercy.

Not to trespass too much on your patience by going over all
the ground which might here be traversed, let me refer you to one
illustration more.   It is from the book of Isaiah.   Says the prophet,
in the second chapter, " It shall come to pass in the last days, that
the mountain of the Lord's house shall be established in the top
of the mountains, and shall be exalted above the hills ;"—that is, the
religion of the only living and true God shall supercede all others ;
—" and all nations shall flow unto it.   And many people shall go,
and say, come ye, and let us go up to the mountain of the Lord,
to the house of the God of Jacob; and he will,"—mark what he
will do,—" and he will TEACH *us of his ways,* and we will walk
in his paths."   Then follows a rapid delineation of the blessings
which would result from this instruction, and from the conformity
to the divine law, which would follow it.   Justice would be every
where maintained : swords would be beaten into ploughshares, and
spears into pruning-hooks ; nation would no more lift sword against
nation ; they would learn war no more.   These precious results
would flow from the instruction in divine things imparted, and are
evidently referred to the influence of that instruction, as its natural
effect.

No one, I trust, will understand me to represent the happiness of the millennial period as springing from a *mere intellectual* perception of divine truth. Knowledge,—not to say theory and speculation,—will probably, in itself, have no more power then to make men love, and obey, and rejoice in God, than it has at present. The intellect will doubtless then fathom depths of which we now know comparatively little; but the sphere of the heart is not to be proportionally contracted. On the other hand, we have reason to expect there will be a vast enlargement of the moral sensibilities. And instead of the operations of the intellect ever drying up, or choking the fountains of feeling, as is too often the case now, the various powers of the soul will then act in harmony. Their reciprocal influence on each other will be such, that an advance of the one will be sure to occasion an advance of the others also. Then, we may expect, the great practical problem, how to adjust the balance between the mental perceptions and the moral feelings, will be solved. It will no longer be true, that those who see the least, feel the most; whilst those, whose field of view is the widest, are seldom found thrilling with emotion.

Besides, we do not overlook the fact that the Holy Spirit,—whose peculiar province is the heart,—is in those days to exert his special influences in an augmented measure. "After those days, saith the Lord, I will put my law in their inward parts, and write it in their hearts; and I will be their God and they shall be my people." No, no; far be it from me to represent that there is any such efficacy in the mere head-knowledge of religion, as to make it only necessary that this be universally diffused, to produce a millennium. It is indispensable that there be the influences of divine grace in order that the facts and principles of religion be ever *seen* in their true character; how much more, that they be *felt*,—that the view of them exert any thing like a subduing, or an exhilarating influence upon the heart. Nor is there the the least conflict in all this with the representation, that religious knowledge,—an intimate acquaintance with the facts and principles of religion,— will hold a fundamentally important place in the glory of the latter day.

The Saviour prayed for his disciples, and *all* those whom the Father should give him through their word, "Sanctify them through thy truth; thy word is truth." Lifeless and inoperative as is that word by itself, it is still the means of sanctification employed by the Spirit; and in the Spirit's hand, "quick and powerful, and sharper than any two-edged sword." And so we must believe it will be in that better age. The truth, unaccompanied by the Spirit's energy, will continue to be inefficient; and yet, as God's instrument, it will be an indispensable and effectual means of securing to our race the joy which shall then gladden the hearts of an obedient world.

It is clearly revealed, however, that when the millennial glory shall have fully arrived, the necessity will no longer exist for those special, extraordinary efforts which the Church is now required to put forth for the diffusion of religious knowledge. "They shall teach no more every man his neighbor, and every man his brother, saying, know the Lord; for they shall all know me, from the least of them unto the greatest of them, saith the Lord." By this we cannot suppose it to be meant, that men will not communicate with each other on religious subjects; but only that the knowledge of the Lord will be so generally promulgated and received, that the demand, before so pressing, to diffuse the light of the Gospel at the cost of exhausting labor and sacrifice, will have ceased. The people will no longer be perishing for lack of vision. Instead of those toilsome exertions which the Church is now called to make for the conversion of the impenitent, the communications of God's people will be chiefly those of mutual congratulations, such as are now to some extent witnessed, and felt to be so delightful, among spiritually-minded and devoted believers.—There will be no further need of those various organizations, the operations of which can be carried on only at a great expense of toil, and privation, and suffering, such as are now maintained for the purpose of extending the Gospel to the unevangelized and benighted portions of our race. Every community will possess within itself, and keep in energetic employment, abundant means for its spiritual culture. In respect to the conversion of men,—for we suppose they will as truly have to be regenerated and converted then as now,—it cannot be doubted that this work will, in most cases, be effected at a very early age ; and that these transformations will take place very much as a natural consequence of the state of things then existing. So deeply will the mass of society be penetrated, and so thoroughly impregnated, with divine truth ; so powerful and extensive will be the force of holy example ; and so effectually will these influences be applied by the mighty operation of the Holy Spirit, that seldom will the sinner fail to be attracted to the cross at a very tender age. In the most literal acceptation of the words, the prediction will probably be made good, "All thy children shall be taught of the Lord ; and great shall be the peace of thy children."—Besides, we are assured, that answers to prayer will not then be deferred, as was often the case in previous times: " It shall come to pass, that before they call, I will answer ; and while they are speaking, I will hear." What a pledge of these results have we furnished in this single prediction !

But, my brethren, that happy day has not yet come. The balance of moral power in this world is yet far from being on the side of Christ. Satan may still claim as his, the title which Inspiration itself has conferred on him. He is still " the god of this world." We cannot believe that more than a very small fraction of the human family have, as yet, been brought under the saving knowledge and efficacy of the truth. Before that day shall have arrived, how many places of the earth, now dark, and full of the habitations of cruelty, must the Gospel have reached! But not only this. Much more is contemplated in the millennial diffusion of evangelical knowledge than we are accustomed to suppose. Were all the nations of the earth at this moment what England and our own favored land are, in respect to the prevalence of religious information, the earth would still be far from exhibiting the latter day glory. It is not the simple fact that in every land the Gospel is preached, and many believers are to be found, which will constitute the millennium. That era will not have come, so long as the nations are little more than nominally christian; so long as there are extensive districts in which the people know hardly more of the Lord Jesus Christ than if they were actually pagans; and so long as in the most favored communities, the simple doctrines and ordinances of the Gospel are corrupted by even many of the hopefully pious; whilst many others profess a faith which is utterly destitute of vitality; and not a few may be found, who have scarcely the slightest conception of the necessity for an atonement, and of the plan by which that necessity has been met. We must believe that, in the millennial age, not only will Christianity have supplanted every other form of religion; but that all classes in all lands will have been rendered intimately acquainted with the principles of divine truth; and that those principles will be received, pure and unperverted, cleared of all those corruptions, which, in former and less happy times, so wofully marred their simple beauty, and neutralized their power.

Let us now see, brethren, how these considerations bear on the proposition with which we started. It was that the universal diffusion of religious knowledge by the Church is the great prominent means by which the latter day glory is to be brought about. We have seen that that era is to be one of intelligence, and that the happiness which will characterize it, will be founded on the knowledge of the Lord, which will then every where prevail. If this view be correct, what does it indicate respecting the nature of the means by which the Church is to labor for the fulfilment of these high expectations? Surely, if the means are to bear any resemblance to the end, they must be such as are adapted to increase the knowledge of Jehovah among men. And we have no more right to expect that the end will be accomplished by any other means than just such as are in their nature fitted to produce it, than we have to expect that it will be accomplished without the intervention of means at all. Unless, therefore, the Church can safely conclude that the regeneration of the world may be abandoned to miracle, and she has only to stand with folded arms, and wait till Jehovah shall, in his own time, work out the transformation, it is obvious what is the duty of the Church. She is to exert herself to the utmost to send to all nations the unadulterated truth as it is in Jesus, with all the facilities at her command for promoting the understanding and the receiving of it. And she is not to content herself with doing this in the mass merely. As far as practicable, she must reach every individual, and render every individual as minutely intelligent as possible in divine things. Society and the truths of revelation are to be brought together particle by particle. Atom by atom the word of God must be made to assimilate with the common mind. Through every vein and artery of the social system the living current must be sent, to the extent of its remotest and most attenuated branching .

But we are not left to inference on this point. Irresistable as is the conclusion to which we have thus come, there is a much more direct way of arriving at the kind of means by which the Church is to labor for the renovation of the world, than by arguing from the nature of the end contemplated. We have explicit testimony on this subject in the Bible. Not only is the fact disclosed that God *has* such gracious purposes in respect to our stricken world, but also the *manner* in which he has ordained that his designs shall be carried into effect. The means are predicted as well as the result. Our text is a specimen of these predictions. " Many shall run to and fro, and knowledge shall be increased." How clear is this testimony, and what a lively picture have we presented before us ! Let us contemplate it a moment. It is the only passage from the Old Testament, to which, in consideration of the time, I shall ask your further attention.

Many shall run. The messengers of salvation shall not be a mere handful. Their number shall be somewhat proportionate to the demand. Doubtless, not one to millions, as now, but enough to bring the glad tidings within hearing of every ear.

And they shall *run.* The angel having the everlasting Gospel to preach, is to *fly* through the midst of heaven. Energy, celerity, despatch, are to characterize these operations. The Church is to prosecute this work with her heart in it. Her resources are to be dealt out not in reluctant driblets. She is to cease sending forth her heralds, manacled and fettered. She is no longer to cripple them by her parsimony. They shall run.

And they shall run *to and fro.* They shall hie in every direction, and from place to place. Wherever there is guilt to be expiated, —wherever there is wretchedness to be relieved,—wherever there is debasement to be elevated,—wherever there is darkness to be enlightened,—in fine, wherever there are souls to be saved, and to be made happy by the knowledge of God, thither shall the eager Church despatch on their embassy of love the faithful representatives of herself, and of her adorable Head.—Thus is it just as true that the age which shall usher in the latter day glory will be one of active, self-denying toil for the spread of the Gospel, as that the millennium is to be a period of comparative rest and enjoyment.

" And knowledge shall be increased." This is to be the effect of the operations we have been considering. In consequence of these vigorous exertions, men shall every where become familiar with the way of life. *Knowledge* shall be increased. It shall *be* knowledge. It shall not be speculation. It shall not be a medley of truth and error. It shall be the pure, unadulterated, unperverted word of Jehovah,—the truth, the whole truth, and nothing but the truth. This is what shall be increased.

It shall be *increased*. It shall come to be more and more largely, and more and more thoroughly understood. It shall be more and more widely spread, until heresy and corruption shall have retreated to their native pit. Truth is the sun, whose glowing radiance shall betoken the millennial dawn ; and the signal for the lark to soar, shall send the owl hooting to his dark recess.

I sometimes think, my brethren, I can discern a few faint streaks in the east. Secular and scientific truth is certainly advancing at an unprecedented rate. I believe it no less unquestionable that religious truth is, rapidly becoming more and more accurately determined, thoroughly developed, and settled beyond dispute. We are now in the transition state between the age of investigation and that of comparison and decision. The very convulsions now agitating the world of opinion indicate this. The truth is daily becoming more clearly discerned. How many there are at the present day, who acknowledge the correctness of views which in practice they still repudiate. It is very different now from what it was a few years ago. It is by no means so general as formerly, for people to profess and practice error, because they believe it, or see no better way. They say " something else will do as well." They talk much about non-essentials. They say, " I own you are right, but I am not quite satisfied that I am wrong." How many heresies now subsist in Christendom, almost exclusively on prejudice, and habit, and party spirit, and worldly patronage. But, thank God ! the sun is coming nearer and nearer,—the light is growing stronger and stronger,—the heat more and more sensibly intense,—and people will soon be able to see how unsightly and injurious are these excrescences. They will soon see that if they do not lop them off, of their own accord, the warm beams of that rising luminary will leave them no choice but to submit to their being *melted off*. Few, comparatively, as yet, are running to and fro ; and they can hardly be said to be running: nevertheless, knowledge is already on the increase, and we have the earnest of a better day. A few years, and a different generation, unwarped to false views, by prescription, private interests, and personal partiality, will have arisen. Even now, we can perceive the bands which hold error o her worldly props, loosening. The age is at hand, which shall pronounce upon the diverse conclusions of the age of investigation. Truth, cleared of those mists, which now so obscure her features, shall speedily stand forth too manifestly truth for the boldest sophist to dispute her claims. Bless

God for it! Roll on, day of her complete manifestation! But, brethren, let us not forget, that many must run to and fro, before that day shall have come.

If now, we turn to the New Testament, we shall find the tenor of its representations the same. Nothing can be plainer than that our Lord designed to set up his kingdom in the world through the agency of his followers, and that he intended they should prosecute this end by the dissemination of his truth. What was the last great commission but a charge to this effect? " Go teach all nations." " Go ye into all the world, and preach the Gospel to every creature." Surely, there is no need of amplification here.— Nor need any thing be said to show how the primitive disciples understood the last injunctions of their Master. Their conduct demonstrates that they regarded themselves as individually consecrated to the work of spreading the knowledge of the Gospel, and as associated together for the express purpose of facilitating its progress.—With equal prominency is this province of the Church brought to view in the writings of the Apostles. Hear Paul: " Whosoever shall call upon the name of the Lord shall be saved. How then shall they call on him in whom they have not believed? and how shall they believe in him of whom they have not heard? and how shall they hear without a preacher?" And when we have reached the close of the sacred canon, we have still ringing in our ears, among the last lingering accents of Inspiration, " The Bride says, come; and let him that heareth, say, come." " The Bride says, come." It is the business of the Church to send out through the world, this invitation, Come! Come! and to point out clearly the way to Christ. " Let him that heareth, say, come!" It is the business of every individual, who has himself heard and heeded this call, at once to join his voice to the general cry, Come! Come to Jesus, the way, the truth, and the life.

Nothing can be clearer than that the New Testament throughout, holds up the Church as a body designed to be constantly engaged in a warfare against the Kingdom of Darkness, and required to subordinate every thing to the grand endeavor to advance the knowledge of Redemption. So conspicuous a place did the diffusion of evangelical information hold in the minds of primitive believers, that they indicated the conversion of sinners by hardly any form of expression more commonly than by that of "coming to the knowledge of the truth." Whilst undoubtedly they had reference to that experimental acquaintance with religion, which can never be had without the operation of the Holy Spirit on the heart, there is still an unquestionable allusion to the fact that it is by means of the truth, as revealed in the Sacred Oracles, the Spirit carries on his gracious work. This instruction it is the office of the Church to impart. How speedily may we believe, would the world be converted, were the Church true to her vocation!

But, brethren, it is needless to carry this argumentation further.

What we want is, not so much to have our duty pointed out, and to be convinced that it *is* our duty, as to drink into the spirit of the holy Apostle, who declared, " what things were gain to me those I counted loss for Christ. Yea, doubtless, and I count all things but loss for the excellency of the knowledge of Christ Jesus, my Lord." When this is the estimation we set upon the knowledge of Christ, there is no danger but we shall be prompt and zealous in our endeavors to disseminate it. We need expansion, we need elevation of soul. We need growth in grace. We need to breathe more of the melting atmosphere of Calvary. I was delighted that our brother, who preached the sermon before the General Association, selected the subject he did, and urged us so earnestly to strive for a higher spirituality. May his effort not prove vain. That is just what we want,—old-fashioned, simple-hearted, primitive piety. In proportion as we increase in that, will our sagacity be deepened, and our energies quickened, to know and to do the will of our adorable Master. Spirit of all grace! descend, and take possession of thy servants. Open our eyes,—enlarge our hearts; then shall we run the way of thy commandments.

The application of what has been said to the object of the Society at whose bidding I have appeared before you, must be obvious. That object is indicated by its name. It is to promote the knowledge of the Gospel by means of Sabbath Schools and religious publications· How happily adapted, and how indispensable these means are, to hasten the triumph of the Redeemer's Kingdom, in accordance with the view that has been presented, of the way in which that triumph is to be brought about, is very apparent. It is true that the immediate sphere of the Society's operations is our own land. That sphere will, however, without doubt, eventually be extended; and just as soon as the liberality of the Churches shall make it practicable. But allowing that it be confined to our own country, or to our own state, nothing need be said to show how essential is just that kind of effort which this Society is putting forth, to render even the most favored portions of Christendom what they must become before the millennium shall arrive, and to fit them to shed forth such a light as shall reach and renovate the benighted nations of the earth.

The precedence of preaching, over all other means for diffusing the Gospel, will not be disputed. But the faithful herald of the Cross will be the last to deny the value and necessity of these auxiliaries. It is vain to think that people who depend exclusively upon the pulpit for their religious instruction will ever be intimately acquainted with the word of God. To a great extent preaching can only pioneer. From various causes, in not a few cases, the most the preacher can hope to effect, is to impress the bare outlines of the Christian System on the minds of his hearers. The studies of the Sunday School, and the deliberate perusal of good religious books, must accompany his labors, in order that the impressions he

produces be not exceedingly meagre and short-lived. These concomitants are indispensable to the filling out and the fixing of his
message in the minds of his hearers.

But the province of the pulpit is a wide one. It includes the
very highest and most difficult walks of scriptural exposition and
discussion. As in the cases just referred to, the school and the
book are needful to *follow up* the instructions from the sacred desk,
so cases exist, in which they are needed to precede and *prepare the
way* for these instructions. It is the preacher's business to bring
forth things new as well as old, out of the sacred treasury,—to
furnish meat as well as milk for the nourishment of his charge.
But how justly may he despair of rendering an exhibition of the
deeper truths of revelation profitable to those who do not read and
study on religious subjects. He cannot expect them to follow him
beyond the simplest statements. How then can he expect them
to feel the force of an extended argument, and retain the process
by which he arrived at his conclusion? It is a hopeless undertaking, for a minister to make a people familiar with the details of
christian doctrine, who do not couple with his ministrations those
means, the employment of which it is the object of this Society to
promote. Without these, it is but a very remote approximation
which any community can make to that state of things which is
foretold of the latter days.

The Sunday School,—why, my brethren, there is nothing in the
world that looks so much like the millennium as a well regulated,
thriving Sunday School. Here we behold persons of all ages,
but especially the young, associated together for the purpose of
diligently searching out and storing up the communications of God
to man. With the utmost propriety has the plan of this institution
been so extended as to embrace adults among the pupils. But,
after all, its *youthful* must ever remain its most charming and hope-
ful feature. No stroke of Christian policy can be happier, than
to take the child before his mind has been pre-occupied by error,—
before time has developed, and habit confirmed depravity,—whilst
his heart is the most susceptible of impressions,—when he learns
the most easily, and what he learns fixes itself the most indelibly,
—to take him at this age, and inculcate on him the invaluable lessons of the Gospel. This looks something like being wise to
win souls. It is acting in harmony with the laws of mind. Only
a very moderate share of sagacity is required to foresee a most
glorious harvest from such culture. The day of Sunday School
results has as yet but just dawned; but already enough has appeared abundantly to justify these natural anticipations. Let no
one withhold his hearty co-operation from this lovely institution of
the Church. Let us nobly sustain this Society, which aims to dot
our beloved state over thickly with these bright spots every Sabbath. Alas that her present destitution in this respect should be
so extensive! May the remedy be speedily applied!

This Society, in its publication department, is auxiliary to the American Baptist Publication Society. Its object is the same, with special reference to the supply of our own state with a pure, complete, and decided evangelical literature. It aims to bring within the reach of all, the means of ascertaining precisely what are our denominational views; and no one who is familiar with the extent to which they are blackened and distorted by our adversaries, as well as misunderstood and *not* understood, by our own communicants, will doubt the desirableness of this.—Still further, it is engaged in promoting the preparation and circulation of works not strictly denominational,—tracts and books, in which the great vital doctrines of the cross are held up and enforced, and which have been so largely honored in the conversion of sinners.—And then, the furnishing and sending out of *colporteurs* is included in its plan,—a most important feature, as the history of this, and of other kindred Societies attests. But these matters have all been laid before you, so fully, by the energetic and indefatigable Corresponding Secretary of the National Society, as to render it superfluous for me to detain you longer upon them. How coincident is this plan with the prediction of our text:—" Many shall run to and fro, and knowledge shall be increased." Hitherto, the history of our Publication Society has been a Record of the day of small things. But we trust that this is to be the case no longer. Let the proposition recently issued by the Board for an extension of its means of operation be met by our churches, and nobly carried out. Let us look at the immense and efficient Book Concerns of our neighbors, and be roused to emulation. Let us sustain this organization, as becomes a great people, contending for the faith once delivered to the saints. Let it be made useful somewhat in proportion to its capabilities of usefulness, or let it *no longer live to be our reproach.*

But I must close. Pardon me, if I have trespassed on your patience.

" God be merciful unto us, and bless us; and cause his face to shine upon us. That thy way may be known upon earth, thy saving health among all nations. Let the people praise thee, O God; let all the people praise thee. O let the nations be glad, and sing for joy; for thou shall judge the people righteously, and govern the nations upon earth." Amen! Amen!

THE POWER OF THE PRESS.

More than one fourth of the professors of religion in evangelical denominations, in our whole country, are members of Baptist churches. The proportion is about two to seven. Consequently, were the present population of our nation (19,500,000) divided amongst these denominations, about 5,500,000 would come under our influence. For this number, at least, we are expected to provide adequate means of grace.

In the Western Valley, the Baptist denomination includes about one fourth of the Protestant church members. The population of that district now exceeds eight millions and one third. We are expected to provide for the spiritual wants of more than two millions in that field. Can this be done, without an efficient Publication Society? This is a solemn and weighty subject. With this work before us, we cannot turn it aside. We have a large class of ministers in the Middle, Southern and Western States, who would make efficient colporteurs; and who, if supplied and commissioned, would perforn the three-fold service of preaching the gospel to the destitute, distributing books and tracts, and exciting the people to read for instruction.

The colporteur system, applied to the Baptist denomination in the United States, through the Publication Society, requires capital, in some degree commensurate with the numbers and the wants of the people to be supplied. A few hundred dollars may put into circulation a single book; but many thousands are requisite to publish the number and variety needed. Books in sufficient quantities, and of considerable varieties, must first be procured, and placed in deposit at convenient points; where colporteurs, missionaries and pastors can obtain them. Depositories for the retail of books (excepting, perhaps, in large cities,) should not be established by the Society. The colporteur system is far better adapted to supply the wants of the people, and cultivate the habit of reading.

The result of the whole is, that we have in all our churches more than 650,000 communicants,—that, by increase, we double in less than twelve years,—that a large proportion of our church members have not the pastoral supervision and training which is indispensable to make them active, devoted Christians, abounding in every good work,—that, in consequence of this deficiency, less than half can be expected to contribute for foreign missions and other benevolent operations,—that a large number of our ministers should receive aid in books,—that one half of the denomination must lend a helping hand to train up the other half for every good work,—and that the circulation of religious books and tracts, providing libraries for a class of our ministers who are destitute, establishing Bible classes for persons of adult age, and Sabbath schools for the young, with a more enlarged system of home missions, and a more liberal plan for the education of our ministry, are measures to be adopted.—*Rev. J. M. Peck.*

THE
BAPTIST PREACHER.

| VOL. III. | September, 1844. | NO. 9 |

THE DECLINE OF SPIRITUALITY IN THE CHURCH.

A Sermon preached by REV. THOMAS HUME, *Pastor of the Baptist Church in Portsmouth, before the General Association of Virginia, June* 1, 1844.

"*Nevertheless I have somewhat against thee, because thou hast left thy first love.*—REV. II: 4.

The peculiar admixture of reproof and commendation, set forth in the text and context, presents us with a striking illustration of the faithfulness and tenderness of Jehovah towards his people. Complacently regarding their steadfast opposition to the enemies of righteousness, he encourages them by intimations of his approval. Yet, discerning some defection of their hearts, which might not be realized by them, he faithfully admonishes them in the pungent terms of the text.

The *commendation* suggests the force and meaning of the *reproof.* The former, describes an external character which involves so much of the true Christian spirit, as to intimate, that the latter refers to an element of vital religion, of which we may be deficient, though the commendation of the text may be entirely just. That element is *a prevailing spirituality of mind*, "the first love" of the converted soul, an inner life, inspiring and beautifying the whole man; for which there can be no sufficient substitute, and which in fact comprehends the distinguishing peculiarity of the gospel of the grace of God.

The text, then, charges upon the church at Ephesus, a declension in spirituality. She was making a kind of laborious effort to resist the encroachments of error and unrighteousness; she had a sort of zeal for the truth, and jealous regard for the glory of the Lord, which kept her enemies in abeyance. But there was already a dying away of those internal fires which were her true and ultimate sources of light and heat, in the absence of which, darkness from without would encroach upon her, and desolation would ensue. O had she humbled herself at this reproof, and

22—Vol. III.

obeyed the salutary prescription of the Divine Jesus ! her life, her glory, would have endured and her mournful epitaph would be unwritten.

Brethren, an honest scrutiny of the churches we represent has forced the painful conviction upon our minds, that this charge of the text applies to them. From many points of observation we see much in their condition to gladden our hearts. Their multi-plication and increase; the augmentation of external means; the spreading influence throughout communities, of our peculiar views; and many kindred considerations; excite in us devout thank-fulness, strengthen our hopes, and seem to justify our claim to the commendation of the text. But we must declare without disguise, that there are many evils in our churches, which appear promi-nent;—above all a radical deficiency in their spirituality, from which these evils chiefly proceed, and which betokens others more fearful. It will be well for us, in view of this serious state of things, to look faithfully into some of its causes; seek out the remedy; and so meditate upon the blessed influence of a prevail-ing spirituality in the church, that even now, for Zion's sake, our hearts shall be moved with earnest supplication at the Throne of Grace.

We shall proceed as intimated—

I. To state some of the causes of a declension of spirituality in our churches.

II. To suggest a remedy for this evil, and enforce the importance of the subject.

I. To state some of the causes of a declension of spirituality in our churches.

1. We find an evident cause of the declension of spirituality among us, in the character of much of the preaching of the pres-ent day.

It is scarcely necessary to say, that the preaching of the word has been appointed, not only as one of the great conservative agen-cies of the church, but as a chief source of her nourishment and her strength. If then there be defect in this, its results must be sadly injurious. And must we not mournfully confess that such is the case in some respects? Has not carnal-mindedness made large demands upon the pulpit, which have been too often honored greatly to the dishonor of God's truth, and the suffering of the church? We must be allowed to say, it has succeeded in very many instances to form and direct our ministrations with reference to one great end, viz: to become *popular ministers.* And can there be a prevailing impulse more injurious to the minister of Jesus Christ, or more fruitful in evils to the church than this? How must he become popular? Shall he open the fountains of eternal truth, the clear streams of which only reflect the full image and form of guilty and polluted man? Rather, must he not affect the eloquence of words, the gorgeous display of language, the polish of manner, the neatly turned period, the fine spun sentimentalism, or the skillful play upon the passions. Truth in the simplicity of her garb, must not be set forth to commend herself to the heart and conscience, but must be decked with meretricious ornament—that she may charm by a vicious loveliness. O how must the spirituality of our churches die under such pestilential influences.

But there are other kinds of preaching, the tendency of which is, injuriously to affect the spirituality of those under its influence. Especially do we refer to that which omits the frequent and clear enforcement of the distinguishing doctrines of the gospel. We need not *preach error*, in order to secure its presence among the people of our charge. Let us *omit to preach the whole truth*, and we shall find error flourishing as in a congenial soil, and under propitious influences. Such omission will itself throw out of joint and proportion, the form of the Gospel; will be an evisceration which will leave a putrid carcass to spread disease and death. Where are the enforcements to practical piety, where are the real and overpowering persuasives to a holy life, if not in the doctrines of the gospel? Shut out these, and we close up the fountains of life, and of strength to the church. We are so "old fashioned," as to desire that the time may speedily return when the ministrations of the pulpit shall be seasoned with sound doctrine as in the days of Flavel, and Howe, and Owen, and Bates. Otherwise we must expect that our church-members will attain at best, but a slender growth, and that feebleness will mark all their demonstrations.

2. Another cause of the declension of spirituality in our churches is the passion for their *mere numerical increase*.

This feeling has a growing tendency in the present day. It needs but little argument to show that it is fruitful in the production of the most radical errors, and the most corrupting practices. Let us instance one error which it begets, viz: that professedly unconverted persons should become members of the church. Where will the evil stop, which proceeds from this mistaken and mischievous sentiment. Through the influence of it, the ordinances of the gospel are perverted,—baptism becomes regeneration,—the Lord's Supper, the elements of which are affirmed to be the body and blood of the Lord Jesus, "is life sustaining," and the administrators of these, are a peculiar race of beings, whose "succession" is a question of life to the human family. Thus, false and ruinous issues upon the subject of religion are made up, and their assumed verity takes the place of every other question. From these things you turn with a disgust which is only checked by the pity you feel for those thus deluded, and assert that the teaching of the Bible is contrary to all this, and that the distinguishing views we hold as a denomination, are very much based upon the sentiment that a profession of faith is essential to participation in the ordinances and membership in the church. We rejoice that this ground is occupied by us, and we are jealous of every influence that may in the least degree tend to remove us from it.   Yet may we not fear that we have in some respects practically affiliated with the errors in question.   Have not the terms of admission been softened, have not equivocal evidences of conversion been too often received, and has there not been indiscretion countenanced in gathering individuals into the church ?   If these things are true in the least degree, they are to be lamented.   And if they have prevailed, we have just occasion for alarm.   Let us be cautioned.   Let us correct the mistaken feeling that a mere numerical increase of our churches is a supreme object, and a real occasion for unmingled rejoicing.   What is the addition of numbers without piety?   As the swelling of the body with diseased flesh produces suffering and death, so must we fear that a similar unwholesome influence exists in our churches, causing their present sad declension, and threatening other and aggravated evils.

3. The evils lamented by us may be justly attributed to some of the means used to promote revivals of religion.

These demand more of specification and careful analization. than we can devote to them at present.

We shall involve a good deal when we say, that some new and eccentric modes of preaching, some novel and attractive measures, and some very startling results, constitute the popular idea of a revival.   The accomplishment of good in the church, whenever spoken of, carries forward the minds of many to "a protracted meeting," when as an integral part of the same, there are to be present some strangers or rather some *strange men.* - Then, without reference to the preparation of the church, and with a kind of confidence which is presumption, the conversion of souls is looked for as a matter of course.   As a sure consequence of these efforts, all other means are apt to be despised, and a vitiated appetite is formed, the certain precursor of leanness and feebleness, because it loathes the substantial food of the gospel.   Pastoral ministrations are rather endured than esteemed, unless, indeed, this perverted state is consulted, and topics of hortatory address, and means of moving the passions, are used to the exclusion of closely studied exhibitions of the doctrines of the gospel, and a plain yet faithful enforcement of "the truth as it is in Jesus."   The great evil of all these peculiarities, is, that they tend to exclude those forms of action and influence, which gradually bring up a church from weakcess to broad and deep efficiency.   A kind of hot house system will be adopted, and plants of an unnatural growth will fill up our churches, which will wither away, and be soon succeeded by desolation.   We might trace these influences and contemplate them in other respects so as, affectingly to confirm us in the opinion that . revivals (so called) are often brought about and sustained, by a course of means calculated seriously to affect the spirituality and real prosperity of our churches.   But we forbear on this point, and proceed to remark upon another and the only additional cause' we shall now mention, of the declension of the spirituality of our churches, which is—

· 4. An undue regard for, and reliance upon mere accessaries,— such as wealth, worldly influence, and others of a like character.

We have no objection that these should occupy their proper places in the church. Let them be subordinated to more assential influences, and sanctified to the advancement of the Divine glory, and then they will have their real importance. But if these are regarded as matters of supreme necessity to the advancement of the cause of truth, there will follow a train of influences, subversive of the true power and glory of the churches of the Lord Jesus. A system of expediency and a religion of formality would work out the ruin of the church sooner than any other given causes; and these will inevitably prevail where there is undue regard for the things of which we now speak.

And in the feeling which prompts to these mistaken reliances, there is a spirit manifested which is fatally sure to secure the destruction of our churches. Does it not entail upon it the curse of Almighty God; is it not a self-sufficiency which his word denounces, the folly and guilt of which his judgments will awfully confirm? O let us be instructed by the sad results which have ensued to others, and whose history teaches us that nothing can more effectually secure the downfall of a people than their undue dependence upon mere worldly agencies.

If we are right in apprehending these as some of the influences operating upon the character of our churches, then we must feel assured that spiritual declension will abound among them. But is there any kind of necessity that these influences should continue, or declension prevail among them?—assuredly not. There is a demand that these things should be corrected, and we proceed,

II. To suggest a remedy for these evils, and enforce the importance of its application, and an increase of spirituality among us.

1. Pastors of churches must enter more fully into the spirit and nature of their work as ministers of the Lord Jesus.

May it not be that we have possessed the minds of the people with such views of the design of our ministrations as have led them off from their great object, and left them to lapse into fearful declension. We are aware that in various ways this may be done. On the other hand, a minister may so enter into the spirit of his station, and so manifest the elevated character of his work, as to drive out from the church all that is contrary thereto, and gather around him hearts that shall beat with holy impulses. Such an one will not be silenced in his faithfulness by the fear of losing his popularity ; he will not virtually distrust the fitness of Divine Truth by a timid statement of some of its peculiar doctrines, nor will he shun to declare the whole counsel of God, though he may be assured it will be responded to by most rancorous opposition of the carnal heart. Pastors must learn to value the spiritual davancement of their churches, and seek to promote this in every scriptural way. For their own comfort, for their own usefulness' and for the desirable increase of their churches, this must be regarded an assential element. Let those who will, pander to the popular taste, cringe around the great of this world, flatter the rich because they are rich, or connive at wrong doing in the church for fear of unpleasant contact with the guilty, but let not the minister of Jesus Christ, who would be faithful in his Master's house, or see the pleasure of the Lord prospering in his hands, or preserve a clear conscience, thus compromise the truth, or degrade his calling.

2. We need more *enlightened* piety in our churches, to correct these causes of evil we have spoken of, and promote their real Spirituality.

Look into the different churches, and you will find their action, and the characteristics of their piety, to be very essentially directed and formed by the popular or prevailing notions of their several communities. Or you will find a readiness to embrace every novelty, and unwillingness to walk in the old paths, or a yearning for some excitable influences, all which indicate a deficiency in religious principle. We must correct these tendencies, and in no way can this be so effectually done as by setting forth clear views of the Gospel, and inciting Christians to a systematic and careful study of the word of God.

3. Lastly, a more efficient discipline in the churches is essential to their spirituality, and a necessary remedy for much of the evil with which they are afflicted.

It would be easy to show that many of the causes of declension in the Churches, which we have referred to, tend to introduce evils which can only be extirpated by an uncompromising discipline. There is often much that is painful in the application of this process, yet where it is faithfully and judiciously used, its effects must in the end be salutary, nay eminently promotive of the spirituality and healthfulness of those that remain in the church. But when we speak of discipline, we do not alone contemplate, as many seem to suppose, those more heinous acts and immoralities of which expulsion is the consequence; we include that necessity which exists in times of declension, for enforcing anew the obligations of church members, and urging on all, a more faithful attendance upon the means of grace, a more particular interest for their individual welfare, and a more direct regard to the spiritual concerns of the whole body. A process like this would diffuse reviving influences throughout the church and there would recur a prevailing spirituality which would draw down an enlarged blessing upon such a people.

In conclusion,—the importance of these remedial influences,

and the value of their peculiar result,—viz: the increased spirituality of thec hurch, must commend this discussion imperfect as
it is in many respects. We repeat it, the standard of piety among
us is too low, the measure of our spirituality is too small. Shall
we, can we then, look at this subject with indifference? Can we
in any sense consent that there should be withheld from us those
peculiar manifestations of the blessed Spirit, which are so specially enjoyed by those who maintain a course of devout, and fervent and consistent piety? Can we be willing to surrender those
scriptural assurances of successful labor in the cause of Christ,
which can be appropriated, or comfortably enjoyed, only by the
devoted, ardent and heavenly-minded christian? Or can we be
willing that our churches shall be divested of that only guarantee of their continued union and harmony, which is found in the
binding power of prevailing piety? No, we cannot, for if cut
off from these comforting, sustaining and conservative sources,
we despair, and are ready to exclaim, We are undone! On the
other hand, only continue to the churches these concomitants of
devout, consistent piety, and they will be "fair as the moon,
clear as the sun, and terrible as an army with banners."

THE COMING OF SHILOH:

A Sermon, by REV. R. B. C. HOWELL, *of Nashville, Tenn.*

" *The sceptre shall not depart from Judah, nor a lawgiver from
between his feet, until Shiloh come, and unto him shall the gathering of the people be.*"—GEN. XLIX: 10.

A proper understanding of some of the most important terms
which occur in this passage, and a comparison of their import
with the events of sacred history, will afford us most gratifying
incidental testimonies of the claims to Messiahship, of Jesus of
Nazareth. He is the Divine Shiloh, and it is of his coming we
here have prophetic assurance. Let us attentively consider these,
and afterwards we will refer, briefly, to the glorious events
which shall characterise the spread of the Gospel—the conversion of the nations,—and the universal dominion of Christ, predicted as the results of his coming.

In the prosecution of this design our attention is first arrested
by the name *Shiloh,* as the most striking in the passage.

This name, as to its literal and grammatical signification, has
been the subject of a debate equally protracted and useless. Some
critics, rendering it into English, read the whole passage thus—
" The sceptre shall not depart from Judah, nor a Lawgiver from
between his feet until *he comes to whom it* [i. e. the sceptre]
belongs." Others give it this form—" The sceptre shall not de-

part from Judah, nor a Lawgiver from between his feet until the
coming of *the Peacemaker.*" Others again understand the name
to mean *prosperity,* supposing that *Shiloh* is derived from *Shalah,*
and should, therefore, receive the same interpretation. The
agreement, however, is general, among both Jews and Christians,
that this is but another appellation for *Messiah.* The Vulgate
renders the name, " *Qui mittendus est,*" and makes it describe
"the Apostle, and High Priest of our profession," Jesus Christ.
Beyond this point, which is on all hands cheerfully conceded,
I need not now extend critical investigation. The occasion demands not recondite exegesis so much, as plain exposition, and
practical application of divine truth. The name Shiloh in our
text, unquestionably designates the Messiah.

Sceptre is another word in our passage, which requires a more
careful and extended examination. This term usually expresses
regal authority. Such is its general acceptation in the estimation
of all writers, sacred and profane. The text, it would therefore,
seem, secures to Judah the regal authority over the twelve tribes
until the coming of Messiah—" The Sceptre shall not depart from
Judah until Shiloh come." This is the exposition which is generally adopted; and historical testimony is zealously sought to
prove that Judah, in the persons of his distinguished sons, either
as kings or governors, continued to reign over the Hebrews, until
Herod the Idumean was placed upon the throne of their nation,
by the Roman Emperor, at which time Messiah came, and the
sceptre departed from Judah.

Could this popular interpretation be sustained by the requisite
facts, it would not on other accounts, be particularly objectionable.
This, however, I imagine, cannot be done. If *kingly rule* must
be adopted as the true sense of the word *sceptre,* as it occurs in
this text, one of two conclusions is inevitable—either Jesus of
Nazareth is not the true Messiah; or the prophecy in the text has
signally failed of its accomplishment; neither of which can for
a moment be entertained. I assume, and shall now attempt briefly
to demonstrate, that the word translated *sceptre* does not predict
the regal authority of Judah, but simply his continuance as a
distinct and separate Tribe, until the coming of the Shiloh.

In support of this proposition I, in the first place, remark, that
the Hebrew word translated sceptre, is *shevet,* or as sometimes
pronounced *shebet.* Judah had the shevet, whatever it was, at
the time the prophecy in the text was uttered. This fact is evident from the form of expression employed—" The sceptre shall
not *depart* from Judah until Shiloh come." Were I, for example, to say of my friend, disease shall not *depart* from him until
he employ a specified remedy, would you not understand me as
affirming that he *is now* sick. Could I with any propriety declare that I will not part with my farm until a designated future
time, unless I now possessed a farm. Judah, then had the shevet,

(the sceptre) at the time of the prophecy. He certainly *had* (for it was by his dying Father in that hour conferred upon him, and the same organization was also simultaneously conferred on his brethren) a separate and distinct existence as a family, or tribe, but no one presumes that he had any regal rule, or the least authority of any kind, over the families or tribes of his brethren, either at that time, or during more than six centuries afterwards. Jacob died in the year of the world, two thousand *three* hundred and fifteen; but David, who was the first king of Israel belonging to the tribe of Judah, did not begin to reign over all the tribes, until the year of the world two thousand *nine* hundred and fifty-six. Judah therefore, although he had the sceptre (the shevet) at the time of the prophecy, had no regal rule until six hundred and forty-one years afterwards The shevet, or sceptre in our text cannot therefore mean the regal authority.

I, in the second place remark, that the kingly sceptre of Israel did not originate in the tribe of Judah. Saul, who was the first king of the Hebrew people, was a member of the tribe of Benjamin. It is written—1 Sam. ix: 16, 17—"The Lord said unto Samuel, I will send thee a man out of the land of Benjamin, and thou shalt anoint him to be captain over my people Israel—and when Samuel saw Saul, the Lord said unto him, "Behold the man whom I spake to thee of! This same shall reign over my people."

I observe, in the third place, that although the tribe of Judah, in the person of the illustrious son of Jesse, succeeded Benjamin in the throne, the sceptre of regal authority did not continue in Judah, over *all* the tribes, but for two generations.

The melancholy death of Saul on the mountain of Gilboa, left the Hebrews without a ruler. David was elected monarch of his own tribe. By degrees he succeeded in extending his authority to the limits of the nation, and reigned happily over the whole house of Israel nearly half a century. His wisdom, moderation and prudence, secured for him unrivaled prosperity, and elevated his country to a high degree of power and wealth. After a long and brilliant administration he died, transmitting the kingdom to his son, the magnificent Solomon, under whose dominion the temple was reared, and the nation enjoyed its most palmy and prosperous days. Solomon, on his demise, transferred the throne peacefully to his son Rehoboam. But a few years, however, passed before this young prince, so unlike his predecessors in every respect, superficial in intellect, and intoxicated with power, by the cruelty of his measures, and the haughtiness of his bearing, lost the confidence, as he had forfeited the regard of his people. Jeroboam, the son of Nebat, seized the advantage offered by the general disaffection, placed himself at the head of the insurgents, who were willing to adopt any expedient likely to extricate them from the iron grasp of tyranny, and thus crushed the power of

Rehoboam. Ten of the tribes who followed this daring and
popular leader, becoming completely dissevered, formed the
kingdom of Israel, and they were never afterwards recovered to
Judah. To you all, I doubt not, these events are most familiar.
It may therefore, in truth be said, so far as *all* Israel was concerned, that the *sceptre* did at this time depart from Judah. Consequently, if it is to be understood as expressing regal authority,
as the Shiloh certainly did not come at that time, the prophecy in
our passage signally failed of its accomplishment.

The sceptre of the native rule of Judah over herself did not
continue until the coming of Messiah. This is a fourth fact of
importance upon the topic before us, and the truth of which, we
shall presently see, is capable of the most satisfactory demonstration.

Judah was prone, like his brethren, to forget God, and rebel
against his laws. His departures were most numerous and criminal. The cup of his iniquity ultimately became full. The
long threatened vengeance of Jehovah so often denounced by the
holy prophets, and so wickedly scorned by the people, could no
longer sleep. The Babylonians became the instruments of the
divine wrath. The army of Nebuchadnezzar, in number like the
locusts, appeared before the walls of Jerusalem and commenced a
vigorous siege. The desperate citizens held out against them for
two years, but subdued at last, more by the ravages of famine,
and the violence of internal broils, than by the arms of their in-
vaders, in the year of the world three thousand four hundred and
fifteen, the city was taken and sacked, the temple was burned to
the earth, and the people who survived the ruthless massacre inflicted by the soldiery, were carried into captivity. The kingdom of Judah here *ended*; native rule over herself *ceased*, and
the sceptre *finally departed.* These events occurred five hundred and
eighty-nine years before the advent of Messiah—the divine Shiloh.

Judah, however, ultimately returned, and it will be asked,
whether the regal authority was not restored; and that this period,
therefore, should not be regarded simply as an interregnum.

I remark, in reply, that the captivity in Babylon continued
seventy years. After the return, which consisted only of a small
remnant of the people, a favor granted them by the clemency of
Cyrus, Judah was ruled a hundred and twenty-eight years by
Zerubbabel, Ezra and Neheimah. The first of these Governors
was o fthe race of David, but both the second and the third were of
the tribe of Levi. During the two hundred and forty-two years
next succeeding, Judah was governed by her High Priests, all
of whom were of the house of Aaron. The nation was, in this
period, successively tributary to the Persians, the Greeks, the
Egyptians, and the Syrians. From the close of this era, until
Judah became a Roman province under Herod, who ascended
the Jewish throne, aided by the power, and subject to the authority
of the emperor, the Jews were under the government of the As-

monean family, known in sacred history as the Maccabees, either as kings, princes, or priests; and the Maccabees, as you are fully aware, were all descendants of Levi, and belonged to the Sacerdotal tribe. Thus it is seen, that after the Babylonish captivity, except for a few years under the government of Zerubbabel, who ruled simply as a governor and not as a king, the *sceptre never returned* to Judah.

The sketch of Jewish history now submitted, with reference to their rulers, proves that the word in the text translated *sceptre* does not in this connection mean the exercise of government, or kingly rule; or if it does, that it is certain, the prophecy wholly failed of its accomplishment, and that Jesus of Nazareth is not the true Messiah; because Judah had the sceptre, or shevet, at the time of the prophecy, but he had no kingly rule; because the sceptre of Israel did not originate in the tribe of Judah; because when Judah obtained the sceptre over all the tribes it was continued in his house but for two generations; because the sceptre of the native rule of Judah *over herself* did not continue, until the coming of Messiah, but departed finally more than four hundred years before the advent of Shiloh. The sceptre therefore, if Jesus of Nazareth is the true Messiah, and this fact no one questions, does not mean regal authority. But if not, what is its meaning? To this enquiry we consider ourselves under obligations to render a full and satisfactory reply.

The *usees loquendi* of the Hebrew language justifies us in assuming for this purpose the postulate that the term is designed to express simply (and nothing more, as we have before intimated) the separate and distinct endurance, or continued existence of the tribe of Judah until the fulfilment of the promise of God with relation to Messiah, the Redeemer and Savior of men. This proposition I shall now attempt by adequate testimony to sustain.

The word *shevet* here translated sceptre, is literally rendered a *rod*, or *staff*. Such is its plain sense. A *rod* or *staff*, is in the Bible very frequently employed as a metaphor emblematical of a tribe or family. Asaph—Ps. lxxiiii: 2, for example, thus utters his prayer to God: "Remember thy congregation, which thou hast purchased of old; the ROD (the shevet, the *staff* the SCEPTRE) of thine inheritance, which thou hast redeemed." Again, Jeremiah the prophet exclaims—Jeremiah x: 16—God "is the former of all things; and Israel is the *rod* (the sceptre) of his inheritance." In both of these instances the rod, or sceptre, is used as a metaphor for the family of Israel.

An event occurred, during the passage of the Israelites from Egypt to the land of promise, which will illustrate still more fully the correctness of our proposition.

A controversy originated between Korah, Dathan, Abiram, and two hundred and fifty others, princes and distinguished men, on the one side, and Moses and Aaron on the other. These men ap

proached Moses and Aaron, and said to them—Numb. 16 : 2—
" Ye take too much upon you, seeing all the congregation are
holy, every one of them, and the Lord is among them.   Therefore then, lift ye up yourselves above the congregation of the Lord."
They thus upbraided their rulers with reference to the priesthood
particularly, and to the officers of the nation, generally, which
they believed Moses was too much disposed to distribute among the
members of his own family.   They demanded to share in these
honors and emoluments.   The excitement became painful in the
highest degree, and the result was most disastrous.   Jehovah in-
terposed, and—Numb. 17 : 1—" Spake unto Moses, saying—Speak
unto the children of Israel, and take of every one of them a *rod*
(shevet—a *sceptre*) according to the house of his Father, of all
their princes, according to the house of their Fathers, *twelve rods*"
(sceptres.)   " Write thou every man's name upon his rod ; and
thou shalt write Aaron's name upon the rod of Levi ; for one *rod*
shall be for the head of the house of their Father.   And thou
shalt lay them up in the Tabernacle of the congregation, before
the testimony, where I will meet with you.   And it shall come to
pass that the man's *rod* (sceptre,) whom I shall choose, shall blos-
som, and I will make to. cease from me the murmurings of the
children of Israel.

" And Moses spake unto the children of Israel, and every one
of their princes gave him a rod (a sceptre) a piece, for every prince,
one according to their Father's house, even twelve *rods*.   And
Moses laid up the rods before the Tabernacle of Witness.   And
it came to pass, that, on the morrow, Moses went unto the Tabernacle of Witness, and behold the *rod* of Aaron for the house of
Levi, had budded and brought forth buds, and blossomed blossoms,
and yielded almonds."

During this whole transaction each family of Israel, as you
have seen, was designated by a *rod*—a *shevet*, which in the text is
called a *sceptre*—as its emblem, and the favor of God was intimated by its flourishing condition.   The use of this term in the several passages quoted, affords us ample means of understanding its
exact import in the passage.   In the oriental style of the dying
Jacob, each one of his sons was considered as a *rod*, or *scion*, all
of whom were to be transplanted into Canaan, and there to grow
and flourish, through different periods.   " Behold," said he, " *I*
die ; but God shall be with *you*, and bring you into the land of
your Fathers.   The patriarch foresaw that all the other tribes
would melt away and be lost, long before the coming of Messiah
—that the several *scions, rods*, of his family, would wither, and
perish, except the favored Judah.   They accordingly shared the
common destiny of nations.   They were scattered, intermingled
with each other, and with the neighboring nations, and finally disappeared among the tribes of the east.   This catastrophe befel them
more than seven hundred years before the coming of Shiloh.   But

the tribe of Judah, while the fulfilment of the promise lingered, continued, like a speck in the midst of the ocean. Although possessing no kingly rule, and perpetually harrassed, and driven before their enemies, they were as indestructible as their own native hills.

These remarks render it, I trust, sufficiently apparent that the word in the passage before us translated *sceptre,* means simply a *rod,* is used not literally, but as a metaphor, and is emyloyed to express only the distinction of the Judean tribe from the other tribes, and to guarantee its safety until God's promise should be fulfilled in the gift of his Son Jesus Christ.

"The promised land"—Bishop Newton very justly observes—"Jacob might divide among all his children, but the promise of being the progenitor of Messiah must be confined to one only. He assigned to each his portion of Canaan, but Judah was honored as the Father of Shiloh." On this account the tribe in question ever occupied a distinguished position, and the utmost care was always exercised in relation to its genealogy. Other means existed, by which Israel was distinguished from surrounding nations, such as their language, and the numerous and striking ceremonies of their religion. But the tribes had all the same manners, language and religion. They were, and could be, known from each other only by their genealogies. Consequently in the days of David—1 Sam. 24: 9—Judah was numbered apart from the other tribes. From Ezra and Nehemiah we ascertain that during the captivity in Babylon, the prophets were particularly careful in regard to the genealogy of this tribe. The Scriptures, and doubtless for this special reason, abound with catalogues, which are continually repeated till Shiloh came. Then arose upon our world the glorious sun of righteousness. Christ came at the time predicted, performed his amazing work of mercy, and ascended up on high, leading captivity captive, that he might give gifts unto men. The prophecy of Jacob was fulfilled. The separate existence, the rod, the sceptre, of Judah as a tribe, was no longer necessary. Jerusalem incurred the guilt of crucifying the Son of man, and principally for this reason, was by the providence of God, soon invaded by the armies of the victorious Romans—"the abomination that maketh desolate." The city was broken up, the Temple was destroyed, the records were lost, the nation was dispersed, and the sceptre—the separate existence of Judah as a tribe—forever departed.

If we have not erred in this statement of facts, and it is presumed we have not, how exactly did the events fulfil the prophecy in the passage! And how perfectly do they establish the Messiahship of Jesus! Shiloh came, and the nation existed no longer! Was not Jesus the Christ? If not, then no Christ can ever come, or if he does, it can never be certainly known to Jew or Gentile. It is conceded that no son of Judah, or other Israelite, even though, perchance, he may be of the family of David, can now trace his lineage, nor for a thousand years past has he been able, to do so. For the correctness of this statement we have the authority of the Jews themselves. The posterity of the tribe of Levi, divided into Priests and Levites, are still distinguished from the other Israelites by the ceremonies and duties of their religion, some of the forms of which, like the ruins of their ancient cities, still linger to impart additional solemnity to their utter desolation. These facts are sufficiently striking, and satisfactorily illustrate the glorious truth that he for whom was ordered the sceptre, and the genealogy of the tribes was preserved, to mark his descent from the seed of Abraham, the tribe of Judah, and the family of David, in whom all the families of the earth are to be blessed, has come, and having fulfilled the object of genealogies, they exist no more.

Such, without question, as appears to me, is the sense of the word in our text translated *sceptre*.

One other word in the passage requires a brief notice. It is the term *Lawgiver*. "The sceptre shall not depart from Judah, nor a *Lawgiver* from between his feet, until Shiloh come."

The enquiry is of some importance whether this title is to be here understood in its usual sense. Solon was a Lawgiver; so was Lycurgus. Was Judah to supply in succession until the coming of Shiloh, men of this class. If so, neither was *this* part of the prophecy realized by the event! Until Shiloh, Judah never, in truth, had a *Lawgiver* in the popular sense of that word. All Israel produces but one, who appeared in the person of Moses, and he belonged to the tribe of Levi. Nor, indeed, can it be said even of Moses, legitimately, that *he* was a Lawgiver, although he is usually honored as entitled to that distinction. Tne laws he delivered were all uttered by the mouth of God himself, and Moses was but the instrument by which they were communicated to his people. It is sufficient for us to state, without entering into any critical investigation in proof of the correctness of the exposition, that the word means simply a *Teacher*, or Prophet, and nothing more, and ought to have been so rendered.

The phrase, "from between his feet," to comport with the genius of the English language should be translated by the word *offspring*, or descendants. This emendation we shall assume as granted.

The sense of this part of the prophecy is obvious. It declares that among the offspring of Judah, a Teacher, or what is the same thing, a Prophet, shall not be wanting, until the coming of Shiloh. Accordingly, the most eminent Teachers and Prophets, of all Israel, were of the family of Judah. Such was David; the immortal melody of whose harp falls upon the senses as—

> "Sabian odours, from the spicy shore
> Of Araby the blest."

Such was Solomon, who breathed divine wisdom, and poured forth the knowledge of God—

"From lips wet with Castalian dews."

And Isaiah who "sung beside Siloa's brook," the glory of Messiah; and most of the noble army, of whom our Saviour bears testimony, establishing the fulfilment of this prediction, in the memorable declaration—"The law and the prophets continued until John" the Baptist, the commencement of whose administration introduced the Gospel of Christ.

If we adopt as correct, the expositions now submitted, and apply them, we shall find that the true reading of the the text is as follows: "*From Judah his distinction as a tribe shall not depart, nor a Teacher from his offspring, until Messiah come;* and unto him shall the gathering of the people be."

Such are some of the testimonies that establish, incidentally, the Messiahship and divine mission of Jesus, and demonstrate the claims of his religion to the faith and obedience of his people.

Let us now refer, for a moment, to the glorious events which will characterize the spread of the Gospel, the conversion of the nations, and the universal dominion of Christ, predicted in our passage as the result of the coming of Shiloh.

These results are expressed in the text in brief, but emphatic language. "Unto him shall the gathering of the people be." It is in another place predicted of him that—"He shall gather together in one all things in Christ; both which are in heaven and which are on earth; even in him, in whom we have redemption by his blood, the forgiveness of sins." This whole world shall be subdued unto him, and

"Jesus shall reign where'er the sun
Does his successive journeys run."

Reference is had in the form of the language in the passage to the military gathering of a tribe to the standard of their leader. The ensign of Judah was a Lion, which marched in the van of their victorious armies. On this account Christ is sometimes called "The Lion of the tribe of Judah." In every movement which characterized the deadly conflict upon the field of battle, the eye of the soldier was fixed upon the advancing standard, around which gathered, for the honor of their country, the noble, the generous, and the brave. Such a centre of attraction, amidst the conflicts and strifes of this world, is Jesus Christ; not to Judah and the Hebrew tribes alone, but to all the kingdoms, and nations, and people, of the earth; not to contend for the honor, and power, and wealth of this world, which will so soon fade away and perish, but for enduring honors, and glory and immortality—eternal life.

God is no respecter of persons. Consequently in Shiloh, the Messiah, the middle wall of partition between the Jews and Gentiles is broken down. In him there is neither Jew nor Greek, Barbarian, Scythian, bond, nor free; but all are one in Christ. He is the supreme ruler, and all of every nation, are invited to him, and those who come and are renewed by his Spirit, are entitled to all the advantages and blessings which belong to citizens of his spiritual kingdom.

As the centre of so great and glorious a union, Jesus Christ is all that is required. He is our prophet, our priest, and our king; to foretell, and consequently to prepare us for every event; to offer for us acceptable sacrifice, and to direct and lead us in every action.

To gather to him all nations, languages and people, of our round earth, various and efficient instrumentalities are to be employed, the principal of which is the preaching of the gospel. "Go ye" said the ascending Shiloh to his ministry—"Go ye into all the world, and preach the Gospel to every creature. He that believeth and is baptized shall be saved, and he that believeth not shall be damned." And for your encouragement, remember that "all power in heaven and on earth is committed unto me." You are my *servants*, sent to do *my* work, and you shall be *successful.* To guide in the accomplishment of this great achievement, he has given his revelation; the Holy Ghost has been sent forth to make effectual his written and preached word; and he has constituted the Church his representative on earth to facilitate the merciful designs of his infinite grace, and to fill the earth with his glory. Through these means shall all the people be gathered unto him.

When we look abroad upon the nations, we cannot but perceive that much of this work yet remains to be accomplished. Eighteen hundred years have passed since the Gospel Kingdom was visibly established. During the primitive ages of the Church, when to profess the religion of Christ was to forfeit honor, wealth and life, religion, in both its doctrines and its practices, remained comparatively pure. No man entered, except in rare instances, the sacred ranks in whose heart the love of the world was a predominant principle. Under these circumstances, notwithstanding the barriers by which it was opposed, the zeal of the Christians by the blessing of God, pushed the conquests of the cross into most of the nations then known to history. Falsely imagining that the victory was now almost gained, religion, hitherto simple and unassuming, began to feel the spirit of ambition, and panting for earthly distinction and honors, she clothed herself in purple, and ascended the throne of the Cæsars. From that hour the receding darkness began to steal back upon the world, and the minds of men to grow more and more shadowy and dark. The Church of God returned into obscurity: the wicked world assumed her name and station; the ministers of iniquity reveled in her forsaken sanctuaries; the Bible was suppressed to give place to the

Missal; and Popery, gaining unresisted rule, locked in the chains of ignorance, the nations of the world.

The true Church of Christ, branded with the odious name of heresy, was hunted, persecuted, and destroyed, for a thousand years, but "the gates of hell" did not prevail against her. The mercy of God was not destined to sleep forever. The sun of what has usually been called the *reformation,* but which was, indeed, not a reformation of the Church, because Popery had no claims to be considered a Church; but of a *revival,* or *resuscitation,* of religion, at last arose. One after another the manacles of superstition have been broken. The Bible has been restored to its place in the sanctuary, and at the domestic altar; the truth has again found admittance to the hearts of men ; sacred learning is attracting interest; his holy word is rapidly going forth in all the languages spoken by the human race; and the Church has once more emerged to view, "fair as the moon, clear as the sun and terrible as an army with banners." Missionaries are penetrating all lands. Still, of the nine hundred millions of inhabitants that at present people our earth, but a small part recognize, even nominally, our heavenly Shiloh. We cannot, however, be deceived as to the fact that the full period of the gathering together to Christ is not distant. The Church, like a mighty army, is deliberately forming herself into battle array. Already at some points, the conflict is raging. The war shout swells from the valleys, and echoes among the hills.

A part of *Europe* has long since submitted, and *all* her teeming nations shall soon throw aside her rosary and her images, and be gathered to Christ. Luxurious *Asia*, forgetting, on the one hand her Koran, and on the other her idols, and sable *Africa*, abandoning her fitishes, shall come. Boodh, and Confucius, and Juggernaut, shall cease to reign, and the millions of China, shall be gathered ; and Hindostan, and Siam, and Burmah, shall bow themselves; and the war-whoop of the American savage shall be strangely transformed into songs of praises. The heathen will have been given to Christ for his inheritance; and the uttermost parts of the earth for a possession. His Kingdom shall fill the universe, and he shall reign forever and ever. For unto him shall be the gathering of the people. How full of delight will be that glorious period ! The earth shall again bloom in the purity and freshness of Paradise!

"One song shall employ all nations, and all cry
Worthy the lamb, for he was slain for us,
The dwellers in the vales and on the rocks
Shout to each other, and mountain tops
From distant mountains catch the flying joy;
Till nation after nation taught the strain,
Earth shall roll the rapturous hosannah round."

We have now examined the most important terms in this passage, and by a comparison of their import with the events of
sacred history, have seen the testimony they give to establish the
Messiahship of Jesus Christ, and we have referred briefly to the
conversion of the nations, and the universal dominion of Christ
predicted as the results of his coming. Did time permit, I would
close this discourse by an attempt to make an APPLICATION of
this subject.

Degraded, fallen, ruined, our sinful world had no claims to the
divine mercy. Our ingratitude was loathsome to him, and our
transgressions had placed our recovery beyond the reach of our
own power. The compassion of our Heavenly Father was not
however exhausted; He pitied our miseries and sent his Son,
who, by the sacrifice of himself upon the cross, redeemed from
eternal death all those who come to God by him. The distinction
of his people is holiness, which is at the same time, the source of
happiness in this life, and the condition of eternal glory with him in
the world to come. Where then, permit me to ask, is the heart
so wedded to misery and death, as to be unwilling, joyfully, as
the only return which it is in our power to make for grace so
boundless, to offer soul and body a living sacrifice, holy and
acceptable unto God. Do you draw back from a service so
reasonable? God forbid. May the declaration of all hearts in
this assembly now be,

> "Here Lord I give myself away,
> 'Tis all that I can do."

Who of this assembly, conscious of your sinfulness, and of the
necessity of religion to save you, have come to Christ? Permit
me once more, affectionately to remind you that out of Christ,
who can be approached only by repentance and faith, there is no
salvation. Eternal death is inevitable. Suffer me to beseech you
then, that you delay no longer your submission to your *only* Redeemer, whose favor is life and whose loving kindness is better
than life.

In the conquest of the world to the dominion of Messiah, I
remark finally, our Heavenly Father has been pleased to honor
his people as the great instrumentality. We recognize in this
arrangement, the same exhibition of grace by which the whole
Gospel dispensation is distinguished. Our aid is not essential to
him. The slightest exertion of his omnipotence would renew in
a moment the face of the earth. But our participation in the conquest at once stimulates us to duty, heightens our joys, and constitutes us partakers of his glory. Who is there among us who
does not burn to enter the work. Let the world, my brethren,
around you in every part, feel your power. Be workers together with God. The event shall elevate your thrones, and add
brilliancy to your crowns, in the world of immortality.

I. Once bring the matter to this point, that the profession you make may be the effect of your solemn deliberate, choice. There is too much reason to recommend this rule to the generality of Christians, amongst whom, it is very apparent, there are too many, whose profession is rather the effect of chance, or fate; or any thing they are thrown into by the concurrence of some external circumstances in their condition; than of a serious deliberate choice. How many are there who profess themselves Christians, as we observed before, merely because it is the religion of their country, or was that of their ancestors! or is established by the laws under which they live! So that it would be very inconvenient, for them, too hazardous it may be, or at least scandalous, to make a contrary profession. Now it highly concerns us once to come to this, that the religion we are of be what we have chosen, and that we profess it upon mature deliberation. We are nothing in religion till we come to this.

2. Endeavor to know God in good earnest. Know him in deed and then you are in no danger of the charge, which the apostle brought against false professors. You have been formerly told, that this phrase of professing to know God, is not to be restrained and limited unto the bare speculative knowledge of him abstractly considered. But though it is not to be thus limited, yet it must include this as the leading, initial thing to all the rest. It is an expression for religion in general, and is sometimes put for the whole of it; and therefore it cannot be supposed to leave out that, which is the leading principle of all, from whence the denomination is taken, and put upon the whole.

3. Ponder well on the dignity and sacredness of this profession. Oh what a mighty thing is this! that whereas the world has been lost in the ignorance of God, through many successive ages, we should take upon us to profess to know him. It is too big a word for the mouth of a profane and irreligious world. That description of Balaam which he gives of himself, is grand and very solemn: "The man whose eyes are opened, that heard the word of God, that knew the knowledge of the Most High, and saw the vision of the Almighty."—Numb. xxiv: 3, 4, 15, 16. And yet the knowledge he alludes to, and which this prophet seems to glory in, was only such as he derived from the spirit of prophecy, and not the spirit of saving holy illumination. However, it was a great thing to come out of such a profane mouth as that of Balaam, when he came to curse the armies of Israel

4. Look upon your profession as an obligation upon you; to a correspondent practice. Every profession is so understood among men; and what an ignominy were it for a man, to wear the name, when there were none of the things to which the name corresponds

Do we look upon professing to know God only as an idle profession? as a thing which no business goes along with, nor is attended with any suitable employment? Theology was well described by him, who reckoned it was not mere knowing for knowing's sake, but was the doctrine of living unto God.

5. Comprehend as distinctly as you can in your own thoughts, the sum of that duty unto which this profession does oblige you. Learn and encompass in your own mind, the whole circle of all those duties, which a professing to know God does engage you to. Run through the Encyclopædia, or the whole system of practical religion, to wit, the duties, to the practice of which you are obliged by virtue of your profession, both internal and external. Duties towards God the Father and his Son, your Creator and Redeemer; such as agree with your acknowledgment of the mystery of God and of Christ, Col. II. 2. Yea, and not only such, but also duties towards man too, which religion ought to influence, and wherein we are to be governed by our knowledge of God.

6. Labor thoroughly to understand the grounds on which you take upon you the obligation to every christian duty. It is very plain that the agenda of religion, that is the things to be performed by us, are grounded upon the credenda, or things to be believed. "I believe so and so, and therefore conceive myself as obliged to do so and so. And the common foundation of both I must reckon to be the divine authority, revealing certain principles and truths as necessary to be believed; and enjoining certain duties as consequences from thence, and equally necessary to be done." Thus go to the ground and bottom of the religion you profess, and then you have it in its original, and truly divine. But if we look upon our religion as merely human, handed down from father to son, and the like, no wonder then if we trifle with it; but no man would be adventurous, with relation to what he apprehended to be divine. Therefore is men's religion usually weak, impotent, and ineffectual, and has not its proper influence in commanding the heart, and governing the life, because the divine original of it is not apprehended. My own things, I am ready to think, may be used as I please, but I may not do so with those which are divine.—*Howe.*

THE
BAPTIST PREACHER.

VOL. III.	October, 1844.	NO. 10

INSUBORDINATION:—ITS CAUSES, TENDENCIES, AND GUILT.

A Sermon by Rev. J. Lansing Burrows, *Pastor of the Fifth Baptist Church, Philadelphia, Penn.*

———

"*The wicked are like the troubled sea, when it cannot rest, whose waters cast up mire and dirt.*"—Isaiah LVII: 20.

The wicked are necessarily restless. An approving conscience is essential to a calm and quiet spirit. The passions of the depraved heart, when left, without the restraints of inwrought moral principles, to their own natural exercise, strengthen in virulence and turbulence, until from the din of their conflict, peace flies and hides. The chambers of the mind, where heavenly guests are not invited and cherished, will be forced and filled by infernal tenants. He whose passions are unsubdued and uncontrolled by divine grace, has within himself all the elements of riot.

Outward manifestations of the inward turmoil may be prevented, by the necessary activity which the business of life demands; by the dread of legal penalties; by the absence of sufficient causes of excitement, or opportunities of their exhibition, in a well governed community; but the elements of insubordination and brawl exist in every unregenerate heart.

. The text describes the natural character of the whole human race. The wicked cannot rest. The waters of the sea are the graphic type of their restless spirits. Occasional calms are no security against sudden and frequent storms. While the "mire and dirt" of sin remain in the uncleansed heart, though for a season in undisturbed deposit, the waves of passion, so easily moved, may at any moment "cast up" the filth, and dash it over the surface of human society.

Fearful illustrations of these truths we have been compelled, recently, and repeatedly to witness in our own city. The blood of murdered citizens still stains our streets, and the bitter tears of bereaved widows and orphans, have not ceased to flow. The terrible sounds of cannon and musketry, and the tramp of armed men, are still resounding in our ears, teaching, by their tremen-

dous utterances, the truth and universality of the inspired descrip-
tions of man's inherent and unmodified depravity. Human
character remains essentially unchanged, notwithstanding the
boasted progress and influence of civilization and refinement, of
education and art.

Believing it to be the solemn duty of the Ministers of Jesus
Christ, to exert the whole of the mighty influence of the pulpit
for the support of law, and for the suppression of popular turmoil,
I invite your attention, in this discourse, to a consideration of
The Causes, Tendencies, and Guilt of Insubordina-
tion.

I. The text suggests the ultimate causes of Insubordination.

Without dwelling upon the secondary causes of particular
scenes of violence, that have distressed and disgraced our community, I remark, at once, that, *selfishness is the prime element in a
riotous spirit.*

The preservation of the personal rights of each member of a
community, while at the same time, the best interests of the whole
body are secured, is the great end of law.   It prohibits men from
pushing their own purposes at the expense of others' interests
and happiness.   It builds barriers around every one's person and
habitation, through which no one has a right to force a passage,
and beyond which no inmate has a right to obtrude.   Every person under a government of law, moves, as in a charmed circle,
which all are forbidden to enter.   A sacred regard for individual
rights and happiness, is essential to general prosperity.   The
body being composed of members, each member must be unrestrained in the exercise of its appropriate functions, or the whole
body suffers.   Human law, so far as perfect, is based upon the
simple precept ; " Thou shalt love thy neighbor as thyself." Thou
shalt regard his rights and means of happiness as sacredly as
thine own.

Against this principle, the selfishness of the natural heart rebels.
It would have others bound indeed, in order that its own ends may
be the more readily gained, but it chafes beneath the cords that
hold back its rapacious hands from a neighbor's rights.   It would
appropriate to itself more than its own share of the means of enjoyment.   It is dissatisfied with its legitimate place, and would
enlarge its own circle, though its circumference may impinge that
of others.   Selfishness would set up another law for its conduct—
its own will.   Desirous of attaining its own ends, reckless of the
interests of others, it groans as in bondage under legal restraints.

· Here originates the restlessness of the unsubdued heart.   Here
commences the struggle for selfish freedom.   The bad man may
regard law, as a bond properly fastened upon others, to prevent
their interference with him—to hold them fast while he plunders
with impunity, but as a preventive of his own designs and aims

he dislikes it. He is bound within limits which he loathes, and beyond which he tasks his ingenuity safely and profitably to pass. Compelled by law, yet struggling to burst its fetters, he is "like the troubled sea, when it cannot rest, whose waters cast up mire and dirt."

Illustrations of this selfish disregard of law are found upon almost every page of the world's history. Our first parents were controlled by wise and benevolent laws. When by the injected suggestions of the Fiend, selfish desires originated in their hearts, they disregarded the law, rose in insubordination against the lawgiver, and with a riotous hand, plucked the "forbidden fruit." The history of our first parents symbolizes the history of the race. At one period, the whole world, with the exception of one faithful family, threw off the restraints of law, and made their own perverse wills the rule of their conduct. "There was no fear of God before their eyes." The world was in riot and rebellion, and God swept them from the face of the earth. So has depraved man ever rebelled against God's authority. His government they have rejected. "We will not have him to reign over us," has been the fixed determination of the world.

The necessary restraints of this selfishness of depraved humanity, originates and fosters *enmity* against the laws. This enmity may not be openly avowed, or even secretly confessed. The heart is very deceitful, and men often conceal, even from themselves, the motives of their actions. They may persuade themselves, that righteousness demands their disregard of law, in avenging or rectifying, real or imaginary evils; that in some circumstances riot is duty.

Neither do I mean that men indulge hostility to law in the abstract. They are willing that it should bind all but themselves, and perhaps the band with which they sympathize. And even its claims upon themselves they acknowledge, in all but pendant circumstances. They would make themselves, for the occasion, exceptions to the general application of the code; and prohibitions of what they desire, awaken restless anger in their hearts. Nothing but fear of the penalty prevents open hostility. And when this fear is allayed by the promise of impunity, the law is as impotent to restrain as a spider's web upon a giant's limbs.

The principle is the same, in its application to human or divine law. The great mass of mankind promise themselves impunity in violating God's law, and exhibit their open hostility and contempt, by an utter disregard of all those precepts that interfere with their depraved appetites and passions.

The next step naturally and easily taken, when opportunity offers, is *violence*. This is the open exhibition of the selfish enmity of the heart. The enmity to law may long be hidden. The valve of public sentiment may be kept closed upon it, too tightly, to permit the escape of the boiling wrath. But let circumstances relax the pressure of public opinion upon these turbulent elements, but for an hour, and a disastrous explosion will be sure to follow.

II. Let us, in the second place, consider the TENDENCIES of this spirit of insubordination.

All manifestations of this spirit, are *destructive of individual rights and safety.*

If men are encouraged in disregarding law, what assurance have I, that an unpopular sentiment, uttered to-day in the discharge of a conscientious duty, may not bring upon me or upon the Sanctuary in which I minister, the wrath of the offended.

Are you a merchant? The purchase or sale of some article, concerning the manufacture of which there is difficulty among the artizans, or concerning the importation of which there is excitement among seamen or citizens, may bring the torch to your store-house.

Are you a mechanic? If you refuse to co-operate with your fellow-mechanic, in demanding an advance of wages, or if jealousy is excited against you, because of the qualities or prices of your wares, what warrant have you, that your property will not be destroyed, and your person assaulted by your opponents.

Are you a physician? The death of a patient under your treatment, though the utmost skill and wisdom may have been exercised, may expose your person or habitation to the wrath of his friends.

Are you a lawyer? The felon you defend, may be convicted; and his associates may visit their rage upon you; or the honest man against whom the popular prejudice is excited, may be cleared by your labors, and the disappointed wrath of the multitude may fall upon you.

Criminals may be torn from our court rooms; our dwellings may become blockaded prisons, and inoffensive citizens may be shot down in the streets. What will be the end of the operation of this principle? Who is safe? Whose rights are secured? If the laws are not competent to protect each class and citizen against popular rage, what encouragement is there, for the freeholder to erect his tenement, or for the capitalist to invest his stock? Unless this spirit be checked and crushed by the overwhelming force of a correct moral sentiment, generally diffused among the people, and encouraged by them, no man can gain a warrant of an hour's safety or enjoyment.

The spirit of insubordination is necessarily *subversive of all national prosperity.* There can be no stability, no enduring prosperity, under a government, the legislation and administration of which is vested in the capricious will of a despot. No subject can be sure, for an hour, of his property, or his life. In oriental nations no permanent foundation can be laid for national greatness. The scimetar and the bow-string are so constantly shaken before

the eyes of the people, that their terror prevents them from looking upon any other object, with the fixed attention necessary for
its attainment.

The administration of a populace, acting according to its own
caprices, under varied causes of excitement, is the most terrific
kind of despotism. Its laws are written, as it were upon the sea
beach, liable to be obliterated by every swelling wave.

" All public improvements require time, and the fixedness and
the security which can be furnished by laws alone. The purposes
connected with the endowment of a college, a school, a canal
company, a banking institution, with manufactures and with commerce, can never be accomplished, rarely more than commenced
in a single generation. They stretch into future times, and demand the continued protection of the laws. They must reach on
beyond the life of an individual, and beyond the capricious will of
a mob, or a despot, or their purposes cannot be accomplished.
They demand the permanence of laws that are known, and the
plighted faith of a whole people, that cannot soon change." " In
our own country there are more rights vested on the presumption of the stability and permanence of the laws, than in any other
on the face of the globe. All our agricultural improvements ;
our farms and plantations ; our banks, colleges, churches, manu-
factories, railroad investments, religious seminaries, hospitals, and
asylums, are founded on the presumption of the permanence and
stability of our laws ; and the announcement that the caprice of a
mob or a despot was to rule hereafter in this land, would cripple
or destroy them all in a day."*

There is nothing that gives assurance of the perpetuity of our
national institutions—nothing that constitutes our glory and greatness as a nation, that may not be swept away by the ruthless hand
of lawless violence. I have no fear for my country from foreign
innovation. The threats of distant monarchs trouble me no more
than the distant rumbling of the thunder, in an eastern cloud, upon
a summer evening. Our distance, isolation, energy, self-esteem,
and jealousy of foreign influence, render our overthrow, impossible, unless the omnipotent aid our foes. But I do tremble before
the gatherings of internal lawless mobs. This startles me like
the near thunder that suddenly breaks close to the roof that shel-
ters me. I remember Jerusalem, before its last destruction, when
its own citizens turned their swords against each other, and in all
the furiousness of popular violence, wrought out their own ruin.
As a man's bitterest and most vengeful " foes, are those of his
own household," so, a nation's most powerful and destructive enemies are marshalled among its own citizens. Let riots be defended and encouraged, as the remedies of wrong, and soon under
their rule would be realized the graphic description of the Poet.†

---

* Albert Barnes.
† Robert Pollock.

" Satan raged loose, sin had her will; and death
Enough; blood trode upon the heels of blood;
Revenge in desperate mood at midnight, met
Revenge; war brayed to war; deceit, deceived
Deceit; lie cheated lie ; and treachery
Mined under treachery; and perJury
Swore back on perJury ; and blasphemy
Arose with hideous blasphemy ; and curse
Loud answered curse ; and drunkard stumbling, fell
O'er drunkard fallen ; and husband, husband met
Returning from each other's bed defiled;
Thief stole from thief; and robber on the way
Knocked robber down ; and lewdness, violence
And hate, met lewdness violence and hate."

The violence of insubordination *strengthens the very evils it is intended to prevent and punish.* Abuse, is not unfrequently a commendation to popular favor. The veriest wretch, whose hands reek with the blood of the murdered, as he passes to the deserved scaffold, looks upon crowds of compassionate faces and weeping eyes. Human nature sympathizes with the oppressed, or with those who seem to be oppressed. Would you enlarge the influence of Romanism? Kindle a fire in its convents and churches, and that light will reveal its most attractive features, while its deformities will all be concealed in the dense shadows, created by that very light. Would you multiply converts to Mormonism? Excite the wrath of the populace against its advocates; shoot down their leaders like wild beasts; and the very sound of your musketry will be most eloquent preaching in their behalf. Would you spread the principles of abolitionism? Give its advocates an opportunity of pointing to the ashes of its ruined halls, the graves of its martyrs, or their own scourged backs, and scarred forms, and you furnish them their strongest appeals to the sympathies of the people. Nuns are more respected in Charleston, and gamblers are more tolerated in Vicksburg, than before riot undertook their suppression. Christianity itself was most rapidly propagated in its purity when most fiercely persecuted.

Evil or good principles—like the fabled Gheber fires—are only scattered to blaze in more numerous places, by every rude attempt to beat them down, and the very instruments used for extinguishing them, become fuel for the flames, and spread wider their light and heat.

Riotous violence generally recoils upon the heads of those who excite and urge it. In the present state of our humanity it is the direct tendency of violence, to rouse a desire of revenge in the oppressed party.

Long protracted oppression may habituate its victim to the hopeless endurance of wrong. The spirit of christian piety

may subdue the resentful passions of the natural heart, and refer
the punishment of injuries to HIM, who has declared " vengeance
is mine, I will repay"—and who has explicitly promised to "a-
venge his own elect." Thus did Jesus, the faithful Stephen, and
many other of the primitive saints, endure with calm and forgiving spirit, the reckless wrath of murderous mobs.

But the number who thus bear injuries, is comparatively small.
Most hearts throb with desire, and most eyes watch with eagerness,
for an opportunity to hurl back the weapons with which illegal
violence has pierced them. Rarely do men attempt to revenge
the punishment of law, by violence against its authorized officers.
An innate sense of right justifies legal penalties. But if even a
just and mild punishment, of great crimes, be illegally inflicted,
the vengeful anger of the victim is aroused, and nothing but want
of power or opportunity, will prevent the blow of revenge. The
criminal who will quietly submit to the sentence of an official
judge, without the consciousness of a passionate emotion against
him, personally, will swear vengeance against an individual, or a
self-constituted clique, even if they inflict lighter punishment for
similar crimes.

> "Spirits of fire, they brood not long,
> But flash resentment back for wrong ;
> And hearts, where, slow but deep, the seeds
> Of vengeance ripen into deeds ;
> 'Till in some treacherous hour of calm
> They burst like Zeilan's giant palm
> Whose buds fly open with a sound
> That shakes the pigmy forests round." *

Not unfrequently do rioters themselves, become the victims of
riot. For an illustration of this principle, we need look no
farther than to the terrible scenes that have recently disgraced our
own city. The clan who in utter disregard of law, armed themselves
to drive from their lawful privileges, those whom they chose to
consider their foes, murdering them, as though they were rabid
dogs, along the streets; were speedily visited by the wrath of a
band, as riotous and more powerful than themselves. The mob
that fired the churches and dwellings of Roman Catholics, was
begotten by the mob that assaulted and assassinated American
citizens, legally and peaceably assembled.

So long as the law maintains its power and integrity, aggres-
sors upon the rights of others will be hunted out, and meet the
penalty of their infractions. The passion of a mob speedily dies
away. Its fire is two fierce to last long. But law, can calmly
and deliberately wait its time, for the infliction of its vengeance.

* Moore.

The penalty not having been threatened in wrath, is not modified by postponement. It can follow transgressors to their homes, watch about their doors, and track their wandering course, with unimpassioned determination, until the favorable opportunity for vindicating its power, and avenging its dishonor, arrives.

And even if the wretches who trample upon law, and upon the rights of their fellows, and stab the peace of others from the throng and darkness of a crowd, escape the eye of Justice in this world; Jehovah has said, "though hand join in hand the wicked shall not go unpunished." They may run and hide from earthly tribunals, but they can take no path that will not terminate at the bar of God. There the record of their crimes has been faithfully kept, and when the judgment is set and the books are opened, there can be no evasion or escape. If the advocacy of Jesus Christ, the only Mediator, be not then secured, the settled sentence of the law will most assuredly be uttered and inflicted; " Depart from me ye accursed; into everlasting fire, prepared for the devil and his angels."

III. We speak in the third place of the GUILT of insubordination.

Violation of human law, involves violation of God's law. Insubordination is direct and positive disobedience against God. At a time when self-interest, and safety, and personal rights, would, if ever, seem to warrant resistance to law ; when the bloody Nero bore the imperial sceptre; Paul's pen guided by the Holy Ghost, wrote to those dwelling in the very city and palace of the tyrant, subject to his capricious and cruel despotism, the following plain and emphatic instructions : " Let every soul be subject unto the higher powers. For there is no power but of God; the powers that be, are ordained of God. Whosoever, therefore, resist-eth the power, resisteth the ordinance of God; and they that resist shall receive unto themselves damnation. For rulers are not a terror to good works, but to the evil. Wilt thou not then be afraid of the power ? Do that which is good, and thou shalt have praise of the same, for he is the minister of God unto thee for good. But if thou do that which is evil, be afraid; for he beareth not the sword in vain ; for he is the minister of God ; a revenger to execute wrath upon him that doeth evil. Wherefore ye must needs be subject, not only for wrath, but for conscience sake. For this cause pay ye tribute also; for they are God's ministers, attending continually upon this very thing. Render, therefore, to all their dues; tribute to whom tribute is due; custom to whom custom; fear to whom fear; honor to whom honor. *

. That it is right, under some circumstances, for a people to abrogate their laws, and change their government, cannot be denied

---

* Epis. Rom. Cap. xiii : 47.

or doubted. That no human law is binding upon man, when it directly contradicts, or counteracts God's law, is also granted. But while the laws are satisfactory to the mass of people, while they are upon the whole willing to live under a fixed administration, and while conscience is permitted its legitimate control of the conduct, the man who manifests or encourages insubordination, rebels against God himself. He denies God's right to rule, by the same speech or action that violates human law.

God governs the universe, in all its departments, by fixed laws. Matter is controlled by unchanging physical laws. For the government of mind he has prescribed a system of moral laws. The administration of civil magistrates forms a part of this system. He has given them authority to punish evil and reward good. They are "his ministers." "These laws are to the moral universe, what the laws of nature are to the material universe, the source and secret of strength and order. Who would tamper with the law of gravitation in the solar system, or try to stop the smallest wheel in the machinery of that system, even if he could disturb them? The very idea of falling stars, or loosened comets would paralyze the boldest hand, or an indignant world would arrest and chain it. He is however a greater enemy to his species and to his own soul, who would destroy or disturb the authority of moral law as a whole, or in any of its parts." *

Disregard of law is the very essence of guilt. "Sin is a transgression of the law." The man, therefore who exerts an influence for the subversion of human law, at the same time sins against humanity, and rebels against God.

If the guilt of human actions be measured by the mischief and woe they procure, then no action can be more guilty, than those which originate and encourage riot. Is man responsible for the evil results of his wicked deeds? He is so held by laws both human and divine. Beside the mischief wrought, by endangering the stability of government, by weakening the confidence of the community in its power and perpetuity, by undermining the foundations of that wall of law which has been erected around the persons and rights of men, there are other terrible results, which necessarily flow from this source.

Riot arouses all the evil passions of the depraved heart. When all these passions are subdued and quiet under the controlling and salutary influence of order, and while religion, under these most favorable circumstances, is laboring entirely to purify the heart, and whilst the members of a community are dwelling together as a common affectionate brotherhood, are not the wretches most fearfully guilty, who turn loose upon society the demons of passion and lash them into fury; who thrust discord and hate in amongst the people, break up all harmonies of peace,

---

* Robert Philip.

interrupt all the communings of mutual confidence; call up from their graves, where christianity had buried them, the horrible ghosts of bigotry and intolerance, and array neighbors against each other in malignant and prolonged feuds? The men who strive and boast in such a work, are allied in spirit and aim to the fiends of hell.

Murder is reckoned the blackest crime which man commits. Insubordination, always awakens the murderous spirit. Life is worthless in the estimation of a mob. Shall we speak of the woe that distracts the family, whose head has been murdered in a riot? Shall we write the guilt of the murderers, in the tears of the widow, and sound it abroad upon the wailings of bereaved orphans!

And those murdered men!! They have been hurried into the presence of their Judge, perhaps, "with all their sins upon their head." Oh! what are all earthly griefs, and wrongs compared with the "eternal destruction" of a soul. I see lying amid the ruins which riot has wrought, the mangled body of an unpardoned sinner! I trace the flight of that spirit to God's bar, and hear the just, though fearful sentence, that pronounces its doom of woe! I can see nothing else!! Oh! tell me not now, of persecuted and flying families, of burning and sacked buildings, of chapels consumed and property destroyed, and law dishonored. All the woe, time can alleviate; all the buildings, clay and stone can replace; the violated law can be avenged; but, the murdered can never be restored to life; their souls, if unprepared for death, are irredeemably lost!!

These things considered, how infinitely beyond all human computation, is the guilt of those who originate or countenance riot.

Among the many important reflections suggested by this subject, I have time, in conclusion, only to allude to the following:—

1. This subject teaches the unspeakable importance of settled and absolute submission to law. For the maintenance of its positive supremacy, every christian and citizen—where an enlightened conscience does not interpose its higher claims—should give his whole, unmodified influence.

2. The constant necessity for the exercise of charity and forbearance, is taught by this subject. Remembering our own lamentable fallibility, let us permit others to hold and defend principles and sentiments, even if abhorrent to ourselves, while our civil and religious rights are secured. And if abused and wronged still let us exercise that forbearance which the gospel teaches, and which Jehovah exhibits toward our transgressions.

3. This subject teaches us that *christianity is the sole conservative influence, upon which we can depend for the preservation and perpetuity of our civil institutions.* The law cannot restrain the sovereign who legislates, if sufficient motives are presented him for disregarding it. The people of this country are its sovereign

legislators and none can call them to account if they violate their own laws. Intellectual culture, unregulated by moral principle, will only give men greater power for mischief. The prevalence of pure christianity, teaching us to " love God with all our hearts and our neighbors as ourselves," is our only hope.

4. In fine, this subject suggests the infinite value of Christ's atoning mediation in behalf of a revolted world. The guilt of insubordination against the divine law attaches to each of us. To its charges we can only plead guilty.

But Christ by his sacrifice repaired the breaches our sins had made, and prevented the ruinous results our rebellion must have procured. Through him we are reconciled to God, our hostility of heart is subdued, and our peace and purity secured. "Great peace have they who love thy law, and nothing shall offend them."

RELIGIOUS APATHY.

OUTLINES OF A SERMON.

"*Is there not a cause?*"—1 SAM. XVII: 29.

These will probably be recollected, as the words of the youngest son of Jesse. He had been taken from the sheep-fold, to carry provisions to his elder brothers, who were encamped in the valley of Elah, and were momently expecting a battle with the Philistines. Censured by his eldest brother, as to the motives which had brought him thither, he defends himself in language of which the text is a part. Into its precise meaning, which is rather doubtful, we propose not to enquire, but we avail ourselves of the words, to state a solemn fact, to enquire into its probable causes, and to recommend means for its removal.

I. *To state a solemn fact.* It is, that the present, is a cold state of religion, in our churches. *Is* this a fact? Allowing it *to be* a fact, it can be *ascertained*, only by comparing the *existing state of things*, with *some other state*, or with some *acknowledged standard:* because it may be alledged, that what we call a *cold* state, or a *declension*, is the *right state.*

We have in the gospel, an infallible standard, of what the church ought to be. And although at our *best* state, we are below that standard, yet at some times we are lower than at others. The present is one of our *lower* positions. Compared with *that* standard, we are deficient; and we *are* below what we *were.* The misfortune and the criminality implied in this fact, are greatly. aggravated, when we consider two things. First, that we have a much more certain criterion, by which to judge of correctness and obliquity in the *moral* world, than we have in the *natural*. And second, that departures from right are much more common in the moral than in the natural. Indeed, we do not know that there are *any* departures from established laws, in physics : for it may be that *our* exceptions, are within the general rules. In the moral world, not so. Although moral philosophy is a complicated science, the Bible is infallible. Judging by this rule; *the world*, the *whole* world is moral chaos ; and the *church but imperfectly reduced to order.*

What an awful picture is this! " Other sorts of evil are kindly circumscribed and have their bounds. The fierce volcano, mars the adjacent fields for some leagues round, and there it stops. The big swollen inundation, buries whole tracts of country, threatening more, but that too has its bounds, it cannot pass. Sin has laid waste, not here and there a country, but a world, despatching at one wide extended blow, *entire mankind.*" *What is* it ? Do we see *a commonwealth dying of starvation ? The population of an entire country confined to lazar-houses ? One whole generation of human beings bereft of reason ?* These would be minor evils. We see our species in array against the great Creator, and bent on self-destruction. And we, brethren, what do we? With scarcely an emotion of pity, we can see our race perish. Ourselves on ship-board, we scarcely throw a rope to our sinking offspring. O, Heavens ! Are we insane, or asleep, or dead ? Let us

II. *Secondly, inquire into the probable causes of this fact.* Perhaps it would be safer in this connexion, to speak of accompaniments, than of causes. Two of these are, unnecessary absence from religious meetings, and the exclusion of religion from topics of ordinary conversation. Under these, a healthy state of the soul is impossible. In some constitutions, irregular meals, produce dyspepsia, but irregularity in partaking of the bread of life, is a certain forerunner of disease. The presence of these two means is itself the versimilitude of revival ; their absence, death.

There is difficulty in tracing any effect, of the kind now under consideration, to any known cause : since in every instance, a cause may be sought for, beyond another cause. If, for example, we trace indifference to religion, to worldly-mindedness, we make worldly-mindedness a cause, and religious indifference an effect. And it may be asked whether there was not a previous indifference to religion which gave rise to the worldly-mindedness. It is presumable that various causes may have contributed to produce the one effect : and some of them beyond detection. A heresy in New England, or in the West, may injure morals in Virginia, as mountains of ice, or stagnant waters, affect the atmosphere in distant regions. The wind may be sown beyond the mountains, and a whirlwind reaped on tide water. Worldly pursuits, party politics, religious innovation, amusements, pleasures, and sectarianism may all have had a share. But there are two causes of this effect, (I use the word in the popular sense, of antecedent and consequent,) to which I may safely refer you.

First, we have been insensible of our responsibilities. I mean comparatively. We have known and felt that it rested somewhere. Ministers have blamed people, and people ministers. The church has blamed the world, the world and the church. And then both have indirectly blamed God himself, by resolving our deficiency into his sovereignty, to the exclusion of our agency. We have not sufficiently felt that we are stewards, and must account for the talents we possess, whether ten, five, two or one.

And, *secondly*, we have not appreciated our privileges. And here we may safely select *one* as the representative of all the rest: the gospel ministry. We do not complain that ministers are not popular. Popularity is not the true exponent of talents, usefulness, or worth. Our complaint is not that the messenger has been neglected, but the message despised. We hasten,

III. Thirdly, *to recommend the means for its removal*. Here it will be said, that the same causes will continue, or *may* continue, to produce the same effects. But we affirm that they *will not*, nay that they *cannot*, if you will throw between them, sufficiently powerful *interrupting causes*. To do this we have the means. Let us see.

It is clear, that all the causes and accompaniments of this evil, mentioned under the second topic of remark, are capable of being so modified as to be changed in their moral character and tendencies. Take for example, party politics. Is there any necessary connexion between my wishing this man rather than that, elevated to political office, or these principles carried out rather than those, and my neglecting the social prayer meeting, or going there in an improper spirit? Properly considered, my civil duties are a part of my religion. Or take for another example, ordinary secular business. Worldly men accuse christians, when industrious and economical, as being equally worldly with themselves. This accusation is not necessarily true. Sometimes it is slander, and should be repelled. Christianity encourages neither idleness, improvidence, nor waste. The worldly character of a man before his conversion, affords no bad criterion to judge of what he will be afterwards. Do you think, that he whose fences are decayed, fields covered with briars, houses unpainted, children uneducated, and debts unpaid, is the man, whose life will be meditation and prayer? Give me the man of business, to make an active christian. Labor, wealth, fame, enterprise, learning, every thing the world calls good, may be made subservient to religion. To conclude, we would sum up, all we have to recommend, in these two items, *devout supplication*, and *scriptural effort*.

out prayer, are self-dependence; prayer without means, is phrenzy. They are combined in the hymns we use.

> "Hasten, O sinner to be wise,
>   And stay not for the morrow's sun,
> The longer wisdom you despise,
>   The harder is she to be won."

.This is the language of exhortation. But the next verse is a prayer.

> "Do thou, O Lord, the sinner turn,
>   And rouse him from his senseless state,
> Nor let him his sad folly mourn,
>   And rue his fatal choice too late."

They are combined in the lessons of Christ, and his apostles:— "Now unto him that is able to keep you from falling, and to present you faultless before the presence of his glory, with exceeding joy, to the only wise God our Saviour, be glory and majesty, dominion and power, both now and ever. Amen." This is a prayer of the Apostle Jude. And the very words which precede it, are a cogent exhortation to personal and relative duty. "But ye, beloved, *building up yourselves*, on your most holy faith, praying in the Holy Ghost, *keep yourselves in the love of God*, looking for the mercy of our Lord Jesus Christ, unto eternal life. And of some have compassion, making a difference; and others save, with fear, pulling them out of the fire."—JUDE 20–25. The use of such means, may expose us to the old charges of fanaticism, human device and innovation.

It is easy to talk of sympathies, and reason and faith, without knowing the meaning of the words. If cavilers mean by sympathies, the *excitement of the moral feelings to action*, we maintain that this is as important as either reason or faith; since without it there can be no religion. As regards *human machinery*, the whole system of gospel effort is a system of human instrumentalities—call it what you please—God converts men, by means of men. And is it any *departure* from the institutions of the gospel, *daily* to reiterate the claims of religion? The Apostles preached not only on the first day and the seventh; our Lord not only on the seventh; they both preached, at the Temple, in Synagogues, on hills and in valleys, by rivers, in upper rooms, from house to house, until midnight, with much entreaty, and with many tears. In a word, wherever and whenever *men* would hear, *they* preached. It is then so far from being a *departure*, from the primitive mode, that it is the precise spirit and practice of the gospel, to reiterate the claims of truth until they are met. As it respects the ill effects of revivals, you can form no better opinion of the value of revivals from a few apostacies, than of the productiveness of a shower by a few washed furrows, or overflowed bottoms. In fact, our Ministers, Deacons, Sunday School Teachers, Missionaries, the strength and glory of our churches, are the fruits of revivals. If these are not *the works* of God; but the effects of *imposture or delusion,* Satan has been unwontedly at work in building up the kingdom of righteousness, and destroying the works of darkness.

For *a revival,* we are dependent on God. *We* can get up *protracted meetings,* and *camp meetings;* but these are no more revivals, than *prayer meetings* are *answers to prayer.* And that there should be various success attendant upon scriptural means to promote religion, resolvable alone into the sovereignty of God, is no departure from the ordinary method of the providential government of God. Temperance and labor promote health; industry and economy, fortune; patriotism and valor, national independence, and vice versa. "But promotion cometh neither from the east nor from the west, nor from the south, God is judge himself: He pulleth down one and setteth up another."—Psalms 75: 6. Such is the way of Providence. Grace is similar. "Do good O Lord, in *thy good pleasure,* unto Zion, build thou," &c. "Thou shalt arise, and have mercy upon Zion: for the time to favor her, yea *the set time* is come," &c.—Psalms 102: 13, &c.

THE GUILT OF UNBELIEF.

Unbelief involves great guilt. The accused can alledge but *one* single plea: this has been made a thousand times—and has been as often answered—and it is still repeated:—that faith is not a voluntary act, and therefore man is not responsible for his belief.*

We admit the premise, but deny the conclusion; because the major proposition, that men are responsible for such acts only as are voluntary, is not true. We admit, I say that faith is not a voluntary act—that you do not in believing, first will or determine to believe, and then believe, as the result of such volition. My coming here to-day was a voluntary act, because I first *willed* to come. Your refusal to pay a just debt, which you *can* pay and won't pay, because you choose to make some other use of the money, is a voluntary act: because you first *will, purpose,* or *decide,* to withhold the payment, and then consequently withhold it. Thus many religious acts are voluntary, but not all. To pray and to restrain prayer, are voluntary acts: but no man loves, or believes, or fears, or hopes, as the result of any *determination* to do it.

* "Volition is the determination of the mind, to do, or not do,—it is the determination or act of choice."—Upham's Philos. § 366, Vol. II.

Plainly then, there are many acts for which we are responsible, and which are not voluntary. Because, in loving my children, I am not conscious of any volition or will, to love them, does it follow that I am under no obligation to love them? There are many duties with which voluntariness or involuntariness has no conceivable connexion.

But " man is not responsible for his belief " is a conclusion of which every rational man ought to suspect the logical accuracy, whether he could discover its fallacy or not. In truth it is one of the most alarming forms of skepticism. Every reason which can by any ingenuity be offered to prove that man may lawfully entertain any *opinions* he chooses, without regard to God, or the immutable principles of truth and holiness, may also be offered to prove that man is not responsible for any of his *acts*, either towards his fellow creature, or towards his Maker. That you may understand what I say, feel its importance, and act accordingly, I insist that *if* it is not your duty to believe the gospel, it must be either because you are *not required* to do it, or because it is *deficient in evidence*, or because you are not possessed of *the faculties requisite* for believing. But,

1st. It is plainly commanded, " He that believeth not is condemned already; *because he hath not believed.*" *&c.*

2ndly. The evidence in this case is, to say the least, as good as has been adduced to sustain any fact, or any truth in moral or natural science. The impediment does not consist in the want of evidence, but in *want of attention to it,* or in *the prejudice with which it has been considered.* *Inattention* itself is sufficient to account for all the unbelief which prevails in the world. This *is voluntary,* and its moral qualities are as bad as those of unbelief. Inattention is, in fact, a prejudgment of the case—a determination not to listen to the evidence for fear of conviction. Hence the awful charge of the Apostle, " Therefore we ought to give the more earnest heed," etc.—Heb. ii: 1—3.

3rdly. The faculties requisite for believing moral and religious truth, are the same as those employed in believing other truth. To suppose otherwise, is as ridiculous as to suppose, that a religious man has *two* memories: one for remembering *religious facts* and *truths,* and another for *other facts* and *truths.* The language of the poet is as theologically true, as it is poetically beautiful :

" Faith was bewildered much, by men, who meant
To make it clear. So simple in itself,—
A thought so rudimental and so plain,
That none by comment, could, it plainer make."

THE
BAPTIST PREACHER.

| VOL. III. | November, 1844. | NO. 11. |

CHRISTIAN STEADFASTNESS,

AND LABORIOUS ACTIVITY IN THE CAUSE OF CHRIST,
URGED, FROM THE CERTAINTY OF SUCCESS AND HOPE OF
REWARD.

*An Introductory Sermon, Delivered at the Second Session of
"The Rappahannock Association," held with Mattaponi Church,
King and Queen County Va., August 3, 1844, by* REV. ADDISON
HALL, *of Lancaster County, Va. Published at the request of
the Association.*

—

" *Therefore, my beloved brethren, be ye steadfast, unmovable,
always abounding in the work of the Lord, forasmuch as you know
that your labor is not in vain in the Lord.*"—1 COR. XV: 58.

The Author of our text, and those to whom it was originally
addressed, have been for about eighteen hundred years, slumbering
in death; and still doth the King of Terrors maintain an undisturbed dominion over their mortal remains. The gloomy
chambers of death, still hold them in prison, and the seal of silence
still remains unbroken. This large assembly, now living and
moving upon the stage of life, with him who now claims their
attention for an hour, will very soon, yea, long before another
cycle of a century shall have revolved, be added to the conquests
of death, and descend to the tomb. Centuries upon centuries
may still roll on, and countless millions of our fallen race, follow
in the train, and swell the conquests of the last enemy; causing
him in hellish triumph to exclaim, *Victory!* VICTORY!! But
hark! I hear a sound, awful and terrific. Whence comes it?
The Angel of the Most High, has received his commission to
summon the pale nations before him. The trumpet of the
Archangel sounds, and its mighty reverberations are heard
through all the earth. In tones of thunder it proclaims the
astounding summons, "AWAKE YE DEAD AND COME TO JUDG-
MENT!" The seal of death is broken, and the long sleep of the
grave has ended. The sinner, trembling with horror, calls for

the "*Rocks and Mountains to fall on him, and hide him from the face of Him that sitteth on the Throne, and from the wrath of the Lamb.*" But the Christian, calm and undismayed, exclaims in the language of the context, "*O Death! where is thy sting? O Grave! where is thy victory? . Thanks be to God who·giveth us the victory, through our Lord Jesus Christ.*" ·

The chapter whence our text is taken, contains a most powerful argument upon the resurrection of the dead, and closes with the words of our text as the corrollory· or conclusion, to which the argument leads.   The purport of the Apostle's language is this:— that, inasmuch as the righteous are to be raised from the dead, and to enjoy unspeakable happiness in heaven forever, they should be steadfast in the belief of the great truths of the gospel, and unmoved in the profession of their faith, whatever sufferings they might endure, abounding. in the work of the Lord at all times; knowing that their labor would not be fruitless, but that they would reap a rich reward for all their toils and sacrifices, in their Master's cause.   The passage therefore, that we design, on the present occasion to improve, contains *an exhortation to Christian steadfastness, and laborious activity in the cause of Christ, from a consideration of the certainty of success, and hope of·reward.*

In discoursing on this subject, we shall apply the first part of the exhortation to our profession: the latter to our practice. The distinction is obvious, and highly important ; for we may be quite firm and orthodox in our opinions, and very lax and careless in our lives, as it is possible also for us to be.consistent and upright in our deportment, and unstable and unsound in our faith.

· First, then, we are exhorted to be "*steadfast and unmovable.*"

There are some words connected with religion, as well as with all other sciences, (if we may call religion a science,) which have various meanings.   There are some such words in the Holy Scriptures, which have a theological or. technical signification, variant from their common or received import, the knowlege of which, is necessary, in order to comprehend the meaning of the writer.   In the passage before us, there is no difficulty on this score.   There is not a word contained in the text, that. requires any other than the aid of a common lexicon, to understand its import.   .

. The word "*steadfast*" whether in a common, or theological sense, means *fixed, firm, constant, resolute.*   The exhortation, therefore, simply requires, fixedness or firmness of purpose, constancy and resolution, in our opinions and efforts in matters of religion. The Apostle does not specify as to the various matters alluded to, though doubtless the great doctrines and precepts of the gospel, and especially the doctrine of the resurrection, so ably maintained by him, and denied by the Sadducees, filled his mind when he penned the text.

We shall not, we trust, wander too far from our subject, if

we shall somewhat amplify, and dwell to some extent, sepa-
rateiy, on several of the great truths of Revelation, to which as
Christians, we should most steadfastly adhere. And we feel the
greater necessity of doing so, from the fact that upon many points
in religion, professed Christians, and especially Virginia Christians, are characterized with great fickleness or instability.* No
people are more ready to embrace good sentiments and principles,
and to act with greater zeal in a good cause, for a time, but, as if
we were lineal descendants of unstable Reuben, we grow tired, and
relax our efforts, as the novelty of the enterprize passes off. Instead of being men, strong in the faith, and persevering in our
efforts, we too much resemble "children tossed to and fro, and
carried about with every wind of doctrine, by the sleight of men and
cunning craftiness, whereby they lie in wait to deceive."—Ephesians iv: 14.

With these preliminary remarks, we proceed to notice some of the
most important doctrines of the gospel, to which it is our duty as
Christians, and especially as a denomination, to adhere, and firmly
to maintain.

I. The doctrine of human depravity. This doctrine is fundamental, and lies at the very foundation of the Christian Religion
insomuch that a practical conviction of its truth, may be considered
as the first step towards the reception of the offered mercy of the
gospel. By it, we understand that man by nature is wholly corrupt and depraved; not only destitute of love to his Creator, but
actually opposed to his laws, and at war with his perfections.
That man's whole nature and attributes, animal, intellectual and moral, are perverted. His understanding is darkened, his imagination
beclouded, his memory impaired, his reason dethroned, his will perverse, his conscience defiled, his affections estranged, his heart
polluted. In his thoughts he is impure, in his words filthy, in
his actions vile. In short, that he is "earthly, sensual .devilish."
Let Paul, with the pencil of inspiration, draw his portrait.
"There is none righteous, no not one: There is none that under-
standeth, there is none that seeketh after God. They are all gone
out of the way, they are together become unprofitable, there is
none that doeth good, no, not one. Their throat is an open sepulchre; with their tongues have they used deceit: the poison of Asps
is under their lips: whose mouth is full of cursing and bitterness:
theie feet are swift to shed blood: destruction and misery are in
their ways: and the way of peace have they not known: there is
no fear of God before their eyes."—Rom. iii: 10–18.

But let another sacred writer fill up the back ground, and
deepen its shades still darker, if possible. "Hear O Heaven, and
give ear O Earth; for the Lord hath spoken: I have nourished
and brought up children and they have rebelled against me: the

*It would be well, if the fluctuations of piety were confined to Vir-
ginia.—ED.

*ox knoweth his owner, and the ass his master's crib: but Israel
doth not know, my people doth not consider. Ah sinful nation,
a people laden with iniquity. a seed of evil doers, children that are
corrupters! They have forsaken the Lord, they have provoked
the Holy One of Israel unto anger, they are gone backward. Why
shall ye be stricken any more? Ye will revolt yet more and more.
The whole head is sick and the whole heart faint. From the sole
of the foot, even unto the head, there is no soundness in it; but
wounds and bruises, and putrifying sores: they have not been closed,
neither bound up, neither mollified with ointment."*—Isa. i: 2–6.
'Tis done—the canvass is full—the picture complete—drawn from
life—*daguerrotyped.* Behold the portrait! Whose is it? 'Tis
yours—'tis ours—'twas Paul's and Isaiah's too, in a state of nature.

Pelagius, in the fifth century, denied the doctrine of original
sin, and asserted that the consequences of Adam's transgression
were confined to himself, and did not affect his posterity; and that
the favor of God was bestowed upon men according to their
merits. A doctrine so much in unison with the feelings and bias
of the carnal heart, found many advocates, and finally obtained
such an ascendancy in the world, that the Church itself was
corrupted, and on the verge of ruin, and would have perished in
the vortex of error, and superstition, and vice, had not God been
her defender and deliverer, As he had raised up Moses, and
Aaron, and Joshua, to be the guides and deliverers of ancient
Israel in the wilderness, so he raised up Luther, and Melancthon,
and others, to oppose and root out this heresy from the Church,
and to establish again the doctrines of grace and truth. This
humiliating doctrine is confirmed by the history of all nations and
religions, whether Pagan, Mahommedan, Jewish, or Christian;
else why those scenes of war, of rapine, and bloodshed, that fill the
pages of history, sacred and profane? Surely, if any record
could be found free from such recitals, it might be found, at least,
in the history of that favored nation, God's peculiar people, the
Jews. Read those records, my hearers, and deny if you can, that
man by nature is totally depraved. Yes, ancient Israel was not
more distinguished for her high and exalted principles, than for
her ingratitude, rebellion, and idolatry. If further proof be necessary, look for a moment at the history of individuals, from the
highest to the lowest station in society; and, without specifying
as to names among so many, you will find, from the king to the
peasant, predominant in the heart of man by nature, pride, malice,
envy, deceit, treachery, and revenge. Nor is this depravity the
effect of education and example. These may tend greatly to augment the evils of sin, but they are not the cause. The disease is
hereditary. We are " *born in sin and shapen in iniquity.*" and
before we can discern to know good from evil, this hereditary bias
is plainly developed. " *The wicked are estranged from the*

womb, they go astray as soon as they be born speaking lies."—
Psalms lviii: 3.* We have dwelt upon this topic quite as long
as our limits will allow, though not longer than its importance
demands, and will close our observations on this subject, by urging
upon our brethren generally, a steadfast conviction of this great
truth; and upon our Ministering brethren in particular, to give it
a prominent place in all their efforts to save souls. Yes, brethren, fail not to tear away from the self-righteous Pharisee, the fig
leaf. covering of his own righteousness, and expose him to himself, in all his native and naked deformity and pollution; so will
you be better prepared to inculcate, and he the better prepared to
receive instruction, upon the second greath truth we design to bring
to your notice, namely:

II. *The Atonement of Christ.*—From the fallen, depraved, and
lost condition of man, arises the necessity of some method or plan,
by which he can be cleansed from his pollution, and saved from
the awful consequences of his guilt. He has violated the law,
and incurred the displeasure of his Maker, and he must die.
The decree has gone forth in righteousness and must be executed,
unless justice can be satisfied, and God's holy character vindicated.
How can this be accomplished? Who will make satisfaction?
Will angels? If they would, they could not. They are created
and accountable intelligences, required themselves, to love and
serve their Great Creator, with all their power, and have, therefore, no surplusage of merit to bestow upon man.

> "Call a bright council in the skies;
> Seraphs, the mighty and the wise,
> Speak, are·you strong to bear the load,
> The weighty vengeance of a God?
> In vain we ask, for all around,
> Stand silent through the heav'nly ground:
> There's not a glorious mind above,
> Has half the strength, or half the love."

Human reason can discover no way of escape for the sinner;
but infinite wisdom and goodness devised, and executed a scheme,
in all respects suited to the occasion. *"God so loved the world
that he gave his only begotten son, that whosoever believeth in him
should not perish, but have everlasting life."* Christ, the anointed,
so pitied our condition, that he condescended to leave heaven, assume human nature, obey the law, and die to make atonement

---

* The author does not mean to convey the idea, that man is so depraved
in *degree*, that he can grow no worse. On the contrary, he believes that he
may, and does in time, and very probably·in eternity *" wax worse and worse,
deceiving and being deceived."* By *total depravity* is meant, that every *faculty*
of man is corrupt. " The whole *head* is sick.and the whole *heart* is faint.
From the sole of the foot even unto the head there is no *soundness,*" &c.

for our sins. The original Hebrew word for atonement, it is said, signifies *covering*, and which was early and aptly typified by the clothing or covering, which God provided for Adam and Eve after their fall, from the skins of beasts. The atonement signifies that satisfaction, or expiation, which was made to Divine Justice, by the sacrifice of Christ, commencing with his birth, and ending with his tragical death upon the cross. This sacrifice, or atonement, was exhibited in the various sin offerings made under the Mosaic dispensation ; hence, says the Apostle, " Christ was made sin" (or a sin offering) " for us who knew no sin, that we might be made the righteousness of God in him." The atonement of Christ and the redemption of sinners, though often used synonymously, should not be confounded. There is more than a shade's difference between them. They stand related to each other as cause and effect ; the atonement having refence to God, as its object, and redemption to man. Atonement is the price paid for our redemption. "He was wounded," says the Psalmist "for our transgressions, he was bruised for our iniquities, the chastisement of our peace was upon him, and with his stripes we are healed." And thus sang also the four and twenty elders that John saw fall down before the Lamb. " Thou art worthy to take the book and to open the seals thereof, for thou wast slain and hast redeemed us to God by thy blood, out of every kindred, and tongue, and nation."— [Rev. v: 9.] Atonement conveys the idea of expiation or satisfaction for sin; redemption of pardon and deliverance from punishment. "In whom we have redemption through his blood, the forgiveness of sins according to the riches of his grace."—[Ephe. i: 7.]

Long, and violent, and we may add, unprofitable, has been the controversy among polemical divines, as to the extent of the atonement; some contending that the covering or propitiation thus provided, extended to the whole human family ; and others, that it was limited to a definite number called the Elect ; and that Christ suffered just so much, and no more, with mathematical precision, as would atone for their sins only. May we not venture the remark, that the atonement is really both general and limited, as we may have reference in the expression to the particular application of our language. In regard to its sufficiency, it knows no limit : its provisions are adequate to the wants of every human being, and would all accept its provisions, the claims of eternal justice would be fully met, and satisfied. But that in its application, it really does cover the sins of all mankind, and thus screen them from punishment, is not true. Its benefits are limited to those who believe and obey the Gospel. Keeping up the distinction before made between the atonement and redemption, we conclude that the atonement, in its true signification is unlimited, being a provision for sinners generally; but that redemption can apply only to those who by faith embrace the Gospel scheme of salvation. In short, by this doctrine, we understand that the cross of Christ furnishes ample satisfaction to the requirements of Divine justice, without the adventitious aid of human merit, whether in the form of obedience, penance or purgatory. As the result of the whole, therefore, we conclude, that as Ministers of the Gospel, we should have no scruples whatever in inviting and urging all men, every where, to come and partake of the gracious provisions of mercy, relying at the same time upon the Holy Spirit to accompany the word and make it effectual in them that believe.

III. *Justification by faith.* Justification is a legal term, and signifies the declaring of a person righteous according to law. It is opposed to guilt and condemnation. When a prisoner at the bar is charged with a crime, if he be found innocent of the charge, he stands justified, is discharged from custody, and is in a state of justification. If he be found guilty he is condemned: still however, through executive clemency, he may be pardoned, and though in such case, the criminal cannot properly be said to be justified, the *guilt* of his crime remaining when the *penalty* is remitted, God (as we shall presently see,) can in the economy of Divine grace "*justify the ungodly*" by taking away not only the penalty but the guilt of sin. And herein appears the transcendent glory of the Divine plan of grace, beyond that of any human economy. Justification, in a theological sense, is either legal or evangelical. If a man could be found who had never sinned, he might be justified upon principles of law. " *This do and thou shalt live,*" said our Saviour to a lawyer, who enquired what he should do to inherit eternal life; referring him to the first great law of love to God; which if a man could and would obey he should live thereby. But alas! there is none righteous, all have sinned and come short of the glory of God, are under sentence of death, and in a state of condemnation, and the question recurs, how shall man be just before God? The Apostle of the Gentiles, in his Epistles to the Romans and Galatians, expatiates largely upon this important topic, and proves that by the deeds of the law no man can be justified; and that it is by faith in the Lord Jesus Christ, that man's guilt can be removed, his sins pardoned, and he reconciled to God; " *Therefore being justified by faith we have peace with God through our Lord Jesus Christ.*" The Apostle James, it has been supposed by some, maintains a doctrine conflicting with that of Paul, inasmuch as James declares that Abraham and others were justified by works. But Paul and James are not thus at variance, else inspiration did not guide their pens. 'Tis true that Paul says we are "*justified by faith without the works of the law,*" and James declares that "*a man is justified by works and not by faith only.*" Observe the precise language of the two Apostles, and the subjects upon which each is treating. Paul is discoursing of the justification of the ungodly, or the way of a sinner's acceptance with God, which is by faith in the righteousness of Christ, without the works of the law, as a cause or means of justification in the sight of God. James is treating of the justification of the godly, or righteous, and shewing how it is made to appear before men, that they are approved before God. He does not say, that we are justified by works of law, without faith, for he says, "*Shew me thy faith without thy works and I will shew thee my faith by my works.*" Nor does Paul, on the other hand, say, that we are saved by faith alone without works, but without "*works of law,*" as the meritorious cause of salvation. The truth is that there is an indissoluble connection between faith and good works, as there is between a good tree and good fruit. If we have faith, we shall evince it by our walk and conversation, hence says the Apostle Peter "*Add to your faith virtue, and to virtue knowledge, and to knowledge temperance, and to temperance patience, and to patience godliness, and to godliness brotherly kindness, and to brotherly kindness charity; for if these things be in you and abound, they make you that ye shall neither be barren nor unfruitful in the knowledge of our Lord Jesus Christ.*"

The misunderstanding, or perverting of these truths, of faith and works, has led to the most unhappy and fatal results, as the one or the other has been abused. The Antinomian, in his folly and the wickedness of his heart, abusing the doctrines of grace and continuing in sin that grace may abound, will find to his eternal shame and discomfiture, that his faith was dead and his "*heart not right in the sight of God;*" whilst the Arminian or Pelagian, in his vain conceit and boasted self-righteousness, expecting heaven upon the ground of merit, when he arrives at the gate of that happy world, and knocks for admission there, will to his utter consternation hear the Saviour say "*Depart from me, I never knew you.*"

But, brethren, let us not in attempting to sustain the justification of a sinner by faith, give to faith a place to which it is not entitled. Even faith itself, though indispensable to, is not the procuring cause of man's salvation. The sacrifice or atonement of Christ alone procures that: faith apprehends, receives, appropriates the merits of Christ. Christ is "*a hiding place from the wind.*" Faith inclines us to resort to its shelter for protection. Christ is "*a covert from the tempest.*" Faith guides and hastens us to its retreat for safety. Christ is "*As rivers of water in a dry place.*" Faith draws us to the cooling streams, and causes us to drink and live. Christ is "*The shadow of a great rock in a weary land.*" Faith urges and directs us to its refreshing shades, and we are protected from the scorching heat, and find rest and security. Finally, to sum up all, Christ is a "SAVIOUR." Faith leads the sin sick soul to Him, and accepts his offered mercy, and he becomes the recipient of pardon and salvation.

These truths, brethren, we cannot too firmly embrace, nor too steadfastly maintain and preach. As "*there is none other name given under heaven whereby we must be saved,*" so there is no species of ministerial teaching, so well calculated to woo and win the sinner, as the simple story of the Saviour's expiatory sacrifice, and the necessity of faith in his blood.

IV. *The nature and necessity of regeneration,* will claim your notice as another grand doctrine of the Gospel. This doctrine though plainly taught in the word of God, is not comprehended by human reason, and worldly philosophy, else the learned ruler of the Jews might not have so misconceived the import of the Saviour's teaching when he said to him, "*Ye must be born again.*" By the term regeneration, we understand that work of the Holy Spirit which is wrought in the soul of man by the instrumentality of the Divine word, by which his heart is changed from its natural unholy and wicked propensities, to a prevailing love of holiness, and hatred of sin. It is a work wrought in and not by us, and produces such a radical change that it is comparable to a birth, or beginning to live and breathe, such a mighty transformation of character that it is called a new creation; "*If any man be in Christ he is a new creature: old things are passed away, behold all things are become new.* (2 Cor. v: 17.)

It is not baptism, as was erroneously thought by some early writers, whose error it seems, was not confined to a former age, but has been transmitted down to the present generation, producing consequences fearful and dangerous. And whilst we would not detract one *iota* from the importance of believer's baptism, as an ordinance of the Gospel, we would in the name of truth and for the sake of the souls of men, protest against the idea of baptismal regeneration. Judas and Simon Magus were both baptized, but the former "*Went to his own place,*" and the latter was still found "*In the gall of bitterness and bonds of iniquity.*" They received the sign but not the thing signified, and so we fear, many professed disciples of the Saviour at the present day, relying upon their outward symbolical "*washing of regeneration,*" will find at last when too late, that they have mistaken the shadow for the substance.

In connection with these truths which as Christians we are required steadfastly to support and practically to experience, we advert briefly, to

V. *Obedience to the ordinances of the Gospel.*

1. *Baptism.* This is not the time and place to treat of this subject in a controversial manner; and we only refer to it on this anniversary occasion as one of those important duties of the Christian, which should command the unwavering testimony of our Churches.

In a spirit of acrimony, bigotry and heated controversy, it does not become us as ministers, or members, at any time to harp on this command, to the neglect of others of equal or greater importance. In urging the doctrine of obedience, we should not make baptism the centre of the circle from which all the lines of duty radiate; but placing LOVE in that centre, make baptism one of those numerous *radii*, which emanate from this divine principle of love. "*If ye love me,*" says Christ, "*keep my commandments.*"

On proper occasions, with respectful regard to the feelings, and even prejudices of our brethren of other denominations, we should "*declare the whole counsel of God;*" but we should endeavor to convince by sound argument, and to win over with Christian love and courtesy, those whom sarcasm and denunciation cannot, and should not, affect. In this spirit, our friends and brethren who differ from us in practice on this subject, will allow us with all candor and affection to say, that we consider it the bounden duty of all believers, here, and every where, who have not hitherto done so, to obey forthwith this interesting and important command of our Lord and Master; and that they cannot comply with this duty except by being solemnly immersed in the name of the Holy Trinity. An argument upon this subject we are not offering, but we feel fortified in the remarks we have made, by the plain letter and spirit of God's word, and stand prepared, on suitable occasions, to prove from the history of the ordinance and the meaning of the terms employed in reference to it, that immersion only is the proper action, and believers only the proper subjects. Contrary to your convictions of duty, permit us to add, we urge no one to conform to our practice, for "*whatsoever is not of faith is sin;*" but we do urge, and that in the name of the gread Head of the Church, whose laws we would enforce, that each of you who are delinquent in this duty, do not fail with all convenient speed, and with a determination to be guided in your course by the light of truth, to examine the word of God on this subject. When you shall, from an impartial investigation, arrive at the conclusion that truth requires you to obey this commandment, and notwithstanding, you find yourself reasoning yourself out of its absolute necessity upon the ground of its being "but an ordinance," a mere "non essential," then tremble, least you be found numbered with the unfaithful servants in the day of God's visitation, and hear the voice of your Master, "ye knew your duty but ye did it not."

2. We proceed in our design to offer some remarks upon *the ordinance of the Lord's Supper.* Like the ordinance of baptism, this institution had its origin in the positive directions of the Great Head of the Church, in the days of his humanity, and was designed to commemorate forever his own expiatory death. Its design was not to create a test and pledge of our love to, and confidence in each other as Christians, but of our love and obe-

dience to Christ. "This do in remembrance of me" It is a church ordinance, and is connected with, and follows in order of observance, the initiatory rite of baptism, as will appear from its history as recorded in the New Testament. It was instituted by our Lord himself; and after his ascension, on the day of pentecost, that memorable occasion when so many were converted, we are informed, that "They that gladly received his word were baptized: and the same day there were added unto them about three thousand souls: and they continued steadfastly in the Apostles' doctrine, and fellowship, and in breaking of bread, and in prayers. (Acts ii: 41, 42.) As baptism, in our estimation, is essential to enable us to enter the Church, and as none out of the Church ought to commune, so none are entitled to the communion who are not baptized. That baptism is a pre-requisite to communion, is not a sentiment peculiar to our denomination. Most, if not all of the prominent evangelical denominations of Pedobaptists, hold the same views, and never do according to their rules of faith and discipline, invite unbaptized persons to commune with them; and yet Baptists are charged with bigotry and want of Christian love, because they, acting upon the very same principle do not extend their invitations to partake of the Lord's supper to unbaptized persons. We believe (and our faith must guide us and not another's,) that immersion only is baptism, and that an individual is just as truly and effectually buried, upon whose head a few grains of sand only are thrown, as he is baptized upon whose face a few drops of water have been sprinkled. Whilst therefore, we cannot open a door that will admit Pedobaptists to the communion table, without yielding the question as to what constitutes baptism, our Pedo-baptist brethren are in no such difficulty, for they all admit that immersion is at least one mode of baptism; they can therefore consistently commune with us without violating their principles, whilst all candid persons must see and admit, that we cannot extend our invitations to them.

The wall of partition is not of our building. Pedo-baptists have reared it, and they only can, without the sacrifice of principle, break it down. It becomes them to do so, or to withdraw the oft reiterated charge against us of bigotry. Could we rend the separating veil as easily as they can, and would not, might it not with more truth and justice be said of us that we were bigoted sectarians, and blinded zealots and separatists.

There are other difficulties in the way of a free and open Church communion with other denominations, besides those growing out of the mode or action of baptism.

Open communion recognizes as members of Christ's mystical body, and invites to the holy ordinance of the Lord's supper those who are without faith and who are enemies to God; unless indeed there be some narrow isthmus between a state of rebellion and a state of grace, on which to place such communicants. It is no answer to this objection to open communion, that wicked men are found in all Churches, and partake of their ordinances. The question is not whether such do not sometimes creep into the Church unawares, but whether they should be invited in, and retained there.

Whilst therefore, we as a denomination are bound by the laws of Christ's kingdom, to adhere to what is called close communion, or the administration of the ordinance to baptized believers only, we are disposed freely to associate and unite with all who love our Lord Jesus Christ in sincerity, by whatever name they may be called, in all those acts of religious worship and Christian intercourse and effort to do good, which after all, will best evince our sincere attachment to Christ's people, though we may in some things deem them in error.

Before leaving this subject, we will notice what we conceive an erroneous view of this institution entertained and acted upon by some of the members of our own denomination, that of failing frequently to commune either on account of a sense of their own failings, or on account of the unchristian conduct of some one or more members of the Church. If this ordinance had been designed for pure and holy beings, then indeed should none of us lay unholy hands upon it, or were it intended as a pledge of our unshaken confidence in, and fellowship towards each other as Christians, we should abstain from the communion table till the Church be purged of all who are unworthy. In regard to the first error, of failing to commune on the ground of our own unworthiness, we would observe that such an unworthiness as causes us to feel no hatred to sin, and no love of holiness, no love to Christ and no faith in his atonement, no discerning of his body and blood, in the elements used, and no determination to crucify our sins and live a holy life, should indeed keep us away from this holy ordinance; and should with equal propriety drive us at once from the pale of the Church. But if our unworthiness consist in a sense of our own depravity and vileness, accompanied with sincere sorrow and repentance for sin, and an humble reliance on Christ as our hope, then we should not fail to come to the feast, where are so affectingly represented the merciful provisions of the gospel for sinners. As to the unfitness of others to partake of these symbols being any bar to our communion, as well might they debar us the privilege of baptism, put a stop to our songs of praise and drive us from the throne of grace and from all public worship; for some of the most unworthy often mingle with us in all our religious services.

We might notice on this part of our subject, as important articles of our faith, *the final perseverance of the saints; the resurrection of the dead* and a *future judgment*; but time would not allow a discussion of the first, namely, the perseverance of the saints; and as the others are truths held in common with all evangelical denominations, we shall the less reluctantly pass them by and proceed to consider the second branch of the Apostle's exhortation, namely, the duty of "abounding in the work of the Lord."

And it is necessary to distinguish under this head between the possession in an eminent degree, personally, a large share of the Divine presence and favor, causing us to abound in the Christian graces of faith, knowledge, temperance, patience, godliness, brotherly kindness and charity; and that industrious and laborious activity in the cause of God, which looks from ourselves and is intended to operate upon others. Man was not created for himself alone, solely that he might be happy. If so, he had not been suffered to fall. But he was formed to honor and glorify his Maker, and is therefore required to find his own happiness in efforts to advance the cause of God. We trust the idea is nearly exploded, that the convocations of Christians in Churches, associations and conventions, have for their main object the personal enjoyment of believers, and that the whole machinery and arrangement thereof should be so ordered as most effectually to rouse up the feelings and fill the souls of Christians with spiritual peace and joy. O 'tis delightful, my good old brethren and sisters, to get upon the mount, and look over into the promised land; and still more so, to pluck and eat of the grapes of Canaan, as we are permitted sometimes to do; but remember, that while Moses was in the mount holding sweet communion with God, sin and idolatry were spreading in the camp of Israel. And notwithstanding the children of Israel were permitted to have a foretaste of the delicious fruits of Canaan, they had yet a tedious journey of forty years before them, in which they had to endure much labor and toil, and to have many conflicts with their enemies. These labors and toils too, be it known, were not to inure to their own temporal good. They were laboring and fighting for posterity, for they all (who had reached manhood) with two exceptions, died in the wilderness. Expect not then brethren, in this life to revel in bliss and to be always happy, but learn that this is the time and place for action, heaven the place of rest and enjoyment. In this life we should "abound in the work of the Lord," in the life to come we shall receive our reward. What are we to understand by the "work of the Lord?" Doubtless the Apostle meant that course of action which would best promote the salvation of sinners. When our Saviour said "Father I have finished the work which thou gavest me to do," He alluded to the completion of the great scheme of redemption, whose design was to rescue and save man from hell, and for which he left the realms of glory, entered our world, labored, suffered and died. We too shall most abound in the work of the Lord, as we labor for the same great end, the salvation of sinners.

In pursuing the enquiry as to the most effectual means of securing this great object, we are happily aided by your own proclamation of the objects of your union. By adverting to your first Minutes, it will be perceived that you have engrafted upon your Constitution, as the very basis of your organization, a declaration of the objects of your Association, and a plan of operations by which the kingdom of the Redeemer may be enlarged, and the happiness and well being of man promoted.

This plan is worthy of minute consideration, but we are admonished of the necessity of bringing this discourse to a close, and shall as briefly as we can, dwell upon the several items as they appear before us.

Here they are, *Domestic Missions, Foreign Missions, The Education of the Ministry, The Bible Cause, Sabbath Schools* and *Temperance.*

On each of these means of doing good, or in the language of our text, of "*abounding in the work of the Lord,*" let us for a short time animadvert.

1. *Domestic Missions.* Within the bounds of our new Association, first, and then within the limits of our State, we are required and pledged to labor for the building up of Christ's kingdom. That there is great destitution of ministerial labor in some parts of our Association, and that there are a number of feeble Churches that need the fostering care of this body, is known to all. Why it is, that any of the Churches are without an under shepherd to guide and feed them with the bread of life, we cannot tell. The cause we fear is to be found in the neglect of our Saviour's injunction, "Pray ye the Lord of the harvest that he will send forth laborers into his harvest," as also in the culpable disregard of the scriptural duty of supporting the Ministry. Whatever may be the cause, the fact is lamentably true, that great destitution does prevail within our bounds. The Committee appointed on this subject will no doubt fully enter into it and propose the most efficient plan for supplying all the Churches with regular preaching. But the Committee can only devise and suggest the plan. The Churches must furnish the men to labor and the means of their support.

In uniting our means and combining our efforts to supply our own destitution, we should not withhold our aid from the General Association, whose operations extend over a much wider and more destitute region. That body has risen from a very small beginning, to a powerful and efficient auxiliary in the general Mission cause; and many a family residing among and beyond the rugged mountains of Virginia, have been made to rejoice through its labors.

2. *Foreign Missions.* On this particular branch of Christian effort we shall not dwell. Its history is familiar to most of you and its claim upon your sympathy and support are acknowledged.

This much we will say, however, that the contributions of the Churches fall very far below their proper standard; and we fear that many professed Christians, who are not ignorant of their duty in this respect, are daily luxuriating upon the bounties of heaven, while they are doing little or nothing towards the support of those who are toiling and laboring in heathen lands.

Brethren and friends, we shall meet those Missionaries whom we neglect to feed, and those perishing heathen for whose salvation we have not labored, at the bar of God!

3. *The Education of the Ministry.* The introduction by a unanimous vote, into your articles of Association, of a distinct clause, requiring an annual report upon this subject, by a committee of your body, marks the progress of public opinion, and the sentiment of our denomination at the present period. When good old mother Dover was constituted, and long since, even within our own recollection, such a proposition would have found no favor, and would have been considered as a most dangerous innovation. In an age when *priestcraft* and *witchcraft* were believed in, and alike dreaded; and when old women held familiar intercourse and chit chat with satan; and could only be kept from entering one's domicil by a rusty nail, an old horse shoe, or a broomstick, no wonder that it was believed that an ignoramus of a minister had but to enter the pulpit, and literally open his mouth and have it filled with arguments. And that when he discoursed allegorically and mysteriously, as well from Paul's "*cloak*" that he left at Troas, the "*rams horns*" which were used as trumpets at the seige of Jericho, or the "*great pot*" in which pottage was seethed for the sons of the Prophets in the days of Elisha, as he could upon the great and solemn doctrines and truths of the Gospel, he was looked upon as an oracle of wisdom, and human learning and acquirements were denounced as dangerous and destructive. But those days of ignorance and superstition have passed away, and the Churches are waking up on the subject of Ministerial Education. It has been discovered that the sacred Scriptures were not originally written and delivered to our fore fathers in plain old homespun English; and that consequently, without the aid of human learning, or a new and direct revelation to us of the Anglo Saxon race, we should forever be debarred from perusing God's Holy Book.

That Education is beginning to be appreciated, is evinced by the growing disposition of the people to hear, and the Churches to select as their spiritual teachers, those men who combine with ardent piety and deep humility, the most thorough knowledge of language and science. Men who can resort to the fountain head of the Scriptures for knowledge, and who can illustrate and expound the Divine precepts plainly and perspicuously.

We would therefore most importunately urge upon the Churches composing this Association the great importance of Ministerial Education, and that they will seek out and furnish with the means of obtaining an education, such promising and pious young men as may feel it their duty to preach the Gospel. By this course you will brethren, as effectually work for God as though you were literally and daily laboring with your hands in his cause.

Closely connected with these remarks is the subject of Ministerial ordination, in regard to which some of the Churches have been very lax and careless; and because a good brother is found to possess the gifts of prayer and exhortation; and exhibits a pious course of conduct, he is hastily ordained to the responsible work of a Pastor or Evangelist, notwithstanding he is wholly destitute of the necessary qualifications to be a teacher in the Church.

The Churches are, and ought to be independant, but a wholesome state of things cannot exist, till both the Churches and candidates for the Ministry are willing to profit, and to some extent, be governed by the wise counsels of their brethren. Why not adopt the plan of (not without example and precedent, for we are told it prevails in several of the Associations) of sending up to our annual Associations such individuals as it is proposed to ordain, to be examined by an experienced and judicious Committee, and if found to possess proper qualifications to be recommended by the Association for ordination. Thus will the associated wisdom and advice of all the Churches be brought into requisition upon so important a question; and the Minister thus sanctioned and approved by his brethren generally, will go forth with greater confidence and with brighter prospects of usefulness.

4. *The Bible Cause.* Another topic deemed worthy of especial regard by yourselves at your organization, is the circulation of the Bible. Whatever some few individuals may think upon the subject of Missions and Education and however they may differ with us in opinion in regard to them, we now approach a subject, upon which we are satisfied, that all lovers of truth will unite. Having imbibed the spirit of God's word themselves and found their peace and happiness in knowing and obeying its precepts, they cannot differ as to the propriety of extending and widening its circulation as much as possible.

In the great multiplication of books of every possible caste that can be imagined, which the facilities of the age has caused, it is to be feared that the importance of reading and studying the Scriptures has been undervalued: and though this Holy Book is found in the library of the affluent and on the shelf of the indigent, yet it is not read with that care and delight that characterized a former, though more unenlightened age. And if we have been led to indulge in a reflection upon the learning and intelligence of our ancestors, we may in candor and justice acknowledge, as a sett off to the charge, that they gave more attention to, and more diligently searched the Scriptures than the present generation. We well remember when our grand-mothers would sit for hours together diligently pondering over the word of God, and making it a part of their religion to teach it to their children and grand-children: and notwithstanding they might occasionally close a tedious winter evening with a ghost or witch story, they employed many such evenings in narrating the interesting histories of Joseph, and Samuel, and Ruth, &c., thereby leaving indelible impressions upon the minds of their youthful auditors. At the present day we fear these instructive Scripture narratives are too often overlooked by parents, and their places supplied with the popular and poisonous tales of romance and fiction which are teeming from the press, and like the locusts and frogs of Egypt blighting the leaves and corrupting the fountains of morals.

One object of this Association will be to encourage the study and promote the circulation of the Bible at home and abroad, as a means of correcting the deleterious effects produced by this great inundation of trifling and corrupting literature.

5. *Sabbath Schools.* Among the numerous instrumentalities employed to advance the cause of God, the Sabbath School holds an important rank, and is an institution which has effected incalculable good. It proposes to carry out the wise maxim of Solomon, "Train up a child in the way he should go, and when he is old he will not depart from it." To give a religious bias to the tender and flexible mind of youth, before its natural propensities to evil become fixed and habitual.

Nature, it is said, abhors a vacuum—a principle which is equally true in mental as in natural philosophy. The mind is never vacant. Awake or asleep, it is ever employed, and although reason itself may be dethroned, and the brain in a state of disorganization and disease, yet it is continually giving birth to legions of ideas—crude and unconnected 'tis true, but yet affording incontestible evidence that there is no vacuum there. Hence the importance of making timely efforts to fill the minds of youth with such wholesome moral and religious truth as will cause the eviction of that which is evil. The mind has been fitly compared to a garden, which while left uncultivated and neglected, will produce a plentiful crop of weeds and briars; so the youthful mind neglected, will be filled with all kinds of mischief and evil. As the spring, in nature, is the most favorable period to weed out and destroy the noxious weeds and plants from the garden, and to fill it with wholesome vegetables and fruits, interspersed with variegated shrubs and flowers, so the spring time of youth is peculiarly propitious to weed out the evil desires and passions of the mind, to supply it with wholesome instruction, and beautify it with the christian graces.

Here is an ample field in which each one of our hearers may labor. From various circumstances, such as a want of the necessary talents and qualifications, you may be debarred the high privilege of proclaiming from the desk, to sinners, the everlasting Gospel; and from a deficiency of worldly means, from contributing much to send the Bible and the Missionary to the Heathen. But the Sabbath School opens an effectual door for you to labor in the cause of God. In searching out and taking from the streets of a city, or from the highways and hedges of the country, a poor orphan boy, and training him up in the Sabbath School, you are doing a noble work, the results of which eternity alone can develope. When the daughter of Pharaoh said to the mother of the infant Moses, "Take this child and nurse it for me, and I will give thee thy wages," neither the real nor adopted mother conceived that they were nursing and raising up a child who was to be the deliverer of Israel from Egyptian bondage, and their great leader and lawgiver whilst journeying through the wilderness to the land of Canaan. Nor can you, my young brethren and sisters, anticipate the tremendous influence that some little urchin of a Sabbath school Scholar, instructed by you and taught to walk in the way of righteousness, may one day wield in the world.

God, in his providence, often effects the greatest results by the feeblest instruments; and secluded from, and unknown to the world, as some of you may be, you may nevertheless be made instrumental in accomplishing the most happy and glorious benefits to mankind, by planting in some youthful mind the germ of religious knowledge.

Robert Raikes little dreamed of the immense benefit that would ensue to his race, when, with trembling sensations of anxiety and doubt, to rescue a few miserable, degraded Sabbath breaking children from vice and ruin, he said, "*I'll try.*" Difficulties and discouragements you may encounter, but if each of you, with the spirit and perseverance of Robert Raikes, will ,'*try*" and do something for God, you will assuredly be successful.

The last item proposed for our consideration, and deemed worthy of a place among the efforts of the day, to promote the happiness of man, and the glory of God, is,

6. *The Temperance Cause.*—This subject, in our estimation, is of such vast importance, that we regret the want of time to give to give to it more than a hasty consideration. And if in this, we shall seem to trespass too much upon your patience, and indulge in, what some of you may consider, too great freedom of remark, we beseech you to withhold your censures, and suspend your verdict of condemnation, till both your own, as well as our opinions and practice, in regard to this, and all other subjects, shall pass through the ordeal of death, and shall be seen in the light of eternity.

To the honor of the Ministry generally, of all evangelical denominations of Christians, it may be said that they are united with few exceptions, and present an unbroken phalanx of co-laborers in this good cause; and with swords unsheathed, and banners flying, are manfully battling against King Alcohol and all his legions.

It is equally due to a host of private members of the different Churches, to say, that they, too, have courageously and heartily enlisted in the cause, and are its practical and consistent friends.

Would that there were no exceptions. But, "Tell it not in Gath, publish it not in the streets of Askelon, lest the daughters of the Philistines rejoice, lest the daughters of the uncircumcised triumph," that in this day of information and light upon the subject, there should be any professed Christians, and especially, any who minister at the altar, in holy things, who still withhold their influence and example—nay, who even oppose this glorious reformation. What do the advocates of Temperance propose to do, that they should encounter the opposition of such persons? Let us enquire.

They propose to save to the nation annually, a sum of money much greater than the whole amount of revenue needed to support our National and State Governments.

They propose to repair and paint the dilapidated and ruined tenements, now inhabited by the drunkard, and to improve and fertilize his barren and neglected fields, thus relieving the distress of his family and giving an agreeable change to the general face and appearance of the country.

They propose to dry up the fountains of tears, and to pour consolation into the wounded spirits, of the wives and children of the inebriates.

They propose to feed, clothe, and educate thousands and tens of thousands, of the children of want and infamy.

They propose to remove the proximate or remote cause of a multitude of diseases to which man is subject, and thus prevent numerous cases of suffering and death: and to banish entirely and forever from the world, and to make obsolete in the vocabulary of Medicine, the very name of that most fearful and terrific disease, *delirium-tremens.*

They propose to put an end to three-fourths of the daring crimes that now abound in society, and blacken the records of our state trials, and which supply tenants for our Jails and Penitentiaries, and furnish employment for the hangman.

They propose to avert the point of the fatal dagger from the bosom, and dash the poisoned chalice from the lips of the unfortunate suicide, whose ruined fortunes and blasted reputation, brought on by intoxication, cause him, in a fit of desperation, to resort to this, as a supposed relief from his woes.

They propose to save from an untimely death, the thirty thousand drunkards, who in our country alone, annually fall victims to intemperance. And finally,

They propose to save these wretched beings from eternal death from the "weeping and wailing and gnashing of teeth" of the DAMNED.

If the prnciples of the Temperance advocates are carried out and total abistinence from all intoxicating drinks, shall universally prevail, who will venture to deny that all of these results will follow? And we here sole mnly propound the question, WHO WILL ESPOUSE THEM?

We call upon every patriot and philanthropist; we call upon the more aged and influential members of society; we call upon the young men upon whom rest the hopes of the country and the Church;- we call upon parents, as they value and desire the temporal and eternal welfare of their children; to lend to this cause their hearty support, both by precept and example.

Again, we call upon the fair mothers and daughters of this large assembly, as they desire to escape the hissings and fangs of the serpent Intemperance, in a drunken husband or besotted child, to give the influence of their names and zealous efforts, as we would fain hope they have already done, that of their example.

And lastly, in more solemn appeals, and louder tones, would we invoke the disciples of our Lord and Saviour, of every name, to espouse this cause. We beseech you in the name of your children, and children's children, yea, of unborn millions. We beseech you in the name of your aggrieved brethren, whose counsels you have disregarded, and whose hearts you have wounded. And finally, we beseech—we implore you, in the name of the blessed Jesus, who died for you, to withhold no longer, your hearty co-operation in the cause of Temperance.

A few closing remarks upon the success and final reward o the steadfast and abounding Christian, and we have done. "There fore my beloved brethren be ye steadfast, unmovable, alway abounding in the work of the Lord, forasmuch as ye know tha your labor is not in vain in the Lord."

The Apostle uses no hypothetical language on this subject. "Ye *know* that your labor is not in vain." Be encouraged then, brethren, and labor abundantly for God, and be assured that success will crown your efforts. As Ministers, you shall not be without "seals to your ministry and souls for your hire," and as private members of the Church, you shall all find the work of the Lord prospering in your hands. Having faithfully discharged the several duties of your station, you shall have a quiet conscience and a peaceful death. Angels will convey your emancipated spirits to the realms of bliss—kindred spirits will welcome you to your eternal home, and your Redeemer, as he places upon your brow "the crown of life," will say to you, "Well done thou good and faithful servant: thou has been faithful over a few things, I will make thee ruler over many things: enter thou into the joy of thy Lord." AMEN.

THE
BAPTIST PREACHER.

| VOL. III. | December, 1844. | NO. 12. |

The mediatorial reign of Christ, an all-sufficient encouragement for the Church to attempt the conversion of the world;

A Sermon, preached by REV. CORNELIUS TYREE, before the Western Virginia Baptist Association, Aug. 28, 1844, and published by the request of that body.

"And Jesus came and spake unto them, saying, all power is given unto me in heaven and in earth. Go ye therefore and teach all nations, baptizing them in the name of the Father and of the Son and of the Holy Ghost : teaching them to observe all things whatsoever I have commanded you: and lo, I am with you always, even unto the end of the world. Amen." MATT. xxviii : 18-20.

These verses contain the great commission of Christ. The circumstances under which it was given, were peculiar and deeply interesting. The great work of human salvation had just been finished. The prophecies had been fulfilled, the atonement made, death abolished, hell conquered, earth redeemed and heaven purchased. The risen Saviour had been for forty days lingering amid his sorrowing disciples, comforting their hearts, enlightening their minds and strengthening their faith. The time had now come for him to leave them. He was about to ascend to heaven and take possession of that glory he had with the Father, "before the world was." Under these circumstances he blessed them, and dismissed them to the great work of converting the world.

This commission contains the statement of a glorious fact; a great command : and a precious promise. The glorious fact is, that Jesus Christ has all power in all worlds: the great command is, that the Church is to convey the Gospel to the world: and the precious promise is, that Jesus Christ is with his Church, in this great work to the end of time. This fact, this command and this promise, constitute "the Gospel of the blessed God," and form that great moral scheme by which the Church is to convert the world. Hence these words are a kind of summing up of all Christ did to save man: the essence of the new dispensation : an epitome of the whole of God's revelation to man. In

Vol. 3.—29.

these words, all the light of the Gospel dispensation is brought to a focal blaze. This commission is the watch-word of the ministry, the law of the Church, and the hope of the world.

Before announcing the theme of this discourse, I wish to premise some two or three remarks :—

First. This commission was given to the Church as such.—It was not given merely to the first Apostles, nor to the ministry in subsequent ages, but to all the redeemed on earth. The position that the propagation of the Gospel should be confined entirely to the ministry, is as unscriptural as it is irrational and mischievous. "To confine the propagation of the Gospel," says Alexander Carson, "to office conveyed by a certain succession, is an artifice of satan to spike the cannon of truth on the Gospel batteries." However important it is that the Church should have regularly ordained *elders* or *bishops*, it is certainly the duty of every Christian, in an enlarged sense, to preach the Gospel according to his abilities and opportunities. In this sense there should be no private Christians. Jesus Christ has ordained that every Christian, from the most talented minister down to the most obscure female, should take a part in carrying out this great commission.

Secondly. That all the aid upon which the Church are to rely in their efforts to convert the world, has been put into the hands of Jesus Christ, as mediator.—After the resurrection he became the official guardian, head, and representative of his Church; "He then became head over all things to the Church." The Father then made over to him, the kingdom of nature, of providence and of grace. All the blessings of the New Covenant, were then taken out of the hands of the pure Godhead and put into the hands of Jesus Christ for distribution. Every agency in the universe, from the highest arch-angel, down to the smallest insect; from the mightiest globe to the most minute particle of dust; together with the Holy Spirit himself, has been committed to Christ for the completion of the world's redemption.

Thirdly. The promise with which this commission closes, extends to the Church in all ages.—There is no propriety in limiting this promise to the Apostolic age. It is literally and in the most unqualified sense true, that Jesus Christ is with his Church till time ends. But for his mediatorial presence, the gates of hell would have long since prevailed against the Church.

We are now prepared to bring before you the proposition that we wish to illustrate and establish. It is this, THE MEDIATORIAL REIGN OF CHRIST, FURNISHES TO THE CHURCH, AN ALL-SUFFICIENT ENCOURAGEMENT TO ATTEMPT THE CONVERSION OF THE WORLD. The truth taught in these verses, is, that the mediatorial government of Christ secures and guarantees to us success in our attempt to evangelize the world. In this day of religious effort; when there are so many benevolent societies that are local and somewhat worldly in their organization and operations, there is danger of losing sight of the great source from whence comes all our help.

This text, like many others, has by many been cut into two distinct parts. Some in their efforts to do good, neither admit nor realize their dependance on divine influence. They disconnect the *command* of the commission from its *preface,* and read, " Go *ye* and convert the world." There are others who would release themselves from the obligation to convert the world. They disconnect the *preface* of this commission from its *command,* and read, " All power is given unto Jesus Christ in heaven and in earth.", therefore " stand still and see the salvation of God." One class hang *their* hopes of the world's conversion on human *instrumentality* and the other on Divine *efficiency.* Now either of these theories is downright presumption. Disunite the first and second parts of this commission, and act on that disunion, and you unhook from the eternal throne, that chain of influences that hangs earth on heaven, and let down the inhabitants of this globe, in one great congregation into hell. Dissever the command of this commission from its preface, and you strike out the link that connects human instrumentality with Divine efficiency and leave us nothing to expect, but disappointment and defeat. No, " What God has joined together let no man put asunder." Let us guard against two fatal extremes. On the one hand, let us never overlook the means in relying on Christ; nor on the other hand, overlook Christ in using the means. In the great work of human salvation, Christ, revealed truth, and Christian agency, are all concerned. There are different senses in which the conversion of the soul is ascribed to each one of them. These three great agencies however are not to change places. Christ will never do for the Church, what he has ordained the Church is to do for herself. Nor can Christians take the place of revealed truth, or revealed truth the place of Christ, without marring heaven's plan. Having stated our proposition, we proceed and remark,

I. THAT THERE ARE TO THE EYE OF REASON VERY MANY AND VERY GREAT DIFFICULTIES IN THE WAY OF THE WORLD'S CONVERSION. The word " *teach* " here means to disciple or make Christians. Hence the import of the command, is that the Church by teaching and baptism, and teaching *after* baptism, is to convert the world. This implies that the world is *unconver-*ted, or that there are many great difficulties in the way of carrying out this commission. Let us mention some of them.

1 *The first we mention is moral death.*—Ascend the mount of vision, and to the spiritual eye, the moral world is one great valley of dry bones. It is true the world is alive, active, physically and intellectually ; but morally, all is still loathsome and

melancholy. The ungodly are as much cut off from the spiritual world, as a corpse is from the natural world. The souls of
the ungodly have none of the spiritual senses. They have no
eye for the light of heaven, no ear for its melodies, no taste for
its pleasures and no energies for its occupations. All are wrapped up in the winding sheets of sin and buried in the grave of
transgression. We have before us a dead world. Nor is it in
the power of all finite beings combined, to raise one of our fellow
men from the grasp of spiritual death. To attempt to raise them
in our own strength, would be as unavailing, as to attempt to
hurl the sun from his position, or turn the angels out of heaven.

2. *Another difficulty in the way of converting the world, is,
ignorance concerning spiritual things.*—As civil and social
beings, mankind may be intelligent, but as moral, immortal
beings, they are ignorant of themselves, of the Bible, of God, and
of Christ. The eyes of their understanding are darkened.
They cannot apprehend spiritual things.

That portion of the world that have heard or read the word of
life, may be regarded as knowing spiritual things *theoretically,*
but ignorant of them *experimentally.* Christ has been revealed
to this class, but not *in* them. The light of the glorious Gospel
shines *around* them but not *into* them. There is outward
light, but inward darkness. The sun of righteousness shines
with healing in his wings, but there is no organ of sight, no power of vision. There is spiritual light, but no spiritual discernment. This is the condition of all unbelievers in christendom.
But the six hundred millions of heathen who live upon the face
of our globe, are ignorant of spiritual things both *theoretically*
and *experimentally.* With them there is darkness without and
blindness within. Their darkness is two-fold. There is neither
eye within, nor sun without. First, their minds are blinded by
the god of this world, and secondly, the moral heavens around
them are palled with impenetrable darkness. Not only does
" darkness cover the earth, but gross darkness the minds of the
people." This deep dense moral darkness then, that covers the
earth is another difficulty in the way, to carrying Christ's great
commission into effect.

3. *Another difficulty is selfishness.*—This was perhaps, the first
sin that ever entered into our world. It consists in supreme self-
love, in making self the centre and circumference of all our
affections, toils, aims and plans. All who are not constrained by
Christ's love, are setting up for themselves to the exclusion of
every other being. This sin splits the world up into as many
contending interests as there are different individuals. Its tendency is to dethrone God and produce misrule and ruin in the moral
universe. It is the great antagonist of the Gospel of Jesus
Christ. It meets the spread of truth at every point, and contests
every inch of its progress. It battles with Christ for dominion

over the human heart. This is a difficulty with which we meet everywhere, in all climes and in all lands. We have to convert a world that is living to itself.

4. *Another difficulty is the world*; not the material globe upon which we stand, but that world which if a man " love, the love of the Father is not in him." Or in other words, the *riches, honors* and *pleasures* of this state of being. These three things are the trinity of the ungodly; and consequently an immense barrier in the way of converting the world to Christ. Riches prevent their votaries from entering into the kingdom of heaven. " It is easier for a camel to go through the eye of a needle than for a rich man to enter the kingdom of God." Honor keeps *its* votaries from believing. " How can ye believe which receive honor one of another?" Pleasure prevents *its* votaries from retaining the truths they hear. " That which fell among thorns, are they which are choked with the *pleasures* of this life." These are God's rivals, for the hearts of the children of men. They wean the affections of men off from God and heaven. Under their influence the impenitent become earth struck. Time becomes their eternity; mammon their god; pleasures their religion; and honor their great reward. Under this triple influence they are spell-bound, held with a grasp of death. This world, as little and as insignificant as it is when brought in comparison with the riches, honors and pleasures of heaven, is keeping thousands away from the cross. It is one of the great obstacles in the way of bringing the soul back to its Redeemer. Where is the minister who has not often been almost overwhelmed in the face of this difficulty?

5. *Another difficulty in the way of the world's conversion is our animal nature.*—If the unconverted world were all soul, all spirit, perhaps our work would not be so difficult; but those whom we have to convert to Christ, are compound beings,— creatures of appetites, passions, and inclinations, which "war against the soul." Their earthly natures sensualize, stupify and embrute the soul. Man's immortal part becomes buried in the senses. His flesh and blood contract and bind the soul down to earth and sin. We have to evangelize those, whose bodies have obtained a complete mastery over their souls. With its ceaseless urgencies and activities, it engrosses the mind and makes it heedless and listless as to a coming judgment and eternity. Men's animal natures conceal from them their high dignity; shut out the prospect of eternity; and make them the mere creatures of time and sense. The corrupting and corruptible nature of men make the whole soul gravitate towards earth. Now to arouse such creatures to a preparation for the other world, is a work too mighty for human powers. It resists the eloquence of the human tongue, and the strength of the human arm.

6. *Another difficulty is the power of habit.*—We have to con-

vert those who not only sin from the natural inclination of their
hearts, but from the power of habit; a habit which has been
increasing and maturing for the last six thousand years. Of all
habits, the habit of sin is the oldest and most inveterate. It falls
in with the current of men's feelings, thoughts and associations,
to sin against God. The world has sinned so long and so much,
that the practice has become a second nature. And humanly
speaking, it is morally impossible to break this habit. How
difficult, if not impossible, it is for the man whose affections have
been set on the earth to transfer them to things above. How
difficult to bring one to tread the valley of humility, who is puffed
up with pride; to inure the lips to prayer, that have been profane; to bring those to walk by faith, that have walked by sight;
to bring those to deny themselves, who have given loose reign to
all their appetites and passions. In a word, how impossible it is
to induce those to walk in the narrow way to heaven, who have
been accustomed to walk in the broad way to hell. No power
beneath the throne of God can break the awful habit of sin.
"Can the Ethiopian change his skin, or the leopard his spots?
then may ye also do good that are accustomed to do evil." This
habit is as universal and confirmed, as it is strange and deplorable.

7. *Satanic influence is another difficulty in the way of carrying
out this commission.*—For the last six thousand years the prince of
darkness has claimed this world as his empire, and mankind as his
subjects. He "is the god of this world," and around his throne all
the millions of his subjects are continually bowing, and worshipping
him with a glowing ardor and burning zeal. He is "the spirit
that now worketh in the children of disobedience." He leads
them captive at his will. He has had such long success and
long experience in the black art of perdition, that he can work
himself into the thoughts and feelings of the sinner and cause
him to sin, while the sinner thinks he is acting out his own volition. By an enchantment, of which the ungodly are unaware,
he is toling them down to hell. He holds his servants bound by
a thousand influences. He blinds their minds, hardens their
hearts and pollutes their imaginations.

8. *Another difficulty in the way of the conversion of the world.
is, aversion for divine things.*—"The carnal mind is enmity
against God." Men are averse to God and his service; and
even opposed to the means which He has instituted for their
recovery. They resist all the attempts that God makes to save
them. He has revealed to them his word, to teach them, and that
they disbelieve. He has caused to be published to them his great
salvation, and that they neglect. He has sent his son to die for
them, and him they reject. He has sent his Spirit to sanctify
them, and him they grieve away. Christ crucified is to an ungodly world a rock of offence. They are displeased with the terms

of salvation. They are too proud . to be saved by the grace of God, abounding through his Son. There are thousands who seem determined to reject Christ even at the hazard of losing their souls forever; who seem willing rather to plunge into hell, than into the bosom of God's eternal love. They would rather lie down in fire for a long eternity, than to love infinite beauty and be thankful for infinite grace. In the bosom of every unconverted man and woman, there is a heart which is averse to holiness and God, and consequently in every unchanged heart there. is a mountainous difficulty in the way to the spread of Christ's Kingdom. As paradoxical as it may seem, mankind are far off from God, and are averse to being brought back. They are sick and dying, and are opposed to being cured; they are lost and unwilling to be saved · they are miserable, and opposed to being made happy. My brethren, not only are the world, the flesh, and the devil, leagued against us in our great work of benevolence, but the heart of the sinner has taken sides against us also. Need another word be said to plunge us in despair? What power can surmount these strong and numerous barriers?

9. *Another difficulty is insensibility.*—Not only is the world depraved, but it is hard-hearted. Those whom we are to win to Christ, have hearts of stone. Amid all the soul-moving motives by which God has surrounded them they are unaffected. Though the cross moved the solid rocks and waked up the sleeping dead, it neither moves their hearts nor disturbs their spiritual slumbers. They are neither charmed by the glories of heaven nor alarmed by the woes of hell. While all the moral universe besides, are deeply concerned in the sinner, he himself is heedless and obdurate. He laughs while heaven weeps. Amid the mingled reverberations of the thunders of Sinai and the death groans of Calvary he is light-hearted. We have before us a hard-hearted world. This difficulty rises before us like a mighty mountain.

We might mention many other difficulties, such as the power of unbelief, the greatness of man's guilt, the love of sin, procrastination, the influence of wicked associates, together with the mighty number who are still under the dominion of satan.

Nor do these difficulties stand alone. They are all interlocked and confederated together. We cannot overcome one without overcoming all. They are all combined, and we have to meet them at once.

Now in view of the *number, magnitude* and *combination* of the difficulties that stand before us, is not the conversion of the world entirely impracticable. Has not enough been said to overwhelm us, and induce us to give up the enterprize of converting the world in hopeless despair? Is it not chimerical to think of carrying out the great commission in the face of such formidable difficulties? Is not this imperfect survey of the obstacles in our path sufficient to cause us to disband our benevolent societies, and spend the balance of our days in taking care of our own souls? Does not the devil stand behind the fires of hell and laugh at our puny efforts to convert the world? Must we give up all in despair? On this spot must the last hope of a dying world be entombed? Must our unconverted fellow-men lie down in ever-lasting burnings? Yes, surely, unless help comes from a higher deliverer. But hark! I hear a sound! it seems to be the voice of encouragement. It comes floating down from the mediatorial throne of our ascended Jesus; listen! *"All power is given unto me in heaven and in earth. Go ye therefore, teaching all nations,"* *&c.* Here is an all-sufficient encouragement to go forth with a bold step in the great work of giving the Gospel to the world. Jesus Christ has taken the salvation of the world into his own hands. The command to go and convert the world is predicated upon the fact, that Jesus Christ has all power in heaven and in earth. This leads me to remark,

II. THAT JESUS CHRIST, IN VIRTUE OF HIS MEDIATORIAL DOMINION AND PRESENCE, ACCOMPLISHES THE CONVERSION OF THE WORLD THROUGH THE INSTRUMENTALITY OF HIS CHURCH.—The entire universe is under the control of Christ. His dominion extends upwards, as high as the flight of the highest archangel; downwards, as low as the bottomless abyss; and outwards, as far as those desolate wilds of immensity, where the wing of an angel never ventured to rove, and whither no created mind ever sent out a solitary thought. Life, death, and unknown worlds, are subject to his command. He shuts the gates of hell and opens the gates of heaven. His frown is hell: his smile is heaven. Now this extent of his power is the reason we should attempt the conversion of the world. As if he had said, "Go, and you shall move under the shield of my omnipotence. I will remove all the mountanious difficulties out of your path. I am not only on the throne of the Universe, to govern, direct and afford you aid, but I will be in your midst, to sustain and encourage you."

His mediatorial dominion, lies back of, and gives efficiency to, our exertions to carry into effect, this commission. We are only the pencil with which he writes his law on the tables of men's hearts. We do not convert the world ourselves, but he does it by us. Some of us plant, and others water, but he gives the increase. And in this way, observe how he removes all the difficulties out of our path, and brings a revolted world back to himself.

Is the world *morally dead?* He is with us to break the grasp of death, and to call the impenitent forth to the resurrection of life. While his Church are, by their prayers, self-denials, and labors, taking away the stone from the tomb of dead souls, he is calling them forth to life eternal. At his command hundreds are daily springing into life. Is the world *ignorant?* He is "the great teacher sent from God." He can open their darkened minds, and can pour into them "the light of the knowledge of the glory of God." He can lift up the heavy eyelids of the spiritually blind, and in a moment, flash light through the whole inner man. He can make the soul "wise unto salvation." He is a prophet to teach the world, as well as a priest to atone for it, and a king to govern it. Is the unconverted world *selfish?* He constrains them no longer to live unto themselves," but unto "him that died for them and rose again." By his invincible grace he can make those who made themselves their centre and circumference, take his cross for their centre and the world of want for their circumference. Is *worldliness* in our way of doing good? There is a power in his cross to crucify the world unto us and us unto the the world. He can throw all the riches of this earth into contempt, by opening to the soul a prospect of the riches of heaven. He can wither, dim, and throw into the shade, all sublunary honor, by bringing before the eye of faith "a far more exceeding and eternal weight of glory." He can cause the soul to turn from the deceitful pleasures of sin with a loathing disgust, and impart to it a desire after the "pleasures which are at God's right hand." How little and mean does this world appear to the penitent sinner, when Jesus Christ reveals to him the charms of his person, and the glories of his cross! Is the world under a *Satanic influence?* He can destroy the works of the devil. He can break the fatal spell by which the prince of darkness holds the ungodly; and translate them out of this kingdom into his own kingdom of light and liberty. Are men's *animal natures* in the way of their embracing the gospel? He can awaken men to a sense of their dignity and immortality, and create a law of holiness in the mind which will overcome the law in the members; and in so doing, the flesh with its affections, becomes crucified. Have the world long cherished *habits* of sin? By his invincible grace, he can revolutionize all the feelings and sentiments of the sinner, and train him to habits of holiness. Have the ungodly a *disrelish for divine things?* He can regenerate the soul, and in so doing, impart to it a relish for himself, the Bible, holiness, and heaven. Are men *hard-hearted?* He is with us to melt their hearts into soft relentings. He can look the obdurate into repentance. He can "take away the heart of stone and give a heart of flesh." He can break up all the springs and deep fountains of tenderness, penitence and love, and cause the sinner "to look on him whom he has pierced, and mourn as one mourneth for an early son, and be in bitterness, as one who is in bitterness for his first born." Are the world *unbelieving?* "He is the author and finisher of our faith." Faith is his gift. Is the *world in love with sin?* He can displace the love of sin, with the love of holiness. By the influences of his Spirit, he can dislodge this passion from the bosom, and fill it with a hungering and thirsting after righteousness. Is *procrastination* an obstacle in the way of the world's conversion? Yes, this is the rock around which the bones of ship-wrecked millions are whitening. But Jesus can arouse men to a sense of their *present* need of salvation, and make them feel that "*now* is the accepted time, and *now* is the day of salvation." Is the guilt of sin in the way? That is removed by the atonement. Are the *power* and pollution of sin in the way? These are removed by the enlightening and sanctifying influences of his Spirit. And is much the larger portion of the inhabitants of our globe still opposed to Christ? Jesus Christ has the power, and he intends to subdue the entire world to himself. "The heathen are given to him for an inheritance and the uttermost parts of the earth for a possession."

In a word, all these difficulties may be grouped together. They may stand before us like mountains piled on mountains. There may be a vast confederacy of evil arrayed against us, but in the strength of our glorified Redeemer, we are an overmatch for them all. "We can do all these things through Christ strengthening us." With him who has all power in heaven and in earth, in our midst, we can move the moral world. "If Christ be for us, who can be against us?" Led on by him, who is the captain of our salvation, we can demolish the strong holds of sin, and storm even " satan's seat." This is the secret of our success, and the source of our encouragement. Christ is in our midst, to support us when faint, to strengthen us when weary, to stimulate us when sluggish, to shield us when assailed, and to make us mighty in pulling down the strong holds of wickedness. "In the power of his might," " we that are feeble, shall be as David, and the house of David shall be as God." O, Brethren! let us think of this great truth, until we feel its importance. Why, not another soul would be converted, but for the power and presence of Christ! But for the mediatorial power of Christ, the Church would never gain another triumph—never have another addition. It is upon this truth the Minister relies, and by it he is encouraged, when he beholds the ministration of the word produce no effect, and not a soul under all the pleadings of divine love, moved to enquire the way to heaven. It is here the missionary finds support and encouragement, while laboring in the dark lands of heathenism. The heart of benevolence, bleeding at every pore, and trembling for the ark of God, can seize on nothing to sustain its hopes, but the blessed truth held out in this text. I preach, only because I firmly believe in the mediatorial power and presence of Christ. But for it, I would close my Bible, and leave the pulpit in despair. In my darkest hour, I can in view of this text, thank God and take courage. Hence we can say, "Now thanks be unto God who always causeth us to triumph in every place." In carrying out this great commission, the victory is ours, but the praise is Christ's.

Having then surveyed the difficulties in the way of the world's

conversion, and having seen also, that the Church, in the strength
of Christ, can overcome them all, let us,

III. MENTION SOME MOTIVES, TO INDUCE CHRISTIANS TO
CONSECEATE THEMSELVES TO CHRIST, IN CARRYING OUT THIS
COMMISSION.

1. *The first motive I bring before you, is the main design of
your redemption.*—Christians have not been redeemed for mere self-
enjoyment. The great design of their conversion to God, is not
answered merely, in their deliverance from sin and hell, and admission into heaven. They have been redeemed and left in this
world, for the purpose of carrying into effect, this commission.
But for this, perhaps, we should have been taken home to heaven
immediately after our conversion. It is the very business and
calling of every Christian, to carry into effect Christ's gracious
designs. Here, many dear brethren are laboriug under an injurious mistake. They seem to think that if they are finally saved
themselves, the great purpose of their redemption has been answered. They forget that the main object Christ had in making
them the *subjects* of his grace, was that they might become the
mediums of that grace. He has blessed us, that we might be a
blessing to others. He has imparted unto us light, that we might
transmit that light to those around us. He has communicated
unto us, the savor of his grace, that we might prevent the world
from going to moral putrefaction. He has been merciful unto us,
and caused his face to shine upon us, that we might make known
his way upon the earth, and his saving health among all nations.
He has restored unto us the joys of his salvation, that we might
teach transgressors his ways, and convert sinners unto him. He
has loved us, given himself for us, and redeemed us from all iniquity, and perfected unto himself a peculiar people, that we might
become zealous of good works, in winning others to him. He
has saved us and washed us in blood divine, that we might be
instrumental in the salvation of others. In a word, he has made
this great commission, the power of God unto our salvation, that
we might convey it to others.

And now, dear brethren, shall the great design of our redemption be defeated? Shall we stay in this world of want, ten, twenty,
thirty, or forty years, after our conversion, without accomplishing
any thing for Christ? While all the works of nature are
answering the end of their *creation*, shall we miss the design
of our redemption? O no. Let this soul-moving motive incite
us to exert our mortal and immortal powers, in conveying to the
world the commission, which was given in love and sealed in
blood.

2. *Another motive which should induce us to consecrate ourselves
to Christ, in carrying out this commission, is gratitude to its
Author.*

Jesus Christ has, upon his followers, a thousand claims—claims not merely derived from creation and providence, but from redeeming love. It is neither a rhetorical nor a figurative, but an actual historical truth, that each Christian has been redeemed by Christ's blood. Our familiarity with this great subject, may have diminished its freshness and fire: it is nevertheless true, that the claims of Christ are just as binding, as if the price had just been paid, and the wonderful scenes of Calvary had just transpired.

Let us, then, approach near the cross. Look at that streaming blood, hear those death-groans, and compute if you can, the sacrifices Jesus Christ once made for you. It was for you he exchanged the bliss of heaven for the agonies of Gethsemane—the adoration of admiring angels for the spitting of Roman soldiers—the diadem of glory for a crown of thorns—a robe of light for Pilate's faded garment—the palace of the universe for the judgment-hall—his body guard of holy and mighty angels for the cruel mockings of puny mortals—the honors of the great white throne for the shameful death of the cross. " He stooped from the height of his throne, to snatch you from eternal flames, to the transports of immortal life; from everlasting contempt, to be kings and priests unto God; to raise you from the turpitude of sin, to the purity of the divine image—from a dungeon to the radiance of his throne—from the society of devils, to commune with angels—from the blasphemies of hell, to the songs of paradise—from universal destruction, to infinite riches—from contraction and degradation, to expand forever in the regions of light." He died the death of the cross, that you might not die the second death. He suffered the penalties of the law in this world, that you might not suffer its penalties in the world to come. He toiled and wept on earth, that you might rest and sing in heaven. He was clothed with a mock-robe and crowned with thorns in this world, that in his Father's kingdom, you might be clad in the white raiment of his righteousnsss, and wear a crown "that fadeth not away." In a word, from his bleeding cross you derive your repentance, your pardon, your regeneration, your justification, your faith, your sanctification, your hope, your joy, and your home on high. He is your help for the past, and your hope for the future.

Nor can you live unto yourself in view of all the benefits you have received from him, who gave you this commission? Can heaven wield a stronger motive to incite you to deeds of goodness, than this? The author of this commission is the being "who loved you and gave himself up for you." He who commands you to exert yourself in giving the gospel to the world, is the being through whom, you are delivered from hell and elevated to heaven. O where is the christian, that can resist this appeal?

3. *Another motive that ought to awaken you to zeal in carrying out the commission, is your covenant vows.*—At the time of your conversion, you voluntarily dedicated yourself to Christ. You stood before your Redeemer, and called heaven and earth to witness,

that until the day of your death, you would love Christ more than
father and mother, and glorify him in your body and spirit, which
are his. You then covenanted to him your all. As you sat by
the cross and wept and sobbed out your heart, you put forth your
finger to the blood that issued from the bleeding cross, and sealed
the covenant. It was recorded in heaven, and ratified in the holy
emblems of baptism. At that deeply interesting hour, you pledged yourself to live for him, who died for you. This covenant you
have never revoked: aye, you have often in your closets and at the
sacramental table, renewed it. These solemn vows are yet upon
you. Will you fulfil them or not? Surely you will. Though
every other covenant be broken, break not the one you made with
your Redeemer. Was your influence *then* given to Christ? Let
that influence be extended to him *now*. Did you *then* make over
to him all your possessions? Let them *now* be held at his disposal. Did you *then* consecrate to him your time? Let every
moment of that time be *now* redeemed and improved, to his glory.
Did you *then* covenant to him your body? Let that body *now*,
with all its members, be employed "as an instrument of righteousness unto God." Did you *then* dedicate to Christ your soul?
Let that soul *now*, with all its powers, be employed in extending
Christ's kingdom. Do *now* what you promised *then*. Christ is
keeping you here, to see whether you will fulfil your covenant
now. Let this covenant that you made under such solemn and affecting circumstances, stimulate you to persevering, strenuous
exertions, to furnish a dying world with the means of salvation.

4. *Another motive that ought to lead you to exert yourselves, in
carrying into effect this commission, is your own happiness.*—Perhaps the most profitable source of *unhappiness* in the Church,
is spiritual inactivity. We never read of the ancient saints com-
complaining of doubts and fears; and the reason was, they wept
and prayed and toiled for Christ. The mercy of the gospel is
twice blessed. It blesses those who impart it, as well as those
who receive it. It is in watering others, that we ourselves are
watered. If the men of this world, in their enterprizes, speak
with enthusiasm of the luxury of doing good, surely there is delight in converting souls to Christ. He who labors and prays for
the salvation of his fellow-men, cannot be unhappy. He opens in
his bosom a source of enjoyment, which will never be fully estimated, till the scenes of the present world are revived in eternity. A
single direct effort to win a soul to Christ, will create a fountain of
enjoyment that will flow on, after the heavens and the earth shall
have been melted down by the last conflagration. I would not
give the small glow of pleasure, that I find amid my severe ministerial labors, for all the delights that earth can yield. While A.
Fuller was preaching a missionary sermon, his own heart was
comforted, his people were revived, and the mourner was converted. The pleasure found in toiling for Christ, is ennobling, satisfying,

and ever-enduring. It is the same kind of pleasure Christ has when he looks from his throne and sees sinners flocking to his cross. It is the same kind of bliss the angels have, when they strike their new and rapturous songs over the conversion of sinners. Brethren, if you would enjoy an anticipated heaven on earth, and ripen for a higher and brighter heaven in eternity—if you would enjoy the approbation of conscience and all holy beings; in both worlds—if from your death-bed-pillow and the last judgment, you would look over your life with delight, make it the great end of your life to do good to the deathless spirits of your fellow-men. Do not so much expect happiness by poring over your past experience, nor alone by contemplating the cross, but by laboring for the conversion of the world.

5. *The last motive I shall mention is the rewards of eternity.*— On the morning of the judgment day, after the resurrection trumpet shall have sounded, we shall stand before our judge. To those, who by patient continuance in well doing, sought to carry out this commission, he will say, " Well done good and faithful servant, thou hast been faithful over a few things, I will make thee ruler over many things; enter thou into the joys of thy Lord." To them on the right he will say, " Come ye blessed of my Father, inherit the kingdom prepared for you from the foundation of the world," and why? Because they, by feeding the hungry, clothing the naked, giving drink to the thirsty, taking in the stranger, and visiting the sick, have carried into effect his last great commission. He will in effect, say to them, " thou hast toiled for me on earth, thou shalt now rest with me in heaven. Thou hast been faithful until death, now receive thy crown of life. Thou hast been occupied in my vineyard, now enter the kingdom I have prepared for you, and employ thyself forever in my praise." This is the last motive I bring before you. It is the " well done" of our final judge; and after this all the undying glories of heaven. It is "a far more exceeding and eternal weight of glory." See that " recompence of the reward." It is all radiant with gold and glowing with saphire. There are golden streets to walk, the river of the water of life to drink, crowns to wear, robes to deck, songs to sing, melodies to hear, pleasures to taste, and splendors to see. All this is held out as a motive to zeal in the service of Christ.

These are the motives with which we are surrounded. If we but open our Bibles, they flash upon us in sunbeams. These motives have already moved two worlds—they have interested heaven and hell, and surely they will move the redeemed on earth. What Christian, surrounded by such considerations as these, does not pant to be useful. Who, with the cross behind him, hell beneath him, sinners around him, and heaven before him, will not rally his last energy, and spend his last breath, that he "may by all means save some ?" Who can live to himself in such a world as this? Who can remain inactive, when souls which God loves, and for which the Saviour bled, are in danger of being lost eternally?

And what we do, must be done quickly. The present scene will soon close. In this field our last blow will soon be struck. The sun of life will soon go down, and that night in which none can work, will close around us. These favorable seasons for doing good will soon have passed for ever. We cannot move the wheels of time backward. Death will put an end to our exertions for the salvation of the ungodly, as well as an end to their space for repentance, and preparation for heaven. Winning souls to Christ, is one privilege that earth has over heaven. Our fellow-men, in vast crowds, are moving on and plunging, uncleansed by Christ's blood, into a dark and dreadful eternity. As they move on to the judgment-seat, they are calling on us for help. The wrath of God, like a dense cloud hovers over them. Soon they will reach the edge of the tremendous gulf:—

> " Oh ! ere the hour of doom,
> Whence there is no reprieve, brethren awake
> From this dark dream.
> The time of hope and probation speed on rapid wings,
> Swift and relentless. What thou hast to do,
> Do with thy might. Haste, lift aloud thy voice,
> And publish to the borders of the pit,
> The resurrection. Then when the ransomed, come
> With gladness unto Zion, thou shalt joy
> To hear the vallies and the hills break forth
> Before them into singing : thou shalt join
> The raptured strain, exulting that the Lord,
> JEHOVAH, God, Omnipotent, doth reign
> O'er all the earth."

And O, Blessed Jesus, let " Thy kingdom come." Let the whole earth be filled with thy glory. AMEN AND AMEN.

A CARD.

The Editor hereby informs his patrons and readers, that in the hope of improving his declining health, he expects to spend the approaching winter in the South; but, that in his absence his place will be supplied, in the editorship of this Paper, by his Christian brethren and particular friends Rev. J. B. Jeter, Rev. James B. Taylor and Rev. Eli Ball. All communications addressed to the Editor, as usual, in this city, whether they appertain to material for publication, or to financial concerns of the Work, will meet with prompt attention.

The close of the third year, brings increased evidence of the utility of the enterprize. To the Baptist denomination and its friends, especially in the South and West, it would be well worthy of support, considered merely as a medium of publicity to discourses preached on extraordinary occasions, on topics of absorbing interest to the churches and to the Redeemer's kingdom everywhere. In the present volume, there are some half a dozen or more sermons of this class, any one of which, is well worth a year's subscription; and several others have been requested of the authors, by the Associations and Conventions before which they were delivered. These are expected to come to hand soon. And although the North, on account of its density of population and its consequent more abundant media of religious intercourse, was not expected to feel so deeply interested in the Work, as the South and West; yet valuable aid is promised from that quarter also.

When the increase of subscribers shall justify it, it is the Editor's design to make each No. consist of at least 24 pages, and to ornament each volume with one or more likenesses of our most distinguished ministers, especially those who have gone to their reward.

At the close of this vol., he would repeat what he has before said—that this Work is not his, but that of the denomination. Its prosperity and even its continuance, with the divine blessing, will depend upon the churches and their pastors. While they furnish the material, and subscribe and read, the Editor will feel encouraged to proceed with his labors, and no longer. May he not hope for a large accession to his subscription list, with the commencement of a new year. It is much easier to double the present list, than it was to attain to what has been done. Success at first, was doubtful. Now there is no doubt. And yet, there are 500 subscribers with only one or two names at the same Post Office, and these for the most part, subscribers who, unsolicited, and without having seen the Work, forwarded their names. In other places where effort has been made, the list is larger than could have been expected..

The Editor solicits again the co-operation of his ministerial brethren; and hopes to meet the approbation of the churches and of heaven.

BAPTIST PREACHER.

ORIGINAL—MONTHLY.

REV. HENRY KEELING,

EDITOR AND PROPRIETOR.

VOLUME IV.

TERMS—ONE DOLLAR PER ANNUM.

RICHMOND:

H. K. ELLYSON PRINTER, MAIN STREET.

1845.

CONTENTS OF VOL. IV.

Page.

JAN.—The Primary Business of the Gospel Ministry, by Rev. J. J. -Finch, of N. C.................................... 1

FEB.—The Success of the Gospel, a ground of grateful triumph to the friends of Christ, by Rev. John O. Turpin, of Va........ 21

The Truth of Christianity Sustained, by Rev. Wm. Carey Crane, of Mississippi 32

MARCH—Remedy for Heart-Troubles, by Rev. Andrew Broaddus, of Virginia 45

APRIL—Perseverance of the Saints, by Rev. Thomas W. Sydnor, of Virginia 61

MAY—The Reasonableness of Faith, by Rev. S. G. Hillyer, of Georgia 85

JUNE AND JULY—Memory, its Influence on the Torments of the Wicked, by Rev. L. A. Alderson, of Va.................. 113

The Importance of a Well Regulated Temper, by Rev. C. D. Mallary, of Ga...................................... 123

AUG.—The Value of Christ's Sacrifice, by Rev. R. B. C. Howell, D. D., of Tennessee 149

The Ministry which God Approves, by Rev. Robert Ryland, of Virginia 158

SEP. AND OCT.—Public Offences, or Church Discipline, by Rev. A. W. Chambliss, of Ala.................................... 173

NOV.—The Fears of the Flock Calmed by the Voice of the Shepherd, by Rev. T. F. Curtis, of Ala.................... 213

The Resurrection of the Dead, by Rev. R. B. C. Howell, of Tennessee 224

DEC.—The Co-operation of the Churches with the Ministry, by Rev. Thos. G. Keen of Kentucky 237

THE
BAPTIST PREACHER.

VOL. IV.   January, 1845.   NO. 1.

THE PRIMARY BUSINESS OF THE GOSPEL MINISTRY:

A Sermon, preached before the Baptist State Convention of North Carolina, in the city of Raleigh, October 20, 1844, by Rev. J. J. Finch, and published by their request.

—

" *Preach the word,*"—2 Tim. iv : 2.

—

The gospel ministry is a divine institution. The same facts which shew that christian churches were organized by divine sanction, also show, that an order of men were set apart to instruct and guide them. If some have made too much of the ministry, indulging in a kind of man worship, and regarding even the circulation of the scriptures as useless, where they are unattended with the living teacher, others have attached too little importance to it as an instrument in the conversion of sinners and the sanctification of believers. In proof of this, we refer to the fact, that many churches content themselves without the living ministry,—to the fact, that so little is contributed to its support,—to the fact, that but little, comparatively, is done to send it to the destitute,— and to the still more astonishing fact, that many professed christians oppose the measures employed to send it to all men.

In searching for the causes which have led to this depreciation of the christian ministry, we are induced to believe that it is to be ascribed, in no small measure, to deficiency in the ministry themselves. Some of them, instead of correcting, have inculcated the very errors referred to; others are so occupied with earthly things, that they do not study to shew themselves approved, and consequently their preaching is not edifying and cannot be much respected; and others are so given to change, heresy and contention, as to render it doubtful whether they do more good than evil; and thus,

through the fault of the ministers themselves, an institution of
God, which is intended to confer the greatest benefits on mankind, is divested of its efficiency and often sinks into contempt.

There are, doubtless, many crying sins in our land that
call for reformation, but the amendment must *begin* in the
pulpit.   It is there that many others take their rise, and
from hence an influence must go out for their correction.
The ministry must throw a sacredness and importance
around their office; they must so act and preach, as to carry
the truth with convincing power to the heart, and make men
feel that they "are the servants of the most high God,
which shew unto them the way of salvation." And believing, as we do, that here lies the principal hinderance to
the progress of our Zion and the general spread of truth,
which we have assembled in convention to promote, we
have concluded to address you, on this occasion, on *the primary business of the gospel ministry.*

I. As to the *object* of preaching, it might seem unnecessary to say that the salvation of souls should be the aim of
every sermon, were there not so many prostituted to inferior
purposes.   There are many pulpit exhibitions, directed to
other ends much more than they are to the salvation of sinners.   It is enough, if they meet a professional engagement,
or fill up the hour allotted to religious worship. It is enough,
if they suit the tastes and wishes of the people, and bring
fame to the speaker.   It is enough, if they make manifest
the party lines and increase the adherents of a sect, whether
any souls are converted or not.   And thus, preaching is perverted from its appropriate object, to others of an exceptionable
character.

We would not have ministers to be indifferent to their
fame, their secular interests, or the success of their party;
but none of these should be the prominent object of their
preaching. How should we feel, to see those who were sent
to effect the deliverance of their fellow-men from some temporal calamity, pursuing other objects, and were entertaining the sufferers to whom they were sent, with discussions
which have no connection with their necessities? But are
not ministers sent to effect the deliverance of souls from
eternal death? Are they not called "ambassadors for
Christ?" (2 Cor., v: 20.) And is not the object of their
embassage said expressly to be, "to turn men from darkness to light, and from the power of satan unto God"?
(Acts, xxvi: 18.) Why, then, do they waste so much of

their time and strength upon subjects which have no proper
connection with their great object? Why is the pulpit perverted from its solemn business of saving souls, to every speculation and contrivance that this stirring age can invent?
It is no justification of such a perversion of the pulpit, to say
that the objects to which it is applied are good. Farming,
merchandise, literature and philosophy are good, but are
these the proper objects for the labors of the pulpit? Is the
saving of men so light a duty, that it leaves leisure to devote
to other objects? Did Paul think so, when he said, "who
is sufficient for these things?" Did he, especially, make
his public discourses subservient to any other end than that
of winning souls to Christ, and establishing christians in the
faith? Paul, though capable of entertaining his hearers on
topics more congenial to their tastes, and which would have
gained him much more popularity, determined to know
nothing among them, save Jesus Christ and him crucified;
because it was the preaching of the cross that saved them
that believed. 1 Cor., i: 18—21; ii: 2. How different, in
this respect, was the strain of apostolic preaching from
much that passes current in the present day? Then it was
directed exclusively to the object of saving souls; now it is
perverted, to the thousand and one projects by which society
is agitated. And the dullness with which sermons are delivered and heard, arises in no small measure from this perversion. The preaching does not bear upon its proper object,—
the preacher is not inspired with the aim of pulling his
hearers out of hell,—the hearers are not made to feel that
the preacher is trying to save,—and hence their mutual apa-
thy. The lawyer is not dull, when he pleads for the life of
his client. The orator is not dull, when he speaks for the
endangered liberties of the people. And the preacher would
never be dull if he always aimed, as he should, at the salvation of his hearers.

II. In accomplishing this object, ministers should "preach
THE WORD," relying upon that for success, and not other
things. The term word, as here used, embraces all the doctrines and duties of christianity. This is the *subject* of the
gospel ministry. On this, the minds of the people are to be
enlightened, and by it their hearts are to be affected, and
their actions controlled. It is not the office of the minister,
the touch of his hand, or the mysterious virtue of ordination, that is to save the soul, or turn the sinner to God; but
the truth which he is employed in carrying to the minds of

the hearers. The truth is affecting, through whatever medium it passes; and without it, no knowledge of mysteries, no gift of tongues, no chain of ordinations, can unite a soul to Christ. This is a fact that merits careful consideration at the present day, when circumstances are tending to turn the attention of the people from the efficacy of truth, and fix it on men and measures. Is it not distinctly avowed at this day, and zealously advocated in our State, that truth is not efficacious, unless attended with certain ministerial attributes, and conveyed through a certain chain of ordinations? Those who have not "what they call apostolical succession," whatever degree of truth they may feel or practice, are regarded by this school, says archbishop Whately, "either as out-casts from the household of faith, or at best, as in a condition "analagous to that of the Samaritans of old," who worshipped on mount Gerizim, or as in "an intermediate state between christianity and heathenism," and as "left to the uncovenanted mercies of God." *

Is not this attaching too much importance to the personal properties of the ministry, and not enough to the truth which they are sent to proclaim? And it certainly cannot be amiss to ask the successors of the Apostles, if their predecessors, the Apostles, taught their hearers this? Did they wilfully make the impression on the minds of their hearers, that truth borrowed any of its efficacy from them? Did they not, on the contrary, oppose all such impressions, and throwing themselves into the shade, point to the truth as the effective agency? As Peter and John went into the temple, on a certain occasion, they were instrumental in curing a man who had been lame from his birth; and "all the people ran together into the porch that is called Solomon's, greatly wondering. And when Peter saw it, he answered unto the people, ye men of Israel, why marvel ye at this? or why look ye so earnestly on *us*, as though by our own power or holiness we had made this man to walk?" And then exhibiting certain facts concerning Jesus, he added: "And his name, through faith in his name, hath made this man strong, whom ye see and know; yea, *the faith* which is by him, hath given him this perfect soundness in the presence of you all." Acts iii: 1—16. The difference, then, to say the least, between the Apostles and their successors, (?) is, that the former thought the people attached too much importance to their agency, while the latter think they attach

*Kingdom of Christ, p. 115.

too little to theirs; that the former insisted upon the efficacy of truth, while the latter insist on the efficacy of ordination.

But those who are far removed from excessive reliance upon the grace of ordination, run into a similar error, by relying too much upon *artificial means,* and not enough upon the power of truth. We·have nothing to do, in this discourse, with the question, whether the Holy Spirit acts only through the medium of the written word, or separately; nor have we any thing at all to do with the agency which is necessary to give the word success, as it is certainly no part of ministerial duty to control such agency. We are concerned, at present, only with the fact that the truths of the gospel are the means appointed to save lost sinners, and that the ministry are charged with the duty of proclaiming them for this end. They are sent to deliver a particular message,—to open a specific subject,—to proclaim the word of life, not human speculations. But how many harangues there are in the pulpit, in which there is precious little, and sometimes not a particle of the gospel. Some preach tradition, the philosophers and fathers, much more than they do Christ and his Apostles. Many continually insist upon metaphysical subtleties, that are far removed from the wants and sympathies of their hearers; while many others fill up their discourses with common tales and anecdotes, which may move the passions for a season, but which leave the mind unenlightened, and the heart unaffected by the truths of the gospel. And what makes this latter expedient the more dangerous, is, it is so taking with the people, it is so favorable to neglect of the study, and is so much better adapted to present effect, than the presentation of substantial truth.

> " The honest seer, who spoke the truth of God
> Plainly, was left with empty walls; and round
> The frothy orator, who busked his tales
> In quackish pomp of noisy words, the ear
> Tickling, but leaving still the heart unprobed,
> The judgment uninformed,—numbers immense
> Flocked, gaping wide, with passions high inflamed,
> And on the way returning, heated, home,
> Of eloquence, and not of truth conversed."

If it be said that sinners will not be affected by the simple preaching of the truth, and that such exciting elements are necessary to secure their conversion, the answer is:

1. That such things are not hereby excluded, in their *proper* use. There is a vast difference between introducing incidents to clear the point of an argument and to give impressiveness to truth, and filling a discourse with startling occurrences, merely for effect. In the one case, the gospel is preached, in the other, stories are related; in the one case, the effect is produced by the truths of the gospel, in the other, by physical causes; by the exciting nature of common facts, and the ingenuity, often, the affectation of the narrator.

2. That it is not for us to decide upon the efficiency of the means, our duty lying only in preaching the word, not in making it effective. If it fall unheeded upon sinners' ears, we have discharged our duty, provided we have truly preached the word.

3. That such a statement reflects upon the wisdom of God, in appointing an instrument to an end, for which it is found insufficient! And

4. That whatever effect may be produced by other means, sinners are only *really benefited* in proportion as they are affected by the truth. Suppose the truth fails to affect the sinner's heart, and to supply the deficiency something else is brought forward, which does succeed in producing an effect, the subject of it is no better off than before, because it is not *the* effect required. And though this may satisfy those who aim only at effect, and who think that good is accomplished whenever there is an effect, by whatever agency it is produced, it cannot satisfy those who feel that their hearers' safety depends upon their subjection to the truth.

A minister, for instance, may wish to produce in his hearers the feeling of penitence, and for this purpose he exhibits their sinfulness and God's goodness; but to his surprise, this exhibition of truth fails to produce this result, and to bring about the desired manifestations of sorrow, he exhibits death-bed scenes, speaks of departed friends, and reminds the hearers of their own approaching destruction, &c., and suddenly their tears begin to flow, and many are ready to assume any posture, or do almost any thing the preacher may suggest;— but is there any penitence in all this? Many are made sad and joyful by the use of such means, who have never been subdued under a sense of their guilt, nor healed by the peace-speaking blood of Christ. And in this way, it is to be feared, many are sent to their graves with false hopes, while many others are hardened in sin. It is for this reason that I

here present the matter to your consideration, and not from
any desire to reflect upon any of my brethren. It is an
awful thought, that the very institution which God has set
apart to *save* men, should be the means of deluding them to
their eternal *ruin!* But that this is the result of that excessive use of artificial means, which is too prevalent in many
sections of our country, no one can doubt. Let it be borne
in mind, that it is not only necessary to produce a change in
the hearts and conduct of men, but a change of a particular
type; and that *this* change can only be produced by the
truths of the gospel. It is not enough, therefore, that the
heart is affected, it must be affected by correct views of truth;
nor is it enough that a change of action is induced, it must
be induced by the motives presented in the word: and before
we pronounce that word insufficient for such purposes, we
ought to be sure that we have fully and fairly exhibited it.
Were the same pains taken in studying the sacred oracles,
that there is in collecting common stories, and even scripture
facts opened with the same clearness, earnestness and force
with which inferior things are narrated, there would be less
cause to complain of the inefficiency of that word which the
Apostle says is " quick and powerful."

III. The word should be preached in its *fullness* and *proportions.* The doctrines and duties of christianity are not
systematically recorded in the scriptures, yet they constitute
one harmonious system. It is the business of the ministry
to comprehend all the parts of this system, and to exhibit
them to their hearers in their proper form and relations. It
is just as important that every part should have its proper position, as it is that its nature should be properly defined. We
may say nothing false about Christ, but if we fail to exhibit
the whole truth concerning him, or should we give him a
wrong position in the scheme of redemption, we may encourage the self-righteous, the Socinian and the infidel. We
may faithfully instruct our hearers respecting the nature of
faith and works, but if either is unduly elevated or depressed, or if the relation which they sustain to each other is not
exhibited, they may become satisfied with faith without
works, or with works without faith. We may present correct
views concerning the nature and form of baptism, but if we
teach it at the wrong place in the christian system, we may
more effectually endanger the salvation of our hearers, than
if we were to expel it entirely, or substitute something else
in its place. That which is salutary in its place, is often de.

structive out of it.   We see this verified daily in the physical
world around us, and it is equally true in the moral. ˙Much
of the heresy, contention and division, with which the christian world has been, and is afflicted, may be traced to this
very fault.   Some parts of scripture doctrine are pushed too
high, and others are sunk too low.   Each minister has his
chosen points, upon which he is all the time insisting, while
others, perhaps equally important, are never touched, or but
slightly glanced at.   Some preach nothing but doctrine, others nothing but duty ; some deal chiefly with the externals
of religion, ordinances, discipline, &c., while others, leaving
their hearers ignorant upon these points, work only upon a
certain class of emotions ; some are always insisting on election, and with apparent zeal for the scripture doctrine on this
point, run into the absurdities of Antinomianism ; others, dis-
gusted with this excess, dwell so much upon human liberty
and ability, as to lead their hearers into the equally absurd
excesses of Arminianism.   And thus, each wrapped up in
his *own* idea, sees and talks of nothing else.

Is not this one cause of the continual rise of parties
among christians, which is one of the greatest curses now
abroad in the land.   What gave birth to the party called
Campbelites, Disciples, or whatever title they choose to be
known by ? It was giving excessive prominence to some few
points, laying too much stress upon baptism, and presenting
it at the wrong place in the christian system.   What produced Millerism, which for the last few years has caused such
disturbance among the churches at the North, but from
which a kind Providence has preserved us at the South ? It
was the pressure of one single idea concerning the end of
the world.   What gave rise to the Perfectionists, as a party ?
Excessive zeal on one view of christian perfection.   And not
to mention a thousand others, which must be familiar to the
reader of history, or the observor of events, we would ask
what is it that divides our countrymen at present, in their
political and ecclesiastical relations, and which, unless it is
checked, must sever the union into bleeding fragments ? It is
the *Abolition mania* on a single point, which blazes in every
newspaper, every pulpit, at every gathering of the people in
a certain section of our country.   This is the one thing
needful which must speak on all occasions, and be heard by
every audience, of whatever materials composed, and for
whatever purpose convened.   Even those general institutions, which were organized for a specific and separate object,

with a view of combining the efforts of christians throughout the Union, on a few points of duty where all are agreed, however they might differ about other things, *these* must become tributary to abolitionism, or they must be *altered* or *dissolved!* It is not enough that they attend to the business for which they were constituted,—it is not enough that they send the word of life to the destitute, by which sinners are converted and believers are built up; they must favor certain movements against slavery or they accomplish nothing worth holding together for.

If the several classes of enthusiasts mentioned, were right in their views on the points referred to, which we are not prepared to admit, still they make them productive of all the vice that can attach to the rankest error, by insisting on them too exclusively, and pressing them beyond proper bounds. There is more than one truth in the Bible to be preached, and more than one form of vice in the world to be corrected. Let us aim, then, at a full exhibition of the truths contained in God's word, and

> "Nothing conceal, nothing extenuate,
> Nor set down aught in malice."

When this is done by all the ambassadors of Christ, the christian family will become united, a healthy circulation will pervade our spiritual system, and every function will assume its proper activity.

IV. The word should be preached seasonably. Ministers should not only look into the word to see what truths it contains, but also into the character, circumstances and wants of their hearers, that they may give to each his portion in due season. Every sermon should, in a certain sense, be personal,—it should come directly to the wants and duties of those addressed.

This was the characteristic of apostolic preaching. On the day of Pentecost, Peter's hearers did not have to guess that they were aimed at,—they did not have to infer that their cases might possibly be embraced in the positions advanced by the Apostle: they were singled out by name,— "Ye men of Israel, hear these words,"—and continuing the personal form of address, he proceeds to specify their crimes: "Jesus of Nazareth, a man approved of God among you by miracles, and wonders, and signs, which God did by him, in the midst of you, as ye yourselves also know: Him, being

*2

delivered by the determinate counsel and foreknowledge of God, *ye* have taken and by wicked hands have crucified and slain." The effect was electrical. "Now when they heard this, they were pricked in their heart, and said . unto Peter, and to the rest of the Apostles, men and brethren, what shall we do?" Acts ii: 22, 23, and 37. How different is this from many discourses of the present day, which seem to be delivered without any regard to the actual wants of the hearers. Some labor hard to prove what their hearers never doubted—to refute objections which they never raised; while others are continually rectifying speculative errors, which their hearers would happily never know any thing about, but for such attempts at their correction. It is sometimes necessary to do this, to guard the hearers against errors and sophistries, by which they *may* be assailed; but as a general thing, it is best to direct the instruction of the pulpit, to the existing wants of the people. As one shot will do more execution, which hits the mark, than ten thousand which miss it, so one word, seasonably uttered, will accomplish more than volumes that are inappropriate. The most successful preachers, have ever been remarkable for the directness of their discourses. Baxter, Bunyan, Wesley, Whitfield and Davis, made their hearers feel that the interests of their souls were pending, from the commencement to the end of their sermons. They aimed not at fine expressions, nor were they satisfied to know, that what they preached was true and acceptable; they aimed to fasten appropriate truth in the living hearts before them, and by it, to draw them to the cross. Hence their success. And if the same directness characterized the pastoral instruction of the present day, there would be less need for calling in revivalists, and resorting to extra stimulants to arouse the people. Nothing is so rousing as truth. The reality in man's condition, is more affecting than any fancied state. Tell man the plain truth of the Bible, concerning his case, press its sharp point upon his slumbering conscience, and no additional stimulant will be needed.

For the want of appropriateness, many discourses, which are rich in thought, are powerless. An audience can generally tell whether a minister's instructions are called for or not, by the circumstances under which they are delivered, and though what is said may be true, yet it excites disgust if presented unseasonably. A minister may preach his distinctive sentiments at proper times and places, but to go out of the way to do it is highly indiscreet, and never fails to bring one's cause into contempt. It is not enough, therefore, that what is preached is the word, it must be dealt out as the varying wants of the hearers require.

V. The word should be preached affectionately. The manner is little less important than the matter; for if the manner be disagreeable, the matter, however important, will often fail to secure attention, and of course, cannot affect the heart. There are some religious instructors, who seem to think that roughness and severity are necessary parts of fidelity, and that the truth cannot be preached without making somebody angry. This is certainly a mistake. Persons are more frequently excited to anger by a needless attack upon their opinions, and a coarseness and violence in their assailants, than they are by a candid exhibition of New Testament sentiments. There is much indulgence of passion—much personal denunciation and invective in the pulpit and press, under the pretence of contending earnestly for the faith once delivered to the saints. We should never shun to declare the whole counsel of God for fear of giving offence, but we should take care that the truths inculcated are not obstructed in their progress by an unbecoming harshness of manner. The *fortiter in re* should be blended with the *suaviter in modo.* "Speak the truth in love," is an inspired injunction and one quite as important as many that are so earnestly insisted on. How often is the greater command violated, while contending for the smaller How often are weighty truths rendered repulsive, through the severe epithets and harsh tones in which they are conveyed? And those who thus defeat themselves often attach all the blame to the bad hearts of the people, or the prejudice that prevails around them against the truth. They are all the time croaking over the unpopularity of their cause, while the obstacle perhaps is found in themselves.

Making allowance for over sensitive minds, which are ready to take offence at every thing that is contrary to their own views, there is no intelligent community that will be offended by the seasonable and affectionate exhibition of a minister's sentiments on any subject that may come within the range of his duty. The common fault is, that ministers are not content with exhibiting their own views, they must needlessly attack the opinions of those who differ from them. It may be proper, in defending truth, to refer to the history of religious opinions, to expose the errors of those who have perverted it, especially when our hearers are in danger of

falling in with such errors, and to avail ourselves of a fair
contrast between opposing sentiments; but it is wrong to be
needlessly throwing out personal reflections, bitterness and
invective; it is wrong to occupy the sacred hours of worship
with the discussion of topics, when diversity is no fault, and
uniformity would be no great virtue.   The better way is to
give a full exhibition of truth, and leave its opponents to
stand if they can.   When the foundation is removed, the
house will fall without any help.   If we convince a man of
the truth of christianity, we most effectually guard him
against whatever may be offered against that cardinal point.
I we establish the divinity of Christ, we need not ridicu e
the Socinians to expose their error.   If we satisfy our
hearers that believers *only* are proper subjects for baptism and
church-relationship, of course, they are then convinced that
unbelieving infants are not proper subjects for this ordinance.
And if we prove by substantial reasons, that immersion is
essential to a valid baptism, we thereby explode the assumption, that other applications of water are baptism.   In this
way all is gained that is desirable, while we avoid the prejudices which are usually aroused by a direct allusion to the
sentiments of others.   It is proper, however, sometimes to
expose the absurdity of opposing views on the points here
referred to; all that we mean is, that as a general thing we
shall most effectually put down error by *establishing* truth.
We do not materialy benefit our hearers by convincing them
that certain opinions are false, any more than we should
benefit a hungry man by convincing him that what was
offered him as food contained no nourishment; we must
furnish the starving with the needed supply, if we would do
them good, and we must establish our hearers in what is
positively right, if we would save them.   And hence those
discourses which deal chiefly with the negative side of subjects, while they communicate but little on the positive,—
which very fully disclose the defects of erroneous theories,
but do not exhibit the nature and evidences of the true,—
may lead the hearers to reject what is false, but will hardly
bring them to embrace what is right.   If, then, it be proper
to exhibit our opinions upon the evident truths of the gospel,
without needless reflections upon those of others, much more
is this necessary upon those endless minor points, when there
may exist an innocent diversity.   As to the dress of ministers while officiating, form and attitude of prayer, manner of
singing and preaching, and many other similar things, the

scriptures give us no specific instruction, and those of, one way in such matters, should not be severe against those of another. The value of a sermon or prayer, does not depend upon its being written, printed, or extempore, but upon the qualities of the matter; the efficacy of preaching does not depend upon the garments or official attributes of the minister, but upon the measure of truth communicated, and the spirit with which it is imparted and received; nor does the acceptance of sacred music depend upon its being vocal or instrumental, but upon its expressing the fervent sentiments of the worshippers. While, then, we aim at the greatest fidelity in preaching the word, let us avoid severity against those who differ from us on points respecting which the word is silent; and while contending earnestly for the faith once delivered to the saints, let us be equally careful to exhibit that truth with love. An opposite course betrays a little mind, violates the express precepts of christianity, and brings the cause of truth into contempt. And in consequence of this very fault, exceedingly prevalent at present in this country, the press and the pulpit have given many a stab to the heart of christianity.

VI. Preaching the word is not the occasional, but the exclusive business of the ministry, to which all their time and energies should be devoted. Under a former head, we have said that preaching should aim at the salvation of souls, not at other things, and under this we say that ministers should give themselves to preaching, not to other things. A minister may aim at the salvation of souls whenever he preaches, but he may preach too little. He may have so many other things to attend to, that preaching may be only an occasional service to fill up time not otherwise employed, not his *primary business.* We do not mean, of course, that ministers should be all the time proclaiming in the pulpit; a large portion of their time must be employed in the study, for them to have something worth announcing from the pulpit. We mean, that the *duties* of their *office,* including studying, visiting and preaching, should constitute their business, and receive their undivided attention.

This is certainly according to apostolic instruction, which is less regarded in relation to this subject, it seems to us, than almost any other. No minister among us feels, at his ordination, that he then consecrates himself to the *business* of preaching, and that he is expected to devote himself *wholly* to it. The call to the ministry, ordination, &c., only mean, it would seem from general usage in our State, that ministers *may* preach occasionally, if they choose, but that the most of their time *may* be devoted to other pursuits.   Hence, a great many of our best preachers are school teachers, agents, farmers, merchants, &c., and many are kept out of the ministry, who feel inwardly drawn towards it, because they see no way to give themselves wholly to its duties, as they conscientiously feel every minister should do.   Now, how does this state of things appear in the light of that precept, which, referring to the duties of his office, says to every minister, " *give thyself* WHOLLY *to them.* 1 Tim., iv : 15.   Doubtless, there is a fault somewhere, and it becomes us to ask, on whom does it lie ?   May it not lie partly on ministers themselves ?   They, like other men, may be too worldly minded, too anxious to accumulate, too distrustful of Providence.   Some, who make their poverty an excuse for ministerial neglect at first, change their plea when fortune smiles upon them, and they must neglect preaching to attend to secular affairs, because of the smallness of their resources ; now they excuse themselves because of the extent of their possessions.   They have so much on hand of a secular nature, that they have no time scarcely for the duties of the study or the pulpit.   Two questions may be put to such cases, to shew the fallacy of such an apology :—1. Why have you become encumbered with so much ? and 2. Finding you are obstructed in the work of the ministry, by your worldly possessions, why do you not relieve yourself of your burden by distributing to those who need ?   If you are weighed down with your earthly clogs, you need not *continue* so.   And we are satisfied, that in such cases, one of two things should be done ; they should throw off their worldly hinderances and give themselves to preaching the word, or surrender the ministry and support others in their place.   The ministry are further at fault in this thing, for not having faithfully instructed the people on the duty of supporting the gospel, as many more are hindered by the paucity, than the abundance of their means, while our membership are amply able, if they were willing, to sustain any competent minister throughout the State.

The sin in question lies, doubtless, most heavily on the churches, in withholding from the ministry an adequate support.   The same authority which requires ministers to give themselves wholly to the business of preaching, has *or-dained* that those who preach the gospel, shall live of the gospel. But the churches, generally, have not enabled their ministers to live of the gospel, and consequently, the ministers have not been able to give themselves wholly to the duties of their profession. And what is the result? The churches supplied have lean preaching, while large sections are uncultivated. The fields are white for harvest, but many who are sent to gather the fruits, are driven by necessity to other occupations. Souls are perishing in crowds, daily, for the lack of vision, and many heralds of the cross, sent to administer the word of life, are immersed in worldly cares!

VII. Finally, we remark, that the business of the ministry will not be discharged, till the word is preached to *all men.* All men have a common nature—have inherited the same depravity—can be saved only through the same Mediator—and are hasting to the same eternity; why should they not all hear the same glad tidings? Why should they not be made acquainted with Him, on whom they must call in order to be saved, but in whom they must believe, before they will call on him, and of whom they must hear, before they can believe on him? Rom. x: 13, 14. If the gospel is necessary for us, why not for other men, and if for some, why not for all?

But we do not rest this duty on simple inference; the Saviour has expressly commanded it,—"Go ye into *all* the world and preach the gospel to *every* creature." This command could not apply only to those immediately addressed, for the duty commanded was more than they could perform, and the promise annexed, which was intended to encourage those embraced in the command, extends to the end of the world. (Compare, Mark xvi: 15, with Matt. xxviii: 20.) And for the same reason, it does not bind any one minister, now, to preach the gospel to every creature. It only binds every one to do what he can for the universal spread of the gospel, and teaches us that the work of the ministry will not be accomplished, till every nation and tribe are made acquainted with the scheme of redemption through Jesus Christ. More than eighteen centuries have passed since this last command of Jesus was announced, and yet the larger portion of the earth's inhabitants, have never heard the gospel! What is the cause of this delay? It is sometimes objected to christianity, that it is known to so few of the human race, and that were it what it claims to be, God would have made it more public. But why is it not more public? Did not the Saviour *sufficiently* provide for its publicity, in the constitution of the church, and the appointment of the christian ministry? And had this great missionary society, the church, and these heralds of the cross discharged their duty, would not the gospel long since, have been preached to all men? Charge not then this fault to God, who gave his Son to die for the world, nor to the Son, who having appeared for the rescue of sinners, has sent his servants to offer salvation to all men: but charge it to the negligence and worldliness of his servants, who have lost sight of the missionary character of the church, who have turned away from the high trust committed to them, and Jonah like, are sailing in pursuit of other things.

In conclusion, we observe, that the duties of the ministry, as now specified, impose a corresponding duty on the church at large. When God commands the performance of any thing, the command embraces whatever is necessary to its accomplishment. He has commanded the preaching of the word,—the preaching of the word to all men. But the word cannot be preached without preachers; how then are they to be obtained? God must provide them, is the answer, and this is true,—but how does he provide them? Has christian instrumentality nothing to do with it? God provides our daily bread, but has our activity nothing to do with its attainment? If we are instructed to pray for our daily bread, we are also instructed to pray the Lord of the harvest, to send forth more laborers into the harvest. Luke x: 2. But what a man prays for, he is bound to use proper means to secure; when a man prays for bread he exerts himself to get it, and looks for an answer to his prayer, in the blessing of God *upon* his labors, which renders them successful. So, when christians ask the Lord to send forth ministers, if they would be consistent, they must seek them. Here is the point where christians fail,—they expect spiritual blessings in a manner totally different from that in which they get their temporal supplies. They offer a few cold prayers to God for ministers and grace, but do not labor for them; while they do not trust to such prayers, unaccompanied with exertion, for food and raiment. While, therefore, we rightly look to God to provide ministers, let us not overlook the means by which he operates in providing them. Christian labor and seminaries of learning, are among these means. God could as easily carry on his work without ministers, as he can provide ministers without christian instrumentality. If, as christians, you say God has no need of your help, why may not ministers say the same? And if God converts sinners through the instrumentality of preachers, why may he not raise up preachers through the instrumentality of christians? Christians, therefore, must admit *their* obligation in this matter, or say that the preaching of the gospel is not a *necessary* instrument in saving the souls of men; but as this would be a direct contradiction of the scriptures, no *christian* can say it.

But, to preach the word, as has been stated, requires certain qualifications. To give a full exhibition of the word, seasonably and in its proportions, demands a vast range and depth of knowledge. A minister must be acquainted with the grammar of his vernacular tongue, for how can he get the meaning of sentences, till he understands the harmony and government of their several members? He must understand the meaning of words, for it is through these the principles are conveyed which he is to unfold to others; and as our language is formed from various other languages, he must have some acquaintance with these foreign elements, if he would safely interpret the lively oracles. Not only is our language formed from other tongues, but the English Bible, which many think English learning all sufficient to construe, contains many transferred words; how then can a minister intelligently preach the whole truth, when a part of it is wrapped up in Greek and Hebrew terms, with which he has no acquaintance? It is on this ground that we urge the importance of an acquaintance with the languages, to the minister; without it, he cannot get the meaning of the Bible, on many points, and what he cannot get, he cannot communicate.

Besides this, such are the local allusions in the Bible, the change in customs and manners, the variety and philosophical depth of the subjects upon which it treats, that one must be well acquainted with geography, history, antiquity, and the sciences, to be able to show himself a workman that needeth not to be ashamed. Eighteen centuries intervene between us and the birth-day of christianity. It has passed through many vicissitudes, and is now variously construed in its doctrines and duties. Papists and semi-papists claim on their side the voice of antiquity, and intrench themselves among the Greek and Latin fathers. How are they to be successfully met and vanquished, but by those whose researches extend over the same period, who can expose their mis-quotations, their fallacies, and false criticisms? The further we get from the apostolic age, the higher must the stand-

*3

ard of ministerial learning arise ; and we are not only getting further off every day, but knowledge is spreading among the people, demanding increasing knowledge in their instructors. Despite of what enthusiasts may say to the contrary, it requires an intelligent, well furnished mind, permanently to influence an intelligent community. There must be an adaptation in the instrument, to the materials upon which it is to operate. Hence, the churches ought to see to it, that those whom they call to the functions of the ministry, are qualified for their work. We do not say that every one should be a graduate, but there ought to be a degree of information, below which no one could be admitted to ordination. Let candidates spend more time as licentiates and in preparatory studies, before they are admitted to the full responsibilities of the ministry. It will be better for them, and better for the cause. Let christians urge them to study, instead of urging them so hastily to the pastoral office, and let them furnish the means to enable them to pursue their studies till they are qualified for their work. Have we not religion enough among us, to say that no young man of promise, who desires to enter the ministry, shall fail for want of means, or be compelled to enter unfurnished for his work? There are many now drawn to the work, and thirsting for knowledge, who are kept back for the lack of means to enable them to advance. Can we suffer them to be kept back any longer, without incurring the guilt of hindering the fulfilment of the Saviour's last command? But, besides furnishing the means to enable them to acquire knowledge, we must furnish the means of support, to enable them to use it for the advancement of the cause. If christians refuse to furnish the necessary support, ministers, of course, will be kept back from preaching the word as they ought, and their excuse will be, Lord we would have gladly obeyed thy command, and given ourselves wholly to publishing the word of life, but *thy people* would not let us; they closed our lips by their parsimony, and compelled us, against our wish, to follow other business.

Here, then, is our business. As ministers, thus to preach the word for the healing of the nations; and as christians, to apply our means and energies to raise up ministers for this work, to send them forth well furnished for their duties, to sustain them under their exhausting toils, and never to cease the struggle, while any portion of our fallen race is ignorant of the great salvation.

It was to aid in this great work, that this convention was organized. It seeks to do this in three ways. 1st. By assisting indigent young men, who are called to the ministry, in acquiring a suitable education. 2d. By sending itinerant preachers to the destitute sections of our own State. And 3d. By contributing to the spread of the gospel among heathen nations. It is to these objects you are now invited to contribute,—objects so clearly scriptural and important, that they need only be clearly stated, it seems to us, to gain the support of every friend of God and man. The aspect of the moral world, and the embarrassed condition of our Missionary Boards, throw a solemn responsibility around the contribution we now make to the treasury of the Lord. Mason and Bennet speak the feelings of many others when they say—"What shall we do? Shall we tell parents and children, they must wait for years, till the churches send aid from America? We have done what we could. If we enter into one field of labor, with all our might, another and another still pressing duty forces itself upon us, and some must be neglected. Which shall it be? An era has dawned upon the Karens, and we feel that we shall be culpable, if we do not plainly lay their case before the American churches. Brethren and sisters, this people are upon our *hearts*, and we come to you with them. We must not, will not, cannot lay down our burden. Will you help us, or see us crushed beneath it?" And in behalf of this convention, the young men coming into the ministry, our struggling College, the destitute sections of our State, and the millions in heathenish darkness, we make the same appeal. "Brethren and sisters, these interests are upon our *hearts*, and we come to you with them. We must not, will not, cannot lay down our burden. Will you help us, or see us crushed beneath it?". Think of God's blessings around you, of your christian vows and professions, and answer this question; think of his example, whose cross opened to you the gate of heaven—who, though he was rich, yet for your sakes became poor, that ye through his poverty might be made rich—and answer it; think of that great day, when you must mingle with domestic and foreign heathens, at the judgment bar, to give an account of all your resources, and answer it.

APPOINTED BY CHRIST.

AN EXTRACT.

We earnestly enjoin it upon you, brother, to remember the Source from which you have received your appointment. It is not the College, it is not the Theological Institution. Your diplomas are not your commission. Nor is your authority derived from any Ecclesiastical Council. Jesus Christ is King in Zion; and if your appointment is valid, you are his ambassador to his rebellious subjects. Your commission is from his lips; your relation to him is direct; by his instructions are you to regulate your whole conduct, and to him personally and immediately are you responsible. No earthly prelate or judicatory is authorized to interpose between you and him. You are yourself a bishop—the highest functionary, subordinate to the Supreme Head, that a church is permitted to recognize. From this station you can rise no higher on this side of heaven. If you leave it for any other which human suffrages can offer, you descend.

As the office was instituted by Christ, and you fill it by his appointment, let us suggest that it becomes you strictly to adhere to the instructions of your great Diocesan. He has left very little to your discretion. The message with which you are charged, is his ultimatum to guilty men; and it is full and explicit, specifying his own rights and human duty; and stating definitively the terms upon which rebels against the divine government may be forgiven and eternally saved. All the duties of your holy vocation are prescribed with great clearness and exactitude. Scrupulously abide by his directions. As his ambassador, negotiate for him, and not for yourself.

Let the conviction be deep and permanent, that for all success in your mission, you are dependent on the sovereign pleasure of your Lord, "*Of whom, and through whom, and to whom are all things.*" You are to perform your duty, and leave it to him to render your ministry effectual just when and where he chooses. "*It is not of him that willeth, nor of him that runneth, but of God that showeth mercy.*"

THE
BAPTIST PREACHER.

VOL. IV.　　February, 1845.　　NO. 2.

THE SUCCESS OF THE GOSPEL,

A GROUND OF GRATEFUL TRIUMPH TO THE FRIENDS OF CHRIST:

The Introductory Sermon delivered at the Sixty-first Anniversary of the Dover Association, at Hampton, Elizabeth City County, Va., October 12th, 1844, by Rev. John O. Turpin, of King William, and published by request of the Association.

"*Now thanks be unto God, which always causeth us to triumph in Christ, and maketh manifest the savour of his knowledge by us in every place.*"—2 Cor. ii : 14.

The cause of the christian is arduous: and he who supinely folds his arms, and looks for a royal road to heaven, has fearfully miscalculated. The word of God abounds with testimony, both expressed and implied, sustaining the truth of this declaration. Were this not so, our Lord would not have informed his disciples that they should be "baptized with the baptism with which he was baptized." Nor would he have urged the exhortation, "Strive (agonize) to enter in at the strait gate, for many I say unto you, shall seek to enter in and shall not be able." Neither would the Apostle have found it necessary, for the encouragement of the Hebrew christians, to refer to that extended line of patriarchs and prophets, "who, through faith subdued kingdoms, wrought righteousness, obtained promises, stopped the mouths of lions, quenched the violence of fire, escaped the edge of the sword, out of weakness were made strong, waxed valiant in fight, turned to flight the armies of the aliens." He had a proper conception of the magnitude of his work; therefore, he urged his brethren to "lay aside every weight, and the sin which most easily beset them:" adding, that they had not yet resisted unto blood, striving against sin. The text looks to this. The term *triumph*, implies the existence of a contest. Yet were the testimony of scripture less abundant, every shadow of doubt would be

dispelled, by contemplating the depravity of human nature
in connection with the purity of God's law. Alas! what a
fearful chasm! A chasm which feeble man can never fill.
The exploit is too arduous. Is not this an affecting view?
But thanks to matchless grace, relief is proposed in the gospel of the blessed God. Vain are all our efforts without the
gospel. This can heal the breach between man and his
Maker. Well, then, might the Apostle exclaim, "Now
thanks be unto God, which always causeth us to triumph in
Christ, and maketh manifest the savour of his knowledge by
us in every place." This, then, appears to be the proposition
contained in the text, namely : *The success of the gospel is
a ground of grateful triumph to the friends of Christ.*

Such is the proposition awaiting our attention ; and may
the spirit of wisdom and grace influence us in its elucidation.

I. What may be considered the success of the gospel?
This is an inquiry of engrossing interest. Properly understood, and exemplified, it would greatly promote the purity
and efficiency of the church. It will then be profitable to
examine this subject in the light of God's word. We must
not hastily conclude, from the great enlargement of the visible church, that the gospel has been correspondingly successful. For there is danger that partizan policy may have
its influence in swelling our ranks at the expense of truth
and righteousness, that we may thus present an imposing
array in the eyes of the world. As there will, in the last
day, be many who shall cry " Lord, Lord, open unto us,"
so may we fear that there are many around our communion
tables, in whose hearts grace has never reigned. We may
safely aver, that the churches may increase in number, respectability and opulence, while yet the gospel is unsuccessful.
Nay, the gospel may be successful, while the church, in
these particulars, is on the wane. We cannot, my brethren,
approach this subject without having increasing convictions
concerning the fearfulness of ministerial responsibility. Ah,
what graces should pervade his heart who is more specially set
apart to guard the interests of the Redeemer's kingdom!
Well may we exclaim with the Apostle, " *who* is sufficient
for these things ? "

Under the denunciations of the law, the sinner may be
filled with alarm and terror, and when these emotions have
been succeeded by a reaction of the animal spirits, he may
fancy he is converted. Under the influence of no better
feelings than these, doubtless, many join the church.

By the exhibition of popular talents, crowds may be drawn into the sanctuary, whose sympathies have been awakened and whose respect has been secured to the external forms of religion, and yet the gospel has not proved successful. In this *negative* view of the subject, might be embraced 'all the appearances of gifts, graces and liberality, and still the gospel may have failed of success. But we must consider this question in the *positive* point of view.

First then. *Whenever the gospel is successful, there are penetrating views of human depravity.* If emotions prevail like those expressed by the prophet, when he said "wo is me! for I am undone; because I am a man of unclean lips," then is there occasion for encouragement, for there is the gospel successful. It has been forcibly declared by another, that a "conviction of this doctrine lies at the root of true religion. It should be regarded as strictly fundamental, and should be considered as the basis of the evangelical system;" insomuch that the blessings of the gospel can never be possessed until there is a practical conviction of its truth. Our lost condition must be recognized or there can be no salvation. The Son of man came to save that which was *lost.* "I never knew a person," says Andrew Fuller, "verge towards the Arminian, the Arian, the Socinian, or the Antinomian schemes, without first entertaining diminutive notions of human depravity, or blameworthiness." Painful as is this truth, it is still interesting and momentous; it is written in the word of God as with a pencil of light. The whole human race possess a state of mind opposite to that required by the law of God. Depravity consists in a want of love to God and our neighbor, or an attachment to some other objects to the exclusion of those contained in the divine law. Man in his conduct has not the glory of God in view. His heart is engrossed by the world. "For all have sinned and come short of the glory of God." "By one man sin entered into the world, and death by sin, and so death passed upon all men, in that all have sinned." "The scripture hath concluded all under sin; that the promise by faith in Jesus Christ might be given to them that believe." "If we say, we have not sinned, we make him a liar and his word is not in us." The scriptures then, teach the doctrine of universal and deep seated depravity; and where this doctrine finds a response in the convictions of men, there we may declare the gospel has been successful. In connection with this we may say,

Secondly. *The gospel is successful, where elevated views of the awakening, convincing and attractive power of the cross are entertained.* We have no relief from the affecting condition we have just been contemplating, but in the cross of Christ. " Christ crucified," has always been and ever will be, the " power of God unto salvation to every one that believeth." " This doctrine is rich in divine efficacy, and radiant with divine wisdom." What but this, my brethren, could have given relief to the trembling jailor, namely: " believe on the Lord Jesus Christ and thou shalt be saved." Clearly as this truth is taught on the inspired page, often as it is opened and illustrated from the sacred desk, yet the views entertained concerning it are fearfully contracted and erroneous, and persons too, from whom we have a right to expect better things, sometimes pursue a course whose tendency is, we humbly conceive, to detract from the glory of the atonement.

Instead of the circuitous and perplexing process through which the awakened sinner is not unfrequently conducted, is it not more rational as well as more scriptural, to present to his trembling conscience the atoning blood,—the all-sufficient merit,—and the prevailing advocacy of our divine Redeemer? Wherever there is a faithful and persevering exhibition of this method, success will crown the endeavor. It was this method, which in primitive times, filled the churches with trophies of grace. A method God will always honor and approve. Human theories and speculations, however dear to the theorist, must be sacrificed to this fundamental principle in the religion of Jesus.

That preacher exhibits diminutive convictions of the magnitude of his work, who supposes, according to the views just given, that there is no room for the exercise of elevated talents—cogent reasoning—and a lively imagination, in his appropriate work. Instead of laying the restraining hand upon these excellencies, the gospel claims them in its proclamation. But I wander. We say, the gospel is successful, when men are aroused, convinced and drawn to the cross, and to that alone. However foolish it may appear to them that perish, to such as are called, it is the power of God and the wisdom of God.

Thirdly. *Wherever there is a self-sacrificing zeal for the advancement of the divine glory, there we may infer the gospel is successful.* Where the service of his master is the nourishment of the believer's soul. When he is so absorbed that the language of the Apostle best describes his feelings: "I am crucified with Christ, nevertheless, I live, yet not I, but Christ liveth in me, and the life I now live in the flesh, I live by the faith of the Son of God, who loved me and gave himself for me." To be brief, the success of the gospel is known by the cultivation of *personal holiness,*—by the overcoming of *remaining sin,*—by the *resistance of temptation,*—by the suppression of any encroachment of the world upon the affections of the believer,—and by an advancement in the divine life. It is further shewn by awakening a spirit of enlarged benevolence. It hushes that maxim of avarice, "let charity begin at home," a maxim which quiets the conscience of

> "The miser who with dust inanimate
> Holds wedded intercourse."

The gospel widens the range of the spiritual vision. It binds the interests of universal man to the believer's heart. It teaches him that every man is his brother. It imparts a soul in harmony with heaven. It leads him to regard the world

> "As one
> Sole family of brothers, sisters, friends,
> One in their origin, one in their rights,
> To all the common gifts of providence,
> And in their hopes, their joys and sorrows one."

'Tis thus he is taught by the gospel to view the universal human race. This principle is implanted within his bosom, "you are not your own." He feels that his interests are identified with those of the church. Does Zion languish? So does his spirit. Do her ways mourn, and few come up to her solemn feasts? He too mourns over her desolations; and cries, when will the time come, yea, the set time to favor Zion? He feels for the spiritual condition of his neighbor. His light shines, enlightening the community in which he dwells. And it is thus that the leaven works its way into the masses of society, until the whole is leavened.

II. How may the success of the gospel be secured? Measures necessary for the diffusion of the gospel will suggest themselves by a consideration of the views already presented. "Every resolution should be wrought out in men's minds, before it takes its shape in action," is an important

remark of D'Aubigne, in his history of the reformation. So
we say,

1. In order to promote the success of the gospel, the
mind of the believer should be enlightened by compiehen-
sive views of the wants of the world. " Lift up your eyes
and look on the fields, for they are white already to harvest,"
is the direction of our Lord. The world is, in a very fearful
sense, under the dominion of satan, and men are his willing
captives. The passions, habits, principles and pursuits of
men, indicate that they will not have Christ Jesus to
reign over them Such is the moral condition of the
world. In the plentitude of divine wisdom, man is chosen
as the instrument to change the moral character of his fellow-
man. He is to bear to the world the tidings of salvation.
How great the honor placed upon him! Men, aided by the
Holy Spirit, have this work to perform ; " go ye and teach
all nations, baptizing them in the name of the Fathei, and of
the Son, and of the Holy Ghost, teaching them to observe all
things whatsoever I have commanded you ; *and lo, I am
with you always, even unto the end of the world.*"

2. *Prayer* is an essential element in rendering the gospel
successful. This exercise evinces that we have some important knowledge ; that we have discovered the secret
where lies the hiding of our power. It recognizes the feebleness of man and the power of God. There is power in
prayer. A praying preacher is an efficient preacher. A
praying church is an influential one. She makes inroads
upon the powers of darkness. Her light is seen and her
influence is felt in community where she exists. Oh, what
a sublime spectacle is presented in that church, all of whose
members hold habitual "fellowship with the Father and
with his Son Jesus Christ!" Does there exist on God's wide
earth such a church? Point her out to me ; and as we look
upon her, we may safely say, there is a church, who, though
oppressed by poverty, and apparently crushed by opposition,
is yet exerting a moral energy which the powers of eatth
and hell combined cannot resist. God clothes prayer with
power.

3. Another important measure is the diffusion of the
sacred scriptures ; I had almost said the preacher has not
much labor among a people who search the scriptures. In
such a position we *may* say his work is superlatively delightful. Under this head it will not be improper to arrange
christian books and tracts, sabbath schools and frequent in-

tercourse with the world upon the momentous truths of religion. It is impossible, in the present state, to know the full
results of these instrumentalities. They have been blest
with success in times past and we look forward with assurance that they ever will be successful. Let all christians,
people as well as preachers, use all possible measures to
" warn every man and teach every man, that every man may
be presented perfect in Christ Jesus."

Finally, upon this head, I remark, that an *example* of
spirituality on the part of believers, is an essential means
in promoting the success of the gospel. No measure of
liberality, or zeal, or activity, can atone for the absence of
spiritual example. " Observation teaches us," remarks an
elegant writer, " the power of example. Good examples
induce to the practice of virtue and holiness. General precepts
present abstract ideas of virtue ; but in examples, virtues are
visible in their circumstances. Precepts instruct us in what
is our duty, but examples assure us that they are possible,
they are practicable. Examples, by secret and lively incentive,
urge us to imitation. We are touched in another manner by
the visible practice of good men, reproaching our defects,
and in a manner obliging us to the same course, which laws,
however wise and good, cannot effect." Now, more than
ever, methinks, the church is called upon to the practice of
sobriety and godliness. In the present unsettled state of the
public mind, when our land is affected from centre to circumference, by agitating questions, where, I ask, is the
patriot, the real lover of his species, to seek repose amidst
this tempest of politics, if he finds it not in the church of
Christ ? The church should ever prove the grand conserva-
tory of moderation and good order. Let the power of example have its influence, and complaints concerning the
languishing condition of the church will cease. The gospel
will have " free course, and be glorified." Believers
will possess a sanctified emulation ; there will be an increase
of christian love ; a heavenly zeal commensurate with the
great objects contemplated by christianity, will be awakened ;
infidelity will be disarmed ; proud hearts will be humbled ;
sinners will be converted ; " Zion will arise and shine, her
light having come and the glory of the Lord having arisen
upon her ; " and the savor of divine knowledge would thus
be manifest in every place."

III. We come to notice, lastly, the *result*, the *triumph
of believers* ; not a mere conquest, but a *triumph ;* not a

heartless, but a *grateful* triumph.   This triumph is not
effected by human agency, " *God* causeth them to triumph."
It is not temporary, " God *always* causeth them to triumph."
It rests upon no mutable basis, He always causeth them to
triumph in *Christ.*

Believers are recognized in the text, as the instruments in
diffusing the savor of divine knowledge.   God is represented
as the agent, and Christ as the medium of their triumph.
As believers can " do all things through Christ, which
strengtheneth them," so in their success and triumph they
recognize him.   No joy can equal that of bringing souls to
Christ; making them " meet to be partakers of the inheritance of the saints in light."   What reward can be richer
than this, " they that be wise shall shine as the brightness of
the firmament, and they that turn many to righteousness, as
the stars forever?"   Well may we be willing to " go forth
weeping, bearing precious seed," if we can return again
with rejoicing, bringing our sheaves with us.   There is supposed to be an allusion in the text, to the triumphal proces-
sions among the Romans.   According to Macknight, the
Apostle represents Christ as a victorious general, riding in a
triumphal procession through the world, attended by his
apostles, prophets, evangelists and other ministers of the
gospel, and followed by all the idolatrous nations as his
captives.   Among these, the preachers of the gospel diffused
the smell [savor,] of the knowledge of Christ, [as fragrant
flowers and perfumes were liberally scattered in a Roman
triumph.] . The conqueror's joy sinks infinitely below that
of the soldier of the cross, who has gathered around him
trophies of grace as seals of his ministry.   The Apostle
refers with heavenly satisfaction, to this source of *his* joy;
" For what," asks he, " is our hope, or joy, or crown of
rejoicing?   Are not ye in Christ Jesus? for ye are our glory
and joy."

The Apostles frequently referred to the results of their
labors as the fruitful source of their bliss.   John says, " I
have no greater joy than to hear that my children walk in
the truth."   Paul says, " ye are our epistles, known and
read of all men."   To the Colossians he says, " for though
I be absent in the flesh, yet am I with you in the spirit, joy-
ing and beholding your order, and the steadfastness of your
faith in Christ."   These grateful joys are realized by the
believer in the present state, but their richest fruition is
reserved for the kingdom of glory.   It is impossible in the

present state, for the christian to know the full results of his labors and influence. Doubtless, very erroneous calculations are made upon this subject. It remains for eternity to disclose these results. The solemn councils of the last day will enable us to form a correct judgment, and to understand and appreciate the richness of that benediction: "They that be wise," &c. Then, while the consistent and laborious christian contemplates the various and happy results of his labors, with a spirit overwhelmed with rapturous astonishment, he will enquire, "can all these be the children which the Lord has given me?" "Now I see," he says, "obscure as I was in yonder world, humble as was the sphere in which I moved, the Lord's eye was upon me, marking my course, and his hand blessing my labors." He will then see, that those exhortations and warnings, made not *only* in the great *congregations*, but under the roof of the humble poor, and in the ears of the stranger upon the highway, the divine Spirit rendered effectual.

While the ransomed spirit contemplates the glorious bearing of all his self-denials, works of faith and labors of love, and as he hears that these are acknowledged as rendered to the person of Christ; with a feeling approaching incredulity, he will inquire, "when saw we thee a hungered and fed thee? or thisty and gave thee drink? when saw we thee a a stranger and took thee in? or naked and clothed thee? or when saw we thee sick or in prison and came unto thee?" Prophets and patriarchs will there see the fruit of their toils. "In the morning they sowed their seed, and in the evening they withheld not their hand. They knew not which should prosper, whether this or that, or whether both should be alike good." All shall be made plain in eternity. Peter will see the seals of his ministry, from among the Parthians, and Medes, and Elamites, and the dwellers in Mesopotamia, and in Judea, and Cappadocia, in Pontus, and Asia, Phrygia, and Pamphylia, in Egypt, and in parts of Libya, about Cyrene, and strangers of Rome, Jews and proselytes, Cretes and Arabians. And if we take into the account the savor these people shed upon their respective countries on their return, how vast the "works following" up this Apostle to the throne of God. Paul will see and know his converts from Rome and Philippi, from Corinth and Antioch, and who can describe his joy as he cries exultingly, but gratefully, "thanks be unto God, which always causeth us to triumph in Christ, and maketh manifest the savor of his knowledge by us in every place.", Coming down to the present generation, how widely is this savor extending itself. Carey, and Boardman, and Judson, and Mason, and a host of others, among them many devoted females, having gone forth toiling and "weeping bearing precious seed, shall doubtless return again with rejoicing; bringing their sheaves with them."

Brethren in the ministry, I feel some reluctance in referring to our prospects in this connection. But if our toils have not been so great as theirs; if we have not been required to spill our blood on account of our faith, still may we not hope that we are the approved ministers of Christ? I know that the conscientious servant of Christ sometimes trembles in view of the present comparative ease and favor connected with the christian ministry. Yet the christian ministry is an arduous work: " To be instant in season and out of season:" " To be an example of the believers in word, in conversation, in charity, in spirit, in faith, in purity : " to " reprove with all long-suffering and doctrine," require a great measure of circumspection and christian integrity and labor. If this be our character and condition, we may look forward with pleasing anticipations to a share in the bliss of those who rejoice in the fruits of their labors. Let us be " faithful unto death, and we shall receive the crown of life." No heart can conceive the joy of the faithful minister, as he looks upon all his toils with the assurance that they are accepted and approved by his Heavenly Father.

> " There on a green and flowery mount,
>   Our wearied souls shall rest,
> And with transporting Joys recount
>   The labors of our feet."

We will conclude this discourse by addressing three classes of persons.

1. *The ministers of the gospel,* if one younger than many of you may address you. How responsible our labors! How bright our rewards! These are placed over against those. Gladly should we perform the labors, for the sake of such a " far more exceeding and eternal weight of glory." Never should we indulge in vain repinings, saying " the burden of the Lord, the burden of the Lord." Let us look forward to the prospect before us. Oh how great a joy, " to convert a sinner from the error of his ways," and thus to

"save a soul from death, and hide a multitude of sins."
Where stands the watchman upon the walls of Zion, who
would not prefer one such jewel to adorn the crown of his
rejoicing, above wearing the diadem of England's queen?

2. A word to you *brethren in Christ*, though not ministers. The part you bear is an important one. If what I
have said be true, and the word of God sustains me, you
can do much in the conversion of the world. None of you
will suppose yourselves released from anxiety and labor,
because you are not ministers. Remember, David was not
clad with sacerdotal robes; he did not serve at the altar.
Amidst all the cares of a crown, he still recognized his relation to God, and the duties growing out of that relation.
He prayed, " restore unto me the joy of thy salvation, and
uphold me with thy free spirit, then will I teach transgressors thy ways, and sinners shall be converted unto thee."

The 3rd class I wish to address, is the *impenitent.* My
unconverted friends, how deep the solicitude felt on your
behalf. If such joy thrills the bosoms of God's people on
your conversion, they have sorrow correspondingly deep,
when they discover their labors for you have been in vain,
while you remain careless and at a distance from God.

When the man of God goes glowing with faith from the
closet to the pulpit, and preaches as one deeply penetrated
with a sense of the fearful realities he proclaims, and, as he
closes finds the sinner still turning a deaf ear to his warnings
and expostulations, alas, how crushing! Under such
painful trials, nothing but almighty grace can sustain him.

Come immortal soul, help us to-day to swell the volume
of thanks, and praise, and joy. There is not only joy on
earth, " but there is joy among the angels over one sinner
that repenteth." Come, will you bear a part with us in
these toils? Share with us, I should perhaps say, in these
blessings. And when we arrive in heaven, there, upon the
banks of everlasting deliverance, we shall all join in the
chorus of the redeemed, and sweep our harps to this rapturous sung, " unto him that loved us, and washed us from
our sins in his own blood, and hath made us kings and
priests unto God and his Father; to him be glory and dominion, forever and ever. Amen."

THE TRUTH OF CHRISTIANITY SUSTAINED

BY THE MIRACLES WHICH REVELATION RECORDS AND THE PROPHECIES WHICH HAVE BEEN FULFILLED.

A Sermon, delivered in Nashville Tennessée, July 7th, and in Columbus, Mississippi, July 27th, 1844, by REV. W. CAREY CRANE.

Thy word is truth.—JOHN XVII: 17.

Incredulity respecting religion is the sin of our race. What is fair and reasonable evidence in anything else, is unworthy of notice when connected with the interests of the immortal soul. No system of religion, true or false, ever found the world, at its introduction, in so credulous a state, that it would or could confide in its pretensions. Man seems to distrust at the very first blush, every thing which sheds light upon the distant future. The various discoveries of the world in scientific pursuits, have never met with half the scepticism with which religion has had to contend. Tell man a new world has been discovered, and he does not ask for evidence that the documents are genuine, which give account of the discovery, nor whether there has not been forgery, nor whether there is not an improbability that any discovery could be made. Man believes it. Tell man that the sun is the centre of a great system, instead of revolving itself around this small planet, which to the natural eye is the most obvious, and man believes it,—actually believes what seems to be contradicted by his senses. Tell man that the world in which he lives is a globe and is continually wheeling on its axis, and at the same time revolving around the sun, and though it appears paradoxical to human reason, unsophisticated, he believes it. Publish a long account from the Cape of Good Hope, affirming that Sir John Herschell has with his forty feet telescope descried land in the moon, and has actually seen living beings of all forms and almost no form; that in that important satellite of this more important sphere, verdure is more luxuriant, and fruits more abundant than on this, he is disposed to believe it, though the most marvellous story of the age. But inform man that Christ, a Divine Being, descended from heaven, was on earth about two thousand years ago, that he wrought miracles and predicted future events, many of which have already come to pass, man is incredulous. At one moment we are led in sorrow to exclaim, how credulous is man, and in the next, how incredulous. He seems to have come into the world so much depraved as almost to be considered a natural sceptic. The first manifestation of evil in the garden of Eden, was the commencement of scepticism. Our primal mother parleyed with the serpent concerning the nature of the forbidden fruit and fell from her high estate. In view of the natural tendency of mankind to atheism, and especially to dissipate the effects of incredulity from the minds of avowed christians, we shall treat the text as a basis on which to found an argument for the religion of Jesus Christ.

I. FROM MIRACLES RECORDED IN THE OLD AND NEW TESTAMENTS.

II. FROM THE EVIDENCE OF PROPHECY.

Upon these the necessity of faith will be based, as well as upon the almost exact fulfilment of the truth contained in the text.

I. *The evidence of miracles.* Fully to set forth all that can be properly said respecting this species of evidence, would require volumes, rather than a few slight and necessarily imperfect sketches of proof. One good and impregnable argument is however sufficient to sustain any cause. One unanswerable truth must be better than a thousand answerable ones. A miracle, in the jewish or christian sense of the term, is a display of supernatural power, in attestation of the truth of a message from God. In order to have credit among men, a message or messenger, before it can become acceptable, must be sealed. Miracles are called the seals of a message. The form, " witness my hand and seal," is as necessary and essential in religion as in the mere concerns of temporary life. Moses was a divinely commissioned and sealed messenger of God ; he exhibited his seal by the miracles which he performed. Christ was a divinely commissioned legate from the skies, and he as well as Moses, sealed his message by miracles and prophecy. Moses and Jesus were, therefore, properly accredited messengers from God ; the former was the minister of the law, the latter was the minister of grace : " For the law was given by Moses, but grace and truth came by Jesus Christ." Miracles, (and among miracles we include prophecy, as there are two sorts of supernatural powers—physical and mental,) are the only direct evidence which can be given of divine inspiration. It

is true that the history of every religion abounds with relations of prodigies and wonders, wrought by *assumed* supernatural powers.   And many are the classic stories of the
intercourse of men with gods.   Read Homer's poetical description of the scenes witnessed upon the plains of Troy ;
gods are seen contending with one another, and with the
Greeks   or   Trojans.   In   the   minds   of   the   ancient
heathen these were miraculous displays; " but the *assumed*
miracles of pagan historians and poets were not even pretended to have been wrought publicly to enforce the truth of
a new religion contrary to the reigning idolatry."   The most
of them   can   clearly   be   shewn   to   have been only   natural
events.   Many are evidently tricks ingeniously contrived for
sinister purposes, either to flatter power or promote the existing forms of superstitious worship.   But compare the immoral character   of   the   divinities, who   are   said   to   have
wrought   such   prodigies,   with   the   pure   character   of those
who acted   by the   influences of our   holy   religion, and the
tremendous disparity is manifest, indeed it were almost unworthy of Moses and Christ, Samuel and Peter, to call for
a comparison.
   Considered abstractly, miracles are not incredible, for they
are capable of plain proof from analogy *indirectly*, and from
testimony directly.   The analogical proof is based upon
nature and reason, the direct proof upon revelation and physical nature.   The christian miracles were objects of real
and proper experience to those who saw them.   Admitting
this, the question sometimes occurs, were miracles necessary ?
and did the end proposed to be accomplished warrant an immediate and extraordinary interference of the Almighty ?
The only reply which we can make to such questions is,
that if their occurrence be established beyond doubt, all
reasoning and speculation concerning their probability, possibility or necessity, is quite frivolous and false.   These are
questions   which   can   perplex   the human   understanding
without benefitting it.   Shall we be shaken in our understanding, or give up our belief because we cannot discover
their origin ?   Shall we assent to the infidel insinuation of
Hume, that our ignorance is God ?   That there is blind cre-
dulity and superstition, when there is want of physical proof,
and reason is at fault in its researches ?
   Blessed be God ! that we do not know every thing ; that it
" is the glory of God to conceal a thing ; " that where our
feeble intellects are unable to come to proper results, there is

" enthroned on high, in sempiternal light divine," an all-glorious Being, who will ultimately resolve all our difficulties. There must be some limit to the human understanding. Why may not that limit be the throne of God? Vain man! attempt not to leap over that boundary! Taking the argument from *effect to cause*, to be a perfectly legitimate mode of reasoning in establishing the fact of God's existence, we can see no just reason why that which to mortal vision is *supernatural*, should not be attributed to him. Where the reason, unaided by divine power, must stop in its grasping, there the supernatural begins and God exists.

Holding that God is infinitely wise, holy and powerful, human reason demands if it was not a supernatural motive which induced him to send his Son to die for a guilty and condemned world. Was not the mission of the Saviour a miracle? Why not make a general proclamation of pardon to penitents? Why not send a legion of angels to accomplish the great purpose? True believers admit that God's plan is miraculous, and of course supernatural. Speculations do not disturb those who confide in the sacred scriptures. From them we learn that the sacrifice of an infinitely holy being was necessary to make atonement for crimes of an infinite nature, as well as to harmonize the attributes of a God who is infinitely and eternally holy, happy and divine. Any divine revelation must be considered a miracle, and though a miracle, the necessity of the revelation through the Old and New Testament may be easily proven by an appeal to reason. Contemplate the state of the world when Christ actually appeared. The first chapter of the epistle to the Romans, is a synoptical portraiture of a large portion of the human race. Examine, if you please, the degraded condition of the Jewish nation at that time. Was not reform loudly called for? Consider the nature and tendency of the christian religion; how admirably was it adapted to the exigencies of the world! Even profane history will admit that a miraculous interposition of Providence was needed. The gracious and important ends that were to be accomplished, will convince mankind, not only that God wrought gloriously and miraculously, and that there was no idle and useless display of divine power, that while the means effected and confirmed the end, the end fully justified and illustrated the means. But we are gravely told by infidels, that a miracle is contrary to experience. Hume, especially, remarks, that " he could not believe any testimony which is

contrary to universal experience," because, says he, it is infinitely more probable that the witnesses are mistaken, than
that the laws of nature have been violated. It is also asserted that the course of nature is fixed and inviolable, and
it is inconsistent with the immutability of God to perform
miracles. Thus, the evidence of the senses is made the
standard by which, from a residence of half a century on
one speck of the illimitable universe, *a very mote* in creation,
we are to deduce the inviolability of God's laws, through
infinite space and eternal duration. To employ the indignant language of one of the distinguished men of the age,
"a mole, a gnat, an insect may then, from the image of this
great world painted on the retina of its eye, philosophically
depose that the universe is self-existent and eternal." If the
being of a God is admitted, the possibility of a miracle must
also be admitted. If the omnipotence of God be conceded,
the possibility, nay even the probability of a change in his
laws must be conceded. Can it be possible to conceive that
God would ordain such general laws for his own operation,
as will effectually exclude a change of those laws, where a
great and important end could be answered thereby. The
very creation of the world was a change in the course of existence, yet what sane man denies that the world was created;
hence, according to infidel logic, the laws of nature were
violated, which is contrary to universal experience. If the
definition of a miracle which has already been given, be
correct, then the creation of this terrestrial planet was a miracle. To prove to common sense that blind chance brought
out of the womb of eternity this footstool of God, will puz-
zle all the infidels and pagans, philosophers and wise men,
from this time until the judgment day.

But let us for a moment, examine the reasoning, that miracles are opposed to experience and the common course of
nature. Is experience the only teacher from whom we
obtain knowledge? If so, our lot is indeed most lamentable. The past is all a fable; historians are ingenious novel-
ists; travelers are arrant liars; to those of us who have not
crossed the great deep, (indeed the very existence of the
" deep " is problematical;) Europe, Asia and Africa are
regions, the fairy creations of a poetical fancy. Alexander
and Cæsar, Washington and Napoleon were not. The
future cannot be, because not experienced. The future ! it
is a horrid, hideous vacuity. Has memory no share in obtaining knowledge? Why then send your children to

schools and colleges? Is faith of no avail in amassing intellectual treasures? Then the world is hardly less than the burning reality of hell, exhibiting all the awful proofs of enormous guilt and distressing crimes; and man is but a single remove from the monkey tribe. But, says the sceptic, we mean "universal experience, when we speak of experience." Who will deny that universal experience is the experience of *all* men, in *all* places, and at *all* times. And what man of three score years and ten, and of no greater dimensions than ourselves, has stood over this narrow world like a mighty colossus, one foot on the plains of Hindostan and another on the wine fields of France, and in all ages and all times has observed all changes and all events, and from this far-reaching point of observation has gathered and concentrated upon his own brain the accumulated treasures of universal knowledge? The wisdom of that conceit which makes experience the only teacher, is well illustrated in the story told of the emperor of Siam. An Englishman, in whose society he delighted, informed him that in England "water congealed into ice and was so hard and thick that men and cattle walked upon it." This was so glaring a falsehood in the eyes of the emperor, and so distinctly opposed to his experience, that he pronounced it a *lie* and refused to believe any thing the Englishman thereafter would say. Surely that emperor must have become a wise man!

Hume, who attempted in all his writings covertly to inculcate his sceptical sentiments, disproves his own theory by his own practice. In his works upon "Human Nature," his enquiry concerning "the Human Understanding," and the "History of England," he very plainly contradicts his own favorite argument from experience, in the credit he attaches to a multitude of facts, of which it was impossible for him to have had any experience. Did he ever see William the Conqueror? Did he ever attend the court of Richard III., and witness the machinations of that wicked man? Did he ever shake hands with queen Elizabeth, or drink wine with queen Anne? If he had not seen them all—been an eye witness of their administrations—how dare he, in the face of his great principle, attempt to describe what he had never personally observed, nor experienced?

But let us dwell, for a brief period, upon the argument from the inviolable and unchangeable course of nature. Infidels have set up geology as their main bulwark, from which they have fulminated their bulls against the truth of Almighty God.   As this is too wide a field for explo-ration at one glance, let us confine ourselves to proofs only, that there have been changes in nature's laws appa-rently as miraculous as the changes in nature's course, which the scriptures affirm and set forth.   We shall con-tend that these must be disbelieved too, if it is indeed true that all of nature's laws are uniform and permanent without the intervention of any supernatural agency. Hence, all things are as they were originally.   Astronomy, geology and every physical and metaphysical science are mere suppositions or base lies, " without fact or reason"—as who will believe?

What man of intelligence doubts that there have been immense changes in the strata of the earth's surface? *Mac-cullock*, in his account of the " Western Isles," has des-cribed a tract of country, which he says, " may be considered as exceeding twenty miles on a line taken transversely to the bearings of the strata, and throughout this space, compu-ting from enumerations taken at different places, there are probably not less than 40 000 strata." *Lyell*, in an address before the British Geological Society, of which he is presi-dent, says, " we can prove man had a beginning, and that all the species now contemporary with man, and many others which preceded, had also a beginning, consequently, the present state of the organic world has not gone on from all eternity as philosophers have maintained." *Laplace*, main-tained the contrary and strove to bolster up the theory of Hume. *Cuvier*, in his theory of the earth, says, that " from the different stratas of shells, sands, ect., ect., it is evident the basin of the sea has undergone one change, at least, either in extent or situation : such is the result of the very first search and of the most superficial examination." He further clearly shows that the present earth was formed under water. How stands Hume's theory of the inviolable course of nature, if this be true. Upon this point science and revelation, geology and the Bible, Moses and Peter all agree. Look at the millions of structures in the vegetable, animal and mineral kingdoms. Have they existed from the beginning without change? Was not supernatural power exerted, when the waters were separated *above* and under the firmament, and when the dry land and pure air were made to appear? Was there not a new suspension, violation or deviation from the *then* laws of nature, when the vegetable genera and species were created—when the earth was pe..pled with animals? Who can describe the series of supernatural *interpositions* which were required to fill the air, the sea and the earth with inhabitants requiring vegetable productions *mediately* or immediately for their subsistence? And when all this was done, there was no being of earthly creation that could read, or understand, or enjoy the Creator and his creation. Another exercise of divine energy was called for, and man was brought into being, the greatest miracle ever wrought. The whole work of creation consisted in a series of miracles opposed to the previously known *laws* of the world. At every step there was a violation of the assumed "inviolable laws of nature." Will any one deny them on this account? Let now the priests of the sublime science of astronomy testify. They alledge, that continually "stars are *forming* and the remote fields of space are filling up with new systems of suns and their satellites: all contrary to our experience and the immutable laws of nature. Sir Wm. and Sir Jno Herschell, have telescopes which penetrate beyond the limits of conception. It is calculated that their glasses can descry objects almost four hundred times more remote than the most distant star, which is about thirty-six billions of miles from our earth. Is nature violated, when these stars are formed, of which these telescopes give such clear account? To what will not the depravity and sophistry of infidels lead them?

It may be well, now, briefly to consider the direct argument which is based upon miracles. In both the jewish and christian dispensations, there are two classes of miracles.

1. Those which consist of a train or combination of events, which distinguish themselves from the ordinary arrangements of Providence.

2. Those particular operations which are performed by agents and instruments incompetent to effect them, without a supernatural power.

Under the first head, may be ennumerated the preservation of the *Israelites*, under all circumstances; the provision made during their many changes and trials, for their protection and their constant supply of *manna* for their sustenance during their long sojourn or wandering in the wilderness. Under the *latter* heard, may be classed the particular miracles of our Lord and Saviour Jesus Christ, and the few supernatural displays of divine power through Moses, the lawgiver of ancient Israel; such as the striking of the rock Horeb, when it became a fountain of water at the bidding of the great prophet; the marvellous preservation of three Hebrew young men, Shadrach, Meshach and Abednego, who being cast into the fiery furnace, walked in it unscathed and breathing in flame; the turning of water into wine at Cana of Gallilee, by our Saviour; the resurrection of Lazarus; the son of the widow of Nain; and the centurian's daughter; and the feeding of the five thousand with five loaves and two small fishes. Besides, there were some other miracles performed by the Apostles. The evidence in favor of their actual performance is as strong and powerful as is adduced in favor of the prodigies of valor recounted of Napoleon Bonaparte. Indeed, the testimony which can be brought against the existence and the exploits of Napoleon, is as great and weighty as can be adduced against the existence of Christ and his miracles.

Sufficient, we hope, has been said, to show that the evidence of miracles is as strong, as clear, as irrefragable, as any testimony which the human mind is capable of even imagining. The obvious deduction then, is, that if miracles are supernatural, the power that works them must be *supernatural*, and that cause they attest is *divine*.

II. *The evidence of prophecy.* Prophecy, it has before been observed, is one species of miracles. For he who foretells a future event, depending on no known or ascertainable cause such as the *fate of a man, the rise or downfall of a nation*, displays supernatural and miraculous mental power. By the evidence of prophecy, we who are under the meridian blaze of gospel revelation, are made equal with those who lived when Christ appeared. The early christians saw some miracles and believed those that were predicted. We see what were predicted and believe what primitive christians saw.

It is an established law of testimony, in religious matters, that the longer the *interval* existing between us and the occurrence of the miracle, and the more numerous the hands through which the miracles have been transmitted to us, the fainter and more obscure is the evidence. He, therefore, who sees the accomplishment of prophecy, as clearly sees a miracle performed, as were a living agent working wonders before his eyes;—as fully does he see a miracle, as those who by their natural eyes saw Lazarus revive and leave the sepulchre at the command of Christ. To exemplify this, let us suppose a case. Some extraordinary individual arises among us and claims to be a divinely inspired messenger: he professes to have a communication for us of infinite importance to our race. He solemnly declares his message, but his solemn affirmation of the genuineness of his mission is not sufficient. He is required to exhibit some token of his power. Physical miracles are performed. Those who witness them are satisfied. The miracles are reported to posterity. Posterity are not satisfied with a mere belief in his divine power or in his miracles. Other evidence is demanded confirmatory of his divine origin. A miracle is called for; therefore, to satisfy coming ages, he repeatedly predicts, and before many witnesses, coming future events. Among many other things, he predicts that the inhabitants of Holland, will in fifty years from this period, possess the North American Continent; that the language, customs and laws of Holland shall here triumphantly prevail; that all the ancient land-marks of republican simplicity and glory shall be swept away, and nothing remain of our pristine glory. Let this prediction be a matter of historic and civic record, and be translated into the various languages of the world. To cap the climax, let us imagine that every jot and tittle of the prediction prove true, the events do actually occur as prophesied. The question arises, then, do not those who live at the time and are acquainted with the prophecy, see as actual and complete a miracle, as others who saw the prophet in his own times work miracles? We, therefore, who are eye-witnesses of the fulfilment of prophecies, as clearly behold miracles as those who beheld the divinely inspired prophet and Saviour walk upon the sea; turn water into wine, and raise the dead. The fulfilment of prophecy makes all prophecies miracles. Let us now specify one or two remarkable prophecies, which in their fulfilment have now become veritable miracles. Moses predicts, Deut. xxviii: 46–68, certain curses which should be upon the Israelites, because of their infidelity to their covenant. These curses would be for a miracle and a perpetual wonder. 1. A far distant nation, of foreign tongue, warlike character, fierce and unrelenting to old and young, should come swift as eagles fly, from the ends of the earth, and should devour the good land, all its products, and then besiege them in all

their cities. 2. The siege should be so distressing throughout its continuance, bringing about such dreadful calamities
and keen famines, that natural ties should be forgotten, and
a delicate lady should kill and eat her own infant secretly.
3. From vast numbers, they should be reduced to a very
meagre band, and driven from their own good land. 4
They should be scattered among all people, from one end
of the earth to the other; should serve other nations and
worship gods of wood and stone. 5. While among these
nations they should have no ease, nor rest for the sole of
their feet, but should be seized with trembling of heart, failing of eyes and sorrow of mind. 6. Though thus oppressed
and pealed by heaven's judgments, they should not be absorbed by other nations; for saith Jehovah, by his prophet
Jeremiah, "They should never, while sun, moon and stars
existed, cease from being a nation before him." The allusion throughout the whole prophecy, is plainly directed to
the Jewish people. Their history seems to have been as
well written by prophetic pens thousands of years ago, as
it could be now. The siege of Jerusalem is plainly described
and the horrid circumstance of a woman eating her own
child is predicted as it happened, with almost aggravating
minuteness. A part of the prediction is now in a course of
fulfilment. The Jews, though not annihilated, are still a
separate and distinct people, scattered to the four winds of
heaven, while other nations which were their tyrants, have
lost their identity and hardly have a "local habitation or a
name." Bear it in mind, that the downfall of the Jews and
Jerusalem, was predicted two thousand years before its
occurrence. Did not prophecy become miracle in this extraordinary case?

Let the enquiring mind compare Paul's prediction in 2nd
chapter of 2nd Thessalonians, and the rise, progress and
general history of the church of Rome and the conclusion
is irresistible, that prophecy and fact were in this case identified, and are now beyond reasonable speculation.

Enough has been said upon these two grand arguments
for our holy religion, without borrowing other illustrations.
With the impregnable arguments already set forth, we might
close this discourse; but in conclusion, let us turn our attention to the prediction of the text, which, though we
have digressed thus far, we have all along had in our mind's
eye. It is David, Israel's distinguished prophet, psalmist

and king, who is speaking: "they gave me gall for my meat, and in my thirst, they gave me vinegar to drink." The whole scene of Christ's trial and cruel crucifixion were before his mind, and almost the exact language which another inspired penman was directed to employ was used by him. Matthew informs us, that the blessed Saviour was taken to "a place called Golgotha, that is to say, a place of a skull. They gave him vinegar to drink, mingled with gall; and when he had tasted thereof, he would not drink." How exactly did these inspired minds agree. The Old and the New Testament are in harmony testifying to our Saviour's divine character.

Shall mere testimony be offered? Who with such undoubted evidence before him, will deny the spiritual authority of our religion, or the divine authority of Christ's mission? Unreasonable must be that man who will hold to a speculative creed. Leaving all such men to the great ultimate ordeal of judgment, we will remark, that the text may be a fruitful theme of reflection. 1. View it as actually setting forth David's severe trials. 2. View it as a prediction of Christ's intense physical suffering. 3. View it as referring to the fiery trials of the church in general. 4. View it as relating to every believer in general. Fully to unfold all these views, would extend this discourse to an unwonted and unreasonable length.

In the light of the beautiful harmony between the light of reason and revelation, which we have established by the humble essayings of human argument: a harmony so fruitful and encircled with such convincing evidence of the wisdom, goodness and divine majesty of our Saviour; let us adore the God and Father of our spirits, that we have so clear a manifestation of his will revealed in the sacred books of inspiration. "What is man that thou art mindful of him, or the son of man that thou visitest him?"

True love for Christ and unlimited faith in the Father, will apply all these glorious truths to our hearts; and in joyous expectation of a triumphant future, we may say, in the burning, intense desires of our hearts—

"There is a world above
Where parting is unknown;
A long eternity of love,
Formed for the good alone,
And faith beholds the dying here,
Transported to that glorious sphere."

AN EXTRACT.

Futurity is known to Omniscience; and it is God's sole prerogative to "declare the things that shall come to. pass. " Prophecy is therefore a miracle of knowledge—and the declaration of future events is so far beyond the power of human discernment or sagacity, that it is justly regarded as the highest evidence that can be produced of supernatural intercourse with the Deity, and of the truth of divine revelation.

Prophecy abounds in the holy scriptures, in such a series, and of a kind so magnificent, that the evidences of its fulfilment may be examined; in numerous instances, by those of the present age, with increasing light and more powerful demonstration of its divinity. Every reader of the Bible perceives that prophecy, in its most sublime revelations, comprehends the whole course of time; commencing with the first prediction, delivered to guilty Adam in the garden of Eden, concerning the appointed Saviour of the world, until the consummation of the mystery of Providence in the kingdom of God. Events and ages, however, yet future, are embraced by the inspired predictions; and while we survey the manifest fulfilment of many of them, relating to various people, extensive countries, and mighty cities, their actual present condition affords evidence that is accumulating in strength, in support of the saving belief of christians.

Contemplating divine prophecy in its original revelation —in its progressive advancement and fulfilment, in relation to numerous tribes and people—in the desolation of ancient cities—in the subversion of mighty empires—in the subjugation of the Israelites—in the advent of Messiah—in the accomplishment of his work of redemption—in the dispersion of his enemies, the Jews—in the establishment of his kingdom—and in the preservation and propagation of his gospel to regenerate our depraved world—no subject can be imagined so elevating to the brightest understanding, or so delightful to the pious mind. Events that are now transpiring in the nations of the world, more particularly the silent, peaceful, revolution which is taking place, especially throughout Europe, manifestly declare the mysterious direction of divine Providence, and a glorious improvement in all parts of the world, by the advancement of pure christianity.

THE
BAPTIST PREACHER.

| VOL. IV. | March, 1845 | NO. 3. |

THE REMEDY FOR HEART-TROUBLES.

BY REV. A. BROADDUS.

" Let not your heart be troubled: ye believe in God, believe also in me.
JOHN, xiv: 1.

Amidst the variety of subjects which, for a considerable time past, have employed the attention of our ministers, whether in the pulpit or from the press, there is one topic which seems to have been almost entirely overlooked:—I mean the consolations which the gospel has provided, as the remedy for the troubles and afflictions of God's people. Important as the subjects of discussion have been and worthy of the deepest regard, they do not supply this "lack of service"—a service which in its place appears to be as pressingly called for as any that we can render to the church of Christ.

Make the best of human life, brethren, it is fated to have its griefs; nor has the highly privileged state of the christian exempted him from this lot. The *aspect* indeed of the church's trial may change with changing times and circumstances,—so also may the *measure* of our sufferings. The afflictions of the primitive christians, in apostolic times, were, in some respects, of a different character from those which are experienced by us, and much more grievous to be borne;— particularly in regard to earthly privations and bodily sufferings: yet have we our measure meted out to us; and so must we expect it will be, while we inhabit this vale of tears, and while we have to conflict with sin and with its train of evils. Christian sufferings, however, are not to be considered in the light of a *curse*—inflicted merely as the penalty of sin. No!—our gracious Master, in his wisdom and covenant love, has given them a disciplinary character;—has infused into these bitter draughts a wholesome quality; and, as a pledge of his kindness, has furnished the means for sweetening the draught, and for sustaining the spirit in its painful struggles.

It is my present purpose, brethren, to throw some contri-

bution into that division of the spiritual treasury which
seems most to need it :—in other words, to present, as I may
be enabled, the remedy which the gospel furnishes for the
troubles of the heart :—" let' not your heart be troubled : ye
believe in God, believe also in me." I shall' not stop here
to enquire whether (as some think,) the translation would
be improved by rendering both these expressions, imperative-
ly—"believe in God, believe also in me." In substance
and effect the two readings amount to the same thing; and
I deem it unnecessary to trouble you or myself with this
criticism.

Our text is a small part of an extended discourse delivered
by our Lord to his apostles—" the eleven," I mean, for Judas
had gone out at an early period in the conversation which
took place at the table. It was his valedictory address—his
farewell sermon to his beloved little band, after the last supper, and just before his separation from them by death.
This circumstance, you can easily conceive, is well calculated to add weight to the things which were spoken, and to
deepen the interest of a discourse in itself so interesting and
so weighty.

"The things concerning Jesus", were now hastening to a
crisis. The dreadful agony was just at hand ;—Pilate's bar
rose in full prospect before him—and death, in its most appalling form was staring him in the face ! Nevertheless, his
heart is on his disciples. His affections still linger around
the little family from which he is presently to be separated ;
and as a rich legacy suited to their need, he leaves them this
his farewell sermon.

Yes, " a rich legacy suited to their need." How admirably ! how sweetly suited ! what wise instructions ! what
salutary admonitions ! what soul-encouraging promises ! and
what soothing and consoling assurances for desponding
spirits ? All bearing the impress of heaven itself, and blended in harmonious keeping, to meet the cases of those to
whom they were addressed. Surely, my friends, we may
well apply to this discourse of our blessed Lord, the character which Solomon gives to a " word fitly spoken :—" like
apples of gold in pictures of silver." Surely these heavenly
truths, these precious promises—grounded on the power, and
love and faithfulness of Christ, are more beautiful to the
view of the soul, than would be to the bodily eye, the rich

piece of needle-work, where figures of glowing apples are wrought with threads of gold on a ground of silver tissue.

But it is with that feature of our Lord's discourse which is more peculiarly adapted to the *consolation* of his forlorn disciples, that we are now particularly concerned. My text is one of those passages which exhibit that feature in a strong light, and is of so comprehensive a character, that it seems capable of a bearing on all cases of suffering to which the christian may be liable. No particular case is here specified— no matter what it may be—here is the remedy : " Ye believe in God, believe also in me." The prospect presented by this divine faith is calculated to brighten the gloom of afflic- tion. " In my father's house are many mansions "—" I go to prepare a place for you."

Enter with me into this subject. "Let not your heart be troubled : ye believe in God, believe also in me."

The doctrine contained in the text may be thus briefly stated : " evangelical faith, or that faith which Christ requires, is the sovereign remedy for heart-troubles."

In the discussion of this general proposition, let us consi- der it under two heads, namely : *The faith which is here required; and this faith, the sovereign remedy for the troubles of the heart.*

And here, brethren, let me remark to you, that if you are not at present tried with any peculiar affliction, you are liable to become so.; and therefore you are interested—*all* interest- ed in the subject now presented to your attention.

I. We propose to consider that important article, the faith which is required or enjoined in the text. And at once we see that this faith has for its object GOD as the supreme source of being, and JESUS CHRIST as the Redeemer of men. " Ye believe in God, believe also in me."

1. Its object is God—the self-existent Being ; the supreme source of all created beings ; and I may add, the fountain of all fullness—the centre and circumference of all perfec- tion. Now faith in God, the great First Cause, is justly con- sidered as lying at the foundation of all religion, whether *natural* or *revealed*. I am aware that some have made it a question, whether the idea of God (or of a First Cause,) could be originated in the mind of a mere child of nature; nay, that they have not merely made this a *question*, but have taken the *negative*, and denied that fallen man, without a revelation, or that tradition, which is the offspring

of revelation, would ever originate the idea; and so they
would deny that in strict propriety there is any such thing as
natural religion. I shall not here attempt to settle this question, nor is it material to our purpose. It is agreed on all
hands, that when the idea of God, as the Creator or First
Cause, is once suggested to the enquiring mind—come from
what source it may—then the universe around stands forth
as the evidence of this great truth, and conviction follows as
the consequence. Faith then, in the existence of God, may
be justly considered as the first link in the chain of religious
truth;—as first in the natural order; or, as before observed,
as lying at the foundation of all religious belief. And with
this agrees the testimony of the Apostle, "He that cometh to
God must believe that he is "—that he *exists.* The phrase
—" He that cometh to God," is expressive of religious exercise;
and it follows that in this case there must be faith in his
existence.

The scriptural idea of God, involves in it all-perfection as
to Himself—all fullness as to his creatures. If we can have
access to this fountain—if we can be allowed to draw from
his fullness, we may find a supply in every case of need:
and hence the necessity, that in the initial stage, in the first
step of religion, we " believe in God; "—believe in his existence, and in his ample fullness to meet all our wants—to
relieve all our woes.

Yes, my brethren—ay, and my fellow sinners *all*, here is
a rich supply for all our needs. Are you *guilty?* Here is
authority to pardon all transgression. Are you *polluted*
with sin? Here is sanctifying influence—the source of holiness. Do you feel your *weakness?* He can " strengthen
you with might by his spirit in the inner man." Are you
" in *heaviness* through manifold temptation? " He can
" make a way for your escape." And is your heart oppressed
with *grief?* He is " the God of all consolation."

I have said—" If we can have access to this fountain—if
we can be allowed to draw from his fullness." But now, be
it observed, that faith simply in the existence of the all-sufficient God, does not present us with the way of access to
Him—does not assure us that we are allowed to draw from
his fullness. Though necessary as the incipient stage of
religion, it does not suffice for the desired object. God is set
before us; but how shall we obtain free and favorable access
to Him? We are brought to the vestibule of the temple;

but how shall we gain admittance? We are in sight of "the fountain of living waters;" but how shall we draw the needed supply? Thanks be to the God of all grace! our text furnishes us with an answer to the anxious enquiry: "Ye believe in God, believe also in me." While faith in God presents before us an object all-sufficient—faith in the Redeemer is the way whereby we come to God and partake of his fullness. And so we remark,

2. That the object of this faith is not only God, as the all-sufficient Being, but Jesus Christ as the Redeemer of sinners. It is through him that we become "reconciled to God"*—by him that "God hath reconciled us to himself" † and so, "by him also we have access by faith into this grace wherein we stand." ‡ The ample supply indeed is treasured up in him; for "in him are hid all the treasures of wisdom and knowledge:" ‖ "in him dwelleth all the fullness of the godhead bodily;" § and "of his fullness have all we received, and grace for grace." ¶

And now, brethren, I trust you see the fitness of one part of this divine prescription to the other;—the fitness of combining these remedies to give them due effect: "believe in God, believe also in me." While God stands before the mind's eye in the fullness of his all-sufficiency, you see in Him all that you can need, whatever your case may be. But you see, at the same time, an awful moral distance between this holy Being and your own sinful souls: "your iniquities have separated between you and your God." You see indeed in his holy nature a fearful hostility to all that is sinful; and well may you enquire with anxious solicitude, how, O how, shall I find access to Him as a reconciled God and Father? Hark! that voice! Behold, Jesus Christ comes forth to answer the enquiry! He declares himself "the way, the truth, and the life:" he asserts the gracious designs and the love of God; and gives the evidence in groans, and tears, and blood! And thus, while faith in God presents us with an assurance of his *ability* to bless—faith in Jesus Christ presents an equal assurance that He is *willing* as well as able. "Ye believe in God, believe also in me."

Before dismissing this part of our subject, it seems proper,

---

* Rom. v: 10.   † 2 Cor. v: 18.   ‡ Rom. v: 2.   ‖ Col. ii: 3.
§ Col. ii: 9.   ¶ Jno. i: 16.

I should remark, that faith is to be considered in regard not only to its *object,* but to its *quality.* Considered in this respect, let me offer a reflection or two on this important exercise of the soul.

That there is something more in evangelical faith than mere abstract passive persuasion of the truth of the fact, is, to my mind, as clear as any thing that is revealed or required in the scriptures. Such an abstract persuasion—such a passive admission of the truth, may exist without any vital operation. And what is *dead* faith, but a faith of that sort? If then it be asked, what more is necessary to evangelical faith—to a living faith in God—in Jesus Christ? I answer, *trust—confidence* in the object is necessary: a casting of the soul on him " who is able to save to the uttermost all that come unto God by him : " I know in whom I have believed : (or trusted,) and I am persuaded that he is able to keep that which I have committed to him." *   When the last idol is resigned, and every dependence given up but Christ the Redeemer—the soul being brought to rest on him alone— then is evangelical faith seated in the heart; and working by love it becomes a vital principle of holy action.

We come now to the other division of our subject; and here we are to consider,

II. That the faith here required-is the sovereign remedy for heart-troubles: " Let not your heart be troubled: ye believe in God, believe also in me."

But here I would caution you against a mistaken view with respect to this point.   Let it not be thought that we are to consider faith *in itself* as possessing this virtue.   No, brethren: here, as in other cases, where the most interesting and important results are ascribed to faith, the *efficient* cause is to be found in the *object,* not in the *act* of faith.   It was thus with regard to the healing of bodily diseases: " Thy faith hath made thee whole."   And it is thus with regard to spiritual healing : " Thy faith hath saved thee; go in peace." In all such cases, the result is ascribed to faith as the *instrument*; and as, in that character, taking hold on the object, and receiving and appropriating the benefit. ' A wonderful instrument indeed is faith!—capable of achieving wonders, through the efficacy of the object on which it acts!   In this

---

* 2 Tim. i : 12.

sense then is this faith to be considered, when we speak of it as the sovereign remedy for the troubles of the heart.

Well, brethren, we have our "songs in the house of our pilgrimage," and here too we have our troubles: for "this is not our rest." And we are now to see how the remedy provided by our heavenly Physician may be brought to bear upon these afflictions. Under the first head of our discourse, this view of the case has been in some measure necessarily anticipated; but we now assign to it a more particular attention.

I am aware, brethren, how much easier it is, calmly to present the remedy for the evils and afflictions of life, and earnestly to press the advice that we should appropriate and apply that remedy—than it is to put this advice into actual practice for our own benefit. But trusting in that grace which can give effect to our feeble efforts—remembering that we ought to "bear one another's burdens," and having a common interest with you in this case, I am encouraged cheerfully to proceed with this part of my subject.

"Many are the afflictions of the righteous." * To attempt an enumeration of them in detail, would be a task which we cannot undertake, nor is it necessary. There are *classes* of affliction which we shall notice, including all the particular cases to which we may be subject, (some of which we may specify;) and if the remedy provided by infinite goodness should be found to cover all these classes of human evil, then may we feel assured that it is sufficient for all particular cases, whether specified or not; whether appertaining to mind or body—whether of a spiritual or an earthly character. Be not discouraged. If "many are the afflictions of the righteous," remember, "the Lord delivereth him out of them all."

These classes of affliction may arise at different times, from different quarters; as the storm arises sometimes from one point of the horizon, and sometimes from another. And I may add, that as in the case of a storm, so here; the clouds of trouble may gather from different quarters at the same time, and meeting and mingling in conflict, what a tempest threatens to crush the sufferer! See Paul "in heaviness through manifold temptations!" and hear the old

---

* Psm. xxxiv: 19.

patriarch exclaim—"All these things are against me!"
Brethren, if amidst your trials you have been spared from
the severity of the tempest, you have reason to bless the
hand divine for milder dealings : and if ever *that* should be
your lot, remember that He who "rides in the whirlwind"
has promised, "as thy days, so shall thy strength be."*
Let us take a view of these classes of affliction, and the fitness of the remedy provided by our gracious Redeemer.

1. There is a class of sore troubles arising from the
temptations with which we may be assailed. Name them
"legion, for they are many;" and various are their characters and the aspects which they assume. But thanks to
divine grace! he who expelled and controlled the legion of
demons, can strengthen us to bear the fiery trial, and give us
the victory over all temptations. What are the characters of
these troublers of our peace? Some are *spiritual*—some
fleshly ; and some partake of a *mingled* character. You
may be assaulted with suggestions of unbelief;—with apprehensions that you are deceived in your best hopes;—with
legal and slavish fears that you may miss at last of the blissful enjoyment of God's presence. And hence may be
induced a despondent spirit—a trouble of the heart, sad and
grievous to be borne. Again, you may experience entice-
ments to an improper, an unlawful indulgence of carnal
appetite : and sore may be the conflict, when " the flesh lust-
eth against the spirit."

In all these temptations—these troubles of the heart, you
will need the prescription of the heavenly Physician, " ye
believe in God, believe also in me." And behold the fitness
of the prescription! Remember, brethren, that as faith in
God presents the remedy in all its fullness and sufficiency, so
faith in Jesus Christ gives you access to that remedy, and
the privilege to take and apply it :—and again I say, behold
the fitness of the prescription! Consider that in looking to
our Redeemer for help, you look to one who " having himself suffered, being tempted, is able to succour them that are
tempted."†

Does your trouble proceed from temptations of a spiritual
character—tending to distrust and despondency? Direct
your attention to the *freeness* of his grace. It is *here* that

* Deut. xxxiii: 25. † Heb. ii: 18.

you are to find relief. Cease to pore over your own unworthiness, to the discouragement of your spirit, and listen to the gracious promise, "Him that cometh unto me I will in no wise cast out."* What a promise! Why not embrace it? Over the head of all your apprehensions, reach forth the hand of faith, and take hold of the grace of the Father manifested in the Son. O, that is a blessed resolution of afflicted Job—"Though he slay me, yet will I trust in him."†

Are you troubled by a conflict with temptations addressed to "the desire of the flesh?" Place before your eyes the bright model of purity presented in the character of our Redeemer; and resolving to imitate that model, take courage from the promise that "Sin shall not have dominion over you; for you are not under the law, but under grace."‡ But do you feel self-condemned, from a consciousness that you have in some grievous measure *fallen* by the force of temptation? If grieved indeed, and penitent for the failure, let not your heart yield to despondency: "If any man sin, we have an Advocate with the Father, Jesus Christ the righteous."‖ And still he says "come;" and still he promises, "Him that cometh I will in no wise cast out." Surely, that is a precious remedy for heart-troubles arising from temptation—"ye believe in God, believe also in me."

2. There is a class of troubles growing out of our connection with *the world;* and the declaration of our Lord, John xvi: 33, is still applicable—"In the world ye shall have tribulation;" and still too is that encouraging word of his applicable—"But be of good cheer; I have overcome the world." The world has its various aspects, as well as the temptations of which we have taken a view. It is itself indeed the fruitful occasion of temptations; although, on account of its peculiar character and influence, we give it here a distinct place in the sources of the christian's troubles.

Yes, brethren, in a greater or less degree, according as circumstances may operate, the world in its different aspects will be found to be a source of trouble. Its blandishments allure—its frowns discourage—and its smiles deceive: various objects of business tax the attention—and cares of dif-

---

* John vi: 37. † Job xiii: 15. ‡ Rom. vi: 14. ‖ 1 Jno. v: 4.

ferent sorts oppress the spirits. But, brethren, our Captain having overcome the world, we through him can conquer too : and " This is the victory that overcometh the world, even our faith." * " Let not your heart be troubled : ye believe in God, believe also in me." The bright example which faith recognizes in him shall encourage your hearts, and that holy influence which faith receives from him shall strengthen your hands.

3. Troubles often arise from *afflicting providences.* The loss of dear friends and relatives—the bodily pains and sickness which you may experience—the operation of adverse circumstances, come from what quarter they may,—all these I class under the head of afflicting providences. It seems to be too common a persuasion, that Divine Providence has nothing to do with those cases of calamity which are brought about by wicked agency. Permit me to say, brethren, that he who cherishes this sentiment, not only circumscribes the range of God's providential government, but *so far* deprives himself of that ground of resignation, and that support, which faith offers to him under the pressure of any such calamity.

All things are in the hand of God. Accidents (so called,) are under his control and management; and even those cases of calamity which are brought about by wicked agency—these too come within the range of his all-pervading providence. " He worketh all things after the counsel of his own will." † For his own wise purpose he *permits* the act of wickedness, and by his wisdom and power he governs its operation. And thus, while he holds the wicked agent accountable for his wickedness, he brings to pass, through his criminal agency, the counsel of his own will. " Surely, the wrath of man shall praise thee : the remainder of wrath shalt thou restrain." ‡ And thus too, I may add, while you or I justly complain of the injury at the hand of the *unrighteous man*, we submit to the hand of the *all-righteous God* —considering the affliction as a dispensation of his providence. Is there something here mysterious and incomprehensible?—Join with me then, and with the Apostle, in the adoring exclamation, " O the depth of the riches, both of the wisdom and knowledge of God ! how unsearchable

---

* 1 John v : 4.   † Ephes. i : 11.   ‡ Ps. lxxvi : 10

are his judgments, and his ways past finding out!"*

In regard to the dispensations of Divine Providence, of every description of character, there is a lesson taught by an eminent teacher in the school of Christ, of deep interest to every believer. Learn it, christians, learn it *by heart*. Rom. viii : 28 : "And we know that all things work together for good, to them that love God, to them who are the called according to his purpose." Learn this lesson, I say, *by heart*; and then you will be enabled to understand that estimate of human affliction which an apostle has made—2 Cor. iv : 17 : "Our light affliction, which is but for a moment, worketh for us a far-more exceeding and eternal weight of glory."

It remains for us to direct our attention to an important object, introduced by our Lord in close connection with the text, and obviously designed to give the crowning effect to the prescription which he has here given, as the remedy for the troubles of the heart. I allude to that blissful prospect opened before the disciples,—their final resting place and home in the future world : "In my Father's house are many mansions: if it were not so, I would have told you. I go to prepare a place for you. And if I go and prepare a place for you, I will come again and receive you unto myself; that where I am there ye may be also." To this prospect I made an allusion in the introductory part of this discourse— as calculated to brighten the gloom of affliction. And surely, brethren, the eye of faith cannot be raised towards such a prospect, without receiving a cheering ray of light from the throne of God.

Shall we undertake, by dressing it in pompous words, to *adorn* this passage—this rich promise of our Saviour to his disciples? 'Twould be "to varnish gold, or paint the diamond." The mind cannot imagine any thing more perfectly finished; and it only requires that our attention should be directed to it, in all its bearings, to see its beauty and to feel its influence.

"In my Father's house are many mansions."—"My Father's *house*." How familiar the expression!—like that of a prince brought up in a palace, and undazzled by the splendors of royalty.—"*My father's* house." Then *you* have an interest in it; for you belong to my family.—

---

* Rom. xi : 33.

"Many mansions." *Here* you may be slighted, uninvited, cast out, as unworthy of a place among the children of this world : but be of good cheer; there is room for you in the mansions above.—"If it were not so I would have told you : " so that you should not be tantalized with the vain hope of a place among the blessed, and then shut out as unwelcome intruders.—" I go to prepare a place for you." To bespeak your future habitation, and see that all is in readiness for your reception.—"And if I go and prepare a place for you, I will come again and receive you unto myself; that where I am, there you may be also." Count upon my return, as certainly as on my departure. "That where I am, there you may be also." Christians, are you not ready to say, Lord, it is enough! Let me be where Jesus is, and I shall be with God, who is the fountain of bliss; for " in his presence there is fullness of joy; at his right hand there are pleasures forevermore." *There* the turmoil of life is hushed in perfect repose, and peace and joy take place of sorrow and affliction. Where is the believer who, in view of such a prospect, will not subscribe to the Apostle's estimate, Rom. viii: 18—"I reckon, that the sufferings of this present time are not worthy to be compared with the glory which shall be revealed in us."

Christians, I commit the subject to the blessing of God, and to your reflection. May you find, by happy experience, the efficacy of that remedy which our heavenly Physician has provided for the troubles of the heart—"Believe in God, believe also in me."—"Grace, mercy and peace!" Amen.

NOTE.—I wish to add here a few thoughts, in regard to the supervision of Divine Providence, (as noticed in this discourse,) in cases of injury in any form, perpetrated by the agency of wicked men.

If we would rightly conceive of any such case, we must view it under two different aspects; namely, as a wicked action on the part of the agent; and as a dispensation of Divine Providence. Viewed in the light first mentioned, we justly abhor the deed and condemn the perpetrator:—in the second point of view, we bow to the Disposer of all events, and own the righteousness of his all-pervading government.

But here it may be asked, if the case above mentioned be a dispensation of Divine Providence, how can the agent be considered culpable, and subject to just condemnation? Or, (*vice versa,*) if the agent be really criminal, how can such a case be considered a dispensation of Divine Providence?

In answer to these queries, and as something towards a solution of the difficulty, I offer the following remarks:

1. That in any such case, the agent acts freely, of his own volition, without any constraint or impulse from God —being left to the exercise of his own wicked disposition and design : Jas. i : 13 : and thus is he responsible and justly subject to condemnation. And

2. God, the sovereign Ruler, removing those restraints which might prove a hinderance, and so laying or ordering the train of circumstances as to permit the perpetration of the deed—the case thus becomes a dispensation of Divine Providence. And thus we exhibit the twofold aspect of such a case, as before mentioned.

The limits, however, of this *permission* on the part of Divine Providence, are marked out by unerring wisdom, and guarded by almighty power. "Hitherto shalt thou come, but no further," is spoken by the voice of Omnipotence, to the turbulent passions of wicked agents, as well as to the tumultuous ocean. See this truth exemplified in the case of satan's power to afflict God's servant Job: and see too that expression of the Psalmist verified: "Surely the wrath of man shall praise thee: the remainder of wrath shalt thou restrain."

It is in this view of Divine Providence, (as I humbly conceive,) that God is said to *do* that which he has seen proper to *permit*—having so ordered the train of circumstances, that it will certainly take place. Thus it is said that "He hardened Pharaoh's heart:" Ex. vii: 13; while Pharaoh, more strictly speaking, "hardened his [own] heart:" ch. viii: 15. So, also, David says of Shimei, while cursing the king, "Let him alone, and let him curse; for the Lord hath bidden him:" 2 Sam. xvi: 11. Examples to this effect abound in the scriptures: I add one more—the case of the death of our Redeemer, Acts iv: 27, 28: "For, of a truth, against thy holy child Jesus," &c. they "were gathered together, to do whatsoever thy hand and thy counsel determined before to be done."

That there rests still an adorable darkness on that link which connects the purpose and providence of God with human freedom and accountability, is readily admitted :—a darkness which checks our presumption, and renders *reverence* more suitable than *speculation.* " O the depth ! "

Nor is this the only mysterious feature in the afflicting dispensations of Divine Providence. Cases occur in which we may enquire in vain, *why* should this be ?—Why such a visitation, so signally distressing, from the Divine hand? The reason rests with the great Sovereign ; and it is the proper office of faith, in such a case, to refer the matter to Him, whose wisdom never errs, whose goodness never fails.

AN EXTRACT

FROM THE LONDON PULPIT, BY JAMES GRANT.

There is another thing which the preachers of the gospel ought most sedulously to guard against, if they would consult their ministerial usefulness : I mean a spirit of levity. Let me not be understood as here proscribing a cheerful disposition, or even innocent conversation of a playful kind. The levity which I condemn is a very different thing : it is that excess of merriment or jocularity which leads the party to forget, for a time, the ministerial character altogether, and to degenerate into a sort of temporary buffoon. To make the proper distinction on paper between undue levity and innocent playfulness, is no easy task ; but every one possessing a discriminative judgment will be able to make it in his own mind. One rule for distinguishing between the two things is this : that whenever a minister perceives that he is carrying his jocularity so far as that those around him are beginning to give unrestrained utterance to *their* fancied witticisms and real or supposed humorous remarks, he must have exceeded the bounds of propriety. There must be something wrong in a minister's conversation or conduct when his presence does not operate as a restraint on any undue levity on the part of even the men of the world.

Of the importance to the preacher of the gospel, if he would be a useful christian minister, of abstaining from anything approaching to laxity either of conversation or conduct, I need not speak. It must be sufficiently evident to all who have ever expended a moment's thought upon the subject. Where is the man who cannot point to cases which have fallen under his own observation, of some of the most able and eloquent ministers he has ever heard, neutralizing, in a great measure, the effects of their pulpit discourses, by looseness of conversation or laxity of conduct? Are there not evangelical ministers who can take as liberal, and seemingly as unrestrained a part in the conversation which is going on in a mixed company, as any of the other persons present? And is there not, on the very face of the thing, something wrong in this? My impression of the sanctity which ought to attach to the character of the christian minister is such, that I conceive he ought not to be any length of time in a mixed assemblage of individuals without something transpiring in his deportment or conversation, if not in both, which will clearly indicate to the rest of the company the profession to which he belongs.

A man, I repeat, may be a first-rate preacher; there may be a peculiar unction in all the services of the sanctuary in which he engages; and yet, if there be anything loose in his words or conduct; anything like levity in his manner, or any appearance of his having caught the spirit of the world, —the efficiency of that man's ministerial labors is sure to be impaired to an awful extent.

I was expressing a short time ago to a Dissenting minister, my admiration of the able and evangelical preaching of the pastor of a Dissenting church; and added, that I was surprised his congregation was not larger. "The reason," said the other, "is, that though an excellent preacher, there is a levity in his conduct which is most unbecoming. For ex· ample,"· he added, " Mr. ——— has been known repeatedly to purchase and eat apples in the streets on the Sunday; and though never charged with any flagrant immorality himself, some of his most intimate acquaintances are very immoral in their conduct." I speak on this point from personal observation. I have known ministers remarkable for their talents as preachers, and whose doctrines were evangelical in the highest degree, but whose conduct, without being positively immoral, was not becoming the gospel,—labor for a long succession of years with but very limited success. I have heard it remarked times without number, of the ministers to whom I allude, " Oh what a pity it is that Mr. So-and-so ever comes out of the pulpit at all; how different he is in private from what he is there!" To guard against misconception, it may be proper to state, that in making these remarks I have no London minister in my eye. I make the observations in the hope that they may have the effect of causing some preacher of the gospel who may feel that they apply in a greater or less measure to his case, to be more vigilant in his life and conversation. And for the encouragement and consolation of such ministers as may be conscious that Providence has not gifted them with those talents which acquire for men what is called popularity, let me here observe, that if they only walk holily and justly and unblameably before their fellow-men, they may be made the instruments of much greater spiritual good than those of far superior talents whose conduct is unbecoming the spirit of the gospel. I am much afraid that there are many christians, both in the ministry and out of it, who have never yet had proper views of the vast importance of a blameless example, to their usefulness in the world. Example, either for good or evil, exerts a mighty influence on the minds of those with whom we associate. I believe and am sure, that many a sinner has been converted through the still small voice of example, if there be not an inaccuracy in the expression, who have heard for years the preaching of faithful ministers without effect. It is a silent but most powerful and persuasive language. You hear not its voice, and yet the results show that it speaks with the tongue of a trumpet.

ial
THE
BAPTIST PREACHER.

| VOL. IV. | April, 1845. | NO. 4. |

PERSEVERANCE OF THE SAINTS:

A sermon, by Rev. Thomas W. Sydnor, preached before the Appomattox
Association, at the Rocks, Prince Edward Co., Va., August 10th, 1844,
and published at the request of that body.

—

*" Being confident of this very thing, that he which hath begun a good work in
you will perform it until the day of Jesus Christ."*—PHIL. i: 6.

—

In compliance with a resolution passed at the last session
of this body, I have selected as the theme of my discourse,
THE PERSEVERANCE OF THE SAINTS. This doctrine, I think,
is clearly taught in the passage before us. In the context the
Apostle expresses his thankfulness to God, and the joy
which he felt in praying for his Philippian brethren:
" I thank my God upon every remembrance of you, always
in every prayer of mine for you all, making request with
joy, for your fellowship in the gospel, from the first day until
now." He then assigns the cause of these emotions—the
confident assurance which he felt that God would perfect
the work of grace which he had begun in their hearts.
"Being confident of this very thing, that he which hath
begun a good work in you will perform it until the day of
Jesus Christ." This *good work* consists in the gradual con-
formation of life to the principles and requirements of the
gospel. The phrase *will perform it until*, is very significant; the full sense being, " will carry it on unto, and finish it at "*—that is, will carry it forward, gradually perfecting
it, until a certain period, and then perform upon it the last,
the finishing process. *The day of Jesus Christ*, may refer
to the period of death or that of judgment—and so far as

---

* Bloomfield.

7—Vol. IV.

the present argument is concerned, it is not material to which the reference is made.

The text teaches us, that in every believer a good work has been begun ; that at its commencement, and at every subsequent period previous to the coming of the Lord Jesus, this good work is incomplete ; that it is nevertheless in progress, and will certainly be carried forward to perfection ; that God is its author, beginning, carrying on and consummating the entire work. Let this last point be distinctly noted : God is the author and finisher of this work of faith and holiness. If he be not, then we abandon the doctrine of the saints' perseverance—there is no security for the believer—there can be no perseverance on the part of any being infected with sin, except in a course of iniquity and destruction ; but if this work be of God, then is the believer safe and his complete redemption certain ; a being of infinite love, and faithfulness, and wisdom, and power, will never abandon a work commenced by His free and sovereign grace.

> " The work which his goodness began,
>   The arm of his strength will complete ;
> His promise is yea and amen,
>   And never was forfeited yet." *

The doctrine is simply this,—*God will complete the work of grace which he commences in the heart of each believer.* I shall endeavor to illustrate the doctrine ; to

---

* Their perseverance must depend entirely on themselves, or partly on themselves, and partly on divine aid, or entirely on the help and purpose of God. Does it depend entirely on themselves? This, I am inclined to believe, no person will affirm. Their progress in holiness is as much the work of the divine Spirit, as regeneration itself. If they work out their own salvation, it is God who worketh in them ; if they live in a spiritual sense, it is " Christ who liveth in them ; without me ye can do nothing." Does their perseverance depend partly on themselves, and partly on divine aid? This, at first sight may appear plausible. But what part of this great and important work is it that depends on themselves? Is it their faith? This is the gift, and the work of God. Their repentance? This is the gift of their exalted Prince and Saviour. Their hope? This is given them through grace? Their love? This is " shed abroad in their hearts by the Holy Ghost." Their peace? This is bequeathed to them by their divine Friend. Their knowledge? The knowledge of God is given them. Is it their hatred and opposition to sin? This is the necessary result of those pious affections cherished in the heart. All these things are of God ; as christians, they are his workmanship.—(*Matthews on the Divine Purpose*)

evince its truth; to vindicate it from objections; and to exhibit its practical bearings.

I. The doctrine has been misapprehended and misrepresented. It is important, therefore, to state it definitely, and to show precisely what we mean when we maintain the final perseverance of the saints.

That all who profess religion, and seem to be christians, will be saved, we do not believe. That many such do fall away and perish, is abundantly évident, both from observation and scripture. But that all who possess religion, who are real christians, united to Christ by a living faith, will be kept in faith and holiness unto eternal life, we steadfastly maintain.

The question before us is not whether real christians may suffer a decline in grace and fall into sin. We admit that they may, and often do. The question is, whether they will be allowed to lose all grace and to perish in sin? We argue they will not. For the entire sinlessness of believers in this world, we do not contend. This is no part of our creed; it belongs to those who deny the doctrine of perseverance. We admit that sin may exist within the christian; we deny that it is dominant within him. "A just man falleth seven times and riseth up again."

Again, when we say that the saints will certainly persevere, we do not mean to affirm that in themselves, and with no strength but their own, they are safe from apostacy. On the contrary, we believe and are sure, that if left to themselves, they would fall away and perish. Without divine assistance, they could not continue a single moment in faith and holiness. We rest their safety upon the promised support of the Holy Spirit. They are secure, because "kept by the power of God through faith unto salvation."*

The question is not whether a true saint, if he fall into sin and die impenitent, will be saved. We know that there can be no salvation, whether of saint or sinner, without repentance. The question is, whether any true saint will be

---

* Dr. Macknight, on this passage remarks: " The word signifies *guarded in a garrison.* The term is very emphatical here. It represents believers as attacked by evil spirits and wicked men, their enemies; but defended against their attacks by the power of God, through the influence of their faith, 1 John v: 4; just as those who remain in an impregnable fortress are secured from the attacks of their enemies, by its ramparts and walls."

allowed to die in impenitence. It is a perversion of the doctrine to represent it as promising salvation to any, irres- pective of a continuance in holy obedience. The point at issue is not whether the believer will be saved, if he do not endure unto the end, but whether he will not, by almighty grace, be "confirmed unto the end,"—not whether he will be saved without his own exertions, but whether he will not be made to persevere in the use of the appointed means of salvation. The question is not whether he will persevere, if grace do not continue. Such a question is absurd. You might as well ask, will a man live if the vital principle be extinguished, or will the sun shine if its light be blotted out? We maintain that grace is so fixed and settled in the soul, that it will never be removed; and that by its operations the believer will be kept from falling, and be made to persevere in holy obedience till the end of life, when grace will com- plete its work and glory crown the whole.

The grand question is this—" whether any who have been born of the Spirit, justified by grace, and adopted as God's children, will be left to utter and final apostacy,"—or whether all such, by the operation of the divine Spirit, will not be preserved from the controlling influence of sin, and be kept in faith and holiness until the end of life, and final- ly, be saved with an everlasting salvation?

Having thus explained the doctrine, I shall attempt

II. To establish it.

1. Our first argument is derived from the purposes of God. It is certainly the purpose of God to save a portion of the human family. Those whom he means to save are termed the elect. I am aware that the opponents of this doctrine, deny also the doctrine of election, in the sense in which we understand it. They admit, however, that believers are the elect. It does not affect our argument whether they are chosen from all eternity or not, until they believe. It is easy to show that it is the purpose of God to save all his elect:—Matt. xxiv : 24. "For there shall arise false Christs and false prophets, and shall show great signs and wonders, insomuch that *if it were possible*, they shall deceive the very elect." *If it were possible,* implying, obviously, that it is not possible so to deceive the elect, that they shall finally perish. Acts xiii : 48 : "As many as were ordained to eter- nal life believed." All believers, then, are ordained to eter-

nal life, and if ordained by an almighty and unchangeable God, will they not possess eternal life? Take another passage: Rom. viii: 29, 30. "For whom he did foreknow, he also did predestinate to be conformed to the image of his Son, that he might be the first born among many brethren. Moreover, whom he did predestinate, them he also called; and whom he called, them he also justified; and whom he justified, them he also glorified." Nothing can be more explicit. Words cannot be put together to express any thought more definitely than these words do convey the truth, that it is the purpose of God to bring all his saints into a state of glory. The passage shows that there is an indissoluble connection between predestination, effectual calling, justification and glorification. There could be no such connection, if it were possible for any of the saints to fall away and perish. It would not then be true, that all whom God predestinates, them he also calls; and whom he calls, them he also justifies; and whom he justifies, them he also glorifies. 2 Thes. ii: 13. "God hath from the beginning chosen you unto salvation, through sanctification of the Spirit and belief of the truth." Eph. i: 4. "According as he hath chosen us in him, before the foundation of the world, that we should be holy and without blame before him in love; having predestinated us unto the adoption of children, by Jesus Christ, according to the good pleasure of his will." Can it be supposed that God will allow his own purpose to be frustrated? Will he suffer those whom he has chosen unto salvation, and predestinated unto the adoption of children, at last to fail of salvation, and to be cast out with the children of the wicked one?

In the scheme of redemption, God requires of Christ, (Is. liii: 10, 11,) that he shall make his soul an offering for sin, and promises as his reward, that he shall have a seed to serve him; that the pleasure of the Lord shall prosper in his hands; that he shall see of the travail of his soul and be satisfied. With reference to this promise, the Saviour says, John vi: 37–40: "All that the Father giveth me shall come to me, and him that cometh unto me, I will in no wise cast out. For I came down from heaven, not to do mine own will, but the will of Him that sent me. And this is the Father's will which hath sent me, that of all which he hath given me, I should lose nothing, but should raise it up at the last day." The Saviour here declares that his purpose in coming into the world was to do his Father's will. He moreover declares, that the will of his Father, with respect to those who were *given to him,* and who, by consequence, should *come to him,* is, that he *should lose* none of them, that he should *bestow upon them everlasting life.* Now, if God has purposed to bestow these blessings upon all believers, and has committed the accomplishment of this purpose to the Lord Jesus Christ, who pledges himself to perform all the will of God, then is it not certain, that no believer will be lost, but that all shall have a glorious resurrection, and a blissful immortality? John x: 27–29. "My sheep hear my voice, and I know them, and I give unto them eternal life, and they shall never perish, neither shall any pluck them out of my hand. My Father which gave them to me is greater than all, and none is able to pluck them out of my Father's hand." Here the omnipotence of the Father, and the faithfulness of the Son, are both pledged for the preservation of believers.

In the covenant of grace, the covenant between God and believers; God engages to be their God, and that they shall be his people: Jer. xxxii: 40. "I will make an everlasting covenant with them, that I will not turn away from them to do them good, but I will put my fear into their hearts, that they shall not depart from me." Here is a covenant which can never be frustrated. God will not violate it. "*I will not turn away from them to do them good.*" He moreover ensures its perpetual observance on the part of his people: "*I will put my fear into their heats, that they shall not depart from me.* God does, sometimes, veil his face and withhold his Spirit from his people; but his word is pledged that he will not utterly forsake them. Is. liv: 7–10. "For a small moment have I forsaken thee: but with great mercies will I gather thee. In a little wrath I hid my face from thee for a moment: but with everlasting kindness will I have mercy on thee, saith the Lord thy Redeemer. For this is as the waters of Noah unto me: for as I have sworn that the waters of Noah should no more go over the earth; so have I sworn that I would not be wroth with thee, nor rebuke thee. For the mountains shall depart, and the hills be removed; but my kindness shall not depart from thee, neither shall the covenant of my peace be removed, saith the Lord that hath mercy on thee." It would be easy, were it necessary, to multiply such passages. To adduce all that are pertinent to the subject, would be to transcribe a large portion of the Bible. I will mention in this place but one other. Heb. vi: 17–19. "Wherein God, willing more abundantly to show unto the heirs of salvation the immutability of his counsel, confirmed it by an oath; that by two. immutable things, in which it was impossible for God to lie, we might have a strong consolation, who have fled for refuge to lay hold upon the hope set before us: which hope we have as an anchor of the soul, both sure and steadfast, and which entereth into that within the veil." In condescension to human weakness, God confirms his counsel by an oath: and if the counsel and oath of Him who is Almighty, and who cannot lie, do not ensure the salvation of the believer, I know not what will. Thus has God declared his purpose with reference to the preservation and complete redemption of his people. Now, if he is a being of infinite perfections, unchangeable in his purposes, and faithful to his promises, then all believers are safe. "The Lord of hosts hath purposed and who shall disannul." "The promises of God are yea and amen in Christ Jesus."

2. We pass to another argument. It is founded on the mediation of the Lord Jesus, and the relations which he sustains to his people. "This is a faithful saying, and worthy of all acceptation, that Christ Jesus came into the world to save sinners." The grand object of his advent into the world—the grand object of his life upon earth, of his death, his resurrection, and re-ascension to heaven, was the salvation of the elect. Yes, he gave himself for his people, to live for them, to die for them, to rise for them, to ascend for them, to intercede for them. Now will he certainly save them? Will he accomplish what he has undertaken?

By his obedient life and his vicarious death, he has made complete atonement for sin, and removed all the obstacles to our salvation, presented by a broken law. "He has redeemed us from the curse of the law, being made a curse for us." God may now, consistently with the holiness of his nature, and with all the principles of justice, bestow pardon and salvation upon all who believe. How is it possible then for any who rely upon the atonement of the Lord Jesus, to perish forever, when he himself declares, "whosoever liveth and believeth in me, shall never die."

Again, by his resurrection, he has furnished a pledge or earnest of the resurrection of the saints,—" Christ, the first fruits, afterwards, they that are Christ's at his coming," and not only of their resurrection, but of their complete forgiveness, and final acceptance with God. Rom. iv : 25. " He was delivered for our offences, and was raised again for our justification." 1 Pet. i : 3, 4. " Blessed be the God and Father of our Lord Jesus Christ ; who, according to his abundant mercy, hath begotten us again unto a lively hope, by the resurrection of Jesus Christ from the dead, to an inheritance incorruptible, undefiled, and that fadeth not away, reserved in heaven for you." " Because I live," saith the Redeemer, " ye shall live also." " When Christ, who is our life, shall appear, then shall ye also appear with him in glory."

More than this. When Christ was raised from the dead, he was received up into heaven, and seated on the right hand of God. This denotes the sovereign dignity to which he was advanced, and the universal power with which he was entrusted. He had humbled himself and become obedient unto death. He is now raised from the dead by the power of God,—he ascends to heaven triumphant over all his enemies, he is received amidst the shouts of angels, exalted to the right hand of the Majesty on high, clothed with dignity and honor, invested with sovereign universal power and authority. And this exaltation is with express reference to the salvation of his people. " He is head over all things to the church." The power which Christ is now exercising in heaven, is different from that which belongs to him as God. It is a delegated power, given to him in view of the work which he had undertaken to accomplish, given to him, that he might the more effectually carry on and complete the salvation of his people. " As thou hast given him power over all flesh, that he should give eternal life to as many as thou hast given him." The believer is under the control and protection of Jesus Christ, who has all power in heaven, upon earth, and in hell. How is it possible then for him to sink in this world, or to fail of eternal life in the world to come ? Nothing can change the love of Jesus, or diminish his power to save.

Nor is this all. Christ is constituted the great intercessor of his saints. " If any man sin, we have an advocate with the Father, Jesus Christ, the righteous." " Wherefore, he is able to save them to the uttermost, that come unto God by him, seeing he ever liveth to make intercession for us." In the prayer which the Saviour offered for his disciples just before he left the world, we find the following petitions: " I pray for them; I pray not for the world, but for them which thou hast given me. Holy Father, keep through thine own name those whom thou hast given me, that they may be one as we are. I pray not that thou shouldst take them out of the world, but that thou shouldst keep them from the evil. Sanctify them through thy truth. Neither pray I for these alone, but for them which shall believe on me through their word; that they all may be one, as thou Father, art in me, and I in thee; that they also may be one in us. Father, I will that they also whom thou hast given me, should be with me where I am, that they may behold my glory which thou hast given me." John xvii: 9–24. You observe that he prays for all whom the Father hath given him, not only for those who were his disciples when he was upon earth, but for all who should believe on him to the end of the world. He prays that God would *keep them through his name*—that he would *keep them from evil*—that he would *sanctify them through his truth*—that they all may be *made perfect in one*—that they may be *with him and behold his glory.*

Now, is the intercession of Christ prevalent or not? Does the Father always hear and answer the prayers of his Son? John xi: 41, 42. " I thank thee Father, that thou hast heard me, and I knew that thou hearest me always." Well, if Christ prays for his people, that they may be kept unto eternal life, and if God always hears his prayers, will they not be kept? Is not their salvation certain? In view of these several considerations, the death, the resurrection, the mediatorial power, and the intercession of Jesus Christ, may we not triumphantly exclaim with the Apostle, " Who is he that condemneth?—it is Christ that died; yea, rather that is risen again, who is even at the right hand of God, who also maketh intercession for us."

The peculiar spiritual union between Christ and his people, ensures their eternal salvation. They are represented as *the possession, the property of Christ, his peculiar people, given to him by the Father, his purchased people, bought at*

8—Vol. IV.

an infinite price, redeemed with his own blood. Will he fail
to take care of his own property, especially that which he
has procured at such immense cost? They are spoken of
as the *members of his body.* Will he allow his own body
to be maimed? Will he suffer any of its members to be
severed and destroyed? They are represented as his *spiritual seed, his sons and daughters.* Will he be so negligent
of his own offspring, as to allow any of them to be torn from
his family, and to be made the children of the wicked one?
It cannot be   The relation of parent and child is indissoluble. The believer is a child of the Most High by a two-fold
title, that of regeneration and adoption, and can never cease
to be a child. 1 Pet. i: 23. "Being born again, not of
corruptible seed, but of incorruptible by the word of God,
which liveth and abideth forever." Gal. iv: 5, 6. "God
sent forth his Son, made of a woman, made under the law,
that he might redeem them that were under the law, that
we might receive the adoption of sons." Regeneration gives
us the nature of sons; adoption the privilege of sons. Nor
is it possible, as in the case of earthly parents, for the love
between Christ and his children ever to cease. His is unchanging love. Having loved his own, he will love them
unto the end. And he "sends forth his Spirit into the hearts
of his children, crying, Abba, Father; and puts his fear into
their hearts, that they shall not depart from Him." They
are represented as his *brethren* also. Heb. ii: 41. "Both
he that sanctifieth and they who are sanctified are all of one,
for which cause he is not ashamed to call them brethren."
And as his brethren, they are heirs of the same inheritance,
"heirs of God, and joint heirs with Christ." Jesus, our
elder brother, has already passed into the heavens, and taken
possession of this inheritance, to hold it and keep it in readiness for us who are to come after him. They are represented as *his spouse,* to whom he is betrothed, *his bride, his
beloved,* over whom he rejoices. Can it be supposed that he
will suffer these objects of his tenderest love to perish? This
union of believers with Christ ensures their perseverance.
They are one with him. Their life and interest are identified with his. "Their life is hid with Christ in God."
Whilst there is life in him, there must be life in them. He
is the vine, they are branches. He diffuses his virtues to
them, as naturally and as freely, as the vine sends forth its

sap into its own branches. Now who can sever this bond of union? Rom. viii: 35–39. "Who shall separate us from the love of Christ? shall tribulation, or distress, or persecution, or famine, or nakedness, or peril, or sword? Nay, in all these things we are more than conquerors through him that loved us. For I am persuaded that neither death, nor life, nor angels, nor principalities, nor powers, nor things present, nor things to come, nor height, nor depth, nor any other creature, shall be able to separate us from the love of God, which is in Christ Jesus our Lord."

3. Our third argument we deduce from the operations of the Holy Spirit, and his continued residence with believers. To console his disciples, when about to take his final leave of them, the Saviour assures them, "I will pray the Father, and he shall give you another comforter, and he shall abide with you forever." It is clear that this promise is made to all, in every age, who should believe. Christ's business upon the earth was not only to make atonement for his people, but to renew them in the spirit of their minds, to sustain and comfort them, and make them meet for the inheritance of the saints in light. This part of his work he has entrusted, to the Spirit, whose efficient aid was promised to him in the everlasting covenant. The peculiar office and work of the Spirit is to renew and sanctify the soul. He is given to believers, *to abide with them forever—to lead them into all truth—to take of the things of Christ, and show them unto them—to seal them unto the day of redemption—to be an earnest of their inheritance.* Now, who can doubt that the Spirit will fully perform his work, and if he does, who can doubt that every believer will be " washed, sanctified, justified," saved.

4. In addition to the arguments already presented, I will now adduce a number of texts, not yet quoted, which clearly establish the doctrine under discussion. "I know that my Redeemer liveth, and that in my flesh I shall see God." "As for me, I will behold thy face in righteousness, I shall be satisfied when I awake in thy likeness." "We know that when he shall appear, we shall be like him, for we shall see him as he is." "The time of my departure is at hand: I have fought a good fight, I have finished my course, I have kept the faith; henceforth there is laid up for me a crown of righteousness, which the Lord, the righteous judge,

shall give me at that day; and not to me only, but to all
them also, that love his appearing." There is such a thing
then as an assurance of salvation, or how could Job, and
David, and John, and Paul, speak so confidently of their
acceptance with God? The exclamation of Paul suggests
another thought. He declares that a crown is laid up for
him in heaven, kept in readiness for him, to be bestowed
upon him at the last day. But what if Paul should fail to
get to heaven? What would become of that crown? On
whom would it be bestowed? Whose head would it fit?
It was laid up for Paul, and would not be suitable for
another. Besides, each individual saint, every one that
loves the appearing of the Lord Jesus, has his own appropriate crown laid up. It can hardly be, my brethren, that
there are crowns in heaven which are never to be worn; and
yet it must be so, if any real saints fall from grace. Again,
it is said of the saints, that their " names are written in
heaven," " written in the Lamb's book of life." Are any
of these names written there to be blotted out again? Are
any of them recorded one day, and the next day erased, and
after a time re-inserted, and yet again expunged? It must
be so, if the names of all believers are inserted, and if any
of them are given over to fatal apostacy. But we are not
left to mere speculation in this matter. The time is coming
when this book will be opened to the universe, and the reve-
lator tells us beforehand, something of the disclosures which
will then be made. Rev. xx: 12–15. " And I saw the
dead, small and great, stand before God; and the books
were opened; and another book was opened, which is the
book of life; and the dead were judged out of those things
which were written in the books according to their works;
and whosoever was not found written in the book of life,
was cast into the lake of fire." The plain inference is, that
none whose names were found in that book, were cast into
the lake of fire. Again, after describing, in superhuman
strains, the great city, the holy Jerusalem, he declares: xxi:
27: " And there shall in no wise enter into it any thing that
worketh abomination or maketh a lie; but they which are
written in the Lamb's book of life." Now, for direct proof
that no name is ever blotted out of this book. Rev. iii: 5.
" He that overcometh, the same shall be clothed in white
raiment; and I will not blot out his name out of the book

of life, but I will confess his name before my Father, and before his angels." Is it objected that the promise is made *to him that overcometh*, and may not be applicable to every christian? Overcometh what? Why, the world and the devil, surely. There can be no greater conquest. And who is it that gains this mighty victory? " Who is he that overcometh the world, but he that believeth that Jesus is the Christ?" 1 John v: 5. "This is the victory which overcometh the world, even your faith." 1 John v: 4. " Whatsoever is born of God, overcometh the world." 1 John i: 14. " I have written unto you young men, because ye are strong, and have overcome the wicked one." Now, every believer overcomes the world and the devil. No one that overcomes the world and the devil, shall have his name blotted out of the book of life. Then no believer shall have his name blotted out of the book of life.

There is one other passage to which I would call attention. It occurs in our Lord's intercessory prayer. " This is life eternal, that they might know thee, the only true God, and Jesus Christ whom thou hast sent." Eternal life, then, is indissolubly connected with a knowledge of God and of his Son Jesus Christ. Christ imparts life to all believers, not a life which is temporary and fluctuating, but eternal and unchangeable. Every christian has " eternal life abiding in him."

From what has been said, it is clear that the doctrine of the fatal apostacy of a regenerate man, is not according to truth. It is against all the purposes of God with reference to the salvation of his chosen; at variance with the design of Christ as mediator, and opposed to the end of the Spirit's mission into the world. It is, however, believed and advocated by many, and the doctrine which I have been preaching has been strenuously opposed, and denounced as unscriptural, unreasonable, and dangerous. Let us

III. Examine these objections, and see whether they do really invalidate the doctrine.

1. It is objected to the doctrine, that it is plainly unscriptural. Numerous passages are referred to as disproving it. Some of the most plausible, and those principally relied on, I will notice. We are referred to Ezekiel xviii: 24: " But when the righteous turneth away from his righteousness, and committeth iniquity, and doeth according to all the abom-

inations that the wicked man doeth, shall he live? All his righteousness that he hath done shall not be mentioned; in his trespass that he hath trespassed, and in his sin that he hath sinned, in them shall he die." Hebrews vi: 4–6. "For it is impossible for those who were once enlightened, and have tasted of the heavenly gift and were made partakers of the Holy Ghost, and have tasted the good word of God, and the powers of the world to come, if they shall fall away, to renew them again to repentance." 1 Pet. ii: 20. "For, if after they have escaped the pollution of the world, through the knowledge of the Lord and Saviour Jesus Christ, they are again entangled therein and overcome, the latter end is worse with them than the beginning." I have brought these several passages together, because their general import is the same, and the remarks which I would make on either one of them, are applicable to all. It will not be expected for me to give a full exposition of the passages. It is sufficient to show that they do not disprove, or, in the slightest degree, invalidate the doctrine under discussion.

In the first place, it is by no means certain, that true believers are referred to in either of the passages. The one in Ezekiel, refers to a matter entirely different from the one under discussion. The prophet is showing the manner of God's dealing with the Jews, in reference to the land of Canaan, and not to the manner of his dealing with his saints, in reference to their spiritual and eternal state. The term *righteous*, may refer to one who is only reputed to be righteous; as persons are often spoken of in the Bible, according to their apparent or visible, and not their real character. That the passage in Hebrews does not refer to real christians, may be inferred from the comparison introduced in the context, in which their character is represented under the figure of the " earth which beareth thorns and briers," whilst that of real christians is expressed under the figure of the " earth which bringeth forth herbs meet for them, by whom it is dressed; " and also from the declaration, verse 9: " Beloved, we are persuaded better things of you, and things which *accompany salvation*, though we thus speak." The persons mentioned in 1 Pet. ii: 20, do not seem to be real christians, for they are represented under the figure of dogs and swine; whereas, christians are uniformly spoken of as sheep and lambs. These terms are used, it would seem, to indicate that their reformation was merely external, that no change of heart had taken place within them. The dog was but a dog, and loved its vomit; and the sow, though washed, was still a sow, and would return to the mire. But we are not strenuous on this point. Suppose the passage to refer to real saints. Then,

Secondly. They unite in establishing an indissoluble connection between total apostacy and eternal perdition. "*In his trespass, that he hath trespassed; and in his sin, that he hath sinned; in them he shall die.*" "*It is impossible to renew them again to repentance.*" "*The latter end is worse with them, than the beginning.*" If these passages teach that true believers may lose all gracious dispositions, and be brought under the reigning influence of sin, they also prove that they can never again experience the pardoning and sanctifying grace of God.

Lastly. The language of each passage is hypothetical. It is not affirmed that a righteous man ever did fall away, or ever will fall away, but that, *if he should fall away*, he would certainly die. The passages which we have adduced in support of our doctrine are plain and positive declarations. They assert unequivocally and unconditionally, that the *saints shall hold on their way, and be kept by the power of God through faith unto salvation.* These before us are mere hypotheses. Supposing a particular event to occur, they assert the consequences. Now, we do not deny that if the event should occur, the consequences would certainly follow. If a truly righteous man should turn from his righteousness and do according to all the abominations of a wicked man, we know that he would die. And it is equally true that if Gabriel should apostatize, he too would utterly perish. The question is, whether the thing supposed will ever take place? There are many such hypothetical expressions in the scriptures, with reference to which, it is certain that the event supposed will never occur. "Ye shall, therefore, keep my statutes and judgments, the which, if a man do, he shall live in them." The meaning of which is, that if a man should obey perfectly the law of God, he would be justified by his own works. Are we thence to infer that any man ever did, or ever will obey perfectly, the law of God? "Though we, or an angel from heaven, preach any other gospel to you than that which you have received, let him be accursed." Must we, there-fore, suppose that an angel from heaven will preach another gospel? With no more soundness of reasoning can we con-clude, because it is affirmed, *if a christian fall away he shall perish*, that therefore he will fall away?

We are referred to Gal. v : 4: "Whosoever of you are justified by the law, ye are fallen from grace." To raise an objection upon this passage is a mere play upon words. Its obvious meaning is, that those who hold to the doctrine of justification by works, reject the doctrine of jus-tification by grace.

We are referred to Heb. x : 29: "Of how much sorer punishment, suppose ye, shall he be thought worthy who hath trodden under foot the Son of God, and counted the blood of the covenant, wherewith he was sanctified, an un-holy thing." The objection is founded on the phrase, *wherewith he was sanctified.* Now, the most natural con-struction of the sentence is, to refer this phrase to the Son of God, and not to the person who had trodden him under foot. Wherewith he, that is the Son of God, was sanctified. The passage then, is not at all in point.

It is argued, moreover, that the doctrine is contradicted by scripture facts. Numerous instances of apostacy, it is said, are recorded in the Bible. As examples, we are referred to Noah, Lot, David, Solomon, Peter, Judas, Hymeneus, Alex-ander and Simon Magus. It devolves upon the objector to prove that all these were real saints, and moreover, that their apostacy was total and final. That some of them were true believers, we readily admit, but that their apostacy was total, we unhesitatingly deny. They were brought to repentance, which could not have been the case, if they had totally apostatized, according to the passage in Hebrews, which declares "If they shall fall away, it is impossible to renew them again to repentance." With regard to those who did not repent, the apostle John settles the question. 1 Jno. ii: 19. "They went out from us, but they were not of us; for if they had been of us, they would, no doubt, have continued with us; but they went out from us, that they might be made manifest, that they were not all of us."

There is another passage which shows us in what light to regard such apostates. Mat. vii: 22, 23. "Many will say unto me in that day, Lord, Lord, have we not prophesied in thy name; and in thy name cast out devils, and in thy name done many wonderful works? And then will I profess unto them, I never knew you, depart from me, ye that work iniquity." But if they had been real believers, Christ did once know them. "My sheep hear my voice, and *I know them.*" "The foundation of God standeth fast, for the Lord *knoweth them that are his.*" These passages also serve to explain the parable of the stony ground hearers, the tares in the wheat, and the foolish virgins. They teach, indeed, in which light to regard all the instances of total apostacy which we read of or witness. *" They went out from us, because they were not of us."* The case of Judas may demand a more particular notice, as it is maintained, that he is expressly included among those who were given to Christ. Jno. xvii: 12. "Those whom thou gavest me, I have kept, and none of them is lost, but the son of perdition." The expression *gavest me*, may be used to denote the gift of the twelve as apostles, and not as real disciples. But supposing it to refer, as it probably does, to all who are given to Christ as true believers, it furnishes no proof that Judas was so given. Let us notice some similar passages. Luke iv: 26, 27. "Many widows were in Israel in the days of Elias; but unto none of them was Elias sent, save unto Sarepta, a city of Sidon, unto a woman that was a widow." The widow of Sarepta is here included among the widows of Israel, by the very same prhaseology as Judas is included among those who are given to Christ, whereas, we know that she was not an Israelitish, but a Sidonian widow; and we know, equally well, that Judas was not a disciple of Christ, but "the son of perdition." "There were many lepers in Israel, in the time of Eliseus the prophet, and none of them were cleansed, saving Naaman, the Syrian:" i. e. none of the Israelitish lepers were cleansed, but Naaman, a Syrian leper, was cleansed. The precise meaning of the passage relating to Judas, may be thus expressed. Those whom thou gavest me, I have kept, and none *of them* is lost, but the son of perdition is lost. Besides, it is clear, that the Saviour never regarded Judas as a true disciple. Jno. xiii: 10, 11. "And ye are clean, but not all. For he knew who should betray him, therefore, said he, ye are not all clean." John vi: 70, 71. "Have not I chosen you twelve, and one of you is a devil."

9—Vol. IV.

It is said, also, that angels fell, and Adam fell, and surely christians may fall. Well, if christians have no other security against apostacy than the fallen angels and Adam had, there is little hope of their preservation. Adam was placed under the law of works, we are placed under the covenant of grace; a covenant established upon better promises. True, he had a better nature than we have, and a stronger inherent power to keep the commands of God, but he had no supernatural help. He had the ability to stand, and precepts requiring him to stand, and promises encouraging him to stand, but not one promise to secure him from falling. Believers are kept by the power of God, Adam was to be kept by his own power. So that they are safer in their state of imperfection, than he was in all his innocence. " Without me," says the Saviour, " ye can do nothing." " Through Christ strengthening me," affirms the Apostle, " I can do all things." Believers are secured by the promise of God, the mediation of Christ, and the influence of the Holy Spirit, which security Adam and the apostate angels never had.

2. It is objected to the doctrine that it is unreasonable and absurd, as the Bible contains numerous exhortations and commands to a holy life, and cautions and threatenings against apostacy, which would be unnecessary and impertinent, if it is already certain that all christians will persevere. Why, it is asked, should Paul caution the believing Hebrews " to take heed, lest there be in them an evil heart of unbelief, in departing from the living God," if they already had the assurance that their faith should never fail? Or why should Peter exhort the Christians to whom he wrote, " to beware, lest being led away with the error of the wicked one, they should fall from their own steadfastness," if it were already determined by God that they should never fall? We reply, that these exhortations and commands are a part of the means which God uses to save his people from apostacy, and ensure their perseverance. The question is, will these means be effectual? Surely, it is not sound reasoning to infer from the existence of a command, that those to whom it is given will disobey it, or from the existence of a caution, that those to whom it is directed will disregard it. Besides, we readily admit that christians are liable to partial and temporary backsliding; and these cautions are ne-

cessary to prevent such relapses. Indeed, we allow that, in some sense, they are in danger of total apostacy. We do not maintain that grace is immutable in its own nature. Its operations may be interrupted, its comforts may be destroyed, indeed, the very principle of grace, so far as its preservation depends upon the believer himself, may be utterly and forever lost. It should be borne in mind, that in the work of salvation, the means are ordained as well as the end. God is the author and finisher of our faith ; yet it is his pleasure that we should " work out our own salvation with fear and trembling," and he, by commands, and promises, and threatenings, as well as by the efficient agency of the Holy Spirit, " worketh in us both to will and to do." When Paul was imprisoned at Jerusalem, an angel appeared to him and said, " Be of good cheer, Paul, for as thou hast testified of me at Jerusalem, so also shalt thou bear witness of me at Rome." Here was a positive assurance to Paul, that he should live to preach the gospel at Rome. The next day, Paul's nephew informed him, that more than forty Jews had bound themselves under oath, that they would neither eat nor drink until they had put him to death. Here was a caution to Paul to be on his guard, that his life was in danger. God had indeed, determined to preserve the life of his apostle, and bring him safe to Rome, where he was to preach the gospel, and this caution of the young man was a part of the means which God used for the accomplishment of his purpose. Accordingly, so soon as Paul heard the intelligence from his nephew, he sent to Lysias, the chief captain, and apprised him of the conspiracy, and as speedily as possible, left the city under the protection of a strong guard. The fact, then, that God has promised to keep his saints from falling, is certainly no reason why exhortations and commands should not be addressed to them, especially since it is by these very means that God intends to effect their salvation.

3. It is objected to the doctrine, that it is of dangerous tendency, rendering christians careless, leading to licentiousness, and affording encouragement to sin. We cannot see how it tends to promote indifference and self-security, any more than other similar promises. Joshua was assured, that no man should be able to stand before him ; but this did not hinder him from using means of defence against his enemies. Hezekiah had the assurance of restoration from his infirmity,

yet he was very diligent in using means of recovery. When Paul was shipwrecked on his voyage to Rome, he had the assurance that not one on board should be lost, and yet, when he saw the sailors letting down the boat to leave the ship, he cried out to the centurion and the soldiers, " except these abide in the ship ye cannot be saved." The death of Christ was plainly foretold. He himself had a perfect knowledge of the time and manner of his death, yet he was as careful, as it was possible for him to be, to avoid all unnecessary exposure to his enemies, and to use all proper means of preserving his life.

If we can prove that this is a doctrine of the Bible, we at once refute the calumny that it affords encouragement to sin. That it may be perverted by ungodly men is not denied ; and what doctrine of the Bible has not been perverted ? False professors may wrest it to their own destruction, and turn the grace of God into lasciviousness, but no real christian will make it an excuse for his sin, or for his negligence in the discharge of christian duties. Show me the man who takes occasion from this doctrine to sin, and I will show you one who has never tasted and seen that the Lord is good. I cannot suppose that for God to assure any one whom he has regenerated by his Spirit, and adopted into his family, that he will be with him and sustain him in all his trials, that he will grant him grace to help him in every time of need, that he will never leave him or forsake him, but will make all things work together for his good, and at last crown him with immortal glory—I cannot suppose, I say, that such an assurance would alienate that child of God from his heavenly Father, causing him to turn aside from his commandments, and to indulge in all manner of sin. If this be the tendency of such promises, I have yet to know what christianity is—certainly, I have not so learned Christ. It seems to me that these assurances of support, and comfort, and grace to the end, would have precisely the opposite effect, uniting the believer the more closely to God, and prompting him continually to holy obedience. Moreover, it is true, in point of fact, that such is the practical tendency of the doctrine? Are those who hold it, less active, less diligent to make their calling and election sure, are they less devoted to the cause of Christ, and do they exhibit less of the spirit of their Master, than those who hold the contrary doctrine? I think not. I ask the question not in the spirit of vain glorious boasting, but to refute the charge, that our doctrine leads to supineness and licentiousness. I ask, where do you find most professors "falling from grace, and turning to the beggarly elements of the world?" Not among those who embrace the doctrine which I am advocating. But let us inquire more particularly,

IV. What is the practical influence of the doctrine? I remark, in general, that it is peculiarly adapted to promote the holiness of the believer.

It promotes his holiness, as it leads him to inquire into the state of his own heart. It teaches him that holiness is a progressive principle, that "the path of the just is as the shining light which shineth more and more unto the perfect day." He learns then, that there can be no good evidence of the existence of holiness in the heart, unless there is an habitual increase of holiness. No one can certainly conclude that the work of grace has been begun within him, unless it is progressing within him. This will naturally lead the professor to look within himself for the evidence of grace, to examine himself whether he be in the faith, to strive against sin, and diligently to use the means of growth in grace.

It gives joyous and admiring views of the grace of God in the great work of redemption. How wretched the condition of fallen man, how guilty, how depraved, how helpless—how malignant his character, how foul his pollution, how dreadful his doom.

> "How sad our state by nature is,
> Our sin, how deep its stains;
> And satan binds our captive minds,
> Fast in his slavish chains."

Now, when we think of the depths of sin into which the believer was sunk, when we "look upon the rock whence he was hewn, and the hole of the pit whence he was digged," with what emotions of joy and wonder do we contemplate the grace that has been displayed in his elevation? This doctrine teaches that salvation is all of grace. That it was grace that contrived the scheme of redemption—that it was of grace that the elect were first given to Jesus Christ—

that it is of grace that they are awakened and enlightened—
that it is of grace that they are brought to repentance and
obedience—that it is of grace that they are pardoned—that it
is of grace that they are kept from falling—that it is of grace
that they will, at last, be brought to immortal glory.

> " Grace all the work shall crown,
>   Through everlasting days;
> It lays in heaven the topmost stone,
> And well deserves the praise."

Our admiration is increased, when we consider that this
mighty work is accomplished in despite of numerous and
powerful opposing influences.   Aside from his own evil passions, all leading him away from holiness and from heaven,
the believer is beset with enemies bent upon his destruction.
" No sooner is grace implanted in the heart, than all the
powers in hell are in arms against it."   Now, what can a
worm of the dust do against principalities and powers? To
see a lawless, infuriated banditti, rushing, with deadly
weapons, upon a little child, holding in its hand a rich jewel,
and yet not able to murder the child or to seize the treasure,
would fill the beholder with unutterable astonishment, and
cause him to extol the invisible, almighty hand that protects
the child and defeats the assailants.   It is a standing miracle in the world, that the devil, with all his allies, is not
able to overcome the weakest babe in Christ, or to wrest
from him that treasure of grace, which he holds as a gift
from his Father in heaven, and as an earnest of a richer inheritance of glory.

Whilst this doctrine leads the believer to admire the grace
of God, it at the same time inspires him with love and gratitude.   It teaches him that God loves him—that he has manifested His love towards him at immense sacrifice—that His
love secures for him an inheritance in heaven—that it is
bestowed upon him, not because of any worthiness in him,
but by God's free and sovereign grace—that this love, like
its author, is unchangeable, eternal, infinite.   Who can
resist the power of such love?   Must it not constrain him
who is the subject of it, to " strive continually to make some
suitable returns of affection and thankfulness."   " We love
Him, because He first loved us."

This doctrine is pre-eminently fitted to promote a spirit of humility. It shows us our sinfulness, our weakness, our utter helplessness. It brings us to see and feel that there is nothing good in us, that there is no help in us, that we are entirely dependent upon divine power and grace for pardon, and sanctification, and every blessing. How must this perception of our abject and helpless condition, check every emotion of pride and self-gratulation?

It inspires the believer with confidence. Whilst it teaches him his weakness, it shows him where his strength is. It points him to the Saviour, who is his righteousness and his strength; who has promised to sustain and comfort, to guard and defend him through all the journey of life, and at last bring him "through the gates into the city, and admit him to that rest which remains for the people of God." Must not this assurance make him strong in the Lord and in the power of his might?

It prompts him to cheerful and active obedience. It appeals to the highest and strongest motives to obedience—his love, his gratitude, his sense of obligation. It shows him what great things God has done for him—that he has redeemed him from death, and hell, and sin. It shows him how great are his obligations to consecrate all the powers of his body and soul, his time, his talents, his property, his influence, his life, his all, to the service of Him who has loved him and given himself for him.

In conclusion, my brethren, suffer a word of exhortation. Are these things true? Is the doctrine which I have preached a doctrine of the Bible? Is its tendency such as I have represented it to be? Take heed, then, to yourselves and to the doctrine. Evince to the world by your holy life, that it is a doctrine according to godliness. I remember a remark made by an esteemed brother at our late anniversaries in Philadelphia. * I shall never forget it, nor cease to feel its force. Much had been said about the evil of corrupting the word of God, especially by covering up and concealing the meaning of terms in a professed translation of the Bible. In all this he sympathised. "But would you know," said he, "what is the worst translation ever given of the Bible? It is that translation which is given of it in

---

* Rev. Richard Fuller, of South Carolina.

the inconsistent lives of professed christians. For that trans-lation, if it be wrong, contradicts the whole tenor of the gospel, which teaches us to deny all ungodliness and worldly lusts, and to live soberly, righteously, and godly, in this present evil world." Christians are witnesses to testify in their lives, as to the truth of the doctrines of the gospel. I beg you, my brethren, not to contradict, by your lives, the doctrine which I have preached to-day. That was a high compliment bestowed upon the Corinthian christians by the Apostle when he said, "ye are our epistle, known and read of all men: for as much as ye are manifestly the epistles of Christ; and a higher still, by our Lord himself, upon his people, when he declared, "ye are my witnesses." I call upon you to bear witness in your lives, to the truth and purity of the doctrine which you profess.

> " So let our lips and lives express,
> The holy gospel we profess,
> So let our works and virtues shine,
> To prove the doctrine all divine."

My heart's desire and prayer to God for you all is, that you may be sanctified through the truth. "And now, unto Him that is able to keep you from falling, and to present you faultless before the presence of his glory, with exceeding joy, to the only wise God our Saviour, be glory and majesty, dominion and power, both now and ever. Amen.

> "Lord, hast thou made me know thy ways!
> Conduct me in thy fear:
> And grant me such supplies of grace,
> That I may persevere.
>
> Let but thine own almighty arm
> Sustain a feeble worm,
> I shall escape, secure from harm,
> Amid the dreadful storm.
>
> Be thou my all-sufficient friend,
> Till all my toils shall cease ;
> Guard me through life, and let my end
> Be everlasting peace." .

THE
BAPTIST PREACHER.

VOL. IV.   May, 1845.   NO. 5.

THE REASONABLENESS OF FAITH:

A sermon, by Rev. SHALAR G. HILLYER, Principal of the Penfield Female Academy, preached in the Chapel of Mercer University, in Penfield, Ga., March 2, 1845.

—

" *We walk by faith and not by sight.*"—2 COR. v : 7.

—

The doctrine of faith is often made the ground of objection against the religion of Jesus Christ. We are asked, what is the propriety of suspending so important an interest as the salvation of the soul upon mere faith? Have we not a right to demand absolute knowledge in relation to *religious truth*? With a view to meet the difficulties suggested by these questions, I propose to offer some remarks upon the subject as set forth in the text.

I. My first remark is, that the sentiment is not peculiar to the subject of religion. It has been often shown that man's absolute knowledge is very limited. And of that which he does possess, very little is available in the details of those operations in which he is engaged. The consequence is, and it is a matter of fact, that in the most important affairs of life, man walks by faith and not by sight. We offer a single illustration. Trade engages the industry of many thousands of the human family; and in its results affects every rank of society : yet this immense business is sustained by faith. The history of one transaction will show this. A merchant in New-York orders from London a quantity of goods. To pay for them, he remits a draft upon his correspondent in Liverpool. To provide for this draft, he has already ordered from New Orleans a shipment of cotton to Liverpool, with instructions to his correspondent to honor his draft in favor of the London house. There is the whole operation, just such as do occur repeatedly in the commercial world. Examine it. At each successive step the intervention of faith is necessary. The post office must be trusted. Letters must be sent to all the aforesaid points; and perhaps a hundred different persons must share the responsibility of their safe transmission. All these must be true to their trust, or the whole plan fails. The London house, the Liverpool correspondent, and the New Orleans factor, together with their respective subordinates, must be trusted. Each in his appropriate place, has his part to perform, essential to the success of the enterprise. Should there be unfaithfulness, or negligence, or fraud, at any of these points great inconvenience,—ruin may result. What a demand for faith? and in whom? In men, who are always fallible, and sometimes corrupt. But the necessity of faith does not stop even here. The dangers of the sea, and the accidents of the land, must be hazarded. The explosion of an engine, or an untimely storm, may overwhelm the whole speculation, and involve in bankruptcy the bold adventurer. Yet in the face of such contingencies, does he confidently embark his capital, and with it all his earthly hopes. Verily the merchant walks by faith and not by sight.

It were easy to show that the same is true of every man of business. But for this we will not detain you. To the reflecting mind, our position is doubtless clear. The use we make of it is this: no one can consistently withhold his assent from the truths of religion, because they are not objects of absolute knowledge, until he is willing to forsake the avocations of life because he cannot predict the results of his operations. If the well known uncertainties of every branch of human industry, presents no objection to its pursuit, neither should the mysteries of religion deter the soul from the pursuit of spiritual blessedness. Such is the conclusion to which this brief comparison has brought us, in favor of that feature in christianity which our text portrays.

But while the sentiment of the text is not peculiar to religion, we admit that in this it most especially applies. Divine truth furnishes its best, its noblest illustration. There is something painful in the thought, that a human heart should refuse to adore the Almighty, because that Great Being does not unvail himself and become an object of sense, that flesh and blood may comprehend him. On the other hand, there is sublimity in the act, when the soul, taught by the silent indications of a teeming universe, and by the still more instructive lessons of inspiration, believes in the existence, and so acknowledges the authority of a superintending and eternal cause. No man hath seen the Father at any time. The eye whose far-searching vision surveys the earth, and sweeps the vaulted sky, hath not found Him; the ear that drinks in the thousand melodies which float along the air, hath not heard Him; and yet there is an inward power, whose holy revealings, when enlightened by sacred truth, pour in upon the soul the idea of Divinity. That power is faith. It lays no claim to demonstration; but relying upon the deductions of moral reasoning, is capable of perceiving those truths which make the bosom of the *seraph burn*; and which, when applied to a human heart, are sufficient to cleanse and sanctify it, and make it a fit habitation of God, through the Spirit.

II. Let us consider, in the second place, how exactly this arrangement, to walk by faith and not by sight, is adapted to our condition as sinners. We shall find that our being shut out from absolute knowledge of those truths which respect God, and our relation to him, is an arrangement of mercy. Remember, more knowledge enriches the intellectual powers only. It is not its *property* to purify the heart. If then God had bestowed upon our race the highest degree of intelligence, so that we could comprehend all mysteries, it does not follow that we should have been any the less sinners. Yet continuing transgressions under such circumstances, must have aggravated, beyond measure, our iniquities. A sinner's knowledge unsanctified, has no other moral power, but to magnify indefinitely the enormity of his guilt; and thus to make him tenfold more the child of wrath.

In proof of what is here stated, let us look at the condition of the fallen angels. We cannot suppose that they were deficient in knowledge. They walked not by faith, but by sight; yet their exalted privileges neither shielded them from transgression, nor inclined them afterwards to repentance. To this hour, with certain knowledge of those great truths, which are to us objects of faith only, they continue the same lost spirits. Nor have we the slightest evidence that a token of mercy was ever tendered to them from

on high. They seem to have sunk unpitied to their eternal
doom. Now, who can say that our condition would not
have been equally hopeless, if we had enjoyed equal knowledge? There are in scripture, impressive intimations that
such *would* have been our unhappy destiny. What mean
the woes denounced upon the devoted cities of Capernaum,
Bethsaida and Chorazin? The judgment shall be more
tolerable for Sodom and Gomorrah than for them. Why?
We do not pretend that their knowledge was perfect; yet
they did enjoy, in the person and conduct of Christ, a light
far greater than that which the little household of Lot was
able to shed upon the benighted regions of the plain.
Therefore they were more guilty. We cannot fail to notice
that while the greater privileges of the Galilean cities do
not seem to have inclined them to the service of God, or to
have excited any wholesome moral effect upon them, yet in
proportion to the superiority of these advantages, the judgment of heaven becomes more fearful and unforgiving.

We infer, that when knowledge of divine truth becomes
so far complete as to remove all occasion for the exercise of
faith, God finds no place for the exercise of forbearance
towards the sinner. This is corroborated by the fact, that
there is no hope for the wicked beyond the grave. When
such an one enters upon the scenes of the invisible world,
he is no longer required to walk by faith—perfect revelation
of the whole truth bursts upon his mind. But *then*, God
will show no mercy. He that is guilty must be guilty still.
Our Saviour gives us another intimation to the same effect,
which is yet stronger. In his dying prayer he said, Father
forgive them, *for they know not what they do.* Satan, who
instigated this deed, did know. The misguided people who
were his instruments, did not. The latter were, therefore,
the objects of his compassion, while satan was the serpent
under his heel, fit only to be trampled. Thus it appears,
that a want of knowledge, when not voluntary, is made a
ground of clemency. Hence, says Paul, I found mercy,
because I did it ignorantly in unbelief. From all which we
conclude, that that very state of things, which shuts out
from the perception of our senses the propositions of religion,
and makes them the objects of enlightened faith, is the only
state of things in which the Almighty would ever have
devised in our behalf, any scheme of redemption. If so,

that we are in such a state, becomes an indication of divine goodness. That we are required to walk by faith and not by sight, is the glory of religion—showing that our God is not an " austere man," but a compassionate father. Surely, then, it is our highest duty, and our best interest, humbly to embrace the plan which God has so wisely adapted to our condition as sinners, and in which he so kindly offers to us eternal life.

III. In the next place, let us consider how this doctrine affects the glory of God. This is a matter of no small moment. It will be conceded by every *pious* mind at least, that the glory of God should be the object of highest esteem with all his intelligent creatures. The scriptures teach us that he is himself jealous in respect to his own honor. He will not give it to another. To promote it, was his ultimate aim in the work of creation. Then we may well suppose that in the work of redemption he would not neglect it. Accordingly, the plan of salvation in all its details, does display the glory of God; and in a very eminent degree is this accomplished, by the arrangement that the redeemed must walk by faith. It is manifestly true, that the sincere faith of a pious man reflects more honor upon God, than the knowledge of an angel, who has never sinned, can do. The reason is obvious. The angel is surrounded by the blaze of heaven; he is in the full possession of all its bless, edness; drinking of its everlasting pleasures; and feeling with every sense which belongs to his nature, that heaven, with all its sublime and holy associations, with its endless duration, and with its triune God, is a glorious reality. I ask, is it strange that such a being, thus situated, should persevere in his allegiance? True he honors his creator with his confidence, but that confidence is exercised where it is impossible to doubt. How different is the case of the christian. He puts his trust in God, and with patience treads the path of obedience, though he is unable to discern a hand's breadth before him. Often, too, his faith is tested by the severest trials; temptations to unbelief and distrust beset him in a thousand forms; inscrutable providences, seemingly opposed to every dictate of kindness, sweep over him, inflicting upon his person inexpressible sufferings, and overwhelming his spirit with the deepest anguish: yet in the very hour of his extremity, he can look up, and exclaim with confiding assurance, "though he slay me, yet will I trust in him." Verily this declaration of Job, uttered amid the dust and ashes of his affliction, rendered unto God more exalted praise, than did the most pompous service, adorned with all the parade of wealth, in the days of his prosperity. A like reflection may be drawn from the history of Abraham. I presume no sinless creature ever honored his maker so highly as Abraham did, when he offered up his son whom he loved. He did not comprehend the divine intentions. He only knew that the Lord had made him the subject of happy promises in reference to this very son. Yet in the face of these promises, as if with a view to defeat their accomplishment, comes forth the demand for the life of Isaac. Does the Lord mean to sport with his own word, and to mock his servant? So one might reason who would walk by sight. So did not Abraham. He walked by faith: sustained by this, we see him repair to the mount of sacrifice; the altar is erected; the wood is laid in order; and now, the darling boy, the center of every earthly hope, is bound; and the fatal knife is stretched forth to slay him. Thus did the pious patriarch render unto God a homage which an angel could not pay. No wonder that such faith should be accounted to him for righteousness.

But what is true of these individual saints, is true of all the host of God's elect. Actuated by the same spirit, they have believed in him whom they have not seen. They have received his word though its doctrines are incomprehensible. They have trusted in his promises, though they do not know the mode of their accomplishment. When the skeptic taunts them with their ignorance, and derides them for believing what they do not know and cannot explain, it is enough to say, "We walk by faith and not by sight." True, we now know only in part and understand only in part, but the time cometh when we shall know even as we are known. True, it doth not yet appear what we shall be, but this we know, that when he shall appear, we shall be like him, for we shall see him as he is. Such is the unshaken confidence with which the whole church, with united voice, honors her eternal Lord. Such is the incense of praise which goes up to heaven from every pious heart. No wonder that the plains of Bethlehem rang with the shout "Glory to God in the highest:" for the angels knew that the Saviour's advent would set up forever the righteousness of faith; which righteousness, is indeed, glory to God in the highest.

IV. But as a further justification of this principle in our religion, let us notice the effect of faith upon the heart and life of the believer. We shall here find another proof of its full efficiency for all the purposes for which it was designed. We will notice, first, its effects upon the *heart.* It is proper, however, before entering upon this point, to premise two things. First. It is not incumbent upon me to discuss the procuring cause of faith. I assume that it is the gift of God, by the influences of his Spirit, and the teachings of his word. Nor, secondly, is it necessary, to the end in view, that I should draw any distinction between proper faith, and a certain *kind* of belief of the scriptures, which seems to be compatible with a state of unregeneracy. Of course, I have reference to that faith only, which is genuine, to that which is expressed by the text. Waiving these two points as not relevent, let us proceed:

The first effect upon the heart, is to disturb the repose of the sinner. So long as an impenitent man can remain inattentive to the claims of religion, he may enjoy comparative composure. He may pursue his business, or his pastime, careless of a hereafter, and heedless of a coming judgment. He may live a prayerless life, with no confessions of sin, and with no supplications for pardon. His maker may not be in all his thoughts: and he is a practical, if not a professed infidel. But let faith impress upon his mind, even a slight perception of divine truth, and its application to his own case, and this careless state can continue no longer. He beholds in the pure word of God, as in a mirror, the reflection of his guilt. Conscience, whose voice had been so long neglected, now wakes up to be his accuser, and in terms of bitter reproach, ratifies the justice of that law, which in every line condemns him. The work of conviction goes on, and at each step he discovers more and more plainly how lost is his condition. He tries to reform, but the evil is not only in his life, it is in his heart, and therefore, pollutes his whole nature. The law, he discovers is spiritual, holy, just and good : but himself is carnal, sold under sin. To will is present with him ; but how to perform that which is good, he finds not. All that he can do is to cry, " God be merciful unto me a sinner." But even his prayers only increase his self-abhorrence. In this condition, one is indeed the subject of deep distress. And the true cause of what is here described is, that the man has begun to believe aright the truths of the Bible. They have found access to his heart, and it is pierced. He can find no more peace in the ways of sin.

But faith not only kills; it also makes alive. By the severe discipline just referred to, under the subduing influences of God's Spirit, the heart is opened to receive the soothing words of redeeming love; he is brought to look on Him who was bruised for his iniquities; and perhaps unconsciously, he finds himself regarding with an interest wholly new, the Lamb of God. The character of Jesus Christ rises up before him, full of all admiration and loveliness. His feelings are drawn towards him as the chief among ten thousand. He delights to think upon the incidents of his life—to dwell upon the proofs of his tender compassion—and to honor his sublime and awful virtues. At length the cross, with its bleeding victim, fixes his attention; there he discerns the atonement; the plan of redemption stands revealed to his understanding; and though he may not yet identify himself with it, his soul is transported with the mighty idea; his sorrows now have passed away; his sense of condemnation has given place to a strange emotion of joy; he is conscious of love to God, though he may not yet dare to call him father; he is conscious of love to Christ, though he may not claim an interest in his atoning blood; and christians too engage his warm affections—for they reflect that glorious image which has just been to him so exceedingly attractive. Faith works by love, and perfect love casteth out all fear, till at length, receiving with gladness the engrafted word, the happy convert being justified by faith, has peace with God, and rejoices in hope of his glory.

We have yet to consider, under this head, the effect of faith upon the life. On this point our proposition is, that faith in supplying the soul with motives to action, is no less efficient than any amount of absolute knowledge could be. This subject is most forcibly illustrated by inspiration, in the eleventh chapter of the epistle to the Hebrews. The band of moral heroes, whose deeds are there recorded, could not have done more, even if the light of eternity had beamed upon their path. Yet, they walked by faith and not by sight. Their history needs no comment. We will therefore pass on, with only this remark: The instruction contained in this chapter, is not only retrospective, but the design of the apostle was to teach us, that such are the natural fruits of faith, and that such fruits are expected from it, wherever it is in exercise. True to this idea, the apostles, and martyrs, and missionaries of the cross, in every age, deserve to be classed with Moses and the prophets, as brilliant illustrations of the triumphs of faith. Nay, this is, at present, the power which sustains the vast machinery of christian benevolence. See the Bible Society, with its multiplied auxiliaries, spreading itself over the length and breadth of christendom, gathering up, from the stores of private charities, the material with which to pour into the dark places of the earth, the glorious light of the blessed gospel. Subsidiary to this, see the patient colporteur, with his little cart, or perhaps with his bundle on his back, making his way towards some obscure hamlet, or destitute region, that he may impart to the poor, the riches of revealed truth. See the Sabbath School, collecting together the neglected children of our cities, towns and country places, rescuing them from the hands of vice, throwing around them the sympathies of christian affection, and leading them by the hand up to the very gate of heaven. See, too, the organized institutions of charity—the Sailor's Home—the Orphan's Asylum—the sick man's Hospital—and the retreats prepared for those who would forsake the paths of infamy and shame. Let it be remembered that these things were not, till faith in God, and in Jesus Christ, whom he hath sent, found its abode in the human heart. Babylon, and Egypt, and Greece, and Rome, even in the days of their magnificence, knew them not. But, under the persuasive, yet controlling power of faith, human selfishness has given way, and man has learned, in some degree, to love his neighbor as himself.

There is one character to whom allusion has been made, that deserves a more extended notice. I mean the devoted missionary. And yet, I feel incompetent to do him justice. With a heart overflowing with the most refined social and filial sensibilities, he turns away from a home endeared by a thousand attractions, and hallowed by sacred associations. Possessed of a love of country that yields to none in purity,

11—Vol. IV.

depth or fervor, he abandons, forever, the land of his nativity. Endowed with a mind cultivated, intellectual and refined, he forsakes the circles of the learned and the halls of
science. For what are all these high and valued blessings
exchanged? For a home on some heathen shore—for a
country where the repose of civilization is unknown—where
the sympathies of human nature are scarcely allowed—and
where Terror, shrouded in a night of clouds, throws upon
the land his blackening pall. What high and holy purpose
hath impelled him forth? It is, that he may plant the gospel banner upon the heights of Paganism, and gather round
it the blest of God. We cannot follow him in all his jour-
neyings, but his steps are seen along the burning sands of
the desert, and upon the frozen regions of the north; amid
the recesses of the mountains, and over the far scattered
islands of the sea. He turns not aside for the riches of the
mine; he enquires not for the merchandise of the trader;
but careless of every personal interest, he seeks only for the
dying souls of his fellow-men. I ask again, what unseen
influence prompts to such self-devotedness? It is faith, that
works by love,—faith in the promises of a faithful God.
And this is the power which, under God, shall finally win
a universal, but bloodless victory, and subdue all the nations
of the earth under the gracious sceptre of our Lord, and of
his Christ. Well did our Saviour say, " this is the work of
God." What? To remove mountains? To stop the mouths
of lions? To quench the fury of the flames? To hush the
roarings of the storm? No—none of these. But this is the
work of God, " to believe on him whom he hath sent."
For, here is an element of power, by whose prevailing energy, virtue achieves her noblest triumphs—the soul secures
her everlasting rest—and God receives his highest praise.

Such are some of the considerations that may be urged in
justification of that feature in christianity which our text
presents. We have seen, first: That we are required to
walk by faith and not by sight, in the common affairs of
life, as well as in religion, although in this the rule finds its
most important application.

Secondly. That this arrangement is exactly adapted to our
condition as sinners.

Thirdly. That it promotes, in a peculiar manner, and in
an eminent degree, the declarative glory of God.

Fourthly. That in its effects, both upon the heart and life, faith is manifestly as efficient as any amount of absolute knowledge could be.

These points being, as we think, established, we conclude that all objections to our holy religion, founded upon the fact that we walk by faith, are in the very HIGHEST DEGREE UNREASONABLE. Let this be well considered by those who are conscious of neglecting its claims. At the day of judgment, the unbeliever will be speechless; for he cannot give a reason for his infidelity. His salvation is sought by his maker himself, in that mode, which, under all the circumstances, is best calculated to secure *all* the important ends. We say, then, to the impenitent, " Why will ye die? "

But this discussion would be incomplete if we did not pay some attention to an enquiry which, possibly, has occurred to many of you. Faith being such as has been described, why are not christians always bright and shining illustrations of its excellency? Why do we see around us so many languishing churches? Why so many sickly christians? Whence comes the worldly-mindedness that spreads through Zion so wide a moral ruin? In answer to these questions, we remark,

First. These melancholy facts are not attributable to any defect in the nature of faith; but to the very small degree of faith in exercise among professors. "O! ye of little faith," may well be addressed to christians of the present day. If it existed among us, even as a grain of mustard seed, far better would be our condition. Its efficacy would be seen in the prosperity and peace of our churches—in the success of the preached word—and in our progress in personal holiness. But,

Secondly. In order to realize all the blessings of this principle, it is necessary that we should actually conform to it. That is: if we would secure to ourselves, and to the church, and to the world, and to the glory of God, the full effect of the gospel, we must, in reality, fulfil its fundamental condition. We must walk by faith. Taking God at his word, we must follow him as Abraham did, when he left Urr of the Chaldees, not knowing whither he went. We may be grateful for whatever light he may please to shed upon our path—but we should follow him, even if required to grope our way in darkness. There are several particulars in respect to which we should especially walk by faith.

1st. We should do so in respect to the *doctrines* of the gospel. These, like their divine Author, are incomprehensible. We cannot fully explain them. And on this account, some have thought that we should let them alone. But the fact that they are revealed, is at once a contradiction of this sentiment. Indeed, the sentiment flies directly into the face of our text, for it implies that what we cannot understand, we may with propriety neglect—that is, it justifies the infidel's demand, to walk by sight and not by faith. While our text plainly teaches us to take the statements of God's word as they are, and to trust where we cannot understand, it is not only our duty, but our interest, to embrace them with all confidence. This will appear if we reflect that these doctrines, collectively, constitute the deep foundation upon which the whole superstructure of religion rests. Take them away, and the fabric falls. Consider, for example, the doctrines of God's existence—his triune nature—his infinite attributes. Take these away, and there remains no object to worship. Atheism is the result. Again,—Consider the doctrines of the incarnation—the eternal love of God for his people—the atonement—the resurrection of the dead—and the general judgment. Let these be removed, and there remains no efficient motive to worship. The result would obviously be fatal to all true religion. But to omit, or to neglect them, or to esteem them lightly, is virtually to remove them, or if not, at least it is to impair their moral effect to the very same degree in which they are neglected or lightly esteemed. These truths, now under consideration, were given by inspiration, and, as all scripture is, they are profitable for doctrine, for reproof, for correction, and for instruction in righteousness, that the man of God may be perfect, thoroughly furnished unto all good works. If, then, we would grow in grace, and in the knowledge of the Saviour—if we would have fulfilled in our own hearts, and illustrated in our own lives, the blessedness of the gospel in its renewing, sustaining and consoling power, we must receive its sublime and holy teachings, with meek confiding assurance of their truth, content to walk by faith and not by sight.

2nd. But again. We should walk thus also in respect to the precepts of the gospel. These show us our personal and relative duties. Now, it is true, that short sighted as we are, we do not always see the end from the beginning, in respect to our duties. Perhaps we may not know why this or that precept was enjoined upon us. Here, then, is an occasion upon which we should especially walk by faith. How pleasing to our Heavenly Father is that obedience which comes forth from a heart that trusts in his goodness. The child of God may reason thus : " I do not understand why I am required to do this, or to abstain from doing that. But I am assured that He who is the author of all my mercies is too wise to make a useless requisition, and too good to make an unkind one—therefore, what He hath required, that will I do." Such obedience, surely, is better than sacrifice, and with it God is better pleased. But there is another sense in which we should exercise faith in respect to our duties. We should, in them, clearly and distinctly recognize the authority of God as the only true source of obligation. I am bound to keep my word, not because it is reputable to do so, but because God hath said, "thou shalt not bear false witness." I am bound to observe the Sabbath, not because it is a rest from toil, but because the Lord hath said, "remember the Sabbath day to keep it holy." And so of all the rest. A neglect of this principle, is productive of much mischief. For just as soon as we lose sight of divine authority, in our duties, we are prone to regulate them by calculations of convenience. And as it is often inconvenient to perform our duties, we frequently neglect them, and still more frequently give them only a partial attention. In this manner we say our prayers—and pay our preachers—and give to the poor. In this way, too, some of us perhaps preach the gospel. Perhaps our prevailing motive for attending to these things at all, may be no better, than to pay an external respect—not to religion—but to ourselves as professors of religion. Duties thus performed are badly done. Nor is it strange that living thus we should be without the divine blessing. The remedy is, to walk by *faith*—to be fully persuaded that they are binding upon us, because God hath actually required them—and to perform them as unto the Lord. Then we shall enjoy sweet consciousness of rectitude, and feel in our own hearts the sanctifying influence of obedience, as we grow in grace and become more and more meet for the heavenly kingdom. And the whole church, thus acting, would come forth stript of her weeds of mourning, fair as the moon, clear as the sun, and terrible as an army with banners.

3rdly. I remark in the last place, and but briefly, that we should walk by faith and not by sight, in respect to the promises of the gospel. I think we may say, if there be any consolation in Christ, any comfort of love, any bowels and mercies, they are all made sure to us in his rich and precious promises. These are the arguments of prevailing prayer—and these are the Ebenezers of triumphant hope. Amid the sorrows of affliction, they hush our moanings—in doubt and darkness, they light up in our habitation the candle of the Lord—and along the weary pilgrimage of life, they offer to our timid and faultering steps, the staff of everlasting strength. But these promises, rich and precious as they are, are yet unproductive of good to any till they are believed and trusted. And they, too, are often mysterious, and sometimes incomprehensible. The saint who is guided to heaven by their life-giving indications, must walk by faith and not by sight. Like Abraham, he must not stagger at the apparent impossibilities which they involve, but receive them upon the credit of God's eternal truth. One who thus believes, takes hold upon the Almighty. The world, the flesh and the devil, have no power to harm him. No weapon formed against him shall prosper. For him, vicissitude can occasion no disappointment—bereavement no unmitigated sorrow. In every conflict he shall come off more than conqueror, and his dying shout shall be, "O death, where is thy sting? O grave, where is thy victory?" Such is the happiness of him who walks by faith and not by sight. Amen.

PROPER OBSERVANCE OF THE SABBATH:

A sermon preached by the late Rev. James Payne, of ————— county, Va.

—

" *Remember the Sabbath day, to keep it holy.*"—Exodus, xx : 8.

—

The Sabbath may be contemplated from many different points of view. It may be considered in its influence on the powers of our nature, exhausted through six days of anxiety and toil; in the necessity which is laid in our very constitution, by the author of our nature, for periodical seasons of relaxation and repose; in its influence on the intellect of an individual, or a people, by directing the attention to topics adapted to elevate and expand the soul ; in the aid which it furnishes to the magistrate in enforcing the observance of law ; in its influence on neighborhoods and families in promoting social feeling and refined intercourse ; in its bearing on the civil liberties of a nation, and its indispensable necessity in preparing for the life to come. Each one of these points would furnish an ample topic of discourse; and by the arguments which might be accumulated on these topics, we could satisfy any reasonable mind of the value and importance of the Sabbath. But I wish at this time to present a different train of thought from what would be furnished by either of these points. I design, particularly, to address christians, and to urge upon their minds some considerations why they should feel a special interest in the proper observance of this day.

I. The first consideration which I shall suggest is, that if the Sabbath is abolished, the christian religion will be abolished with it. The question whether this day is to be observed or desecrated, is just a question of life and death in regard to christianity. This is so obvious, that it scarcely needs any attempt to prove it. Without a Sabbath, our public institutions, designed to promote and perpetuate religion, would cease; our Sabbath schools would be disbanded ; family instruction would soon come to an end ; the sanctuaries would be closed; the ministry dismissed and discarded ; the current of worldly affairs would be unbroken ; plans of evil would meet with no interruption ; and all the means of grace would be at once arrested. Christians might meet at irregular and distant intervals for prayer and praise, but the number of such meetings would rapidly decrease, and soon the last vestige of christianity would disappear. The books containing its defence would be forgotten, and the Bible soon cease to be read with interest or gratitude. If the Sabbath be abolished, what hold can christianity have on man ? What way of access can it have to the heart and conscience ? How should the arguments for its truth be brought before the mind? How should its moral precepts be urged ? How should its high hopes and its solemn appeals and sanctions be presented ? And how should its stern rebukes be made to fall on the ear of the guilty? If you close your churches and your Sabbath schools, there can be no other effectual way. Nothing can be plainer than this ;

and nothing can be more manifest, than that he who violates or disregards the Sabbath, is taking the most effectual means of obliterating the christian religion from the world.

The whole history of christianity shows, that where the Sabbath is observed religion flourishes; where it is not, religion dies away and becomes extinct. We might appeal here to any man's observation, and ask him to recall the memory of a place where there is no Sabbath, and the scenes which he witnessed there. Was the voice of prayer heard there? Was God feared and honored? Were children and youth trained in the way of religion, and taught to worship and honor their maker? Did meekness, and temperance, and chastity, and justice, and honesty, abound? Or, was the place distinguished for riot and disorder; for falsehood and profaneness; for intemperance and licentiousness; for indolence and brutal scenes of violence and strife? Was there ever a place in which the Sabbath began to be observed, in which there did not revive the love of truth and order; industry and intelligence; urbanity and benevolence; temperance, purity and the love of God—like streams breaking out in the desert, and like the lilly and the rose springing up in waste and sandy places! Has there ever been an instance where this day has been observed, that it has not been followed by blessings which industry, and temperance, and intelligence, and piety, carry in their train? This appeal is made with the utmost confidence, and the friends and foes of christianity are invited to examine the point at their leisure.

Well do the enemies of christianity, in these times, know what they are about. In former generations, attempts were made to destroy the gospel, by the sword and the faggot—but all such attempts were foiled. Imperial power attempted to crush it; but imperial power found its arm too weak to contend with God. Argument and sophistry were then employed; ridicule lent its aid, and contempt pointed the finger of scorn; but all was in vain. Christianity survived all these, and rose with augmented power and more resplendent beauty—and would do so to the end of time. But there is one weapon which the enemy has employed to destroy christianity, and to drive it from the world, which has never been employed but with signal success. It is the attempt to corrupt the christian Sabbath; to make it a day of festivity; to cause christians to feel that its sacred and rigid obligation has ceased; to induce them, on that day, to mingle in scenes of pleasure, or the exciting plans of ambition; to make them feel that they may pursue their journeys by land and water—by the steamboat and the car—regardless of the command of God; and this has done, and will continue to do, what no argument, no sophistry, no imperial power, has been able to accomplish. The "Book of Sports," did more to destroy christianity, than all the 10 persecutions of the Roman Emperors; and the views of the second Charles and his Court, about the Lord's Day, tended more to drive religion from the British nation, than all the fires that were kindled by Mary. Paris has no Sabbath, and that fact has done more to banish christianity than all the writing of Voltaire; and Vienna has no Sabbath, and that fact has done more to annihilate religion *there*, than ever did the scepticism of Frederick. Turn the Sabbath into a day of sports and pastime, and not an infidel any where would care a farthing about the tomes of Volney or Voltaire; about the scepticism of Hume, the sneers of Gibbon, or the scurrility of Paine.

The great enemy of God and liberty, in this western world, understands how to meet christianity here. *He* knows that it will not be possible to kindle the flames of persecution. *He* knows that the friends of Christ cannot be turned over by the sentence of the Inquisition, to the tender mercies of the civil arm. *He* knows that he cannot get up an *Auto-de fe*, and that the garden of the capitol cannot be illuminated by the burning bodies of the saints. *He* knows, too, that there is too much science and learning; that there are too many schools and colleges, to attempt to attack it by sophistry and argument. It has passed through too many such trials, and has come out of them all unscathed. But was there no new form of opposition, by which religion could be met in the new world; no vital part of christianity that could be hacked; no blow that could be struck that would wither its rising power and lay it prostrate in the dust? There was one experiment that could be made. Over these broad and ample States and territories, men might be sent in search of gain, regardless of the Sabbath. Our majestic streams, winding along for thousands of miles, through the richest lands on earth, might be ascended,

12—Vol. IV.

regardless of the sacredness of the day. Young men might be led away, by the hope of wealth, from the peaceful scenes where a Sabbath sheds repose on a village, or the Sabbath bell summons an entire population to the worship of God. The nation might be roused by the love of *gold;* and new facilities for intercourse, and the love of travel, might unsettle almost the whole population, and transform them into wandering tribes or families, and lead them to trample down the barriers of virtue and the institutions of religion. The experiment was one of vast moment, and as fearful in its results as it was vast. It involves the whole interest of this nation. Its results will settle the fate of christianity in this land, and perhaps throughout the world. If we can have a Sabbath, sacred in its stillness and its associations; maintained by a healthful popular sentiment, rather than by human laws; *revered* as a day of holy rest, and as a type of heaven; a day when men shall delight to come together to worship God, and not a day of pastime, christianity is safe in this land, and our country is safe. If not, the Sabbath, and religion, and liberty, will die together.

In the experiment going on in this land, not a few hands are engaged, but many. It is not the mere work of thoughtlessness and recklessness, but it has all the marks of purpose and plan. It has evidence of being under the control of that master mind that is the author of all evil, and the father of all the embarrassments that christianity has ever met with. The attempt to blot out the Sabbath from this land, evinces more knowledge of human nature, and more tact and skill, than the persecutions of the Roman Emperors or of Mary. For who is engaged in the work of blotting out the Sabbath? Every atheist is engaged in it, and here places his main hope of success. Every sceptic is engaged in it, and anticipates more from this than all his arguments. Every profane man is engaged in it, every intemperate man and every licentious man is engaged in it, for in this way they hope that all restraint will be removed from unlimited indulgence and vice. And a multitude of men, who are not professedly atheists or infidels, but whose heart is with them in opposing the sacredness of this day. In one word, the mass of busy, active, unprincipled, infidel mind, in this nation, in high life and low, in office and out of office, in city and country, that for various reasons would desire christianity to be extinguished, has made war on the Sabbath, and is prosecuting that war by all the means within its reach, and it is to be feared, with augmenting prospects of success. The question now, is just this: Is christianity worth preserving, or can we afford to see it driven from the land? Are we so secure without it, in our individual and national interests, that we can part with it without regret? Or, is it worth an effort to save it? Has christianity such a connection with pure and wholesome morals as to make it desirable to retain it in the commonwealth, or will our morals be equally pure without it? Can this great nation be governed and defended without a God, or will it be best to yield obedience to his laws, and retain the religion of "peace and good will toward men," among us, and transmit it to posterity? These are questions connected with the Sabbath; and the course which is pursued in regard to this day will settle them all.

II. The second reason why this subject demands now the special attention of christians, is, that if the Sabbath is not regarded as *holy time*, it will be regarded as *pastime ;* if not a day sacred to devotion, it will be a day of recreation, of pleasure, of licentiousness. The Sabbath is not essentially an arbitrary appointment; for it is required in the very nature of the animal economy, that there should be periodical seasons of relaxation. Nature cannot always be taxed to incessant effort. We *must* have periodical rest in all the functions of our nature. Bonaparte once passed three entire days and nights without sleep, but he could no longer contend against a great law of nature, and sank to sleep on his horse. There is not a muscle in the animal economy that does not demand rest after effort, and that will not have it. If it is not granted *voluntarily*, it will be taken. If the powers of nature are overworked, they *will* take relaxation by disease, and perhaps when too late to repair their exhausted energies. This great law of nature must and will be obeyed. If the frame is worn out and exhausted without this relaxation, the consequence must be sickness or rest in the grave. Mr. Wilberforce declared, that at one period of his parliamentary career, his duties were so multiplied and exhausting, that his health must have been utterly prostrated but for the seasonable relief which the Sabbath afforded him. There is not an animal that can endure unceasing effort, without repose.; and God, in requiring that the " cattle " should be allowed to rest on the Sabbath, has spoken according to the laws which he originally impressed on the brute creation. If the question were simply one of interest, and a man wished to make the most of the noble horse or the patient ox, he would allow him to rest according to the commandment. For every such day of periodical repose, he will secure more than an equivalent in augmented strength and length of days. If rest is not allowed them, their powers are exhausted and they expire. The universe is fitted up, so far as we know, for the purposes of alternate action and rest, from the first beating of the heart in infancy, to the mightiest effort of the mature man ; from the insect that flutters and dies, to the *lion* of the forest, the mighty elephant, and the monarch on the throne.

In demanding, therefore, that the animal and mental economy shall be allowed a day of periodical repose, God has acted in accordance with a great law of nature. There is nothing arbitrary, except in designating the particular day which should be observed ; and all that is arbitrary in this, is a consultation of convenience, that we may not be disturbed by the toil and action of another, while we seek repose— just as he has so ordained the animal functions, that all are disposed to sleep at night.

Further, all nations have had, and will have, periodical seasons of relaxation from the severity of toil. The *Jews* had their weekly Sabbaths ; the *Greeks* and *Romans* had numerous festivals in honor of their gods, and many a day in the year for riot and disorder ; the followers of Mahommed observe a weekly Sabbath ; the heathen nations observe numerous festivals, frequently occurring ; and even the actors in the French Revolution were constrained to bow to this great law of nature, and appointed one day in ten, as a day of relaxation from toil. Hesiod and Homer said, " The seventh day is holy." Josephus says, " There is no city, however barbarous, where the custom of observing the seventh day, which prevails among the Jews, is not observed." Whatever may be the time selected, whether a day in honor of an idol, or in honor of the Saviour ; whether one day in seven, or one day in ten ; whether it be in honor of a saint, a hero, or the birth day of a prince, or of a nation, such days *will* be observed. In our country, it is settled that this day of periodical rest is to be the first day of the week.

This is settled by custom; by the statutes of the land; by universal understanding among all classes of society. This custom is settled, moreover, by the belief of the religious portion of the nation, that this is *holy time*, and by the lingerings of conscience among those who have been trained in the ways of religion. It is to be the settled custom in this nation, that on this day toil is to cease, and men are to give themselves to other purposes than to the ordinary employments of life. As a general habit all over the land, the store-house is to be shut; the school is to be disbanded; our courts will be closed; the student will lay aside his books; and the farmer will lean his plough in the furrow. The day is to be one of relaxation and rest. It is either to be devoted to religion, or to such pastimes as the general public sentiment shall demand.

Since this is to be so, the question is: What is to be the effect if the day ceases to be a day of religious observance? What will be the effect of releasing a population of several millions, one-seventh part of the time, from any settled business of life? What will be the result if they are brought under no religious instruction? What will be the effect on morals; on religion; on sober habits of industry; on virtue, happiness and patriotism? Can we safely close our places of business, and annihilate all the restraints that bind us during the six days; can we turn out a vast population of the young, with nothing to do, and abide the consequences of such a universal exposure to vice? Can we safely dismiss our young men, all over the land, with sentiments unsettled and with habits of virtue unformed, and throw them one day in the seven, upon the world, with nothing to do? Can we safely, as we do, open the fountains of poison in every city, town, village, hamlet and neighborhood, and invite the young to drink there with impunity? Can there be a season of universal relaxation, occurring fifty-two times a year, when all restraints are withdrawn, and when the power of temptation shall be plied with all that art and skill can do to lead the hosts in the way to ruin, and to drag them down to hell? One would suppose that the experiment already made in our land, particularly in our cities, would be sufficient to remove all doubt from any reasonable mind on this subject. As a nation, we are making the experiment on a large scale. The Sabbath is an institution of tremendous power, for good

or evil.   If for good, as it is designed, and as it easily may
be, it is laid at the foundation of all our peace, our intelligence, our morals, our religion.   If for evil, it strikes at all
these ; nor is there any possible power in laws or in education, that can, during the six days, counteract the evils of a
Sabbath given to licentiousness and sin.   And the question
before the nation is not, whether this is to be a day of labor
and sober industry, for that is settled, but whether it is to be
a day of religion or licentiousness ; a day of virtue or of sin ;
a day for God, or a day for the *devil?*   It is whether the
nation can *afford* to have one day in seven a day of riot and
disorder—a *saturnalia,* occurring more than fifty times in a
year—when Rome, in the most palmy days of her virtue,
could scarcely survive the effects of one.   No graver question
can occupy the attention of our nation than this.

Further, the Sabbath is favorable to the spread of pure
morality.   This assertion is made with the utmost confidence, and you are invited to test the truth of it.   Go
through the country and examine the cities, the towns and
villages ; mingle with the inhabitants of every class, and
converse with them freely ; learn their opinions and their
habits ; examine the prisons of the land, and then tell me
where you find most industry, most sober habits, most con-
tentment, most sobriety, most intelligence, most freedom from
low and debasing vices.   Tell me in what place you would
prefer to place a son, and where you would wish a daughter
educated.   Is there here a parent who would hesitate a moment in regard to this?   The virtues which go to adorn
domestic intercourse, and to cement society ; the mild and
gentle charities that are connected with the fire-side, with
the sick-room and the bed of death, flourish pre-eminently
among those who regard the sacredness of the Sabbath inviolable.   Can you point me to one idle and dissolute family ;
to one disturber of the peace ; to one vicious neighborhood ;
to one community in which licentiousness reigns, where the
Sabbath is habitually and generally observed ?   And can
you point me to one community where it is not observed,
which does not become riotous and vicious, and where intemperance, and gambling, and licentiousness, do not sooner
or later abound?   Sir M. Hale, (one of the brightest ornaments of the English bench,) says : "That of all the persons convicted of capital crimes while he was on the bench,

there were few who were not ready to confess that they had begun their career of wickedness by a neglect of the duties of the Sabbath."

Now, if the Sabbath be abolished, it will become a day of immorality. In particular, I wish to say, that this remark specially concerns young men. I do believe, if I could collect around me all the young men of this land, and if I could get their ear for a short time, I could convince the mass of them that the only security for their correct moral character, and their future usefulness, success and happiness, will be connected with the proper observance of this day. I could show them that the temptations which are spread out to beguile the unwary, are designed by cunning, unprincipled and avaricious men, for them. I could satisfy them that when they go forth from their father's dwellings on this day, unless it be for the purpose of attendance on the worship of God, they are exposed to temptations where no young man is safe. For be it remembered, that no young man leaves his father's dwelling, and devotes this day to amusement and revelry, without flying in the face of an explicit command of the *Most High*. He tramples beneath his feet one of the solemn mandates that were given amidst flames and thunders on Mount Sinai, and when one command of God is basely and contemptuously trod beneath his feet, the other nine will soon cease to be regarded. Be it remembered too, that the laws which God has ordained, tend only to promote human virtue and happiness. Go to the *penitentiaries* of our land, and walk along from cell to cell, and enquire of the inmates, *when* their career of guilt commenced. Go and converse, in his sober moments, with the drunkard, and ask him, *when* he first trod that downward way, and the answer will be, in a majority of cases, on the Sabbath day. It is by a violation of this day, that many a young man, in thoughtlessness, commences a career which terminates in breaking a mother's heart, and in the early wreck of all the hopes of a family, and in the extinction of their peace, as they weep over a drunkard's grave.

III. A third reason why this subject demands the attention of christians in a special manner now, is, that there is a state of things in this land, that is tending to obliterate the Sabbath altogether. The events to which I refer, are these: In every direction the mail is carried, and the example of the violation of the day, is thus set by national authority. Every post office is required by law to be kept open, and a public invitation is thus given to obtain the political and commercial intelligence, and to divert the mind from the sacred duties of the day, by the reference to the cares of this life. In every part of our land, also, the facilities for inter-communication have been augmented to an extent that excites the surprise of the world. By canals and rail-roads distant portions of our country have been brought together, and the earth trembles as the *car of commerce* rolls on, and the long lines of majestic improvements are crowded with the results of our toil, and with the traveling community. Against these national improvements the language of com-plaint, assuredly, is not to be urged. In many respects they are the glory of our land; and they should be sources of gratitude to God, who has thus signally blessed our country. But can any be ignorant that each canal and each rail-road furnishes increased facilities for Sabbath violation, and that they are fast tending to blot it out of the land? Where, in these public conveyances, is the Sabbath regarded? Where is the rail-road car that is arrested by the return of this day? Indeed, they are generally more crowded on this day than on any other. Had it been the purpose of the people of this land to abolish the Sabbath altogether, and to furnish the most rapid and extended means of its entire obliteration, it would have been impossible to have devised a more cer-tain and effectual way than that which is now employed.

In the mean time, there is an augmenting desire for *mo-tion*, in this land. The population is becoming migratory ; and few pause, whether christians or not, to rest on the Sab-bath. The merchant hastens on his way to the commercial emporium, as if the saving of a day for wordly business were of more value than the observance of the laws of God; the legislator pursues his journey to the captiol, as if anxious to exhibit a specimen of breaking the laws of God, while he goes to make laws for man ; the party of pleasure urge their way to the scenes of revelry and amusement; our friends and relations in the far west, are traveling beyond the inviting sound of the gospel ; and the idle and the dis-sipated, the profane, the atheist, the christian, in their public vehicles, pursue the business of gain, of pleasure, or conve-nience, or ambition, as if there were special merit in forgetting all the usual distinctions in society, and each and all were showing how they can most effectually disregard the obligations of this day. For one man in the community who *conscientiously* and *strictly* observes this day, there are hundreds' who not only disregard it, but make it a special day of business, convenience or pleasure. In the high places of our land there is an increasing looseness of principle on this subject. During the times that tried men's souls, in the war of independence, our fathers would have been alarmed had the ordinary business of legislation been pursued on the Sabbath, and the voice of indignant remonstrance would have been heard throughout our land. Yet, nothing has been more common of late years, than for the national legislature, after wasting months in needless and profitless ` debate, to close their labors on the Sabbath, and amidst such scenes of disorder as to be a disgrace to themselves and the nation, on any day. It is not easy for men, in any situation, to cast off respect for the laws of God, and at the same time maintain a character for sober virtue and order; and in legislatures, as elsewhere, a disregard for God's laws is but the beginning of evil.

I will close by repeating a remark already made. It is this. The warfare which christianity is to wage is here. The opposition to religion is here. The *Sabbath* has more enemies in this land, than Baptism, than the Lord's Supper, than the Bible, than all the other institutions of religion put together. At the same time it is more difficult to meet the enemy here than any where else, for we come in conflict, not with argument, but with interest, and pleasure, and the love of indulgence and gain. The conflict is to rage here. The wish of the atheist, the infidel, the scoffer, the man of vice, is to blot out the Sabbath. The attempt will not be made in this land, to destroy christianity by persecution, for that has been often tried elsewhere, and as often failed. It is to see whether the Sabbath can be obliterated from the memory of man; and if it *can*, it will be done. If this day, with its sacred institutions, can be blotted out, the victory will be won. Infidelity will achieve what the faggot and the stake, the force of argument, and the caustic severity of sarcasm and ridicule, have never been able to accomplish.

We repeat, this is the ground on which are marshalled the
13—Vol. IV.

contending armies. Under the ample folds of that dark flag, which waves over the heads of the enemies of religion, the eye of fancy discovers the grim visage and fiend-like carriage of the master spirit; the enemy of God, of religion, and of the Sabbath; stimulating his adherents to make a desperate rally upon this point. Among the many legions who recognize his authority, and in addition to his *avowed* followers and liege subjects, we see, occupying a conspicuous station near their leader, a numerous company of professing christians, whose hearts, notwithstanding their decent exterior, are "enmity against God," "vessels of wrath fitted for destruction." "Verily, they shall have their reward." But whilst from their numbers and unceasing zeal, the christian may for a moment tremble for the issue of the conflict, yet, when we cast our eye upon the numerous hosts composing the armies of Israel, whose captain is "Emanuel, God with us;" when we reflect that "as the mountains are round about Jerusalem, so is the Lord round about all them that fear him," and that they have always come off victorious; when we reflect that his church, with all her hallowed institutions, is built upon Him, the rock of ages, and that he has said "the gates of hell shall never prevail against her;" when we reflect that the King of kings and Lord of lords is our God, we may defy the utmost fury of our opponents, and with the Psalmist exclaim, "We will not fear, though the earth be removed and though the mountains be carried into the midst of the sea."

So far, I have confined my remarks to the subject as involving our national interests. I cannot close without making a remark of a practical nature, and designed for our individual and personal good. Well does the text begin with the word "*remember;*" seeing that thoughtless mortals are so prone to forget it. The word "*remember*," seems to intimate the necessity of preparing for it. We should *remember* on Saturday, that the Lord's day is at hand, and prepare accordingly. On this day, the command of Jehovah is, "Thou shalt not do any work, thou, nor thy son, nor thy daughter, nor thy man-servant, nor thy maid-servant, nor thy cattle, nor the stranger that is within thy gates." Our worldly business, whatever it be, must be laid aside. It is not to be supposed that *manual labor* alone is interdicted. Traveling, walking or riding for mere pleasure, trifling visits, paying or receiving wages, frequenting public houses, writing letters, settling accounts, reading books on ordinary subjects, yea, conversation of a worldly kind, is here forbidden. Again, the Sabbath is as much profaned by *idleness* as by *active labor*. Mere rest of *body* is the Sabbath of a *beast*, not of a *man*. We have immortal souls, and this is the day on which their eternal welfare is to be sought.

But some will say, "Is nothing to be done on the Sabbath?" I answer. Works of *necessity* and *mercy* are *allowed*. For spending the Sabbath in that manner which we have endeavored to point out, we have the authority of God, who so commands it; the goodness of God; the example of God; and the blessing of God. As we spend our earthly Sabbaths, even so shall we spend the eternal Sabbath, to which we are fast hastening.

AN EXTRACT.

"The great truths of the gospel not only commend themselves to the understanding of mankind, but ought to affect and influence the heart. Their infinite importance and eternal bearings, ought surely to awaken the deepest interest in the minds of all; especially of those who, from their professedly applying themselves to their constant study, may be presumed to be more alive to their unutterable momentousness than mankind generally are. That ministers, therefore, should talk of the great verities of the gospel with as much coldness and languor of manner as if they were speaking on topics of the most trifling interest, is not only surprising, but is a positive anomaly. What avails it that they expatiate on the infinite importance of the doctrines they deliver, when their manner does not correspond with their words? If, I repeat, they would impress the reality and the importance of divine truth on others, they must show that they feel its importance and reality themselves. They must not deliver their sermons in such a way as would lead their hearers to suppose that they considered themselves engaged in the performance of an irksome task. They must preach in such a manner as will convince those to whom they address themselves that their heart is in the work—that they speak, because they *believe*—that they expostulate and exhort, because they *feel*.

"It was one of the happiest and truest things that ever Horace gave utterance to, when he said, 'that those who would convince others, must first show that they are themselves convinced.' If this observation holds good in every case, it applies with special force in the case of ministers; inasmuch as the unbeliever or sceptic is apt to suspect them of preaching a certain class of doctrines merely because they live by the ministerial profession. When such persons see the preachers of the gospel delivering their sermons with coldness and indifference, they only become the more confirmed in their ungenerous suspicions. Let the christian minister only evince that warmth of feeling and that earnestness of manner, which I am recommending, and neither the deist nor the sceptic will be able to resist the conviction that there is a truth and reality in religion. When a great orator of antiquity was asked what was the first requisite of effective oratory, his answer was, 'action;' when asked what was the second, his reply was, 'action;' and when the question was put to him what was the third, his answer was still the same. His meaning was, that action was every thing in oratory. I cannot say of earnestness of manner, that it is every thing in preaching sermons; for preaching truth is of greater importance; but I do say, that next to sound evangelical doctrine, an earnest or impassioned manner is that from which the christian minister may anticipate the happiest results. * * * * * *

"If the preachers of the gospel would only make a point of meditating more frequently on the inexpressible importance of the truths they are about to deliver, the circumstance could not fail to conduce in a great degree to the warmth and earnestness of manner which I am so anxious to see universally exhibited by those who are called to minister in holy things. In their own minds, and in their moments of calm reflection, they are fully persuaded of the unutterable importance of the doctrines of the gospel; but the very circumstance of being called habitually to preach those doctrines, has so necessary a tendency to familiarize the mind with them, as to render them at times, in so far as mere appearance goes, less alive to their infinite momentousness. This ought to be carefully guarded against."

London Pulpit, by James Grant.

THE
BAPTIST PREACHER.

| VOL. IV. | June, 1845. | NO. 6. |

Bro. Keeling.—I find but few of the sermons that have appeared in the Preacher, are addressed to the unconverted. Hence, in preparing a discourse to be at your disposal, I have selected the subject presented in the following pages. Permit me humbly to express the hope that, if it should be read by any one unprepared for eternity, it may awaken him to see the fearful end to which he is hastening, and induce him to seek safety in the Saviour of sinners.

With christian regard,   L. A. ALDERSON.

Palestine, Greenbrier, March, 1845.

MEMORY ; ITS INFLUENCE ON THE TOR-MENT OF THE WICKED :

A sermon, by L. A. Alderson, of Greenbrier county, Virginia.

" Son, remember that thou in thy life-time receivedst thy good things, and like-wise Lazarus evil things : but now he is comforted, and thou art tormented."—Luke xvi: 25.

Memory is the depository of all our knowledge. It is a faculty essentially necessary for the transaction of even the most ordinary business of life. It is also the source of both pleasure and pain. It is pleasing to recur to the days of youthful innocency, and to bring up before us the scenes of our childhood, together with the many little events that caused the current of life to glide so smoothly. It is pleasing to think of those kindly friends who cheered us in prosperity, and who smoothed our pathway in adversity. It is still more pleasing to recount the merciful dealings of that Friend above, who has prospered us in health, who has sustained us in sickness, who has rescued us from destruction, and who is now our only hope of salvation. But have we intentionally injured a fellow-being? Have we needlessly oppressed the poor? Have we filled our coffers through

14—Vol. IV.

treachery and dishonesty? Have we committed some secret sin, too dark for the light? Ah! how painful the recollection!

The rich man "lifted up his eyes, being in torments." Memory was the source of his keenest pangs. To Lazarus, who rested in the bosom of Abraham, it was the source of much pleasure. The rich man remembered the splendor in which he once lived, and the honor that was then paid him. Having had Moses and the prophets, he remembered the neglected opportunities once enjoyed of securing his salvation. He remembered, too, that even under the blessings of God, he had not only ruined himself, but had exerted a pernicious influence upon his five brothers, in leading them on to the pit of destruction. The language of Abraham, " son, remember," though the language of affection, must have pierced his soul through with pain inconceivably great. On the other hand, Lazarus, reclining in Abraham's bosom, and enjoying the bliss of heaven, could cast his eye down to the gate of the rich man, from which he had been borne by angels in triumph, and exclaim: " There, I was a poor beggar, sustaining life by the few crumbs that fell in my reach, and gladly receiving the friendly offices of dogs; but God was even there to bless me. Though my body was an offensive mass of corruption, and my soul was at one time still more corrupt, he enabled me to stay that soul upon him, and in my bodily sufferings he made me happy in the enjoyment of his abounding love and mercy. He conducted me safely through the valley and shadow of death, and his messengers conveyed me to this world of glory. To his name be all the praise." " Son, REMEMBER that thou in thy life-time receivedst thy good things, and likewise Lazarus evil things: but now *he is comforted,* and *thou art tormented.*"

In this discourse, it is our design to offer a few remarks upon MEMORY *as it exists in a future state, and then show that it will tend to aggravate the torment of the wicked in the world to come.*

I. IN A FUTURE STATE, THE EVENTS OF THIS LIFE, EVEN SUCH AS MAY HERE BE FORGOTTEN, WILL BE BROUGHT TO OUR REMEMBRANCE.

A few circumstances in the course of life, make such a strong impression upon our minds that they are never forgotten.~ Such, particularly, is the case in regard to the things with which we were familiar in the days of our childhood. But such is our frailty, that most circumstances, however important, in the course of time, are forgotten. Numerous other things, of daily occurrence, receive so little of our attention, as not to be remembered a single hour. They are erased from our memory as the writing of the ancients from their waxen tablets, to give room for the recording of new events. But, in the future world, thousands of circumstances connected with our present life, however unimportant they may now appear, and how long soever they may have been buried in oblivion, will be revived.* " For there is

---

* Even in this life, there is sometimes such a revival as that to which we have alluded. An intimate friend of ours, who has gone the way of all the earth, gave us the following remarkable fact : When a youth, pursuing a course of study in England, his native country, he, with several others, was skating upon an ice-pond. Unfortunately, he broke through, and was from five to ten minutes under water. When rescued he was entirely insensible, and he remained in that state a length of time. When he came to himself, he remembered distinctly breaking through the ice, and being under water. While there, he remembered that in his last moments of sensibility, thousands of thoughts rushed upon his mind, producing such an influence as he could not describe. Said he, " the whole history of my impenitent life was presented before me at one view, and such was the impression made upon my mind, that I shall never forget it as long as I live."

Many cases have been mentioned, which show the influence of disease in restoring past thoughts. " An eminent medical friend informs me," says Dr. Abercrombie, in his inquiries concerning the Intellectual Powers, " that during fever, without any delirium, he on one occasion repeated long passages from Homer, which he could not do when in health." p. 124.

" A Lutheran clergyman of Philadelphia, informed Dr. Rush that Germans and Swedes, of whom he had a considerable number in his congregation, when near death, always prayed in their native languages, though some of them, he was confident, had not spoken these languages for *fifty or sixty years* "—*Abercrombie, Intel. Powers, p.* 124.

The following is abridged from Upham's Mental Philosophy. The facts in the case were made known to S. T. Coleridge, when on a tour through Germany. `In a catholic town of Germany, a young woman who could neither read nor write, was seized with a nervous fever during which she was incessantly talking Greek, Latin and Hebrew. The case attracted much attention, and many sentences which she uttered were taken down, and were found intelligible. Ignorant and harmless, as this young woman was known to be, no one suspected any deception ; and no explanation could for a long time be given, although inquiries were made in different families where she had resided as a servant. A young physician, however, in tracing her history back to her childhood, ascertained that at nine years of age, she had been kindly taken to be brought up by an old protestant minister. He was a very learned man. The passages which had been uttered by the young woman, were found by the physician to agree precisely with passages in books of different languages which had formerly be-nothing covered that shall not be revealed, neither hid that shall not be known."* It may be that this revival of forgotten events will take place at the dissolution of the soul and body. For illustration,—suppose I wish to address a letter to a friend in captivity. The contents of the communication must be carefully concealed. I write with sympathetic ink. Not a trace of the pen is visible. The prisoner receives the letter—he dips it into a solution prepared for the purpose—he holds it up before him—the whole is perfectly legible. May not the separation of the soul from the body produce a similar change? May not the record of those innumerable circumstances which time and infirmity have erased from the memory, be restored by that event, so as to be perfectly legible? Let it be remembered that, in our present state, the activity of the mind is greatly encumbered by its union with the body. Then, it will be completely divested of this encumbrance.

But it may be that the more perfect revival will take place at the time of the general judgment; that with the resurrection of the body, which the scriptures inform us will be immediately connected with the judgment, there will also be a resurrection of all the deeds, words and thoughts, which, in this life, have been buried in forgetfulness. That we shall have a lively remembrance of the whole history of our lives on that fearful day which God has appointed for the judgment of the world, is evident from the following scriptures: "Therefore judge nothing before the time, until the Lord come, who both will bring to light the hidden things of darkness, and will make manifest the counsels of the hearts."† "But I say unto you, that every idle word that men shall speak, they shall give account thereof in the day of judgment."‡ "God shall bring every work into judgment, with every secret thing, whether it be good, or whether it be evil."|| "And I saw the dead, small and great,

---

longed to him. But this was not a full explanation. The young woman knew nothing of Hebrew, Greek or Latin. On further inquiry, it appeared that this aged minister had been in the habit of walking up and down a passage of his house, and of reading to himself with a loud voice, out of his favorite books. These passages made an impression on the memory of this unlettered girl, and though beyond the reach of her recollection when in health, they were, after several years, vividly restored by the influence of disease.

*Luke xii: 2.   † 1 Cor. iv: 5.   ‡ Matt. xii: 36. || Eccl. xii: 14.

stand before God ; and the books were opened : and another
book was opened, which is the book of life : and the dead
were judged out of those things which were written in the
books, according to their works."* When the book of memory shall be opened, the wicked will be convicted of their
guilt. Their numerous and their aggravated offences brought
to their remembrance, they will feel the weight of the just
sentence of condemnation before it is pronounced by the
Judge seated upon his throne and clothed in terror.

The events of this life being once revived in our memory,
it appears to us that not one of them can be again forgotten.
We are to be judged, not according to the general tenor of
our conduct, but for every particular action ; nay, more, for
every word, and for every thought. How can the criminal
forget the crimes that were alledged against him, on account
of which he was condemned, and for which he is now suffering ? How can the pardoned rebel forget the offences for
which he received a reprieve ?

To the views we have advanced, it may be objected that,
if the righteous in a future state remember their sins, it will
interfere with their happiness ; besides, the scriptures represent the transgressions of the righteous as " *blotted out*,"—
" *covered.*" Can any suppose that the penitent thief, now
in heaven, has forgotten the crime for which he was crucified ? Or, that Paul does not still remember that he once
persecuted the people of God ? But, as it regards the latter
part of the objection, we would remark that the *blotting out*
and *covering* of sin, are only other expressions for the *pardon* of sin. Although the sins of the righteous will be
remembered in eternity, it is very evident they will be remembered so as not to interfere with their enjoyment. If I
have injured my friend, and am convinced of the fact,
knowing at the same time that he is angry with me, I am
unhappy. But if I have the magnanimity to go to him and
confess my fault, and if he receive my acknowledgment,
and we are again restored to friendship, then am I relieved
of my distress ; I enjoy peace of mind. The christian,
standing before the throne of God, and looking back upon
his past offences, sees how numerous and how inexcusable
his transgressions were. But now they are all pardoned.

* Rev. xx: 12.

O! amazing love!—boundless mercy! that a creature so richly deserving the wrath of God, should be plucked from the pit of destruction, and made a trophy of redeeming love. As the angels join in one general burst of praise to the honor and glory of God, he strikes his harp to a newer and more noble song—a song which none but the hundred and forty and four thousand who were redeemed by the blood of Jesus, can sing. A view of his pardoned sins inspires him with fresh motives of gratitude to God. But should he ever forget the events of this life, then would his motives to honor and glorify God, be greatly diminished.

II. MEMORY, IN THE WORLD TO COME, WILL TEND TO AGGRAVATE THE TORMENT OF THE WICKED. "Son, *remember* that thou in thy life-time receivedst thy good things."

1. We have already said that *the wicked will remember the sins they committed.* Transgressors frequently violate the laws of God without feeling the pain of guilt. For most offences, however, their consciences condemn them, and, for awhile, they are miserable. But time too often heals these painful wounds. It will not be so with the ungodly in the world of misery. There, their sins will ever appear before their eyes, written in living characters. They will have a painful view of all their wicked deeds—their fraud, their treachery, their intrigues, and their unholy indulgencies. There, too, will be written their profane oaths and their blasphemous expressions. Their envy, their malice, their wicked desires, and all their unhallowed thoughts, will also be recorded, never to be blotted out. Oh! what a fearful catalogue. If, my ungodly friend, all the secret workings of your wicked heart, even for one day, were recorded, would it not present a dark page from which you would turn away with horror? But think, O think, if you continue an enemy to God, in that prison of woe, a similar record for every day of your life will be presented before you, and in the bitter anguish of your soul you will have to gaze upon it to all eternity.

2. *They will remember the character of the Being against whom they sinned.* If such laws were now in force as existed under our colonial government, and we, by these laws, were thrust into prison for preaching the gospel, we would be convinced that the laws were *oppressive,* and that

the sentence pronounced upon us was *unjust*. Hence, we should be enabled to bear our sufferings with some degree of patience and resignation. The transgressor of the laws of God, who is condemned to writhe in torment, will have no such consoling reflections as these. He will remember that God was represented to him as a God of justice, and now he will be convinced of the fact. He will consider that the sentence pronounced upon him is just, and that he is receiving the due reward of his deeds.

Again,—his sins were committed, not against a Being who took pleasure in inflicting punishment, but against Him whose name is LOVE, and whose dealings towards him were dealings of mercy; who watched over him with more than a parent's tenderness; who ministered to him all his earthly comforts; who often delivered him from impending danger, and who even provided a Saviour that he might live. Will not the reflection of having sinned against such a Being increase the pangs of his torment?

3. *That they were often urged to turn and live.* The Bible, ah! the Bible which is here so much forgotten, will there be remembered. Hear the lamentations of a condemned sinner destined to spend an eternity in misery: "That book which I so much slighted, was my best friend. It pointed out my sins; it told me of a Saviour; and it bid me seek that I might find, and knock that it might be opened unto me. There, too, was the faithful minister who portrayed to me the glory of heaven, and the awfulness of perdition; who pointed me to Jesus, 'the way, the truth and the life,' and who, in his melting appeals, called upon me to escape for my life. There, too, were my parents, now with angels before the throne of God. O, that I could blot out from my recollection their affectionate counsel and their oft repeated prayers that ascended up in my behalf! As if God, too, would hedge up my way, he warned me by his providences, and drew me by his Spirit. Then I was 'almost persuaded;' but my deceitful heart whispered, 'there is time enough;' and now my doom is eternally fixed."

4. *That the way to heaven was once plain, and the requirements reasonable, but now that way is closed forever.* If the sinner had been destined to a life of wickedness, and his condition unalterably fixed without any provision whatever for his escape, his pain would be more tolerable. Christ,

however, was presented to him as an all-sufficient Saviour, and all that was required of him, was to renounce his sins and accept of him as his Saviour.. But he wilfully rejected the Son of God, choosing the pleasures of sin for a season, and, in the end, eternal destruction, rather than the mild sceptre of the Prince of peace, and that endless joy which is unspeakable and full of glory. Having refused the plan of salvation which was offered to him on such reasonable terms, his destiny is now forever fixed. Between him and heaven, there is a great gulf, across which none can pass. No invitations to turn and live, will again salute his ear.

> " In that lone land of deep despair,
>   No gospel's heavenly light shall rise,
>   No God regard *his* bitter prayer,
>   No Saviour call *him* to the skies."

The gates of heaven now barred against him forever, hope, that sustains us amid the trials of life, and that cheers us in our final separation from friends and kindred—hope, that sheds a light around the dark walls of the prisoner's cell, and that even casts a smile upon the pale countenance of death, takes her everlasting departure, and leaves him in the blackness of darkness to brood over his melancholy condition.

5. *That having rejected the gospel plan of salvation, and persisted in sin, they were their own destroyers.* That man who, by a life of dissipation, has brought on himself some mortal disease, as he lies upon his bed contemplating his wretched condition, and the speedy termination of his present existence, must be miserable beyond description. There is no one that he can blame for his misfortune. His miserable end is the result of his own imprudence. If he had contracted a lingering disease from exposure to an unfriendly climate while disseminating the truths of the gospel, or even while engaged in patriotic services to his country, he could endure it with fortitude. Can you imagine the anguish of the miserable sinner in perdition, when he reflects that there are none upon whom he can charge the guilt of his destruction?—that they were his own sins that closed the door of mercy—that dug the pit of hell—that reared its walls, and that kindled its flames?

6. *That they not only ruined themselves, but aided in the destruction of others.* It has been justly observed, "that we are so linked together in society, that we almost necessarily communicate our dispositions one to another. We draw and are drawn, in both good and evil. If we go to heaven we are commonly instrumental in drawing some others along with us; and it is the same if we go to hell."* How painful must be the reflections of that accomplished sinner, who, in his career of wickedness, beguiled the innocent and unsuspecting youth, and led him into the vortex of destruction. There, too, the universalist, the infidel and the atheist, will remember that they did not only close their own eyes to the truth, but blinded the eyes of others. Behold the ungodly parent withering under the hot indignation of God, and surrounded by his offspring, who reprove him for his wicked example, and for having withheld from them the light of truth. Hear them exclaim: "You were an indulgent parent—you loved us, and you were concerned for our happiness: Why did you not tell us of Jesus? You taught us the value of riches: Why did you not tell us of a treasure in heaven? You relieved us when in distress, and guarded us against danger: Why did you not warn us of the pit of destruction?

7. *Finally, the wicked in torment will remember with pain their enjoyments in this life.* "Son, remember that thou in thy life-time receivedst thy good things." The Siberian exile, as he wanders alone amidst the dreariness of almost perpetual snows, thinks of the sunny plains of his own native country—he thinks of the friends whose society he once enjoyed—above all, he thinks of his beloved children and her to whom he pledged his vows, and whose smiles so often cheered him in the hour of despondency. Can you conceive the anguish that rends his soul? Much less can you conceive the pain endured by the exile from heaven, when he reflects upon the comforts he was once permitted to enjoy. Once, when afflicted and distressed, he had friends to share his sorrows; but now, not a single tear of sympathy is to be found in all the regions of despair. Once, he could quench his thirst with the cool and refreshing draught just from the fountain; but now, even a drop

---

* A. Fuller.

of water is denied him to cool his tongue. When he returned home, wearied with the toils of the day, he was
welcomed around the domestic hearth, and was permitted to
rest in quietness upon his pillow; but now, his troubled
soul finds no rest, day nor night.

But we turn away from this frightful picture. It is a
theme upon which we take no pleasure in dwelling, further
than it may be beneficial to those whom we address. But
in taking our leave of the subject, we must observe that we
have not led you to the brink of the *"lake,"* whence you
might have a glimpse of its awfulness; we have merely led
you to the bank of one of its tributary *streams.* What
then must be the "lake" itself? We leave you to imagine.

And now, thoughtless sinner, we affectionately entreat
you to pause one moment, and consider the ground you
occupy. You have long persisted in the violation of the
laws of God. You have treated with the grossest ingratitude, your very best friend. You are now under his displeasure. In the court of heaven, sentence of condemnation
has already been pronounced against you. You are in danger of lifting up your eyes with the rich man in torment.
Do you ask how you may escape? Look to Jesus:—he
died that sinners might live. He endured the wrath of God,
that they might escape that wrath, and secure eternal happiness. He is now seated on the right hand of the throne of
the majesty on high, and says: "Come unto me all ye that
labor and are heavy laden, and I will give you rest."[*] Will
you not go to him, humbly confessing your sins, and exercising
confidence in his merits? "He is able also to save them to the
uttermost that come unto God by him, seeing he ever liveth
to make intercession for them."[†] O that you were wise,
that you understood this, that you would consider your latter end.[‡]

---

[*] Matt. xi: 28.   [†] Heb. vii: 25.   [‡] Deut. xxxii: 29.

THE
BAPTIST PREACHER.

VOL. IV.	July, 1845.	NO. 7.

THE IMPORTANCE OF A WELL REGULATED
TEMPER:

A SERMON, BY REV. C. D. MALLARY, OF GEORGIA.

" He that is slow to anger is better than the mighty ; and he that ruleth his spirit, than he that taketh a city.—PROV. xvi: 32.

Man, in his original constitution, was most happily tempered. Reason and righteousness swayed their sceptre over all his powers—there was no discord in his bosom, no war in his members, no irregularity in his intellectual and moral movements. Sin broke the sweet harmony of his nature; reason lost its mastery over the affections, and those instincts and passions, which, in their original condition, were not only sinless, but highly subservient to the happiness and perfection of man, were turned loose to contend with each other in confused and bitter strife, and to prey upon their once happy and exalted possessor. Man becomes malignant, contentious, implacable, revengeful. His passions, once obedient and helpful, but now corrupt and rebellious, become his unmerciful dictators.

To rectify this disorder, to restore man to the right government, and proper enjoyment of himself, is one of the great designs of grace; and to gain this desirable and happy end, should be his own high aim, and ceaseless endeavor. The proper subjugation of the impetuous and wrathful feelings, the establishment of a well balanced and healthful temper, it must be allowed by all considerate minds, is an important part of this great design, and must naturally, and necessarily, be embraced in this high aim, this rational and noble endeavor.

" *Keep your temper,*" is a plain, vulgar precept; yet, it is one in every respect entitled to the consideration of those who would live happy, useful and consistent lives. It is sometimes said, that "*temper is every thing.*" This is a maxim, which, in the *letter*, may seem somewhat hyperbolical, but which, in *spirit*, exhibits a salutary and momentous truth. Who can estimate the advantages of a *well regulated temper*? It is worth more than paternal legacies—more than mere worldly greatness. He that has not learned to rule his spirit, has not learned to be happy, though he may be surrounded with innumerable comforts, calculated in themselves to minister to his peace; whilst he who has acquired thoroughly this blessed art, cannot well fail to be happy, though surrounded with circumstances of disappointment, affliction and peril.

In the prosecution of our present aim, we shall consider:

I. What is implied in a WELL REGULATED TEMPER.

II. Its great IMPORTANCE. And

III. The MEANS by which it may be secured.

.I What is implied in a WELL REGULATED TEMPER?

Temper is an expression often applied to the condition and qualities of the mind, and in various acceptations. It is sometimes employed, with a qualifying epithet, to designate some particular trait or disposition;—thus we speak of one quality as a *good temper*, of another as an *evil temper.* It is sometimes used, in an extended import, to express the more general condition of the affections;—thus a person, who exhibits in his conduct a well ordered state of pious feelings, is said to manifest a *christian* spirit, or temper; whilst a different course of conduct is spoken of as an indication of an *unchristian temper.* Again—it is sometimes used to express the condition of the irascible passions, in connection with those of a sweet and gentle nature, which are regarded as their opposites. A person in whom the former are easily excited, is said to be *quick tempered ;* one in whom they are frequently roused to an intense and unreasonable degree, is said to be *high tempered ;* and if in any one their natural tendency, when excited, is to a malignant and revengeful state of mind, he is said to possess a *bad*, or an *evil temper.* When the kind and gentle passions of the soul habitually predominate—are so exercised and cultivated as properly to soften, regulate and control the fiery qualities of our nature, we see an exhibition of what we frequently denominate a *good temper*, or a *well regulated temper.* And this is the acceptation in which we propose, for the most part, to use the expression in our present discussion.

Our text, we conceive, describes an individual characterized by such a temper. He is *slow to anger ;* he *ruleth his spirit.* The expression *slow to anger* does not seem so much to describe the natural temperament of the individual, as that well balanced state of the irascible passions, which is the result of proper discipline. The phrase which follows, (he that *ruleth* his spirit,) may be regarded as both a parallel and explanatory expression, and will consequently justify the exposition we have given of the preceding clause. But to be more particular.

1. A well regulated temper implies *habitual self-control.* Its possessor is one who has subjected his spirit to a steady, judicious and permanent rule. His will acts with promptness, vigor and effect—it stands a well trained sentinel by the crater of passion, to keep down the rebellious fires beneath. Amidst the temptations and excitements with which he may be brought into collision in the prosecution of his various duties, he is in a peculiar sense his own master ; maintaining a calm and solid jurisdiction over the turbulent portion of his nature. It is not a temporary, but a permanent victory that he has gained over himself. There are some, who, for a season, manifest great equanimity of spirit ; they parry the edge of many successive provocations ; the bitterest insults seem not to cast them down from an apparently calm and settled equipoise ; but the will, unaccustomed to long and well established command, relinquishes at last its grasp upon the passions, which, like a torrent that gathers force from a temporary obstruction, now rush forth with augmented violence, scattering abroad mischief and confusion. We see not here the operation of a well regulated temper. These are not the individuals who have learned to rule their spirits. They are like a city with broken walls— like a magazine whose train is open at a hundred points, to the falling sparks of a neighboring conflagration.

As occasional and temporary self-control is not all that is needful to constitute a well regulated temper, so the government of the irascible passions, in some of their modifications, but not in others, leaves the spirit but imperfectly defended. Our self-control must maintain a *broad,* as well as a *permanent* jurisdiction. Unreasonable anger assumes many forms.

There are some who in their wrath are sullen and silent; there are others who are blustering, noisy and impetuous. There are some who kindle into vexation in a moment; whilst there are others who are constitutionally slow to be moved, but when excited are like a furious bear, or a raging tempest. Some there are who can bear with a good degree of patience and fortitude, the more cumbersome and distressing afflictions of life, whilst a thousand petty provocations worry them into an unamiable and fretful humor. And strange to tell, we sometimes discover in the same individuals, at different times and in varying circumstances, more or less of these various modifications of disordered and angry feeling. That self-control, of which we are speaking, must rear its munitions at all these vulnerable points, and protect us against the insidious and imposing, as well as the more open and violent assaults of our unhallowed passions.

This self-control must itself be controlled by right reason. Reflection must be its hand-maid and its guide. We may sometimes meet with those who, on some occasions, display much self-possession and energy of will, who are nevertheless, unhappily, defective in judgment. Now is it reasonable to suppose, that the proper management of the temper will rise higher than the dictates of judgment? That it should often fall below these dictates, is by no means strange. Superficial reflection will often allow us to palliate, if not applaud, many of the little sallies of petulence and passion, and even the wilder outbreaks of wrath, which sober reason must condemn. The man of a well regulated temper is a thoughtful, considerate man. He ponders well his goings. He avoids temptation when he can, and where duty calls him into the strifes of the world, he moves on with wise forecast and deliberate caution. If at any time he allows in himself the expression of indignation, he sees to it that the occasion which provokes his displeasure is a just one, that the motives which prompt him are in themselves pure and heavenly, that his anger does not rise to an unreasonable height, nor dwell long in his bosom, and that the expression of it be moderate and well timed.

2. A well regulated temper is one that is habitually free from bitter, malignant and vindictive feelings, and is sweetened by a due admixture of meekness, gentleness, forbearance and love. We suppose that there may be a lawful

expression of anger. This is implied in the declaration "be ye angry and sin not." We may receive injuries that may awaken a just and holy resentment. We may witness folly and sin that may demand the expression of open, decided and intense disapprobation. It is not the possession of that attribute of character, that renders us capable of indignant feelings, which constitutes our sin, but the perversion of that attribute. This perversion, in a greater or less degree, is almost universal. There is a strong and fearful tendency in the irascible passions to wrath, hatred and revenge. Our hatred of an injurious and provoking act is apt to be transferred to the person who performs it, and thus, instead of pursuing him with our pity and our prayers, we follow after him with malediction and spite. To struggle resolutely against this perversion, is the imperative duty of all; and a high degree of success in this struggle, secures to us one happy item of a well regulated temper. Our anger, to be without sin, must be like that of our Father above, blended with tender benevolence and endearing compassion; like that of Christ, our great and spotless exemplar, who wept over those whose hard-heartedness provoked his indignation. It must be under the control of that wisdom which is from above, which is first pure, then *peaceable,* gentle and easy to be entreated, and full of mercy. It must be tempered and sweetened with that heaven-born charity which suffereth long and is kind, is not *easily provoked,* beareth all things, believeth all things, hopeth all things, endureth all things.

3. A well regulated temper, in a high, evangelical sense, implies a proper state of mind with reference to the adverse providences of God. The turbulent nature of man, does not allow him to confine his unhallowed resentments to his fellow-man. It were far less to be blamed, if this were the case. But alas! it rises up in an indignant attitude against the allotments of heaven, and calls forth the Almighty to the field of battle. His dispensations are questioned with the spirit of bitterness and anger. The afflictions which seem to fall, as it were, visibly from his hand, disconcert, and irritate, and enrage. It is occasionally so, at least for a season and in some degree, with the people of God. Look at peevish and fretful Jonah. The smiting of his fondly cherished gourd, fills him with vexatious disappointment. The very compassion of Jehovah, that rescued for a season a mighty

city from destruction, was the occasion of angry disquietude. Such was his strange and unreasonable selfishness, that in the unhallowed excitement of the moment, he would seem to prefer that all Ninevah should perish, rather than that he should run the risk of suffering in his prophetic reputation, by the interposition of mercy in behalf of that guilty city. Surely he was a badly tempered believer! Happy would it be, if querulous Jonah had no imitators in this unreasonable controversy with the providence of God. A well regulated temper is a quiet, meek, submissive temper. "The Lord gave, the Lord hath taken away, blessed be the name of the Lord." "Surely I behaved and quieted myself," says Daniel, "as a child that is weaned; my soul is even as a weaned child; I was dumb and opened not my mouth, because thou didst it." Here then we have a lovely exhibition of a right temper, with reference to the providence of God.

In concluding our remarks upon this point, we may be allowed to say, if the views just presented be correct, a well regulated temper is one which is habitually governed by the Scriptures of divine truth. It implies self-control—this self-control must be guided by right reason; reason to guide us right, must be enlightened from on high. The Scriptures constitute the only safe guide to the understanding, and in them are to be found those motives and restraints which are the most effectual to subdue the rebellious spirit, and bring it into sweet and habitual subjection to the teachings of an enlightened judgment. A proper temper of mind is only to be found under the powerful and sanctifying operations of divine truth. The Spirit, like a peaceful dove, must brood upon the heart, and infuse into it his own lovely and harmonizing nature. Many persons, it is true, are naturally amiable and self-possessed; we have read of heathen philosophers who advanced far in the art of self-government, and whose example might well reprove the childish petulence, and hasty wrath, of many of Christ's professed disciples; yet, if the testimony which the Scriptures present of the native malignity of the human heart, is to be received; if the evidence afforded by our own consciousness of the secret, subtle, malignant workings of our depraved nature, is entitled to consideration; what right have we to say that human nature, unaided by grace, undisciplined by the effectual influence of divine truth, is able to attain to the highest attributes of a well regulated temper.   Its existence, therefore, in any individual, implies an humble reverence for the word of God. It implies that the motives and precepts of the gospel have thrown their restraints upon his impatient and unruly spirit; tempering his anger with moderation, his displeasure with gentleness, his indignant resentments with forgiving and heavenly meekness.

II. We are now to consider the IMPORTANCE of a well regulated temper.

1. In estimating its *importance*, it is natural that we should reflect upon the advantages it brings to its truly fortunate possessor.   It contributes greatly to his happiness; his spirit dwells in a peaceful calm; in adversity, as well as in prosperity, a delightful sunshine rests upon his soul; the fountain of comfort within is deep, and well sealed up from external intrusions; he is the master of his own comfort, because the ruler of his own spirit; he is better prepared than other men for temptation and for duty; and he partakes, with a pure and undisturbed relish, of the sweet enjoyments of life.   On the other hand, the passionate man robs himself of comfort; he is not his own master; he is like a badly equipped vessel upon the driving surge; like the troubled sea, whose waters cast up mire and dirt; he is the servant and the prey of circumstances; he gives his enemies ten thousand advantages over him; the pure joys of domestic life, of neighborhood intercourse, and more especially of communion with heaven, are to him often embittered, and perhaps destroyed.   After the bitterness of the storm, comes the bitterness of the calm, the reproaches of his better judgment, the stings of a disquieted and condemning conscience. " What a fool have I been," exclaims the poor man in the hour of reflection—" what a fool to yield so needlessly to the impulse of passion, and cherish for such slight provocations the feelings of revenge.   I have justly exposed myself to the reproaches of friends and enemies, and what is worse, to the condemnation of my own bosom."   But his complaints do but little good: as he has not learned to rule his spirit, he is soon hurried again to the same foolish excess, and compels himself again to repeat the same humiliating sentence of self-condemnation.

He that has gained a decided and permanent victory over his spirit, possesses a friendly and effectual safe-guard against

16—Vol. IV.

many dangers; where others stumble, he moves with a firm
step; where others are pierced with fiery darts, he stands
clad in bright, impenetrable armor : in times of aggravated
excitement and provocation, he appears erect in calm dignity,
like a rock amidst the angry billows.   But what is the security of a man who possesses a hasty and ungovernable spirit?
To what folly, to what calamity—may not heaven abandon
a man in the hour of his wrath?   At such an hour, he may
not only inflict a deep wound upon the cause of the
Redeemer, but may embitter the slumbers of his whole subsequent life : he may utter some fearful imprecation ; he
may raise his hand in violence, and wound or slay an enemy :
but if mercifully restrained from such extremes, there is one
fearful danger to which a man of an undisciplined spirit is
peculiarly exposed.   Passion, unsubjected to wholesome restraint, is likely to wax worse and worse.   It adds gall to its
own wormwood—it casts fuel upon its own unhallowed
fires.   Many that were once mild and amiable, have gradually become sour, and sullen, and hateful.   In prosperity
they seemed all smiles and loveliness ; scarcely a ripple of
anger moved over the surface of their bosom.   But temptations, disappointments, vexations came ; their equanimity
was disturbed ; their spirits were ruffled, and they ruled them
not ; misfortunes and provocations multiplied ; sorrow, de-
jection and wasting disease came on, and those once gentle
and amiable tempers, yielding by degrees to the increasing
and long continued pressure, and unchecked in their descent
by any firm and well directed efforts, have at last sunk down
into unmingled bitterness.   Whilst living in a world which
sin has so fearfully cursed—where ingratitude, selfishness,
and injustice on all sides multiply their provocations—where
sad and sudden reverses so often blast the fondest hopes of
men, have we any right to look for exemption from vexation
and trial, and if we are not duly prepared for such emergencies by habits of self-government, what is to prevent us from
gliding along the same declivity, and settling down at last in
wormwood and gall!

2. Shall we estimate the influence exerted by a man of a
well-regulated temper upon those around him.   This influence is most salutary.   The calm, self-collected man, not
only dwells himself in a pure sunshine, but he reflects
abroad the sweet radiance.   Wife, children, neighbors rejoice

in the light. His spirit falls with subduing influence upon his enemies. What reason, entreaty, remonstrance and force cannot do, he often accomplishes by the might of a meek and quiet temper. His gentleness makes him great; his soft answers turn away wrath. But how is it with the passionate man? He is not only shaded himself, but he often casts a gloomy shade upon others. In his calmest moments, the ripples of his spirit are scarcely so much allayed as to allow a bright and unbroken reflection—and even if the light seems bright and perfect for a time, there is the chilling apprehension in the bosom of his friends, that the storm will soon rise and mar the beauty of the scene. His repulsive demeanor increases the displeasure of those who are already partially estrayed; and often, by a hasty and unreasonable discharge of his bitterness, he makes a friend an enemy forever.

In arresting the collisions which frequently occur in soci-ety, the man of a well governed spirit is of great value. He, of all men, is the best peace-maker, who maintains an un-broken peace in his own bosom. Whilst the man of an angry, nitric soul, stirreth up strife where it is not, and aggravates every little contention that already exists, the influence of that man who has thoroughly mastered himself, distils like reviving dew upon the languishing plants of tranquility and affection, whilst it descends upon the fields of strife, like copious rains upon a burning forest. Who can estimate the worth of such an individual in the church of Christ? Conflicts will often occur amongst unamiable and querulous professors, and on such occasions he is like the healing branch in the waters of Marah. For the want of such members, many churches have fallen into remediless ruin.

A well regulated temper aids essentially in the exercise of authority. It is indispensable to the master, the parent, the ruler. He that cannot govern himself, is not fit to govern others. A passionate ruler resembles a lion amongst the tender flocks, rather than a kind shepherd who knows how to carry the lambs in his bosom, and gently lead those who are with young. What considerate and patriotic American has not blushed for the disgrace inflicted upon our country, by the petty squabbles and furious contests of peevish, angry, boisterous legislators! The history of the world testifies, that important political measures are often moulded in the heat of personal animosity; and that empires have been involved in war, and drenched with blood, to gratify the spleen of a few poor petulent mortals!

In our domestic governments, we often fail for the want of a good temper. In our peevish, angry haste, we make unreasonable laws, and inflict unreasonable punishment; and even if the laws be just, and the punishment deserved, a bitter, repulsive administration of them often destroys their salutary influence. In our moments of reflection we sometimes retract the decisions of our passionate mood, and thus our government becomes uncertain and fickle. We soon lose our influence, and our capricious authority perhaps at length becomes positively hateful. We impart our own spirit to our servants and children; they drink in the gall; their brows gather up and reflect our angry frowns; they learn and repeat the phraseology of petulance and passion. We may lecture them very eloquently upon the value of calmness, and the beauty of a sweet temper; but in vain do we reach out the hand to smooth the brows of our children, when our own are darkened with the clouds of anger. He that can habitually rule himself, is well calculated, in the exercise of his authority, to give to reason its proper sway; he can blend discretion with law; mildness with reproof; and kindness with needful severity. Such authority will be respected; it gains its object; it conciliates those whom it controls; and sweetens those whom it vanquishes.

3. A well regulated temper is one very important part of our preparation for religious duties. That such services may be acceptable to God, and profitable to ourselves, they must be spiritual; that they may be spiritual, they must of course be performed with a temper of mind in accordance with the pure and peaceful dictates of the blessed comforter. That frame of mind is ever to be dreaded, which unfits us for prayer, religious conversation, reading the word of God, and for the services of the sanctuary. But hands that are lifted up in *wrath* and doubting, cannot reach the heavens; a tongue that often speaks in anger, is illy trained for pious discourse; the inflamed and agitated bosom derives but little sweetness from the pages of divine truth; and he that goes to the sanctuary with an angry and wrathful spirit, will seldom find solace in compassing God's altar. In these sacred

services, especially in the duty of prayer, calmness and self-possession are peculiarly needful. What hypocrisy, to offer up the pretended sacrifice of penitence, confession and praise, upon a heart burning with indignation! What presumption, to seek and expect forgiveness from that God whom we owe ten thousand talents, when we reflect with a revengeful and unforgiving spirit upon the petty injuries we may have received from our fellow men! Is this the way to come into the presence of a holy and jealous God? We need the preparation of a calm, pacified and humble spirit. But this preparation should not be that of a momentary calmness, which is forced as it were grudgingly upon the heart, just as the hour of worship draws near. If the soul stands still but for an hour, a dark, poisonous sediment will settle down upon our devotions. The dregs of our long and oft repeated resentments will be likely to mingle with the sacrifice, and it will rise in no grateful odor to the God of peace and consolation. Habitual quietude and self-possession are what will the most effectually clarify the soul, and thus prepare it to let in the beams of permanent blessedness, and reflect with a steady light the image of Jehovah. Is it strange that those persons should often complain of deadness in their meditations, and want of comfort and success in their prayers, who are peevish and petulent in their families, and are often aroused to intemperate heat in their intercourse with the world at large?

4. In illustrating the importance of a well regulated temper, may we not speak of the honor which it brings to Christ and his blessed gospel. The gospel, in its spirit and inculcations, is most directly arrayed against all the boisterous and malignant passions of men. It is gentle, and kind, and dove-like. It inculcates the entire subjection of all the turbulent feelings, to sober reason, to calm, steady, righteous control. It requires us to live in peace with ourselves, and with all around us. The charity which it inculcates, is not easily provoked; the wisdom which it teaches, is pure and peaceable; the temper which it enjoins, is that of the Prince of Peace, " who when he was reviled, reviled not again ;—who did not strive, nor cry, neither did any man hear his voice in the streets." Its injunction is, " let all bitterness, and wrath, and anger, and clamor, and evil speaking, be put away from among you, with all malice." And whilst the gospel urges upon us these divine precepts, it aids us, as has already been

intimated, by its motives and instructions, to obey its commands. It claims to be the power of God. It claims for itself
the abiliy to regulate effectually the jarring machinery of our
natures ;—to make "the wolf dwell with the lamb, the leopard lie down with the kid, and the calf, and the fatling, and
the young lion together." It denies this ability to every other
system which has ever been devised for the improvement and
government of man. He therefore that has thoroughly learned
in the school of Christ, the blessed art of ruling his spirit, in
one very essential and prominent point, honors the holy requirements and sanctifying power of divine truth. He lets his
light shine, and God receives praise. As the sky, and the
forests, and the hills are reflected in their sweet and unbroken harmony, from the bosom of the calm lake; so Christ,
and holiness, and heaven, are sweetly reflected from his calm
and peaceful spirit, and well regulated life. This is what
our Saviour, so to speak, reasonably expects; this is what the
world have a right to expect from the advocates of the gospel, and this is what we have virtually promised by the solemn
profession we have made. To meet this expectation, to redeem this sacred pledge, is indeed a mighty and honorable
achievement.

And yet how different is the conduct of multitudes! How
many peevish, fretful, passionate professors are there in the
churches! Go to their families, and how many harsh looks
will you see, and how many angry speeches will you hear!
Follow them to the public concourse in market places, and
at political convocations: they lift up their angry voices in
the streets, and mingle in the strifes of the clamorous and the
revengeful! Follow them to the churches—to associational
councils—and even there, whilst deliberating upon the interests of the blessed kingdom of righteousness and *peace,*
they are often ready to bite and to devour. You would scarcely suspect that they had owned the meek and lowly Lamb
of God as their guide and Saviour, and the Heavenly Dove
as their sanctifier. They fall out with their children, their
servants, their neighbors, their brethren, with almost every
thing around them. Like poor fretful Jonah, they are sometimes angry even unto death, and when reproved for their
unchristian conduct, the are ready to say like him, "*we do
well to be angry.*"

It is truly melancoly to reflect, that there are some whose

characters are dignified with many substantial virtues; who possess much real kindness, generosity and good will; who would make many sacrifices to aid a friend, and even to benefit an enemy; who are the advocates of pious undertakings, and perhaps liberal contributors of their substance to the cause of Christ, at home and abroad; who, nevertheless, exhibit more or less of the sad deformity of a hasty, unsubdued temper. Their very benevolence seems, at times, embittered. Their pious services, which flow from a heart really kind and compassionate, not unfrequently go forth with an uninviting air. And some we find, whose hearts seem effectually purged from bitterness, upon whose exterior, nevertheless, rigid and antiquated habit has entailed the forms of moroseness and anger, and they seem to us like unlovely crucibles that we are afraid to touch, though we know that the fiery liquid they once contained, is all evaporated. Thus, the characters of many worthy christians are marred in their symmetry, and the heart of the Saviour is made to bleed in his own spiritual members. O Jesus! when will thy professed friends cease thus to pierce thee! O Jesus! when shall these unseemly spots be washed from thy sacred vestments! O ye professed disciples of the Lamb! how long will ye cast these stumbling blocks before your families, your brethren, and the feet of blind, perishing sinners! Look at pure, heaven-born christianity: is there one unlovely wrinkle upon her countenance—one drop of bitterness in the cup which she presents to the lips of her followers? Why, then, will you dishonor your profession, grieve your Saviour, and reproach his sacred cause, by your unlovely conduct?

But we hasten to consider,

III. In the third, and last place, the MEANS to be employed for securing a WELL REGULATED TEMPER.

1. It must be settled in our minds, that such a temper, by the grace of God, is attainable, and that, by the assistance of that grace, we must attain it. Unless this point is well established in our plans and purposes, further instruction will scarcely be needful; for who is properly prepared to use those maxims which may be prescribed for the accomplishment of an important end, so long as that end is regarded as unattainable, or for which he has not resolved diligently to labor. In many cases, perhaps I may say in most, the victory is difficult; and I am not unwilling that the arduous-

ness of the conflict should be fully apprehended. Some are
by nature so happily constituted, and are thrown by the
providence of God into circumstances so favorable to the
preservation of their natural equanimity, that they know but
little of the pain and ardor of the strife. But few, very few,
are thus highly favored. Most persons, in getting the mastery over themselves, are compelled to wrestle with many
stubborn, mighty influences—with angry enemies in high
and fortified places. We often flatter ourselves that our
spirit has been subjected to a wholesome and effectual discipline, when in the very temper which we have long trained,
and which, on the whole, we may humbly and honestly
approve, a careful inspection will occasionally detect somewhat that savors of childish fretfulness, hasty resentment, or
unreasonable indignation. We may drive the enemy from
one lurking place, but soon he entrenches himself in another. He may slumber for a long time; we may congratulate ourselves that we have at last obtained the victory;
but some unexpected occurrence rouses him from repose,
and calls us forth to a new and desperate encounter. How
difficult to lay up all that amount of strength and self-control, which will stand the test amidst the numberless, sudden
and powerful provocations of life. Some are constitutionally hasty and wrathful; how hard to struggle against the
strong, deep tide of nature. Some are thrown by accident,
or the calls of duty, into irritating company and perplexing
occupations: how difficult to rise superior to the force of
adverse circumstances. In some cases, an irritable spirit is
deposited in an afflicted, irritable body: how difficult to harmonize a jarring soul, amidst the discord of disordered, contending nerves! A man may be wise, and learned, and
powerful, and yet never have acquired the art of ruling
himself. Napoleon, that towering colossus of military power, that resistless conqueror of nations, was often as peevish
and indomitable as a spoiled child. How true is the inspired
sentiment of the text: "He that is slow to anger is better
than the mighty; and he that ruleth his spirit, than he that
taketh a city." He is better, he is greater; for the course
of action, which leads him to this victory, demands, in most
cases, more circumspection, watchfulness and self-denial; a
more refined and exalted exercise of true wisdom, that those
which conduct the military chieftain over prostrate cities,

and blood-stained battle fields, to victory and a throne. Behold, my brethren, the nature of the conflict! Are you fully ready for the struggle? Some seem to regard the conquest as a thing impossible, and therefore do not attempt it in serious earnest. " We admit," say they, " that our tempers are stubborn and unruly; we have suffered all our lives long, from their unholy dictation; a hasty spirit is our besetting infirmity; we have often struggled, but in vain, for the mastery; all else seems comparatively easy and practicable, but the truth is, *we* CANNOT *keep our temper.*" Is this the language that should ever fall from the lips of a christian? It indicates both an unbelieving and an indolent spirit. There is a criminal want of faith in the power and grace of God, which are ever equal to our necessities; and a slothful indisposition, most highly culpable, to encounter that labor and self-denial, through which only, we may confidently look for the blessing of the Almighty. And besides, who does not see that, in this very confession, there is a covert defence, or at least a palliation, of the very sin acknowledged. Our guilty stubbornness is made a plea for non-resistance. The sin is to be tolerated, because it is so sinful; the enemy is to be submitted to, because he does us so much harm! But all this is wrong. The christian has not so learned of his Master. The gospel requires us to believe, that all things are possible with God; that every evil temper is to be encountered and subdued; that the prayerful and persevering struggles of faith, will terminate in certain victory. The gospel allows us not to palliate sin, by its own enormity, but to hate it according to its hatefulness, and resist it according to its strength. Let this resolution, formed with an humble dependence on divine grace, be our starting point, *the Lord being our helper, our evil, rebellious tempers, must be, and shall be, effectually subdued.*

2. Watch, my brethren, the first risings of unholy feeling, and raise up, at once, a barrier against it. Nip anger in the bud. " Let not the sun go down upon your wrath." Anger, when indulged, ministers, as we have seen, to its own bitterness. When the passions are up, the imagination is busy in magnifying the causes of disquietude; in the mean time, we allow our resentment to boil and expand, that it may correspond with the imagined enormity of the provocation. This fomentation being often repeated, and allayed, not by reflec-

tion and prayer, but by its own violence; our feelings will be
likely to subside in settled malignity. What a fearful issue!
Surely, beginnings that may possibly tend to such a consummation, are not to be tampered with. Let the spark be
quenched—let the little rivulet be dammed up. It is easier
to extinguish a spark, than a mighty conflagration; to check
the rippling Kidron, than to arrest the swellings of Jordan.

3. We should study well our characters, and learn what
are the things which most easily excite us. No man can
govern himself, unless he *knows* himself. Individuals are
variously constituted; all are not equally exposed at the same
points. That which would be to one man a weak and unsuccessful temptation, might prove to another a keen and
fiery dart. "Know thyself," and then carefully avoid those
things which you know to be dangers. A wise man will
not rush needlessly into temptation; he will turn away his
eyes, and search out some other path. But if duty lead
him into exciting and dangerous scenes, every step will be
well pondered; the shield of watchfulness will be thrown
before every weak point of his nature; his eye be steadily
fixed upon his subtle enemies, and his hand upon the strength
of the Eternal.

Intimately connected with these remarks, is another suggestion which I would beg leave to urge, viz: that we should
carefully watch our peevish moods. Our evil humors have
their periods, their ebbs and their flows. The same temptations do not always operate upon the same individuals alike;
at least, this is the case with many, particularly those in
feeble health; and of a nervous temperament. Many occurrences take place which have a tendency, at certain times,
to play severely upon our natural sensitiveness. We are
busy, and no not wish to be disturbed; or we are weary, and
desire repose; or we are sick, and desire to be left in quiet;
or we have met with disappointment, and, for the present,
we have no relish for the pleasantries of social intercourse;
or, perhaps, it is a cloudy and dark day, and our inner man
sympathises with the external dreariness. At such times, if
our wishes are incidentally crossed, it is difficult to be composed. The crying of a child, the barking of a dog, or a
rap at the door, may throw us from a just balance, and call
forth some foolish expression of discontent. We vent our
spleen upon the horse we ride, or the kind domestic animal

which fawns upon us, or even upon senseless and inanimate objects. On all sides, the eye sees provoking things; and to our excited nerves, even the ministrations of friendship and love seem acrid and unwelcome. On occasions like these, prudence suggests to us the necessity of great circum-spection. Here are revealed to us the weak points of weak-ness itself. Our besetting temptations have now a tenfold advantage. Now are we to summon to our aid our best judgment, and our firmest resolutions ; now should we watch unto prayer. We should at such times avoid, as far as pos-sible, all those trains of thought and conversation, which would be likely to aggravate our ill humor. If we cannot speak peaceably, let us not speak at all ; if we cannot act with moderation, let us forbear acting. Let us be much by ourselves, and commune with our hearts, with the meek and lowly Saviour, with the Scriptures of divine truth, and with the solemnities of an eternal world. Saturdays and Mondays are often trying days to ministers ; on the former they are generally busy in their more immediate prepara-tions for the pulpit ; on the latter, they are often enfeebled by their Sabbath labors ; and, on these occasions, they are frequently liable to be impatient and fretful ; they would do well to consider this, and watch and pray that they enter not into temptation.

4. It might often be profitable for us to imagine ourselves acting in the presence of a friend or a neighbor, and especi-ally to realize that we are ever in the presence of God. Much of our peevishness, in its more visible and unlovely exhibition, is confined to a narrow circle. We wish to be thought amiable and good natured, by our neighbors. Home is the principal store-house of hard looks and angry words. How many there are, who appear to the public eye gentle, lovely and slow to anger, that assume a very different aspect in the eyes of their fire-side associates. In the crowd, their brows seem clothed with the serenity of a fine summer morning, but at home, it appears the citadel of storms. All are not such ; but a majority are apt to be more unguarded at home, than abroad ; before the members of their own households, than visiting friends, or strangers. If a neigh-boring window is open, they scold in a suppressed and guarded tone ; if a tap is heard at the door, the excited voice mellows into sweetness, and as the visiter enters, the

countenance is robed in smiles. One would think that they breathed the atmosphere of perpetual peace. And is the presence of a neighbor sufficient to restrain us? This shows that we have power to keep our temper, or at least greatly to modify the expression of it. We would do well, therefore, often to imagine a neighbor near, and act, in some measure, as though his eye were perpetually upon us.

But if the presence of man will restrain us, how should we be affected by the presence of Jehovah? God, our maker and our judge, is ever near; and a realizing sense of this, will do much to bridle our unhallowed anger. "Thou God seest me." What a solemnizing thought! "Thou under-standest my thought a far off; there is not a word in my tongue, but lo, O Lord, thou knowest it altogether." What a motive to circumspection and self-government. Shall we dress our countenance in wrath, under the very gaze of Je-hovah? Shall we utter passionate and revengeful words, in the very ear of our Maker? Shall that heart, which is every moment pierced through and through by the glance of omnis-cience, nourish its unhallowed resentments? We live so far from duty, because we live so far from the presence of God. We are not fully prepared to sin. till we forget that the eye of the Lord is upon us. Cherishing a constant and solemn sense of his purity, majesty and nearness, we shall be *slow to anger*, and learn to *rule* our rebellious spirits.

5. The lovely character of the Saviour, should be the sub-ject of distinct and frequent contemplation. Let us ever keep it before us in its full-orbed brightness, that in its sweet-ness and glory our own evil tempers may be called into sub-jection. Were the Saviour to visit our families in person, and mingle with us in the various walks of life, his presence would no doubt often fill us with shame and confusion. He would find us not only like Martha, careful and trou-bled about many things, but perhaps like her, peevishly com-plaining that some of our pious friends should remain so long at the feet of their master, and leave us to serve alone. Per-haps he would often have occasion to say to us, as he did to some of his disciples of old, "ye know not what manner of spirit ye are of." But although the Saviour is not per-sonally with us, yet, his holy image visits us in his word, and he is ever looking down upon us from his lofty throne, to see if we make that image our study and our model. We

know what manner of spirit he was of, and we know that his spirit must be ours; "for if any man have not the spirit of Christ, he is none of his." Did the patient and lowly Saviour ever utter a peevish word? Was his meek brow ever darkened by a resentful frown? He was indeed once said to be angry; but his anger was not fretfulness, it was not resentment, it was not malice; but that strong, vehement displeasure, with which infinite and insulted holiness looks upon incorrigible transgression. Neglect never irritated him; insult never provoked him; hunger, weariness and want, never made him peevish. When in their scorn his enemies mocked him, and in their spite they spit upon him, and in their wrath they scourged and crucified him, there was no scorn, no spite, no wrath, in his spirit. What unparalleled meekness! What unspeakable forbearance! "He was led as a sheep to the slaughter, and like a lamb dumb before his shearers, so he opened not his mouth." Christians, this is your pattern, this is your Saviour. Behold the man! You have taken upon you his name; his image you profess to bear. Then take upon you, daily, his yoke, and learn of him; let the same mind be in you which was also in Christ Jesus; be ye followers of him, as dear children.

6. We have already hinted at the importance of prayer, but this must be urged as a distinct point. That we may prevail over own evil spirit, we must know how to prevail with God, at the mercy seat. Without prayer, all other prudential maxims for the regulation of our temper, will lose much of their efficacy. It is in the near and frequent communion with the King of kings, that the heart receives its salutary and abiding impressions. In that devout and spiritual exercise, a powerful antidote is conveyed to the very fountain of disease. The Holy Spirit draws near in his gentle, soothing, dove-like influence, and enlarges and strengthens his dominion in the inner man. It is then the soul receives that precious, heavenly annointing, which causes the vexations of life to glance off without penetrating and poisoning; or if they should inflict a partial wound upon the spirit, the healing oil is present to arrest the inflammation, and effect a speedy cure. He that has an irritable nature, and would thoroughly rectify its disorders, has the most urgent occasion for pondering, and practicing the law of inspiration, "*pray without ceasing.*" Whenever he

may feel the fire of wrath kindling in his bosom, he
should take the alarm, as though his habitation were in
flames, and lift up his cry for the quenching influence of
grace.   When the great Robert Hall, on a certain occasion,
became unduly excited, he withdrew to the opposite side of
the apartment, and ejaculated in a suppressed tone, "Lamb
of God, Lamb of God, calm my perturbed spirit."   How
admirably appropriate!   How appropriate the occasion : he
was gliding off beyond his own strength and resources, and
needed divine help.   How appropriate the phraseology of
his petition ; he needed the help of the Saviour, in its soothing, lamb-like influence.   We would do well, on similar
occasions, to withdraw, if possible, from the scene of conflict, and silently, at least, invite the assistance of heaven.
We would do well, also, at such a time, to contemplate the
Saviour, in our petitions, in the character of the meek, patient, inoffensive Lamb of God.   Is any danger foreseen?
Let us anticipate it with prayer.   And what, though there
be no visible cause of alarm, a thousand secret perils lurk
around, and we should still, most fervently, bespeak grace
and help for our unknown times of need.   How do we
know but that a prayerless frame was the prelude to that
rash offence, which barred the feet of Moses from the land
of Canaan ; and to that unhappy contention of Barnabus
and Paul, which has been recorded for the caution and reproof of all succeeding generations.   Where the spirit
proves incorrigible, occasional fasting should be joined with
prayer.   "This kind," said the Saviour, on a certain occasion, "goeth not out, but by prayer and fasting."   From
this it would seem, that in ancient times, some evil spirits
were more formidable and malignant than others ; and that
their expulsion from their unhappy victims demanded extraordinary means.   In some individuals, nay, in many, an unruly temper may be likened to one of those malignant, indomitable spirits.   If fasting, in connection with strong crying and tears, would aid in its subjugation, what individual
that truly hungers and thirsts after righteousness, would refuse to set his face unto the Lord with sackcloth, and fasting,
and ashes.

   7. Proper reflections upon own imperfect and sinful conduct, will furnish us with weighty motives for meekness and
moderation.   If we had never sinned ourselves, we might,

with less inconsistency, cast abroad our hasty and bitter resentments. If we had never been the occasion of provocation to others, we might find some excuse for bearing with so little equanimity the insults which are cast upon ourselves. If we had never insulted our Heavenly Father, we should be less guilty in quarrelling with his afflictive and mysterious providence. But how stands the case? In a thousand instances, perhaps, have we unreasonably provoked our fellow-men; in ten thousand instances of unreasonable and wanton rebellion have we provoked Jehovah. We are irritated by the little follies of our children: have we forgotten that we were once thoughtless and wayward children, and that often our kind parents were annoyed by our intractable tempers, captious complaints, and insubordinate behavior? We are sore vexed with our neighbor for some little slight, or impertinence, or unkind expression: how often may that neighbor have had equal cause to complain of our impertinence, neglect, or unkind expressions? We fall out with the dispensations of heaven, and, like Jonah, are ready to say, "it is better for us to die than to live." O have we forgotten that our compassionate and indulgent Father in heaven has registered against us an infinite debt of forgetfulness, ingratitude and insults; that the smallest of our numberless provocations, if visited upon as it merits, would subject us to his insupportable, eternal wrath? Such reflections, frequently and solemnly indulged, will teach us calmness and moderation. They will hush the storms of anger. They will rebuke and quell our corroding resentments. They will suggest to us, that as we desire and expect forgiveness for our own sins, we must look with forbearance upon the follies of others; and that least of all should the sin-polluted culprit, that merits eternal death, fret against that being, whose mercy and goodness have followed him all his days, and whose almighty and gracious arm has been every moment extended to ward off this merited destruction.

Lastly, we should cherish frequent and solemn thoughts of a dying hour. This will naturally lead us to reflect upon that frame of mind which would be most suitable for death, and an eternal state. It would lead us to realize the force and solemnity of the truth, that no disposition of heart should be cherished for an hour, which would be unfit for that hour, were it to be our last. Under the influence of proper views of death and judgment, and that eternity which rolls beyond, could we give loose reins, as we too often do, to our angry passions? Would wrath, and malice, and revenge find entertainment in our bosoms? The hour of passion may be death's hour; death heeds not our moods and our temper. Who would die in his wrath, and be carried to the grave with a frown congealed upon his brow? But though we might be certain that a calm hour would usher in our dissolution, yet surely the uniform composure of a whole life is a sweeter preparative for death, than the calmness of a few transient moments. Must not the recollection of angry disputes, of wrathful indulgence, diminish the blessedness of dying? "Those servants—how often have they listened to my needless and unchristian-like threatenings! Those dear children that I am so soon to leave behind—how often have I provoked them to anger, to their discouragement and injury! This beloved wife that is now weeping in anguish her long, her last farewell—how often has my petulence planted deep stings in her affectionate bosom! This husband, my prop, my solace, my earthly all, from whose arms death is now tearing me away! O how often has he been pierced by my angry looks; how often has he wept in secret over my harsh words, and unreasonable contentions!" Ye saints of God, why will you treasure up for your dying beds such melancholy reflections?

With some practical reflections and appeals we shall now conclude. From the foregoing views which we have presented of the subject, we are confident that it must appear to all as one of great importance. The theme has been too frequently overlooked in our hours of meditation, self-scrutiny and prayer, and too seldom has it been urged from the sacred desk.

Need I say, my younger brethren, that it is one which claims your special consideration. You are now forming your characters for future life—how important that these characters be shaped in the mould of the gospel of peace. Now learn, my dear young friends, to be *better than the mighty—than he that taketh a city.* Be *slow to anger;* learn thoroughly to *rule your spirit;* and you have gained this honorable, and, I might say, this enviable distinction.

If youth is allowed to be passionate, manhood may be wrathful, and old age malignant.

Parents, cultivate and exhibit at all times a well balanced temper; then will you not needlessly *provoke your children to anger.* Husbands love your wives and be not *bitter* against them; wives obey your husbands, not with a reluctant and peevish air, but with an affectionate and winning demeanor. Masters, mingle a good temper with the exercise of your authority, *forbearing threatening.* Teachers, rule well your own spirit; then will you more successfully control and fashion the minds and tempers of your pupils. Legislators, banish afar your undignified and hurtful contentions—write down, in massive capitals, upon the walls of your council chambers, the instruction of a wise monarch of Israel, " HE THAT IS SOON ANGRY DEALETH FOOLISHLY—ANGER RESTETH IN THE BOSOM OF FOOLS." Christian Editors, be careful to manifest in your discussions and controversies, a *good temper ;* be courteous, kind, magnanimous; pour not abroad upon the public mind the streams of bitterness, to irritate and distract; but the oil of gentleness and peace, to soothe and to gladden.

Brethren in the ministry, consider well, we entreat you, what we have said. In the pulpit, in your families, in your social visits, in deliberative councils, be careful to maintain a well regulated temper. *"Not soon angry,"* is one of the scriptural qualifications of him that is to take the oversight of souls. He is to be neither *"a striker,"* nor a *"brawler."* He must avoid those things "that gender strifes." The servant of the Lord must not strive, but be gentle unto all men,—in meekness instructing them that oppose themselves. The plea of christian faithfulness and zeal for the truth, should never be urged in defence of a harsh and petulent manner in reproving sin, and enforcing the injunctions of the gospel. "Speaking the truth in love,"—this is the inspired exposition of that temper which is to accompany all the communications of the ambassador of Christ.

A minister must not obstinately stand upon every unimportant punctilio; nor catch and quibble at every little roughness that comes in his way. He must, in the true sense of the phrase, be a *high-minded and honorable man.* With a generous forbearance and noble magnanimity, must he pass over a thousand slights and provocations, which may

18—Vol. IV.

be thrown before him by the forgetful, and the inconsiderate, as well as by the captious, designing and inimical. His duties are too urgent and too sacred to allow him to come down, and fritter away his time and his strength in brooding over his childish grudges, and contending for hair-breadth rights, which, if gained, would add nothing to his reputation and usefulness. The magnanimous conduct of Abraham, on a certain occasion of difficulty and vexation, may furnish a lesson which christians in general, and ministers in particular, would do well to remember. "And Abram said unto Lot, let there be no strife, I pray thee, between me and thee; and between my herdmen and thy herdmen; for we be brethren. Is not the whole land before thee? Separate thyself, I pray thee, from me: if thou wilt take the left hand, then I will go to the right; or if thou depart to the right hand, then I will go to the left." Is it not to be feared that the want of a well regulated temper amongst many of the ministers of Christ, has greatly aggravated those unhappy contentions, which are now agitating the churches, and even threatening the safety of our country. *Money* is said to be the *sinews* of war:—the *mercury* of the soul may, with equal truth, be said to be at least *one* of the sinews of theological strife and ultraism. An unruly temper, connected with blind zeal and a misguided conscience, with an adequate seasoning of pride and self-consequence, will soon generate ultraism enough to turn the world upside down.

Sinners, impenitent sinners, can I close without a word to you? Aim at securing, as a most important and desirable possession, a well regulated temper. That you may be successful, learn in the school of the meek and lowly Saviour; submit at once to the discipline of the gospel. Possibly, without the grace of God, you may live what is generally called an amiable and harmless life. But I beg you to remember, that nothing is entitled to the name of a well regulated temper, which is connected with enmity against God. And I beg you further to remember, that all which you may consider amiable and lovely, you will leave behind you at the grave, if you die impenitent; that you will go into eternity with nothing but the unmingled dregs of your fallen nature; and that, with the tormented victims of your own malignity, and spite, you will forever

" Curse
Almighty God, and curse the Lamb, and curse
The earth, the resurrection morn, and seek,
And ever vainly seek, for utter death."

What cheering results should we witness from the universal prevalence of that temper, which we have been endeavoring to describe. Happiness, on all sides, would be greatly increased. Many domestic trials, neighborhood conflicts, and even national calamities, would be warded off. Religious controversies would be softened down into kind, courteous and useful discussions. Church and associational difficulties would, in a great measure, come to an end; a dark cloud would be rolled away from the prospects of Zion; new brightness would be imparted to the christian name; our prayers would have more free access to the throne of grace; and the God of love and peace would be more abundantly honored.

Brethren, friends, one and all; let us, like good soldiers, rush to the conflict. Let us be men; let us be christian men. In that encounter, which is carried on in the name and strength of the Most High, for the mastery over our spirits, we see human nature struggling for its just rights. It is reason contending with madness. It is man striving to be man. It is the sublime struggle of an immortal spirit, endeavoring to re-establish in the bosom, the reign of primeval harmony which sin had destroyed. It is not the contest of brute force, but of wisdom, faith, prayer, patient endeavor, and holy courage. It is sustained by pure motives, elevated desires, and rational, holy principles. The victory, which crowns such a course of conduct as this, cannot but be great and ennobling, fully worthy the aims and efforts of an intelligent, immortal being.

But I must close. Come my hearers, go with me to an humble dwelling, and let me introduce to your acquaintance an individual, whose example, in my conclusion, I beg leave to present, as well worthy of your imitation. He lives in a retired vale, far from the pomp of cities. His name is Pacificus. He is unknown to fame; genius never owned him as her favorite son; wealth never saw him in her glittering train, nor science in her academic groves. His name never echoed beyond those little hills which bound his rural prospect. Yonder is his lowly cot. Retired, contented, pious, happy, he cultivates his paternal acres. But he is a great man. When young, he possessed a wrathful, ungovernable spirit. If there was clamor, if there was con-tention, if there was confusion, he was in the midst. But grace at length awakened in his bosom, the contest between the flesh and the spirit. He commenced a christian life. Long and doubtful seemed the conflict with his hasty temper. He resolved, and wept, and wrestled in prayer. Often did he seem discouraged; sometimes was he nigh the borders of despair. But deriving fresh vigor from the promises of the Most High, he renewed and prosecuted the battle. At length he prevailed. He is now meek, peaceable and love-ly—he is one that can rule his spirit. A sweet serenity ever rests upon his brow; peace reigns at his fire-side, and his rustic neighbors rejoice in the influence of his gentleness. Immortal man! Though the proud, busy world knows thee not, thou art known in heaven. There thy name is enrolled amongst the illustrious, and precious, and eternal will be the fruit of thy victory.

Beloved friends, whoever you may be, go ye and do like-wise. In a word, " whatsoever things are true; whatsoever things are honest; whatsoever things are just; whatsoever things are pure: whatsoever things are *lovely ;* whatsoever things are of good report; if there be any virtue, if there be any praise, THINK OF THESE THINGS.

PLAGIARISM, SOMETIMES ONLY APPARENT,— NOT REAL.

The sermon published in our May No. as original, pur-porting to be from the pen of the late Rev. Jas. A. Payne, of Albemarle County, Va., turns out to be an exact copy of a sermon, published a year or two since in Philadelphia, by Rev. Albert Barnes. It is due to the memory of Mr. Payne to say, that we have no evidence that he preached, or otherwise used it;—that it was found among his manu-scripts after his decease, whether in his own hand-writing or that of another we know not; and that it was furnished by his executor for this work. It was published in our absence; but had we been present, we might not have detected the mistake, as we do not read every thing good, nor recollect all that we read. We hope this explanation will be as satis-factory to Dr. Barnes, to the friends of Bro. Payne, and to our readers, as it is to ourselves. EDITOR.

THE
BAPTIST PREACHER.

VOL. IV.   August, 1845,   NO. 8.

THE VALUE OF CHRIST'S SACRIFICE:—

A sermon, preached in the ordinary course of his ministry, to his people, April 27, 1845, by Rev. ROBERT BOYTE C. HOWELL, D. D., Pastor of the First Baptist Church, Nashville, Tennessee.

—

" Every priest standeth daily ministering, and offering oftentimes the same sacrifices, which can never take away sins: but this man, after he had offered one sacrifice for sins, forever sat down at the right hand of God; from henceforth expecting till his enemies be made his footstool. For by one offering he hath perfected forever them that are sanctified. Whereof the Holy Ghost also is a witness to us.—Heb. x: 11-15.

—

The value of Christ's sacrifice for sins, is infinite. This is the proposition affirmed in the text, and which, in the present discourse, I shall attempt to sustain, and illustrate.

The sacrifices and offerings, which under the former economy, were of so frequent occurrence, could never take away sins. Their design was not of themselves to purify, but simply, and alone, to direct the faith of the worshipers to Messiah, their true and great antitype. In his sacrifice only, true and inherent virtue was found; and from it all others derived whatever of efficacy they possessed. "It is [evidently] not possible that the blood of bulls and of goats *should* take away sins;" and yet, "without the shedding of blood there is no remission." A sacrifice was required more efficacious than any of those prescribed in the formularies of the Levitical priesthood. But where can such a sacrifice be found? by whom can it be offered? whence is to be obtained the victim? whither, for an answer to these inquiries, shall we look, but to Christ? He, "*by one offering*, has perfected forever, them that are sanctified." He "has appeared to *put away sin* by the *sacrifice of himself.*"

The provision is ample. Those who, by repentance and faith, become partakers of its rich blessings, are thenceforward, " meet to be partakers of the inheritance of the saints in light."

Such is the excellency, the magnitude, and the power of Christ's sacrifice for sins. Nothing more is needed. It is perfect; it is effectual; it is sufficient.

The unspeakable value of Christ's sacrifice for sins, may be seen in the fact that *God has appointed it especially to be the medium of our cleansing and salvation.*

" It pleased the *Lord* to bruise him." He it was, who made " his soul an offering for sin." Although " with wicked hands he was crucified and slain," yet it was done "according to the determinate counsel and foreknowledge of God." For this reason the Redeemer said to his followers, who were astonished that he did not overwhelm and crush his persecutors: " I lay down my life of myself ; no man taketh it from me." Having been, therefore, previously ordained as the means of pardon by Jehovah, can he fail to accept it for that end, when its merits are pleaded by the guilty, but penitent offender.

But what is a sacrifice, properly so called ? It is, I answer, the solemn infliction of death, by the shedding of blood, upon a living being, with the forms of religious worship, and the presentation of the victim, life, body and blood, to God as a supplication for pardon. All this occurred in the offering of Christ. Death was inflicted upon him ; " his life was cut off from the earth ; " the last drop of blood in his heart was poured forth ; his *body* was exposed upon the cross. If, in this appalling deed, the scourge, the nail and the spear, were in the hands of sinners, who were moved to the infliction of his sufferings by malignant envy, this serves but the more plainly to set forth the grace which could impel him to bear the curse for his *enemies*, as well as for his friends. His *life*, his *body*, his *blood*, his *soul* and his *divinity*, by himself, our great High Priest, were offered to God, a supplication of boundless efficacy, for the remission of our sins.

Upon this sacrifice, so appointed by the Father, and so consummated by the Son, we lay hold, in every acceptable prayer we utter, and thus wield all its power. It is not, therefore, surprising, that "Prayer moves the hand that moves the world."

But let us also consider *the dignity of the offerer*, and we shall be able to perceive, still more fully, the value of the sacrifice. Whom do we now behold at the altar? Not the High Priest of an earthly lineage, with his glittering breast-plate, and his flowing robes. Not the most exalted of the sons of men. It is God himself, incarnate. *He* it is (amazing condescension and grace!) who becomes our priest; and *he*, because no other victim of sufficient virtue could be found, on earth, or in heaven, offers *himself*, as the precious sacrifice! The sword of justice raised for our destruction, he receives into his own bosom, and bids *us* but *love our deliverer*, and live, and be happy!

Of this overwhelming scene, the sons of Aaron, in the tabernacle, and in the temple, exhibited but types and symbols. They "stood daily ministering, and offering, oftentimes, the same sacrifices, which can never take away sins." We now behold the illustrious antitype! His character and work are shadowed forth to the eye of faith, not only in all the victims which bled in sacrifice upon Jewish altars, but also in the blood of Abel; in the offering up of Isaac; in the contumely received by Joseph from his brethren; and in the guidance which Moses gave to the children of Israel; and he it was who inspired the songs of the patriarchs, and the predictions of prophets, who through "the dim vista of coming years, saw the day of the Son of man and were glad."

The ministry of angels, fearful exhibitions of the power of God, and appalling expressions of the sympathy of nature, attested *the dignity* of Messiah in his humiliation. There hung the sacred victim upon the cross, quivering in every nerve with anguish, and bleeding from every gaping wound! Angels, aghast, hovered around in anxious suspense and astonishment. Fiendish men, in whose bosom fear and envy mingled with the spirit of revenge, scowled upon the scene. Hark! the agonized sufferer "cries with a loud voice—It is finished!" Look! "he bows his head, he gives up the ghost!" Pale, mangled, all gory, he dies! The earth, as if seized with astonishment and fear, shook and trembled; the veil of the temple was torn asunder throughout, exposing the most holy place; as a flickering candle, the sun in mid-heaven went out, and the universe, from the sixth to the ninth hour, was shrouded in thick darkness. The multitude, although intoxicated with rage, as they groped their way from Calvary, exclaimed, this, this *is*, he is *the Son of God.* Kind friends, with aching hearts, took him down from the cross, and laid him in the grave. But he was not destined long to remain a prisoner there. The third morning came, and with it his glorious resurrection! Behold him, as he comes forth from the sepulchre, " leading captivity captive " at his chariot wheels, a triumphant conqueror! Again, the earth and the heavens trembled with agitation! Angels passed swiftly about the tomb; and many bodies of the saints arose, and were seen in the holy city! And now joy and gladness mingled everywhere, with the amazement of his people. Forty days he conversed with his disciples, and having, at Olivet, given them his final commands, as he blessed them, he arose in their presence and ascended up into heaven. They gazed upon him until a cloud received him out of their sight. He is gone to take possession of the mansions of glory in our behalf, and " sits at the right hand of God, until his enemies are made his footstool." Thus, so great is his dignity and glory, that when he offers *one* sacrifice for sins, it is enough. He thereby " perfects forever them that are sanctified." All other sacrifices and priesthoods are instantly abolished. His *one* offering is ample for all ages; and his priesthood is thenceforward perpetual.

When the infinitely glorious God descends to be the offerer, and at the same time, the victim, accompanying the sacrifice with events so illustrious, the value of the offering must correspond in magnitude to the grandeur of the transaction.

We will, however, if you please, look for a moment at *the great object which it secures,* and we shall be able to perceive, in a still more striking point of light, the value of Christ's sacrifice. We always estimate causes by their effects. They are considered of little consequence, except for the results they produce. Apply this rule of judgment in the case before us. What objects are secured by the sacrifice of Christ? Jehovah, I reply, was moved to pity by the woes of men, whose whole moral nature was poisoned and embittered by transgression. He *loved* us, and determined to institute means for the removal of human guilt. It was in pursuance of this gracious design, that he sent his Son into our world, the abode of wretchedness and woe. He "brought life and immortality to light, by the gospel." In consideration of his sacrifice, God the Father is reconciled, justice is appeased, and the way of salvation opened to men. We may now approach him with confidence, and obtain all our desires.

Another object secured is the mission of the Holy Spirit. Pardoned indeed, we might be, without his regenerating work. This, however, would avail us little, since, as our depraved nature would remain unchanged, we should still be unqualified for happiness, and incapable of the glory of heaven. Through the satisfaction offered by the Redeemer, the Spirit comes into our world, whose prerogative it is, in the individual application of his merits, to purify the soul. That "he by one offering, has perfected forever them that are sanctified," the Holy Ghost, the sanctifier, "is to us," the ever present and best "witness." Yes, blessed be his name—

"The Spirit answers to the blood,
And tells me I am born of God."

Yet another object secured, is the all powerful, ever successful, and perpetual mediation, and advocacy on high of Jesus Christ. He, our adorable High Priest, sympathizing with all our infirmities, has entered into heaven, with his own priceless blood, for us; thus establishing a glorious medium of communion in all our worship with the Father of our spirits, and through which we may receive continually, unceasing supplies of grace. Now, therefore, we may come boldly unto the throne of grace, and there obtain mercy, and find grace to help us in time of need. Since, therefore, the objects secured by the sacrifice of Christ are, to speak of no others, the pardon of our sins, the sanctification of our natures, and the salvation of our souls, who, judging only by these, can fully comprehend the extent of its value?

Again, the value of this offering is shown in the fact, *that from it all the forms and ordinances of religion,* whether under the patriarchal, Mosaic, or christian dispensations, *receive their life and energy.* The sacrifices of the fathers, as we have already seen, were efficacious only as the worshipers exercised faith in Christ, the great antitype. Take away the sacrifice of Christ, and the Mosaic priesthood, and all its offerings were destitute of significancy, or energy to move the heart. They all pointed to Messiah, and told, in letters of blood, that " the wages of sin is death, but that the gift of God is eternal life, through Jesus Christ our Lord."

What without Christ's sacrifice, could we accomplish by preaching the gospel? The callous heart of the sinner is untouched by mere moral lessons, however sublime. Appeal to him in terms the warmest and most impassioned, to consult his spiritual safety and happiness, it passes by him all unnoticed as the idle wind. Take him to Sinai ; show him the terrors of the law ; let the thunders of divine vengeance burst, and the lightnings of his wrath flash and blaze along the gathering storm ; he stands amid the fearful scene unmoved. Nothing, *nothing*, but *the love of God as seen in the sufferings of Jesus Christ upon the cross*, will, *can* subdue and melt the obdurate heart of the sinner. This is omnipotent. None can be so hard as to resist the power of the cross. Here, blessed Redeemer,

> " By dying love *compelled*,
> We own thee conqueror."

From the sacrifice of Christ, baptism derives its form and expressiveness. Jesus died for our sins, was buried, and rose again for our justification. And "know ye not that so many of us as were baptized into Jesus Christ, were baptized into his death? Therefore we are buried with him by baptism into death, that like as Christ was raised up from the dead by the glory of the Father, even so we also should walk in newness of life."

The Lord's Supper also is an equally affecting representation of the same great scene. This bread, said the Redeemer, is my body, given for you ; this cup is my blood, shed for you. " As oft as ye eat this bread and drink this cup, ye do show the Lord's death till he come. Do this in remembrance of me." Thus it is seen, that the sacrifice of Christ is the great centre to which points every institution, doctrine and ordinance of religion, and from which they derive all their life and energy.

And yet more. The value of Christ's sacrifice for sins, is seen in *the instruction which it affords us for the formation of christian character.* "Brethren, if Christ so *loved* us, (that he died for us,) we ought also to *love one another.*" He is our illustrious example. To be like his, how pure should be that love; how disinterested; how expansive; how fervent! He has taught us, too, in his life, and in his death, with what freedom and cheerfulness we should *forgive our enemies.* Heard you that prayer, solemn, devout, impassioned, which he uttered with his dying breath? And for whom? For the persecutors and murderers about him, whose garments were reeking with his blood. "Father forgive them, they know not what they do." Here is "compassion like a God." So he *endured* the scoffs, and so he *forgave* his enemies. Can we do less? In our daily prayers he instructs us to say, "forgive us *our* trespasses, as *we forgive* those who trespass against us." And how much more should we exercise the same spirit towards our brethren.

> "———How beautifully falls
> From human lips, that blessed word, *forgive!*
> *Forgiveness,* 'tis the attribute of God;
> The sound which speaketh heaven; renews again
> On earth, lost Eden's faded bloom; and flings
> Hope's halcyon halo o'er the waste of life!"

Readily and cheerfully he *suffered* for us. Shall we then shrink from suffering, whenever the honor of the cause, the triumph of the truth, or the salvation of sinners demands it? God forbid! Let me bear the cross after my Redeemer. Come persecution, contumely, death,—come what will— blessed Saviour, I will follow thee.

In a word, what quality is there which gives excellency and perfection to christian character, in relation to which we do not find ample instruction in his own illustrious example?

The sacrifice of Christ for our sins will, finally, *constitute a theme to myriads for delightful contemplation, and a source of the purest enjoyment forever.*

Heaven without Christ would lose its most radiant charms to the redeemed. And what is it, but his glorious sacrifice, which renders him so precious to the hearts of all? His love fills every bosom with overflowing delight. The triumphal song of the glorified, which the bright inhabitants of paradise will sing unceasingly, has direct reference to his great sacrifice. "Worthy is the Lamb that was slain, to receive power, and riches, and wisdom, and strength, and honor, and glory and blessing." "ALLELUIAH." For, "he hath died to redeem us, out of every nation, and kindred, and tongue, and people, under heaven."

Angels themselves learn, from his sacrifice, more of God than they before knew, or ever, otherwise, could have known. Its mysteries were to them most profound and amazing; but when they saw the benevolence which it evinced, they, the more readily, tuned their harps and swept the golden chords, in unison with the hosannas of the saints on high.

A perpetual flood of love, and grace, and glory, and happiness, pours forth from his sacrifice, which fills, and will continue to fill, all heaven, with delightful rapture, *forever.* This is the true "river of the water of life, the streams whereof make glad the city of God."

These are some of the considerations, feebly and very inadequately presented, which sustain and illustrate the value of Christ's sacrifice for sins. It is evinced by the fact that it was offered by the appointment of God; it is seen in the personal dignity of the offerer; it is proved by the magnitude of the objects which it secured; by the consideration that it gives, and ever has given, form and life to all the institutions, ordinances and doctrines of religion; by the instruction it affords us in the formation of christian character; and by the joy which it gives, and will continue to give, to the countless myriads of heaven, forever. The value of Christ's sacrifice for sins, is therefore, *infinite, inconceivable, boundless.*

It remains only, that a brief APPLICATION be made of our subject.

1. We cannot but perceive, unless we greatly err in our conceptions of the topics now brought in review, that in the sacrifice of Christ, we have a full and perfect antidote for sins.

Moral disease has indeed laid its withering hand upon us all. But there "is balm in Gilead; there is a physician there." The ransom price is paid. No man, now, need remain in his sins, and under the power of death. Infinite

love invites you to repentance, to faith, to pardon, to salva- ·
tion. Will you, *can* you resist the kind entreaty of him
who died for sinners? What more can the inquirer ask,
than is presented to him in Christ's satisfaction? Here is
fullness and freeness of redemption. Here alone the wretched
backslider can find a cure for his miseries. Sinners, inqui-
rers, backsliders, all, *all*—come to the Saviour. He asks
but your love, your faith, your obedience. Can you possibly withhold them? Would you *give him* less? Why
then do you thus waver, hesitate and delay? Come to this
full fountain, drink of its purifying waters and live forever.

2. The sacrifice of Jesus Christ for sins, teaches us the
unreasonableness of attempting to reach heaven by any other
means. Philosophers may cavil, and waste their learning
in metaphysical discussions as to the nature of God, of the
soul, and of the relations that subsist between them;
moralists may exhaust their powers of reason in speculations
regarding their favorite theories; the legalist may watch,
may study, may employ ceaseless diligence; the sombre
ascetic may afflict himself with woes innumerable; it is all,
if relied upon for salvation, utterly in vain. "There is no
other name given under heaven among men, whereby we
must be saved," but the name of Jesus. He himself has
said, "I am the way, the true way, and the living way; no
man cometh unto the Father but by me."

"None but Jesus, none but Jesus,
Can do helpless sinners good."

Deceive not yourselves, I entreat you, by indulging the
supposition that you may possibly be saved in some other
way. Salvation without an application to the soul, by the
Holy Spirit, of the merits of Christ's sacrifice for sins, is and
will remain forever impracticable.

3. This subject instructs us that the sacrifice of Christ for
sins, is entirely sufficient to accomplish all the purposes for
which it was designed. Can the all-wise and omnipotent
God fail in his purposes of love to us? This is his own
expiation, appointed, executed and accepted by him. Is it
adequate? How *can* it fail?

"A faithful and unchanging God,
Lays the foundation of my hope,
In oaths, and promises, and blood."

19—Vol. IV,

Nor can he who relies upon it be disappointed. Never, *never.* If 1 am upheld by his sacrifice I am safe, I ask no more.

4. If such be the value of Christ's sacrifice for sins, it is infinitely important that we shall keep it continually before our minds, that upon our character and life as christians, it may produce its full effect. Thence we derive alike, our hope of salvation ; our strength to surmount the impediments that obstruct our spiritual progress ; and exalted motives to the performance of every duty. Let its hold upon our thoughts and our affections, not relax and become enfeebled, but grow daily more and more strong. The foundation upon which you, my brethren, stand, is firm as eternity. The prospect before you is all bright and glorious. Courage, then, beloved brethren ; it is Christ your Redeemer, who speaking from heaven, says to each of you, " Be thou faithful unto death ; and 1 will give thee a crown of life." Amen.

THE MINISTRY WHICH GOD APPROVES :—

A Sermon, preached May 31, 1845, in Lynchburg, before the Virginia Baptist Education Society, by Rev. Ro. Ryland, President of Richmond College. Published at the request of the Society.

" *Study to show thyself approved unto God, a workman that needeth not to be ashamed, rightly dividing the word of truth.*—2 Tim. ii: 15.

The relation of Paul to Timothy was alike solemn and endearing. Under the labors of the one, the other had been converted, baptized, and inducted into the ministry of reconciliation. They had journeyed together for the purpose of announcing the glad tidings of the kingdom of God. A community of toils, perils, hopes and triumphs, had thus strengthened the mutual sympathy which the gospel had implanted in their minds. While Timothy regarded Paul as a father in years and in affection, the latter looked upon the former as his " dearly beloved son " in the gospel. With such feelings he dictated to him the two epistles which bear his name ; epistles in which the authority of an apostle, and the solicitude of a father are beautifully blended. But the Spirit of inspiration did not design these letters exclusively for one man. They were written for the instruction of all the ministers of the gospel who should live on the earth to the end of time. To each one of *us*, that Spirit is now saying, "study to show thyself approved unto God, a workman that needeth not to be ashamed, rightly dividing the word of truth." This language evidently refers to the account which all the servants of God will have to give in the final day. Earnestly strive to present thyself to the judge as an approved minister; as a workman that needeth not to be ashamed when his work is reviewed; as a teacher who rightly divides the word of truth. To enable you in some degree to appreciate the importance of this precept, and to aim at a rigid conformity to its spirit, I propose to answer the following inquiry: What kind of a minister will God approve?

1. The first and most essential requisite in his character, is a renovation of the heart. It is not sufficient that the aspirants to this office should merely possess a decent morality. To educate one from childhood for "holy orders;" to endow him with all the intellectual furniture necessary to the attainment of human eloquence, and then to invest him with the pastoral functions, regardless of his spiritual tastes and aptitudes, is utterly abhorrent to the spirit of the gospel. We have no such custom, neither the churches of God. The minister whom heaven approves, has intelligently felt his guilty and lost condition; has acquiesced in the justice of his condemnation; has cordially embraced Jesus Christ as his Savior; and has realized the power of divine grace to purify his nature and to regulate his life. Of all the arts of hell, none are so malicious as that of inducing ungodly men to assume the garb of religious teachers. "Unto the wicked, God saith, what hast thou to do to declare my statutes, or that thou shouldst take my covenant in thy mouth, seeing thou hatest instruction and castest my words behind thee?" This practice is fraught with peril to the eternal interests of the incumbent of the office, and of those who come under his influence. Much as I value extensive learning, I would rather see all our pulpits occupied by unlettered, but warmhearted, thorough, experimental christians, than to see them filled with men destitute of vital piety, though adorned with splendid talents and profound erudition.

2. But conversion alone is not sufficient. The motive that should impel one to assume this responsibility, must be single and disinterested. It is possible that even good men may, from unworthy impulses, and without due caution, seek this awful avocation. They may suppose it less toilsome than their previous calling, or more respectable in the world's estimation, or a door of entrance into greater notoriety, or even more promotive of pecuniary interests. All such incentives to the public ministry of the word, God will condemn. He requires supreme love to Him, and expansive benevolence to his creatures, as the all-constraining motives to this service. Nor do we conceive that this remark is needless. The purity of the churches depends mainly on the character of their respective bishops, and to preserve this character from reproach, we must scrutinize the grounds on which it is coveted. Time was when persecution was a safeguard to the ministerial office. Hypocrisy had no idea of exposing herself to odium and contempt, yea, moreover, to bonds and imprisonment. But the gospel has so far prevailed, as to divest wicked men of the power to persecute, and the world now bestows its smile on what once excited its frown. Still it is the world, and its spirit is yet hostile to true holiness. There is danger of mistaking our anxiety to attract that smile, for sincere love to God and devotion to his cause. Let us aim to exclude this feeling from the church, and especially from the ministry. Let no selfish policy; no sordid love of ease, wealth, or honor; impel men to this holy enterprise. And when the work shall have been begun from correct principles, there is need of perpetual caution lest these principles should degenerate. The temptations to indolence, jealousy, self-esteem and ambition, are peculiarly strong, and demand our constant vigilance. Our exhausting labors leave us with languid affections, which can be quickened only by reading, meditation and closet devotions. Nothing can sustain a minister of the gospel, in a course of uniform self-sacrificing application to his great work, but a spirit of elevated piety.

3. Having these fundamental traits of character, the candidate for the ministry should resolve to acquire as much mental training as his circumstances will allow, and the spirit of the age may demand. Our churches, very wisely, have not insisted on extensive education, as always and every-

where essential to the preacher of the gospel. A man of strong native sense and meagre attainments, may be converted after he is encumbered with the cares of a family. He may be residing in a destitute region, and may be urged by the benevolence of his heart and the inspiration of truth within him, to persuade his fellow-citizens to turn to God. To pursue a course of elementary study now, is impossible. What shall he do? Let him confer with judicious counsellors; observe the indications of Providence; and adopt that course which he may deliberately and prayerfully approve. Should he conclude to preach, let him give himself to such reading and meditation as shall bear immediately on his design; confine himself to such subjects as he fully comprehends; and seek such spheres of action as he can appropriately fill. In all newly settled countries, such men have been eminently blessed. They have been called from their retirement by the emergencies of society, and God has crowned their self-denying labors with signal success. And when to original genius they have added the treasures of knowledge, accumulated by long continued research, they have acquired an influence which time has only enlarged, and death itself has only consecrated. The writings of a Bunyan and a Fuller, will be felt as long as the English language shall be a vehicle of thought. But to infer from such examples, that young men of the present day need no special cultivation for the ministry, would be to refuse to plant because the earth brings forth some spontaneous fruits. It would be to shut our eyes on the improvements of the age; to adhere to the obsolete modes of traveling, when the power of locomotion has been, by the discoveries of science, so much augmented. The young man who now meditates the work of the ministry, must compare himself, not with the fathers of the present or of a bye-gone age, but with those who are to be his living competitors. He will have to combat error under new forms; to operate on more cultivated minds; to maintain a fiercer rivalry for the attraction of the public ear. He will need all the native and acquired capacity he can bring to the cause, to sustain himself when the novelty of his manner shall have worn away. Parents of every class are now giving their children better education than they themselves enjoyed, and those children, when grown to maturity, will demand spiritual guides of a

higher order of intellect than their fathers required. Hence
the churches everywhere are beginning to ask, not merely
for good men, but for well trained, well read men to occupy their pulpits. And, observe this prophecy, they will rise
yet higher in their requisitions. And young men may at
once determine either to seek thorough preparation for their
calling, or to be left unemployed. One thing is certain—
ignorance dressed up, however decently, in clerical robes, will
not long be tolerated by intelligence. Illiterate young men
may immodestly thrust themselves into the office ; churches
of the same description may give them their sanction ; pastors may, from wrong views, or false delicacy, unite in their
ordination, but public sentiment, as it becomes enlightened,
will gradually doom them to silence. If, however, they
still retain their stations, it will be by an electioneering,
underbidding process, while their influence will be diminished
in the ratio of the diffusion of general knowledge. Far
be it from me, however, to intimate that such a spirit
animates our young men. They see the fields already white
to harvest ; they long to thrust in the sickle, but conscious
of their incapacity, they are resolved to seek adequate preparation. To aid them in the execution of such a purpose
(for they are generally the poor whom God calls to this
work,) the Virginia Baptist Education Society was formed.
It proposes to receive such youths as the churches approve
and recommend, and to conduct them through a course of
elementary study. The plan is to furnish tuition gratuitously
and to allow a credit, when necessary, for board, at $80 per
annum. In carrying out this plan, the Society has contracted a debt of about $1,000. This has been occasioned by
the backwardness of the churches to contribute means, and
of the early students to refund the amount credited. Prudence has dictated the necessity of abandoning the credit
system, until the debt shall have been canceled. It is important that this shall be speedily done, and the Society
furnished with means to educate every young man in the
State, whom the churches may sanction. Already have they
received ninety, and imparted to them various degrees of
instruction. One of the greatest obstacles to the complete
success of the enterprise, has been the readiness of some of
the churches to obtain pastors before they were qualified,
and the consequent tendency of the students to falter in

their course. Public sentiment among us, is not yet sufficiently decided in its demand for able ministers. Our pulpits are too accessible in many portions of the State, to men who cannot teach and will not learn. Another obstacle has been, the want of means to conduct our students through a full range of study. Whenever circumstances seemed to justify it, we have urged them to resort to other institutions, after going through our course. It is but just, however, to say that many who could not avail themselves of any higher advantages, have become efficient and acceptable pastors. The institution established in the vicinity of Richmond, by this Society, should not be suffered to languish for want of encouragement. It has been called into being by Virginia Baptists, and they are responsible to the community for its enlargement and support. It is alike their duty and interest, to unite their counsels and efforts to make it worthy of the denomination. We need not here recite the causes, which have led to the change of the school from a theological to a collegiate institution. The most important were these :— that there was a well known and a long cherished opposition in our Legislature to grant charters to theological schools ; that the tenure by which all unincorporated societies hold property in Virginia, was insecure ; that our theological course was too brief and likely to continue too brief, to justify its retention at such a sacrifice ; that many of our sacred studies could be incorporated into a collegiate course, without violating the charter ; that many of our brethren who were opposed to *theological* education, would second our efforts to impart to licensed ministers the elements of general science and literature ; that the State would, perhaps, at some future period, assist a college, but never would assist a theological school ; and that our young men generally, not prepared for theological studies and too far advanced in life to go through both branches of learning, would do better to expend their time on one department, than to divide it between the two. For these reasons, the Society have transferred their school to the " Trustees of Richmond College," on the express condition, that they would educate, free of charge, for tuition, forever such candidates for the ministry, as the Society should recommend. The *original design* of the institution, therefore, has never for a moment been abandoned. The mode of executing that design has been

modified by the dictates of prudence, and the manifest
indications of Providence.   *The speedy endowment of
Richmond College, is now the most important object that
presents itself to the enterprise of Virginia Baptists.*
Funds thus contributed, will not be sent out of the State
and subjected to the control of irresponsible strangers. They
will not be diverted from the object contemplated by the
donors, but will be appropriated with all the caution that
human law may allow, and divine law may demand. They
will not be consumed at once, but will continue from age to
age to diffuse the blessings of a wholesome literature, and
of an enlightened ministry. The institution has thus far
been conducted with rare economy. It has sustained itself,
and avoided the gulf of pecuniary embarrassment into
which so many kindred enterprises have fallen. But its
operations have been comparatively circumscribed. Could
it obtain an endowment of, say $50,000, sufficient to employ
two additional professors, it would be enabled, by conferring
degrees, to hold out inducements to youth to remain and
complete their studies. And will not our friends furnish this
amount? Look at the signs of the times. Every religious
denomination in Virginia has a college under its influence.
With a proportion of wealth and a numerical strength equal
to the largest, shall we be excelled by the smallest? Or
shall we surrender the education of our children to men
either of no religious principles, or of principles with which
we cannot sympathise? Shall we stand with indifference,
and see our country studded all over with papal establish-
ments, built by European wealth, and occupied by imported
teachers? Shall we do nothing to supply the 250 Baptist
pulpits that are vacant every Lord's day in this Commonwealth? Shall we do nothing to raise up a host of primary
school teachers, who shall go through the length and breadth
of the land, to diffuse a love of books, and to instruct the
rising generation? We are wont to boast of having been
born in Virginia; but it is high time to examine the grounds
of this boasting. Who of us does not *blush* to own that
there are now in the borders of our State 58,789 white persons over 20 years of age, that can neither read nor write?
And that, counting those under that age, who are still at the
reading period of life, there are at least 100,000 in the same
condition? Whence shall we obtain evangelists and school

masters to remove this appalling mass of ignorance. The critical attitude now assumed by the extremes of the Union, will render it more and more inexpedient to send our youth to the North for instruction, or to receive thence educated minds for our various spheres of religious and literary activity. We must prepare for the crisis that is approaching, by giving permanency and enlargement to our own institutions. After studying the claims of all our benevolent associations, and examining the wants of our citizens generally, I am fully prepared to avow my deliberate belief, that popular and ministerial education, is now *the great work, which above all others, claims the regard of the patriot, the philanthropist and the christian.*

4. When the requisite attainments shall have been secured, nothing short of a diligent and skilful devotion of them to his cause, will satisfy the demands of God. This is evident from the phraseology—"a workman that needeth not to be ashamed, rightly dividing the word of truth." The ministry is styled a *"work,"* those who sustain its duties are called "workmen," "laborers," "co-workers" and "builders." These and similar epithets, imply the need of laborious activity in propagating the gospel. The end of all true knowledge is right action. Perish the thought, that the cause we now plead is designed to furnish a race of intellectual idlers, of elegant drones for the church of Christ. Learned indolence is the most criminal kind of indolence. Time is too short; souls are too precious; the retributions of eternity are too awful; for men who are suitably qualified for noble achievements, to sit down in inglorious ease. And yet the most able ministers are sometimes the least known. They have a nervous modesty; a morbid aversion to exposure; which confines them to small and obscure fields of action. Do such men forget that reputation, mental endowments and spiritual gifts, are talents committed to their trust for the glory of God? How will they answer at the coming ordeal, for the concealment of the light of life within their own minds? Brethren, you who are competent, should preach wherever Providence opens a door; in season, out of season, you should seek opportunities, and thus make it appear that preaching the gospel is your *great business.* If you have no charge, go into destitute regions, and gather up ·

a band of disciples." " *Aut viam inveniam aut faciam.*" *
If you really have a heart to work, you can always find a
vineyard. But if you determine not to labor until you find
a wealthy church,—meeting in a tasteful edifice—occupying
a healthy location—and exactly suited to your wishes, then
you deserve some other office than that of the christian ministry. But the divine requisition extends to the *manner* of
expending this labor—" *rightly dividing the word of truth.*"
Does the apostle here allude to the action of the priest, in
dividing the victim to be presented as a sacrifice to God?
Then he would teach us, that the great system of revealed
truth should be skilfully analyzed into its component parts,
when it is laid on the altars of the sanctuary. What God
has united we should not separate, and what He has left
disjoined we should never forcibly unite. Every link in the
grand chain of doctrines should retain its heaven-appointed
position. Every duty should have its relative importance
in our religious code. All the parts of the system will thus
be blended in their true proportions and will contribute to
the symmetry, and force, and beauty of the whole. Some
ministers dwell exclusively on one class of subjects, others
on another class. Some acquire the reputation of being
doctrinal, others of being practical, and others still, of being
experimental preachers. Such a reputation, however, is of
doubtful praise, because it indicates a habitual disregard to
the collateral branches of the great system of truth. Was
Paul a great doctrinal, or a great practical, or a great experimental preacher? Did he address either the judgment or
the affections exclusively? Did he not aim, by appealing to
the *whole man*, and by expatiating on the *whole gospel*, to
exhibit such a *combination* of excellencies as should constitute him a model to all posterity? It is a sure evidence of
an ill-poised mind to be carried away with one idea. Such
men are usually unstable. For a time, they are wholly
absorbed with one darling theory—making the salvation of
the world depend on its reception. Then, vibrating with
fearful violence to the other extreme, they will applaud their
discovery of new truth, and pity those who may hesitate to
follow them in their erratic course. The remedy for this
evil, is first, to acquire a liberal education, and then to form

---

* I will either find a way or I will make one.

upon that basis, a uniform habit of studying the *entire volume of inspiration* in all theological researches.

Does the apostle refer to the carving and distribution of meats at a feast? Then the duty here enforced is to allot to each guest such a portion as his peculiar condition demands. In another place, he tells us that he fed the babes with milk and the men with strong meats. It is a delicate task to adapt the diversified truths of the Bible to the ever-varying characters of men. To comfort the deluded; to intimidate the desponding; to confirm the self-righteous; and to discourage the sincere but feeble, is alike injurious to men, and offensive to God. The preacher is bound, not only to utter general truth, but so to delineate the various shades of character; so to discriminate between the genuine and the spurious; so to enter into the hidden recesses of the heart, as to carry to each hearer a consciousness that he is the very individual addressed. The apostle commended himself to every man's conscience in the sight of God. I understand from this, that he not only exhibited the gospel in general terms, but that he so adapted the truth to every class of hearers as to make it difficult for them to evade its force. Conscience told them that he was *talking to them and that he was speaking the truth.* This is the highest attainment of sacred oratory—an attainment infinitely superior to the graces of style and elocution. He who reaches this point hides himself behind his subject, and turns the people from admiring the sermon to feeling their sins. How much wisdom then is needed by him who deals with human souls! We place important causes in the hands of the most able jurists. We demand skill and judgment in the physician to whom we commend the sick and dying child of our affections. But oh! who can estimate the wisdom needed, and the responsibility assumed, by him whose very words are to influence the everlasting destinies of the soul! Compared with this, all earthly interests sink into annihilation. The minister of the gospel, in every public exhibition of truth, touches chords in the heart that must vibrate in eternity. To all his hearers he is either a savor of life unto life, or of death unto death. Should he preach false doctrine; cherish groundless hopes; suppress wholesome fears; bring down the Bible standard of holiness; and by gross ignorance throw contempt on the whole subject of religion, God will hold him accountable.

Brethren, what are you doing to render yourselves able ministers of the New Testament? Long has been exploded the dogma, that ministers are to preach by inspiration. The absurdity of such a dogma was equalled only by the indolence and arrogance from which it originated. To associate the most varied reading, and the most patient thought in the preparation of sermons, with the most fervent prayer for divine aid, and with the most sincere reliance on the divine blessing, is the only rational and consistent course. If then, you would rightly divide the word of truth, you must meditate upon these things; give yourselves wholly to them, that your profiting may appear to all.

To the *churches* here represented by their several delegates, permit me to say, that all your operations are, under God, dependent on a cultivated and faithful ministry. You are building neat edifices for the worship of God, but whence will you derive men capable of attracting to those houses listening crowds? You have organized yourselves into an association to supply the desolate portions of Virginia with the preached word, but where are the efficient evangelists to commission for the blessed work? You see around you the advocates of error striving, some of them with learned ingenuity, to conciliate public esteem, and to spread their respective opinions. How will you sustain the conflict? Especially, how will you sustain the approaching contest between popery and protestantism, which is destined to draw the line between the friends and the enemies of Christ, and to agitate this whole continent? In view of these facts it is your duty,

1. To pray the Lord of the harvest to send forth more laborers into the harvest. The world with all its population belongs to God. He is pleased, by the foolishness of preaching, to save them that believe. It is his province to raise up and send forth messengers of mercy to the lost and guilty sons of men. It is our duty to importune Him to carry on his work until his glorious schemes of grace shall have been accomplished, and the earth shall have been filled with the knowledge of the Lord.

2. To look out from among yourselves, young men of retiring worth and sterling piety, and encourage them to exercise their gifts in your social meetings. If they are promising, send them to school; extend to them a generous

sympathy; relieve them, if it is necessary, from the anxieties of poverty. If you are judicious in the selection, and will conduct the process of mental discipline to a proper extent, it will prove to be a wise and benevolent expenditure of your means. If you find no such materials among yourselves, you can aid those churches who have the young men, but not the means of educating them. Should not every church in Virginia take up a collection once a year for educational purposes?

3. To allow your pastors such compensation as will enable them to devote their whole time to the ministry. I plead not for an idle, pampered race of clerical gentlemen, but for a working, devoted and faithful ministry. This you never can have until you give such remuneration as will justify prudent men in doing little else than the duties of the episcopal office. No church deserves or should expect an efficient pastor, until they say to him in substance : " Occupy your whole time in serving us, and we will supply all your reasonable wants." It is indeed miserable economy to permit an able preacher to toil in the school-room or on the farm, for the support of his family, when a few hundred dollars would enable him to preach far more frequently and profitably. To pray for an increase of ministers; to educate them for their calling; and then to confine them to extraneous pursuits, is most inconsistent and unwise. Let ministers cultivate habits of frugality in themselves and families; let them be content with moderate salaries; let them convince their churches that the only motive that impels them to ask a support is a desire to do more faithful and more abundant service in the cause of Christ; and then let the churches willingly extend that support and enjoy that service.

But to conclude: Brethren in the ministry! yours is a fearful responsibility! In the final day you will stand with your respective charges before the great white throne of judgment, and render an account of your stewardship. *Why* did you preach? Was it from a constraining love to Christ and pity to the souls of men? *What* did you preach? Was it the whole counsel of God, neither mixed up with human philosophy, nor modified to suit the corrupt tastes of men? *How* did you preach? Was it with plainness, and solemnity, and zeal, and faithfulness, and a tender importunity? *How often* did you preach? Was it

whenever and wherever you could find an auditor? In the
sick chamber; in the social parlor; in the workshop; on
the high-way; in the mansion of wealth; in the hovel of
poverty; as well as in the pulpit? Above all, did you
preach by your example as well as by your discourses?
These will be subjects of investigation in the great day. If
here you study to show yourselves approved unto God, *there*
you will be found to be workmen that need not to be
ashamed. If here you are faithful unto death, then you
shall receive a crown of life. Yes! for every tear you have
shed; for every honest, well directed effort you have made;
for all your toils, by day and by night, through cold and
heat, through drought and storms; for all your sacrifices of
ease, and wealth, and domestic joys; God will give you an
accurate reward. Every sinner saved by your instrumentality will augment your bliss. They that be wise shall
shine as the brightness of the firmament, and they that turn
many to righteousness as the stars forever and ever. Nor
is this consummation far remote. I look round me in vain
for the dignified forms of the devoted Rice; the warm-
hearted Kerr; the decided Mason; the affectionate Jones;
and the eloquent Daniel. Fourteen years ago we held our
anniversaries in this house, when they mingled in our counsel and we heard their voice. Where are they now? They
have gone to their reward. You too will soon die.

> " The time of hope
> And of probation speeds on rapid wings,
> Swift and returnless. What thou hast to do
> Do with thy might. Haste, lift aloud thy voice,
> And publish to the borders of the pit
> The Resurrection . . . Then, when the ransomed come
> With gladness unto Zion, thou shalt joy
> To hear the vallies and the hills break forth
> Before them into singing; thou shalt join
> The raptured strain, exulting that the Lord-
> Jehovah, God omnipotent, doth reign
> O'er all the earth."

Even so. Amen.

MISCELLANEOUS ITEMS BY THE EDITOR.

Ministerial qualifications. No other man, in whatever profession or pursuit employed, has more use for mental discipline, and attainments of the highest order, than has the gospel minister. Things deemed final, by other great men, in responsible stations, are with him only instrumental for nobler purposes. History, philosophy, belles-lettres, logic, rhetoric,—every department of science and literature,—whatever is useful,—whatever is ornamental,—is imperiously demanded by his every-day avocations. He needs, to begin with, not only an accurate and familiar acquaintance with the language he speaks, but some knowledge of the languages in which the Bible was originally written. This is a profession which actually includes all other professions.

Go to the most distinguished university you please. Consider the aggregate of the talents and acquisitions of its twenty learned professors. It were desirable, were it possible, that the preacher possess them all; he has daily use for all. These are not indeed the most important parts of the endowments his office demands, as has been shown in Mr. Ryland's sermon before the Education Society; but they nevertheless have their own intrinsic and relative value. Geology is not so valuable to the geologist himself, as it is to the interpreter of the Bible. The mere philologist, to whatever department of language or thought he intends to appropriate the results of his labors, cannot have so valuable a purpose to which to apply them, as has the minister of the gospel. Were he familiar with every translation, of every text, ever made by the greatest linguists, so much the better. Unbounded resources may be made tributary to the duties of his office, in every conversation; in every epistolary correspondence; in every meditation; as well as in every sermon or prayer. The higher his ascent in metaphysical and moral studies, the better is he qualified to converse with a child, or to instruct a servant.

Ministerial pursuits. And yet, notwithstanding the truth of the foregoing remarks,—and while the peculiar and appropriate duties of the pastor, or the evangelist, are so various, absorbing and overwhelming as they are, all christendom, with here and there an exception, concurs in the opinion, that the business of a preacher requires only *a por-*

tion of his time.   Nay more, that *that* portion is so small as
to justify his dependance upon other than ministerial pursuits
for his support:—in other words, that the labors of a gospel
minister, in his official capacity, demand only such shreds of
time as other men devote to their amusement.   We heard it
asserted by an individual, who ought to know, that the
salaries of the ministers of the Episcopal churches in Virginia, do not average more than two hundred dollars.
Those of the Methodist churches, including the circuit
riders, are not probably greater.   Of the Presbyterian
churches, we cannot speak advisedly.   But of the Baptists,
we affirm, and we can demonstrate it if required, that there
is no known body of men in existence, among whom there
is so much unemployed, inactive, or misemployed capital.
There are known to us personally, not a few, men of varied
learning, fair reputation, sterling abilities, and indefatigable
zeal in their master's cause, whose main employment is
farming, teaching, merchandize, surveying, the practice of
medicine, anything else than the ministerial profession,
while to ·the latter they apply what time they can *conve-
niently spare.*   In the mean time, the churches are praying
to the Lord of the harvest to send forth laborers into his
harvest.   They pray for the multiplication of those whom
they are already *unwilling* to employ.

One of the saddest effects of this state of things is this:
The impression is made upon the world, upon the whole
non-professing community, that christians themselves consider religion a merely secondary, or third rate thing.   Intel·
ligent men, and men of business minds, *cannot* be made to
believe, that any human being considers *that* to be of the
first importance, in support of which he is unwilling to make
some sacrifice.   Other professions *are* supported.   There is
no congregation in christendom which does not support its
medical faculty, its advocates at the bar, its police officers,
and every thing else, but its preachers.   The inference is
irresistible, and too plain to need to be stated in words.

Ministerial Candidates.   One tendency of the evil
exposed in the foregoing paragraph, is, to exclude from the
pulpit the greatest and best men:—men of talents, attainments, honest convictions, and fine moral feelings.   Such
men know, there are other duties, besides that of preaching
the gospel.

THE
BAPTIST PREACHER.

VOL. IV.   September, 1845.   NO. 9.

PUBLIC OFFENCES, OR CHURCH DISCIPLINE:

A sermon, by Rev. A. W. CHAMBLISS, Tuskegee, Alabama.

NO. I.

" Now, I beseech you, brethren, mark them which cause divisions and offences, contrary to the doctrine which ye have learned, and avoid them : for they that are such serve not our Lord Jesus Christ."—ROM. XVI: 17, 18.

In a former discourse, we labored to show the distinction between public and private offences; and we hope we were not unsuccessful in explaining the divine law in relation to those who have trespassed against us, in our private capacity. The offence was between us as individuals, and we had the right, nay, it was our duty, to settle the matter between ourselves. We may not, until every other expedient has failed, introduce it before the public. To bring it into the church, is the very last resort. The language of the " Baptist Confession of Faith " is, " should any private matter be brought into the church, before the previous steps (described in Matt. xviii,) have been taken, the person that brings it in ought to be severely reproved and admonished, and that publicly, before the whole church, for his irregular and injurious conduct therein," * (p. 221.) " Let all things be done decently and in order."

Having, therefore, disposed of private offences, we shall in this, and the following discourse, invite your attention to those that are public. To such, our text has allusion. " Now, I beseech you, brethren, mark them which cause

---

* " The Baptist Confession of Faith." This volume, of about 300 pages, was first adopted in London, A. D. 1699 : and afterwards by the Charleston Association, S. C., A. D. 1831 ; and as a summary of ' Faith and Practice,' may be said to represent the views of the Baptist churches generally : although neither this, nor any other confession or formula, is considered binding on the conscience of any, the Bible being the only acknowledged standard.

divisions and offences, contrary to the doctrine which ye have learned, and avoid them : for they that are such serve not our Lord Jesus Christ." Or to use the paraphrasis of the learned and pious Dr. Scott, on this place : " those persons must be marked with decided disapprobation and avoided, who aim to prejudice believers against each other,— to draw them off from faithful pastors,—or to seduce them into strange doctrines and practices, contrary to the simple truths of God's word."

The discipline of the church, in primitive times, was exceedingly strict. In the estimation of the apostle, who was inspired to prescribe rules for the regulation of the house of God, it was a sufficient ground of excommunication, that a member was the cause of dissentions and factions in the church : or that his deportment was calculated to bring scandal and reproach upon the cause of the Redeemer. Nor could it have been otherwise with him, who charged it, as a crime, upon the Jews, that "the name of God had been blasphemed through them." He who taught others, must needs teach himself. He who blamed the Jewish church for so acting as to bring dishonor upon the divine glory, could not allow such conduct in christian churches, as would cause the name, and "the way of Christ to be evil spoken of."

In the apocalyptic vision, the Spirit said to the Ephesian church, by way of commendation, "thou canst not bear them which are evil." (Rev. ii : 2.) This was honor enough for one church : and it formed a striking contrast to the rebuke which the same spirit administered to the church at Pergamos. "I have a few things against thee, because thou hast them there which hold the doctrine of Balaam, who taught Balak to cast a stumbling-block before the children of Israel, and to eat things sacrificed unto idols, and to commit fornication. So hast thou also them that hold the doctrine of the Nicolaitanes, which things I hate." (v. 14, 15.) In this church were some base, mercenary souls,—of a covetous, temporizing spirit, similar to ancient Balaam, who, for the sake of gain, did not scruple to sacrifice the best interests of the people of God. Also, were retained in the communion, some, who, under the notion of "christian liberty," did not hesitate to run into licentious indulgences— a set of anti-nomians, who "despised all rules and all authority"—or to use a modern phrase, who, because "they were free, claimed the privilege to do just as they pleased." The retention of such characters in the church, the Son of God said, "I hate." "Such serve not our Lord Jesus Christ." "Wherefore," said he, "repent, (that is, reform, turn them out,) or else I will come unto thee quickly, and will fight against them with the sword of my mouth."

It is a striking fact, which has doubtless occurred to every one familiar with ecclesiastical history, that the periods of the declension of *pure and vital religion* in the church, in all ages, and in all countries, have been characterized by a corresponding laxness in discipline; and that the revival of religion, has been similarly characterized by a revival of the wholesome discipline which God has instituted for the government of his house. An example of this, worthy of attention, is recorded by Milner, the historian, in relation to the condition of the church in the third century. "It deserves to be remarked," says he, "that *the first grand and general declension*, after the primary effusion of the divine Spirit, should be fixed about the middle of this century." (Vol. 1, p. 165.) The cause of this declension, was the neglect of church discipline, as the Decian persecution was esteemed by Cyprian to be its chastisement. Cyprian was elected bishop of Carthage, A. D. 248. He found the church, at that time, in a wretchedly lapsed and declining condition; and in a treatise concerning the lapse, he said: "If the cause of our miseries be investigated, the cure may be found. The Lord would have his family to be tried. And *because long peace had corrupted the discipline divinely revealed to us*, the heavenly chastisement hath raised up our faith, which had almost lain dormant: and when, by our sins, we had deserved to suffer still more, the merciful Lord hath so moderated all things, that the whole scene rather deserves the name of a trial, than a persecution." (Ib. p. 165.) Here was the cause of the persecution; and here the consequences of inattention to the discipline of the church. Let it be neglected, and a blighting and a mildew will result, which will not fail, ere long, to induce the divine judgment upon us.

If, therefore, the apostolic injunction—if the authority of the Son of God—if the testimony of ecclesiastical history—if all these together, have any weight—then, by them,

" I beseech you, brethren, mark them which cause divisions and offences, contrary to the doctrine which ye have learned, and avoid them : for they that are such serve not our Lord Jesus Christ."

We propose, in this discourse, to describe the characters whom the scriptures represent as public offenders; and in the next, to inquire what discipline the scriptures prescribe for such.

I. We are to describe the characters whom the scriptures represent as public offenders.   In the text, a general description of two classes of these, is specified : those who produce anti-scriptural schisms in the church, and those who occasion scandal to the cause of Christ.   " Mark them which cause divisions and offences, contrary to the doctrine which ye have learned."

1. *Captious and contentious persons cause divisions contrary to the gospel.*   " Now the end of the commandment is charity out of a pure heart, and of a good conscience, and faith unfeigned : from which *some* having swerved, *have turned aside unto vain jangling*, desiring to be teachers of the law ; understanding neither what they say, nor whereof they affirm."   " If any man consent not to wholesome words, even the words of our Lord Jesus Christ, and to the doctrine which is according to godliness, he is proud, knowing nothing, but *doting about questions and strifes of words*, whereof cometh envy, strife, railings, evil surmisings, perverse disputings—from such withdraw thyself."   1 Tim. i: 5—ib. vi : 4, 5.

Seest thou a man heady and high-minded ? Seest thou one who refuseth to submit to the authority of the great body ? Seest thou one whose whole spirit and deportment are an everlasting protest against the decisons of the majori-- ty ? One who loveth to have the pre-eminence in all things, who would sooner rend the peace of the whole body, than yield the most trifling matter? Such an one causeth division, contrary to the doctrine which ye have learned.

The entire spirit and letter of the sacred volume, so far as relates to the demeanor of christians, is that of mutual forbearance, concession and submission. In all questions of mere opinion and education—of mere policy and custom— of mere pleasure and expediency—in all questions *where it is perfectly immaterial to our innocence which side we adopt :* as whether we eat one thing or another—whether we follow one fashion or any other, in our dress—whether we worship God in a finely finished house or a log cabin—whether we adopt one mode or any other in the defrayment of our church expenses—whether we assemble on Saturday or any other day, for the transaction of the business of the church—in all such questions as these, *the law of charity,* and the *voice of the majority,* are to be the rule : and any dissention from this, which is persisted in to the grief and annoyance of the body, is a violation of the principles which Christ has laid down for the regulation of his church. Yes, we repeat it, to adopt any indifferent opinion or practice : that is, any opinion or practice which we may either hold or let alone, and still be innocent, and to maintain and pursue this, to the pain and injury of the church, is not only an infringement of the laws of republicanism, which the Bible teaches, but is in fact a sin against Christ. "Let not him that eateth despise him that eateth not ; and let not him which eateth not, judge (or condemn) him that eateth." "But if thy brother be grieved with thy meat, now walkest thou not charitably." "It is good neither to eat flesh, nor drink wine, nor any thing whereby thy brother stumbleth or is offended, or is made weak." "When ye sin so against the brethren, and wound their weak consciences, ye sin against Christ." "Let nothing be done through strife or vain glory, but in lowliness of mind let each esteem others better than himself." "Submit yourselves one to another, in the fear of the Lord." "But if any man seem to be contentious, we have no such custom, neither the churches of God." (Rom. xiv : 3, 15, 21—1 Cor. viii : 12—Phil. ii : 3—Eph. v : 21—1 Cor. xi : 16.)

2. There is a class of persons, a little dissimilar from these, whom, for the sake of distinction, we denominate, factious. *All factious persons cause divisions, contrary to the gospel.*

The distinction which we draw between a "captious" and a "factious" person, is this : The one is a man of mere prejudices and prepossessions—the other is a man of party. The one would exclude himself from the society of the faithful, on account of some favorite notion of his own—the other would lead away as many as possible with him. To the latter, allusion is made in the Acts of the Apostles,

(xx: 29, 30,) in these strong and impressive words: "I
know, that after my departure, shall grievous wolves enter
in among you, not sparing the flock. Also of your ownselves
shall men arise, speaking perverse things, to draw away disciples after them." Not satisfied to occupy their position
alone, they will lead away captive as many souls as may
fall under their influence. They are men of sour and bitter spirit, and who strive to infuse the same malaria into
other hearts also. Their work is discord; and unless restrained, they will diffuse "the leaven of malice and wickedness into the whole lump." Unless suppressed, their evil
communications will corrupt the entire body.

Perhaps a faithful minister is the object of their malig-
nancy. In this event, nothing will escape their observation,
which may serve to destroy his influence—render useless his
preaching—or weaken the force of his example. Haman
like, nothing can satisfy their hatred, until they have aliena-
ted all hearts, and even compelled the removal of the man
of God. Their distempered senses can see nothing good in
his best example, nor hear any thing good in his soundest
doctrine. Like certain contemptible birds, they pass over
all that is sound and wholesome, and alight only on such
putrid matter as best suits a vitiated appetite. Ever seeking
occasion, they delight to turn all hearts from the truths of
his lips. To such, the rebuke of St. Paul, to Elymas, the
sorcerer, is not too severe: "O full of all subtility and all
mischief, thou child of the devil, thou enemy of all righteousness, wilt thou not cease to pervert the right ways of the
Lord." (Acts, xiii: 10.)

Perhaps the wholesome discipline of the church is the
object of their rage. It may have fallen on them, as a
chastisement of their own wrongs: or it may have touched
some favorite friend. In either event, their malignant spirit
is aroused, as the lion in his den, and nothing can be satisfactory but vengeance, wreaked in the injury of the church.
They can see no reason—no justice—no religion, in the
act. Their discontent is hastily communicated from soul to
soul. They devise mischief on their bed; when they awake,
they execute it. A faction to rescind that act, is the object;
and partly of weak members, and partly of men of the
world, a faction, if possible, they will create, and labor to
reverse the decision, at least in public sentiment. No expe-

dient, that can be of the least avail, will be left untried, to
rend the peace of Zion, or to stain the fair escutcheon of the
church with disgrace.

My brethren, do not imagine that such men are the creatures of our idle fears. Would to God this were so! Would
to God this had always been so! If you have no such characters among you at present, you know not how long it
shall be e're such may arise. *We* have seen the church of
God bleeding at every pore, under the ungodly deeds of such
ungodly hands. *We* have seen the pious and faithful ministry crippled and cut down by such men. *We have* seen
the unity and the peace of God's house laid waste by such
unhallowed influence. Need you, then, be told that such
may arise again? Need you be told that they are grievous
and dangerous wolves? Need you be told that you should
strictly mark and avoid them? "Of your ownselves may
men arise, speaking perverse things, to draw away disciples
after them." To retain such perverse speakers in the bosom
of the church—to lend the weight of your fellowship to their
pernicious course, is to be partaker of their sin. No, my
brethren; mark them who cause such divisions, contrary
to the gospel, and avoid them.

But were we to confine this caution to those who are, or
have been, members of the same church with yourselves,
perhaps we should be unfaithful, both to you and to the
sense of the Apostle. Perhaps he would have you cautioned against the unhallowed influence of those without your
communion also, by whom it is attempted to alienate your
hearts from the right way. If the Apostle said, that of your
ownselves would bad men arise to draw away many; he
also said, that "grievous wolves would enter in among you,
not sparing the flock." Against such you need to be admonished. For although they may not now infest your
fold, you can never tell how soon they may do so. These
are strange times on which we have fallen. The spirit of
party is rife in the land; and it is the disgrace of the christian name, that it is so common in the church of God.
Every year attests instances, in which, from motives of jealousy or suspicion, or dread, some faithful minister is publicly or privately abused—the church of God abused—members set against their pastor, or against each other, and eventually, the harmony, the strength, and the success of the

whole, impaired and destroyed. Mark those who perform such unholy deeds, and avoid them. "They zealously affect you but not well ; yea, they would exclude you, that ye might affect them." (Gal. iv : 17.) It is not your good which such seek; it is not the good of your church which they seek. Yes, lay it down as a truth, when men whisper a word to the disparagement of the pastor of your church, when the drift of their words is to set brother at variance with brother, whatever may be their pretensions toward you or your church, they are insidious enemies to both. "Mark them and avoid them." But

3. Our text has reference to heretics. *Heretics cause divisions contrary to the gospel.* By a heretic in this place, we mean those who would subvert the well known and established doctrines and practices of the church.*

Every society of christians is formed upon the supposition of a certain unity, in regard to some leading points, both of faith and practice. "How shall two walk together, except they be agreed?" (Amos iii : 3.) And while, from the difference of education, and customs, and association, it can hardly be expected, that all should precisely agree in every little matter; yet, surely we have the right to expect those who connect themselves with our communion, to adopt all the leading, the essential and vital points, both of our practice and our doctrines. Has the blessed God laid down the same maxims for the whole human race—an innumerable multitude, and required all, upon the severest penalty, to adopt them? And shall not we require, at least those who connect themselves with our church, to adopt all the leading of those maxims? Surely this is not too much. "If then, any man come unto you and bring not this doctrine, receive him not into your house; neither bid him God speed." (2 John, 10.)

Let no man imagine that our peculiar form of goverment forbids us to say, what a man *shall hold,* and what he *shall not hold* to do. This is not so. True, ours is a republican form of government; and we rejoice—we boast in it. But is it any part of republicanism to have no laws—no system—

---

* "It is worthy of notice," says the excellent Rev. A. Fuller, "that the only passage in the New Testament, wherein heresy is introduced as *an object of discipline,* makes no mention of any thing, but *what relates to the principles of the party.*"—(Works, vol. ii : p. 465.)

no rule—no regulations? Or, to allow its laws and regulations to be disregarded? Our civil government is also republican: and if history is faithful, it was formed after the model of a Baptist church. But will any one say, it has no laws—no constitution defining the limits and powers of all the members of the great confederacy? That is not part of republicanism, allow us to say, where every man makes his own laws—where every man does just what he pleases— and where every man, whensoever it suits his private feelings, or his private interest, protests against the will and the voice of the majority. That is licentiousness—that is antinomianism—that is lawlessness—that is anarchy, confusion and misrule—that is what we have heard the Son of God say, "I hate." No sirs. Republicanism is the peaceable submission of the minority, to the will of the majority—it is the government where the people, the great body of the people rule—where the wisdom of the mass is the standard*—where the many decide what is right, and where all, both the many and the few, adopt and do it. And as we say in civil matters, let that hand wither and die, which shall dare demolish a principle which the majority shall establish—let that tongue cleave to its jaws, which shall attempt to move against it—and let the man go a despised leper from the camps of the faithful, who shall presume to resist what the great body shall decree: so we say in ecclesiastical things, note that man, who, taking advantage of the republicanism of the church, shall claim the privilege to speak to the injury of its doctrines, or in contempt of its established practices. "Now, I command you, brethren, in the name of our Lord Jesus Christ, that ye withdraw yourself from every brother that walketh disorderly, and not after the tradition which ye have received of us." "As we said before, so say I now again, if any man preach any other gospel unto you, than that ye have received, let him be accursed." (2 Thes. iii: 6—Gal. i: 9.)

Beloved brethren, I know not how I shall sufficiently impress this point upon your minds. If our mode of government does not in fact afford no plea for licentiousness, on

---

*It is evident, from the general tenor of this discourse, that the author does not intend to deny, that majorities in church, as in State, may err. In all such cases, redress is to be sought, constitutionally. A majority has no more right, than an individual, to oppress.   Ed.

the one hand, it surely does lay us very liable to abuses, on the other. Under its wide waving banner, not a few find a crouching place, and sometimes to our injury; and nothing but your sleepless vigilance can protect the church, in the peaceable enjoyment of those "heaven born" doctrines and practices, which the Son of God bequeathed to us from the cross, as his last will and testament: and which apostles and martyrs have died to propagate. Innumerable multitudes find an asylum in the bosom of our Zion; and giving a loose rein to their heated imaginations, may gather up any set of whims and notions, and upon the broad basis of our republicanism, may claim the privilege to diffuse the poison of their dogmas. Nor are we wanting in striking examples of this. As there were false prophets in olden times—as there have been false teachers in our times—so there may arise "false teachers among you, who shall bring in damnable heresies, even denying the Lord that bought them, and bring upon themselves swift destruction: and many shall follow their pernicious ways, by reason of whom the way of truth shall be evil spoken of." (2 Pet. ii: 1, 2.) Shall we allow this? Surely it cannot be right to do so. Not right to allow men to think? We said no such thing. To think, is a right which heaven has bestowed on man, nor would we dispossess him of it. But because he has the right to think, has he the right to disturb others with his thoughts? Shall he be allowed to rend the peace of Zion, under the pretence of liberty? Man has the right to think, and to speak too, *what* he pleases; but he has not the right to speak *where* he pleases. The abolitionist has the right to think: but let him not think to the injury of the South. He has the right to speak: but let him not speak fire-brands into the civil and social institutions of whole communities. Let him think, and let him give utterance to his thoughts: but let him not impose them upon those who claim to be as enlightened and as liberal as himself. Let the heretic think and speak what he pleases: but will he demand our pulpits in which to do it? Will he require us to hear him? Will he ask the influence and authority of our communion, to give weight to his pernicious words? Surely he cannot ask all this.

Another thought presents itself here, which may well serve to impress upon your minds the importance of vigilance on this subject: it is the present condition of our churches. Large multitudes are joining us every year; some from other societies, and some from the world. Many of these bring with them certain peculiarites, which we do not admit into our creed, and which would be fatal if they were ad-mitted into it. Not a few of our members are but partially instructed—some of our ministry, either for the want of ed-ucation, or time to devote to it, fail, sufficiently to expound and establish some of the leading points held by us—we have, comparatively, but a few copies of our " Confession of Faith," where, in a small compass, an inquirer may learn what we hold, with the reasons of it—some there are who would destroy even those few: and from all these facts together, it must appear obvious that our whole body lies bare to here-sies.* Every man reads for himself, (or rather, conjectures for himself, for few read sufficiently,) with scarcely the slightest aid, and with multitudes of prejudices and prepos-sessions upon him. Under such circumstances, what but the palpableness of our doctrines, together with the blessing of heaven upon us, can account for the fact, that we have not long since been riven to a thousand atoms? But, breth-ren, let us not presume too far upon the goodness of God. " Let us watch diligently, lest any root of bitterness spring-ing up, trouble us." " An heretic, after the first or second admonition, reject." " His words will eat as doth a canker." " With good words and fair speeches, he will deceive the hearts of the simple." " Many shall follow his pernicious ways, by reason of whom the way of truth shall be evil spoken of." " Mark them which cause divisions and of-fences, contrary to the doctrine which ye have learned, and avoid them : they that are such serve not our Lord Jesus Christ." (Heb. xii: 15—Tit. iii: 10—2 Tim. ii: 17—Rom. xvi: 18—2 Pet. ii: 2.

---

*The utter incompetency of written formularies, to secure denomina-tional unity, is attested by universal experience. Within a few years past, the Presbyterians and the Methodists, in this country, have proved their in-efficiency ; and the Episcopal church, in England, is now passing through the same ordeal : while the Baptists in both hemispheres have been com-paratively united, with the Bible alone as their umpire. But these instru-ments, in the sense of our author, may not only be harmless, but useful. The Baptist churches in Pennsylvania and South Carolina, with their Con-fessions, and those in Virginia and Kentucky, without them, are equally free, and equally united. Those put upon paper as statutes liable to be amended or abolished, what these class with the common law. ED.

Permit us, beloved brethren, before we dismiss this branch of our discourse, to call up again, to your recollection, the positions we have assumed, and the declarations we have made. We said that *captiousness* should not be indulged in members of the church : and that however trifling or indifferent might be the requisition of the church, if its peace and happiness depend upon it, the law of charity requires each and all of its members to comply ; and that an obstinate refusal of any member to do so, would be censurable offence. We said also, that *factiousness* must be guarded against : and that in all or every instance, either in the church or out of it, that person must be " marked " and " avoided," who should labor to prejudice the members of a church against their pastor, or against each other. And, lastly, we said we should use all diligence to suppress any heresies that may appear among us, whether they respect our established usages, or our doctrines: that no confidence— no friendship which we may entertain for the person, the motive, or the ability of the offender, can justify a neglect of duty in these things.

II. Let us now proceed to the consideration of the *second* general description of offenders, specified in the text. They are such as bring scandal upon the cause of Christ. They are such as cannot be retained in the communion, but at the sacrifice of the reputation of the church. Whatever may seem to be the present and immediate bearings of such persons, on the cause of religion, they serve not our Lord Jesus Christ—their ultimate bearings are against christianity. The immediate and particular consequence of their retention, may be a larger number in the church, or some worldly influence to the denomination : but the general and remote consequence, will be the practical abolishment of the principle which requires all church members to live humbly, holily, and unblamably—to " let their light so shine before men, that others may see their good works and glorify their father which is in heaven." Therefore, mark them which cause offences, (scandals) also, contrary to the doctrine which ye have learned, and avoid them.

Under this general description, are included all those who openly and intentionally violate the principles contained in the decalogue. The ten commandments embrace all the fundamental articles of the moral government of God. They are the basis—they are the rule and measure of all the moral and religious conduct in the universe. Hence they can never be abrogated. As a rule of action, they can never be abolished. Although the law is not the terms of salvation, still, all those who are redeemed, and those who are not, will be under perpetual obligation to observe it. Never can it be right to do what it forbids, or neglect to do what it requires. It can never be right to worship idols—to profane the name of God—to lie—to steal—to kill—to commit adultery—to desecrate the Sabbath—to covet that which belongs to another. These principles are equally binding on christians, as on others: and equally binding on all now, as though Jesus Christ had never come into the world to redeem mankind. No redemption price which heaven has bestowed on man—no price of redemption which heaven can bestow on man, can purchase for him the privilege to violate them. It were presumption—it is not piety, to say, that "inasmuch as we are not saved by works of the law, therefore we are under no obligation to keep the law." To assume the liberty to sin, because "we are not under the law, but under grace," is to "turn the grace of God into lasciviousness." Shall we sin because grace hath abounded, or in order that grace may yet more abound? "This were iniquity to be reproved."* "I have written unto you," said

---

* "The ten commandments," says a distinguished author, "being the substance of the law of nature, a representation of God's image, and a beam of his holiness, behooved forever, unalterably, to be a rule of life to mankind in all possible states, conditions and circumstances. Whatever covenant was introduced, whether of works or of grace, or whatever form be put upon them, they behooved still to remain as a rule of life." (Boston's Works, p. 854.)

Says the learned and celebrated Vitringa: "When Paul affirms that believers, being under grace, 'are free from the law,' he must not be understood as asserting that they are loosed from obligation to observe the precepts which constitute the substance of those moral laws, which are contained in the writings of Moses." (Observ. Sac. Tom. II, lvi. c. 18, §1.)

"If the moral law be not a rule of life to believers," says the Rev. Abraham Booth, "either there is some other and a new rule given in its stead, or there is not. If *another*, it may be presumed, that it is *more* or *less* perfect, than that contained in the moral law. But *more* perfect it cannot be, without supposing that the old, the eternal law, was *imperfect;* to suppose which, is absurdly blasphemous. If it be *less* perfect, the consequence is plain. It is not a complete system of duty. It admits of imperfections. It connives at sin. But for any one to imagine that infinite wisdom would contrive, and that infinite holiness would give *such* a rule, for the conduct of rational creatures, is absolutely inconsistent with the divine character,

the apostle, " not to keep company, if any man that is a
brother be a fornicator, or covetous, or an idolater, or a railer,
or a drunkard, or an extortioner : with such an one, no not
to eat." (1 Cor. v : 11.)

By the terms of the law, then, we are forbidden to worship idols. "Thou shalt have no other gods before me,"
saith the Lord, (Ex. xx : 3,) and this coincides with the
apostolic decree, addressed to the gentile christians, from the
council at Jerusalem : "that they should abstain from the
pollutions of idols." (Acts, xv : 20.) By this command we
are required to give to God the supreme place in all our
affections, in all our purposes, in all our conduct. To love—
to delight in—to desire—to expect good from any forbidden
indulgence—to suffer any, the most valuable and excellent
of creatures, to rival the Divine Being in our affections, is
an infringement of this law—is to give the glory to the creature, and not to the Creator. Whensoever such condition of
heart becomes manifest—whensover it is admitted—whensoever it becomes the scandal of the church—it then calls
for your action as promptly, and as loudly, as if images were
set up in the house of the offender.

Profane swearing is also forbidden by the decalogue.
"Thou shalt not take the name of the Lord thy God in
vain : for the Lord will not hold him guiltless, that taketh
his name in vain." (Ex. xx : 7.) This law is violated, by
all that light, thoughtless and irreverent use of the titles and
attributes of the Deity, which we hear in common conversation : and it requires that we abstain from their use, except
in the most solemn and religious manner.

Again, the law demands, that one-seventh of our time be
set apart to the exclusive worship of the great God : and although the wretched disregard of the Sabbath, in this country, would almost lead one to think it a virtue to violate this
command, still, until it can be shown conclusively, when,
and where, and how, the fourth commandment has been
abrogated, we should continue to protest against such practices ; and maintain, that *it* is not less binding upon us than

---

and pregnant with blasphemy. Such a rule, therefore, condemns itself, and
sinks of its own weight. But if *not another*, then it follows, necessarily, that
there is no rule to regulate the conduct of believers : they can neither obey
nor disobey. Sin and duty are unmeaning names and empty words." (Death
of Legal Hope, pp. 72, 73.)

the others among which it stands—and that the scandalous sin of transgressing *it*, is not less than is the transgressing the fifth, the sixth, the seventh and the eighth commandments. God is not man, that we may make our interests, our feelings, or our pleasure, a pretext for the violation of his law: and if such pretexts can be allowed in one case, we see not why they may not be allowed in any other. If, because our interest requires it, we may break the Sabbath, then, when our interest requires it, we may steal or tell a lie. If, because we feel like it, we may disregard the Lord's day, then, when we feel like it, we may kill, or commit adultery. If our pleasure can justify us in a violation of the fourth commandment, then, our pleasure will justify us in violating any law that God has given. No. To break the Sabbath is a crime—a crying sin—a scandal upon the church of God: and whether the offender can be reached by any authority, civil or ecclesiastical, still, it is a crime, which will not fail to meet condign punishment ere long.

The law, again, requires that children should honor their parents—that they attend to them when old and infirm—that they provide for them when poor and in distress—that they forbear to use to them any unkind or insulting language—that they obey them in every reasonable and just command. "Children obey your parents." "Honor thy father and thy mother, which is the first command with promise." "If any provide not for his own, and especially for those of his own house, he hath denied the faith, and is worse than an infidel."* (Eph. vi: 1 Tim. v: 8.)

Another article of the law is, "thou shalt not kill." (Ex. xx: 13.) Murder, fighting, quarreling, and causeless anger,

---

* It is because *this text* has been so wretchedly perverted and abused, that we ask the privilege to append the following note from the able pen of that inestimable prize essayist, the Rev. John Harris: "The sacred writer is giving directions relative to the maintenance of widows, and distinguishes between such as the church should relieve, and such as should be supported by their own relatives: and concerning the latter he makes the statement in question. Whence it follows, *first*, that the provision contemplated by the apostle, is not the laying up beforehand, for future contingencies, but a present supply of present necessaries, a simple maintenance of needy relatives, from day to day. And *secondly*, that instead of countenancing parents in the accumulation of great fortunes for their children, is speaking of the maintenance, which children, if able, should afford to their aged and destitute parents. With the subject of *providing for families, the text in question* has nothing to do. Rightly interpreted, we see that it enjoins, not *accumulating* but *giving*." (Mammon, p. 104.)

or anger cherished in the heart, are modes by which it is violated. " Whosoever is angry with his brother, is a murderer, and ye know that no murderer hath eternal life." (1 John, iii: 15.)

" Thou shalt not bear false witness against thy neighbor." " Lie not, one to another." " Speak every man the truth, with his neighbor." (Ex. xx: 16—Col. iii: 9—Eph. iv: 25.) Such also is the requisition of the law. It looks at perjury—at prevarication—at detraction—at deception. It forbids " double dealing"—it forbids dishonesty in our business transactions: it requires that we excite no expectations which we do not intend to satisfy—that we leave no impressions on the mind of another, which we will not comply with—to make no promises—no appointments, which we do not strive to fulfil. It is violated when these things are neglected. It is transgressed by neglecting to pay our debts, *if possible :* and to pay them punctually and promptly. No laws which Congress or any other authority can enact, can render just and honest, a refusal to pay any debt we may create, if we ever become able, by industry and economy, to do so. Congress may, if she pleases, pass " bankrupt laws," and men may avail themselves of them, and call it lawful ; but we ask, what power has Congress to repeal the divine law, which still thundereth, " pay what thou owest." " Owe no man any thing." " See that no man go beyond and defraud his brother in any matter." (Rom. xiii: 8— 1 Thes. iv: 6.)

Lewd and lascivious practices, in our intercourse one with another, are also forbidden by the decalogue. If these crimes are not so common among christian people, as some others, yet they have been too frequent, in some places of late, to be passed in entire silence. This was the leading sin of the Nicolaitanes, " which thing," said the Son of God, " I hate." Fornication and adultery are crying sins, which it behooves every christian and every good man, in the community, to frown down in the most uncompromising manner. Such offenders have no inheritance in the kingdom of heaven. " Therefore, put away that wicked person from among you." (1 Cor. v: 13.)

Drunkenness is another public offence, that must not pass unnoticed. " Drunkenness," said the excellent Andrew Fuller, " is a sin which involves in it, a violation of the whole law, which requires love to God—to our fellow-men and to ourselves. The *first*, as abusing his mercies. The *second*, as depriving those who are in want of them, of the necessaries of life, as well as of setting a bad example. The *third*, as depriving ourselves of reason—of self-respect—and common decency." (On Gen. ix: 20–3.)

Idleness, laziness, neglect of business, is also a violation of the divine law. That law which requires us to do no work on the Sabbath, we nor our son, nor our daughter, nor our man-servant, nor our maid-servant, also commands that six days we shall work and do all our business. (Ex. xx: 9.) Under the new dispensation, the principle was repeated, thus: "Be not slothful in business." (Rom. xii: 11.) It has been quaintly said, "an idle man's brain is the devil's work shop"—and every body knows the truth of the old adage, "idleness produces want, vice and misery." Hence, in the apostolic style, to be an idler was to be "disorderly." "We hear," said he, "that there are some which walk disorderly among you, working not at all, but are busy bodies. Now, them that are such we command and exhort, that with quietness they work and eat their own bread." (2 Thes. iii: 11, 12.) It is true the Bible does not define the particular employment which each must pursue. This is left to every man's choice, and to every man's necessities. But it does require that every man, adopting some honest and moral pursuit, should "be diligent in business." "Let him labor, working with his hands, the thing which is good, that he may have to give to him that needeth." (Eph. iv: 28.)

Once more: extortion is a public offence, which requires the act of excommunication. Extortion is to take advantage of a fellow-man's necessities, and compel him to pay more than is lawful for money, or to part with his property for less than its value. It is to take of thy neighbor without giving him an equivalent for that which you receive. It is "to grind the face of the poor"—"to oppress him in his cause," whether by usury or other means. The apostle says, "if there be a man who is a brother, and guilty of such an act, class him with idolaters, railers and drunkards, and have no company with him, no not to eat." (1 Cor. v: 11.)

Such, then, are the public offences which the moral law, and the whole christian economy, regard as sinful. Which of them is there, which a religious man may commit, and

23—Vol. IV.

not bring scandal upon the cause of Christ? Is it idolatry?
profanity? lying? stealing? murder? lewdness? dishonesty?
drunkenness? extortion? Which is it, that is not disgraceful
to the christian name? Mark them which cause such offences, contrary to the doctrine which ye have learned, and
avoid them.

Nor is it necessary that all these sins should be found
upon any one member of the church. If any one of them
attach to his character, it is sufficient for all the purposes of
discipline. Note how the apostle speaks: "I have written
you not to keep company, if any man that is called a brother, be a fornicator, *or* covetous, *or* a railer, *or* a drunkard, *or*
an extortioner, with such an one, no not to eat." This is
the general style of the scriptures. When they enumerate
the virtues necessary to christianity, they connect them by
copulative conjunctions: but when they describe the vices
to be avoided, they connect them by disjunctives. To be a
good man, one must add all that is good in his composition:
but to be a bad man, one evil is sufficient.

Nor is it even necessary that *one offence be habitual.* As
in common life, *one criminal act* is enough to convict a
man, so in religion. To kill once, to lie once, to get drunk
once, to steal once, to commit any scandalous offence once,
is sufficient to demand your action. The Bible no where
rests the excommunication of a gross and willful transgressor,
upon habitual wickedness. But throughout, it inculcates
the sentiment of the text: "Mark them which cause divisions and offences, contrary to the doctrine which ye have
learned, and avoid them: for they that are such serve not
our Lord Jesus Christ."

THE
BAPTIST PREACHER.

| VOL. IV. | October, 1845. | NO. 10. |

PUBLIC OFFENCES, OR CHURCH DISCIPLINE:

A sermon, by Rev. A. W. CHAMBLISS, Tuskegee, Alabama.

NO. II.

"Now, I beseech you, brethren, mark them which cause divisions and offences, contrary to the doctrine which ye have learned, and avoid them : for they that are such serve not our Lord Jesus Christ."—ROM. XVI: 17, 18.

It has been said, that "it is the utility alone, of any moral rule, which constitutes the obligation of it." Although this may not be strictly true, either philosophically or morally considered, yet, the idea of utility ought not to be left out of the account. It is an important item in the calculation. This seems the sentiment of the apostle, in the text before us. Do you ask why we should sedulously "avoid" those who perpetrate the offences described in the preceding discourse? Do you inquire why we should separate them from our communion? We will tell you, the cause of Christ requires it—"they that are such serve not our Lord Jesus Christ."

It seems to have been a settled maxim in the mind of St. Paul, that *whoever was not decidedly beneficial to the cause of the Redeemer, was decidedly prejudicial to it :* that there is no middle ground which a man may occupy—that the church of Christ can better. prosper without the encumbrance of an unholy member, than with it. The reason was, he regarded the maintenance of the principle which requires true piety in members of the church, as an indispensable desideratum. He felt that its success in the world, depended, not so much on human agency, as on the divine power : that it had favor with men, not so much because of the paraphernalia thrown round about it, as because the unseen arm of Almighty God rightly disposed the hearts of men towards it : and that, if we would propitiate the divine favor, and secure the divine agency on our behalf, it must be done by carefully maintaining the spirit of piety in the church. And who has not seen this abundantly exemplified? Who has not seen the influence of even a solitary man of stern, uncompromising piety? Who has not witnessed the gradual, but steady enlargement of a small church, which was careful to avoid all evil? "The kingdom of heaven is like unto leaven, which a woman took and hid in three measures of meal until the whole was leavened." (Matt. xiii: 33.) Keeping free of alloys, its purifying influence will be onward and continuous, until "a small one shall have become a thousand, and a little one a great nation." The strength of the church does not consist in her numbers—nor in her wealth—nor in her talents—nor in any worldly accomplishments: but in the depth and fervency of her piety.

It is, perhaps, our weakness, that we are so apt to look at things in a different light: and to fancy our condition greatly improved by the addition, or greatly injured by the exclusion, of this man, or that, of influence in the world, although it is most evident, that he is not decidedly beneficial to the cause of Christ. Yes, we too frequently identify the abundance of what the church possesseth, with the very life and power of christianity. We suffer ourselves to feel too dependant on these things for success. The evil consequence is, we seize hold on all these with too much avidity, and hold on to them with too great tenacity. We receive almost all who apply for admission to our communion; and let none go, so long as the least possible pretext remains. Forgetting that a bad member will prove seriously injurious— "that a little leaven leaveneth the whole lump"—"that evil communications corrupt good manners," we sometimes cleave to those whom inspired wisdom cautions us to "mark" and "avoid," and that to the lamentable detriment of religion. "Now, I beseech you, brethren, mark them which cause divisions and offences, contrary to the doctrine which ye have learned, and avoid them: for they that are such serve not our Lord Jesus Christ."

I. We are in this discourse to inquire: "What is the discipline which the scriptures prescribe for public offenders?" And here permit us to remark, that the solution of this question must be sought, partly in the person: partly in the offence: and partly in the objects of discipline.

First. Who is the offender? This is the first question that bears on the mode of discipline—this is the first which the scripture rule would teach us to ask.

"Omnibus paribus," that is, all things being equal, the scriptures recognize no distinctions between persons. But all things are not equal in the conditions of men. Religious servants have not the same opportunities to perform the duties required by religion, which their masters enjoy. Children in Christ, have not always the intelligence which their seniors possess. Wives are sometimes influenced by their husbands. Differences of education induce a liability to regard the same act in a different manner.

This inequality in the condition and circumstances of the different members of the same church, would render the same discipline, on some oppressive and intolerable, and on others, light and trifling. "Unto whomsoever much is given, of him shall much be required." (Luke, xii: 48.) A neglect of his family, on the part of a religious master, would be a highly censurable offence: whereas, the same neglect on the part of the servant, should be treated with less severity. For a pious wife, or mother, to *frequently* remain from the house of God, might be excusable: but for the husband to do so, would be without excuse. An ignorant christian should frequently receive our pity, where one of intelligence should be seriously reproved. In all cases, therefore, let the age—the intelligence—the opportunities—and the condition of the offender, be calmly and deliberately considered. "And on some have compassion, making a difference: and others save with fear, pulling them out of the fire: hating even the garment spotted with the flesh." (Jude, 22, 23.)

"The sum of our instructions on this subject, (says the Rev. Jos. S. Baker, than whom no man stands higher among us, as a writer,) appears to be this: that gross, willful and obstinate offenders, are to be promptly excluded from the church: while such as have been misled by them, and have sinned inadvertently—not through a settled purpose to do wrong, or any perverse disposition of the heart, but through the weakness of their frail natures and the infatuation of the moment—should be treated with greater lenity. If they are tractable and can be made sensible of their faults—if they are ingenuous enough to confess their faults, and honest enough, not only to reform their conduct, but also to seek to make some adequate reparation for the wrongs they have done—they should be retained in the communion. But even in such cases, it is necessary that the church proceed in such a manner, as to clearly evince, that while she retained the offender in fellowship, she held his sin in utter abhorrence." (Bap. Chronicle, vol. 1, no. 5.)

Secondly. The character of the offence should have an influence upon the mode of discipline.

If there is great inequality in the circumstances of different offenders, the dissimilarity in their crimes is still greater; and this renders necessary, a careful discrimination of the class of offences under consideration at any given moment. In all cases where the offensive act arose, not so much out of an evil intention, as out of some extraneous influence: as ignorance, erroneous education, &c. ; or where the act concerns a thing about which the Bible is silent, and there may be a difference of private judgment: as in attending a ball, a theatre, a circus, playing at drafts, or playing on a violin; or where the act has been so common in the community, as hardly now to be esteemed a fault: as traveling on the Sabbath, or otherwise desecrating the Lord's day— the neglect of the conference, or other days of public worship—the moderate use of ardent spirits, or the refusal to sustain a proper proportion of the church expenses; or where the evil consequences of the act may be easily remedied by a diligent use of the proper method: as in the case of false, or otherwise injurious doctrines, started in the congregation; or lastly, where the fault is so novel, and so unlikely to become common, as not soon to affect others: as in the case of idleness, neglect of parents, &c.,—in all such cases as these, the church should *first* labor to better instruct her members, and thus, if possible, to reclaim them. If by this means they are reformed, let the past be forgiven, and let the offender be retained in the communion. If, however, he refuse to receive instruction, let him be seriously rebuked before the whole church, for an obstinate persistence in a course which is at once injurious to the peace of God's house, and derogatory to the cause of the Redeemer. If still he refuse, let the church proceed to *publicly* excommunicate him from the society of the faithful. "If he will not hear the church, let him be unto thee as an heathen man and a publican." "An heretic, after the first or second

admonition, reject." " If any man consent not to wholesome words, even the words of our Lord Jesus Christ, and
to the doctrine which is according to godliness, he is proud,
knowing nothing: . . . . from such withdraw thyself."
" Them that sin rebuke before all, that others also may fear."
(Matt. xviii : 17—Tit. iii : 10—1 Tim. vi : 3-5—ib. v : 20.)

You will, we hope, distinctly remark the class of offences
which we have specified : for there is a different description
of crimes, where a widely dissimilar mode of discipline is
indispensably necessary. There are acts which are highly
scandalous, and which every one the least familiar with the
subject, is obliged to know are at variance with the whole
spirit and genius of the christian religion. Murder, fighting,
lying, stealing, drunkenness, adultery, and such like, are so
palpably wrong, that no age—no education—no condition in
life, can be pleaded as their excuse. Were it possible that
the Bible should be blotted out of existence, and yet man
be a christian : still he would know and feel that such practices are criminal. The implantation of the " divine nature " in the heart, is the obliteration of such feelings from
the soul. The christian carries a heavenly monitor within,
which reminds him that the opposite of such conduct is the
path for his feet. There is no compromise between such
acts and religion. They are the antipodes of each other.
They are as irreconcilable as light and darkness. When,
therefore, a man that is called a brother is detected in such
scandalous offences, the church is called upon at once to
express her decided, and most uncompromising detestation
of them. Delays in such cases, and least of all, apologies,
excuses and confessions, as are sometimes received, are unquestionably wrong and injurious. They are injurious to the
offender, and to the cause of christianity : and at the same time
a violation of the laws of Christ's kingdom, as laid down by
the apostle. " Mark them which cause divisions and offences, contrary to the doctrine which ye have learned, and
avoid them." " In the name of our Lord Jesus Christ, when
ye are gathered together with my spirit, and the power of
our Lord Jesus Christ, deliver such an one to satan for the
destruction of the flesh." " I have written unto you not to
keep company, if any man that is called a brother be a fornicator, or covetous, or an idolater, or a railer, or a drunkard,
or an extortioner, with such an one, no not to eat." " There-

fore, put away from among you that wicked person." "Now I command you, brethren, in the name of our Lord Jesus Christ, that ye withdraw yourselves from any brother that walketh disorderly, and not after the traditions which ye have received of us." "If any man obey not our word by this epistle, note that man, and have no company with him." (Rom. xvi: 17, 18—1 Cor. v: 4, 5, 11, 13—2 Thes. iii: 6, 11.)

Such are the words of an inspired apostle. They were uttered with divine authority, and with exceeding emphasis. And permit us to say, beloved brethren, they look with a frowning face upon much of our conduct in the discipline of the church. Do they afford any precedent for that tardiness which characterizes so much of our action? When the apostle says, with so great solicitude and tenderness, "in the name of our Lord Jesus Christ, when ye are assembled with my spirit, and the power of our Lord Jesus Christ, deliver" the scandalous offender to "the kingdom of satan" in this world, did he intend that the church should meet and adjourn from week to week, and from month to month, and yet not exclude him from the communion? Or, when he so frequently commanded, exhorted and admonished, in the name and with the authority of the Lord Jesus, "to withdraw from,"—"to avoid,"—"to put away," and "have no company with the wicked person," did he mean that we should set all these laws aside with apologies, excuses, confessions, &c.? Is there in the context where any of these commands occur, a solitary word about apologies and such like? No: not one syllable.

We said, *that delays in the case of notorious scandals, are decidedly wrong and injurious:* and in this judgment we are sustained by our best authorities. John Angel James, whose "Church Member's Guide" has received so wide a circulation among us, says: "Where the crime is highly scandalous, and very notorious, it is necessary for the honor of religion—for the credit of the society—and for the good of the offender, to *proceed immediately to excommunication, as soon as the fact is proved.*" (p. 155.) In precise coincidence with this, is the direction laid down in the "Baptist Confession of Faith," to which we made a former reference. It says: "Where a member has been found guilty of some gross act of immorality, and which is notorious and scandalous, *the church should proceed to this censure (excommunication,) in the first place,* (i. e.) *without the previous steps of admonition and reproof,* in order to vindicate the credit of their holy profession, and to manifest their abhorrence of such abominations." (p. 223.)

What language can be more to the point than this? It is perfectly plain and simple, and easy to be understood. It is the testimony of those whose praise is in all our churches, and it precisely harmonizes with the declaration of the apostle, that when we are *first* assembled after the perpetration of the act, " as soon as the fact is proved," " by the power of our Lord Jesus Christ," " put away that wicked person."

We said also, *that least of all should confessions, acknowledgments and hasty professions of repentance, be received as a satisfaction for public offences.* In this position also, we are supported by the judgment of the wise and the good. The language of the Rev. Jos. S. Baker, whose piety and ability entitle him to a high place in the confidence and affection of the churches, is : " This practice which is very prevalent, seems to us to savor of the Romish practice of forgiving sins, granting indulgences, &c. If there be any difference, we know not but that it is in favor of the Romanist : for he receives an actual compensation, something substantial, for the injury done his church : but we receive nothing but a wordy acknowledgment. We would have it established as a general principle in our churches, that every member guilty of public, scandalous offence, should be excluded, and kept out until he had sufficient time to evince the sincerity of his professions of penitence, and restore himself, in some degree at least, to the confidence of the community." (Bap. Chron. vol. 1, no. 6.)

To the opinion of Mr. Baker, let us add that of the Rev. Andrew Fuller, of England. The name of Mr. Fuller deservedly stands among the first authorities of the christian world. He was the Paul of modern times, and in all cases of question, we rejoice to have his judgment.

In 1779, Mr. F. wrote the " Circular Letter " for the Northamptonshire Association, on the " Discipline of the Primitive Churches," &c., which letter was published with the authority, and under the sanction of that body. From that " Circular," we extract the following language : " We cannot but consider it an error in the discipline of some

24—Vol. IV.

churches, where persons have been detected of gross and aggravated wickedness, that their exclusion has been suspended, and in many cases omitted, on the ground of repentance." "Allowing that repentance, in such cases is sincere, it is not of such account as to set aside the necessity of exclusion." "The end to be answered by this measure, is not merely the good of the party, but the clearing of a christian church from every appearance of conniving at immorality, which cannot be done by repentance only." (Fuller's Works, vol. 2, p. 466.)

Again: we ask what is proven by these authorities, from which no appeal will probably be made by any Baptist church? We have seen the most positive, emphatic and unqualified declaration of the apostle. To this we have added the judgment of the wise and the good, whose names are held in high and tender esteem among us—names brought from different centuries and from different countries, and all conspiring to prove the same, the identical point, viz: that the good of the offender and the credit of religion, demand an immediate exclusion of a public offender from the church: all concurring to say, do not postpone your action from week to week and from conference to conference: all concurring to say, that no apologies, excuses and repentance, however sincere, are a sufficient satisfaction for the injury done to the cause of Christ, by a public offence. Brethren, if we will not hear all these, neither would we be persuaded though one should arise from the dead. But,

Thirdly. The objects of church discipline must be allowed to have an influence upon its mode.

The discipline of the church is not a matter of whim and of caprice. As it rests on the divine authority, so it contemplates high and holy purposes. The good of the offender— the good of the innocent—and the honor of christianity, are the objects which it is to subserve.

It is designed to benefit the offender. Yes, we repeat it, it is to promote, not so much the momentary gratification— so much the short-lived worldly advantage—not so much the imaginary, as the real, the spiritual and eternal good of him, who has fallen into the snare of the devil. It is to teach him "not again to blaspheme"—it is "that the spirit may be saved in the day of the Lord Jesus." (1 Tim. i: 20—1 Cor. v: 5.)

The good of the innocent is another object which it con-templates. It is at the same time to be admonitory to those who are also in the flesh, and to deliver them from the infectious influence of a notorious transgressor. " Evil communications corrupt good manners." " Know ye not that a little leaven leaveneth the whole lump? Therefore, purge out the old leaven, that ye may be a new lump." " Them that sin rebuke before all, that others also may fear." (1 Cor. xv: 33—ib. v: 6—1 Tim. v: 20.)

We said also, that *the honor of religion generally must be sought in the discipline of the church.* This is, perhaps, the highest, as it certainly is the ultimate object which is to be secured by it. As the apostle said, " let God be true, but every man a liar:" so we say, let the honor of Christ's cause be secured, though every man on earth should stand condemned. This is to be " the alpha and omega, the first and the last," in all our actions. Since men are to form their estimate of religion, by the conduct of the church, "let your light so shine before them that they may see your good works, and glorify your father which is in heaven." " In all things *walk worthy of the Lord* unto all pleasing." (Matt. v: 16—Col. i: 10.)

Beloved brethren, it is impossible that we should impress this observation upon your minds with too much point or emphasis. We fear it is too frequently lost sight of, in our discipline. In our overweaning anxiety for the offender, we sometimes fail to do what his real good, and the glory of the church require. When we throw open the doors of our communion to unworthy and scandalous workers—when, from motives of private friendship, of popularity or worldly advantage, we fellowship those who bring reproach upon the cause of Christ—those to whom the world can point as evil doers—those " disorderly walkers " who trample the laws of God and religion beneath their feet, do we in all this seek the good of the church and the honor of christianity? We fear it might sometimes be said of us, with too much propriety, " the name of God is blasphemed through you, as it is written."

Let no one imagine, that we are not to be influenced in our action, by what the world will say or think. This might be so, if public sentiment were opposed to religion—and if men were to speak against you falsely, for righteous-

ness' sake. " It is praise-worthy if a man, for conscience toward God, endure grief, suffering wrongfully. But what
glory is it, if when ye be buffeted for your faults, ye shall
take it patiently." If the church of God shall faithfully
discharge her duty, and this shall be the occasion of mal-
treatment from the world, let her rejoice—let her not care
for it. But no such indifference is justifiable where duty is
neglected : and least of all, may such indifference be pleaded as a pretext for the neglect of duty. Where the whole
moral tone of society is in favor of religion, and where
every man, if from no other consideration, than because his
parents and friends are its members, supports and advocates
the cause of pure religion and the church, it cannot be right
to disregard public sentiment. In fact, if as a church we
may do so, then we may, in like manner, as individuals.
Nay, it is infinitely worse, in our church actions, to contemn
the opinions of the public, than to do so as individuals : because, in the one case, we act in a private capacity : while
in the other, we do so as a public, organized body. When
men, as individuals, act, they do so upon their own private
responsibility : but when they act as a church, they do so
upon the responsibility of religion—of the Bible—and, (if
I may so say,) upon the responsibility of God and of
heaven. It is because we act in the name, and under
the authority of our Lord Jesus Christ, that it is said,
" whatsoever ye shall bind on earth shall be bound in
heaven : and whatsoever ye shall loose on earth shall be
loosed in heaven." (Matt. xvi : 19.) It is this which gives
such weight—which gives such awful sacredness to the actions of a church. It is this which renders circumspection on
the part of the church, so infinitely momentous—it is this
that gives eternal weight to the apostolic exhortation, " walk
worthy of the Lord unto all pleasing." Shall our responsibilities be abused ? Shall the authority vested in us, be employed to sanction that which God has forbidden ? Shall we,
clothed upon with the vestments of divinity, connive at sin ?
Shall we, in the habiliments of the great God, wink at iniquity ? Shall we so act that men shall not see the distinction
between the good and the evil—that men shall regard sin to
be only a trifle ? It does appear to us, that, if in the world
of despair, there be one place deeper and more wretched,
than any other, it must be the appointment of that church
which shall so abuse the divine authority. No, brethren :

let us ever remember, that when in the capacity of a church we act, we are called upon by every consideration of reason and religion, *so to act,* as to honor the cause of Christ in the world.

From the objects of church discipline, which we have stated, we learn : *First, that great tenderness should be used towards the offender.* We do not mean by tenderness, that effeminate weakness, which cringes and shrinks from a faithful discharge of duty : but the faithful performance of duty, in a mild, gentle and affectionate manner. Love, on the one hand, prompts to fidelity : and on the other, checks rashness and precipitancy. It forbids us to accuse and condemn without sufficient evidence : but when this is produced, requires that we dispose of the offence according to the law of righteousness. It cautions us not to provoke to resentment, or drive to despair, him whom we would save : but while we would censure the offence, to do it in such a manner as to evince that we love him who hath done wrong. "Let us not do evil that good may come." Let us be guilty of no wrong ourselves, while we would correct it in another. Let us bear in mind, that he is a brother, perhaps a truly converted man, but in this instance, *unfortunately, guilty.* Let us not seek his destruction, but his timely restoration : and let meekness and gentleness characterize our whole action. The maxim of St. Paul, to his "son Timothy," affords a delightful rule in all such cases : "The servant of the Lord must not strive : but be gentle unto all men, apt to teach, patient ; *in meekness* instructing those that oppose themselves ; if God peradventure will give them repentance to the acknowledging of the truth ; and that they may *recover* themselves out of the snare of the devil, who are taken captive by him at his will." (2 Tim. ii : 24, 5, 6.)

Another lesson, suggested by the objects of discipline, is, *that it must be conducted in perfect concert on the part of the church.* It is not the business of one man, or of two men : it not the business of the pastor, nor the pastor and deacons conjointly, to transact such important affairs of the house of God. It is the business of the church, the whole church. The duty is equally imperative on one, as on any other : on all, as on any, to see to it, that "the old leaven be purged from the lump"—to see to it, that "the wicked person be put away" from the body. No man may, from a mere indisposition to act—no man may,·from feelings of delicacy—no man may, from considerations of private friendship, of interest or popularity—no man may, from motives of moral cowardice and fear, neglect to co-operate with his brethren. There is no excuse which can be pleaded for a neglect of duty in this place, which would not prove fatal if admitted as a principle. If the good of the offender, and the glory of God, are reasons sufficient to justify any one in a prompt and decided action, they are sufficient to justify all; and if any worldly consideration is a proper excuse for one, it is no less so for every one. But least of all, are parties to be admitted for or against the offender. To bring private animosities, or private advocacies, into the discipline of the church, would be to subvert all order and all rule— would be to subvert all the beneficial purposes which it contemplates. That moment it ceases to promote the good of the offender—the good of the innocent—or the glory of God: that moment the church ceases to be the habitation of order, and harmony, and love: and becomes the theatre of strife, and malice, and ill-will. In the language of the Rev. Mr. Fuller: "Beware, brethren, of both these extremes, which, instead of assisting us in our work, would be doing the utmost to counteract us. We may almost as well abandon discipline entirely, as not to act in concert." (Works, vol. 2, p. 474.)

Again: we are taught by the objects of discipline, *to observe the strictest impartiality in all our actions.* In the church, we are to " know no man after the flesh." (2 Cor. v: 16.) " There is neither Jew nor Greek; there is neither bond nor free; there is neither male nor female; but all are one in Christ Jesus." (Gal. iii: 28.) Here all are alike— here all stand on equal footing—here all have equal rights and privileges. In the church of God, we are to know neither father nor mother; neither husband nor wife; neither son nor daughter; neither brother nor sister. (Deut. xxxiii: 9.) As no man should fear he will be condemned, if he remain innocent: so no one should expect he will go free, if he commit transgression. No one is too high, and no one is too low—no one is too honorable, and no one is too dishonorable, to avoid censure, if he be guilty of sin against the laws of Christ. No age—no position in society—no sex—no condition in life, can throw sanctity enough around the offender to cover his sin, or protect him in it. The rich and the poor, the male and the female, the white man and the black, the old and the young, are all alike amenable for their acts; and pursuing the proper method in their arraignment and trial, should receive the same treatment. We may bear with none, where we would not bear with all; and we should condemn none, where we would not condemn all. To depart from this rule, also, is to destroy all the beneficial effects of church discipline. It then ceases to be a terror to the innocent, or to be a punishment for transgression. Nay, it then ceases to promote the good of the church, or the glory of God.

But once more: The objects of church discipline require, that *the excommunicating* ACT *be pronounced against the offender publicly*, (i. e.) *in the presence of the whole congregation.* Excommunication is a recognition of gross and aggravated wickedness, in the actions of church members: and is at the same time, the church's censure of such criminality. If, then, the honor of christianity is a sufficient reason why we should censure the offence at all, it is a no less sufficient reason why we should censure it publicly. "Let your light so shine *before men*, that they may see your good works and glorify your father which is in heaven." (Matt. v: 16.)

The language of the "Baptist Confession of Faith," on this subject, is: "If the offence be private, the censure may, and in some cases ought to be laid on before the church only: but *if the crime is public and very notorious, the honor of Christ calls for the censure to be public.*" (p. 156.) This, too, is the judgment of the Presbyterian church. In the "Form of Government for the Presbyterian church of the United States, adopted by the General Assembly, in Philadelphia, A. D. 1840," we have the following decision: "When any member has been adjudged to be cut off from the communion, *it is proper that the sentence be publicly pronounced against him.*" (p. 122.) To these authorities, from the "Baptist" and "Presbyterian" churches, let us add one from the "Methodist" church. Says Dr. Martin Ruter, of the Methodist Episcopal church, "from the Historical Works of Dr. Gregory," of the Church of England: "*Ecclesiastical censures*, (in the 2nd cent.,) which are so necessary for the honor—the order—and even the preserva-

tion of the regular society, *were publicly denounced against .
the offender,* who had relapsed into idolatry,.or fallen into
gross sin." (History of the Church, p. 43.)

Such, then, is the concurrent judgment of all the leading
denominations of christians, in this country. Let it be distinctly remembered, that the two former are from " official
documents," and that the last, while it is both Methodist and
Episcopal authority, is at the same time, evidence adduced
from the practice of the churches in the first ages—the practice of Ignatius, Polycarp and Justin Martyr, who received
the management of the affairs of the house of God, at the
hands of the apostles. If to such accumulated testimony,
any thing more is necessary, to give *divine authority* to this
practice, it is only the apostolic command which we have so
frequently quoted, " *them that sin rebuke before all, that
others also may fear.*" (1 Tim. v : 20.)

Is it difficult, beloved brethren, to see what influence this
practice would have upon the objects contemplated by the
discipline of ·the church? Do we seek the good of the
offender? How can this be secured, but by annexing such
penalty ·to transgression as shall at once impress his mind
with the magnitude of crime, and at the same time humble
his proud and rebellious ;spirit under it? Do we seek the
good of the innocent? How can this be secured but ·by
throwing the terrors of a public censure before them? Do
we seek. the honor of christianity ? Then let all men see
distinctly, that " we have no fellowship with the unfruitful
works of darkness, but rather reprove them." (Eph. v : 11.)
When this practice shall be rigidly pursued in the case of
notorious and public offences ; if men become more careful
how they connect themselves with the church ; they will be,
also, much more careful how they act after they have
joined it.

What objection then can there be alledged against it? Is
it novel? No. We have seen that it was practised in the
early ages of christianity. Is it without divine authority?
No. We have seen the apostolic declaration in regard to it.
Is it peculiar to us? No. We have seen that Presbyterian,
Methodist and Episcopalian authorities all sustain it. Will
it be injurious? No. We have seen that it will subserve
all the beneficial purposes of church discipline.

It is a great, a pitiable weakness of ours, beloved brethren, when we fear to do our duty, lest it should be injurious. What have we to do with such consequences as that? Duty is ours; consequences belong to God. To adopt again the language of Mr. Fuller: "with regard to the neglect of discipline, lest it should *injure the cause;* what cause must that be, which requires to be thus supported? Be it our concern to obey the law of Christ, and leave him to support his own cause. If it sink by a fulfilment of his commandments, let it sink. He will not censure us for not supporting the ark with unhallowed hands." (Works, vol. 2, p. 465.) Seek the will of God in the scriptures; in the practice of the apostolic churches; in the judgment of the wise and the good; and faithfully discharge it; fear no evil. "God's ways are not as our way; and God's thoughts are not as our thoughts." He will accomplish his purposes only by his own ways. Be faithful and he will do it. "Now I beseech you, brethren, mark them which cause divisions and offences contrary to the doctrine which ye have learned, and avoid them: for they that are such serve not our Lord Jesus Christ."

From the principles stated and advocated in these discourses, we deduce the following reflections:

It is an error in our discipline, that we look not so much at the general, as at the particular bad consequences, of the conduct of church members. We regard them as individuals, and their actions as isolated, instead of considering that a principle is involved in every instance. The particular bad consequence of overlooking any of the offences which we have specified, may be a trifling matter: but this cannot be done in a solitary case, without being done in every case, except upon the principle of partiality; and then it becomes disastrous and fatal. To permit one member to speak contemptuously of the doctrines and practices of the church— or to detract from the standing and influence of the pastor —or to neglect the conference or other days of public worship, might be, so far as his case extends, a comparative trifle: but it cannot be allowed in one without being allowed in all; and who can estimate the evil which would then result? Hence, the force of the rule we have stated; viz: " We should bear with none where we would not bear with all." We should allow no conduct, in any case, which we would not allow in every case. Whatever we should condemn in all, we should condemn in any. Whatever would be injurious and destructive, if permitted as a general thing, is too injurious in a particular case to pass unnoticed.

Again, it is an error in our discipline, that we have too few criminal laws. That is to say, we regard too few things worthy of the censure of the church. Disregarding the apostolic injunction, " now I command you, brethren, in the name of our Lord Jesus Christ, that ye withdraw yourselves from every brother that walketh disorderly, and *not after the tradition* which ye have received of us." (2. Thes. iii: 6.) " *If any man consent not to wholesome* words, even the words of our Lord Jesus Christ, and to the doctrine which is according to godliness, from such withdraw thyself." (1. Tim. vi: 3, 5.) Overlooking these directions, we have decreed by our usages, that no man is to be excommunicated, except for most notorious and aggravated wickedness: nor even then, except upon certain sweeping conditions. Although it is most manifest that his general deportment is most unlovely; that his influence is in no wise favorable to the cause of religion, if he avoid certain specific scandals, he is to be retained a deathly incubus upon the vitals of the church. This is decidedly an error. It was a sufficient reason with the apostle, why we should " avoid" a man, that he " served not our Lord Jesus Christ."

Again, it is an error, that we place too many acts, which are criminal in themselves, under the head of acts indifferent. Indifferent acts, it will be recollected, we have said, are such as a man may either perform, or let alone, and still be innocent They are such as the Bible neither commands nor forbids: and which have no criminality in them, except when they occasion injury to others. This, however, cannot be said of Sabbath breaking—of coveteousness—of extortion —of neglect of the church—neglect of family piety—the habitual use of ardent spirits—a refusal to support the gospel, &c. In all such cases there is a moral and religious obligation resting upon every church member. They are commanded by the Bible, and enforced by considerations of an eternal character. To regard such acts as indifferent; to say to all our brethren, you may either do them or let them alone; to hold no man accountable for the violation of the numerous passages of scripture where they are taught, is unquestionably an error, a grievous error. It is to recind very many commands of the great God. To do such things is not to serve our Lord Jesus Christ.

Another error is, that we observe too much ceremony and formality with notorious offenders. However scandalous may be their sin, our custom is never to touch the case until the next regular conference. If then, perchance, he is not there, " a committee must be appointed to cite him to appear at the next, &c." And sometimes through divers causes, the case receives not the action of the church for months. It is impossible, brethren, that we should express, the deep sense of pain which we feel at the recognition of this error in the churches. Such custom had no existence in primitive times. Says Mosheim, the historian, *" It is worthy of particular notice, that the custom of excluding bad characters from the society of christians, was at first a simple process, or attended with very little formality."* (Vol. 1, p. 160.) It was a short work. "As soon as the fact was proved ; " when they were first assembled after the commission of the offence, he was excluded.

Another error is, that of pardoning a public offender, on the ground of repentance. In addition to what has been said on this subject, allow us to instance one other authority from the history of the church in the first ages. Dr. Ruter, says, " whatever the excuses of the public offender might be, he was deprived of every part in the oblation ; avoided by the whole church ; and excluded from the assemblies of the faithful. In vain did he implore even for *re*-admission into the society, until by a public confession of his sins, he had given solemn assurances of his intention to conform to the christian laws, and undeniable proofs of the sincerity of his repentance." (His. of Ch., p. 43.)

Again, it is an error that we do not act with sufficient concert. To say nothing of the want of uniformity in the discipline of different churches, by which circumstance we greatly enfeeble each other : and to say nothing of the occasional culpable interference of members of other churches in their private capacity, by which the good effects of discipline are sometimes lost : it frequently happens, that squeamishly sensitive members of the same church remain from the conference, lest they should be compelled to act in what they feel to be a painful case : others again remain silent, lest they should be thought to act against the offender : and others still, as though nothing had taken place; carry it so freely toward the offender, even after the action of the church has been had, as to render the censure of none effect. Those persons, says the excellent Andrew Fuller, who behave in this manner, will be considered by the party as his friends, and those who stand aloof, as his enemies, or at least as being unreasonably severe ; which will work confusion, and render void the best and most wholesome discipline. We must act in concert, or we had as well do nothing. Members who violate this rule, says he, are partakers of other men's sins, and deserve the rebukes of the church for counteracting her measures. (Works, vol. 2, 465.) But,

Finally : it is an error, that we are not sufficiently strict in our discipline. We allow too many things to pass unnoticed. As the strength and success of an army depend largely upon the strict and systematic discipline which it observes—as the health and prosperity of the body, require a strict and careful regimen—as the order and happiness of the community demand a close and vigilant observance of the laws and regulations prescribed for the government of its members : so the strength and success—the health and prosperity—the order and happiness of the church, call upon us to have a strict and constant watch over the deportment of all its members. " Now I beseech you, brethren, mark them which cause divisions and offences contrary to the doctrine which ye have learned, and avoid them."

Beloved brethren, the reason for this injunction, is peculiarly pertinent and impressive. " For they that are such serve not our Lord Jesus Christ." The Apostle, with exceeding jealousy, seemed to watch the principle which had been laid down long before by his blessed master. " He that is not with me, is against me; and he that gathereth not with me, scattereth abroad : (Math. xii : 30 :) and he reasoned logically upon the ultimate bearings of a man's influence upon the cause of Christ. He never seemed to think that every name that could be added to the church book, was so much clear gain ; and that every name blotted out, was so much dead loss to that best of causes. He seemed to consider, that the abolishment of the principle, which required true piety, as an indispensable condition in members of the church, would prove more fatal in the end, to the cause of the Redeemer, than the present advantages, derived from the retention of a bad member would be worth. When he contemplated a man in connection with the church, he did not look at his influence for this year, or for this congregation alone; but he looked at his influence for life; and as it bore upon the principle which requires all church members to be holy, unblamable and unreprovable, I fancy he reasoned thus: "If he is admitted or retained in the communion, it is true he will do something fine, so far as the size of the congregation is concerned; or so far as building a meeting house, or supporting the pastor goes: and on the contrary if he is turned out, we shall lose all this, and perhaps have a great deal to suffer from his excited spleen. But, then, if he is retained, it must be at the sacrifice of what is most vital and dear to the cause of Christ; at the sacrifice of the principle of piety in the church. The consequence will be, that we shall eventually have a church full of men, professing to be christians, but really not so. Either there will be none pious, or those who are will go off and set up anew. What now shall I do? Why, I will mark them which cause divisions and offences contrary to the doctrine which I have learned, and avoid them: because they that are such serve not our Lord Jesus Christ."

Allow us to enforce it upon your minds, beloved brethren that when you receive a member into the church, or when you retain one, to ask yourselves this question: not how far it will affect our list of names; not how far it will promote some sectarian purpose; or subserve some ambitious design: but how far it will advance the cause of Christ. How much of the salt of true piety; how much of the savor of godliness does he bring with him. He may have a name; he may have a family; he may have wealth; he may have influence in the world: and if to these he add piety, rejoice and be exceeding glad, that so much is sanctified to the Redeemer. But if the piety is wanting, he will be a dangerous acquisition. By how great may be his influence, if this is not for Christ—if it is against him—by so much will he prove rather a curse than a blessing. I tell you, my brethren, the apostle looked at this subject with inspired wisdom, when he said, "mark them which cause divisions and offences contrary to the doctrine which ye have learned, and avoid them: because they that are such serve not our Lord Jesus Christ.

THE APOSTLES WERE MISSIONARIES.

Deplorable, indeed, was the state of the world when the apostles, in the name of the Lord Jesus, commenced their holy labors. The nations were sunk in the depths of idolatry the most gross, and of superstition the most abominable. The gods, they professed to adore, varying in power and office, and restricted to particular elements or nations, were exhibited in lights too human, too fallen, to secure from degradation and neglect the common dictates of morality. Mysteries were cherished too obscene for description. The heavenly orbs and departed heroes were worshipped with extravagant honors; and the absurd religion of pagan Rome was spread through the nations which her arm had vanquished. Religious observances, if they deserve the name, originated in the policy of States, as with the Egyptians and Persians; or in an appetite for war, as with the Celts, the Germans, the Britons, and the Goths. If into the popular mythology a supreme deity were admitted, his character was dishonored by his committing the foulest offences, and his authority ever considered as controllable by an eternal *necessity*.

For removing these evils the efforts of philosophers were feeble and unavailing. If occasionally they presented sublime ideas, more frequently they offered notions too subtile for general comprehension, or too absurd to secure belief. Some doubted whether gods existed at all; others supposed the doctrine of the immortality of the soul a fable; and a third class represented it as uncertain whether vice or virtue were more favorable to the best interests of man. The philosophers themselves were corrupted; and it were as vain to expect that corruption would purify itself, as that a fountain should rise higher than its source.

But "after that, in the wisdom of God, the world by wisdom knew not God, it please God by the foolishness of preaching, to save them that believe." The apostles went forth without wealth, without arts, without influence. Sustained by divine qualifications, by the force of truth, and by the spirit of Christ, they accomplished wonders, which in the history of our race are without a parallel. Unassuming in their manners, plain in their attire, with the idiom of Galilee, they were sent as sheep into a forest of wolves. The prejudices of the Jew, the craft of the heathen priesthood, the policy of rulers, and the bigotry of the people, were in array against them. It is said that in the arsenal of Bremen there are twelve pieces of cannon, which are called the twelve apostles, as if to insinuate that by such means men are to be convinced. But the apostles of Christ knew nothing of weapons that are carnal. They employed such only as are mighty through God. To their hearers they could promise no earthly emoluments and honors. Contempt, persecution, confiscation, banishment, martyrdom, attended an acceptance of the gospel. Yet modest, fearless, incessantly they pursued their course, gloriously turning the world upside down, until Rome, the arbitress of the nations, bowed to the doctrine of the Cross. They preached the gospel on the very soil which had been stained by the blood of their master; entered the largest cities, disputed with the most insidious and malignant adversaries, and loved not their lives even unto the death.

Little more than a century had passed, when Justin Martyr declared, " there is not a nation, either of Greek or Barbarian, or of any other name, even of those who wander in tribes and live in tents, amongst whom prayers and thanksgivings are not offered to the Father and Creator of the universe, by the name of the crucified Jesus." Tertullian, who succeeded Justin, says: " We were but of yesterday, and we have filled your cities, islands, towns and boroughs, the camp, the senate, and the forum." This victory of holy truth was the more surprising, inasmuch as the apostles and their fellow christians were everywhere calumniated. They were represented as enemies to government. Earthquakes, pestilences, calamities of any kind, were ever charged on them, and considered as indicating the anger of the gods that such monsters as christians were permitted to live. Because they worshipped without temples, images, priests and sacrifices, they were contemplated as a *class of atheists,* and such as killed them imagined themselves rendering a public service.

Had Mahomet, with his followers, been called to conflict with difficulties such as the apostles surmounted, his religion could never have prevailed. It must have been blasted in its bud. With all the advantages which family connections, riches, assuasive manners, and courtly policy supplied him, only fourteen followers were the fruit of the first three years of his mission. The labor of seven years scarcely augmented his disciples to the number of a hundred. Perceiving no possibility of advancing his religion and reputation by the tedious process of persuasion, in the thirteenth year of his mission he declared that he had received an order from heaven to propagate the doctrines of the Koran by the terrors of the sword. To these he had recourse, and his system spread in proportion. to his victories. . To become Christians, was to become exposed to. " deaths oft,"—to become a Mahomedan, was to avoid them.—*Lat. Day Lum.*

" *Touch me not, for I am not yet ascended to my Father.*"—JOHN xx : 17.

This translation supposes the body of Christ will be more susceptible of touch in heaven, than on earth after his resurrection ; or that to touch him before his ascension was improper : neither of which can be true. The word aptomai, means not only to touch, but to lay hold of, to embrace, to cling to. With such a translation, the passage is beautiful and affecting. " Do not cling to me ; you will have other opportunities to embrace me ; for I am not yet ascended ; my brethren are anxious respecting my fate, go to them and announce that I am risen.—*Ibid.*

THE
BAPTIST PREACHER.

VOL. IV. November, 1845. NO. 11.

THE FEARS OF THE FLOCK CALMED, BY THE VOICE OF THE SHEPHERD:

A Sermon, by Rev. T. F. Curtis, of Tuscaloosa, Alabama.

"Fear not little flock, it is your Father's good pleasure to give you the kingdom.."—Luke xii: 32.

John the Baptist, the forerunner of our Lord, preached, saying: "The kingdom of heaven is *at hand*." Jesus, at the commencement of his ministry, told his disciples to proclaim, "The kingdom of God is *come nigh* unto you." All, therefore, were now waiting for the Messiah-to establish his kingdom,—and *most* were expecting it to be one of great splendor and temporal power. Even the mother of James and John had petitioned that her two sons might sit, one on the right hand, and the other on the left hand of Christ, "*in his kingdom.*" How great then must have been the anxiety of the disciples, when they found no general flocking of the people to the standard of their leader? Or, if for a while a few thousands gathered round him, while he fed them with miraculous bread, they soon "dispersed, every man to his own home," until he turns, even to the twelve, and demands, "will ye also go away?"

Indeed, it was soon quite evident, that their mysterious Master, neither *sought* nor *expected* the popular suffrage; but that he avoided pomp, and eschewed every assumption of temporal dignity. "When he perceived that they would take him by force, and make him a king, he departed into a mountain, himself alone." He even exhorted to pay tribute unto Cæsar, and would not speak to a brother to divide an estate. He, who used so little temporal authority himself, could bestow but little on his followers. And if Christ were indeed to be their king, it must have mightily surprised them, that so few flocked to his standard, and acknowledged his claim. Where was the pharisee? the scribe and the rabbin? where the levite. and the doctor? where the priest, whose "lips should keep knowledge?" Are twelve poor fishermen to prove more learned in the prophecies, than the sanhedrim? Shall seventy men, "without purse or scrip," whose leader "hath not where to lay his head," establish a kingdom, such as Daniel foretold,—that "shall break in pieces every other kingdom," and shall itself "never be destroyed?" Doubtless, many an unbidden *"fear"* must have harrowed up their breasts, as thus they meditated. I think I see one or two of Christ's "little flock" anxiously conversing apart, on these difficulties, when suddenly, their gentle Master, knowing their thoughts, resolves their disquietude by the words of my text, *"fear not* little flock, it is your Father's good pleasure to give you the kingdom." The scribes and pharisees hate and persecute you, as if he had said, but your Father will not neglect you. Though so poor, so few, so insignificant, it is his good pleasure to give you the kingdom,—to confer upon each one of you the rights of *a spiritual citizenship* and brotherhood with all holy beings,—to form you into *the visible kingdom,*—the church of God on earth; yea, to set "you twelve" upon the "thrones" of judgment and authority in that kingdom, and finally, to receive you into *the heavenly kingdom,* "the rest that remaineth unto the people of God," above,—there to be "kings and priests to God and to the Lamb."

Such was the assurance given to those who first heard these words. How faithfully it was accomplished, brethren, you are all aware. Even in his dying agonies, our Lord did not forget his promise. At the last supper, in instituting the sacrament, he solemnly declared this kingdom founded and established. "*I appoint unto you* (he saith,) *a kingdom,* as my Father hath appointed unto me, that ye may eat and drink at my table, *in my kingdom,* and sit on thrones, judging the twelve tribes of Israel." (Luke, xxii: 29, 30.)

No sooner had Christ arisen from the dead, than the Spirit was poured out, and thousands, by their baptism, on the day of Pentecost, proved their *spiritual citizenship;* and taking the oath of allegiance, entered *the visible kingdom* on earth, anticipating the time when they should reign with Christ, above the sky.

. Wonderful was the promise when first given! Glorious its primary fulfilment! But bear with me, dear brethren, while I further enquire,

I. *Who now are Christ's little flock?*

II. *What is the kingdom promised them?* and

III. *Finally, why this promise should dispel their fears?* "Fear not little flock, for it is your Father's good pleasure to give you the kingdom."

I. *Who now are Christ's "little flock?"* Surely, this endearing appellation, or the assurance that accompanies it, is not to be confined to the little handful of disciples which first flocked round the Son of God. Equally sure is it, that if all nominally Christian nations, are to be included, it is now no longer a "*little* flock." We are not left to conjecture on this subject, since, in many other places, Jesus makes use of this same figure, of a flock of sheep, in denoting his disciples. Thus, in the tenth chapter of John, he says, "I am the good shepherd, and know my sheep, and am known of mine; and other sheep I have, which are not of this fold, them also I must bring, and they shall hear my voice; and there shall be one fold and one shepherd." Since this latter clause plainly alludes to the call of the Gentiles, into the fold of Christ, it shews, that whether Gentiles or Jews, *we may be* included in this little flock. It does not, however, intimate, that all the Jews, or all the Gentiles, who are called by his name, *are* thus included. Indeed, even to many of those who attended constantly upon his own personal ministry, he said, "ye are not of my sheep,—my sheep hear my voice, and I know them, and they follow me." They "hear his voice" then, and they "follow him" as the worldly do not. Providence, the word of God, the means of grace, speak to them with authority, in the name of Jesus, —a voice which they receive as his.

When lost in the thick, dark woods, or wandering in a strange city, how cheering to hear the voice of a well known friend! You recognize his voice at once, from a thousand other sounds,—amidst—above them all you hear him—him alone. Though you see him not, you know him, and his voice directs your course. And thus is it with the disciples of Jesus, bewildered and astray amid the entanglements of this world. There is still always a spiritual perception, that enables them to recognize the Saviour. They know his voice, and a stranger will they not follow." By means, which the worldly can neither see nor appreciate, he "manifests himself" unto them,—comforts and directs them.

"They find access, at every hour,
    To God, within the veil;
Thence they derive a quickening power,
    And Joys that never fail."

They thus are spiritually intimate with him, as a friend, and they also "*follow*" him as *a teacher*, by listening to his doctrines. *In their imaginations* they follow him personally, delighting in spirit to retrace all his course while on earth:—to Gethsemane, where he prays and is betrayed—to Herod's palace, the scene of mockery and buffeting—to Calvary and the cross—from the cross to the tomb—that wondrous sepulchre, *for a while*, of his dear body—*forever* of our sins. They trace his glorious pathway to the skies, the right hand of the Father. They follow him in *heart*, embracing him as their surety, their advocate, their intercessor, their friend. They follow him *in their lives*, by imitating his virtues, and in preference to dear friends, strongest interests, father or mother, yea, "through much tribulation;" so as to justify the description of them, given by the angel, "these are they that follow the Lamb, whithersoever he goeth."

Not only do they thus recognize and follow him; he, in like manner, recognizes them. " I *know* my sheep," he says; so that no one of them is overlooked,—though extending over every "kingdom, and nation, and tongue,"—over hundreds of generations—not one, however poor, despised, friendless, but he marks and knows, individually. "He calleth his own sheep by name." There is a holy *intimacy* between the true sheep and Christ, indicated, when it is said, "I know my sheep, and am known of mine;" and it is this high and spiritual intimacy which characterizes the flock of Christ.

We have then here, but to inquire further, how this can now be truly described as a *little* flock? Doubtless, it was so when it consisted but of the twelve and the seventy; and it is but a *little* flock still. We do not here take in, you perceive, the number of *nominal christians* through the world, and compare it with that of pagans and mahomedans; though that would leave us but a sad minority. Christ's flock is small, compared with the number of nominal christians. Even among protestants, how small a portion pretend to any thing like an experimental knowledge of Christ, and how many that do, will not at last be found among his true followers! Truly then, does the text still denominate the band of Christ's disciples, "*a little flock.*"

II. We are thus prepared for our second enquiry, i. e., "What is the kingdom here promised?" "It is your Father's good pleasure to give you *the kingdom.*"

No temporal kingdom this. When the dying thief prayed "Lord remember me, when thou comest into *thy kingdom,*" he at least could have had no idea of an earthly throne; while the Saviour, in granting his prayer, taught him to look into "paradise" as the great seat of his great government. He himself, elsewhere declares " *my kingdom* is not of this world." At the same time, it is not so exclusively in heaven, that the saints, even while on earth, may not enjoy a perfect membership in it.

1. Indeed, this phrase means, first of all, *Christ's spiritual kingdom or reign in the hearts of his followers, here.* Hence, when the pharisees demanded of him, "when the kingdom of God should come?"—he answered them, "the kingdom of God cometh not with observation; neither shall they say, lo here, or lo there, for behold, *the kingdom of God is within you.*" "The kingdom of God is not meat and drink, but righteousness, and peace, and joy in the Holy Ghost." Each one thus becomes a member of this spiritual kingdom, at the moment of his conversion,—when Christ first subdues and reigns over his rebel lusts; long before he reaches heaven.

2. But this kingdom extends further. It refers, not only to his spiritual, but here, more particularly, *to his visible kingdom or church below.* In all ages of the world, God has had *a spiritual kingdom ;* for he has ever preserved a pious race upon the earth. Among the Jews, for instance, from Abraham downward, there were always many individuals whose hearts were right with God.

Indeed, it was thus prophesied by Daniel, "*in those days* shall the God of heaven set up a kingdom that shall never be destroyed." (Dan. ii: 44.) This visible kingdom then,

was not "set up" *until the days of the Messiah ;* so that it
is to be carefully distinguished from the spiritual kingdom,
which had long existed, to which all the prophets belonged.
This was, as it was prophesied it should be, "diverse from
all kingdoms," (Dan. vii: 23,) before or after, and perfectly
instituted only by Christ, as we have already seen, at the
celebration of his last supper. To this he particularly referred, when speaking to his avowed disciples in the text, he
said, "it is your Father's good pleasure to give you the
kingdom."

3. Doubtless, however, the promise of the text included
much more than any thing which, on earth, can be bestowed, even upon the believer. It includes the paradise which
was promised to the dying thief; yea, all the perfection of
glory which believers shall enter upon after the decisions of
the judgment day. Then it is that Christ will say to his true
sheep, "come ye blessed of my Father, inherit *the kingdom*
prepared *for you* from the foundation of the world." Then
it is that "they shall be made *kings* and *priests* to God and
to the Lamb," and "shall reign with him forever and ever."
Not until that happy day shall we know all that is included
in the promise of my text.

Behold then, my brethren, what a glorious assurance is
here-spread out before us! It were much for Christ to promise his flock, that they should be considered as a part of
his great, spiritual and invisible kingdom—a kingdom which
numbers in its ancient archives, such men as Enoch and
Noah, before the flood ; Abraham, Isaac and Jacob, among
the patriarchs; such legislators as Moses and Samuel; such
kings as David and Hezekiah ; such prophets as Isaiah and
Daniel. This were much ; but in the new testament, Jesus
offers to all his little flock, far more, a seat in his *visible
kingdom ;* privileges so great, that "many prophets and
righteous men have desired," but not obtained them. True,
the prospects of his kingdom may at times, be dark and
gloomy, as they were when these words were first spoken ;
but it shall "*never be destroyed.*" Oh, let us anticipate its
"latter-day glory," when "it shall break in pieces and subdue all other kingdoms;" when through the length and
breadth of this wide world, it shall be proclaimed, "now is
come salvation and strength, and *the kingdom of our God,*
and the power of his Christ." Happy time this! when "the

house of the Lord shall be established upon the top of the mountains, and *all nations shall flow unto it;*" when "the knowledge of the glory of the Lord shall cover the earth as the waters cover the sea." What though paganism be bulwarked by the walls of China? It shall totter! it shall fall! What though mahomedanism in India, and Roman catholicism in Europe, and many a vile and corrupt thing in the lands of protestantism, be still found? What though vice lay waste our cities, and ignorance the country? "The stone cut out of the mountain, without hands," shall dash all this in pieces. Glorious day, when "from the rising of the sun, to the going down of the same, thy name, oh God, shall be great among the heathen;" when the voice of the archangel shall proclaim, "the kingdoms of this world are become the kingdoms of our Lord and of his Christ."

How vast then is the kingdom of Christ! how triumphant in its prospects! yet, "it shall be possessed by the saints of the Most High," given by the good pleasure of their heavenly Father, to the little flock.

But even this, though much, is not all. This world shall be dissolved, with all that it inhabits,

> " And like the baseless fabric of a vision,
> Leave not a wreck behind."

But "this kingdom is an everlasting kingdom," and shall "never be destroyed." It extends into the eternal world, and embraces the abodes of the blessed dead! All the unspeakable delights of paradise, which St. Paul was "caught up" to behold—the new Jerusalem, with its walls of jasper and its gates of pearl, the river of life, the sea of gold, and of glass, the throne of God and of the Lamb—all that is intimated in this bright imagery, is included in the declaration of the text, "it is your Father's good pleasure to give you *the kingdom.*"

III. *It now but remains for us to enquire, lastly, how this promise dispels the fears of the people of God.*

Let us look at the sources of that fear which presses so heavily upon them.

1. *Is the fewness of their numbers* a cause of anxiety to the people of Christ—that they are such *a little flock?* This was unquestionably a source of great discouragement

to the first disciples. So it is now, even to christians, often-times. The dread of singularity, and of being despised, is often a test of character severely felt, even by the most pious. As the christian looks round upon the dense masses of ami-able sinners—whose only fault is worldliness of mind—it is hard for him to assent to that declaration of St. John, "we know that we are of God, and the whole world lieth in wickedness." Is it possible, the trembling believer will say, that we alone are right and all else wrong; are only the people of God to possess the kingdom, and so many to be lost?

The Saviour seems perfectly to have understood and an-ticipated this difficulty. The terms, therefore, which he uses in the text, are singularly intense. There is a double diminutive, which might be rendered, "fear not POOR little flock, or very little flock," as if Christ was determined *to meet the discouragement in its extremest form.* Fear not, as if he had said, "though so extremely little and weak, it is a *Father* with whom you have to deal; though poor, he will make you rich, he will *give* you the kingdom."

But still you object: "Why then are we not more favor-ed? If not in the wrong, why not more blessed with num-bers? How is so small a flock to take possession of so extensive a kingdom? Shall the little band of christians ever triumph over heathenism and infidelity; mahomedanism and worldly-mindedness?" "Fear not." If, indeed, suc-cess depended merely on *our exertions,* the cause never could prevail. But it does not. Success arises from the sovereign gift of God. "It is your Father's *good pleasure* to give you the kingdom." The purpose, the power, the "good pleasure" of God, ensure final triumph to this cause. Were the flock not so "little," the assurance of success would not be so great; as Gideon's army could not conquer the host of Midian, till reduced to three hundred.

2. What, then, shall alarm the believer? *Shall worldly troubles?* Fear them not. What though religion seems to be your temporal enemy, in becoming your eternal friend; and you are subjected to desertion of friends—to poverty—and to shame, for Christ's sake? Truly there is more moral dignity—there is more princely happiness, even on earth, enjoyed by the believer who follows implicitly his conscience and the word of God, with all the world against him—there

is more triumph, more manifestation of kingly power, in such a life as this, and in a life of self conquest, than in that of any earthly sovereign on his throne. Jesus confers on you an eternal kingdom : murmur not, if for a moment you have to wear the crown of thorns. Who would care about a few dollars, with *a kingdom at stake?* And "it is through much tribulation we must enter into the kingdom of God."

What though pain racks the body—though a fever parches up the skin—or a cancer eats out the flesh—or consumption knaws away the vitals—what though dear friends wither—though death lays his icy hand upon the breast of the believer? " In all these things we are more than conquerors." They take us not away *from our* kingdom, *but conduct us to it.* "There *remaineth* a rest for the people of God." There is an incorruptible inheritance, and an unfading crown, "*reserved* in heaven" for them. This bright kingdom, in the fullness of its development and glory, is kept in " reserve " while they tarry here below; it " remaineth " in " waiting for the manifestation of the sons of God." Not until after death do they perfectly enter into their kingdom. Let the storms of affliction, disease, or death, pursue the christian ever so closely, they will but waft him over the boisterous sea of life, and land him the sooner on the shores of his heavenly inheritance. " When Christ, who is our life, shall appear, *then* shall we also appear with him in glory."

3. *But is there no danger lest some of the members of this little flock should be parted from their good Shepherd, and thus lost?* If left to ourselves, we should be sure to stray. How often are we cold, and negligent, and formal, in prayer—how often neglectful of our Bibles and the means of grace? But that " he restoreth our souls and leadeth us in the paths of righteousness, and maketh us to lie down in green pastures," we should be always straying. But he stands in a peculiar relation to his people, and *therefore* they need not fear. He is their shepherd—they are his little flock. The particle, in the Greek, is often used for the possessive pronoun, and has here an affectionateness in its meaning ; as if it were translated, " Fear not *my* little flock—*my poor* little flock." However poor, and weak, and despised, Christ *identifies himself* with each individual believer, and engages to carry him through; to "give" him

27—Vol. IV.

his heavenly "kingdom." "I know my sheep," he says, "and am known of mine, and I give unto them eternal life, and they shall never perish ; neither shall any pluck them out of my hand." What then shall we fear. " What *shall separate* us from the love of Christ? Shall tribulation, or distress, or persecution, or famine, or nakedness, or peril, or sword? Neither LIFE, nor DEATH, nor angels, nor principalities, nor poweis, nor things present, nor things to come, nor height, nor depth, nor any other creature, shall *be able to separate us from the love of God*, which is in Christ Jesus our Lord."

The last fear of the people of God, is thus triumphantly repelled, by the assurance of the text, " it is your Father's good pleasure to give you the kingdom."

But I may not conclude, without remarking, that *Christ's true sheep are the only persons who have not great reason to fear.*

What are men without grace? " As sheep without a shepherd," at each step wandering further from the fold, led on without end or aim, towards eternal ruin, by every thing that promises, be it but a scrap of pleasure. What security—what hope is there—for such, but that they will be led astray, with only sense to wander, but none to return ?

Such, unconverted man, is your deplorable condition! What ground have you for any thing but fear? Have you any refuge that the sheep of Christ have not, since you have none that they have? In what do you confide ?

In numbers, perhaps!—that you at least are not " a LITTLE flock ;" you have so many, in such a city as this, like yourselves ; and can say, " I am as good as the most ;" " no worse than the rest of the world ;" " better than many who profess more ?" But can numbers save you? Alas ! what a poor consolation will it be at last, that you only went *with the multitude* to eternal ruin. " Broad is the road that leadeth unto *destruction*, and many there be that go in thereat. But strait is the gate, and narrow is the way, that leadeth unto life, and few there be that find it." In what then do you confide ?

In present prosperity? That you are not a *poor* little flock—are not afflicted, see no danger, are " not in trouble, nor plagued like others,"—increase in honor and ease—that you have your portion—your kingdom in worldly pleasures, and have no compunctions of conscience—no disquietude or fear? But does your indifference prove that you have no reason to fear? Alas, no! All the sources of your security and ease will be soon dried up. Your happiness is not permanent, your honors will decline, your beauty will fade, your health will pine and waste, your friends must die. Yea, *death*, the king of terrors, will soon approach your own couch, and you will have no angel, and no Saviour near, to say "fear not." No kingdom, but that of darkness, reserved for you.

And, at the morning of the resurrection, will you not fear then? Though there be such a multitude of you, no one will be overlooked—not one misplaced. The rocks and the hills will refuse to cover any one of your poor souls: but you must meet the eye of the Lamb, when the great day of his wrath is come: and who shall be able to stand? When the Son of Man shall come in his glory, and before him are gathered all nations, as he proceeds to divide the sheep (his "little flock,") from among the goats; when "he calleth his own sheep by name," and leadeth them to the right hand, and you see one after another of your companions and friends on earth thus called away, while you are still left behind—a pious parent, who had prayed for you—a pious brother, or sister, or child, whose eyes you had closed in death—the friend who used to sit next you in the pew—who warned, who wept, who prayed for you; when all these are one by one forever separated from your side, and the Lamb leads them to the "still waters" of bliss, and the green pastures of the heavenly hills; when to them he says, but *not to you*, "come ye blessed of my Father, inherit *the kingdom* prepared for you from the foundation of the world"—will you not fear then? and wish you had joined the little flock, and entered in at the strait gate, and walked in the narrow way? And when, with an eye fixed witheringly on you, and from which you cannot turn, he proceeds to pass sentence on those who are left, "depart from me into everlasting fire, prepared for the devil and his angels,"—oh tell me, have you limbs of iron—have you sinews of brass—have you flesh of adamant, that you will not fear then?

Awake, awake, my dear impenitent friends, nor expose your poor souls to so shocking a fate. He who will then be your Judge, would now be your Saviour. Place yourselves among his children: "He leadeth his flock like a shepherd— he beareth the lambs in his bosom—and gently leadeth the young." Permit us to see the happy time, when it may be said appropriately, to each one of you, in the language of scripture: "Ye were as sheep going astray, *but have now returned to the Shepherd and Bishop of your souls.*"

THE RESURRECTION OF THE DEAD:

A sermon, preached, in the ordinary course of his ministry, to his people, September 21st, 1845, by Rev. ROB'T BOYTE C. HOWELL, D. D., Pastor of the First Baptist Church, Nashville, Tennessee.

"*There shall be a resurrection of the dead.*"—ACTS, XXIV : 15.

A RESURRECTION OF THE DEAD! And shall there be *a resurrection of the dead?* There *shall be*—the dead *shall,* one day, arise from their graves.

The resurrection of the dead, is an event which never would have suggested itself to the mind of man, unenlightened from on high. All the appearances in nature are against its truth. It found a place, therefore, in none of the systems of Greek or Roman philosophy, nor in the theology of ancient paganism. It was reserved for the *Bible*—the revelation to man of the designs, and will of God—to announce to us the glorious assurance, that "there shall be a resurrection of the dead."

The first aspect in which this subject presents itself to us, is, simply, as *a question of fact.*

Assuming the Bible to be true, and this, I trust, no one in this assembly doubts, than the resurrection of the dead, nothing is more incontrovertibly certain. "This I confess unto thee,"—said Paul, in our context, while defending himself before Felix, against the accusations of the Jews— "that after the way which they call heresy, so worship I the God of my fathers, believing all things that are written in the law, and in the prophets; and have hope toward God, which they themselves also allow, that there shall be a resurrection of the dead, both of the just and unjust." Our Lord himself said: "The hour is coming, in the which

all that are in their graves shall hear his voice, and shall
come forth : they that have done good, unto the resurrection
of life, and they that have done evil, unto the resurrection
of damnation." (John, v : 28, 29.)   "The dead," says an
apostle, "shall be raised." (1 Cor. xv : 52.)   But why recite passages in proof of this fact? The resurrection of the
dead is stated, and affirmed, and defended, in all parts of
the word of God, and in a manner the plainest and most
emphatic.   It is impossible to believe the Bible, and not
assent to the doctrine of the resurrection.

Is the religion of Christ a reality? So, then, must be the
resurrection.   The former rests upon the truth of the latter.
The apostolic argument on this proposition is obvious and
conclusive. Addressing the Corinthians, he says : "If there
be no resurrection of the dead, then is not Christ risen : and
if Christ be not risen, then is our preaching vain, and your
faith is also vain.   Yea, and we are found false witnesses
of God, because we have testified of God that he raised up
Christ, whom he raised not up, if so be that the dead rise
not.   For if the dead rise not, then is not Christ raised :
and if Christ be not raised, your faith is vain, ye are yet in
your sins.   Then they also which have fallen asleep in
Christ have perished." (1 Cor. xv : 13 -17.) But the proof,
to use inspired expressions, is " infallible" of Christ's resurrection.   He was *seen*, after he arose, by all the apostles,
and by many of them frequently and closely scrutinized ;
and he was seen by more than five hundred others, at one
time, multitudes of whom were, when Paul wrote, living,
and ready to testify to the fact before any tribunal.   No
rational man, therefore, dare doubt the resurrection of
Christ.   It is, also, equally certain that, as a consequence,
all *men* shall arise.   "For, as in Adam *all* die, even so in
Christ, shall *all* be made alive." (1 Cor. xv : 22.)   The
wicked will come forth, alas ! to an awful fate, but the
righteous to eternal life.   "For, if we believe that Jesus
died, and rose again, even so, them also that sleep in Jesus,
will God bring with him." (1 Thess. iv : 14.) If, then, triumphantly we may exclaim :

"An angel's arm can't snatch us from the grave ;
Legions of angels can't confine us there."

It has been imagined, that the resurrection of the body is

a doctrine taught only in the New Testament. Those who have entertained this opinion, have, surely, not examined the subject. We have only to look into the Bible, and we shall be convinced that the resurrection, as an article of faith, was held, by the patriarchs and prophets, with a confidence as unwavering, as it now is by christians.

Did not Paul say, as we have seen, that "the resurrection of the dead, both of the just and unjust," was a doctrine "allowed" by the Jews to be true? Upon what testimony did they admit it? Look into the prophecy of Isaiah, and, as his vision reaches forward to the consequences of the resurrection of Christ, you will hear him beautifully exclaiming: "Thy dead men shall live, together with my dead body shall they arise. Awake, and sing, ye that dwell in dust, for thy dew is as the dew of herbs." (Isa. xxvi: 19.) The promise of our Lord, by Hosea, is definite: "I will ransom them from the power of the grave; I will redeem them from death. O death, I will be thy plague: O grave, I will be thy destruction." (Hosea, xiii: 14.) It is to this declaration that Paul refers, when he says: "Then shall be brought to pass *the saying that is written*—Death is swallowed up in victory. O death, where is thy sting? O grave, where is thy victory?" (1 Cor. xv: 54, 55.) Daniel, too, said to Israel: "Them that sleep in the dust of the earth shall awake: some to everlasting life, and some to shame and everlasting contempt." (Dan. xii: 2.) The Sadduces, who, in the days of our Lord, denied the resurrection, were, on that account, regarded as heretics;* and Martha, at the grave of her brother, said to the Redeemer: "I know that he shall rise again, in the resurrection at the last day." (John, xi: 24.)

Ancient saints had, as you must now see, from the texts we have presented, and, were it necessary, we could readily adduce many others, the amplest evidence of the resurrection of the dead. Surely no reasonable man can think otherwise, than that this has been an established article of the faith of all ages.

We now see that,—*as a matter of fact*,—the resurrection of the dead is, beyond question, true. It is a most animating reality—a glorious triumph! Paul contemplated it

---

*Matt. xxii: 23.

until his full soul exclaimed: "Death is swallowed up in victory. For this corruptible must put on incorruption, and this mortal must put on immortality."

Let us now, *in the second place*, consider the nature of the resurrection.

It is a magnificent exhibition of *the power of God*. He *alone*, who created all things, is *able* to call forth our bodies, after a sleep of thousands of years, from their dusty beds. His omnipotence is pledged, and shall bring to pass this astounding result.

But what sort of a body shall be the body of the resurrection? This is the great question. Will the same corporeal matter of which we are now composed, be raised from the grave, and form the body of the resurrection? In other words: will the resurrection be an actual physical resurrection of our present bodies? I answer the question, emphatically, in the affirmative. It will, in every proper sense. The accidents of the body—such as age, and disease, its impurities, and corruptibility—will be removed, and, thus changed, it will be a pure and glorious spiritual body; still, it may be accurately predicated, that the bodies we shall have in the resurrection, will be the same bodies in which we now "live, and move, and have our being."

The correctness of this opinion is, however, warmly contested. It is alledged that,—for several reasons,—the bodies of the resurrection cannot be the same, in any correct sense, with those we now have. Let the reasons in question be briefly considered.

It is confidently maintained, that the known facts in physiological science disprove our conclusion. Our present body, it is fully ascertained, is in a constant process of waste, and reparation, so that, in a few years, it entirely changes its substance. There is not a particle of matter in them now, of which they were composed seven years ago. Very well; this is all true; we admit it; and what then? Why, it is now triumphantly asked: What body is it, in the series, that is raised from the dead? That which we now have: or that which we had twenty years ago, or some one possessed in the intermediate time?

This argument may appear, at first view, to present an impassable barrier; but, when more closely examined, it will be found to offer, really, no difficulty whatever. Three brief statements will make this sufficiently apparent.

1. It rests upon a refinement of reasoning which, when taken out of its proper sphere, is sophistical, inapplicable, and " darkens counsel, by words, without knowledge." What is there, in relation to which we may not, by such a process, involve ourselves in an inextricable labyrinth of mystery? What! the bodies of the resurrection not our present bodies! Then our bodies never arise. There is, therefore, after all, really no resurrection of the dead! Our text is not true; and we may take up the lamentation:

> " Alas! the tender herbs, and flowery tribes,
> Though crushed by winter's unrelenting hand,
> Revive, and rise, when vernal seasons call:
> But we, the brave, the mighty, and the wise,
> Bloom, flourish, fade, and fall;
> And then succeeds a long, dark, oblivious sleep,—
> A sleep, which no portentous power dispels,
> Nor changing seasons, nor revolving years."

But no; our faith is not so readily shaken; it is inspiration which assures us, that " there shall be a resurrection of the dead."

2. I remark, that the identity of our present bodies with the bodies of the resurrection, is not the same in a strict philosophical, that it is in a theological sense.* A thing may be theologically true, that is scientifically inaccurate. Do you doubt this? Ponder the proposition, and you will see that it must necessarily be so. It arises, inevitably, from the fact, that the language of the Bible is *popular*, not scientific, language. The word of God, for example, says: " The sun *ariseth*, and the sun *goeth down*, and hasteth to the place whence he arose." (Eccl. i: 5.) Now we have the means of *demonstrating* that this statement is philosophically inaccurate. The sun is really a fixed body, and never moves. Does any sensible man conclude, therefore, that the Bible is not true? By no means. The language is popular,—such as is constantly employed, by all classes of people, learned and unlearned. It is theologically true; and sufficiently accurate for all the purposes of life. Apply these

---

*Vide Christian Review for Sept'r, 1845, art. 1.

deductions to the subject before us. In the resurrection, I shall be conscious that I am the same man that I am now. I know that I am, this moment, notwithstanding physiological changes, the same man that I was twenty years ago; so shall I know, notwithstanding spiritual changes, that I am still the same man. This is identity enough to satisfy the desires of the most fastidious.

3. I observe, lastly, that if this physiological argument proves any thing at all against the resurrection of our present bodies, it proves greatly too much, and, therefore, defeats itself.

We are expressly taught, in the divine word, that " we must all be judged, in the last day, according to the deeds done in the body." But, I ask, according to the deeds done in what body? In the first, or the last, or what intermediate body, in this same physiological series? "The continuity of the vital operations [our learned objectors tell us,] has nothing to do with physiological identity;" and that "it cannot be affirmed, with scientific accuracy, that the body any man has now, is the same which he had ten years ago." You will, therefore, instantly see, that, upon this ground, it is as impossible that there can be any *judgment*, as that there can be any resurrection; for the plain reason, that it is impracticable to identify the body in which the deeds were done, for which we are to be judged! There is, therefore, no such thing as moral accountability! All religion is, of course, fabulous—a mere dream of the fancy! If the objection be allowed as valid, all these absurdities irresitibly follow. You cannot repel them, nor turn them aside. But we are morally accountable, the arguments of "science, falsely so called," to the contrary notwithstanding. We must be "judged according to the deeds done in our [present] body." If so, these very bodies must be raised from the dead, and, in the full popular sense which attaches to all the teachings of the word of God, form the bodies of the resurrection.

You are now, I trust, convinced that this physiological argument against the identity of our present bodies, with the bodies of the resurrection, is wholly baseless, because it is a hypercritical refinement of reasoning; because it takes for granted, in relation to scripture, that which is not true; and because it involves collateral absurdities fatal to the whole system of rational religion.

But a second objection is offered, of a kindred character. It is assumed that our present bodies cannot be identical with the bodies of the resurrection, because, when men die they mingle with the earth, and the matter of their bodies is formed into vegetable life; these vegetables are eaten by animals, and the vegetables and the animals are eaten by men, and constitute parts of other bodies: thus, the body of one man goes to form the body of another man; and so the bodies of multitudes of men may consist of precisely the same matter! It is presumed, as a consequence, that, in the resurrection, there may be hundreds of souls all claiming the same matter—the same bodies—and that there will be those who, if not provided with other bodies than those they had here, will have no bodies! Therefore, it is concluded, that the identity which we contend for is physically impossible.

All this apparently formidable array of argument, is but a mist, and is dissolved by a single touch of divine truth. Do you not see that it limits omnipotence? Besides, it is all built upon *supposition*, and stands like a mighty pyramid upon its point. Its suppositions, too, are all plainly at war with the providence of God, who watches over our bodies, as well as our souls, and will keep them both uninjured until that day. Our souls are immaterial, and, when separated from their present tenements, have no ligatures to bind their parts together. You might as well suppose that God's providence will permit them to be dispersed, and to commingle with each other, in such a manner that they never can be separated and be prepared for their respective bodies! Why not presume this of the souls, as well as of the bodies? It is just as reasonable.

To *our* objectors we may say, as *Christ* did to the *Sadducees*, who proposed to him a similar difficulty: " Ye do *err*, not knowing the *scriptures*, nor the *power of God*." Is it a *falsehood* which you have just sung of Jehovah, or is it a glorious truth?

> " God, the Redeemer lives,
>   And, ever from the skies,
> Looks down, and watches all our dust,
>   Till he shall bid it rise."

Well, then, responds a third opposer: if the bodies of the resurrection are identically the same bodies that we now have, some of them will be in childhood, and some in hoary age; some in helpless infancy, and some in the vigor of years; some in disease, and others maimed, and others still, imperfect. No sir, no; pause, if you please. Infancy is not a part of the body; nor is age a part of the body; nor is health, or disease, or any of the others, a part of the body. These are merely its circumstances, or accidents. The resurrection brings up the body; not the accidents in which it may have been temporarily placed. Paul anticipated the same objection. "How are the dead raised up, and with what body do they come?" His reply is to our purpose, entirely: "Our conversation is in heaven, from whence, also, we look for the Saviour, our Lord Jesus Christ, who shall change our vile body, that it may be fashioned like unto his glorious body, according to the working whereby he is able to subdue all things unto himself." (Phil. iii: 20, 21.) John also answers, in a manner equally satisfactory, the same question: "Beloved, *now* are we the sons of God, and it doth not yet appear what we *shall be :* but we know, that when he shall appear, we shall be *like him,* for we shall see him as he is." (John, iii: 2.) Whatever, then, may have been our physical form, or condition here, in our change from a *natural* to a *spiritual* body, we shall assume, with eternal youth and health, the general appearance which characterizes the Redeemer himself.

But "flesh and blood cannot inherit the kingdom of God." So saith the scriptures. We are now flesh and blood. How, then, it is objected, *in the fourth place,* can the bodies of the resurrection be identical with our present bodies?

We have already stated, that a change occurs in the body to fit us for heaven; which, in inspired language, is described thus: "This corruptible must put on incorruption, and this mortal must put on immortality." "It is sown in dishonor; it is raised in glory. It is sown a *natural* body; it is raised a *spiritual* body." By a *natural*—a mortal, or corruptible—body, is meant the present animal body of "*flesh and blood.*" In other words: a body governed by the laws of physical economy; composed of solids and fluids; in a constant process of change, and requiring to be repaired by nutrition; dependent for its preservation, upon the presence of that

mysterious agent which we call animal life. Such a body
is necessarily *mortal* and *corruptible*. To fit it for heaven,
it must be changed into a *spiritual* body. And, when we
speak of a *spiritual* body, what do we mean? We describe
by it a body to which the presence of the rational spirit
alone is necessary; a body not now " of corruptible " flesh
and blood, and, therefore, not subject to the laws of physical matter; not dependent upon natural productions for its
support; and not subject to mutation, decay, or death, but
governed by the laws of the spiritual world. It is a spiritual
body.

We thus learn the precise extent of that *change* through
which the body passes in its ascent from its present state to
eternal glory. It consists *in its form*—which is changed
from its present vileness, into the glorious dignity, beauty,
and majesty, of our Lord Jesus Christ; and *in its charác-
ter*—from a natural to a spiritual body. Am I told that
this change is so great as to make it quite another, and not
the same body? It is very certain that the change is no
greater than that which takes place in the soul in regeneration. And is not the soul of the christian the same soul that
he had before? Our glorified body is as surely the body
that we now have, as refined gold, purified, and wrought
into a beautiful jewel, is the same gold that it was when al-
loyed in the dross of its original mine; yes, and in all its
brilliancy, it shall sparkle forever in the Saviour's crown.

Not the same body! What, then, means the Redeemer,
when he says: " All that are in their graves shall hear his
voice, and come forth? " (John, v : 28, 29.) This can possibly relate only to the matter of those bodies which were laid
in the grave. That which never was in the grave, cannot
come out of it. Not the same body! What means an apostle,
when he says: " We must all appear before the judgment
seat of Christ, that every one may receive the things done
in his body, according to that he hath done, whether it be
good or bad? " (2 Cor. v : 10.) Can these words be understood of any other body than that in which the things were
done? We must, then, all appear at the judgment seat of
Christ, in the bodies which we now have. " *This* corruptible [body] must *put on* incorruption; and *this* mortal
[body] must *put on* immortality." (1 Cor. xv: 51.) If on
this body I put a royal robe, is it not still the same body?

This mortal and corruptible body, therefore, that we now have, not another, becomes the immortal and incorruptible body of the resurrection, raised from the dead, in virtue of Christ's atonement, by the power of God, and shall shine forever with radiant joy and happiness.

Indulge a few observations, *thirdly,* regarding *the time of the resurrection.*

"There *shall be* a resurrection of the dead." This great event, our text teaches us, is yet in the future. Other texts speak of it as one of the solemn transactions of *"the last day."* "In a moment, in the twinkling of an eye, *at the last trump*, the dead shall be raised." Again: "This is the Father's will, which hath sent me, that, of all which he hath given me, I should lose nothing, but should raise it up at the last day." (John, vi: 39, 40.) And again: "That every one that seeth the Son, believeth on him, may have everlasting life; and I will raise him up *at the last day.*" And again: "Martha said unto him, [the Saviour,] I know that he [her brother,] shall rise again in the resurrection at *the last day.*" (John, xi: 24.)

A few individual cases of resurrection, as also some bodily translations to heaven, have already occurred. When Christ arose, some of the pious dead arose with him. But the *general resurrection* is reserved until *"the last day."* Then shall spring into new being, all who have ever lived; "they that have done good, unto the resurrection of life, and they that have done evil, unto the resurrection of damnation."

The body dies, and is laid in the tomb; the soul "returns to God, who gave it," and happiness or misery begins; but the full award cannot be received, because of the imperfect manner of our existence, until the resurrection. For this reason, till that day, the judgment, although it is fully known, is suspended, which will determine our everlasting destiny. Then, the trumpet sounds; Christ descends from the mediatorial throne; the body arises, and unites with the soul; the teeming millions of earth are assembled; the sentence is pronounced by Christ; the wicked depart; the righteous assume their thrones, and harps; heaven rings with rapturous hosannas; time ceases; and nothing remains but boundless eternity.

Thus have we considered the resurrection of the dead—as a question of fact; as regards its nature; and respecting

the time when this great event shall occur. It remains only
that we make a practical APPLICATION of our subject.

Beloved friends, and brethren :—To what an amazing
destiny are we all reserved! Every one of us will arise from
the dead, and continue to exist, soul and body, forever!
How should we be affected by this solemn fact?

1. What should be its influence upon the wicked?

You, too, dear friends, must "hear his voice and come
forth." Will it be to "the resurrection of damnation?"
This question you will yourselves decide, by your conduct
in this world. If you continue in your sins, how, at the
judgment seat of Christ, will you be able to bear the *shame*
of your sins, and the *contempt* which they will bring upon
you? He who is "the resurrection and the life," now offers to receive and pardon you. Will you now go to him?
He will, and he alone can, deliver you from impending destruction.

In view of this condition of our friends, does it appear,
brethren and sisters, that we have no duty to perform in relation to them? Do not their future prospects alarm you,
and call forth your sympathies? Many of those who are
dearest to your hearts, are yet in sin. Trace in thought,
their fearful future. See, they die, impenitent and unpardoned; they arise, all polluted, and criminal, and at the bar
of God,

> "———— unveil their aspect! On their brow
> The thunder scars are graven; from their eyes
> Glare forth the immortality of hell!"

Up then, dear christians, and seek to save them. O, plead
their cause before your God; plead *with them* to turn and
live; give them no rest until they are won—until they repent, believe, and are made with you participants in the
grace of Jesus Christ.

2. To those of you who seek salvation, our subject, to-
day, must present a theme singularly full of encouragement.

You are laboring to gain a glorious resurrection, eternal
life, and the companionship of happy saints and angels, in
the skies. To sustain you, there are innumerable motives,
all of boundless strength. The merits of the Redeemer are
ample for you. You cannot fail in your purpose. Victory—

a glorious *victory* over death, hell, and the grave—shall be yours. Trust in Christ, and fear not.

> "Death shall never harm thee,
> Shrink not from the blow,
> For thy God shall arm thee
> And victory bestow.
>   Then death shall bring
>   To thee no sting,
> The grave no desolation;
>   Tis sweet to die
>   With Jesus nigh,
> The rock of our salvation."

3. Upon the heart of the christian, how excellent is the effect of the doctrine of the resurrection.

It reconciles us to the loss of friends. Contrast our condition, in this respect, with that of those who are shrouded in the darkness of paganism. The affectionate parent, or friend, upon whose mind the word of God has never shone, carries to the tomb those, who, of all others, are dearest to him in this world—say, for example, an only, and affectionate son, in the bloom of life. He gazes for the last time, with a bursting heart, upon those wan features, cold in death. The grave closes over him, and he is gone! No hope enters his agitated bosom, that he shall ever again behold that countenance, as he has so often seen it, glowing with life, and lighted up with the beams of love. With unutterable anguish he turns away, exclaiming—*Farewell*, forever—farewell, my dear boy, *forever*, FOREVER! With us, how changed is the scene! "Life and immortality are brought to light, by the Gospel." Our thoughts are irresistibly carried forward, from the grave, which swallows up all our earthly joys, to a day, not very distant, when our friends shall be fully restored to us. Then shall we be able to say :—

> "*See*, truth, love, and mercy, in triumph descending,
> And nature all glowing in Eden's first bloom;
> On the cold cheek of death, smiles and roses are blending,
> And beauty, immortal, awakes from the tomb."

Our *farewell* is but for a few days. As we look upon the grave, we can exclaim: Lightly rest the clay upon thy bosom, my son—we shall meet again! *Then* death can no more reach us. We are beyond the boundaries of his dominions. We are safe—forever safe.

The doctrine of the resurrection enlarges our conceptions of the grace of God; regulates our affections for earthly things; and moderates the desires that might injure our spirituality. Why should this world engross our love, when the prospect is so near us of a better, and an eternal life?

The resurrection reconciles us to death—it does more—it really makes death desirable. The putrescence of the tomb is robbed of its repulsiveness, by the recollection that it is a part of the process through which our bodies are sanctified and fitted for heaven. There is no path to glory, but through the grave. Nor shall our bodies be long detained in that dark valley. It is a short sojourn, and the iron dominion of the last enemy is broken. Come, then, death, we will not shrink; come the day of judgment, we will not fear; since it will awaken our pale slumbers, and bring us to heaven, where we will rejoin all those we have loved; and where we—

> "The sons of ignorance and night,
>   Shall stand in *uncreated light*,
>   Through the *eternal love*."

Glorious consummation! "This corruptible shall put on incorruption, and this mortal shall put on immortality. Then shall be brought to pass, the saying that is written—Death is swallowed up of victory. O death, where is thy sting? O grave, where is thy victory? Thanks be to God, who giveth us the victory, through our Lord Jesus Christ." Amen.

THE
BAPTIST PREACHER.

VOL. IV.   December, 1845.   NO. 12.

THE CO-OPERATION OF THE CHURCHES
WITH THE MINISTRY:

A sermon, delivered before the Bethel Association, at its annual meeting, held in Russellville, Kentucky, September 27, 1845, by THOMAS G. KEEN, Pastor of the Baptist Church, Hopkinsville, and published by request of the Association.

—

" That we might be fellow-helpers to the truth."—3 JOHN, 8.

The church, my brethren, is Christ's representative on earth. He sacredly bequeathed to her the honor of appearing in his behalf, amid the desolations of a sinful world. While he was on earth, he was the light of it—the embodiment· of the divine effulgence, scattering his healing rays upon the surrounding darkness. When he ascended up on high, he gave to his people the elements of the same light, and now they stand forth as the light of the world. Light, in the presence of which, all material splendor is eclipsed and dies away. And this light was imparted with a solemn charge to dispense it, that the world may rejoice in its beams. The fiat has long since gone forth—"Let your light so shine among men, that they may be so dazzled and charmed with your brightness, as to glorify God." To accomplish this purpose, christians are brought together into a social compact; they are collected around the standard of the cross. Their forces separated could effect but little; yet when detached from the world and formed into a visible society, they are at once elevated into the rank of power. If we wish to render an object conspicuous, we take it from surrounding objects and place it apart. The light of the sun is composed of particles inconceivably minute, which, if taken separately and placed at a distance from each other,

29—Vol. IV.

would be lost in the surrounding darkness; but when brought together into the great orb of day, it attracts the notice of ten thousand worlds, and becomes a fit image of the glory of God himself. Believers are to shine as lights in the world; they are to throw off the gloom of surrounding darkness; but they can best secure this end when they become fellow-helpers, by bringing their respective lights into the orb of a christian church.

We should never lose sight, my brethren, of the aggressive character of the church. She is to throw her rays upon the darkness of earth. In her militant state, she is engaged in a war of extermination; nothing short of universal triumph will meet the aspirations of the sacramental host; the kingdoms are all to be given to Christ for his inheritance, and the uttermost parts of the earth for his possession; and in this conflict, the leagued forces of satan are to be fairly met and vanquished. The victory will be so signal as to excite the applause of a wondering universe. It is a mischievous error to suppose that christians may remain at ease and look for triumph. To conquer, they must fight. God promised Canaan to Abraham; but Israel must fight for it. God has promised to the church complete victory; but christians must fight for it.

That the church may bring the encounter to a speedy and successful issue, she has appointed her proper officers to execute her plans. This is her policy, and this is the arrangement of Christ himself. The commission which he gave when he stood fresh and triumphant from the tomb, was given to his own church—"Go ye into all the world and preach the gospel to every creature." Every one could not, in person, execute this order; but as a community, they appoint such as are competent to carry out the design—to present the claims of religion, and to refute the errors of an infidel world. As a well regulated soldiery select their leaders, under whom they are marshaled, so the church appoints her officers, who lead on the forces to contest and to triumph. He who is thus set apart—

> " 'Stablishes the strong, restores the weak,
> Reclaims the wanderer, binds the broken heart;
> And arm'd himself in panoply complete,
> Of heavenly temper, furnishes with arms
> Bright as his own, and trains by every rule
> Of holy discipline, to glorious war,
> The sacramental hosts of God's elect."

In coincidence with this, ministers are the servants of the church, "whether Paul, or Apollos, or Cephas, all are yours;" "For we preach not ourselves, but Christ Jesus the Lord, and ourselves your servants, for Jesus' sake." This relation implies the mutual assistance of the churches with the ministry—"That we might be fellow-helpers to the truth."

The assembly met this morning, my brethren, is no ordinary one. I see before me the messengers from more than forty churches; and I am called upon to address these churches through their respective delegates, now convened. Follow me, then, with your prayers, while I endeavor to present the ways by which you may co-operate with your ministers, and the influence of such co-operation.

I. You may co-operate with your ministers by your sympathies. No position is so trying as that of the christian minister. A thousand cares press upon him with crushing weight, and extort from him the thrilling question, "who is sufficient for these things?" Who is competent to acquit himself honorably as an ambassador for Christ? He is entrusted with a message that an angel might tremble to convey; he treats on subjects of such mighty import, as will require an eternity fully to comprehend; he has to do with the soul, stamped by its author with incalculable worth. Does the physician tremble under the weight of his responsibility, when treating a malady, which may be healed by human skill; to mitigate the sufferings of a body, which at best, must soon fall into corruption? Is the touch of the surgeon most delicate when probing or severing the organs of our bodily frame? And what is the fearful responsibility of him who has to treat with the soul, so easily and irremediably injured; that soul which is to sparkle as a gem in the Mediator's crown through eternal ages, or writhe under the pangs of the second death. Little do christians ordinarily appreciate the number and magnitude of the temptations, trials, difficulties and discouragements of the minister.

> "'Tis not a cause of small import,
> The pastor's care demands;
> But what might fill an angel's heart,
> And fill'd a Saviour's hands."

How eminently fitted are the sympathies of christian

brethren to encourage and enliven their minister, under circumstances so depressing? Who that has not felt the power of human sympathy? What care so pressing that is not
lightened when conscious that we share the affections of
warm-hearted brethren? That when we weep, they weep—
when we mourn, they mourn—when we rejoice, they
rejoice. Let the minister be followed in all his toils and
cares, by the warm sympathies of those whom he is leading
on to glory and immortality; and his pillow is softened; his
sorrows alleviated; and his delight increased.

Look at the missionary of the cross: he breaks away from
ties that bind him to country, to kindred, and the endear-
ments of friendship, to proclaim salvation and to throw himself amid the darkness of pagan night; he encounters perils,
suffers fatigue, endures ignominy, and exposes himself to
the hottest persecution: but he cheerfully prosecutes his
labors, conscious of the approving smiles of heaven and the
christian sympathies of pious friends; and when he sends
his reports full of tales of immense suffering, they touch a
chord which vibrates throughout the churches, re-assuring
him of the prominence which he holds in their affections
and sympathies. This influence, my brethren, he prizes
more dearly than gold or silver.

As *christians*, we have trials peculiar to ourselves. Christianity nowhere assures us of an exemption even from the
common sufferings of human nature. But there are spiritual sorrows, spiritual anxieties, known only to the believer.
Where do we look for an alleviation of these afflictions?
Where do we go to have our cares lightened? To the sympathising heart of the Son of God? And is it the glory of
religion, "that we have not an high priest who cannot be
touched with the feelings of our infirmities, but was in all
points tempted as we are; yet without sin?" Enjoying
such sympathies, our burden is lightened and we advance
with quicker and readier step toward the end of our pilgrimage.

Let your ministers, in the midst of their toils, enjoy your
sympathies, and a power is thrown into their hands, by
which they may surmount innumerable obstacles; their
preaching will assume a more earnest and faithful manner,
and thus you become "fellow-helpers to the truth."

II. By your prayers. According to the economy of grace,

prayer is the means of power which every one may secure; a power which may be wielded by all who are in a state of reconciliation with God. Although disqualified to defend the truth from the gross attacks of the infidel; yet he may make an effectual appeal to Him in whose hands are the destinies of all men. It is the instituted medium through which the littleness and meanness of man may prevail with Omnipotence. By words, by entreaties, by petitions, we move man; and by prayer, we move the great President of the universe; and we know of no other power throughout the vast empire of God to which the great Jehovah yields.

The labors of the pulpit are blessed only as they are accompanied by earnest prayer. I care not what may be the eloquence of the preacher, the soundness of the argument, the conclusiveness of the demonstrations, the effort will be poor, without prayer. And here, my brethren, we have a key which unlocks the secret of many a minister's success. How is it, that oftentimes a minister of limited attainments, is far more successful than one equally pious, of superior genius and mental endowments? Why is this? I am not speaking of something that does not exist; why the difference? Ah! my brethren, the answer is written in the history of their respective churches: one has been followed by the earnest and persevering prayers of his church; while the other has secured no such co-operation. While one church is agonizing in prayer, and imploring the author of salvation to grant repentance; the other stands off and charges blame upon the minister, for his ill-timed and ineffectual efforts.

Let us remember, that he whom we serve, is jealous for his honor; that he regards every power in the universe as more or less opposed to him, but that of prayer; that he views it as an attempt to do without him; as a hostile endeavor to contravene the great principles of the gospel of Christ. "If we look into the censer of the angel standing at the golden altar which is before the throne, and if we there mark what it is, of all human instrumentalities which ascends to heaven, we shall see it is only that which is sanctified by prayer." This is all that lives to reach the skies—all that heaven receives from earth—all that is ever permitted to ascend before God. We have no right to expect that the labors of our ministers, however assiduous, will be effective, unless associated with our devotions—unless accompanied by our prayers. It will appear amid the developments of the last day, that many a christian, who once excited the public gaze with his active deeds and burning zeal, will be comparatively unnoticed; while the man of prayer will be drawn out from his closet obscurity and proclaimed in his stead: and it will there appear, that while the one was only moving earth, the other was moving heaven.

The apostle understood the efficiency of prayer, as a way of co-operation with him in his ministerial work; hence he called upon the churches in all the tenderness of his heart, *" brethren, pray for us."* He ascribes his deliverance and preservation from persecution, to the prayers of christians: " You also helping together by prayer for us." Surely then, if this illustrious man was so dependent upon, and indebted to the prayers of christians, how much more the ordinary minister of Christ. Do we hear an apostle pressing this duty? How much more should the minister, who labors amid discouragements now, enjoy the prayers of his church. " Now I beseech you, brethren, for the Lord Jesus Christ's sake, and for the love of the Spirit, that ye strive together with me, in your prayers to God for me.".

When the minister stands forth, as the herald of the cross and the servant of the church, let him feel conscious that the prayers of the church are ascending in his behalf to the throne of God; and thus his brethren become " fellow-helpers to the truth.

III. You may co-operate with your ministers in the enforcement of discipline. The church is a social organization, and has, necessarily, laws promotive of the good of the compact and the glory of God. These regulations are frequently overlooked and forgotten—the peace of the church interrupted—the cause of truth impeded, and the Saviour left bleeding in the house of his friends with a fresh crucifixion. Now the design of the church is to perpetuate her harmony; to throw away every thing that would mar her communion, and to benefit those who violate her laws. The church which neglects this duty, is said to represent a State in which the administration of justice is omitted and crime is committed with impunity. A law which has no penalty, is a burlesque on legislation; and to pass over an infraction without notice, is to endanger the interests of community. Christ, the head of the church, has instituted laws and demands conformity to them. He has invested the church with executive power to enforce them; and when this is neglected, his displeasure is seriously incurred—the progress of Zion impeded—her prosperity darkened—and her light eclipsed. See the hosts of Israel pressing on towards the promised land : their course is suddenly checked ; their efforts to advance are ineffectual ; a diligent search is instituted to determine the cause of their hindrance, and it lies in the sin of Achan : the law is enforced ; the offender thrown out ; and the people of God march on. Here the sin of one man detained thousands from advancing to their destined home.

How is the progress of the christian Israel retarded by retaining in her communion, those unworthy her trust? How is her reputation tarnished? And how does infidelity triumph over her imperfections? She must assert her rights, and thrust from her embrace, the man who would check her course. It has been well said—" that a great part of our duty consists in cultivating what is lovely ; but this is not the whole of it—we must prune as well as plant, if we would bear much fruit, and be Christ's disciples. One of the things applauded in the church of Ephesus, was, that they could not bear those that are evil. " The free circulation of the blood, and the proper discharge of all the animal functions, are not more necessary to the health of the body, than good discipline is to the prosperity of a church." A little leaven leaveneth the whole lump. Sin is communicative, and unless the disease is checked, it will spread itself over the whole body, and enfeeble, sicken and destroy the whole community ; and in this state of imbecility, no manly energies can be exercised—no vigorous efforts put forth for the glory of God.

Where are the enemies of christianity to look for living illustrations of the power and excellency of religion, but to the church? She stands out as the embodiment of true religion. But when her purity is stained by holding in her midst gross offenders, her power is weakened and her glory is departed. The immoral spots must be wiped out, that she may "stand forth, fair as the moon, bright as the sun, and terrible as an army with banners."

Now to whom does the duty of enforcing discipline belong? Is it the exclusive province of the officers of the church? Or of the private members? Or of both. The formularies of discipline made out by Christ, were undoubtedly presented to the church. The last appeal was not to the ministry, nor to the session composed of the officers, but to the church :—" Not to keep company : if any man that is called a brother, be a fornicator, or covetous, or an idolator, or a railer, or a drunkard, or an extortioner, with such an one, no not to eat; put away from yourselves that wicked person." "A man that is a heretic, after the first and second admonition, reject." " I would they were cut off that trouble you." " We command you, brethren, in the name of our Lord Jesus Christ, that ye withdraw yourselves from every brother that walks disorderly." Here are commands which can only be met by the church. She alone has the power to excommunicate such as are disorderly. But while all this is admitted in a chain of reasoning, how few are the churches that carry it practically out. If an unruly member tramples upon the laws of Christ, months and even years elapse, before the offender is brought to the tribunal of the church. Few seem to have sufficient moral courage promptly to notice the offence and adjust the difficulty. The minister warns; he alludes delicately to the evil of loose discipline, and exhorts the church to a faithful execution of the instructions of the King in Zion ; his appeals are passed carelessly by. Conscious that his pulpit efforts are weakened and neutralized by retaining unworthy members, he speaks plainly out and presents the offender. Many, from various motives, are silent, and the minister, with a small portion of the church, is found struggling alone ; the offender, taking shelter under the silence of brethren, retires palliating his crimes, and charging the minister with undue forwardness and temerity. Now what we contend for, is, that discipline should be enforced by the church ; and that the troubler of Israel be excommunicated by a decided concurrence of a respectable portion of the church. In this way, there will be a more efficient co-operation between the members of the church and the pastor, and thus, they will become " fellow-helpers to the truth."

4. You may co-operate with your ministers by defending their characters from false imputation. " If any man will

live godly in Christ Jesus, he shall suffer persecution." This truth has been strikingly illustrated in every age of the christian church : a truth, written with the blood of martyrs, and proclaimed by the dying groans of saints.

The world has no sympathy with christianity; it has no respect for its Author, nor its friends; it has, in every possible mode, shewn its utter abhorrence to the will of God: wherever the standard of truth has been planted, it has been severely and contemptuously assailed; wherever the triumphs of the gospel have been pushed, fresh and powerful obstacles have been encountered; satan and his allies have disputed every step of territory over which the hosts of Zion have advanced. If these things be true, (and who is prepared to dispute them,) the ministry must expect to be the most prominent object at which the darts of the enemy will be aimed. As the leaders in a military engagement, are those whose death is the most eagerly sought—so the leaders of the sacramental host, will be the objects of the most speedy and pointed attack. If they can be destroyed, little is to be apprehended before success. The forces will be thrown into confusion—the banner of the cross torn down—the places of Zion laid waste, and the enemy exulting in triumph. To effect this, the most vigorous efforts are made. As the influence and moral power of the preacher rest essentially upon his character, they make it the object of assault. If his reputation can be blasted, he is at once disarmed and powerless. Hence, in the days of primitive christianity, all the followers of Christ were the subjects of persecution, but the ministers were pre-eminently such. Who were so repeatedly and violently assailed as the apostles? We see them dragged before princes, governors and councils, falsely charged and imprisoned. Why all this? Why direct their severest invectives and malice at them? Because they conceived, if the champions of religion were destroyed, little remained to be done, before the achievement of the most signal victory. And the same feelings exist still, and the same policy observed by those who array themselves against the progress of the gospel; and the more efficient and daring the advocate, the stronger and more frequent the efforts to destroy him. Who among ministers have been the most bitterly opposed? Have they not been uniformly the most able and uncompromising pleaders of the truth? In

30—Vol. IV.

the reformation, we find Luther singled out from all his co-
temporaries, as the subject of contumely and persecution :
and why, my brethren ?   Because he was the most efficient
instrument in beating back the tide of papal superstition—
in exposing the corruptions of an ecclesiastical hierarchy
and setting in motion a train of efforts which threatened the
complete overthrow of the established priesthood.   And
from that day to the present, and all through preceeding
ages, the most effective ministers have been the subjects of
the hottest persecution.

    In a country like our's, where the Inquisition has never
yet gained a footing—where there are no conventional forms
—where no mitred heads frown upon the humble and un-
tiring herald of salvation—the opposition to the ministry
assumes another form.   The great adversary is well qualified to fit his plans to the circumstances and condition of his
antagonist ; therefore his most successful measures are carried by innuendoes—by indirect attacks upon the moral
standing of the preacher.   Satan has an innumerable company of vassals—creatures so destitute of moral principle
and ready to make the most desperate attempts, who are
busily employed in trying to undermine the integrity of the
pulpit.   Now, let the churches repel with indignity and
promptness these shafts of calumny.   Let them take their
posts by the side of their ministers, ready to stand or fall
with them.   Let them be ready to express their warmest
indignation against the witling that would make them ridiculous ; the scorner that would make them contemptible ;
and the defamer that would brand them as immoral.

    My brethren, do not misunderstand me here ; I do not
plead for the defence of bad ministers—for those who ought
to be deposed.   "When a preacher of righteousness has
stood in the way of sinners, and walked in the counsel of
the ungodly, he should never again open his lips in the pulpit, until his repentance is as notorious as his sin."   But
while his conduct is irreproachable—his character untarnished
—you should preserve it with as much care and watchfulness, as you would his life against the hand of the assassin.
The character of your minister is the lock of his strength,
and if that be aspersed and sacrificed, he will be like Samp-
son shorn of his hair, a poor, feeble, faltering creature, the
pity of his friends and the derision of his enemies.

V. You may co-operate with your ministers, by affording them a liberal support. The system of advancing religion on earth, of sustaining the life and purity of the church, and of foiling satan in his efforts to subvert the truth, is a system of means. While we look to the agent whose province it is to give efficacy to instrumentalities, we should see to it, that the means are in use. It would be absurd to complain of a laborer whom we had employed to fell a tree, for not performing the task, while we, according to the provision, failed to furnish the axe; so while we look to a divine power to wield the sword, we must be certain, that the sword is in place. Now "this sword of the Spirit, is the word of God," and it is only ready to be wielded when it is preached, or "held forth." This is God's own economy: "Faith cometh by hearing, and hearing by the word of God. But how shall they believe in him of whom they have not heard, and how shall they hear without a preacher, and how shall they preach except they be sent?" The church, then, is to present the truth—to publish terms of reconciliation through her ministers—ministers of Christ, and servants of the church. Standing in this relation, to whom do they look for support? To whom should they look? Unquestionably to both Christ and the church, for they are responsible to both. The minister looks to Christ for spiritual strength—for an advancement in holiness, and for those moral qualifications which fit him for his responsible trust. He has promised and fulfils it—"Go ye therefore and teach all nations, baptizing them in the name of the Father, and of the Son, and of the Holy Ghost, teaching them to observe all things whatsoever I have commanded you; and, lo, I am with you always, even unto the end of the world." And He invariably performs his part of the contract: he inspires consolation, he emboldens, encourages, strengthens and sustains. But the minister is not all spirit; he is a man, and has wants which belong to his physical nature. The gospel is deposited in earthen, not heavenly vessels; men, not angels, are the ministers of the church; angels sustain no such relation, and have no claim upon the church for support. Here is a man who holds an extensive slave estate —he directs their labor—he counsels them—they are responsible to him. Now, to whom do they look for protection and support? To their own planning—to the world at large—or to him in whose service they live? He it is who feeds them, clothes them, and provides for their necessities. We present this thought uniformly in illustration of the enviable condition of the slave in America. Now, shall a man feel obligated to support his servants that labor on his plantation, and the church feel no obligation to sustain and protect her servants? We should regard that man as deficient in the proper feelings of humanity, who should compel his servants, after toiling all day for him, to spend the night in providing for their own sustenance: and is it not even more cruel for a church to require her servants, after spending their best energies in her employ, to go out and gather materials for their support? Is it reasonable that the church should hold ministers responsible to them—advise and direct their labors—enjoy and feast upon their services—and then cast them off as unworthy their support? The support of the ministry, my brethren, is founded on principles of justice and equity. We are not, as many imagine, objects of charity. We claim it, not as a charitable donation, but as a just debt. "If we have sown unto you spiritual things, is it a great thing if we shall reap your carnal things?" We have given our time, and talents, and attainments, and are entitled to a reward, and that cannot be withheld without robbery. We are not, then, "clerical pensioners upon mere bounty." Our appeal is merely to justice, and if our claims are rejected, we refuse to present them before any other tribunal, and refer the matter to the "Judge of all, who will do right."

But to refuse the ministry an adequate support, is to violate the palpable laws of the New Testament, and to stamp with folly the conduct of Christ himself. When the Saviour sent out his seventy disciples to labor in his harvest, he said in relation to this subject, "the laborer is worthy of his hire." The apostles, having reference, beyond all doubt, to this subject, asserted and defended ministerial support in the plainest instructions. See the conclusiveness of his reasoning, and the force of his appeals, and the clearness of his illustrations: "Let him that is taught in the word communicate to him that teacheth, in all good things—remembering them which have the rule over you, who have spoken unto you the word of God: and the laborer is worthy his reward—have we not power to eat and to drink." *Hear it, my brethren :* " Who goeth a warfare at any time at his own charges? Who planteth a vineyard and eateth not of the fruit thereof? Or who feedeth a flock and eateth not of the milk of the flock. Say I these things as a man; or saith not the law the same also? For it is written in the law of Moses, thou shalt not muzzle the mouth of the ox that treadeth out the corn. Doth God take care for oxen? Or saith he it altogether for our sakes? For our sakes, no doubt this is written—that he that ploweth should plow in hope, and that he that thresh eth in hope, should be partaker of his hope. If we have sown unto you spiritual things, is it a *great thing* if we should reap your carnal things? Do ye not know, that they which *minister* about holy things, *live* of the things of the temple—and they which wait at the altar, are partakers with the altar? Even so hath the Lord ordained, that they which preach the gospel, should live of the gospel." (1. Cor. ix: 7–14.) The churches that violate such express injunctions, do it at their peril.

But the obligation to pay the promised amount, is not always appreciated. Many are prompt to promise, but slow to fulfil. And there is a fatal mistake in the minds of many, in relation to whom, such are responsible. It is evident to the mind of every one, that the contract is between the pastor and the church. There is no recognition of any individual bargain. The church resolves to pay a fixed salary, which is thought to be a fair remuneration for the services rendered, and the minister accepts it. A real and specific contract is now made. The minister is not to know individuals in the transaction; he holds the *church* responsible for every dollar of the salary—and the *church* looks to him for his ministerial services. The individual member, then becomes responsible to the *church*, and the church to the minister. The church is not released until the amount is paid. Let no member suppose that the pastor is rewarded till the fixed sum has been faithfully paid.

The churches, may co-operate, therefore, with the ministry, by promptly supplying their wants, and fulfilling with them a sacred engagement. They will be released from numerous entanglements and enabled to give themselves "to prayer and the ministry of the word;" and thus you become "fellow-helpers to the truth."

VI. You may co-operate with your ministers, by an

exemplification of christianity. Here, my brethren, is the most effectual aid. In truth, it is so comprehensive, as to include the ways which I have already named. For it is difficult to conceive how a truly pious church can withhold from her minister, her sympathy, her prayers—can refuse to enforce proper discipline—to defend his character from false charges, and contribute to his support.

But we would press the thought upon you as of the most essential importance, that *religion is pre-eminently practical.* It is to be seen in every action : and its divine Author calls upon the world to look at his followers as living illustrations. of the truth and power of the gospel. The apostle's arm was freshly nerved, when he could look at his Corinthian brethren and say " ye are our epistles, written in our hearts, known and read of all men." Your lives form a lucid and standing commentary on the transforming efficacy of revealed religion.

The great evil to be overcome is sin. What but holiness is its proper antagonist? The persons to be benefited by the church are sinners. Who, but holy men, can essentially benefit them? The character of the agency, must be adapted to the nature of the object to be accomplished. That object, the recovery of lost sinners to God, is spiritual, and they who would promote it, must be spiritual. How insufficient were the primitive christians before the day of pentecost : how fearful and irresolute? After the diffusion of the Spirit's influence upon them, how bold, and resolute, and effective were they? They went forth, holding in their hands the weapons of truth, equipped in the armory of heaven, and soon achieved for the cross a thousand bloodless victories. Aiming at a holy end, and prompted by holy motives, and governed by a holy rule, they made the world feel their power. Wherever they raised their standard, they could exclaim, " Thanks be unto God, who always causeth us to triumph in Christ; and maketh manifest the savor of his knowledge by us in every place."

The world did not see religion exemplified by the ministry alone ; but by all who had enlisted as soldiers of Jesus Christ. Ministers require the same co-operation now. Believers should all and everywhere, show themselves controlled by the purifying and elevating principles of the christian faith. Religion should be manifest in every thing.

In all intercourse with men, the badge of discipleship should stand conspicuously out. For religion is like the blood of our corporeal frame, which does not confine itself to two or three large arterial ducts, but diffuses itself through a thousand different channels, conveying life and health throughout the whole body. The true christian is ever ready to be met as the friend of the Redeemer—in the shop, in the counting-room, in the office, in the field, at home or abroad, the same pervading principle impels him to works of righteousness : such form living monuments to the divinity and glory of the gospel. My brethren, how effective and happy such co-operation. The minister feels himself surrounded by living witnesses to the truth he is preaching; and while the infidel may evade the force of his reasoning, he cannot resist the power of practical godliness.

Let us notice next, *the influence of such co-operation.*

I. It emboldens the minister. What is better adapted to inspire courage, than the assurance that he is sustained and upheld by his congregation; that he shares their sympathies—has an interest in their prayers—his character sacredly cherished—the discipline of the church kindly and promptly enforced—his temporal wants supplied—and a practical and living illustration of the truth defended, and urged from the pulpit. How is his arm nerved for the battle? What obstacles so great, that he is not ready to encounter? What enemy so inveterate, that he is not ready to meet? His whole soul is fired with fresh and heavenly zeal for the diffusion of the gospel. What commander has any apprehensions of defeat if all his troops are faithful to their trust? The minister fears no enemy, however formidable, if he can enjoy the spiritual presence of Christ, and the hearty co-operation of the church. But let him fail to secure this co-operation, and his energies are relaxed; he is conscious of the honesty of his motives, the divinity of his cause, and the certainty of final triumph—yet he hesitates to advance; he feels that on earth he is alone; he looks before him and there stand the opposing forces, skilfully marshaled and ready for the encounter; he looks around him and sees the friends of Christ abandoning their posts, and unwilling to proceed to the engagement. Oh, how his courage fails! And should he recognize in the ranks of the enemy, his professed friends, his spirits flag and he gives up in comparative despair.

Look at Cæsar in the senate chamber at Rome: he contends manfully for his supposed rights; and when pressed by the murderous throng intent on his death, he fights with all the earnestness of one conscious of his integrity; but when recognizing among his enemies, a professed friend—one that had promised him the most cordial support—his spirits gave way, and he gently awaits his destiny: looking steadily at the conspirators, he exclaims "and thou Brutus" —enwraps himself in his cloak, falls and expires. So the minister is ready to meet the attacks of the enemy; but when recognizing among them, those that pledged their sympathy and aid, his courage fails.

See St. Paul on his way to Rome. Assembled with a number of prisoners, who were accused of different crimes, he was going to the tribunal of Nero, by whose sentence he might be deprived of his life. No honor could result from a connection with such a man; and his friends might be involved in trouble and danger, by the suspicion and jealousy of government. But it was the glory of the disciples of Jesus in those early ages, that they were united in the bonds of affection which the severest trials were not able to dissolve, and they gave a co-operation which nothing but death could break up. They did not selfishly and pusillanimously abandon him who was singled out to encounter the hostility which the world entertained against him; they gathered around him in the hour of adversity, to sustain his courage and alleviate his sorrows by their presence and their counsels. And what was the effect, my brethren, of this unexpected visit? What influence did it have on his feelings and subsequent conduct? We read it in the impressive language of him who recorded the event—"that he thanked God and took courage." He was emboldened—his resolutions were confirmed in prospect of the troubles which might befal him at Rome. By the simple presence and approving looks of his brethren, as well as by their exhortations, the great apostle of the Gentiles was sustained in the severest trials of his patience and fortitude.

II. Such co-operation increases the happiness of the churches. This is one of the great purposes for which we are called into being. God is glorified in the rational enjoyment of his intelligent creatures: he delights to see the workmanship of his hands happy. And it is the creed of the christian, that while the world presents no sources of substantial and permanent happiness, the service of God opens to the soul innumerable streams of the richest enjoyment. The crystal rills of true pleasure, emanate from the throne of God, in which the christian allays his thirst and satisfies his cravings: every other delight, is regarded ephemeral; all other objects perishable; but those connected with the destinies of the righteous. This is the economy of God, and is the acknowledged belief of every believer. But it is virtually falsified oftentimes in actual practice. We look too often for the increase of joy by reposing in indolence; while pressed hard by innumerable foes, we rest at ease.

It is the order of heaven, that true happiness is connected with real service; that the truly active man, is the truly happy man. And it is with the spiritual as the physical constitution, that health is essential to enjoyment. The weak, the afflicted, cannot, in the nature of things, be joyous. The pressure of disease, dries up every channel of worldly delight. Let then, our corporeal frame become disordered; let our animal functions be suspended for a moment; and the world, with all its charms, will be poor indeed. Hence, it is that the worldling studies to preserve his constitution unimpaired, that he may the more greedily drink in this world's pleasure: and he conceives a proper exercise of his physical energies as essential to the preservation of the animal frame. Laziness, inactivity, will bring on disease, and disease will cut off every communication of worldly pleasure. This is true spiritually. Let our moral constitutions become impaired, and we are ill prepared to enjoy moral pleasures. The gate is closed—the avenue shut up—and nothing but clouds hang with their darkening folds over the horrizon of the soul. I apprehend, my brethren, we have become spiritually sickly, and are unprepared to share the joys of religion. We must preserve pure and unweakened our spiritual constitutions, or there will be the dulness and gloom of disease. Now it is evident, that spiritual activity is the great preservative of spiritual health. An indolent christian must ever be, from the very laws of his moral nature, a sickly christian, and as an inevitable result, an unhappy christian. I care not how much he may repose on the almightiness and sovereignty of God—in the promise that

31—Vol. IV.

the universal jubilee will ere long be proclaimed—that victory is the sure result of the encounter; yet if he is not marshaled himself, what enjoyment can he expect from the spoils of triumph? It is the privilege of the soldier to share in the joys of conquest. Look at the history of the church for numerous illustrations of this truth. In what age do you find the churches most happy? When they have been supine and slothful? When they have been laggards in their Master's service? When they have left the ministers to embattle the hosts of darkness alone? No, no! Look at christians immediately under the teaching of the apostles. How could a community be more happy? When has the air resounded with more rapturous notes, than ascended from the lips of the early saints? And was this an age of sluggishness and ease? No, my brethren—every man who was a friend, showed himself to be such; every one felt that he, as a part of the great posts of the christian Israel, was the guardian of the most sacred rights in the universe; that he was the almoner of Christ, to distribute peace and quiet throughout a desolate and disordered world; he was, in the strictest sense of the word, active and happy. Then, let the churches seek an increase of spiritual enjoyment, by hearty co-operation with the ministry in pushing forward the victories of Emanuel to universal triumph.

III. Co-operation with the ministry, impresses the world with the seriousness and importance of religion. One object which the church has to accomplish, before her ends are fully secured, is to convince the world that she is in earnest. The salvation of men is a serious work, and the course pursued should be proportionally serious. The world does not call so loudly now for logical disputations; for demonstrations of the divine authority of the Bible; but she does look for the proof of christian devotedness—of individual consecration. In lieu of this, the men of the world will receive nothing, not even the most convincing arguments and cogent appeals. Give us, say they, practical proof that you yourselves believe, and are in earnest. And to whom do they look for this illustration? To the instructions of the pulpit—to the diffusions of the press? No; but to the lives of individual christians. Let them see that all the strength of Zion lay in the ministry; let them see no proper union or co-operation between the ministry and the churches; and they would regard themselves as objects merely to be played and sported with.

What do you suppose would be the feelings of a vast and powerful military force, when seeing a *few officers* approaching to make an attack? There pity and derision would be excited at men who would rashly invade the territory of an enemy, and make battle, without having first secured proper discipline and co-operation between the various posts and sections. And as an army becomes powerful, as its posts act in concert; so would it be with the christian church. The world would not long be left to speculate and wonder. Men would find that the pulpit was sustained by a mighty host—that christians were standing close at the side of their standard-bearers, resolved to conquer or to die. The Spirit himself would be their leader—his sword, the weapon they employed—his inspirations animating them to the fight, and his power crowning them with success. The enemies of the Redeemer would resolve such a co-operation into a heavenly cause, and feel that religion was from above. Scenes of apostolic triumph would be witnessed afresh, and Jesus would see of the travail of his soul, and be satisfied.

IV. Such co-operation sustains and elevates our denominational respectability. It is the glory of our communion, that it has always opposed the combination of civil and religious associations. And we have no hesitancy in affirming, that it has never yet symbolized with any political power. " My kingdom is not of this world," is an inscription which stands boldly and plainly out. And while we have stood aloof, and asked not for State power or State sympathy; we have professedly kept in view, the policy established by the legislator of the christian church. We have contended for, and maintained, church independency. We bow to no spiritual hierarchy—to no established priesthood—no popish dictations, and to no universal church domination. Ours is a community of believers, brought into social compact, by conformity to ordinances established by the Head of the church. His instructions form our statute book—his authority is invariably paramount. No power is lodged in the ministry to institute laws, and demand conformity to them ; it is for them to preach—to interpret laws already given—and not to legislate. Our church is emphatically an independent body. And in all the essential features of our organization, is recognized the model prescribed in the New Testament. Even Luther, and Melancthon, and Calvin, and Mosheim, and Neander, and Archbishop Whately, testify, that our principles and ordinances are those of the primitive churches. The voluntary principle which pervades our churches, while opposed to the oppression of dictatorial authority, is consistent with the spirit and genius of christianity. All that come into our ranks, come there with full and free hearts. This, my brethren, is our acknowledged policy.

Now, it will be seen that such a form of church organization, implies the hearty concurrence of all connected, in carrying forward the design of the compact. All necessarily have something to do. No one surrenders his rights to an appointed priest. No one hails another as his father-in-god. All are elevated to the same spiritual platform, where they are to stand shoulder to shoulder in fighting the battles of the Lord. This is our theory. This is the glory of our church.

But when the ministers are left alone ; when they step forward, unaccompanied by their brethren to engage in the salvation of sinners; there is a practical denial of our policy. We become virtually an establishment, where the care of the soul is thrown into the bosom of the clergy. And follow this course to its legitimate end, and we should see some vast, encroaching and domineering hierarchy, standing forth as the vice-gerent of God himself. Let not the minister be elevated above the post assigned him by Christ and the church—nor let him be depressed below his appropriate level. Let us stand closely with him in all his toils—commiserate him in all his afflictions—sustain a portion of his load—" become fellow-helpers to the truth "—then will the glorious independency of our churches stand out, challenging the respect and admiration of the world.

In conclusion, my brethren, how abundant are the encouragements to animate you to a more ready and efficient co-operation with your ministers. You are engaged in a contest which must end in victory. Christianity is destined to triumph. Its history is replete with facts indicative of the eventual prevalence of pure religion. And it is with thrilling delight, that we can to-day look back on the past achievements of the gospel. Look at the standard of Christ, as first raised by the early christians. See Rome, the great metropolis of the world—earth's master and tyrant—falling prostrate before it. Nor Goth, nor Vandal could stay its pro-gress. Nor even Nero, bent on obliterating every vestige of re-ligion from the face of society, could kindle fire hot enough to burn up the energies of the church. Nor could the vari-ous implements of torture and death daunt the christian heart. The philosophic infidel has toiled in vain to subvert the foundations of the church—to overthrow the majestic pillars of Zion—and the shafts of the satirist have fallen powerless from her adamantine shield. The hostility of earth has marshaled every power, in every possible form, and yet she has stood. When we see the idols of Ephesus, of Athens, and of the Pantheon crumbling at the approach of Christ—can we apprehend that the powers now at work can undermine the institutions of Jesus, and overthrow our religion. When we have seen philosophers, and poets, his-torians and statesmen, all directing their energies to destroy us, and have seen them retire from their deeds of darkness, defeated and ashamed, shall we not feel encouraged by the success of the past and the prospects of the future?

1. Look at the rapid progress of the gospel in our own land, within a few years. We have seen revivals of religion multiplied ; the progress of the Redeemer's cause advan-ced, seemingly over every obstruction, until the whole coun-try was alive to its interests. In our own borders, within the precincts of our own Association, how constant have been the triumphs of the cross? A few years ago, and you numbered but a few hundred. Many of them were dis-pirited and inefficient. But now look! How vast this as-sembly of delegates! How thronged are now our meetings for business! How many prompt to take manfully the post assigned them by the Captain of salvation. Let us here, my brethren, raise a fresh Ebenezer and proclaim : "Hitherto hath the Lord helped us." Let our past success move us to more vigorous and united efforts for the still further diffu-sion of the gospel among us. Let us embody a light, whose brightness shall irradiate the gloom of thousands, who are now involved in all the darkness of moral night.

2. But while eventual success is certain, we have now approached a period in the history of our Association, which calls for prompt and efficient action. The tone of piety has undergone an essential change. The characteristic of

the religion of the present day is *inconstancy*. That which was once steady and uniform, has become fitful and impulsive. And instead of the regular and persevering effort bent on success, we see the periodical development of christian energy. We have evidently fallen upon times of peculiar change. Our yearly or stated meetings, now seem to offer the only occasion for strong and united labors for the accomplishment of good. The ordinary assembly presents a theatre too contracted to command our attention and to inflame our zeal. Nothing short of a *great occasion* can arouse our energies and nerve us for the contest. Our mode of operation must assume more uniformity. Instead of making a desperate onset, once a year in the great congregation, we should feel the importance of steady effort. Let us proclaim no truce. Every moment should be devoted in some way, to the extirpation of sin and the advancement of our cause.

There has been on our part, my brethren, a too great conformity to the spirit of the times. This is, undoubtedly, an age of novelty, innovation and excitement. Every thing must be carried by storm—and when that subsides, there is a calm which too closely resembles the stillness of death.

In addition to the fitful character of our efforts, is the peculiar adroitness and management of our adversaries. Our churches have assembled to-day, through their respective delegates, to relate their progress during the past year. But, my brethren, how megre are our reports. We are again reminded of the inveterate hostility of the human heart against the truth, and the constant effort of resisting the Spirit's influence. We must meet this crisis by bolder, and stronger, and more persevering efforts. O! let us here, in this consecrated place, resolve afresh, that our light shall no longer be the unsteady flickering of a dying taper; but the constant and uniform brilliancy of a guiding star.

Brethren, what we do to promote the interests of society, must be done quickly. Look over this audience—how numerous are the habiliments of mourning! Death has invaded our Zion and has thinned the ranks of the sacramental host. Who of us may, at the next anniversary, be found lying in our resting-places, is an event known only to God. The angel of death may already have been commissioned from on high, to enter our dwellings, to spread forth his unsparing desolations! God grant, that we may be found battling with the enemies of darkness and fall honorably in the field. May it be said of us :

> "The pains of death are past;
> Labor and sorrow cease;
> And life's long warfare closed at last,
> Our souls are found in peace.
>
> Soldiers of Christ, well done;
> Praise be thy new employ;
> And while eternal ages run,
> Rest in thy Saviour's joy."

3. Brethren in the ministry, let *us* act worthy the confidence and co-operation of the churches. We sometimes complain of desertion, while perhaps, there are elements in our own bosoms which quickly repel the sympathy and aid of brethren. We may oftentimes merit their censure, rather than their praise. We, who are bearers of the ark, should see to it, that we never hold it with unhallowed touch. Let us appreciate the dignity of our calling. We are engaged in no mean service. Our work is intimately associated with ends of incalculable worth. We are soldiers; but we are soldiers of the cross. We are fishers; but we are fishers of men. God has stamped the pulpit with the highest honor. Although we are in ourselves insignificant, yet, as connected with our office, we occupy the most elevated sphere. Here is a piece of blank paper, of no value in itself, but by an impression of the commonwealth is converted into a bank-note, and becomes current for a thousand dollars. See Raphael, with his scroll of canvass, of which the weaver thought nothing, and the seller nothing, but throwing down upon it his immortal tints, made it the object of the world's admiration. And thus our office rises into greatness, as it has affixed to it the divine seal of heaven; the soul of man for its subject; and eternity for its aim. Here is an employment too high and holy, to allow the existence of unholy passions. Here is a calling too dignified, to permit us to condescend to weakness and sin.

My brethren, let no feelings of jealousy interrupt the harmony of our brotherhood. We have all to contend, more or less, with the secret workings of pride. Aspire to be clothed with humility. O may we never be found thirsting for human applause,—pursuing a trimming policy, designed to please the world,—trumpeting our own fame and vaunting parade of our own success. Let us be found enquiring, not "who shall be the greatest? who shall stand upon the highest pinnacle of the temple? but who shall be most lovely—most like Christ—the least in the kingdom? Let humility, as a rich and ample robe, envelope the entire man—veiling his intellectual powers,—his varied acquirements,—his self-denying and successful efforts, from the too intense and admiring gaze of the human eye; and presenting to view, only those features which shew the emptiness and nothingness of the creature, while God is glorified and praised."

Dear brethren, yet a little while and our work is done. The dying are perpetually around us. They listen to our appeals. We meet them at every turn. If they are saved, the work of reformation must quickly commence. We too must die. We are from eternity; for it we live; of it we testify; and to its grand realities are we rapidly passing. Our kindred are already there. The former occupants of our pews are there. Ears that were once open to the voice of our teachings, are now filled with the music of the seraphim, or thrill with the groans of the damned. Eyes that gazed into ours as we looked down from our pulpits, have already seen the Judge of all.

O let us review the history of our ministry! Perhaps the stain of blood—blood—the blood of souls, is lying upon our neglected and deserted altars; upon the floors of our pulpits; and in our addresses. O may we wipe it off with the tears of penitence; while we bathe afresh in the blood of atonement. Let us rely on the aid of the Spirit,—on the guidance of Christ, and advance to the work. Let the prospects which gild the future cheer and animate us for the toil. While we may be pressed down with a sense of our own nothingness and insufficiency, let us look up and catch the notes of the redeemed around the throne, and see the crown of gold and palm of victory gleaming in the distance. And may we all, after the morning of the resurrection, who have labored as "fellow-helpers to the truth," join together in the triumphant song—"Thou art worthy, for thou wast slain, and has redeemed us to God by thy blood, out of every kindred, and tongue, and people, and nation; and hast made us unto our God, kings and priests; and we shall reign forever and ever."